Effective Reading in a Changing World

Second Edition

❖

Rose Wassman and Lee Ann Rinsky
De Anza College

❖

Prentice Hall, Upper Saddle River, New Jersey 07458

Library of Congress Cataloging-in-Publication Data

Wassman, Rose.
    Effective reading in a changing world / Rose Wassman and Lee Ann Rinsky. — 2nd ed.
      p. cm.
    Includes bibliographical references and index.
    ISBN 0–13–348798–9
    1. Reading (Higher education)   2. Reading comprehension.
3. Study skills. I. Rinsky, Lee Ann. II. Title.
LB2395.3.W374 1997
428.4´071´1—dc20

                                      96-20137
                                         CIP

Editor-in-Chief: Charlyce Jones Owen
Acquisition Editor: Maggie Barbieri
Editorial Assistant: Joan Polk
Director of Production and Manufacturing: Barbara Kittle
Managing Editor: Bonnie Biller
Project Manager: Shelly Kupperman
Manufacturing Manager: Nick Sklitsis
Prepress and Manufacturing Buyer: Mary Ann Gloriande
Art Director: Anne Bonanno Nieglos
Line Art Coordinator: Michele Giusti
Interior Design: Lorraine Mullaney and Nancy Wells
Cover Design: Bruce Kenselaar
Cover Art: Theo Rudnak, Stock Illustration Source, Inc.
Photo Research: Rona Tucillo
Electronic Art Creation: Mirella Signoretto and Maria Piper
Marketing Manager: Gina Sluss

Credits and acknowledgments appear on pages 542–545, which constitute a continuation of this copyright page.

© 1997, 1993 by Prentice-Hall, Inc.
Simon & Schuster/A Viacom Company
Upper Saddle River, New Jersey 07458

Printed in the United States of America
10 9 8 7 6 5 4 3 2 1

ISBN 0-13-348798-9

Prentice-Hall International (UK) Limited, *London*
Prentice-Hall of Australia Pty. Limited, *Sydney*
Prentice-Hall Canada Inc., *Toronto*
Prentice-Hall Hispanoamericana, S.A., *Mexico*
Prentice-Hall of India Private Limited, *New Delhi*
Prentice-Hall of Japan, Inc., *Tokyo*
Simon & Schuster Asia Pte. Ltd., *Singapore*
Editora Prentice-Hall do Brasil, Ltda., *Rio de Janeiro*

Contents

Preface

The second edition of *Effective Reading in a Changing World* has been strengthened and improved thanks to the incisive suggestions of instructors and reviewers as well as the helpful comments of many students who have used this text. *Effective Reading* has been expanded with new selections and practice activites, but its primary purpose remains the same: to help students view reading as a positive experience and to help them develop the essential strategies needed for successful college and life-long reading. These strategies address literal and inferential comprehension, critical thinking, study techniques, and vocabulary development.

❖ Goals and Purpose of the Text

Designed for adult readers with varying backgrounds, *Effective Reading in a Changing World* again strives to strengthen the cognitive abilities of students and to help them develop both a positive attitude toward learning and a love of reading. The mature and high-interest reading selections focus on many of the issues students face today in a rapidly changing world. We have designed in-depth practice activities together with a broad spectrum of reading comprehension questions, as well as suggested discussion questions and journal-writing assignments, thereby integrating reading and writing holistically. Chapters 2 through 9 each include a topical essay, a textbook excerpt, and a literary selection, since these reading genres have unique styles and structures. Our aim is to help students read effectively in all their college studies and to become informed, literate citizens who will want to continue reading and thinking critically throughout their lifetimes.

Features New to the Second Edition

Rather than simply using isolated paragraphs to develop reading efficiency, this new edition intersperses throughout the text twenty-two additional essays and textbook passages. The new activity passages vary in length from 300 to 700 words. Also, to encourage critical thinking and lively discussion, we have chosen social, political, and philosophical topics appealing to adult readers: misuse of personal information, "political correctness," gang violence and hate crimes, women's issues and minority issues, sexual harassment, censorship, sports and society, repressed memory, welfare reform, anger, and procrastination.

Also, we have expanded the subject areas of textbook excerpts so as to cover a variety of college courses. Students will use practice materials that focus on business, intercultural communication, geography, history, psychology, biology, sociology, political science, multicultural law enforcement, the criminal justice system, and global perspectives on health care.

There are a number of other changes and new features.

- The section on **sentence structure** has been reorganized and expanded.
- A section has been included to help students distinguish **major and minor details.**
- **Vocabulary review quizzes** have been added at the end of each chapter.
- **Word analogy** has been introduced and practice provided in Chapters 7, 8, and 9.
- Explanations, examples, and practice activities have been expanded for the sections on *context clues, word parts, organizational patterns, fallacies in reasoning, test-taking strategies, dictionaries,* and *reading rate.*
- Seven new cartoons are used to encourage critical thinking.
- Most literary selections are **complete short stories** or chapters of **award-winning books.**

Continuing Features

The following features of the first edition have been strengthened.

- *Vocabulary* words in each chapter include phonetic pronunciations and definitions.
- A major *topic-related selection* in most chapters includes an *essay,* a *textbook excerpt,* and *short story* or an excerpt from a *novel.*
- Each chapter ends with *journal-writing* suggestions that connect concepts.
- Chapter 10 teaches how to interpret information presented in *graphics.*
- *Versatile content reading* includes the types of questions found in textbooks, quizzes, and exams.
- Skills are presented in a hierarchy of learning, but *each chapter is self-contained* to provide flexibility and individualization in teaching.

❖ Structure and Organization

Instructors who teach developmental reading courses have, in the past, had to choose primarily from three basic types of texts: (1) those that teach discrete reading skills, using short drills and exercises and short essays; (2) study/reading textbooks that focus principally on textbook and academic reading; and (3) texts that emphasize essay reading, followed by multiple-choice and/or short-answer questions. By leading students through a sequential development of skills and strategies that promote critical reading and thinking, together with providing varied reading selections, we combine the best characteristics of these basic reading approaches. Additionally, we present critical reading skills holistically, and we ensure that strategies learned in one chapter are expanded, reinforced, and incorporated into subsequent chapters. This structure, in addition to a detailed chapter on study techniques, gives our text its unique format.

Questions

As in the first edition, in the development of questions, we have incorporated recent research. In addition to answering comprehension questions, students must *always* *apply* the author's thesis or main ideas to their own lives and experiences. In so doing, they become truly active readers. The questions can be used in writing and discussion and for evaluative purposes.

Vocabulary

An in-depth chapter on vocabulary development and extended practice reinforce the vocabulary in the reading selections. To make the readings more meaningful and to help students increase their vocabulary knowledge, definitions have also been provided.

Critical Thinking

All of the twenty-four reading selections in Chapters 2 through 10 include questions that focus on inferential and critical thinking. Additionally, more than fifty activities in the text, using both short and longer passages, help guide students to develop inferential and critical thinking. Chapters 7 through 9 specifically emphasize inference, fact and opinion, bias, connotation, persuasive language, author's tone and purpose, author's reliability, and point of view.

Adapting the Text

Chapters 3, 6, and 10 can be presented in any sequence. Chapter 3, "Reading and Organizing for More Effective Study," and/or Chapter 6, "Refining Reading Style and Improving Rate," can be presented at either the beginning or the end of a semester, depending on instructor preference. All selections of more than 250 words are identified and can be used for reading rate practice.

❖ Instructor's Manual

The comprehensive Instructor's Manual includes a reading comprehension pretest, quizzes for each chapter, sample midterm and final exams, suggestions for each teaching unit, readability information, and suggested answers for all activities and practices. Additionally, sample summary maps are provided for some of the chapters.

❖ Acknowledgments

Many people have provided invaluable assistance, giving generously of their time, talent, and expertise in the preparation of the second edition. We are very grateful for the helpful suggestions and ideas of our reviewers: Karin L. Suttle, Miami-Dade Community College; Beth A. Childress, Armstrong State College; Anna-Marie Schlender, Holy Names College; Rose Stewart-Fram, McClennan Community College; Betty Scearce, DeVry Institute of Technology; Dorothy C. Miller, Kentucky State University.

For their assistance at Prentice Hall, we are indeed indebted to Maggie Barbieri, Senior Editor of Developmental English, for her editorial assistance and support throughout the project. Our special thanks and gratitude also go to Joan Polk, editorial assistant, whose patience, efficiency, and cooperation have helped us to complete this revision; to Kathy Graehl for her detailed manuscript copyediting and Shelly Kupperman for her astute suggestions and impeccable judgment in the book's design and production.

We also wish to thank the many students whose comments and suggestions as they used the text helped to shape the direction of the second edition. Last, and of special note, we wish to thank our husbands, Bob and Harry, for their support and patience and many hours of proofreading.

Rose Wassman
Lee Ann Rinsky

You Make the Difference

- ◆ Review your present reading habits.
- ◆ Determine your reading needs.
- ◆ Learn how to become an effective reader.

❖❖❖

- ◆ Think about the chapter's title and try to predict what its contents might include.
- ◆ Ask yourself some questions based on the title and your predictions since questioning can help you to focus your reading.

❖❖❖

- ◆ How do you feel about reading?
- ◆ How often do you read newspapers, magazines, and books?
- ◆ What do you think your field of study in college will be?

❖❖❖

Jot down your responses to the above questions in the

space provided. _____

_____

_____

_____

As the twenty-first century approaches, our knowledge about the world is accelerating at an **unprecedented*** rate. We are living in what has been called the "Information Age." Much of the information on the ever-expanding "Information Superhighway" is recorded and communicated through the printed word. In the United States alone, approximately 50,000 books are published each year. This print explosion also applies to newspapers and **periodicals** (over 12,000 of each are published), paperbacks, pamphlets, brochures, "junk mail,"ᵗ and the explosion of computer services such as America Online and the Internet. It takes an effective reader to make sense out of the print with which we are bombarded daily; therefore, the primary purpose of this text is to help you become an effective reader for this Information Age.

As a college student, you will encounter in your introductory courses some of the heaviest reading loads of your academic career. For example, textbook chapters for such courses as Introduction to Psychology, Accounting, and American Government average thirty-five pages, and often, students are required to read more than one chapter per week in each course. The effective reader knows how to read, how to understand, and how to organize this **prodigious** amount of information for a successful college experience.

❖ The Effective Reader

You do not have to be a genius or have an exceptionally high IQ to read well. Rather you need an understanding of the reading process and an understanding of how to go about reading different types of printed information. In this way you can practice techniques that will help you to succeed in becoming an effective reader. Two main ingredients are needed: the willingness to change those reading habits that interfere with or limit your reading ability, and the willingness to practice, practice, practice.

Practice

Think back to when you first learned to play a particular sport or when you learned to play a musical instrument. Think what your ability was as a beginner and then think of your skill as you became more **proficient.** You probably practiced almost daily, and the more you practiced, the more confident you became. To become a

---

unprecedented (un pres´ ə dent´ əd) unheard of; never happened before
periodicals (pir ē od´ i kəlz) publications issued on a regular basis, such as magazines
prodigious (prə dij´ əs) impressively great in size or intent
proficient (prə fish´ ənt) expert in an art or skill

*All boldfaced words are defined at the bottom of the page to assist you with comprehension and vocabulary growth. Chapter 2 focuses on specific strategies for improving vocabulary and using context clues.
ᵗ*Statistical Abstract of the United States* (Washington, DC: GPO, 1994) Bureau of the Census 574, 576.

skillful reader takes the same kind of effort and practice. The fact that you are reading this textbook shows you have taken the first step toward wanting to become that effective reader.

Organize Yourself for Reading and Study

One of the first requirements for effective reading and study is to understand the importance of *disciplined* study. You must plan undisturbed blocks of time to devote to reading and study. However, after arranging such a schedule, realize the need to be flexible when something unforeseen occurs. Essentially, however, consistency in maintaining a schedule as much as possible is invaluable to success. After reading the brief instructions for a weekly schedule, complete your plan for developing a realistic schedule.

❖ Weekly Schedule

1. Block out your school/work schedule and any other of your scheduled responsibilities.
2. For each unit of class time, try to block out a minimum of two hours of study. For a three-hour class, plan on about six hours of study per week.
3. Be specific. Do not write "study," for example, but write "study American History." Use colored ink or pencil to highlight study hours.

	Mon.	Tues.	Wed.	Thurs.	Fri.	Sat.	Sun.
7:00 A.M.							
8:00							
9:00							
10:00							
11:00							
12:00 P.M.							
1:00							
2:00							
3:00							
4:00							
5:00							
6:00							
7:00							
8:00							
9:00							
10:00							

❖ Improve Your Concentration and Develop a Positive Attitude

The inability to concentrate while reading is experienced by many students. The difficulty, however, rarely has a **neurological** basis. The mind is not faulty; rather, the inability to concentrate is generally a problem of attitude toward a reading assignment. A selection may be extremely challenging or one in which you have no immediate interest. However, having a positive attitude and a commitment to learning can go a long way toward improving your ability to concentrate. Commitment and attitude can also lead to success when students regard the task as a rewarding learning experience.

Things that might interfere with concentration, such as thirst or hunger, should be taken care of prior to the reading/study session. Try to resolve or put aside temporarily any personal difficulty, remove as many distractions as possible, and give your full attention to reading and study. Two things done at once are rarely successful!

Generally, a forty- to fifty-minute reading/study session is recommended. A good idea that adds to reading efficiency is to take a short break of five to ten minutes after a reading/study period. Remember to have all needed supplies such as marking pens and notepaper close by, so it will be unnecessary to break your concentration.

❖ Maintain Confidence

Confidence in reading is chiefly the result of preparedness. If you take good lecture notes, complete assignments on time, and maintain your reading/study schedule, you will set in motion a pattern that builds your confidence.

When personal and career goals are established, confidence also develops. Check with your counselor or find out about taking an interest inventory if you are undecided about a career goal. Most counseling centers have an excellent book called the *Occupational Outlook Handbook* with information on careers and the future of specific fields. Having a career goal can be a great motivator for a positive outlook on the future and the desire to excel in school.

❖ Maintain Curiosity

There are a number of factors to consider regarding your attitude toward reading. Some students ignore reading assignments because they consider the subject bor-

---

neurological (noo rō läj´ i kəl) related to the nervous system and its diseases and disorders ing. The boredom, you should realize, may stem from the person doing the reading, not in the assignment to be read. Right now, you are probably interested in some things that do not appeal to some of your friends. On the other hand, you probably have lost interest in some subjects that once absorbed you or have acquired an interest in areas that formerly did not appeal to you at all. Try to maintain a curiosity about the exciting, **dynamic** world about us, developing interest in many subjects. The prodigious amount of reading materials available can not only help you learn about these subjects but can also help you experience a wealth of satisfaction and pleasure.

❖ Acquire a Framework of Knowledge

Reading is always easier, always faster, and comprehension is always higher when you have some familiarity with the subject. Writers of articles often make reference to people, events, and ideas unfamiliar to you. This, at times, may be why you find a reading assignment uninteresting. But the very same people, events, or ideas may appear repeatedly in print. Learning about them helps familiarize you with their particular contributions or importance. With broad reading, you begin to acquire a framework of knowledge into which you can fit additional information as you read. As one authority has explained it by the use of a **metaphor,** "The head is not really like a pot—the more empty it is of ideas, the more difficult it is to put anything in it! . . . The fuller it is with a wealth of background information, the more you can add to it, retain, and remember."

❖ Be an Active Reader

To be an effective reader, be an *active* reader—one who mentally engages in a dialogue with the writer. While reading, active readers agree and disagree, applaud and criticize, weigh and reconsider what the writer is saying. They involve themselves with the ideas, responding intellectually and/or emotionally to what they read. One prominent writer has stated that what he puts on paper is "a transaction between himself and the reader," sharing who he is. Active readers involve themselves in that transaction, which in turn becomes a valuable aid to both improved concentration and comprehension.

---

dynamic (dī nam´ ik) marked by energy and vigor

metaphor (met´ ə fôr) speech in which a term that ordinarily describes an object or idea is used to describe a dissimilar object or idea, in order to make a clearer comparison

❖ Develop a Flexible Reading Rate*

Perhaps the most serious misconception about reading is that everything should be read at the same rate: cartoons, an editorial, and a legal contract! Certain types of reading demand a slower, more careful approach, with every piece of information critical to comprehension. The key is to be a flexible reader, varying your rate according to how difficult the material is and your *purpose* for reading. To become aware of the wide range in reading rates, study the suggested rates for various types or **modes** of reading material in the following table.

The average person reads the newspaper, magazines like the *Reader's Digest,* and popular novels at a rate of about 250 words per minute with about 75 percent comprehension.

Mode, Examples, and Purpose

Reading Rate Means Reading Flexibility

Mode	Purpose	Rate	Recommended Rate Range
1. Analytical reading (Legal documents, persuasive essays)	To analyze information for **inference,** language, tone, bias; to evaluate logic and writer's craft.	Usually the *slowest* rate. Varies with complexity of material. May require more than one reading.	150–250 wpm
2. Study reading (Textbooks)	To learn, **synthesize,** and retain information; gaining complete understanding of text material.	Rate varies with amount to be learned and type of material.	150–300 wpm
3. General reading (Newspapers, magazines, novels)	To read as a leisure-time activity for pleasure and general information.	Rate varies with material, purpose, and familiarity.	250–500 wpm
4. Skimming (Initial research)	To get a general idea of the material and some details; to get a mental outline of material's organization.	Can be twice as fast as general reading rate.	500–1000 wpm
5. Scanning (Phone numbers, airline schedules)	To locate specific information and answer questions as quickly as possible.	*Fastest* rate with no specific wpm determined.	1000 + range

Decrease ← BASE RATE → Increase

modes (mōdz) forms or variety of things

inference (in´ fər əns) to conclude by reasoning from what is known or assumed

synthesize (sin´ thə sīz) to combine parts to form a whole idea

*Reading rate will be dealt with in more detail in Chapter 6.

❖ Other Factors

After examining the various rates, you should also be aware that your rate is always affected by

Your familiarity with the topic.
Your interest.
The difficulty of the vocabulary and sentence structure.

Consider how the factors in the following table may affect your rate.

Gauging Reading Difficulty

Selection/Purpose	Topic Familiarity	Interest	Difficulty
1. A quick look at an essay in *Sports Illustrated* (recreational reading)	I'm very comfortable with this topic.	High	I recognize all the vocabulary. Sentence length average. Frequent paragraphs.
2. A contemporary novel (an English assignment)	I have read another novel by this author.	Neutral	Some difficult words. Sentences are somewhat long.
3. A textbook with technical material, needing 100% comprehension (will be tested)	I know nothing about this subject.	I have some interest.	Vocabulary is quite difficult. Sentences are average.

Obviously, you could read an essay in *Sports Illustrated* much more rapidly than the others. To understand a technical book, you would certainly have to modify your reading rate.

Examine the following list of selections and purposes for reading. Fill in the blanks, determining the rate at which you would read each: rapidly, at an average rate, or more slowly.

Selection/Purpose	Topic Familiarity	Interest	Difficulty	Selected Rate
1. "Capital Punishment: Does It Work?" (class assignment)	_____	_____	Easy words, short sentences	_____
2. *Domina*, a novel about one of the first woman doctors (recreational reading)	_____	_____	Difficult words, long sentences	_____
3. "States of Consciousness," a psychology chapter (study purposes—will be tested)	_____	_____	Very difficult vocabulary, long sentences	_____

❖ A New Commitment

Check those areas in which you need to work. Write in your journal (page 22) explaining how you plan to carry out your goals.

Practice Needs

 _____ 1. I need to read meaningful selections from a variety of materials.
_____ 2. I need to read on a daily basis.

Organize for Study

_____ 1. I need to establish a weekly schedule.
_____ 2. I need to establish self-discipline and maintain a reading/study schedule.
_____ 3. I need to improve my concentration by increasing my attention span.

Maintain Confidence and Develop a Positive Attitude

1. I need to develop a positive outlook by
   _____ Taking good lecture notes.
   _____ Completing assignments on time.
   _____ Being prepared for class.
2. I need to set some personal or career goals by
   _____ Seeing a career counselor.
   _____ Checking the _Occupational Outlook Handbook_.

Develop a Flexible Reading Rate

_____ 1. I need to be aware of the difficulty of the reading material.
_____ 2. I need to determine my purpose when reading.

Maintain Curiosity: Acquire a Framework of Knowledge

 Below are titles of some articles in current periodicals. Place a check mark next to those topics with which you are unfamiliar. Read some articles in these areas.

_____ 1. Animal Experimentation: Is It Right?

_____ 2. Drug Enforcement

_____ 3. Gene Splicing Comes of Age

_____ 4. Law Enforcement Under Attack

_____ 5. Music and the New Technology

_____ 6. New Careers for the Twenty-First Century

_____ 7. Pros and Cons of Nuclear Energy

_____ 8. The Space Program's Expanding Horizons

_____ 9. Stereotypes in the Cinema

_____ 10. Violence in U.S. Cities

Write a summary paragraph of some of the most interesting articles you read. In writing a summary, state the most significant points the author has made. See page 15 for a chapter summary to use as a model.

❖ Question Types

Before you read the selections in this text, we want to review the three types of questions you will be asked to answer after you read. Basically, these are the same kinds of questions you are asked on tests in your various courses.

Literal Questions

Literal questions are the easiest to answer because you find the answer expressed directly. These questions generally ask you to recall the kind of information that is directly stated as dates, names, places, or reasons for or steps in doing something. For example,

> Why is it important to develop a flexible reading rate?
> What is an active reader?

Interpretive Questions

The answer to this type of question is not directly stated. You are asked to analyze and think about what you have read and to use your own background knowledge about the subject to answer the question. These answers are sometimes called inferences and require you to understand what the author suggests or implies. Sometimes an interpretive question requires you to both analyze and synthesize, that is, to put certain bits of information together before drawing an inference. When synthesizing, we reorganize our thinking to reach a conclusion. For example,

What is meant by the expression "The head is not really like a pot; the fuller it is, the more you can put into it"? What does this have to do with improving reading ability?

Application and Discussion Questions

This type of question asks you to go a step further than literal or interpretive reading and apply the information you have just read to another situation. You must think critically about what the writer has said and make a judgment about it before applying it to something else. For example,

Write the steps you will need to take to enable you to adjust your reading rate when reading for purpose and mode.

❖ The Importance of Previewing Before Reading

The importance of previewing cannot be overstated.

1. Leads to better comprehension and gives you a quick picture of the overall idea and some supporting points.
2. Helps you determine the topic and the organization of the passage.
3. Helps you note what parts of the material justify a more careful reading.
4. Is like consulting a map before leaving on a trip; you develop confidence and interest because you know where you are going.

Previewing Procedures

When previewing, you will note that the written patterns of many articles and essays usually follow this sequence: the topic may be suggested in the title; the main idea may appear somewhere at the beginning of the passage in the first, second, or third paragraph; the remaining paragraphs support the main idea; and the conclusion often summarizes or restates the main idea. Therefore, in previewing the essay, you should read

1. The title (see if it gives you a clue to the topic; then turn it into a question and read to answer it).
2. Any introductory information—usually the first paragraph or two.
3. The first sentence or part of the first sentence of the remaining paragraphs.
4. The last paragraph or two.

With any preview, it is likely you will have to *modify* our suggested procedure to accommodate the writer's style. For example, if there are many one-line paragraphs, you do not have to read each of them. Also, sometimes the first sentence of a paragraph is simply a transition; so you need to read the second sentence too.

Before you begin reading, you should think about what you have previewed to try to *predict what the author's message or viewpoint will be* and to sort out what you already know and think about the issue at hand.

The model page that follows demonstrates how you might preview an article written on the subject of previewing.

Read the title and turn it into a question. How do you learn to preview? Then read to find the answer.

Learning How to Preview

Rose Wassman/Lee Ann Rinsky

Read the entire first paragraph at your normal speed. It may contain an introduction to the main idea. The first paragraph, however, can be merely an introduction with the author trying to get your attention.

Sometimes you may have to read the second paragraph. Here the main idea may be expressed or important clues presented.

Start reading the first sentence or two of each paragraph. _____

_____

_____

_____

The writing patterns of most reading selections, whether articles, textbooks, or essays, follow a pattern of stating the main idea of each paragraph first.

_____

_____

_____

_____

Sometimes the first sentence of a paragraph is just a transition or introductory sentence. You have to read the second sentence.

_____

_____

Look for key ideas as you preview. _____

_____

_____

_____ read only what's important.

Sometimes the main idea of the paragraph is implied. You may have to read

_____

_____

_____

much of it to make sense _____

_____

On the other hand, you may have to skip some paragraphs _____

They are simply transitions _____

_____

_____ or one-line paragraphs.

Previewing enables you to decide _____ whether the material

justifies more careful reading. _____

_____

_____

You can cover a lot of material to find what you wish to use. _____

_____

_____

_____

Previewing is like consulting a map before leaving on a trip. _____

_____

_____

_____

Speed up as you read, but _____

_____

_____ slow down if the information is puzzling or needs

more careful _____

_____

Expect lower comprehension _____

_____

_____

_____ 50 percent is about right _____

_____

Practice is essential. As you practice previewing, you learn to preview. Remember, your purpose is *to get the main ideas as quickly as possible* so you have some familiarity with the material when you give it a more thorough reading.

Practice previewing now with a short selection excerpted from a speech that points to some issues facing us in the coming century, issues that necessitate effective reading. The author, the president of World Trend Research, delivered this speech to a graduating military class.

Follow the suggested previewing procedures by first changing the title into a question and reading to answer the question. By previewing, you should be able to answer the first question. Then, complete reading the selection and answer the questions that follow.

A New Frame of Reference

William Van Dusen Wishard

The profusion of scientific information has, as we all know, generated a Niagara of information. Hence the vaunted information age. . . .

The danger now is too much information. If you were to read the entire Sunday edition of *The New York Times,* you would absorb—or at least be exposed to—more information in that one reading than was absorbed in a lifetime by the average American living in Jefferson's day. The number of books in our leading libraries doubles every fourteen years. There's a bookstore in Reston where I live that carries 100,000 volumes and 5,000 newspapers and periodicals.

Microsoft's CD-ROM encyclopedia has surpassed all printed encyclopedias in sales. This is the greatest shift in the presentation of encyclopedias since Diderot published the first encyclopedia over three hundred years ago. . . .

This cascade of information has brought us to a point of what some corporations call "negative information"—so much information that, in some cases, the quality of decisions made by managers actually decreases. The same thing is happening on Wall Street. Brokers have so much information available that they no longer know when they have accumulated sufficient information to make a wise decision. *The Wall Street Journal* suggests that it is information overload, not ignorance, that's . . . creating a sense of numbness and discouragement.

We're told that the amount of information an individual uses in a lifetime is equivalent to 20 billion bits of data. That amount of data can be sent around the world in seven seconds. In other words, everything you will ever think or say in your entire lifetime can be flicked around the globe in seven seconds. . . .

And we haven't seen anything yet. . . . The president of the Communication Workers of America said that in terms of technology, the telecommunications industry is going to see more change in the next six years than it's seen in the past ninety-four years.

It's becoming clear that the more information we amass, the more important context and meaning become. We live in two worlds—the world of data and the world of meaning. Meaning requires reflection and time-consuming thought. . . .

In my judgment, what this means is that we've got to give fresh meaning and content to what America's all about in an interconnected, global age. . . . And our future depends on what enduring meaning we now infuse into our journey as a people.

approximately 380 words

William Van Dusen Wishard, "A New Frame of Reference," *Vital Speeches,* Dec. 1994: 153–58.

1. Does the writer foresee great or limited change ahead in the next few years of the Information Age? Support your answer with an example.

   _____

   _____

Answer questions 2 and 3 after reading.

2. What are some difficulties the writer states businesspeople face in the Information Age?

   _____

   _____

3. What does the writer suggest that Americans must do in the Information Age?

   _____

   _____

❖ Summary

Reading effectively is a necessity in our Information Age and to keep pace on the Information Superhighway. Repeated practice together with a willingness to modify your former reading habits can ensure success. An effective reader must organize study time by maintaining a schedule. A positive attitude and a commitment to learning will make you a more effective reader and improve your concentration. Things that might interfere with concentration need to be addressed prior to the reading/study time. Additionally, being prepared for class builds and maintains confidence. That confidence is enhanced when personal and career goals are established. Try to maintain a curiosity about our dynamic world, developing interest in many subjects and building a framework of knowledge. Reading is always easier, always faster, and comprehension always higher when you have some familiarity with the subject.

Previewing the material before you read generally leads to better comprehension, helping you get a quick picture of the overall idea and some supporting facts. As you read, your rate should be adjusted according to your purpose for reading, the difficulty of the material, and your familiarity with the subject.

Three types of questions are generally asked by instructors: literal, interpretive, and application questions. Literal questions are the easiest to answer because the expected answer is expressed directly. Interpretive questions ask you to analyze and synthesize information you have read. Application questions ask you to go a step further, applying the information to another situation.

☛ Preparation for Reading

The next selection, "Illiteracy in the Information Age," is followed by a set of questions that is typical of material found with longer selections at the conclusion of each chapter. Preview the selection first, then read and answer the questions. Note the following words before reading the essay. They are underlined in the text.

to the **viability**	ability to live or develop
maneuvering through . . . a service	using skill to arrive at a goal
writes **eloquently**	movingly expressive
deleterious effect	injurious; hurtful
pundits have even coined	learned or authoritative persons
becoming a quaint **anachronism**	something out of its proper time
revert to a pre-**Renaissance** model	the great revival of art and learning in Europe from the fourteenth to the seventeenth century
cognitive skills	involving learning through mental processes
is **ineluctably** linked	inevitably; must take place

Illiteracy in the Information Age

Marcia Kaplan

1 Since I write about and work with the computer industry, people frequently ask me if I think that electronic distribution of newspapers, magazines, articles, and books will mean the death of the publishing industry as we know it.

2 I tell them that they have little to fear from electronic distribution. The biggest threat to the <u>viability</u> of the publishing industry—and our society—is illiteracy, something that is increasing at an alarming rate in our country.

3 Each year, 700,000 people who graduate from high school can't read their diplomas, U.S. education officials say, while one in five American adults is functionally illiterate. Educators sensibly no longer measure literacy by the simple ability to read and write. Rather, they view literacy as a continuum of skills integral to functioning in society—certainly a more useful assessment.

4 While functional illiterates can read words, they cannot comprehend their meanings, synthesize information, or make decisions based on what they read. Few of them own computers, and they are as unlikely to go searching for reading materials on-line as they are to sit down with a newspaper or novel. <u>Maneuvering</u> through a commercial on-line service, a BBS, or the Internet requires an intellectual dexterity that poorly educated people lack. Marginally literate people feel most comfortable receiving information in a visual format, relying more on television than print media for information.

5 At the same time that Americans' skills are declining, entertainment, computer, and telecommunications companies are creating new, technologically advanced methods to amuse and educate us. In the excitement about the information superhighway and new com-

munications gadgets, businesses are ignoring a troubling fact—a substantial number of Americans are not intellectually capable of using their technologies.

Peter Drucker, a noted management expert, writes <u>eloquently</u> about the advent of the knowledge society and the knowledge worker—the individual who relies on technology and intellect rather than brawn to accomplish work. **6**

Perhaps Drucker has not visited a typical workplace recently. "Workplace literacy" projects have sprung up across the United States. To obtain a skilled work force, businesses have to devote substantial resources to duplicate the efforts of our school systems. In many cases they are teaching basic reading, writing and arithmetic. If our future need for knowledge workers is to match Drucker's expectations, our country will have to rely on immigration or robots. **7**

Technology actually may be contributing to our declining capabilities because it has made us intellectually lazy. Our collective attention span gets shorter all the time. We "channel surf" and "Net surf," looking for content that will hold our interest for more than a few minutes. Only short sound bites or brief written summaries appeal to us. We seem to want to run our lives by remote control, fast-forwarding through the dreary parts, and replaying the brief moments that engage us. **8**

The educational system has arguably suffered the most <u>deleterious</u> effects of technology. Children no longer use pencil and paper to learn math; they use machines. But when they rely on calculators and computers for mathematical outcomes, children memorize a series of keystrokes instead of learning a deductive process. Similarly, instead of learning to write well, children with computers depend on software programs to check their spelling and correct their grammar. Some parents and educators have endorsed the philosophy that **9**

unless learning is fun, children are within their rights to decline to participate. Only a multimedia extravaganza of audio, video, and graphics is worthy of children's attention.

<u>Pundits</u> have even coined a fashionable term for this trend. They glorify our "post-literate" society, as if the inability to comprehend the written word is a great accomplishment. Important skills are the ability to manipulate a joystick, a mouse, or a remote control. It should be deeply disturbing to anyone who cares about the future of our society that literacy is becoming a quaint <u>anachronism</u>. **10**

In the 21st century we may very well revert to a pre-<u>Renaissance</u> model in which only an elite class—the clergy in that era, the technical specialist in ours—will know how to read and write. Rather than having a multitude of knowledge workers, we will have a narrow knowledge elite that others will seek out for assistance. **11**

Already, across industries, writing is considered a specialized task. Marketing communications, or "marcom" is a recently created sub-specialty of marketing that focuses on the dissemination of written information such as press releases and product descriptions. Apparently, a marketing generalist cannot be entrusted with the important task of writing. Some companies have turned this task over to public relations firms. Technology businesses entrust technical writers with the task of writing manuals to explain how their products function. Although this specialization creates more jobs, it also relieves others of the responsibility of communicating in a written form that people can understand. **12**

Publishing is not the only industry that will suffer if literacy is relegated to a narrow segment of the populace. Any business that sells products or services that require a user's ability to exercise <u>cognitive</u> skills will face a shrinking market. As for electronic distribution, my own experience has been that people who read avidly are the most intense users of commercial **13** on-line services and the Internet. They use electronic media as a supplement, not as a replacement for hard copy materials.

No other industrialized country treats liter- 14 acy with such contempt as the United States. We haven't grasped that our society's future is <u>ineluctably</u> linked to the preservation of the written word. We will suffer for our disregard.

approximately 1100 words

Marcia Kaplan, "Illiteracy: A Looming Crisis in the Information Age," *San Francisco Sunday Examiner* 7 May, 1995: B5–7. Reprinted by permission of the author.

COMPREHENSION CHECK

Part I
General Comprehension Questions: Literal and Interpretive

Write the correct letter in the space provided.

_____ 1. The author writes chiefly about
- a. social ills.
- b. education in schools.
- c. the computer industry.
- d. the publishing business.

_____ 2. As defined by U.S. education officials, functional illiteracy refers to
- a. alarming illiteracy.
- b. a particular assessment.
- c. the ability to read and write.
- d. skills necessary to function in society.

_____ 3. According to the author, people who are only marginally literate would prefer getting the news from
- a. radio.
- b. TV.
- c. magazines and newspapers.
- d. friends and family.

_____ 4. The writer and Peter Drucker are
- a. writing together.
- b. in agreement.
- c. in disagreement.
- d. none of the above.

_____ 5. The writer believes that what causes Americans to be "technologically lazy" is
- a. a need to watch only what engages them.
- b. a shortened attention span.
- c. their stressful life-style.
- d. both a and b.

_____ 6. A "marcom's" major task is to
- a. find a good public relations firm.
- b. engage in handling written communication.
- c. entrust technical writers.
- d. create more jobs.

7. Would the writer be in favor of software programs in schools that check spelling and correct grammar?

_____

Why or why not? _____

_____

_____

8. Why does the writer suggest we may need increased immigration and the use of robots?

_____

_____

_____

Part II
Application Questions for Writing/Discussion

9. Imagine that you are an advisor to our government in Washington. What are some suggestions you might make about the effects of a decline in literacy, and how might these problems be remedied?

_____

_____

_____

10. What are some of the writer's predictions regarding literacy and social class in the twenty-first century?

_____

_____

_____

11. What is your prediction? Are you in agreement with the writer?

_____

_____

Part III
Extend Your Vocabulary

Can you match these words from the essay with their respective meanings?

_____ 1. eloquently   a.   learned or authoritative persons

_____ 2. deleterious   b.   injurious; hurtful

_____ 3. viability   c.   movingly expressive

_____ 4. cognitive   d.   ability to develop normally

_____ 5. pundit   e.   acquiring learning through
                                       mental processes

Chapter 1 Vocabulary Review

A. Select the appropriate word for each of the sentences in the paragraph from the boldfaced words below and write it in the space provided. Use the sentence context* to help you determine the word's meaning.

inference   dynamic   prodigious   periodicals   synthesize

For some time, we have needed a/an (1) _____ leadership in Washington to bring about some needed reforms in our court system. Recently, our government held hearings on the need to change some court procedures reported as particularly unfair. Essay writers in newspapers and other (2)

_____, in response to citizen dissatisfaction, have been criticizing many court practices. It will require a/an (3) _____ effort to

(4) _____ the best ideas for court reform into a final plan. But

based on what has happened, we can make the (5) _____ that some reforms in our court system will take place.

B. Write the correct word in the space provided.

neurological   unprecedented   metaphor   proficient   mode

1. Related to the nervous system

_____

2. A form or variety of something

_____

3. Words used figuratively to compare things

_____

4. Having expertise at doing things

_____

5. Never happened before

_____

*Context is discussed in detail in Chapter 2.

JOURNAL ENTRY

This is your first journal entry. Write how you plan to carry out your goals and become a more effective reader. You may wish to refer to page 8 to note the areas you checked.

2

Building Vocabulary Through Context and Structure

This chapter will help you to

- Recognize the importance of vocabulary to improve reading comprehension.
- Use the context effectively to determine the meaning of unknown words.
- Learn the meanings of the most common word parts: prefixes, roots, and suffixes.
- Transfer knowledge of word parts to unknown words.
- Develop a personal word collection.
- Use mnemonics (memory devices) to retain word meanings.
- Strengthen use of the dictionary and thesaurus.

❖❖❖

Before reading, think about these questions.

- What can you do to improve your vocabulary?
- Why does a strong vocabulary improve reading comprehension?
- Why is vocabulary important today?

❖❖❖

Jot down your thoughts in the space provided.

_____

_____

Chapter 1 indicated that the *more you read, the better you read*. Reading more is also the best way to increase your vocabulary. It gives you a background of knowledge and helps you experience life through others, or **vicariously.** In turn, this background and these experiences give you the ideas and concepts associated with words. This helps you to understand words better, remember them longer, and use them correctly.

As you recall, definitions of challenging words were included at the bottom of the same page in the previous chapter. This same format continues here. You should look over these words before reading, but study those unfamiliar to you *after* you have finished reading a section.

Students are often surprised to learn how many English words there actually are. At present, in our **burgeoning** technological age, English can boast a total of over 1 million words. A paperback dictionary generally includes about 100,000 entries, representing, perhaps, only about 10 percent of all the words in the English language! Look through an **abridged** dictionary such as *Webster's New Collegiate* or the *American Heritage* to see how many words even a shortened version contains.

❖ Several Types of Vocabulary

All of us have several kinds of vocabulary: one each for speaking, writing, reading, and listening. Your speaking vocabulary tends to be the most limited since you have to feel very comfortable with a word to say it. Your writing vocabulary is somewhat larger because here you have time to think and select words. Still greater is your reading vocabulary. Finally, your broadest vocabulary includes the words you understand when listening, since a speaker often clarifies a word by **inflections,** physical gestures, or facial expressions.

❖ Conversational vs. Formal Vocabulary

We also have a conversational vocabulary and a more formal one. The first consists of those words we use every day in speaking and listening. They **emanate** from words with roots in our Anglo-Saxon heritage, those early English words such as *childish, break,* and *frighten.* The second kind includes **erudite** words used in more formal

---

vicariously (vī kâr ē əs lē) experience through participation in the feelings of another
burgeoning (bʉr´ jən ng) developing rapidly
abridged (a brijd´) shortened
inflections (in flek´ shənz) alterations in tone or pitch of the voice
emanate (em´ ə nāt´) originate or come forth
erudite (er´ yōō dīt´) very learned; scholarly

reading, writing, and speaking. These words are less familiar and often have their roots in Greek and Latin.

The following two lists of words with similar meanings, called **synonyms,** show the difference in difficulty between "everyday" or conversational words and more formal words. Knowing a substantial number of the latter makes the difference between a marginal vocabulary and a superior one.

Conversational Words	Formal Words
begin	commence
free	emancipate
name	appellation
fire	conflagration
large	gargantuan

ACTIVITY 2.1

How many of the two sets of synonyms can you match correctly?

Conversational Words	Formal Words
_____ 1. end	(a) covenant
_____ 2. speed	(b) nuptials
_____ 3. fat	(c) avarice
_____ 4. greed	(d) terminate
_____ 5. wedding	(e) velocity
_____ 6. promise	(f) corpulent
_____ 7. shorten	(g) assuage
_____ 8. funny	(h) abridge
_____ 9. soothe	(i) minuscule
_____ 10. tiny	(j) jocular

❖ Stages in Learning Vocabulary

Is there such a thing as "Ten, twenty, or thirty days to a more powerful vocabulary"? Not really. We learn words best through a series of stages, often over a period of time. The following **paradigm** suggests the varying stages of word recognition.

---

synonyms (sin´ ə nimz´) words similar in meaning to other words
paradigm (par´ ə dīm´) example or model

1. I never saw this word before.	← →	*The <u>ablation</u> has been scheduled for tomorrow.*
2. I've heard or read this word, but I don't know what it means.	← →	*His comments are too <u>sanctimonious</u>*
3. In this sentence, I think I recognize the word.	← →	*His actions were quite <u>uncouth</u> and his manners disgusting.*
4. I recognize and know the meaning of this word when I read or hear it.	← →	*They argued there had been no <u>mandate</u> from the people for the president's actions.*
5. I recognize this word when I read or hear it; I can use this word in my speaking and writing.	← →	*It can only be described as a <u>courageous</u> act.*

ACTIVITY 2.2

Classify your knowledge of each of the following words according to the stages of vocabulary development. Do not use a dictionary, and rate your own knowledge by placing a check mark in the appropriate space.

Word	STAGE 1 I never saw this word.	STAGE 2 I've heard or read this word but don't know it.	STAGE 3 I think I recognize this word.	STAGE 4 I know this word.	STAGE 5 I can use this word in speaking and writing.
1. adversity					
2. candid					
3. demise					
4. efficacious					
5. graphite					
6. insousiant					
7. omniscient					
8. tantalize					
9. theology					
10. valid					

Now that you have completed this activity, you can see that as you improve and increase your vocabulary, you will be at different stages of development.

How many words do you think you know and can define? Recent surveys of vocabulary knowledge indicate that the average high school graduate can recognize anywhere from 30,000 to 45,000 words, or fewer than 5 percent of all the words in the English language! However, because researchers define words and word knowledge differently, statistics about word knowledge can vary. Steven Pinker, a language researcher, claims that between the ages of one and eighteen, high school graduates must have been learning a new word about every ninety waking minutes.* But, unless we continue to make a **conscientious** effort to learn new words, our command of language remains limited.

❖ Developing a Superior Vocabulary

Just as there are mistaken notions about the reading process, there are also mistaken ideas about how to develop a strong vocabulary. Looking up words in the dictionary is not necessarily the best way to learn the meaning of unfamiliar words. While the dictionary is an important tool for vocabulary growth, it is not the only, or even the first, approach to finding word meanings. Why? When you stop to look up a word's meaning, you disrupt the flow of ideas and interrupt your comprehension of the reading. You can't read and look up words in the dictionary **simultaneously!**

Listing words in a notebook or memorizing lists of words also does not necessarily increase your vocabulary. **Rote** learning is difficult to retain! It is the concept or idea of the word that must be understood. Equally important is an understanding of the word's general context. For example, *murky* means "dark and gloomy" and is often used to describe water, as in the phrase "The water looks *murky*." But we

---

conscientious (kon´ shē ən´ shəs) careful to do what is right; thorough and painstaking
simultaneously (sī´ məl tā nē əs lé) existing or done at the same time
rote (rōt) memorized by repetition without understanding
*Steven Pinker, *The Language Institute: How the Mind Creates Language* (New York: Morrow, 1994) 150.

would never say "The costume looks *murky*." The word is not used in the context of describing a *costume*.

While there is not an instantaneous way to acquire a superior vocabulary, certain strategies can help you to improve it. Remember, however, that prodigious *reading always remains the best way to expand your word knowledge.*

❖ Strategies to Improve Your Vocabulary

There are at least six ways you can increase your vocabulary.

1. Learn to use the context efficiently.
2. Use the word parts (prefixes, suffixes, and roots) you already know and apply them to unknown words. Learn additional common word parts.
3. Develop a *systematic* way of your own to collect words you read and hear but whose meaning is unclear.
4. Use mnemonics with visualization and association.
5. Use the dictionary to help you pronounce words and understand their meanings.
6. Use the thesaurus to find synonyms and **antonyms.**

❖ Using the Context—A Powerful Strategy

What is context? To be more specific, what is the context of a word? Conte*xt* is often confused with the word conte*nts*. The contents of a book are the pages within that book. Context, however, refers to the writing—a word or group of words—surrounding a word. This writing can be a phrase, a sentence, or sometimes even a paragraph. Context may help you determine the meaning of an unknown word *if you take advantage of all available clues.* Moreover, it is the context that gives a word its exact meaning. For example, what is your understanding of the word *bank?*

Bank means _____ .

Its actual meaning is determined only by its use.

She placed all her money in the *bank*. (a place to deposit money)
The river*bank* overflowed from the storm. (the earthen sides of a river)
A plane appeared out of the fog, *banked*, and stopped. (tilted and caused to turn)

---

antonyms (an´ tə nims´) words opposite in meaning to other words

Remember, it is the context surrounding the word *bank* that gives this word in each sentence its **unique** meaning.

How Well Do You Use the Context?

How well do you use context? To find out, follow a two-step procedure. First, complete Activity 2.3A without any context to assist you. Write your answers in the A column. Then do Activity 2.3B, where the same words are used in a sentence. Write your answers in the B column. You should have more correct answers in the B column because the sentence context helped you with the unfamiliar word.

ACTIVITY 2.3A

Choose the correct definition and place its letter in column A.

                                                           A   B

1. inadvertently
   a. deviously
   b. approvingly
   c. indeed
   d. accidentally

2. endemic
   a. mysterious
   b. in a particular area
   c. unknown
   d. peculiar

3. impede
   a. spoil
   b. anticipate
   c. set apart
   d. hinder

4. halcyon
   a. cool
   b. stormy
   c. calm, peaceful
   d. rainy

5. indolence
   a. revision
   b. lacks dignity
   c. clumsiness
   d. laziness

---

unique (yo͞o nēk´) the only one of its kind

6. abrogated
   a. removed by authority   _____   _____
   b. amended
   c. strengthened
   d. ignored

7. sanctioned
   a. disliked   _____   _____
   b. approved
   c. amended
   d. repealed

8. vacillate
   a. waver   _____   _____
   b. agree
   c. try
   d. prove

9. officious
   a. official   _____   _____
   b. good-natured
   c. cheerful
   d. meddlesome

10. facile
   a. creative   _____   _____
   b. long
   c. easy
   d. boring

ACTIVITY 2.3B

Using context, now choose the correct definition from the list in Activity 2.3A. Place your answers in column B.

1. In the course of regulating business, the Congress, perhaps **inadvertently,** caused delay in setting up small businesses.
2. The disease seems **endemic** to that section of the country.
3. Officials believe the committee is using delay tactics to **impede** progress.
4. The resort, which is known for its **halcyon** climate, pleasant all year long, attracts visitors from around the world.
5. The sudden warm weather increased our **indolence;** we failed to complete the job.
6. When the rebels took over, they ruled by their own laws and **abrogated** the constitution.
7. They have **sanctioned** the proposed law because they know it will benefit the environment.
8. Each day she **vacillated** about whether to take the job; she could not make a decision.
9. The **officious** clerk interfered in things that were not his concern and often annoyed his co-workers.
10. A **facile** assignment is completed easily and quickly.

❖ Types of Context Clues

Two types of context clues are useful in understanding unknown words.

1. A **semantic** clue provides "meaning" information about the unknown word.
2. A **syntactic** clue provides grammatical information about the unknown word, indicating whether it is a noun, a verb, an adjective, or an adverb.

Although context clues are not always obvious and may require detective-like thinking, their use constitutes an important strategy in vocabulary development. The two types of clues are interdependent, and together they can help you in anticipating and confirming the meaning of a word. For example,

The flood was a **calamitous** event and resulted in the loss of many lives.

Recognizing the syntactic or grammar clue, you can see that the word *calamitous* is an adjective—calamitous event. By noting the semantic clue, "resulted in the loss of many lives," you can judge that the phrase *calamitous event* has something to do with a major misfortune.

Although context clues do have limitations and do not always clarify the word's **precise** meaning, their usefulness in helping to determine the general meaning of a word cannot be overemphasized.

Here are five major context clues to look for when you are puzzled by an unfamiliar word in print.

❖ Kinds of Context Clues

Definition: Direct Explanation

The easiest clue to spot, and the one most commonly used, especially in textbooks, is the definition clue. Some writers explain words directly by giving synonyms—other words that mean the same thing—and by using signal words such as *that is, is, for example, namely, in other words,* or *for instance* to direct you.

---

semantic (sə man´ tic) pertaining to the meaning of words
syntactic (sin tak´ tik) referring to the way in which words are put together grammatically
calamitous (kə lam´ i təs) distressful; disastrous
precise (pri sīs´) clearly expressed; exact

> In the skeletal system, a *foramen*, that is, an opening through a bone, serves as a passage-way for blood vessels, nerves or ligaments.
>
> John W. Hole, Jr., *Human Anatomy and Physiology*

Sometimes the writer uses punctuation marks to provide a signal to the reader that a word is being defined. The most common marks used are two commas. Dashes and parentheses are occasionally used.

> A *numismatist*, a collector of gold medals, needs considerable capital to get started in business.

Contrast

Often, words such as *but, however, yet,* or *in contrast* signal an opposite meaning.

> Her sister was always at ease with everyone she met; Minette, *however,* was quite gauche in social situations.

The word *however* indicates that a contrast will follow the first statement; therefore, *gauche* must mean the opposite of having the right manners. The dictionary definition is "lacking social grace."

Past Experience—Making an Educated Guess

You can use your own familiarity with situations to help understand or clarify a word or predict its meaning.

> Scrooge was such a *skinflint* that he wouldn't give any of his employees a Christmas gift or even the day off from work.

Even if you did not recognize the character Scrooge from Dicken's *A Christmas Carol,* your own experience could suggest that anyone unwilling to give employees time off during Christmas is miserly or stingy, a skinflint.

Summary

Sometimes, an unfamiliar word is explained in summary form.

> There was bitterness in her voice, a scowl on her face, and then an angry reply—as usual, she was in a *captious* mood as she spoke to the children.

The meaning of *captious*—quick to find fault—can be deduced from the summary preceding it.

Examples

Often, the author will give examples that relate [...] Noting these examples can help you determine the word's m[...]

> *Dieseling* happens when you shut off the engine a[...]ill chug, jump, smoke and cough, and, if you turn the key back [...]eep running.
>
> Dorothy Jacl[...] *Know About Her Car*

ACTIVITY 2.4 Practice with Context Clues

Read each of the following sentences, underline the context clues for the boldfaced words, and then write a definition for the word.

Example: Default, <u>or failure to pay the interest or principal amount of the promissory note on its due date,</u> can result in bankruptcy.

Walter Meigs et al., *Accounting: The Basis for Business Decisions*

Definition: <u>failure to pay the interest or principal amount of a promissory note on its due date.</u>

1. But it is a long leap from a matrilocal home where the father is absent, to a **matriarchal** one, in which the females take total charge from the males.

Gloria Naylor, *"The Myth of the Matriarch"*

Definition: _____

2. **Ethics**—the standards of conduct and moral judgment accepted by society—has a strong influence on business communication.

David Popenoe, *Sociology*

Definition: _____

3. **Interdiction** involves efforts aimed at stopping drugs from entering the United States. The Coast Guard, Border Patrol and Customs agents have played the most visible roles in interdiction efforts over the last few decades.

Frank Schmalleger, *Criminal Justice Today, p. 619*

Definition: _____

4. The debate revolves around a computer programmer and author of "Pretty Good Privacy," a program that lets computer users **encrypt** or "scramble" their files.

"Subpoena Follows Articles on Encryption," *San Francisco Examiner,* 12 March 1995

Definition: _____

clarify (klar´ ə fī) make or become clear

5. The most ignored fact of all about pain is that the best way to eliminate it is to eliminate the abuse. Instead, many people reach almost instinctively for the painkillers—aspirins, barbiturates, codeines, tranquilizers, sleeping pills, and dozens of other **analgesics** or desensitizing drugs.

Norman Cousins, *"Pain Is Not the Ultimate Enemy"*

Definition: _____

ACTIVITY 2.5

Look at these sentences with context clues taken from several sources: essays and articles, literature, and a textbook. After you complete the exercises, decide which area may present the most difficulty for you in using context clues. In the space provided after the exercise, explain why you think this is so.

ESSAYS AND ARTICLES

Determine the meaning of the boldfaced word from the choices. Underline the clues in the sentence and write the correct letter in the space provided.

_____ 1. Radon gas is a **carcinogen** which the EPA and others consider to be, next to cigarette smoking, the most widespread cause of lung cancer.
(Hint: What suggestion is made about cigarette smoking and lung cancer?)
(a) medicine   (b) test   (c) cancer-causing agent   (d) painkiller

_____ 2. It proved to be a campaign of **egregious** brutality, killing people and destroying their cities.
(Hint: What do words like *brutality* and *killing* suggest?)
(a) controlled   (b) outstandingly bad   (c) harmless   (d) newsworthy

_____ 3. The car bomb was the start of **carnage** in the holy city, and among the many killed were women and children.
(a) massive killings   (b) understanding   (c) renewal   (d) plans

_____ 4. A **dilemma** faces battered wives: reporting a beating might stop their mates from repeating the offense, but it might also cause them to become violent.
(a) physical exam   (b) choice between   (c) dangerous trip   (d) debt

_____ 5. The congressman has been attacked by a **barrage** of criticism because of his involvement with the scandal.
(a) explanation   (b) rapid outpouring   (c) quiet strength   (d) victim

_____ 6. The parents of an embassy guard found shot in a bar in El Salvador have had his body **exhumed** twice in an attempt to prove he was murdered.

Newsweek, 19 Sept. 1994

(a) blessed   (b) moved   (c) dug out   (d) hidden

_____ 7. The horror movie **titillated** the audience and kept them on the edge of their seats throughout the showing.

San Francisco Chronicle, 28 Sept 1994

(a) excited   (b) bored   (c) confused   (d) annoyed

_____ 8. There are many ways to **disseminate** information. One of the most effective means of getting a message across involves an easy trick, known to schoolteachers for years and years: Make learning fun.

Television Producing and Directing

(a) contradict   (b) assemble   (c) distort   (d) spread widely

THE TEXTBOOK

Determine the meaning of the boldfaced word from the choices below, and write the letter of the correct word in the space provided.

_____ 1. The most effective approaches so far have been group-oriented programs like Alcoholics Anonymous, which focus on the individual's recognition of their problem, total **abstinence,** and the emotional support of fellow alcoholics.

Psychology

(*Hint:* What does an alcoholic need to do to help solve his or her problem?)
(a) argument   (b) refraining from drinking   (c) overindulgence
(d) compromise

_____ 2. Doctors often prescribe them [drugs] for hyperactive children to lengthen attention span and control restlessness, to **narcoleptics** to keep them awake, to sufferers of short-term depression.

Psychology

(*Hint:* Why would doctors give drugs to people to keep them awake?)
(a) salesmen   (b) people who sleep excessively
(c) excessive eaters   (d) rock stars

_____ 3. Under that doctrine, wives were **chattels** of their husbands; they could not legally control their own earnings, property, or children unless they had drawn up a specific contract before marriage.

America, Past and Present

(a) partners   (b) slaves   (c) novices   (d) friends

_____ 4. Susan B. Anthony, a veteran of many reform campaigns, tried to vote in the 1872 presidential election and was fined $100 which she refused to pay. In 1890, she helped form the National American Woman Suffrage Association to work for the **enfranchisement** of women.

America, Past and Present

(a) right to vote   (b) job opportunities   (c) right to compete
(d) persuasion

_____ 5. Private **philanthropy,** born of the large fortunes of the Industrial Age, also spurred growth in higher education. Leland Stanford gave $24,000,000 to endow Stanford University.

America, Past and Present

(a) separation of desirable elements   (b) donations to a worthy cause
(c) practical attitudes   (d) new ideas

_____ 6. In addition, natural events such as earthquakes and volcanoes give the ocean a dull background rumble. **Superimposed** on this are the sounds made by the sea's many inhabitants.

Oceanography: An Introduction

(a) communicated   (b) settled beyond   (c) placed over   (d) silencing

_____ 7. Most current researchers adopt an **eclectic** approach in studying species, employing the theories and techniques of morphology, ecology, biochemistry, behavior, growth, and genetics.

Oceanography: An Introduction

(a) from one source   (b) from many sources   (c) frequently changing
(d) patterned

_____ 8. A group's culture includes its patterns of behavior as well as its possessions. An object of material culture is called an **artifact,** which means, literally, "a thing made by skill."

Edward F. Bergman, *Human Geography*

(a) diverse culture   (b) bright sunrise   (c) handmade tool
(d) fierce loyalty

CONTEXT CLUES FROM LITERATURE

Read the following sentences from literary novels and short stories. Again determine the meaning of the boldfaced word from the choices provided. Underline the clues in the sentence and write the correct letter in the space provided.

_____ 1. They had come to believe he was **invincible,** a strong muscular man with a drill sergeant's booming voice and a bricklayer's hands. . . .

Isabel Allende, *"A Discreet Miracle"*

(**Hint:** Look at all the descriptive words that help explain his personality.)
(a) hard to see   (b) hard to resist   (c) impossible to overcome
(d) easy to change

_____ 2. The frock coat (he never wore an ordinary coat) was **piebald.** That is to say, it had been black originally but now it was studded with yellowish-brown and gray spots.

Nikolai Gogol, *"The Nose"*

(**Hint:** "That is to say" is a definition clue.)
(a) torn and grimy   (b) having spotty or patchy markings   (c) ragged
(d) stolen

_____ 3. James went out into the snowy night and his thoughts were **inchoate,** unclear, but still miserable; they had nothing to tell him except rain . . . .

Taylor Caldwell, *Bright Flows the River*

(a) generous   (b) interesting   (c) undeveloped   (d) surprising

_____ 4. I felt that she was not bored, but her **reticence** puzzled me, and I wished to make her speak.

Henry James, *"Four Meetings"*

(a) unwillingness to speak   (b) abuse   (c) costume   (d) talkativeness

_____ 5. Yet Samantha remained **dauntless.** With each rejection her determination grew.

Barbara Wood, *Domina*

(a) agreeable   (b) prosperous   (c) fearless   (d) worn out

_____ 6. He lived **parsimoniously,** was frugal in food and drink, his clothes were beyond description; he looked like a beggar, but kept on saving and putting money in the bank."

Anton Chekhov, *"Gooseberries"*

(a) extravagantly   (b) far away   (c) stingily   (d) alone

_____ 7. The real truth was that I was not . . . a sissy and there had never been anything **effeminate** about me.

Anne Rivers Siddons, *Peachtree Road*

(a) careful   (b) distant and cool   (c) mistaken   (d) like a female

_____ 8. She had fallen in love with Jatin. It was **inexplicable;** she did not know how it happened, for she had known Jatin for years, at least three, and she had not thought of loving him.

Pearl S. Buck, *Come, My Beloved*

(a) bound to happen   (b) difficult to avoid   (c) easy to explain
(d) difficult to explain

In using context clues, which of the three areas—essay and articles, literature, or the textbook—proved most difficult for you, and why?

_____

_____

ACTIVITY 2.6 **Context Clues in Short Reading Selections**

As you read each of the following selections, underline the context clues that assist in explaining the meaning of each of the boldfaced words. Write your definitions in the spaces provided. Your definitions do not have to be worded exactly like those in a dictionary.

PASSAGE 1

Most of the world's 6,000 languages will be either extinct or on the road to **extinction** by the end of the next century, **linguistic** experts say.

The loss is especially acute in California, which has been called the world's third most linguistically diverse region, after New Guinea and the Caucasus.

"There are still 50 native American languages being spoken in California but not a single one of them is spoken by children. The vast majority are spoken by less than 10 individuals over 70 years old," . . . said a U.C. Berkeley linguist at the University of California, who also said native American languages were **suppressed** until the 1960s. Indian children sent to boarding schools were punished for speaking their parents' language. Now, a movement exists among California Indians to learn the elders' tongue before it's too late.

Michael Krauss, a language researcher at the University of Alaska, warned that the rate at which native tongues were dying would cause **irreparable** damage to human civilization. "I call this a catastrophe—the rate of loss of mankind's linguistic diversity," he said.

Between 20 and 50 percent of the world's languages are no longer being learned by children, he said. "For the next century, something up to 95 percent of mankind's languages will either become extinct or become **moribund** and headed toward extinction."

"World's Languages Dying at Alarming Rate," *San Francisco Examiner* 15 Feb. 1995.

1. **extinction** _____

2. **linguistic** _____

3. **suppressed** _____

4. **irreparable** _____

5. **moribund** _____

PASSAGE 2

In the spring of 1938, on the eve of his greatest triumphs, Adolf Hitler entered his fiftieth year. His physical appearance was unimpressive, his bearing still awkward. The falling lock of hair and the smudge of his moustache added nothing to a coarse and curiously undistinguished face, in which the eyes alone attracted attention. In appearance at least Hitler could claim to be a man of the people, a **plebeian** through and through, with none of the physical characteristics of the racial superiority he was always **invoking.** The quality which his face possessed was that of **mobility,** an ability to express the most rapidly changing moods, at one moment smiling and charming, at another cold and imperious, cynical and sarcastic, or swollen and **livid** with rage.

Speech was the essential medium of his power, not only over his audiences but over his own temperament. Hitler talked **incessantly,** often using words less to communicate his thoughts than to release the hidden spring of his own and others' emotions, whipping himself and his audience into anger or exaltation by the sound of his voice.

Allan Bullock, "The Dictator," *Hitler: A Study in Tyranny,* Chap. 8, 1962.

1. **plebeian** _____

2. **invoking** _____

3. **mobility** _____

4. **livid** _____

5. **incessantly** _____

PASSAGE 3

Belisa Crepusculario had been born into a family so poor they did not even have names to give their children. She came into the world and grew up in an **inhospitable** land where some years the rains became **avalanches** of water that bore everything away before them and others when not a drop fell from the sky and the sun swelled to fill the horizon and the world became a desert. Until she was twelve, Belisa had no occupation or virtue other than having withstood hunger and the exhaustion of centuries. During one **interminable** drought, it fell to her to bury four younger brothers and sisters; when she realized that her turn was next, she decided to set out across the plains in the direction of the sea, in hopes that she might trick death along the way. The land was **eroded,** split with deep cracks, strewn with rocks, fossils of trees and thorny bushes, and skeletons of animals bleached by the sun. From time to time, she ran into families who, like her, were heading south, following the **mirage** of water. Some had begun the march carrying their belongings on their backs or in small carts, but they could barely move their own bones, and after a while they had to abandon their possessions.

Isabel Allende, *The Stories of Eva Luna,* p. 10

1. **inhospitable** _____

2. **avalanches** _____

3. **interminable** _____

4. **eroded** _____

5. **mirage** _____

PASSAGE 4

Control of population growth and the selection of population groups for growth or decline in numbers is at the core of the politics of families, clans, communities, and states. The **imperative** to survive and multiply is coded into our genes. Individuals, families, communities, and states **grapple** with, and strive to control, this imperative. At this time in history, global population growth is often **denounced** as a threat to the survival of humanity. The pressure on resources in certain parts of the world causes endemic famine, disease, and misery. Discontent causes people to **migrate** on a large scale to where they believe life is better. A wide array of political measures have been used for controlling population growth worldwide. In this century they range from the violent anti-semitism in Central Europe in the 1930s and 1940s and, presently, in the violent ethnic clashes in former Yugoslavia, to peaceful programs emphasizing sex education and distribution of contraceptives. Some types of population policies have been **implemented** by drawing on military knowledge and practices; others have drawn on medical knowledge and practices.

Eugene B. Gallagher and Janardan Subedi, *Global Perspectives on Health Care* (New York: Prentice Hall, 1995) p. 312.

1. **imperative** _____

2. **grapple** _____

3. **denounced** _____

4. **migrate** _____

5. **implemented** _____

ACTIVITY 2.7 **Context Clues in a Longer Passage**

Read the following selection, noting the boldfaced words, all of which have context clues. The main clues have been underlined. After you complete the reading, answer the questions that follow.

Sydney Harris was a well-known syndicated columnist. His essays are collected in two books, *Best of Sydney J. Harris* and *Pieces of Eight* and frequently deal with that branch of semantics concerned with how the meaning of words affects our communication with one another. This essay examines one such word, *love*, how it was used by the ancient Greeks, and how we use it today.

Using Love in Whatever Way We Like

Sydney J. Harris

The word that has been most cheapened and **devalued** in our language is "love." We use it for everything—we "love" our mothers, we "love" our new car, we "love" ice cream and Mozart and picnics and being left alone. **1**

Most people suppose that first we think, and then we find words to express our thoughts. Actually, we think in and with words, and the words we have at our command shape our thoughts, rather than the other way around. **2**

Although the ancients had fewer words (because there were fewer things in the world), they discriminated more than we do among the ones they had. **3**

They had at least three different words to express what we call "love"—there was **philia,** for love **4** of family and friends and countrymen, there was **eros,** for love between the sexes; and there was **agape,** for love of God.

They did not apply the word "love" to objects **5** such as chariots and clothing and food and drink and worldly pleasures, for love is not a univocal word. A **univocal** word is one that has only a single specific meaning, and cannot be attached loosely to a wide variety of objects.

Obviously, we do not love our children in the **6** same way we love our wives or sweethearts. We do not love our country in any sense that we love the color blue or the taste of peppermint or the smell of roses. We do not love God in the way we love our pet cockatoo.

Our failure to make these verbal distinctions is **7** more than "a manner of speaking"; it is a manner of **conceptualizing** of <u>defining</u> and <u>distinguishing</u>. The words we use control and direct and limit the thoughts they express. We are spurred to action by slogans and catchwords rather than by the concrete realities they embody.

If we "love" the things that give us pleasure, **8** because they give us pleasure, we will stop loving them when they give us pain. But Job's "love" of God had nothing to do with pleasure or pain, happiness or unhappiness; it was wholly on another level of <u>trust</u> and **fealty.**

Because we use words so <u>loosely</u> and **indiscrimi-** **9** **nately,** we are able to justify almost anything we want to do. People who are willful call themselves "independent" and take their defect for a virtue, people who are **predatory** <u>call their greed</u> "enterprise" and are proud of what should shame them.

If so distinctive a word as "love" is invariably mis- **10** used and abused and flattened and coarsened, imagine what we do with language generally, every day in every way. Like Humpty Dumpty, when we use a word, it means just what we choose to make it mean, because the "meanings" are not in the words themselves, but in the people who use them.

approximately 475 words

Sydney J. Harris, excerpt from "Using Love in Whatever We Like" from *The Best of Sydney J. Harris* (New York: Houghton Mifflin). Originally appeared in the *Chicago Sun-Times.* Copyright 1986 by Sydney J. Harris. Reprinted with the permission of the *Chicago Sun-Times.*

Vocabulary Review

Write your answers in the spaces provided.

_____ 1. A **univocal** word
  (a) has two meanings.   (c) has one meaning.
  (b) has three meanings.   (d) lacks meaning.

_____ 2. The meaning of the sentence "We are spurred to action by slogans and catchwords rather than by . . . realities" means
  (a) we act too slowly and this causes problems.
  (b) we act without really understanding a situation.
  (c) we act by shouting slogans and catchwords.
  (d) both a and c.

_____ 3. According to Harris, we react more to which kind of words?
  (a) catchwords.   (c) slogans and catchwords.
  (b) newly coined words.   (d) loving words.

_____ 4. Something that is **devalued** is
  (a) praised   (c) given less worth
  (b) ignored   (d) given more worth

_____ 5. When we **conceptualize** an idea, we
  (a) blame   (c) predict
  (b) confuse   (d) think

_____ 6. Someone who is **indiscriminate** is
  (a) not careful   (c) too careful
  (b) an alarmist   (d) a racist

7. To show **fealty** to someone means to _____

_____

8. The difference in meaning for the Greek between the words **philia** and **eros** is

_____

_____

Questions for Writing/Discussion

9. Explain the meaning of this sentence: "People who are willful call themselves 'independent' and take their defect for a virtue; people who are predatory call their greed 'enterprise' and are proud of what should shame them."

_____

_____

_____

10. In what ways do you generally use the word *love?* Give three examples of things you believe you love. Show how your idea of love varies in each case. Then try to think of other words in our vocabulary that are used loosely.

_____

_____

_____

_____

_____

_____

❖ Using Word Parts

Some linguists claim that language contributions from Latin and Greek word parts outweigh all others and give meaning to over 50 percent of our words. Another way, therefore, to develop a superior vocabulary is to acquire a general knowledge of these word parts, the source particularly of many of our academic words.

To illustrate, let's examine how *benediction* differs from *malediction,* how *prediction* differs from *contradiction.* All four words share the Latin root *dic/t,* meaning "to speak or say," and a suffix ending *ion,* whose general meaning is "the condition or state of." The difference in meaning lies in the first syllable which gives each word its distinct meaning.

Word	Prefix + Root + Suffix	Word Meaning
benediction	bene ("good") + dict + ion	"speaking good"; a blessing
malediction	mal ("bad") + dict + ion	"speaking bad"; a curse; speaking evil
prediction	pre ("before") + dict + ion	"speaking before"; saying something before it happens; foretelling
contradiction	contra ("against") + dict + ion	"speaking against"; saying the opposite of something

The words *benediction* and *malediction* consist of two roots and a suffix. *Prediction* and *contradiction* consist of a prefix (*pre* and *contra*), a root (*dic/t*), and a suffix (*ion*). For some words, the literal meaning and the definition are exactly the same, as in *prediction* and *contradiction.* Although the literal meaning may not necessarily give you a word's exact meaning, it will help suggest the general sense.

Let's examine how each word part functions. We will use a variety of words.

Prefix: *Pre* means before. The prefix (a group of letters) always comes *before* the main part of the word and changes the word's meaning.

use **re**use   place **mis**place   sure **un**sure

Root: All words must have a root or stem. It is the main part of the word and carries the basic meaning of the word.

vitamin   **vita**lity   re**vita**lize   (vita = life)

Suffix: The suffix (a group of letters) comes *after* the main part of a word. Often, the suffix indicates what part of speech the word is, that is, whether it is a noun, verb, adjective, or adverb. The suffix carries only limited word meaning.

amaze amaze**ment** (n)   nation nation**al** (adj.)

special   specia**lize** (v)

Suffixes may sometimes modify a root word's meaning, as in *shape* and *shape*less (without shape). The major role of the suffix, however, is to alter the part of speech of the word.

Prefix	Root Word	New Word	Suffix	New Word
mis ("wrong")	judge	misjudge (v)	ment (n.)	misjudgment (n.)
dis ("not")	obedient	disobedient (adj.)	ly (adv.)	disobediently (adv.)
re ("again")	place	replace (v.)	able (adj.)	replaceable (adj.)

The term *affix* is sometimes used to refer to either a prefix or suffix since it means "to add" or fix to something.

Commonly Used Word Parts

The following charts list some of the most commonly used word parts. Becoming aware of their meanings will enable you to determine the definitions of many seemingly difficult words.

Write one example of your own for each word part listed in the column "Your Example." You may wish to work with a group.

ACTIVITY 2.8

PREFIXES

WORD PART	MEANING	EXAMPLE	YOUR EXAMPLE
Prefixes with negative meaning			
a, an	not; without	atheist; anonymous	_____
anti	against; opposite	antifreeze	_____
dis	not; opposite	disown; disconnect	_____
in (im before b, m, p,)*	not	inactive; immature	_____
(il before l; ir before r)		illegal; irresponsible	_____
mis	wrong	misnomer	_____
non	not	nonessential	_____
un	not	unavailable	_____
Prefixes that change time			
ante	before	antedate	_____
post	after	postgraduate	_____
pre	before	precondition	_____
re	again; back	reactivate	_____
retro	backward	retrogress	_____
Prefixes that concern placement or direction			
ab, a	away from	abduction; amoral	_____
ad (ac; af; ag; as; at)*	to, toward	admit; accept; affect; agree; assist; attend	_____
circum	around	circumstance	_____
de	down	descend	_____
ex (e, es)	out	expand; eject; escape	_____
inter	between	interview	_____
intra	within	intrastate	_____
per	through; thoroughly	perfume	_____
pro	forward; for	projection	_____

*Sound/spelling changes make the pronunciation of words easier.

sub	below	subnormal	_____
syn (sym)	together	syndrome; sympathy	_____
super	above	superhuman	_____
trans	across	transcend	_____

ROOTS

WORD PART	MEANING	EXAMPLE	YOUR EXAMPLE
audi	to hear	audition	_____
bio	life	bionics	_____
cap, capt	to take or seize	capricious	_____
cide	to kill	genocide	_____
cred	to believe	credulity	_____
dic, dict	to speak; tell	dictate	_____
duc	to lead	educate	_____
fac	do; make	artifact	_____
graph, gram	write	graphite; cardiogram	_____
luc, lum	light; shine	translucent; luminous	_____
miss, mitt	to send	dismiss; transmit	_____
ology	study of	microbiology	_____
path	feeling; suffering	pathos; pathologist	_____
phobia	fear	xenophobia	_____
phono	sound	megaphone	_____
port	carry	portable	_____
scrib, script	to write	scribble/scripture	_____
spec, spic	to look	spectator	_____
tort	to twist	distortion	_____
vers, vert	to turn	conversion; divert	_____
vita, viv	life	revitalize; vivify	_____
voc, voke	to call; voice	vocal; evoke	_____

SUFFIXES

WORD PART	WORD ROOT	EXAMPLE	YOUR EXAMPLE

Noun suffixes—usually mean "the state of," "the quality of"

ance	attend	attendance	_____
cy	constant	constancy	_____
ence	prefer	preference	_____
ion	agitate	agitation	_____
ism	true	truism	_____
ity, ty	superior; loyal	superiority; loyalty	_____
ment	astonish	astonishment	_____
ness	great	greatness	_____

Noun suffixes that refer to a person

ee	nominate	nominee	_____
ary	vision	visionary	_____
er, or	teach; instruct	teacher; instructor	_____
ist	pharmacy	pharmacist	_____

Verb suffixes usually mean "characterized by"

ate	stimulus	stimulate	_____
ize	drama	dramatize	_____
ify	class	classify	_____
WORD PART	**WORD ROOT**	**EXAMPLE**	**YOUR EXAMPLE**

Adjective Suffixes—a few have meaning as below

able, ible "capable of"	accept; sense	acceptable; sensible	_____
ful ("full of")	beauty	beautiful	_____
less ("without")	shape	shapeless	_____
ous ("full of")	courage	courageous	_____

Adverb suffixes—in most cases, _ly_ is simply added to the adjective suffix

ably	acceptable	acceptably	_____
fully	beautiful	beautifully	_____
lessly	shapeless	shapelessly	_____
ously	courageous	courageously	_____

 Check your examples with your instructor.

❖ Applying What You Know About Word Parts

ACTIVITY 2.9

A. Add one of these prefixes to the following words _to change time._

pre   post   retro   re   ante

1. active   _____

2. locate   _____

3. existence   _____

4. natal _____

5. bellum _____

B. Add one of these prefixes to the following words *to make them mean the opposite.*

im   mis   un   il   dis

1. enchanted _____

2. representation _____

3. natural _____

4. mobile _____

5. logical _____

C. The following words contain the root *vers/vert,* meaning "to turn." Match each word with the definition given; refer to the prefix list if necessary.

revert   aversion   introvert   extrovert   perverse

1. _____   turn away from what is right; disobedient

2. _____   one who turns outward; outgoing

3. _____   to turn back; return

4. _____   to turn away from; strong dislike

5. _____   one who turns within himself or herself; directs thoughts inward

D. Add a suffix meaning "one who" to the following words.

Example: **piano**   pianist

1. dermatology _____

2. reaction _____

3. tutor _____

4. alarm _____

5. cinematography _____

ACTIVITY 2.10

Completing the table below should help you realize that you already have a working knowledge of some of the most common word parts and can transfer this knowledge to new words you meet. The first one is done for you.

Prefix and Meaning	Familiar Word	New Word in Context	Your Definition of the Word
anti ("opposite")	antifreeze	The preacher and the sinner were the **antithesis** of each other.	*extreme opposite of each other*
dis ("not")	distrust	The **dissonance** from their argument awakened him.	
post ("after")	postdate	Years after his death, the firefighter was awarded the medal **posthumously.**	
circ ("around")	circle	He frequently strayed from the point, and his **circumlocution** caused him to lose the argument.	
inter ("between")	interview	**Intermediaries** from both labor and management settled the dispute.	
per ("through")	perspire	Bloodstains **permeated** the glove.	
pro ("forward")	propel	The doctor's **prognosis** made Ida optimistic; she would have a full recovery.	
re ("again")	rejoin	**Reconstruction** of the eroded highway, littered with potholes, began in January.	
sub ("under")	subway	Because of the ice storm, the frozen **subterranean** soil could not be penetrated.	
trans ("across")	transport	Still angry, John could not **transcend** his feelings.	

Complete the table in the same way as the one previously. Again, transfer your working knowledge of the roots to new words. The first one has been done for you.

Root and Meaning	Familiar Word	New Word in Context	Your Definition of the Word
dict ("speak")	dictator	The woman whispered **maledictions** at the accused kidnapper.	*saying bad things: curses*
fid ("faith")	confide	Her **infidelity** and recklessness led to a divorce.	
tort ("twist")	distort	The CEO's **extortion** of funds caused the company to collapse.	
vers ("turn")	invert	Don't travel by plane if you have an **aversion** to flying.	
vid ("see")	video	Can you **envision** the beautifully decorated tree in your mind?	
voc ("call, voice")	vocal	An **irrevocable** decision to leave home caused him loneliness and unhappiness.	
mitt/miss ("send")	dismiss	We canceled the game because of **intermittent** rain.	
spec ("look")	spectator	In **retrospect,** considering his decision, he was happy.	
chron ("time")	chronic	Mainframe computers are an **anachronism** today.	
dem ("people")	democracy	**Demographic** studies give us an insight into people's lifestyles.	
graph ("write")	graffiti	According to the **seismographic** reading, it was a 6.6 earthquake.	

More About the Suffix

Recall that the major role of the suffix is to derive a new word that is usually a different part of speech from the root word.

ACTIVITY 2.11

Write the derived or suffixed word and the new part of speech. You may have to adjust the spelling of words marked with an asterisk. The first one is done for you.

Suffix and Part of Speech	Root Word	Suffixed Word	Part of Speech
ible (adj.)	access (v.)	*accessible*	*adj.*
ance (n.)	repent (v.)		
ate (v.)	active*(v.)		
ent (adj.)	fraud* (n.)		
ity (n.)	vulgar (adj.)		
ion (n.)	rebel* (v.)		
ive (adj.)	decision* (n.)		
ize (v.)	immortal (adj.)		
ial (adj.)	torrent (n.)		
ly (adv.)	adept (adj.)		
ment (n.)	denounce (v.)		
ous (adj.)	harmony* (n.)		

❖A Personal Word Bank

How can you remember the meanings of new words? Which words should you remember? You need to be selective in your choices and concentrate on those words that appear repeatedly in your reading, words you see frequently but whose meaning is unclear.

Often textbook terms will be given in a **glossary** or printed in boldface type or italics to signal their importance. Instructors frequently point out words that you must commit to memory. Learning just 10 new words a week increases your vocabulary by 500 words a year.

Starting a Personal Word Bank

Many students create their own personal vocabulary system for mastering new words by using index cards. Such a system is likely to be best suited for your needs because

1. *You* decide which words you want and need to add to your vocabulary.
2. *You* collect them from your reading or listening.

Just selecting words **randomly** from the dictionary and noting their definitions is not productive, as the definitions are unrelated to a context. Again, when you read, find words that appear frequently but whose meaning is unclear. Have a stack of 3″ by 5″ index cards handy for your word notations. Also carry a few extra cards with you to class to jot down important lecture terms you hear.

In building your own word bank, follow these steps.

1. On the front side of the card, neatly write or print in large letters the word you want to remember and the part of speech.
2. Beneath it, write the **phonetic** spelling to help you with pronunciation.
3. Beneath that, copy the context phrase or sentence in which the word appeared. This phrase/sentence will help jog your memory and help you to retain the meaning of the word.

Sample Front Side of a Vocabulary Card

> *adjective*
>
> *immutable*
>
> *i myōō´ tə bəl*
>
> *Laws of nature, immutable and lasting, have challenged scientists for centuries.*

---

glossary (glos´ ə rē) list of specialized words with their definitions
randomly (ran´ dəm lē) having no particular pattern or purpose
phonetic (fə net´ ik) the way it actually sounds

4. On the back of the card, write a short definition of the word, the definition that applies to the phrase or sentence context.

5. Beneath the definition, write a sentence of your own, using the word.

Never-changing; unchanging

The CEO's decision remained immutable—the company would not modernize.

Sample Back Side of a Vocabulary Card

When you have five to ten cards, begin practicing with them every day, pronouncing and defining the words.

Choosing Your Words to Begin

Construct your first vocabulary card by choosing a word from the following remarks by Howard Cosell, a well-known former sports broadcaster.

HOWARD COSELL SPEAKS

- "Arrogant, pompous, obnoxious, vain, cruel, verbose, a showoff. I have been called all of these. Of course, I am."
- "There's one thing about (broadcasting): There is no place for talent. That's why I don't belong. I lack mediocrity."
- "Boxing is the only sport in the world where the clear intention is for one person to inflict bodily harm upon the other person, mainly to the head where brain damage must ensue . . . I don't think improvements or controls are the answer. I think the answer is abolition."
- "If ever there was a trailblazer, a broadcaster sought to bring sports out of the juvenile, out of the banal—this, you see, is my mission. I have been an electronic first, and I don't mean that egotistically."
- "Working with two ex-jocks (on 'Monday Night Football'), I had to pick my spots, knowing when to make observations and editorial comments with maximum impact, and rescue viewers from being bored to tears with an endless stream of nonsensical football jargon."

San Jose Mercury, 24 Apr. 1995: 11A

Can you define *arrogant, pompous, obnoxious, verbose, mediocrity, abolition, trailblazer, banal, egotistically,* and *jargon*? If not, select some of these words and begin your vocabulary card collection now.

Vocabulary Sheet

Copy your words on the Vocabulary Collections sheet on page 54 for practice. Each time you define a word correctly, record a plus (+). Each time you cannot recall its meaning, record a minus (−). Three successive pluses for each word indicate you probably know that word. You may wish to photocopy the sheet.

❖ Using Mnemonics

Visualization and Association

One way to remember new words is to repeat a word and its definition while studying your vocabulary card collection. Another effective memory technique is to make vivid associations or to visualize information. Two principles of memory training apply in learning unfamiliar words.

1. It is always easier to remember things that have meaning than to remember things that do not.
2. The mind can think in pictures.

When you come across a new word you want to remember, associate or relate it to a word or idea you already know. For example, suppose you wanted to learn the word *arduous* from the sentence "Learning vocabulary words need not be an arduous task." Here is how you might use association: *arduous* sounds like *harduous.* Even though there is no such word as *harduous,* you can use this made-up term as a **mnemonic** to help you associate the new word, *arduous,* with one you already know, *hard.* Once you have made an association, try to create a visual image. If you exaggerate the image somewhat, you will recall it more easily. Picture yourself, perhaps, with stacks of vocabulary cards and several dictionaries, trying to learn a new word: *arduous.*

Study the following table to see how this technique works.

---

mnemonic (ni män´ ik) of or helping the memory

VOCABULARY COLLECTIONS

Name_____

Word	Practice Dates										
1											
2											
3											
4											
5											
6											
7											
8											
9											
10											
11											
12											
13											
14											
15											
16											
17											
18											
19											
20											
21											
22											
23											
24											
25											
26											
27											
28											
29											
30											

Plus (+) = Correct   Minus (−) = Incorrect — Study Again

VOCABULARY COLLECTIONS

Word	Practice Dates									
31										
32										
33										
34										
35										
36										
37										
38										
39										
40										
41										
42										
43										
44										
45										
46										
47										
48										
49										
50										
51										
52										
53										
54										
55										
56										
57										
58										
59										
60										

Plus (+) = Correct   Minus (−) = Incorrect — Study Again

Word You Want to Remember	Definition		Association
callow (kal´ ō)	inexperienced; immature	sounds like	*shallow.* If something is shallow, it's not very deep.
jounce (jouns)	the compression of a suspension spring (auto-tech term)	sounds like	*bounce.* When something bounces, it springs.
eschew (es chōō´)	to shun, evade, or avoid	sounds like	*shoo.* If you shoo something away, you want to avoid it.
libelous (lī´ bel əs)	an act that can injure a person's reputation unjustly	sounds like	*lie.* When you lie, someone can get hurt.

Practice with Visualization and Association

Examine the definitions for the following words and then make up some associations and visualization clues. Compare your responses with those of your classmates.

1. hirsute (hur´ sōot) hairy
2. impale (im pāl´) to pierce with something pointed; to torture or kill by fixing on a sharp stake
3. stupefaction (stōō pə fak´ shən) the act of being amazed or astounded
4. myopic (mī äp´ ik) lacking insight; nearsighted
5. insipid (in sip´ id) tasteless, flat, bland

Sketching the Meaning on a Card

Another way to use visualization and associations in trying to remember words is to sketch out ideas on your vocabulary cards to help illustrate a word's meaning. Examine the sample illustrating this procedure on page 57 and then make a sketch for one of the words you have chosen to learn with your own vocabulary cards.

❖ Etymology

Studying a word's etymology, that is, its origin or history, is another method to aid recall. Once you associate the word with a story or visualize an interesting situation related to a word's history, you make it easy to learn the word permanently. The word *bowdlerize*, for example, means to expurgate, or to leave out or change offensive words in a passage. *Bowdlerize* derives its meaning from a person. Dr. Thomas Bowdler was an English editor who in 1818 published an edition of Shakespeare's works in which he left out words or phrases he found personally offensive. To

Sample Vocabulary Card Sketched

remember the meaning of *bowdlerize,* you might picture someone cutting out the words in a book with a huge pair of scissors and you should easily recall the word's meaning.

Investigate any of the following words, each derived from a person's name. You may consult an **unabridged** dictionary or a book such as Nancy Sorel's *Word People.**

boycott	macadam	narcissism
chauvinism	malapropism	nicotine
gerrymander	maudlin	protean
guillotine	mausoleum	pyrrhic
machiavellian	mesmerize	sadism

❖ The Dictionary

You will not always be able to figure out a word's meaning from the context or the word parts and may need to use the dictionary. The key to using a dictionary successfully is to be aware of the aids it provides a reader: a word's correct pronunciation, spelling, parts of speech, various meanings, and derivation or word history.

---

unabridged (un´ ə brijd´) not shortened

*Nancy Caldwell Sorel, *Word People* (New York: American Heritage Press, 1970).

GUIDE WORDS: Two words, generally printed at the top pages of the dictionary, indicate alphabetically what words are included on a page; the left word signals the *first* word and the right one the *last* word on a page.

Assume the following guide words are at the top of a dictionary page.

flood   **flounce**

Place a check mark next to each word that would be listed on the page.

_____ 1.   florid
_____ 2.   flotilla
_____ 3.   flourish
_____ 4.   flout
_____ 5.   fluent

PRONUNCIATION KEY: Helps you to say the word correctly. For a word to actually be "yours," not only should you know its meaning, but you should feel comfortable using it in writing and speaking. The dictionary gives you the phonetic spelling immediately following the listing of the word, either in parenthesis or between slanted lines. The pronunciation key may be found at the front of the dictionary and, sometimes, at the bottom of pages. If you consult more than one dictionary, you may find a slight variation in pronunciation.

Three special markings **facilitate** pronunciation.

1.   *Long and short vowels:* Long vowels are marked with a line (¯) called a *macron*, for example, āimless (ām lis). Short vowels have a curved mark (˘) called a *breve*, for example, ăgony (ăg ə nē). Some dictionaries do not place any mark over short vowels; therefore, in these dictionaries all unmarked vowels are short. A long vowel (so called because it takes longer to say) is simply the name of the vowel: *a, e, i, o, u.* The short vowel takes less time to say, hence its name.

2.   *Stressed and unstressed syllables:* Stress means the degree of loudness or harshness with which a syllable is spoken. Stress is indicated in one of three ways.

     a.   An unmarked syllable indicates the weakest stress.

     b.   A bold mark (´) indicates the strongest stress.

     c.   A lighter mark (´) indicates a light stress.

     Which pronunciation is correct, moth ER´ or MOTH´ er? With any word, if you cannot decide what syllable to stress, try using the word in a sentence.

3.   *Schwa:* This mark is written like an upside-down *e* (ə). Its sound, "uh," often replaces the sound of the short vowels *a, e, i, o,* and *u* in unstressed syllables. The sound is "shorter" and less definite than even that of short vowels. Try pronouncing each of the following words, listening for the "uh" sound:

     a̲stonish   unrave̲l   qualit̲y   pard̲on   s̲uccess

---

facilitate (fə´ sil´ ə tāt) make easier; aid

FIGURE 2-1

Entries in *The American Heritage Dictionary of the English Language,* edited by Peter Davies (New York: Dell, 1987) p. 83. Copyright © 1983, Houghton Mifflin Company. Reprinted by permission of publisher.

---

bourbon/boycott

box·car (boks kar) *n.* An enclosed railway car used to carry freight.

box·er¹ (bŏk´ sər) *n.* One who boxes, esp. professionally.

box·er² (bŏk´ sər) *n.* A short-haired dog with a brownish coat and a square-jawed muzzle. [G. < BOXER¹.]

box·ing (bŏk´ sing) *n.* The sport of fighting with the fists.

box office *n.* A ticket office, as of a theater.

box·wood (bŏks´ wŏŏd´) *n.* The box³. 2. The hard wood of the box tree.

boy (boi) *n.* A male child or a youth. *–interj.* A word used as a mild exclamation. [ME boi.] **—boy´hood´** *n.* **—boy´ish** *adj.* **—boy´ish·ness** *n.*

boy·cott (boi´kŏt´) *v.* To abstain from using, buying, or dealing with, as a means of protest. [< Charles C. Boycott (1832-97).] **—boy´cott´** *n.*

Let's assume you need to find the word *boycott.* Look at Figure 2.1, which was reproduced from a dictionary. Note the guide words **bourbon | boycott.** The entry word is printed in boldface type with a centered dot separating the two syllables. Note the pronunciation in parentheses. The next item in this entry is a small italicized *v.,* indicating the word is a verb. The definition follows, and next, in brackets, is the etymology or word history. Then the entry word is repeated, followed by *n.* for noun.

ACTIVITY 2.12

Practice with a dictionary entry. To strengthen your ability to use the dictionary, study Figure 2.2 and answer the following questions about the word *carnivorous.*

1. List what the guide words might be.   _____

2. How many syllables does the word have?   _____

3. Does *sit* or *hive* rhyme with the second syllable of *carnivorous?*   _____

4. What part of speech is it?   _____

5. What language does the word come from?   _____

6. What is the difference between *carnivorous* and the word that precedes it?   _____

car·ni·val (kär′nə-vəl) *n.* 1. The season just before Lent, marked by merrymaking and feasting. 2. A traveling amusement show. [Ital. *carnevale.*]

car·ni·vore (kär′nə-vor′, -vōr′) *n.* A flesh-eating mammal, esp. one of a group including dogs, cats, and bears.

car·niv·o·rous (kär-niv′ər-əs) *adj.* 1. Belonging or pertaining to the carnivores. 2. Flesh-eating or predatory. [Lat. *carnivorus.*] **—car·niv′o·rous·ly** *adv.* **—car·niv′o·rous·ness** *n.*

car·ny (kär′nē) *n., pl.* **-nies.** Also **car·ney** *pl.* **-neys.** *Slang.* 1. A carnival. 2. One who works with a carnival.

car·ol (kär′əl) *n.* A song of praise or joy, esp. for Christmas. *—v.* **-oled** or **-olled, -ol·ing** or **·ol·ling.** 1. To celebrate in song. 2. To sing joyously. [< OFr. carole.] **—car′ol·er** *n.*

car·om (kär′əm) *n.* 1. A billiards shot in which the cue ball successively strikes two other balls. 2. A collision followed by a rebound. *—v.* 1. To collide with and rebound.

FIGURE 2-2

Entries in *The American Heritage Dictionary of the English Language,* edited by Peter Davies. (New York: Dell Publishing, 1987), p. 107. Copyright © Houghton Mifflin Company. Reproduced by permission of publisher.

Finding the Exact Meaning

To use the dictionary to improve your vocabulary, you need to find the *exact* meaning of the word as it is used in context. The problem, however, is that the dictionary often lists several meanings for given words and even several parts of speech. Dictionary word entries such as these are called combined entries.

Below is such a word entry from the *American Heritage Dictionary* for the word *say.* Notice the different parts of speech for *say,* all italicized.

v	= verb
tr.	= transitive verb (a transitive verb takes an object)
intr.	= intransitive verb (an intransitive verb does not take an object)
n	= noun
adj.	= adjective
adv.	= adverb

say (sā) *v.* said (sĕd), say-ing, says (sĕz).—*tr.* 1. To utter aloud, pronounce. 2. To express in words. 3. To state: declare. 4. To repeat or recite: *say grace* 5. To report or maintain:

allege: "*They say that falling in love is wonderful*" (Irving Berlin) 6. To indicate: show: *The clock says it's 5:00 P.M.* 7. To estimate or suppose: assume: *Let's say that you're right—intr.* To make a statement or express an opinion.—*n.* 1. A positive assertion or assurance: *We're risking this on your say.* 2. A turn or chance to speak. 3. The right or power to influence a decision; voice: *have one's say:—adv.* 1. Approximately: *There were, say, 500 people present* 2. For instance: *a woodwind, say an oboe—idiom,* that is to say. In other words. [ME *sayen* < OE *secgan.*]

The different definitions are numbered, each pointing out a very specific meaning for *say.* Note that separate definitions are given for *say* when it is used as a verb, noun, and adverb. The first definition indicates that *say* means "to utter aloud, pronounce."

ACTIVITY 2.13

Find additional meanings for *say.*

1. If one says grace, the word *say* means _____

2. What is the meaning of *say* in "They say that falling in love is wonderful"?

   _____ What part of speech is it? _____

3. How many noun definitions are there? _____ List one of them. _____

   _____

4. What part of speech is *say* in "There were, say, 500 people present"?

   _____

5. What is the meaning of *say* in "Let's say you are right"? _____

   _____ What part of speech is it? _____

As you can see, one word can have several different meanings, while several can sometimes mean the same thing, such as *car* and *automobile.*

Review the following list of 100 ways to express the word *said,* each with a slightly different meaning. Were you to make a point about something in a gentle way, you might choose to use the word *suggested* rather than *said.* If you wanted to indicate anger, you might use *warned* rather than *said.*

One Hundred Ways of Saying Said

1. acknowledged	26. confessed	51. expressed	76. recited
2. admitted	27. confided	52. foretold	77. recounted
3. advised	28. confirmed	53. growled	78. reiterated
4. affirmed	29. consented	54. hinted	79. related
5. alleged	30. considered	55. imparted	80. remarked
6. announced	31. consoled	56. implied	81. repeated
7. answered	32. contended	57. indicated	82. replied
8. argued	33. countered	58. informed	83. reported
9. asked	34. crowed	59. inquired	84. requested
10. asserted	35. cursed	60. insinuated	85. responded
11. avowed	36. declaimed	61. insisted	86. retorted
12. bellowed	37. declared	62. intimated	87. revealed
13. blasted	38. denied	63. jabbered	88. specified
14. blurted	39. described	64. maintained	89. spoke
15. boasted	40. dictated	65. mentioned	90. stated
16. cautioned	41. disclosed	66. mumbled	91. stressed
17. charged	42. discussed	67. murmured	92. submitted
18. chattered	43. divulged	68. muttered	93. suggested
19. chuckled	44. emphasized	69. noted	94. told
20. cited	45. encouraged	70. notified	95. urged
21. claimed	46. exaggerated	71. pleaded	96. uttered
22. commended	47. exclaimed	72. predicated	97. verbalized
23. commented	48. explained	73. proclaimed	98. viewed
24. conceded	49. expostulated	74. pronounced	99. voiced
25. concluded	50. expounded	75. reasoned	100. warned

Suffixed Forms in the Dictionary

One difficulty with using the dictionary is that you often are searching for a word with a suffixed form, words such as cruel*ty*, astonish*ment,* or obedient*ly*. The paperback dictionary, usually an abridged or shortened form, does not always have the suffixed form as an entry word but instead places it at the very end of the definitions. Therefore you may have difficulty finding it as an entry word.

> **as·ton·ish** (ə stăn´ĭsh) pf. [<L. exintens. + *tonare*, to thunder] to fill with sudden surprise; amaze —**as·ton´ish·ing** *adj.* —**as·ton´ish·ing·ly** *adv.* —**as·ton´ish·ment** *n.*
> **o·be·di·ent** (ō bē´dē ənt) *adj.* obeying or willing to obey — **o·be´di·ence** *n.* — **o·be´di·ent·ly** *adv.*
> **cru·el** (krōō´əl) *adj.* [see prec.] causing pain and suffering; pitiless — **cru´el·ly** *adv.* — **cru´el·ty** *n., pl. -ties*

A change in the pronunciation of the word can occur when a suffix is added since the stress on particular syllables changes. Three common pronunciation changes are with the suffixes *ic, ity,* and *ion.* Adding these suffix endings to words places the stress on the syllable *before* each of these suffixes. Abridged dictionaries do not usually show these stress changes.

Examples: ANgel   anGELic   FEASible   feasiBILity   DOMinate   dominAtion

❖ The Thesaurus

Unlike the dictionary, which gives the definitions of words, the thesaurus lists synonyms, words meaning almost the same thing, and antonyms, words opposite in meaning.

Before you view a sample entry from a thesaurus that lists words related to *talk,* write as many synonyms as you can for this word.

Words Similar in Meaning to *Talk*

_____   _____

_____   _____

_____   _____

_____   _____

Compare your listing now with the one from *Roget's Thesaurus* on page 64. How many of the synonyms listed in the thesaurus for *talk* did you recognize? Did you know, for example, words such as *discourse, repartee,* or *banter?* These words are synonymous with *talk,* but each word has its own shade of meaning.

As you can see, the dictionary is the source to use when you want the meaning of a word clarified, while the thesaurus is the source to use for finding substitute terms for a particular word.

TALK.—I. *Nouns,* talk, speech, soliloquy; somniloquy, somniloquence, ventriloquism; nasalization, rhinolalia.

reference, allusion, advertence, innuendo, insinuation, insinuendo, hint. conversation, converse, tête-à-tête (*F.*), chat, chitchat, confabulation, commune, causerie (*F.*), colloquy, dialogue, duologue, interlocution, parlance, repartee, pleasantries, small talk; banter, chaff, badinage, persiflage, raillery, *blague* (*F.*), discussion, argument, conference, consultation, deliberation, negotiation, palaver, parley, panel discussion, ventilation, *Kaffeeklatsch* (*Ger.*), *pourparler* (*F.*), symposium.

discourse, disquisition, monologue, descant, dissertation, expatiation, oration, exhortation, peroration, epilogue, screed, harangue; lecture, chalk talk, speech, address, allocution, prelection, declamation, recitation.

oratory, elocution, expression, eloquence, rhetoric, grandiloquence, magniloquence, multiloquence, command of words (*or* language), gift of gab (*colloq.*).

talkativeness, garrulity, loquacity, volubility, logorrhea (*med.*)

talker, speaker, spokesman, mouthpiece, prolocutor; soliloquist, somniloquist, ventriloquist; converser, conversationalist, conversationist.

discusser, discussant, conferee, consultant, deliberator, negotiator, negotiant; chairman, chair, leader, symposiarch; panel, round table.

discuss, talk over, deliberate, argue, canvass, palaver, parley, thrash (*or* thresh) out, ventilate; confer with, advise with, consult with, negotiate.

chatter, babble, chaffer, drool (*slang*), gab, gabble, gibber, gossip, jabber, jargon, jaw (*slang*), maunder, patter, prate, prattle, rattle on, tattle, tittle-tattle, twaddle, twattle, whiffle, yammer, blab, blather, blether, burble, cackle, clack.

discourse, hold forth, descant, dissertate, expatiate, stump (*colloq.*), speechify (*jocose*), spout, orate, perorate, harangue, spellbind; lecture, speak, prelect, deliver a speech, declaim, recite; ad-lib, extemporize, improvise; sermonize, moralize, preach, pontificate.

discourser, public speaker, orator, elocutionist, rhetor, speechmaker, rhetorician, Hermes, Demosthenes, Cicero, spellbinder, lecturer, prelector; monologist *or* monologuist, interlocutor.

II. *Verbs.* talk, speak, say, utter, pronounce, soliloquize, ventriloquize, somniloquize, rhapsodize; drawl, chant, drone, intone, nasalize; talk about, comment on, describe, give voice to, noise of, premise, broach. mention, cite, enumerate, specify, itemize, recite, recount, rehearse, relate; refer to, advert to, allude to, harp on.

talk to, address, apostrophize, buttonhole, accost, harangue; *tutoyer* (*F.*); salute, hail, call to, greet; invoke, appeal to, memorialize.

converse, chat, chitchat, collogue, commune, confabulate, confab, coze, talk together, hold (carry on, join in, *or* engage in) a conversation.

whisper, susurrate, stage-whisper, murmur, mumble, mutter.

spout, gush, slobber, hedge, equivocate, blarney, palter, prevaricate, snuffle, vapor.

growl, grumble, mutter, bark; rant, rave.

stutter, stammer, stumble, falter, lisp, splutter, sputter.

III. *Adjectives.* spoken, oral, unwritten, noncupative (*chiefly of wills*), parol (*law*); phonetic, phonic, voiced, lingual.

eloquent, rhetorical, grandiloquent, magniloquent; Demosthenian, Ciceronian, Tullian.

conversational, chatty, colloquial, communicative, conversable.

talkative, loquacious, gabby, chattering, chatty, garrulous, mouthy, voluble.

See also ABSURDITY, EXPRESSION, GREETING, HINT, INFORMATION, LANGUAGE, RUMOR, STATEMENT, TEASING, VOICE, WORD, WORDINESS. *Antonyms*—See SILENCE.

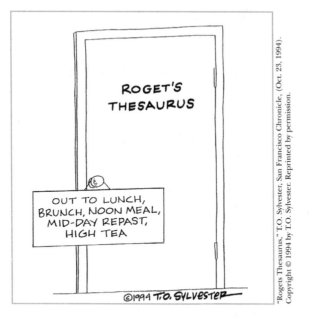

ROGET'S
THESAURUS

OUT TO LUNCH,
BRUNCH, NOON MEAL,
MID-DAY REPAST,
HIGH TEA

©1994 T.O. SYLVESTER

"Rogets Thesaurus," T.O. Sylvester, San Francisco Chronicle, (Oct. 23, 1994). Copyright © 1994 by T.O. Sylvester. Reprinted by permission.

❖ Figurative Language

While reading, you may encounter words that instructors refer to as "figurative language." The term is sometimes confusing because it has nothing to do with figures or numbers. Rather, in figurative language a particular word or phrase is not used literally but is used in a different way. Figurative language, then, consists of words or phrases departing from their usual meaning. Included in this type of language are *similes* and *metaphors,* which compare dissimilar things, making statements more vivid and thereby capturing the reader's attention. Sometimes another form of figurative language called *hyperbole,* or deliberate exaggeration, is used for emphasis. Figurative language is dealt with in more detail in Chapter 8, along with the denotation and connotation of words.

For now, these brief definitions and examples are given to help you recognize figurative language as you read.

ACTIVITY 2.14

The figurative language is underlined.

Simile: A comparison between otherwise dissimilar things using the words *like* or *as.* "Lolling, singing, and rehearsing speeches in his tub, Churchill <u>flopped about like a hefty porpoise.</u>" *Smithsonian,* "Cleanliness Has Only Recently Become a Virtue"

Explain what this means. _____

_____

Metaphor: A comparison between otherwise dissimilar things without using the words *like* or *as:* "<u>Americans are wedded by proximity to a common culture.</u>"
"Does America Still Exist?"
Explain what this means. _____

_____

Hyperbole: A deliberate exaggeration for emphasis. "<u>Only a polar bear could live in that house</u>; everyone walked about with heavy sweaters, scarves, and gloves."
Explain what this means.

_____

❖ Summary

English has over 1 million words, but most of us use only a fraction of that number. Words consist of two types: informal words used in everyday conversation and formal words used in both reading and writing in more academic settings. Formal words often have their roots in Latin and Greek; knowing how to use them leads to a superior vocabulary.

Words are learned in stages; therefore, in order to improve your vocabulary, you must make a conscientious effort to add new words to your existing vocabulary. Wide and varied reading continues to be the best approach, but additional strategies are important.

Using the context while reading is one of the best methods, as writers provide several kinds of context clues that can help unlock the meaning of unknown words. Learning the meanings of the most widely used word parts—prefixes, roots, and suffixes—can also boost vocabulary. Other aids include developing a personal word bank, visualizing and associating words through the use of mnemonics, and finding out the etymology or history of particular words. The dictionary helps you focus on the exact meaning of a word, while the thesaurus aids you in finding synonyms or antonyms for particular words.

While reading, you will encounter figurative language—words and phrases that depart from their usual meaning—used to enhance language and capture your interest.

Chapter 2 Vocabulary Review

Using the Context: Select the appropriate word from the words given below and write it in the space provided. Use the context to help determine the word's meaning. You will not use all the words.

abridged	conscientious	inflections	rote
antonyms	erudite	mnemonics	synonyms
clarify	glossary	phonetic	unabridged

The instructor was determined to help make her students more knowledgeable or

(1) _____ through vocabulary study. First, she suggested that

everyone buy an inexpensive, portable (2) _____ dictionary for

everyday use. It would be more practical than an (3) _____ one, which would have more words than could be learned in a brief school term. She said students would find a portable dictionary useful whenever they needed to

(4) _____ or understand the meaning of unfamiliar words. Then, she suggested that everyone also buy a thesaurus, which is a book mainly of

(5) _____ so that the students could substitute new words for those they already know and may overuse. Both the dictionary and the thesaurus often

list word opposites, called (6) _____.

The teacher taught them how to use memory tricks called (7) _____.

She emphasized that they needed to make a (8) _____ effort not only to learn the meanings but also to learn how to pronounce these words. She

discouraged (9) _____ learning, or memorizing without understanding. Now, all she had to do was sit back and enjoy the sophisticated tones, or

(10) _____, emanating from her students as they spoke.

Selection 1: **ESSAY**

 Preparation for Reading

The following essay, *Double-Talk,* was written by William Lutz, a professor of English at Rutgers University and the author of *Doublespeak,* a classic text concerned with the misuse of language in both business and government in order to conceal the truth.

Note the meaning of these boldfaced words before reading. They are underlined in the text.

euphemistic language	substituting inoffensive words for offensive or harsh ones
visual **acuity**	sharpness or keeness of vision
aggregate living community	entire amount
consensus among all users	general agreement; collective opinion
camouflage our problems	conceal or disguise
outright **bigotry**	attitude of intolerance or prejudice
prove to be **irreparable**	incapable of being repaired or mended

Preview, then read the selection.

Double-Talk

William Lutz

William Lutz

1 Lately I have become fascinated with the growth of a new kind of <u>euphemistic</u> language called "politically correct," or P.C. Since the words we use reveal how we see the world—and how we want others to see it—people who use P.C. language want us to see the world their way—and act accordingly. Just for instance: In everyday usage fat people may be called *stout, stocky, overweight, heavy* or even *fat.* But in P.C. language they are *calorically disadvantaged, differently sized,* or are *size-acceptance advocates.* Going even further, P.C. language has created new oppressions: *sizeism,* the bias against the *differently sized* that is practiced by *sizists;* and *lookism,* the belief that some people are easier on the eyes than others. (I guess I'm guilty of *lookism;* I do indeed find some people easier on the eyes than others—my wife, for example.)

2 I call my two cats pets, but in P.C. language they're *animal companions, friends* or *protectors.* Well, in some ways, cats *are* friends and companions, but they're still pets, and I don't treat them the same way I treat my friends (nor do my friends treat me the way my cats do). Thanks anyway, but I'd like to reserve "friend" and "companion" for the important human relationships in my life.

3 In my youth I spent some time at a Shriners Hospital for Crippled Children in Chicago.

Most of us in that hospital had had the same bad experience with polio. Sure, we were crippled in one way or another, and we knew we were, but the word *crippled* never bothered us. What bothered us were the people who treated us as if we were untouchables. It was the *actions* of others, not their words, that hurt. Now, of course, thanks to P.C., we would be described as *physically challenged, uniquely abled, differently abled, orthopedically impaired,* or as having *differing abilities.* Just as blind people have become *differently sighted, visually impaired, print handicapped,* or have *reduced visual acuity,* and people who stutter are *speech impaired.* (What's next: Will someone who's dead be called *differently alive?*)

I have never been fond of the term *senior citizen,* but its meaning is certainly clearer than *chronologically gifted.* And I have no problem with *retirement community;* what is gained by calling it a *senior aggregate living community?* In my language, kids misbehave sometimes, but in P.C. they *engage in negative attention-getting;* and they don't just learn to read any more but to *interact with print.* 4

Racial and ethnic groups have always been sensitive to the terms applied to them, and surely we should call them what they want to be called. But to avoid chaos they need to agree among themselves; and we need a consensus among all users of the language as to what words mean. In P.C., for instance, *Indian* and *Native American* have been replaced by 5 *Indigenous People, Amerind* or *Abo-American,* short for *Aboriginal-American.* How many people really know what these terms mean? And are they really an improvement over the terms they are supposed to replace?

To their credit, many people who insist on P.C. usage believe that changing our language can eventually change our thinking and thus our behavior—thereby eliminating racism, sexism and all the other isms we deplore. I disagree. We can camouflage our problems, ranging from thoughtlessness to outright bigotry, with fancy "correct" words, but we can't cure them. Instead, we lull ourselves into the false sense that, in calling a rose by another name, we've changed it. 6

I find much of P.C. language absurd and funny—so why do I care? I am concerned, as I said, that its users want to force their view of the world, its people and its problems, on the rest of us. But I have another concern as well: P.C. language attempts to gloss over and distort truth—to prettify it. As George Orwell warned us, "if thought corrupts language, language can also corrupt thought." Compassion must temper truth and reality at times, as when we call mentally retarded children *exceptional* children; but compassion and sensitivity must never be the reason for compromising truth and reality as we experience it. The damage we do to our words, to our minds and to our society may prove to be irreparable. 7

approximately 600 words

William Lutz, "Double-Talk," *Family Circle* 26, Nov. 1991: 168. Reprinted by permission.

COMPREHENSION CHECK

Part I

General Comprehension Questions: Literal and Interpretive

Write the correct letter in the space provided.

_____ 1. *P.C.* stands for
   a. perfectly correct.   c. practically correct.
   b. politically correct.   d. precisely correct.

_____ 2. According to the essay, *lookism*   a. using foul language.
            actually refers to   b. stockiness or stoutness.
                                            c. attractiveness or unattractiveness.
                                            d. women and not men.

_____ 3. Insofar as the words *friend* and   a. use more appropriate words for
            companion are used, the author   them.
            wishes people would   b. refer to their pets by these terms.
                                            c. treat one another more civilly.
                                            d. use them only to refer to human
                                               relationships.

_____ 4. In his youth, Lutz evidently had   a. an accident.
            become crippled because he   b. been engaged in street fights.
            had   c. a diving accident.
                                            d. polio.

_____ 5. The writer believes that P.C. can   a. sexism.
            help eliminate   b. racism.
                                            c. both a and b.
                                            d. none of the above.

_____ 6. The P.C. phrase "engage in   a. misbehaving children.
            negative attention-getting" refers b. cranky adults.
            to   c. stubborn pets.
                                            d. angry ethnic groups.

7. What is meant by this statement: "If thought corrupts language, language can

   also corrupt thought"? _____

   _____

8. P.C. terms are used to describe people who are (a) overweight, (b) impaired in
   some way, (c) older, and (d) racially or ethnically varied. Which category of P.C.
   terms used to characterize groups do you find most inappropriate, and why? Are
   there any which you believe are appropriate? _____

   _____

Part II
Application Questions for Writing/Discussion

9. Lutz states that some advocates of P.C. believe that changing our language can eventually change our thinking and behavior. Do you agree with this statement?

   Why or why not? _____

   _____

   _____

10. A host of terms such as *letter carrier, chairperson,* and *fire fighter* have changed from words formerly ending in *man.* Do you believe this has brought about any

   improvement in women's status, roles, and careers? _____

   _____

Repressive Celibate and the Seven Politically Correct Height-Challenged.

What does this cartoon say about political correctness? Have we gone too far with

its usage? _____

Part III
Extend Your Vocabulary

Use the context of the sentences to help you supply the correct word from those listed below. You will not use all the words.

euphemistic   acuity   camouflage   irreparable   consensus   aggregate

1. Humans cannot begin to match the hearing _____ of most animals.

2. Soldiers daub paint on their faces, wear uniforms that resemble forests, and

   place small twigs and branches in their helmets, all in order to _____ their positions.

3. With no _____ on how to proceed, the two attorneys continued bickering with one another.

4. Politicians are masters in the use of _____ language because they wish to convince us of their views.

5. The Oklahoma City bombing resulted in _____ damage to the Federal building.

Selection 2: **TEXTBOOK**

☛ Preparation for Reading

In this textbook selection, you will read about the building blocks of language and some theories about how children learn language. In reading this selection, you will meet some terms used by linguists and psychologists that pertain to language. As in most textbook writing, the authors have defined many important terms in context, such as *natural language, syntax, phonemes, morphemes,* and *operant conditioning.*

Before reading, note the meaning of the boldfaced words. They are underlined in the text. Note the authors' use of boldface to introduce important terms in the text.

the relation ... is **arbitrary**	selected at random and without reason
within the **constraints** of these rules	restrictions or limitations
theories of language **acquisition**	something gained by one's own efforts
generate increasingly complex sentences	bring into existence
this approach seems **plausible**	appearing true or reasonable
use only for **autistic** children	condition in which a person is withdrawn in self-centered mental activities, like daydream and delusions
are biologically ready, or **predisposed**	made susceptible to something in advance

Preview, then read the selection.

Language Properties and Processes

John G. Seamon/Douglas T. Kenrick

LANGUAGE AND COMMUNICATION

If you think of all the languages you have ever heard, it is easy to be impressed by 1 their differences. . . . Given that there are over three thousand languages in use today, do these languages have anything in common? Underneath their differences are there any similarities? The answer is *yes* to both questions.

A language is a system of gestures, sounds, or written symbols that embodies 2 units of meaning (*words*) arranged according to set rules (*grammar*) for the purpose of communication. Languages may be *natural* or *artificial.* Natural languages—for example, English and French—arose from everyday communication between people; artificial languages such as those used for computer programming were constructed to interact with machines. . . . The science of **linguistics** studies natural languages and their grammatical rules. **Psycholinguistics** is a branch of psychology that examines language as an aspect of behavior involving speaking, writing, and thinking. Together, linguists and psycholinguists have revealed many of the common properties that all languages share.

Properties of Language

To many native English speakers, foreign languages such as Chinese or Greek sound **3** more like a meaningless rush of sounds than an organized sequence of words. Yet all languages use words and sentences to represent thoughts. In order to represent thoughts, all natural languages share a number of fundamental properties. Languages are **productive, structured,** and **referential.**

To say that language is productive means that there is no limit to the number of **4** novel sentences we can generate. Every time we speak, we can express ourselves in new ways. The same is true for writing. Try as hard as you might, you are unlikely to find any sentence repeated in this text. Better yet, if you were to select any sentence at random, you would have a very difficult time finding it repeated in any book in your school library. From only 26 letters and approximately 100,000 words, we can produce literally trillions of novel sentences. And although these sentences are all different, we can read and understand them because we share an understanding of our language and its rules. This leads to the second fundamental property—language is structured.

Language is structured through the rules of **grammar,** the knowledge that **5** enables native speakers to form acceptable sentences, know what they mean, and know how to pronounce them. Although we invent new sentences all the time, the new sentences are constrained by our **syntax,** grammatical rules for combining words into phrases and sentences. For example, grammatical rules organize a list of words—*ship, the, tiny, distant, on, the, landed, planet*—into a meaningful sentence—*The tiny ship landed on the distant planet.* As we will see in the section on language acquisition, we learn these rules implicitly at an early age in life.

In addition to being productive and structured, language is also referential. The **6** term referential describes the relation between words and their meanings. The *babbling* of a brook and the *quack* of a duck are termed *iconic referents* in that these words sound like the things they refer to. By and large, though, the relation between words and meanings is arbitrary. **Words** are symbolic and arbitrary referents for things, and they enable us to refer to those things in their absence. As a consequence, we can learn from the experiences of others because words can convey information about events that occurred at another time.

The Units of Speech

All languages use a limited number of distinct speech sounds. These sounds, **7** which are used to distinguish one word from another, are called **phonemes.** Most languages use less than 100 phonemes. For example, the English language has about 45 phonemes, while the Hawaiian language has roughly 13. Phonemes include vowels, consonants, and blends. The word *tin*, for instance, is composed of three separate phonemes corresponding to the sounds for *t, i,* and *n*. Obviously not all combinations of phonemes are possible within any language (*tpc*, for example, cannot be spoken in English) and not all languages use the same set of phonemes. This is part of the reason why learning a foreign language and sounding like a native speaker is so difficult. Some of the phonemes that are used in English will not be used in another language, and some of that language's phonemes will have to be learned from scratch. Moreover, some languages do not distinguish between sounds that are treated as different phonemes in English. For example, the English sounds corresponding to *l* and *r* are treated as the same phoneme in Japanese. This is why native Japanese speakers have trouble pronouncing such English words as *lollipop* correctly. In addition, all languages have their own rules for how phonemes can be combined. English does not permit words to begin with the letters *tl* (they can occur in the middle of a word—*battle* or *bottle*), but it does allow *sl* as in *slip* or *slide* and *pl* as in *play* or *please*. Although there are restrictions, the 45 phonemes can be combined to yield an enormous variety of sounds.

Sounds, however, are not language. Sounds must be combined to produce   8 meaningful units called **morphemes.** A morpheme is defined as the smallest language unit that possesses meaning. A morpheme could be a word (as in *like*), a prefix (as in *un*), or a suffix (as in *ly*). When combined, these three morphemes yield the word *unlikely.* There are more than 100,000 morphemes in the English language. In different combinations, they can produce over one million words. If we count words like *big, bigger, biggest* as separate words because they are based partly on different morphemes, then most adults have a vocabulary of hundreds of thousands of words. As with phonemes, there are rules for combining morphemes (*teacher* not *erteach*, for example). Even so, the number of combinations is staggering. Looking back, we see that there are grammatical rules for each of the levels of language we have discussed. Phonemes are organized into morphemes, morphemes are organized into words, and words are organized into sentences to express different thoughts, as illustrated in Figure 2.3. By keeping within the <u>constraints</u> of these rules, an inexhaustible supply of speech is possible. This is what gives our language its incredible flexibility and diversity.

ACQUIRING LANGUAGE

Children all over the world are born without the ability to produce language. But by   9 the time they are five, they have mastered enough of their native tongue to carry on a conversation. In only five years, they learn to make the proper speech sounds, to combine these sounds into words, and to organize the words they have learned into meaningful and grammatically correct sentences. We continue to acquire language after early childhood, but the first five years set the foundation for later development.

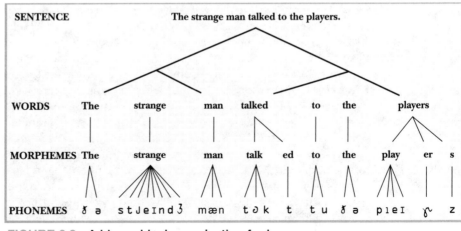

FIGURE 2.3 **A hierarchical organization for language**

All human languages can be hierarchically organized. At the top of the hierarchy is the sentence, which is composed of words, and the morphemes (the smallest units of language that have meaning), and phonemes (the distinct speech sounds of a language). The phonemes are represented by phonetic symbols because English words are not always spelled the way they sound.

Theories of Language Acquisition

There is an orderly progression in the child's acquisition of language. Children listen to the sounds they hear, they begin to babble and later to emit the particular speech sounds from their environment, they use gestures and single words, and finally they <u>generate</u> increasingly complex sentences. This progression describes the child's behavior, but it does not explain how language is acquired. At present, psychologists have a number of theories about how we acquire language.

Language Acquisition by Operant Conditioning   One possibility, put forth by psychologist B.F. Skinner, is that language is learned by operant conditioning, an elementary form of learning in which responses are shaped by reinforcement. Early in life, speechlike sounds may be reinforced by parental attention and may increase in their frequency, while nonspeech sounds are ignored and thereby decrease in frequency. Speechlike sounds might then be shaped into words and words into sentences, again by parental reinforcement. Though this approach seems <u>plausible</u>, research indicates that language is not generally acquired in this way. As a rule, parents do not shape their child's utterances into grammatical sentences. Tapes of parent–child interactions show that parents are more apt to respond to the truth of a child's statement than the manner in which it is stated.

Two-Year-Old Child:	"Mama isn't boy, he a girl."
Mother:	"That's right."

| Two-Year-Old Child: | "And Walt Disney comes on Tuesday." |
| Mother: | "No, he does not." |

R. Brown and Hanlon, 1970

Of course, parents do occasionally correct ungrammatical statements, especially if the meaning of the utterance is unclear. But these corrections are relatively infrequent. Children are very rarely told, "No, you said that wrong."

Language Acquisition by Imitation   Similarly without wide support is the view that children learn language by imitating the speech of adults. Certainly children are capable of learning by observing (and listening to) others, but imitation is not the primary basis of language acquisition. The problem is that not all children imitate.   **12**

Child:	"Nobody don't like me."
Mother:	"No, say 'Nobody likes me.'"
Child:	"Nobody don't like me." (Eight more repetitions)
Mother:	"Now listen carefully. Say 'Nobody likes me.'"
Child:	"Oh! Nobody don't likes me."

McNeill, 1966

In a study of 30 young children who were recorded talking with their parents at home, roughly 20 percent of the children imitated their parents 30 to 40 percent of the time. The remaining 80 percent of the children imitated their parents less than 10 percent of the time. Imitation is not a frequent occurrence, and there is wide variation among children in their willingness to imitate. The fact that children are creative in their use of language is also at odds with the imitation theory.

From a child who plans to drop a piece of paper on his sister—"I'm gonna fall this on her."
From a child asking his mother to make a piece of paper smooth—"How would you flat it?"

Bowerman, 1974

Because these sentences were unlikely ever to have been uttered by an adult, they cannot be explained as due to imitation. To date, research has shown effects of conditioning and imitation on language use only for <u>autistic</u> children working to overcome speech deficits and for children who are delayed in their language development.

Language Acquisition as a Biological Predisposition   If language is not normally   **13** acquired through conditioning or imitation, perhaps it is a part of the biological heritage of the developing infant and child. One view, put forward by linguist Noam Chomsky, holds that children are biologically ready, or "<u>predisposed</u>," to learn any language with ease. Chomsky has argued for the presence of a "language acquisition device" (LAD) that is supposedly responsible for this process. While Chomsky's views have been influential, hard evidence for his position has been lacking.

One fact that linguists like Chomsky use to support their belief that language   14
learning is an innate quality of mind is that young children from many different cultures acquire language in virtually the same manner and with virtually no formal
instruction. Children are exposed to only a limited number of examples out of the
enormous range of permissible utterances from which they learn their language.
From these examples, children figure out the rules of their language and quickly
begin producing understandable speech. Even deaf children who learn sign language go through this same process. They first sign one word at a time, then two,
and so on. Linguists argue that the complexity of the task, coupled with the age of
the children and their cultural differences, implies that children must be biologically prepared to acquire language. Consistent with this view of preparedness . . . is
the research that shows that deaf children go through the same stages of babbling
that speaking children do, except that they babble with their hands. Other
researchers have shown that deaf children who were never exposed to any form of
language instruction (including signing) spontaneously made up their own gestural
systems, called "home signs." It seems that language is so central to the human mind
that it emerges in all people with normal intelligence, whether they can speak or
not.

Language as Social Interaction

Most psychologists currently believe that humans are biologically predisposed to use   15
language, but that the details of a language are acquired through social communication. There is still disagreement over the extent to which a child has to be directly
taught to speak. Most psychologists believe that children take an active part in this
process. Rather than being specifically taught by adults, children become competent speakers by listening to examples of adult speech and then generating the rules
of their language on their own.

Parents do play an important role in their child's acquisition of language, how-   16
ever. Language develops out of the social interaction between parent and child, as
the following interaction illustrates:

Mother:	"Hello. Give me a smile" (then gently pokes infant in the ribs).
Infant:	(Yawns)
Mother:	"Sleepy, are you? You woke up too early today."
Infant:	(Opens fist)
Mother:	(Touching infant's hand) "What are you looking at? Can you see something?"
Infant:	(Grasps mother's finger)
Mother:	"Oh, that's what you wanted. In a friendly mood, then. Come on, give us a smile."

Clark and Clark, 1977

Early on, the infant interacts with the parent (or primary caregiver) by looking at
this person and vocalizing in this person's presence. Later, the infant will make reference to the same things as does the parent. For example, parent and child will

look at the same toy, point to it, and touch it. The parent, in turn, will naturally use language to describe what is going on. Ever-increasing demands for greater specificity and clarity force the child to progress from one-word utterances to two-word sentences to expressions of complete ideas. Without other people to talk to, there would be no impetus for this to occur.

approximately 2400 words

John G. Seamon and Douglas T. Kenrick, "Language and Thought" from *Psychology*, pp. 253–62. Copyright © 1994 by Prentice Hall. Reprinted with the permission of the publisher.

COMPREHENSION CHECK

Part I
General Comprehension Questions: Literal and Interpretive

Write the correct letter in the space provided.

_____ 1. Artificial languages are
    a. spoken, not printed.
    b. used by linguists to communicate with one another.
    c. used to interact with machines.
    d. spoken by people in Asian countries.

_____ 2. "Language is structured" refers to
    a. language as productive.
    b. language as referential.
    c. both a and b.
    d. rules of grammar.

_____ 3. English, like other languages, permits its sounds to occur
    a. in any order.
    b. in a restricted order.
    c. in an unknown pattern.
    d. none of the above

_____ 4. A morpheme may be defined as the
    a. lexicon of English.
    b. smallest language unit possessing meaning.
    c. unit of sound.
    d. both b and c.

_____ 5. Examples of single morphemes include
    a. unlikely, unsettled, unseemly.
    b. big, bigger, biggest.
    c. pre, re, ly.
    d. battle, bottle, bagel.

_____ 6. Symbols for phonemes
    a. use cursive letters.
    b. differ from standard letters.
    c. are not written the way they sound
    d. include a total number of 26.

7. Paraphrase this sentence from the end of paragraph 12:
   a. "To date, research has shown effects of conditioning and imitation on language use only for autistic children working to overcome speech deficits and for children who are delayed in their language development."

   _____

   b. What phrase in the sentence describes one of the problems autistic children

   must try to overcome? _____
8. Why has research failed to support both the imitation and operant conditioning

   theories of language acquisition? _____

   _____

Part II
Application Questions For Writing/Discussion

9. How does Noam Chomsky's theory of language acquisition differ from B.F. Skinner's? Do you agree with the linguists and psychologists who do not fully accept Chomsky's theory? Why or why not?

   _____

10. What is the present theory of language acquisition? What advice would you offer parents of young children if they wish to maximize the language potential of their children?

   _____

   _____

Part III
Extend Your Vocabulary

Study the boldfaced words below. Using the context, write the correct word in the blank provided.

predisposed   plausible   generate   arbitrary   constraints

1. The developers abandoned plans to build the mall because of many legal

   _____ .

2. In writing, the writer's ability to _____ varying sentences makes the task much easier.

3. From childhood, many future mechanics seem _____ to tinker with machinery.

4. In the study of language, many of its rules appear to be without reason and seem

   _____ .

5. Hypotheses may be _____ ; that, however, does not make them factual.

Selection 3: **LITERATURE**

☛ Preparation for Reading

Gang culture in the 1990s reflects to some extent the complexity of our society. We have become accustomed to newspaper accounts that report on the violence that accompanies many gang encounters.

The effect of violence on the life of just one gang member is the focus of the short story that follows. It was written by Evan Hunter, an author best known for his novel on teen violence, *The Blackboard Jungle*. To create the mood of the story, the author uses many explicit details and sets it on a late rainy night outside a dance.

Note these boldfaced words and their meanings. They are underlined in the text.

excruciating pain	intensely painful
a fierce **rumble**	a gang fight; this slang term was popular in the 1950s
lurched away	made a sudden swaying, tipping movement
relentless tattoo	unyielding; persistent
searching and **foraging**	looking for food
an enormous **loathing**	detestation; very strong dislike
ran **hysterically**	with excessive or uncontrollable fear or emotions

As you read, note the author's use of the term *The Royals*. Why might he have chosen this particular term, and what effect did it have on Andy's fate?

On the Sidewalk, Bleeding

Evan Hunter

The boy lay bleeding in the rain. He was sixteen years old, and he wore a bright pur- 1
ple silk jacket, and the lettering across the back of the jacket read THE ROYALS. The boy's name was Andy, and the name was delicately scripted in black thread on the front of the jacket, just over the heart. *Andy.*

He had been stabbed ten minutes ago. The knife had entered just below his rib cage and had been drawn across his body violently, tearing a wide gap in his flesh. He lay on the sidewalk with the March rain drilling his jacket and drilling his body and washing away the blood that poured from his open wound. He had known <u>excruciating</u> pain when the knife had torn across his body, and then sudden comparative relief when the blade was pulled away. He had heard the voice saying, "That's for you, Royal!" and then the sound of footsteps hurrying into the rain, and then he had fallen to the sidewalk, clutching his stomach, trying to stop the flow of blood.

He tried to yell for help, but he had no voice. He did not know why his voice had deserted him, or why the rain had become so suddenly fierce, or why there was an open hole in his body from which his life ran redly, steadily. It was 11:30 p.m., but he did not know the time.

There was another thing he did not know.

He did not know he was dying. He lay on the sidewalk, bleeding, and he thought **5** only: *That was a fierce <u>rumble</u>. They got me good that time,* but he did not know he was dying. He would have been frightened had he known. In his ignorance, he lay bleeding and wishing he could cry out for help, but there was no voice in his throat. There was only the bubbling of blood from between his lips whenever he opened his mouth to speak. He lay silent in his pain, waiting, waiting for someone to find him.

He could hear the sound of automobile tires hushed on the muzzle of rainswept streets, far away at the other end of the long alley. He lay with his face pressed to the sidewalk, and he could see the splash of neon far away at the other end of the alley, tinting the pavement red and green, slickly brilliant in the rain.

He wondered if Laura would be angry.

He had left the jump to get a package of cigarettes. He had told her he would be back in a few minutes, and then he had gone downstairs and found the candy store closed. He knew that Alfredo's on the next block would be open until at least two, and he had started through the alley, and that was when he'd been ambushed. He could hear the faint sound of music now, coming from a long, long way off, and he wondered if Laura was dancing, wondered if she had missed him yet. Maybe she thought he wasn't coming back. Maybe she thought he'd cut out for good. Maybe she'd already left the jump and gone home. He thought of her face, the brown eyes and the jet-black hair, and thinking of her he forgot his pain a little, forgot that blood was rushing from his body. Someday he would marry Laura. Someday he would marry her, and they would have a lot of kids, and then they would get out of the neighborhood. They would move to a clean project in the Bronx, or maybe they would move to Staten Island. When they were married, when they had kids. . . .

He heard footsteps at the other end of the alley, and he lifted his cheek from the sidewalk and looked into the darkness and tried to cry out, but again there was only a soft hissing bubble of blood on his mouth.

The man came down the alley. He had not seen Andy yet. He walked, and then **10** stopped to lean against the brick of the building, and then walked again. He saw Andy then and came toward him, and he stood over him for a long time, the minutes ticking, ticking, watching him and not speaking.

Then he said, "What's a matter, buddy?"

Andy could not speak, and he could barely move. He lifted his face slightly and looked up at the man, and in the rainswept alley he smelled the sickening odor of alcohol and realized the man was drunk. He did not feel any particular panic. He did not know he was dying, and so he felt only mild disappointment that the man who had found him was drunk.

The man was smiling.

"Did you fall down, buddy?" he asked. "You mus' be as drunk as I am." He grinned, seemed to remember why he had entered the alley in the first place, and said, "Don' go way. I'll be ri' back."

The man <u>lurched</u> away. Andy heard his footsteps, and then the sound of the man colliding with a garbage can, and some mild swearing, and then the sound of the man urinating, lost in the steady wash of the rain. He waited for the man to come back.

It was 11:39.

When the man returned, he squatted alongside Andy. He studied him with drunken dignity.

"You gonna catch cold here," he said. "What's a matter? You like layin' in the wet?"

Andy could not answer. The man tried to focus his eyes on Andy's face. The rain spattered around them.

"You like a drink?"

Andy shook his head.

"I gotta bottle. Here," the man said. He pulled a pint bottle from his inside jacket pocket. He uncapped it and extended it to Andy. Andy tried to move, but pain wrenched him back flat against the sidewalk.

"Take it," the man said. He kept watching Andy. "Take it." When Andy did not move, he said, "Nev' mind, I'll have one m'self." He tilted the bottle to his lips, and then wiped the back of his hand across his mouth. "You too young to be drinkin'," anyway. Should be 'shamed of yourself, drunk an' layin' in a alley, all wet. Shame on you. I gotta good minda calla cop."

Andy nodded. Yes, he tried to say. Yes, call a cop. Please. Call one.

"Oh, you don' like that, huh?" the drunk said. "You don' wanna cop to fin' you all drunk an' wet in a alley, huh? Okay, buddy. This time you get off easy." He got to his feet. "This time you lucky," he said. He waved broadly at Andy, and then almost lost his footing. "S'long, buddy," he said.

Wait, Andy thought. *Wait, please, I'm bleeding.*

"S'long," the drunk said again. "I see you aroun'," and then he staggered off up the alley.

Andy lay and thought: *Laura, Laura. Are you dancing?*

The couple came into the alley suddenly. They ran into the alley together, running from the rain, the boy holding the girl's elbow, the girl spreading a newspaper over her head to protect her hair. Andy lay crumpled against the pavement, and he watched them run into the alley laughing, and then duck into the doorway not ten feet from him.

"Man, what rain!" the boy said. "You could drown out there."

"I have to get home," the girl said. "It's late, Freddie. I have to get home."

"We got time," Freddie said. "Your people won't raise a fuss if you're a little late. Not with this kind of weather."

"It's dark," the girl said, and she giggled.

"Yeah," the boy answered, his voice very low.

"Freddie . . . ?"

"Um?"

"You're . . . you're standing very close to me."

"Um."

There was a long silence. Then the girl said, "Oh," only that single word, and Andy knew she'd been kissed, and he suddenly hungered for Laura's mouth. It was then that he wondered if he would ever kiss Laura again. It was then that he wondered if he was dying.

No, he thought, *I can't be dying, not from a little street rumble, not from just getting cut.* 40 *Guys get cut all the time in rumbles. I can't be dying. No, that's stupid. That don't make any sense at all.*

"You shouldn't," the girl said.

"Why not?"

"I don't know."

"Do you like it?"

"Yes."   45

"So?"

"I don't know."

"I love you, Angela," the boy said.

"I love you, too, Freddie," the girl said, and Andy listened and thought: *I love you, Laura. Laura, I think maybe I'm dying. Laura, this is stupid but I think maybe I'm dying. Laura, I think I'm dying!*

He tried to speak. He tried to move. He tried to crawl toward the doorway where 50 he could see the two figures in embrace. He tried to make a noise, a sound, and a grunt came from his lips, and then he tried again, and another grunt came, a low animal grunt of pain.

"What was that?" the girl said, suddenly alarmed, breaking away from the boy.

"I don't know," he answered.

"Go look, Freddie."

"No. Wait."

Andy moved his lips again. Again the sound came from him.   55

"Freddie!"

"What?"

"I'm scared."

"I'll go see," the boy said.

He stepped into the alley. He walked over to where Andy lay on the ground. He 60 stood over him, watching him.

"You all right?" he asked.

"What is it?" Angela said from the doorway.

"Somebody's hurt," Freddie said.

"Let's get out of here," Angela said.

"No. Wait a minute." He knelt down beside Andy. "You cut?" he asked.   65

Andy nodded. The boy kept looking at him. He saw the lettering on the jacket then. THE ROYALS. He turned to Angela.

"He's a Royal," he said.

"Let's . . . what . . . what do you want to do, Freddie?"

"I don't know. I don't want to get mixed up in this. He's a Royal. We help him, and the Guardians'll be down on our necks. I don't want to get mixed up in this, Angela."

"Is he . . . is he hurt bad?"

"Yeah, it looks that way."

"What shall we do?"

"I don't know."

"We can't leave him here in the rain." Angela hesitated. "Can we?"

"If we get a cop, the Guardians'll find out who," Freddie said. "I don't know, Angela. I don't know."

Angela hesitated a long time before answering. Then she said, "I have to get home, Freddie. My people will begin to worry."

"Yeah," Freddie said. He looked at Andy again. "You all right?" he asked. Andy lifted his face from the sidewalk, and his eyes said: *Please, please help me,* and maybe Freddie read what his eyes were saying, and maybe he didn't.

Behind him, Angela said, "Freddie, let's get out of here! Please!" There was urgency in her voice, urgency bordering on the edge of panic. Freddie stood up. He looked at Andy again, and then mumbled, "I'm sorry," and then he took Angela's arm and together they ran toward the neon splash at the other end of the alley.

Why, they're afraid of the Guardians, Andy thought in amazement. *But why should they be? I wasn't afraid of the Guardians. I never turkeyed out of a rumble with the Guardians. I got heart. But I'm bleeding.*

The rain was soothing somehow. It was a cold rain, but his body was hot all over, and the rain helped to cool him. He had always liked rain. He could remember sitting in Laura's house one time, the rain running down the windows, and just looking out over the street, watching the people running from the rain. That was when he'd first joined the Royals. He could remember how happy he was the Royals had taken him. The Royals and the Guardians, two of the biggest. He was a Royal. There had been meaning to the title.

Now, in the alley, with the cold rain washing his hot body, he wondered about the meaning. If he died, he was Andy. He was not a Royal. He was simply Andy, and he was dead. And he wondered suddenly if the Guardians who had ambushed him and knifed him had ever once realized he was Andy? Had they known that he was Andy, or had they simply known that he was a Royal wearing a purple silk jacket? Had they stabbed *him,* Andy, or had they only stabbed the jacket and the title, and what good was the title if you were dying?

I'm Andy, he screamed wordlessly. *For Christ's sake, I'm Andy!*

An old lady stopped at the other end of the alley. The garbage cans were stacked there, beating noisily in the rain. The old lady carried an umbrella with broken ribs, carried it with all the dignity of a queen. She stepped into the mouth of the alley, a shopping bag over one arm. She lifted the lids of the garbage cans delicately, and she did not hear Andy grunt because she was a little deaf and because the rain was beating a steady <u>relentless</u> tattoo on the cans. She had been searching and <u>foraging</u> for the better part of the night. She collected her string and her newspapers, and an old hat with a feather on it from one of the garbage cans, and a broken footstool from another of the cans. And then she delicately replaced the lids and lifted her umbrella high and walked out of the alley mouth with queenly dignity. She had worked swiftly and soundlessly, and now she was gone.

The alley looked very long now. He could see people passing at the other end of it, and he wondered who the people were, and he wondered if he would ever get to know them, wondered who it was on the Guardians who had stabbed him, who had plunged the knife into his body.

"That's for you, Royal!" the voice had said, and then the footsteps, his arms 85
being released by the others, the fall to the pavement. "That's for you, Royal!" Even in his pain, even as he collapsed, there had been some sort of pride in knowing he was a Royal. Now there was no pride at all. With the rain beginning to chill him, with the blood pouring steadily between his fingers, he knew only a sort of dizziness, and within the giddy dizziness, he could only think: *I want to be Andy.*

It was not very much to ask of the world.

He watched the world passing at the other end of the alley. The world didn't know he was Andy. The world didn't know he was alive. He wanted to say, "Hey, I'm alive! Hey, look at me! I'm alive! Don't you know I'm alive? Don't you know I exist?"

He felt weak and very tired. He felt alone and wet and feverish and chilled, and he knew he was going to die now, and the knowledge made him suddenly sad. He was not frightened. For some reason, he was not frightened. He was only filled with an overwhelming sadness that his life would be over at sixteen. He felt all at once as if he had never done anything, never seen anything, never been anywhere. There were so many things to do, and he wondered why he'd never thought of them before, wondered why the rumbles and the jumps and the purple jacket had always seemed so important to him before, and now they seemed like such small things in a world he was missing, a world that was rushing past at the other end of the alley.

I don't want to die, he thought. *I haven't lived yet.*

It seemed very important to him that he take off the purple jacket. He was very 90
close to dying, and when they found him, he did not want them to say, "Oh, it's a Royal." With great effort, he rolled over onto his back. He felt the pain tearing at his stomach when he moved, a pain he did not think was possible. But he wanted to take off the jacket. If he never did another thing, he wanted to take off the jacket. The jacket had only one meaning now, and that was a very simple meaning.

If he had not been wearing the jacket, he would not have been stabbed. The knife had not been plunged in hatred of Andy. The knife hated only the purple jacket. The jacket was a stupid meaningless thing that was robbing him of his life. He wanted the jacket off his back. With an enormous <u>loathing</u>, he wanted the jacket off his back.

He lay struggling with the shiny wet material. His arms were heavy, and pain ripped fire across his body whenever he moved. But he squirmed and fought and twisted until one arm was free and then the other, and then he rolled away from the jacket and lay quite still, breathing heavily, listening to the sound of his breathing and the sound of the rain and thinking: *Rain is sweet, I'm Andy.*

She found him in the alleyway a minute past midnight. She left the dance to look for him, and when she found him she knelt beside him and said, "Andy, it's me, Laura."

He did not answer her. She backed away from him, tears springing into her eyes, and then she ran from the alley <u>hysterically</u> and did not stop running until she found the cop.

And now, standing with the cop, she looked down at him, and the cop rose and said, "He's dead," and all the crying was out of her now. She stood in the rain and said nothing, looking at the dead boy on the pavement, and looking at the purple jacket that rested a foot away from his body.

The cop picked up the jacket and turned it over in his hands.

"A Royal, huh?" he said.

The rain seemed to beat more steadily now, more fiercely.

She looked at the cop and, very quietly, she said, "His name is Andy."

The cop slung the jacket over his arm. He took out his black pad, and he flipped it open to a blank page.

"A Royal," he said.

Then he began writing.

approximately 3000 words

Evan Hunter, "On the Sidewalk, Bleeding" from *Happy New Year Herbie, and Other Stories,*
Copyright © 1963 by Simon & Schuster. Reprinted by permission of the publisher.

Questions for Writing/Discussion

1. Why do you think the author chose the word *Royals?* When does Andy begin to rebel against his association with it?

2. What is the meaning of the sentence "I never turkeyed out of a rumble with the Guardians" (paragraph 79)? Why is there a reference to a turkey and not another type of bird? What can you tell about Andy on the basis of this particular thought of his?

3. Three people could have helped Andy but failed to do so. Who were they? Why did they not help Andy? How does the young couple's attitude toward Andy contrast with Laura's attitude?

4. Why was Andy anxious to get the jacket off his back (paragraphs 90–92)?

5. Do you think Freddie's refusal to help Andy (paragraph 78) is a typical human response? Why or why not?

JOURNAL ENTRY

In the essay by William Lutz, you learned that language is sometimes misused in both business and government to conceal the truth. In the textbook selection, you read about theories on how children learn language. In the short story "On the Sidewalk, Bleeding," you saw that the gang's name *The Royals* was significant in developing the plot and theme; wearing the name embroidered on his purple jacket led to Andy's death.

Write a journal entry reflecting on how your awareness of the significance of the words we use and their impact on our lives may have been increased by these readings. Then, describe a situation in which language has played a role in shaping some important event in your life.

3

Reading and Organizing for More Effective Study

This chapter will

◆ Explain the differences in the organization of essays, textbooks, and novels.

◆ Discuss differences in purpose in reading essays, textbooks, and novels.

◆ Suggest different organizational approaches for study that complement your unique learning style.

❖❖❖

Before reading, think about these questions.

◆ What steps do you now take when reading an essay or studying textbook material?

◆ What are your study habits when you want to retain and recall information for quizzes and exams?

◆ What do you look for in reading a novel?

❖❖❖

Jot down your thoughts after considering your own study habits and reading techniques.

_____

_____

❖ The Essay

In Chapter 2 you read and responded to three selections: an essay on political correctness, a textbook excerpt on the development of language, and a literature selection dealing with gang violence. This chapter will focus on how to organize these three reading **genres** for study and learning, for answering questions, and for test taking.

Differences Between the Essay and Article

Some people use the terms *essay* and *article* **interchangeably.** An essay, however, differs somewhat from an article. An article is simply a nonfictional composition, but the essay is generally considered a **literary** composition on a single topic, usually presenting the *personal view* of the author.

Essays are often found in magazines and editorial sections of newspapers, whereas articles are usually newspaper presentations of current events. Articles are generally informational in nature, while essays are essentially opinionated arguments on **topical** issues. Additionally, in some essays, the author may evaluate a problem and, perhaps, offer a solution. Since the writer gives his or her personal viewpoint on the topic, you must decide whether or not the viewpoint is logical, well presented, and believable.

The Thesis Statement

All the paragraphs within an essay should support a unifying thought or central viewpoint. This is called the *thesis*. Sometimes the thesis is suggested in the title or stated plainly in one general sentence of the essay's introductory paragraphs. However, often the thesis is stated indirectly or **implied,** weaving in and out of the essay. In this case, the reader has to determine the thesis from the supporting details or evidence given. One way to do this is to jot down in the margins of the essay various points from important paragraphs to see how they develop into one major point, then mentally compose a thesis sentence that encompasses those ideas.

---

genres (zhan´rəz) kinds or types

interchangeably (in tər chan´ jə blē) capable of changing places

literary (lit´ ər er ē) writing with permanent value and excellence of form (Do not confuse with *literal,* meaning "based on the actual words in their ordinary meaning.")

topical (tăp¢ i kəl) current or local

implied (im plīd¢) suggested but not stated directly

Is There Support for the Essay's Thesis?

The major purpose of reading an essay, after determining the thesis, is to see if the author presents sufficient information to support it and then to decide whether you agree or disagree with the author's viewpoint. Since the essay is a *literary* composition, you must also note how the author's language is used to strengthen or **diminish** the thesis statement.

Reading the Essay

There are specific steps you can take to help you read an essay effectively. Sometimes, the essay's title is simply one word such as "Beauty" and is quite general. In other cases, the title may be in the form of a phrase such as "The Meaning of Marriage," offering clues to the topic and thesis statement. With this title, the writer may try to prove what marriage should be like. Sometimes, the title is in the form of a question such as "Anglo vs. Chicano: Why?" Here, the writer may suggest *why* he or she feels the conflict between the Anglos (Anglo Americans) and the Chicanos (Hispanic Americans) came about and why.

Thinking about the essay's title prior to reading may help you predict the thesis.

ACTIVITY 3.1   Examining the Essay's Title

Examine the following titles, and in the space provided, write what you might predict the author's thesis will be. The first one is done for you.

1. "Courts Overburdened with Cases"
   We need to reform our court system because the courts have too many cases, and people wait a long time before their cases are heard.

2. "Gun Lobby's Influence Blocks Needed Changes"

   _____

   _____

3. "Government Funds Needed for Ailing Transit System"

   _____

   _____

---

diminish (di min¢ ish) to become smaller or less important

4. "The Drug War Must Be Won at Home"

_____

_____

5. "Legal Battle Brews on the Internet"

_____

_____

Identifying the Thesis and Supporting Statements in Essays

In order to identify the thesis and supporting statements in college essays, you may often need to take additional steps after considering the title, previewing, and careful reading. These steps include

1. Identifying the main ideas of important paragraphs.
2. Writing brief marginal notes for these paragraphs.
3. Examining how the notes relate to a single point.

After you have identified the author's main point, you will find it much easier to understand the supporting information.

ACTIVITY 3.2   Identifying the Thesis and Supporting Statements in Essays

Preview, then read to find the author's thesis in the essay that follows, dealing with one's attitude toward failure. Then examine how the marginal notes help you to quickly identify the thesis statement.

Reversal of Fortune: Attitude Can Reroute Adversity

Alice Steinbach

It was a few minutes before air time and the talk-show   1
host was about to begin his daily radio program. He
poured himself a cup of coffee and then, turning to   talk-show host still fearful
me, said something surprising:

"You know, this job never gets any easier," said   2
this **erudite** man who for years has presided over an
extremely popular call-in show. "Every time I go on

_____

adversity (ad ver´ si tē) misfortune
erudite (er´ yōō dīt) scholarly; having much knowledge

the air, I have to overcome a fear that I'll fail; that the show won't be any good."

He paused. "But I've found out something interesting about failing. And that is, you can build on success but you really learn only from failure."

3 *can build on success but learn from failure*

A few days later, a letter arrived that seemed, in a way, to continue this line of thought. Written by a young man I know quite well, the letter concerned itself with the idea that adversity might offer, in the long run, more rewards than getting what you thought you wanted. My correspondent wrote:

4

"What I guess I'm learning from my difficult situation is a deeper sense of who I am. And what I'm capable of when it comes to handling disappointment. I think—at least I hope—I'll come out of this a stronger person."

5 *difficult situation can make one stronger*

Then last week, in what seemed a curious completion of the philosophy lurking beneath both these remarks, I came across this unattributed quotation in a book on mountain climbing:

6

"Today is a new day; you'll get out of it just what you put into it. If you have made mistakes, even serious mistakes, you can make a new start whenever you choose. For the thing we call failure is not the falling down but the staying down."

7 *failure is not the falling down but staying down*

Few among us can claim the distinction of not knowing the sting of falling down, of "failure:" the promotion not gotten; the honor not won; the job lost; the praise denied, we've all known the loss of self-esteem that comes with such moments. And because the wound of failure is a deep one, we seldom risk sharing our feelings about such moments.

8

"Success does not necessarily build character—sometimes it doesn't even build self-confidence," says a friend, one judged by the world to be successful. "But most people I know—including myself—can point to a disappointment or a failure that resulted in what I would call a **quantum leap** of self-knowledge and self-confidence. The confidence comes from knowing that you can get through 'failure' and come out stronger on the other side."

9 *confidence comes from knowing you can get through failure*

Still, she admits that it is a "painful process to go through."

10

Some successful people find that they become

11

---

quantum leap (kwän´ təm lēp) a leap of powerful dimension; breakthrough

"addicted" to honors and **accolades.** And when they don't get them—when they're just doing well at their job—not sensationally well—they feel depressed.

"It's taken me a long time to understand that prizes and honors, while wonderful to receive, have a short shelf life," says one successful journalist. "I have found that the sense of achievement you get from 'winning' needs to be constantly renewed. It's easy to feel good about yourself when you're winning. It's not winning that's hard. But that's when you learn to dig deeper and do your best work. Not for the rewards of success but for the rewards of self-respect."   **12**

not winning can make you work harder for self-respect

A few years back, I found myself needing to dig down deep (and not for the first time in my life) to find a firmer foundation upon which to build my understanding of what success is and what failure is. And my friend was right: It is quite a painful experience to confront the loss of some trapping or another that seems bound up with success.   **13**

But eventually what emerged from the digging was a sense of something akin to freedom. A realization that there's a feeling of accomplishment and success that comes from mastering the pain of failure. And then getting on with the job.   **14**

mastering the pain of failure gives a feeling of accomplishment and success

Honors and **accolades** are wonderful. Promotions are wonderful. Success—however you define it—is wonderful. But none of them, in my experience, really teaches you anything of lasting value about yourself.   **15**

Adversity, on the other hand, can be an inspirational teacher.   **16**

in life we can expect adversity but adversity can be an inspirational teacher

It is written somewhere that you stand on the summit for only a few moments, then the wind blows your footprints away.   **17**

Life's like that, too.   **18**

Harvard Business School probably doesn't teach that to its MBA's. But you know what? Maybe it should.   **19**

approximately 850 words

---

accolades (ak´ ə lādz) approval; awards

What is the author's thesis? Remember that a thesis or thesis statement is the *unifying thought* or *central viewpoint*. What examples does the author present to support the thesis? Write your responses on the lines below, and then compare them with those of a classmate. Are you in agreement?

Thesis: _____

_____

_____

Support: _____

_____

_____

_____

Now compare your answers with the suggested ones at the bottom of this page.

Your answers do not have to be worded exactly like these but should include the general idea.

Thesis: A positive attitude toward failure can turn it into a rewarding learning experience; working through a failure can make you a stronger person and give you renewed self-confidence.

Support: The talk-show host said he only learns through failure.

The correspondent wrote that his failure had made him a stronger person.

The quote from the book on mountain climbing indicated how failure can lead to success.

A successful businessperson claimed coping with failure made her a stronger person.

ACTIVITY 3.3   **Practice Writing Marginal Notes**

How well do you take notes? Test yourself by writing marginal notes on the short essay in the following activity. Using your notes, write a summary of the essay. Compare your summary with the work of a classmate, then with the original essay. Did your notes explain the thesis? Did you include sufficient support? Think about how you might improve your note-taking ability.

TEAMWORK VS. COMPETITION

Gary Heil/Tom Parker/Rick Tate

Teamwork. We're all for it! Many of us have taken part in expensive team-building exercises where we've climbed rope ladders, built boats, gone on challenging photo safaris, . . . and solved mysteries. Over and over, we've been told we have to learn to work together more effectively. And for good reason. Today's world is too complex for any one person to manage the value proposition alone. This is particularly the case in companies where individuals from different functional areas, departments, and physical locations have to work in harmony to meet the unique needs of their customers. If we hope to succeed, there is, in fact, no real alternative for many of us *but* to work as a team, to *cooperate.*

Unfortunately, it is this alternative that most organizations are least well equipped to implement. We are simply not prepared to cooperate—culturally, structurally, or philosophically. We are, after all, a nation that makes heroes of individuals who distinguish themselves competitively. From corporate raiders to rock stars, from baseball's Most Valuable Player to the most famous heart surgeon, we've focused on individual winners. Looking out for #1 is not only expected, but rewarded.

Nowhere is winning (and losing) more a part of everyday life than in our organizations. Here, the thrill of victory or the agony of defeat is relived by many on an almost daily basis. Unfortunately, the primary field of battle may not be in the marketplace, but in our hallways. The arena where the most intense competition in business is often waged is *within* the corporation itself, among its employees. The costs of unnecessary internal competition are prohibitive in most organizations.

We talk about being part of a team but, instead of cooperating in a system that encourages teamwork, we are pitted against one another to compete and win as individuals. As much as we claim we want cooperation, most of our structures don't reward it, our corporate culture doesn't support it, and our leaders are reluctant to embrace it—though it is often in the best interests of the organization to do so.

approximately 330 words

Gary Heil, Tom Parker, and Rick Tate, *Leadership and the Customer Revolution*, pp. 101–102.

Summary: _____

_____

_____

Complete this sentence: "I can improve my notetaking skill by _____

_____

_____

Summary: In reading and studying essays: Preview. Read and then make marginal notations about important paragraphs. See how the notations add up to the author's thesis. Locate the thesis and then find the supporting information. Decide whether you agree or disagree with the author's thesis.

As you read the essay that follows, jot down the main ideas in note form for each important paragraph. You will find it easier to identify the thesis of the essay and answer the questions. Sometimes, questions are stated in such a way that the word *thesis* is not included in the question. A question about the thesis, however, is generally included because it is the main point the author is making.

Selection 4: **ESSAY**

☛ Preparation for Reading

The following essay, "How Women and Minorities Are Reshaping Corporate America," was the subject of a speech given by the author, a corporate vice-president for a utility company. She delivered the speech to the Women's Bureau Conference in Washington, D.C.

Before reading the essay, note these words and their meaning. The words are underlined in the text.

an **impoverished** one	poor
legal **impediments**	things that get in the way
the **homogeneous** work force	composed of identical parts
by an **infusion**	the act of imparting
will seek out **diversity**	variety; difference
more **introspective**	looking into one's own feelings

Preview, then read the essay.

How Women and Minorities are Reshaping Corporate America

Linda Winikow

There's no question in my mind—none whatsoever—that we have an opportunity today to tap a huge reservoir—the pool of cultural diversity. Our challenge is not only to *accommodate* diversity, but to actually use it to bring new and richer perspectives to our jobs, to our customers and to our whole social climate. 1

But we have a long, long way to go. For generations, our view of women and minorities in the workplace was an <u>impoverished</u> one, and that narrow focus resulted in incalculable harm. 2

Think about the intellect, the cultures, the ideas and the creativity that was wasted by ignorance and by prejudice. 3

The fundamental question we have to ask ourselves, of course, is "How much has changed in the last eighty or ninety years?" The answer is mixed. 4

On the one hand, civil rights legislation and labor laws have done an enormous amount to wipe out the legal <u>impediments</u> to inequality. And the Department of Labor has played a key role in our progress. 5

But while the *laws* to combat discrimination have changed, all-too-many of the *attitudes* that prevented the flowering of diversity still exist. 6

But the issues aren't clear cut—there are no simple "rights" and "wrongs." 7

Recently, the Supreme Court heard a case where in 1982 Johnson Controls said that women of childbearing age couldn't work in certain jobs because their exposure to lead 8 would exceed the limits believed to cause fetal defects.

9 The company said that it had a duty to protect its employees from health and safety hazards. On the surface, this sounds like responsible corporate policy.

10 Many women employees, along with labor unions, on the other hand, claimed that this action was discriminatory, resulting in their losing their jobs or the opportunity to advance. So they sued, claiming that *all* employees should be adequately—and equally—protected from lead exposure.

11 Whatever the merits of either side, this is a classic case of the difficulty of managing diversity—where issues of fairness, equity, competing rights, multiple standards, ethics and law meld together in confusion—where the difference between right and wrong is not as absolute as we would hope for in an ideal world.

12 In corporate America, this is an era of remarkable change. It's no longer the homogeneous white, male-oriented workforce it once was. Today, our business world is being enriched by an infusion of different cultural perspectives. Today's coworkers bring new ideas—whether from Japan or from the inner city.

13 A culturally diverse workforce will mean *less* bias, not more. As minorities make up more and more of the workforce, people will become less and less tolerant of bigotry and discrimination. And the smart employers will seek out diversity; they will recognize that *everyone* can add value to the companies' ability to do its job—and to do it well.

14 Just as the United States was made great—not by making everyone the same but rather by respecting their differences—so, too, can corporations achieve new levels of greatness. Cultural, religious and ethnic diversity in both the corporate boardroom and in the corporate trenches make that company better understand and more in tune with its customers.

15 Today, workers deserve to be recognized for what they *are*, as well as what they *produce*. If management learns to understand the *whole* person, the corporate culture will be enriched beyond imagination.

16 This is no easy task.

17 But regardless of how difficult the issues are, we as corporate executives have an obligation to recognize that these aren't simply side issues to running a business. It's really the opposite: These are the *fundamental* management issues—to bring people to their full potential—to encourage employees to grow, to take risks, to be comfortable with who they are and to be able to learn from their own mistakes and from other people's achievements.

18 I believe that it's the obligation of corporate managers to *learn* about the people who work for them. To *understand* the Orthodox Jewish holidays; to *appreciate* the Chinese New Year; to *reflect* on the Hispanic heritage. Each of these—and every other culture—brings something enormously valuable to the workplace, and we'll never tap it if we don't understand it.

19 Further, I believe that corporate managers must *respect* those cultural differences. If we don't respect them, who will? If we don't value differences, can we expect harmony among others?

20 Finally, I believe that corporate managers must *communicate* with those above—and below—them. All the understanding in the world is for nothing if we don't act on our convictions.

21 As we progress as a society, that ladder becomes increasingly crowded. But it certainly comes as no surprise to learn that women are still being excluded from the top, any more than it's a surprise to learn that women and minorities hold a disproportionate share of the menial or lesser-paying jobs.

22 But the real measure of progress is not taken only by counting those at the top and those at the bottom; another real measure is

the increasing numbers of women and minorities in *middle*-management positions. These are the people with the greatest opportunity. And, unhappily, they are also the ones who most acutely feel the disadvantage of their gender or heritage or color in today's workforce.

Too often, non-traditional middle managers get squeezed by the doubtful expectations of their superiors on the one hand and by the cynical views of those reporting to them on the other.   **23**

Too often, minorities are stereotyped as less assertive or more emotional, less mathematical or more artistic, less persuasive or more sensitive, less open or more <u>introspective</u>, or any one of a hundred generalities without foundation.   **24**

My job as a woman executive—and the job of *every* executive, regardless of sex—is to dispel the myths and get on with the business of managing.   **25**

That's not easy. Women executives—and   **26**

minority executives—have to be very secure, because managing diversity really means managing the unknown.

And to do that, you have to be willing to take risks. You can't be afraid of having people grow in their jobs. You can't feel threatened. You have to recognize that *our* job is *not* to make a widget. *Our* job is to make a *difference*. And in American industry, there's still plenty to be done.   **27**

—We must guarantee equal opportunity in our hiring, and this must go *beyond* affirmative action; it must truly recognize the *value* of ethnic, racial and sexual diversity;   **28**

—We must understand the cultural diversity of the workforce;   **29**

—We must ensure that there's equal pay for equal work.   **30**

These aren't just *business* issues. These are *societal* issues, and how we deal with them will affect every person in this nation.   **31**

approximately 1350 words

Excerpted from Linda Winikow, "How Women and Minorities Are Reshaping Corporate America," *Vital Speeches of the Day*, 57, no. 8 (Feb. 1, 1991), pp. 242–44. Copyright © Linda Winikow. Reprinted by permission.

COMPREHENSION CHECK

Part I
General Comprehension Questions: Literal and Interpretive

Write the correct letter in the space provided.

_____ 1. The author believes that cultural diversity in the business world will

    a. improve the climate of business.
    b. lead to job loss.
    c. lead to increased prejudice.
    d. increase immigration.

_____ 2. The author points out that changes in the business world for women and minorities have

    a. dramatically improved.
    b. remained the same.
    c. stagnated recently.
    d. come about through laws.

_____ 3. Fairness in business
dealings is an issue that

a. is clear-cut.
b. should be decided by the government.
c. cannot be easily decided.
d. women and minorities should decide.

_____ 4. The author believes cultural
diversity in the workforce

a. will diminish.
b. will become bogged down in legal
battles.
c. will grow.
d. none of the above.

_____ 5. The author's thesis is that
the opportunity presented
by a culturally diverse
workforce is

a. a side issue of business.
b. a fundamental issue of business.
c. a management issue of business.
d. both b and c.

_____ 6. Women and minorities
seem to be

a. disproportionately in lesser-paying jobs.
b. predominately in middle management
positions.
c. in top management positions.
d. moving in large numbers to top
management.

7. Explain and give examples of the author's statement in paragraph 15, "If
management learns how to understand the whole person, the corporate culture
will be enriched beyond imagination."

_____

_____

_____

_____

8. The author mentions "fetal defects" in paragraph 8. What are fetal defects? Why
would this be an issue for government?

_____

_____

_____

_____

Part II
Application Questions for Writing/Discussion

9. Do you agree with the author that women and minorities "feel the disadvantage of their gender or heritage or color in today's workforce" (paragraph 22)? Why or why not?

_____

_____

_____

_____

10. Compare your present view of minorities, particularly women in business, with what the author claims to be true.

_____

_____

_____

_____

_____

Part III
Vocabulary

These words were included in the essay. Use the sentence context to place the appropriate word in the blank provided. You will not use all the words.

impoverished	impediments	disproportionate
infusion	diversity	introspection

1. Only a/an _____ of money and renewed activity will make a real difference.

2. A/An _____ society would not be too concerned about democracy.

3. Many _____ stand in the way of creating a society with fairness for all.

4. Because the _____ of the workforce is growing, changes are inevitable.

5. Very sensitive people are also often _____.

❖ The Textbook

Textbook Reading

Differences Between Reading the Textbook  Essay

When reading textbooks, we are sometimes asked to evaluate the information presented. This evaluation generally differs from analyzing ideas developed in essays because textbook writers usually present *both sides* of an issue and tend to be **objective,** whereas essayists usually present their own view and are **subjective.**

Another difference is in the organization of material. The textbook chapter is usually arranged for ease of study with headings and subheadings, but essays usually omit this organizational aid. Additionally, the writing style of a textbook is generally straightforward—facts and events are presented clearly and directly. Essay writing, on the other hand, being more literary, may use **nuance** and **metaphorical** language that is not as easy to understand.

A textbook chapter, however, is much longer than most essays and contains much detailed information as well as specialized vocabulary particular to that discipline. Moreover, college textbook reading assignments are followed by quizzes, midterms, and final exams, to test whether the information has not only been understood but *retained*. So, an important part of textbook reading is the more detailed study you must do, which enables you to remember extensive amounts of information over extended periods of time.

Table of Contents

The importance of a textbook's table of contents cannot be minimized. It can quickly provide you with

An *outline* of the book's contents.
An *overview* of the book's contents and organization of major topics.
Chapter-by-chapter *headings*, breaking the chapter into smaller units, revealing the main ideas and important points of each chapter.

---

objective (əb jek´ tiv) not influenced by personal bias; impersonal
subjective (sub jek´ tiv) personal; resulting from feelings of self
nuance (noō´ äns) a slight degree of difference in meaning, color, or tone
metaphorical (met´ ə for´ ə kəl) using a figure of speech in which dissimilar things are compared, or where a word may depart from its usual meaning, for example, "the *evening* of life"

Surveying the Entire Textbook

Surveying an entire textbook is important to do before you begin to read a text for any course. To become familiar with the book that is central to the course you are studying, you should follow certain procedures.

ACTIVITY 3.4   **Surveying a Textbook**

Use a textbook you are currently using in another class, or use this textbook to answer the following questions and complete a textbook survey.

1. Think about the title to determine what it suggests about the book's contents. Think about what you already know about the subject matter. This will tell you a great deal about how you must plan for study.

    I know _____

2. Look at the table of contents to note the major divisions. Most undergraduate courses are survey courses, so authors select the areas to emphasize. The table of contents will give you a clue as to where the author is taking you.

    Areas emphasized: _____

3. Skim the preface, wherein you will find the author's philosophy—why he or she wrote the book, and what the author hopes the book can accomplish for you. If there is a section called "To the Student," read it.

    Comments: _____

4. Note how the chapters are "introduced." Is there a preview? Are there objectives or quotes?

    Comments: _____

5. Glance through the index, then the glossary. What kinds of terms will you be learning? Is the vocabulary difficult or easy? Does the glossary help you with key vocabulary and specialized terms, or will you frequently have to refer to the dictionary?

    Index: _____

    Glossary: _____

6. Check the appendix—what supplementary material or information is given? Often this information is extremely helpful.

    Supplementary material: _____

7. Find the answer key—if the text provides one. Where is it? At the end of the chapter or in an appendix?

The answer key is found _____

8. Skim to see whether the author uses many graphs, charts, and tables that you will need to integrate as you read. What does the inclusion of these visuals mean for your study?

Comments: _____

9. Read a few pages of text at the beginning, in the middle, and at the end of the text. What is the author's writing style? Is it straightforward with explanations or detailed and complex?

The style is _____

10. What other helpful study aids are provided for you? Are there summaries or chapter questions at the end? How will you use these?

Comments: _____

Reading and Study of the Textbook: SQ3R

A common misconception is that reading and study are identical processes. Reading—in preparation for study—is the process we use to understand the main ideas of the textbook assignment. On the other hand, studying is the process we use to interpret, retain, and recall more detailed information, in order to answer questions, participate in class discussions, and succeed in tests or examinations.

A second misconception is the idea of how much time is needed to study a textbook. Many students underestimate what *real* study involves. *Study steps are essential* in order to transfer what you have read and learned to your long-term memory. Using a study system enables you to study "smarter" and with greater efficiency.

What is the best reading/study system? Research has not identified any one of the following study systems as superior to any other. We do know that using any one of them is far superior to *merely reading and rereading, which is not a study system at all!*

Note the variety of study systems and what their **acronyms** stand for.*

---

acronyms (ak´ rə nimz) words formed from the first letters or syllables of other words

*Most study systems are based on the initial work of Francis Robinson, a psychologist who developed SQ3R: Survey, Question, Read, Recite, Review.

SQ4R: Survey, Question, Read, Recite, Review, Reflect
Survey to get an overview; raise questions as a result of the survey; read with understanding; recite by restating in some way; review the information; and reflect on what you have read.

POINT: Purpose, Overview, Interpret, Note, Test
Have a purpose for reading; get an overview; interpret what you read; take notes; test yourself.

OK5R: Overview, Key ideas, Read, Reword, Recite, Review, Reflect
Get an overview and look for key ideas; read with understanding; reword important ideas; recite as you study; review important ideas; reflect on them.

Reading and Study of the Textbook: A Simplified System

The study steps we suggest in this text—*survey* (or preview), *read, restate,* and *organize*—incorporate the essential features of the best study systems and are easy to use.

1. *Survey* to get an overview of the chapter and raise questions as you do.
2. *Read* to understand and select what needs to be remembered.
3. *Restate* and *organize,* then study the information to retain it.

These steps will be described in detail in the following section.

Step 1: Survey a Textbook Chapter to Focus Your Reading/Study Time

Surveying a textbook chapter is simply an extension of previewing and well worth the five to fifteen minutes it takes. It enables you immediately to see the chapter as a whole and how various parts relate to the central idea. When surveying, you should

1. Check the outline of the chapter in the table of contents for a quick overview. Return to the chapter and really think about the title, raising some questions about what you will read. This helps you focus on the main point immediately.
2. Quickly read the introduction (if there is one) or the first paragraph or two to find out the main concepts and key terms stressed. Reading all the headings and subheadings can reinforce the outline you noted in the table of contents.
3. As with previewing, dip into the text here and there, reading some of the first and last sentences of paragraphs, familiarizing yourself with the author's emphasis.
4. Read the summary or concluding paragraphs, which often restate the important points covered in the chapter.

5. Notice any visual aids such as graphs, charts, diagrams, maps, tables, photographs, cartoons, and illustrations. These often present information to clarify **concisely** portions of a text.*

6. Note where definitions of important words are given—at the beginning or end of a chapter, or in the glossary.

7. Read any questions provided at the end of the chapter before reading the chapter. This will prepare you for what the author thinks is important.†

Step 2: Read to Understand

The survey familiarizes you with some of the main points of the chapter, its specific purpose, and how the information is organized. Also, you learn how the chapter is divided. After you finish the survey, go to the chapter's beginning and apply the following steps to the first section. Remember to search for major concepts, and, again, you will find the supporting points much easier to remember.

1. Read the entire section to get an overall view, actively searching for answers to questions you read or raised before reading, based on the title and survey.

2. Think about what is really important. Do not dwell on trivial details.

3. Selectively mark your textbook as you read. Have a pen or pencil in hand, placing marginal symbols next to key lines. Develop a simple coding system for these marks, such as

= (main idea)	– – – (important support)	* (important)	1, 2, 3 (specific points to recall)
K (key term)	ex. (example)	? (difficult)	

Read the entire section before underlining, highlighting, or making extensive marginal notes. After you make your original brief marginal markings, you will have a better idea as to what is important. Initially everything may seem important, but after reading the entire section, you should realize this is untrue. Do not underline or highlight too much—you might as well not underline at all! Be selective and underline in thought units, using key words and phrases.

Step 3: Restate and Organize for Retention

Most students wish they could read their textbook assignments once, and highlight or underline while reading, and remember everything they read. Although this is not possible, following Step 3 will enable you to retain much more of what you read. When you find a logical or natural break, after you have read several pages, take time for this **critical** step. Paraphrase, or restate the ideas in your own words, so

---

concisely (kən sīs´ lē) expressing much in a few words

critical (krit´ i kəl) of major importance

*Chapter 10 will give you further assistance with this important reading skill.

†Some textbooks do not follow this exact format; you may have to modify your survey to accommodate your particular textbook design.

as to **heighten** your concentration. This shows what you remember, a sure way to test what you have understood and learned.

The form of organization you choose depends on your familiarity with the reading material, your learning style, and the type of textbook you are reading. You may choose to use notetaking, write an abbreviated outline, answer some key questions, write notes on index cards, create a divided page, or map **salient** features.

Remember, you must restate the material in your own words and "make" the knowledge yours by paraphrasing in order to retain it. Be certain, also, that in organizing your information, you have included some of the important supporting details. Realize that instructors can compose dozens of questions from just one section of a textbook chapter. Plan additional study time for reviews of the information you have organized instead of cramming before a textbook test.

ACTIVITY 3.5

Practice Step 3, the restatement step, now with this short textbook passage. Read and make marginal symbols of the information you will need to restate later. Then, go back and paraphrase in the margins or on your own paper.

Westward expansion changed the nature of American politics. The new western states extended the right to vote to all white males over the age of twenty-one. . . . By 1820, most of the older states had followed suit, acting less out of democratic belief than for the practical purpose of attempting to **dissuade** disgruntled nonvoters from moving west. There were laggards—Rhode Island, Virginia, and Louisiana did not liberalize their voting qualifications until later—but by 1840, more than 90 percent of adult white males in the nation could vote. And they could vote for more officials: Governors and (most important) presidential electors were now elected by direct vote, rather than chosen by small groups of state legislators. As Martin Van Buren proved in New York, these changes transformed politics.

Nowhere in the world, at the time, was the right to vote so widespread as it was in the United States. The extension of suffrage to the common man marked a major step beyond the republicanism advocated by the revolutionary generation. Jefferson, as we have seen, **envisaged** a republic of independent (that is, property-owning) **yeoman** farmers. Now, however, propertyless farm workers and members of the laboring poor in the nation's cities could vote as well. European observers were very curious about the democratization of voting: Could "mob rule" possibly succeed?

Nevertheless, even in America voting was not a universal right, and the extent of suffrage tells us something about the limits of American democracy in the early nineteenth

---

heighten (hīt´ ən) make stronger or greater; intensify
salient (sāl´ yənt) prominent; standing out
dissuade (di swād´) to discourage a course of action by persuasion
envisaged (en viz´ ijd) conceived of; had an image of
yeoman (yō´ mən) an independent farmer

century. The right to vote was limited to adult white males: Neither free black men nor women of any race could vote.

approximately 265 words

John Mack Faragher et. al. *Out of Many: A History of the American People,* Copyright © 1994 by Prentice Hall p. 275. Reprinted by permission.

Check your notes with your instructor. Do you know the meanings of *laggard* and *suffrage?*

Laggard means _____ . *Suffrage* means _____ .

Ways to Organize and Restate Information

Some examples of the organizational restatement step follow. A short chapter excerpt has been used as a basis for the examples. Read the chapter excerpt first, noting the many concepts to understand from just one page of a textbook. Without good notes, the information would be extremely difficult to remember.

The New Immigration

Figures from the 1990 census confirmed what many Americans had observed over the previous decade in their communities and workplaces. The face of the nation was **perceptibly** changing. The Census Bureau estimated that 6 million legal and 2 million undocumented immigrants entered the country during the 1980s, second only to the 8.8 million foreign immigrants that arrived between 1900 and 1910. More than a third of the nation's population growth over the decade—from 227 million to 248 million—came from immigration. This proportion of increase caused by foreign migrants was greater than any since the decade between 1910 and 1920, when immigration accounted for 40 percent of population growth. Seven states, headed by California, New York, Texas, and Florida, received 75 percent of the newcomers.

    Hispanics and Asians led the accelerated trend toward cultural diversity. The Hispanic population increased by more than 50 percent, from 14.6 million to 22.4 million. One out of every five immigrants living in the U.S. was Mexican-born, and Mexican

Annotations:
= U.S. changing

‑ ‑ ‑ 6M legal; 2M undocumented immig. in 1980s

‑ ‑ ‑ more than 1/3 pop. growth in 80s from immig.
‑ ‑ ‑ greatest prop. of increase for decade exc. 1910–20

ex.

= Hispanics & Asians lead

‑ ‑ ‑ Hisp. increased 50%—22M Mex.—largest group

---

perceptibly (pər sep´ ti blē) noticeably; understandably

Americans overall composed more than 60 percent of the Hispanic population identified in the 1990 census. **Demographers** predicted that by the middle of the next century Hispanics would replace African Americans as the largest minority group in the nation.

    The decline of world oil prices had a devastating impact on the Mexican economy, worsening poverty and unemployment and spurring more people to seek a better life in North America. Most Mexican Americans struggled in low-paying jobs and fought to hold onto their distinctive cultural heritage. They worked on farms, in garment sweatshops and high-tech assembly plants, and as gardeners and domestics. Through education and business success, a significant number achieved middle-class status and wealth. But almost 20 percent of Mexican Americans lived below the poverty line.

    The number of Asian Americans more than doubled, from 3.5 million to 7.3 million. Nearly two out of every five Asian Americans lived in California. The population of Koreatown in Los Angeles approached 300,000 and the area seemed a world unto itself. Like earlier immigrant groups, new Americans from Korea, Vietnam, and the Philippines tended to cluster in their own communities and maintain a durable group identity. As a whole, Asian Americans made **mobility** through education a priority, along with pooling family capital and labor to support small businesses. Newcomers selected communities with job opportunities or where families and friends had settled. This social network, for example, explained the large numbers of Hmongs, a tribal group from Laos, drawn to Minneapolis and St. Paul.

    The Immigration Reform Act of 1965 had eliminated quotas based on national origin. It also gave preferential treatment to highly educated foreigners seeking professional opportunities in the U.S. The 1965 act set limits of 120,000 immigrants per year from the Western Hemisphere and 170,000 from countries outside the Western Hemisphere. By the mid-1980s, growing concern over "illegal aliens" had become a hotly debated political issue, particularly

Margin notes:
– – – prediction—Hisp. largest minority by 2050
– – – struggled
    some middle class many poor
– – – Asian Am. pop. doubled—7M
– – – cluster in own communities; maintain group identity
– – – seek ed. for upward mobility
– – – pool resources for fam. bus.
= Ref Act 1965
    preferential—highly educ.
    limit—120T—W. Hemp.
    170T—outside W. Hemp.

---

demographers (di mog´ rə fərs) experts in statistics and human population
mobility (mō bil´ ə tē) ability or readiness to move or be moved

in the Southwest. The Immigration Reform and Control Act of 1987 addressed the concerns of Anglos worried about "illegals" and the increasingly influential Mexican American community. It required employers for the first time to vouch for the legal status of their employees. At the same time, it offered an **amnesty** to all undocumented workers who had entered the country before 1982. The law, critics charged, led to discrimination in hiring. And no matter what Congress did, the desperate economic realities in Mexico and Central America continued to encourage the flow of illegal immigration.

= Ref Act 1987—pol. issue (illeg. & Mex. Am. influence)
employer must vouch for employees
amnesty—before 1982

* immig. will continue
desperate econ. of Mex. & Cent. Am.

approximately 580 words

John Mack Faragher, et. al., *Out of Many: A History of the American People,* Copyright © 1994 by Prentice Hall, pp. 1018–1019. Reprinted by permission.

As illustrated, the study strategy using marginal notes, suggested for the essay, may also be used effectively for textbooks. Here are four other ways to organize and restate information you will need to retain.

Simplified Outlining

A formal method of outlining with Roman numerals and letters is unnecessary. Simply

—List main ideas or main headings, relating all subheadings to the main heading they follow.

—Indent to separate important points.

—Use phrases, omit unnecessary words, and abbreviate when possible.

The New Immigration

Face of U.S. changing
    6M legal and 2M undocumented immigrants entered U.S. in 1980s
    More than 1/3 of population growth in 1980s from immig.
    Proportion of growth greater than any other decade except 1910–20
Hispanics and Asians lead
    Hispanic population 50% increase—now 22M
        Mexicans largest Hispan. group
        Demographers—Hisp. largest minority by 2050
        Have struggled but some achieved middle-class status
        Many still poor
    Asian-Am. pop. doubled to 7M in 1980s
        Cluster in own community to maintain group identity
        Generally seek education for upward mobility

---

amnesty (am´ nə stē) pardon for past offense

Pool resources to support family business
Form social networks
Immig. Reform Acts
   1965 Ref. Act eliminated quotas based on national origin
      Preferential treatment for highly educated
      Limited immig. per year to 120,000 from West. Hem., 170,000 outside W. Hem.
   1987 Ref. Act a political issue over illegals and Mex-Am. influence
      Employers must vouch for employees' legal status
      Amnesty for undocumented workers if here prior to 1982

Conclusion: Illegal immigration will continue due to limited economies of Mexico and Central America.

Using Cards

Although it is easier to underline and write notes in the margin of your text, sometimes you are unable to do so because you intend to sell the book. There are other alternatives for study. You can use index cards and write your restatement notes after reading each section. Use the lined side, and, on the blank side, write the chapter heading or subheading. Number the cards so they are organized and write a summary card.

Index cards have certain advantages.

Example of a Study Card

Immigration Reform Acts

1965— eliminated quotas based on nat'l origin
Preferential treatment for highly educ.
Limited immig. per yr. to 120,000 from W. Hemp.; 170,000 outside W. Hemp.

1987— a political issue over illegals and Mex.Am. influence
Employers must vouch for employees' legal status
Amnesty for undoc. workers if here prior to 1982

1. You can integrate class notes with them.
2. They are convenient for study purposes.
3. It is easy to separate cards to determine what information is known from what information is not known.

The Divided Page

The divided page, or Cornell method, is still another way to organize for study. In one column of a page, record important questions to answer or key concepts or terms to learn. As you study, jot the answer or information in the column to the right. The dividing line makes it possible to fold your answers underneath or cover them completely as you study. This method is often used together with other methods, such as mapping, which follows.

Example of a Divided Page

The New Immigration

U.S. changing	6M legal and 2M undoc. immig. entered U.S. in 1980s more than 1/3 of pop. growth in 1980s from immig. proportion of growth greater than any other decade except 1910–1920
Hispanics	50% increase—now 22M Mex.—largest group prediction—Hisp. largest minority by 2050 some achieve middle class; many poor
Asians	pop. doubled to 7M in 1980s cluster in own community—maintain group identity gen'ly seek ed. for upward mobility pool resources to support family business form social networks

Immigration Reform Acts	1965 quotas elim. on nat'l origin
	        preferential treatment for highly educ.
	        limited immig. per yr.; 120T in W. Hem., 170T outside W. Hem.
	1987 political issue—fear illegals & Mex. Am.
	        employers must vouch for employees' legal status
	        amnesty for undoc. workers if here prior to 1982

Conclusion: Illegal immigration will continue due to limited economies of Mex. and Central Am.

Mapping

Mapping is the creation of a graphic chart or word picture so that all pertinent information is visible at one time. The major and minor supporting information to remember is placed in a form that resembles a map or chart, hence the term. For some students, this visualization enables them to recall the textual information much more readily.

Most chapters divide into three or four major sections. You can map each section separately, or if there are many small headings, you can sometimes combine them into one map. When mapping a textbook chapter, you can proceed initially by

1. Surveying the chapter, then previewing each section.
2. Reading, marking, and organizing the important parts.
3. Producing the map, as explained below.

Guidelines for Mapping

1. Write the main chapter section or title (or the thesis if you are reading an essay) in the center of the paper and build the rest of the information around it.
2. To highlight the main chapter section or thesis, draw a square or circle or any other shape around it.
3. Add key words that express the major points. Write these points as branches off the central hub and box or circle them. If the selection is already divided into labeled sections, your task is easy. If there are no divisions, you must group and label the information.
4. Complete the map by adding minor important details off the branches. Try to do some of this from memory.

Example of the Main Idea and the Major Headings

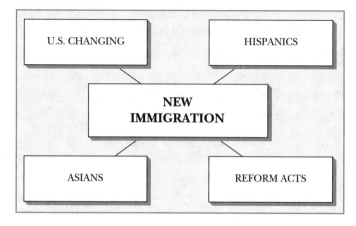

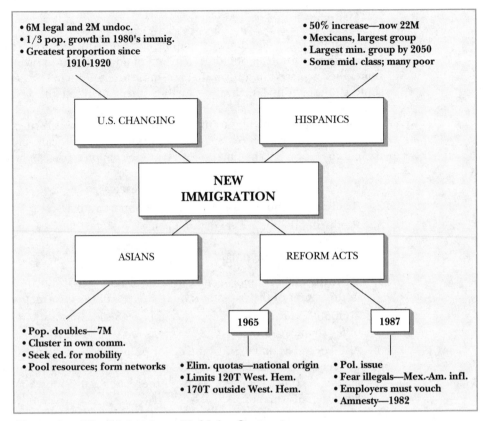

Example of the Main Idea with Major Support

5. Use larger print for important ideas, decreasing size with items of lesser importance. Turn your paper sideways so you can use the width of the paper for your major headings.

The survey/preview and markings or underlining should be done before the mapping so that you reduce the information placed on the map to key ideas. You are creating a study guide so that, before a quiz, you need only spend a brief amount of review time. Moreover, while you are creating the map, you are actually doing further organizing, reconstructing for yourself what needs to be remembered in a **hierarchy.**

---

hierarchy (hī ə rär´ kē) arrangement in a graded series of importance

Frequently, students use mapping in conjunction with the divided page. They place the vocabulary they need to remember, or particular details, on the divided page. This prevents the map from becoming too cluttered. With mapping, you want to show the relationships so details can be more easily visualized and recalled.

An additional mapping technique that aids retention is to use color, separating important ideas and details. You can color-code any map if you wish rather than simply using a black or blue pen. Color is a powerful linking device that can help you remember related information. When you add color, the map, rather than being simply a graphic representation of printed information, actually becomes a picture of ideas—something your mind can see rather than merely read; *this is at the heart of mapping*. If you wish, you can actually draw or paste a picture in the center of the page to represent the topic or thesis of the selection.

Study the maps below, noting how the key ideas about mapping have been organized.

Example of Mapping Format

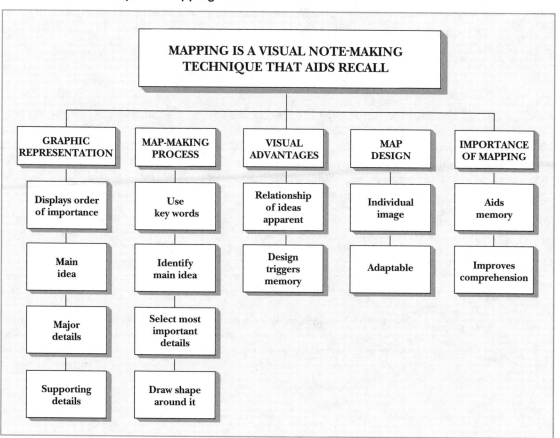

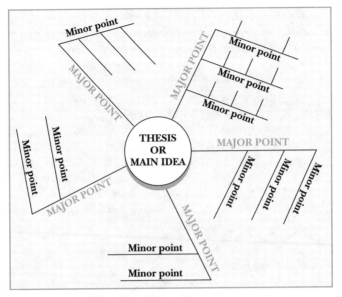

Example of a Mapping Format

A Final Step with All Study Systems: A Summary

The final step with all study systems is to write a good summary of the chapter. Remember, with all summaries, first write a general statement of the main idea. Show the *connection* between the main idea and support. Avoid unnecessary words and include only the most important details. Write your summary in an organized way. If necessary, use some connecting words such as *first, second, additionally.* Here is an example that summarizes the main points of "The New Immigration."

> The U.S. population changed during the 1980s, with dramatic increases in the number of Hispanic and Asian Americans, both legal and undocumented. Mexican Americans continue to be the largest Hispanic group, with predictions that Hispanics, now 22 million, will represent the largest minority by 2050.
>
> The Asian-American population doubled to over 7 million. Asian-Americans generally achieve upward mobility through education and by pooling family resources in business.
>
> The Reform Immigration Acts have been unable to lessen the continuing influx of undocumented immigrants because of the worsening economic conditions in various parts of the world, especially Mexico and Central America.

Practice in Reading and Study of the Textbook

Following is a somewhat longer textbook chapter section. Read and study it by choosing any one of the study methods suggested, paraphrasing in your own words, and then recording the pertinent information. You may also use marginal notes as you did with the essay. If you wish, experiment with several methods to learn which best suits your learning style. Then see how well you can answer the questions that follow.

Selection 5: **TEXTBOOK**

 Preparation for Reading

Read the following textbook chapter excerpt dealing with women and their problems in the workplace and in business. Find out what the E.R.A. stands for, and why it has been controversial for many years. Before reading, note these words, underlined in the text.

feudalism ended	a social system in Europe based on lords and serfs
an **intimidating** environment	causing fear
a male **bastion**	strong defense
experiences **marginality**	being on the border or edge
ascribed status	regarded as belonging to someone
practice of **endogamy**	custom of marrying within one's tribe or clan
thought **deviant**	turning aside from a course or principle
parity with men	equality; equivalency

Preview, then read the textbook selection. Mark important and key ideas. Organize the information before answering the questions with the method that works best for you.

Sexual Harassment

Vincent N. Perrillo

1 For years sexual harassment continued because it was kept secret and considered to be an individual, personal problem. Supposedly, a male, attracted to a particular female, made sexual advances and received a positive, negative, or "maybe" response. Until 1976, women kept mostly silent, thinking the experience an individual encounter and not realizing it was part of a larger pattern connected to their subordination and vulnerability in the occupational structure.

2 *Redbook* magazine's 1976 survey of 9,000 women defined the extent of the problem, as 90 percent reported having experienced sexual harassment at work. The woman's movement brought heightened awareness of the group basis of this problem. Then the federal government's Merit System Protection Board, in a 1978–1980 study, reported a $189 million cost in hiring, training, absenteeism, and job-turnover expenses caused by harassment. When private industry costs are included, the figure probably runs into billions. The government survey also estimated that 1 percent, or about 9,000 female federal employees, had been victims of attempted rape by supervisors or coworkers.

3 In 1979, attorney and university professor Catherine A. MacKinnon wrote the first book on this subject, *Sexual Harassment of Working Women: A Case of Sex Discrimination.* She identified sexual harassment as either a single occur-

rence at work or a series of incidents, rang-ing along a continuum of varying intensity, including:

> verbal sexual suggestions or jokes, constant 4
> leering or ogling, brushing against your body
> "accidentally," a friendly pat, squeeze or pinch
> or arm against you, catching you alone for a
> quick kiss, the indecent proposition backed by
> the threat of losing your job, or forced sexual
> relations.

Some men's assumption that their superior 5 position at work also involves sexual privileges is rooted in centuries of male domination.

> Sexual harassment by a boss or supervisor 6
> harkens back, in a way, to the medieval practice
> of *droit du seigneur*, which gave the feudal lord
> the right to sleep the first night with the bride
> of any of his vassals. Although feudalism ended
> many centuries ago, some people still feel that
> to be a boss is to be at least semi-divinely
> ordained—to have certain inalienable rights.
> . . . The idea of using a paycheck as a license
> for sex seems ludicrous, if not sick, but it hap-
> pens all the time. Men who would never think
> or at least never follow through on, the idea of
> pinching a woman's breast in a bus or on the
> street, feel free to subject their secretary to this
> humiliation as if it were a job-given right.

Prospects for reduction of this type of 7 harassment seem promising. Official guidelines formulated by the Equal Employment Opportunities Commission set standards pro-tecting employees from certain forms of sexual harassment, defined as follows:

> Unwelcome sexual advances, requests for sex- 8
> ual favors, and other verbal or physical conduct
> of a sexual nature . . . when submission is
> made a condition of employment, or rejection
> of the advance is used as the basis for future
> employment decision, or interfering with the

individual's performance or creating an intimi-dating, hostile, or offensive working environ-ment.

Although this sounds formidable it does 9 not encompass many obnoxious and question-able behaviors found in everyday examples. California's Fair Employment and Housing Department has established more down-to-earth guidelines: unsolicited written, verbal, or physical contacts; suggestive or obscene notes; continual leering; obscene gestures; display of obscene objects or pictures; blocking move-ments by physical touching; and forced involve-ment in obscene joking. Because these forms of sexual harassment are not specifically men-tioned in the EEOC guidelines, they can escape definition and punishment. A General Motors representative, however, has suggested a good "rough measure" of sexual harassment: "Would you be embarrassed to have your remarks dis-played in the newspaper or actions described to your family?"

SEXISM AND THE LAW

Stereotyping females as passive and in need of 10 protection became institutionalized in law. Many labor laws, originally intended to prevent the exploitation of women, became a means of restricting their job opportunities and income potential. A vast array of state laws, assuming certain female inabilities, ran counter to reality. As sociologist Rosalind J. Dworkin wryly com-mented:

> A mother can carry her 40-pound child, move 11
> furniture in her home, and finish her house-
> keeping chores late at night. But the same
> woman, working outside the home, legally
> could not carry more than 30 pounds of weight
> or work overtime in some states. . . . [T]hese
> protective laws . . . degrade women to a child-
> like status by assuming they are unable, or not

wise enough, to protect themselves, individually or collectively, from exploitation.

Though many of these laws are changing, 12 compliance does not necessarily follow. Many women do not know their legal rights or find the difficulties involved in securing them outweigh the rewards. Moreover, the courts are hardly free of sexism themselves. In 1983 New Jersey became the first state to complete a self-review of sexism in the state court system. Among other findings it discovered the following:

1. Women received lower personal injury set- 13 tlements, especially if they were housewives, because juries failed to recognize the value of their work.
2. Judges failed to enforce the new law against wife beating and domestic violence.
3. Judges set child-support payments in divorce cases too low, with no strong enforceable sanctions against nonpayment by fathers.

Female attorneys also complained that 86 per- 14 cent of their colleagues and 66 percent of the judges had made demeaning jokes or hostile remarks about their sex. As New Jersey acts to eliminate such practices, some of the other forty-nine states are beginning to conduct similar self-reviews, as pressure for change mounts from the growing number of female lawyers nationwide.

Because changing hundreds of state laws is 15 a long, difficult process, Congress approved the Equal Rights Amendment (ERA) in 1972, intending it to extend full and legal rights to women. The proposed Amendment's wording was brief: "Equality of rights under the law shall not be denied or abridged by the United States or by any state on account of sex." Required to be ratified by three fourths of the states, a total of thirty-eight, it only gained approval by thirty-

five. The failure of the ERA was caused by the opposition of numerous groups, including many women, labor leaders or activists, as well as conservatives, religious groups, and insurance companies.

Is the ERA dead? Many feminists have not 16 given up, vowing to replace state and federal legislators opposed to the measure. Others argue the Amendment is unnecessary, that full property and credit rights for women, and more equal divorce and child custody rights for men, for example, are simply evolving through changing societal norms. The issue remains highly controversial, sometimes surrounded by emotion-charged fears and myths, but with well-intentioned people on both sides of the argument. If an ERA does pass, one thing is certain: It is still years away.

WOMEN AND POLITICS

Earlier we noted that, once they secured voting 17 rights, women did not use their political power to improve their lives or win their proportional share of elected office. Only a handful of women have been elected governor; only a few of the one hundred U.S. senators are female; and only several of 435 Congressional representatives are women. With women constituting slightly over 51 percent of the population, with more female than male registered and active voters, they nevertheless remain vastly underrepresented in elected, decision-making positions.

What accounts for this lack of female polit- 18 ical involvement? The question has intrigued both sociologists and political scientists, with emerging explanations many and varied. Most political careers evolve out of training, experience, and leadership in law or business careers, areas in which women have participated only slightly. Males control the political parties, often resisting placement of women in organizational power positions or as viable candidates for "serious" offices. Politics has been a male bastion for so many generations that male politicians tend to view the female politician as a stranger, one whose feminine values and way of life appear incompatible with the world of politics. Therefore both men and women also prefer male leaders, placing more confidence in them.

A woman seeking a political career experiences marginality; she is unable to retain her past "feminine" ways if she is to be an active political participant, yet unwilling to reject them either. Both choices present threats to her self-esteem, and the simpler choice is avoiding disorientation and personal isolation by not running for office. Women also do not form a voting bloc, because they are not residentially segregated and tend to vote along socioeconomic lines.

RETROSPECT

American society has only recently recognized sexism as a social problem, although it has existed for centuries. Minority-group characteristics—ascribed status, physical and cultural visibility, unequal treatment, and shared-group awareness—apply to women, as they do to various racial and ethnic groups. The practice of endogamy does not apply, but in marriage the dominant-subordinate roles are often quite obvious.

Throughout much of American history, male dominance patterns prevailed. Women lacked voting, contract, and property rights, and were even denied the right to enjoy sex without being thought deviant. After a long struggle women gained the right to vote nationally in 1919, but did not harness any political power to effect change or elect many women to office. During World War II many women worked, but peacetime brought an emphasis on the home as a "woman's proper place." In the 1960s the feminist movement began anew, fostering social awareness and still unfolding social change.

Despite some biological differences between the sexes in size, strength, and longevity, socialization is what shapes gender identity and sex-role behavior. Entrenched value orientations result in a conditioning process producing differential behavior patterns and life goals. The resultant sexual inequality is evident throughout society, and doubly so among minority women. In education, employment, income, legal status, and political power, women's status has improved but still remains far removed from parity with men.

19

20

21

22

approximately 1700 words

Vincent N. Perrillo, *Strangers to These Shores: Race and Ethnic Relations in the U.S.,* 3rd ed. Copyright © 1990 by Macmillan Publishing Company, pp. 501–4. Reprinted with permission.

COMPREHENSION CHECK

Part I
General Comprehension Questions: Literal and Interpretive

Write the correct letter in the space provided.

_____ 1. The first book on sexual harassment of women at work was written

    a. at the turn of the century.
    b. fifty years ago.
    c. about two decades ago.
    d. in 1990.

Source: Wayne Stayskal, *Peninsula Times Tribune* (December 7, 1991).
Reprinted by permission.

"WATCH IT... I HEAR HE JUST TOOK OUT SEXUAL HARASSMENT INSURANCE!"

_____ 2. A rough measure of sexual harassment was defined as

    a. Fair Employment guidelines.
    b. being embarrassed by having the remarks printed.
    c. having the remarks repeated to family members.
    d. both b and c.

_____ 3. Laws that treat women more fairly are being passed but do not secure them their rights because

    a. there is a lack of compliance with the law.
    b. the courts have been sexist.
    c. women aren't aware of their legal rights.
    d. all of the above.

_____ 4. Passage of the Equal Rights Amendment would entitle women to

    a. most legal rights.
    b. some legal rights.
    c. all legal rights.
    d. abridged legal rights.

_____ 5. It appears that the ERA

    a. will pass soon.
    b. will not pass soon.
    c. is a dead issue.
    d. is unnecessary.

_____ 6. According to this selection, most women have not been active politically because

    a. men control the political parties.
    b. women are primarily interested in business.
    c. women form a segregated bloc.
    d. none of the above.

7. Explain how some laws intended to help women actually limit their business opportunities.

_____

_____

_____

8. According to this selection, what has been the position of the courts in recent years when they are presented with women's rights issues?

_____

_____

_____

Part II
Application Questions for Writing/Discussion

9. The ERA failed to be ratified because certain groups, including women's groups, opposed it. Why do you suppose this was so?

_____

_____

_____

_____

10. Name several women who have government positions at the state or national level. Are they, or have they been, effective? If so, is this in contradiction to the article?

_____

_____

_____

_____

_____

Part III
Extend Your Vocabulary

Underline the prefixes and suffixes in these boldfaced words. Look at the root. Can you tell the meaning of the word in the phrase? Write the meaning and the part of speech of the bold-faced word.

1. an **inequality** of opportunity   _____

2. **inalienable** rights   _____

3. **absenteeism** at work   _____

4. protect from **exploitation**   _____

5. **residentially** segregated   _____

❖ Test-Taking Strategies

Success or failure in college is determined in large part by your ability to perform well on tests and examinations. Several suggestions follow regarding effective test-taking.

Rule 1: Come to the test with a positive attitude that you will be successful.

Rule 2: *Always preview and skim a test* so as to plan the time you will need to answer certain sections. Don't plunge in and start answering question 1. When you preview and skim, note the point value of each question. Often instructors give more points or credit for answers to essay questions. Planning ahead will help you make the maximum use of your time.

Tests sometimes include choices, asking students to answer *some* of the questions. If you do not preview the test first, it is easy to overlook such important information as choice.

Rule 3: *Read the directions slowly and carefully.* Directions can sometimes be different from what you expect. For example, in some multiple-choice tests, an instructor might want you to mark *two* correct answers instead of only one, the way most tests are designed.

Rule 4: *Answer the easiest questions first.* Some of the answers you failed to remember will become obvious through reading other test questions, which may jog your memory.

Answering Multiple-Choice Questions

1. Multiple-choice questions may include three or four choices.

    Example: The decade of the 1990s is called the Information Age because
    a. the twenty-first century is almost here.
    b. we are bombarded with information from many different sources.
    c. information is important to know.
    d. our technology has improved tremendously.

    Often, you will note immediately that two choices are incorrect, so you can disregard them. See choices a and c. In most multiple-choice questions, it comes down to one of the two remaining answers. Cross out the incorrect answers a and c now. Concentrate on the two you must decide between. Before you read either of the remaining choices again, think about what the stem, the statement part you need to answer, is asking.

    Read the stem, "The decade of the 1990s is called the Information Age because," and one of the choices, b.
    Read the stem and the second choice, d. This makes it much easier to decide on one of the two. Choice b is the correct one.

2. Often, a word or term you have never heard of may be incorrect; it may have been included simply to distract you.

    Example: A substance found in the red blood cells which binds and transports oxygen and carbon dioxide is
    a. hemoglobin (the correct answer)
    b. tripepglobin (made-up word to distract you)

3. In the stem (the statement part you need to answer) watch for words like *not*, *except*, *incorrect*, or other negatives. These words make a tremendous difference in what answer you should select.

    Example: Which name was not mentioned as being part of the myth machine?

4. The phrase *all of the above* is used frequently by instructors and often, but not always, is the correct answer.

    Example: The author believes that most women in the marketplace
    a. do not earn as much as men.
    b. are held back on the corporate ladder more than men.
    c. must still juggle housework and their job.
    d. all of the above.

5. The most complete and longest statement is sometimes the correct one.

    Example: The introduction of New Math in the 1960s
               a. led to an end of the "back to basics" movement.
               b. was meant to improve reasoning and problem-solving skills.
               c. was embraced by math teachers.
               d. was welcomed by parents.

Answering True-False Statements

You will not encounter this form of questioning in this text, but many instructors, especially in the sciences, frequently use the true-false format.

1. *For statements to be true, all parts must be true.* Therefore, if any part is not true, the statement is false.

    Example: Hemoglobin is found in the white blood cells and transports both oxygen and carbon dioxide. (Hemoglobin is found in the red blood cells—therefore you must choose *false* as the answer even though part of the answer is correct.)

2. As with multiple choice, if you have never heard a word mentioned in class or seen it in your text, the statement is probably false. Similarly, absolute statements with words like *always, all, none,* and *never* are often false.

3. Words like *frequently, probably, some,* and *generally* are different from words like *always* and *never.* These words signal that the statement may be true.

Answering Matching Questions

Although either column may be used to match statement and matching term, it is best to begin with the column having the longer statements because this eliminates a lot of rereading. Also, match everything you are certain is correct first, because making one error generally means you are going to make another. Complete the following example now.

    Example: _____ antonym   a. a word very similar in meaning to another word
             _____ glossary   b. a word opposite in meaning to another word
             _____ synonym   c. a list of specialized words with their definitions

Answering Essay Questions

1. Know the meaning of the terms used by instructors who test with essay questions.

Terms	Meaning
analyze	point out the strong and weak points
compare and contrast	give similarities and differences

enumerate	provide a listing
evaluate	judge whether positive points outweigh the negative
identify	give the characteristics and importance of something or someone
illustrate	make clear by example
interpret	explain the meaning
justify	give reasons for
relate	show how things are connected
trace	describe how something developed

Note how each of the following essay questions on the same topic requires a different type of answer.

Analyze the lobbying efforts by TV producers to keep violence on their programs.

Compare and contrast the TV violence in the United States with that of England and Japan.

Enumerate the TV shows that continue to exploit violence.

Evaluate whether TV producers feel pressure to make changes in shows that promote violence.

Identify the lobbies that pressure Congress to withhold action on TV violence.

Illustrate why there is a need for action on the part of the TV viewing public in regard to TV violence.

Interpret the suggested law to curb TV violence.

Justify or argue against the actions of parents who have brought lawsuits against TV stations that schedule programs with undue violence during prime time.

Relate how changes in our society correspond to the rise of violence on TV.

Trace the rise of violence on U.S. TV.

Be certain to include necessary supporting information.

2. Questions posed by instructors are not always specific, so students are sometimes unsure what answer is expected. For example, look at these two questions.

Describe the effects of poor nutrition.

Describe the effects of poor nutrition *on the developing fetus*.

When answering essay questions, note whether the instructor is looking for a general answer or a very specific one.

Eliminating Test Anxiety

1. The best way to eliminate anxiety is through preparedness. Organize the information, study the information, and review it. Spaced reviews are always better than just one long session. There are few shortcuts!

2. If it's an important test such as a midterm or final, try to relax before the test. Avoid situations that create anxiety such as being late for the test or talking with classmates who habitually are nervous before tests and convey that feeling to you.

3. Reread your essay answers. Ask yourself whether you have recorded everything correctly and whether you have answered *all* the questions. Grammar and spelling checks are strongly recommended.

4. Relax! You've done a great job.

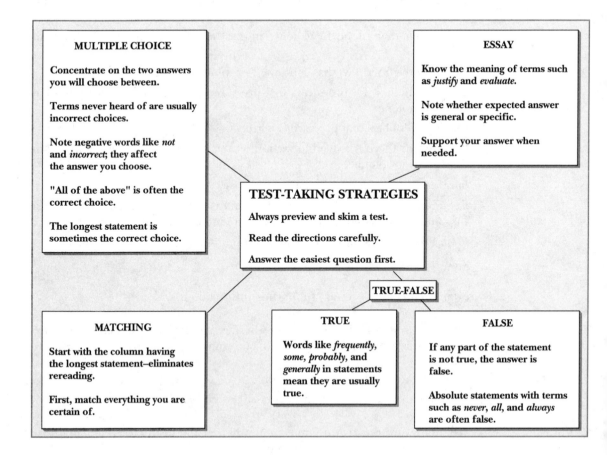

MULTIPLE CHOICE

Concentrate on the two answers you will choose between.

Terms never heard of are usually incorrect choices.

Note negative words like *not* and *incorrect*; they affect the answer you choose.

"All of the above" is often the correct choice.

The longest statement is sometimes the correct choice.

ESSAY

Know the meaning of terms such as *justify* and *evaluate*.

Note whether expected answer is general or specific.

Support your answer when needed.

TEST-TAKING STRATEGIES

Always preview and skim a test.

Read the directions carefully.

Answer the easiest question first.

MATCHING

Start with the column having the longest statement–eliminates rereading.

First, match everything you are certain of.

TRUE-FALSE

TRUE

Words like *frequently, some, probably,* and *generally* in statements mean they are usually true.

FALSE

If any part of the statement is not true, the answer is false.

Absolute statements with terms such as *never, all,* and *always* are often false.

❖ Literature

Why do we read and study literature? Reading literature differs from reading essays and textbooks, which deal primarily with information. We read literature for pleasure and, in part, study it to learn the elements of character, conflict, plot, setting, and theme to determine how good the storyteller is at his or her craft. Perhaps more important than the study of the structure of literature, however, are the reasons described in the following paragraph.

> Literature with a social consciousness speaks out against social, economic and political injustice; it exposes the many faces of racism, sexism, militarism, and elitism; literature extends our capacity for compassion . . . its social conscience reminds us of our commitment to the real democratic covenant—the real meaning of the 4th of July and the flag—that what unites people is not color or gender or religion but moral conscience. . . . Literature therefore becomes crucial in the struggle to activate people.*

In studying literature we learn to mentally interact with characters so as to understand human experiences or what is often called "the human condition"— what it is that makes people, including ourselves, behave in certain ways. We understand ourselves better when we become aware of and analyze the motives, **aspirations,** successes, and failures of others. Through identification with particular characters, we can learn values.

What happens—the plot or the narration—while important, is usually secondary to the development of character through which we better understand the writer's theme. Our focus with literature, therefore, is not the same as with essays or textbooks; your reading strategies should be modified to reflect that difference.

Some Literary Elements Defined

It is important to be aware of the terms frequently used in discussing literature. These include

Character: Three techniques are usually used by writers to create a character. A writer may describe a character's physical appearance and situation, reveal a character's words and thoughts, or show the reaction of other characters toward him or her.

---

aspirations (as pə rā´ shənz) desires for high achievement

*Arthur I. Blaustein, "A Novel Idea to Keep America Afloat," Perspective, *San Jose Mercury News*, July 1, 1990, pp. 4–6.

Conflict:	The conflict or problem must be resolved. It may be an internal conflict of the character or a conflict between people, nature, society, or the unknown. There may be more than one conflict.
Plot:	The plot pattern consists of a series of related events. A problem or conflict is presented; events take place leading to a **climax** and eventually to a resolution.
Setting:	The setting consists of the time and place in which the action occurs. At times the setting directly controls the plot's development, and at times it helps in a better understanding of character.
Theme:	A theme is the underlying main idea of a literary work. It involves a statement or opinion about the subject, sometimes stated, more often implied. Mysteries or adventure stories, often written entirely for a reader's entertainment, do not always have a theme.

A Comparison of How to Study the Essay, the Textbook, and Literature

	Essay	**Textbook**	**Literature**
Organization	A series of literary paragraphs on a single subject; usually presents the author's viewpoint.	Uses boldfaced headings and subheadings; divides and subdivides a lot of detailed information; major and minor topics.	A narrative that depends on the plot and consists of a conflict, a climax, and a resolution.
Purpose	To see whether you agree with the author's thesis; to note whether the thesis is supported; to be aware of language that strengthens or diminishes it; to develop social awareness.	To understand and retain information so it can be used for discussion purposes and for further written evaluation such as quizzes, tests, and exams.	For pleasure and to learn the elements of character, conflict, plot, setting, and theme; to determine how good storytellers are at their craft; to raise social consciousness.
Study Methods	Preview, and then read. Write in the margins the main idea of each important paragraph. Note how all these add up to the thesis. Find support for the thesis. Note the nuances of the language, subtle expressions. Evaluate what you read. Does the writer have a point?	Survey the chapter. Read and mark each section, using coded notations in the margin. Highlight only what is important. Organize and restate, using any of these methods: summary, answering questions, outline, note cards, a divided page, or map. Include summaries with each method. Evaluate what you read to determine its reliability and usefulness.	Ask what will happen to the characters and how they develop as you follow the plot. Look for metaphorical language, often a part of good fiction. Ask yourself if the author has a higher purpose than to entertain. What is the theme? What does it say about life? Evaluate and form a critical opinion of the novel.

climax (klī´ maks) the part in a series of events marked by the greatest intensity

❖ Summary

This chapter has focused on reading and organizing for more effective study and learning. Three genres of reading—the essay, the textbook, and literature—have unique structures and, therefore, particular study strategies enhance organizing their contents for discussion purposes, for answering questions, and for test taking.

An essay's thesis must be identified and evaluated together with its supporting information. Its more literary style differentiates it from the textbook, and it usually does not include the more helpful graphic organizers and headings found in a textbook.

The textbook, on the other hand, usually has a unique vocabulary peculiar to its discipline that sometimes may be equated to learning a second language. Textbook chapters, moreover, are long, with many concepts to retain and remember, and quizzes and tests follow, necessitating a more detailed kind of study and organization so that the information is retained. Study strategies suggested included note-taking, simplified outlining, using index cards, using a divided page, and mapping.

Test-taking strategies used in answering various types of essay and textbook questions require that students first preview or skim a test for content, read the directions carefully, and answer the easiest questions initially. Multiple choice and true-false statements often include particular words that can alert the student to the correct answer. Essay questions have a particular terminology, and students should know the meanings of the most common terms used.

Literature study focuses on certain elements of a narrative: character, plot, setting, style, and theme. The study of literature raises our social consciousness in a unique way as we identify with particular characters and situations.

Chapter 3 Vocabulary Review

Write the correct answer in the space provided. The first one is done for you.

1. If an item is **topical,** is it dated or current? _current_

2. When something **diminishes,** does it grow smaller or larger? _____

3. Would most people like to receive more or fewer **accolades?** _____

4. Who would most likely use **nuance,** a classroom instructor or a writer?

5. Does one who speaks **concisely** usually use many or few words? _____

_____

6. Are **salient** features important or unimportant in notetaking? _____

_____

7. Is a boss at the top or the bottom of a **hierarchy?** _____

8. Does a **demographer's** work generally concern weather trends or people and

statistics? _____

9. Does **amnesty** refer to a conviction or to a pardon? _____

10. Should college students have low or high **aspirations?** _____

_____

Selection 6: **LITERATURE**

☞ Preparing for Reading

Bharati Mukherjee was hailed as "a writer of grace and powerful imagination" when she was inducted into the American Academy of Arts and Sciences in 1993. Since she arrived from Calcutta in 1961, the basis for her fiction has been the immigrant experience in America. In her writings, she explores how immigrants and their adopted country change one another. Their transformations are often very painful, but, with sympathy and insight, she creates a vision of hope. Mukherjee herself has been transformed from an obscure writer into one of America's most respected novelists. She currently resides in California and is a professor at the University of California, Berkeley. *Jasmine,* her third novel, was published in 1989 and continues to receive accolades from both critics and readers.

In this excerpt, Jasmine finds herself in an unknown area of Florida. At eighteen, she has left India, her birthplace, after her husband, Prakash, whom she loved passionately, was savagely murdered by a gang of hoodlums. Jasmine unknowingly puts her trust in an evil sea captain, Half-Face, who promises to bring her to America after she pays him all the money she has. He subsequently rapes her, and filled with both hatred for him and self-loathing with herself, she kills him, then flees from the motel where she had been violated.

You will meet some terms used in Indian culture, defined below. As you read the selection, think about the kind of person Jasmine is becoming.

Jasmine

Bharati Mukherjee

Bharati
Mukherjee

I found Taylor and Wylie Hayes through Lillian Gordon, a kind Quaker lady who res- **1**
cued me from a dirt trail about three miles east of Fowlers Key, Florida. In my fake American jacket, ***salwar-kameez,*** and rhinestoned ***Jullundhari sandals,*** with only a purse, Ganpati and forged documents, I had walked out of an overpopulated, deserted motel and followed a highway headed north; that's all I knew. In India, I would have come upon at least a village or two, but in Florida there was only the occasional country store or trailer park. I hadn't a penny.

Honoring all prescriptions for a purified body, anticipating only release from **2**
this world, I had not eaten in two days. I had taken no water, especially not in the glass that Half-Face offered.

Around noon, I could go no farther. My swollen festering tongue was an agony, **3**
nearly choking me. A sandy trail tunneled through a distant row of mossy trees. Battered trucks full of produce kept pulling out. More trucks, filled with laborers, turned in. It was as though I'd never left India. After a few minutes, a station wagon

---

salwar-kameez clothing
Jullundhari sandals name-brand sandals

driven by a lone woman followed. Fields on either side of the highway were dense with tomatoes, eggplants, and okra (still aubergines and ladies' finger in Masterji's English). I had traveled the world without ever leaving the familiar crops of Punjab. Thinking I was among farmers, that I might find food, water, and work, I decided to follow the trail.

Trash cans lined one edge of the clearing. So much trash in America! Bony dogs **4** leaped and snarled at the end of short chains. Mangy hens scuttled in and out of dried-out tire ruts. Short, thick, dark-skinned men with vaguely Asian features— Nepalese, I thought at the time, *Gurkhas;* can this torture all be a dream? where have I come to?—shadowed the windows and doorways of an old barracks, and a wingless parrot hopped on a rusty bar.

A boy whistled at me from behind a tree. I couldn't tell his age. He had a child's **5** body: fat stomach and thin legs with crusting sores, but a wrinkled, cynical face. I had been in America nearly a day and had yet to see an "American" face. He carried a plastic Uzi, not that different from the hardware of the Khalsa Lions, and he had the Uzi pointed at me. He did impressive sound effects, too. Kssss! Kssss!

"Water," I tried to say. "Pump." Blood still drained from my mouth.   **6**

The boy dropped down into a sniper's crouch and sprayed me one more time.   **7**

I made a pumping, drinking gesture.   **8**

At the far end of the clearing, by the trash cans, a man was teaching two others **9** to drive a low-sprung old sedan. I waved my hands over my head, then pointed to my mouth. "Wah-huh!" I shouted at them. The man behind the steering wheel got out of the sedan. He mimicked the way I talked and walked. The boy and all three men laughed.

The driver of the sedan kicked a cola can and sent it clanking toward me. "No **10** work!" he snapped. "This Kanjobal crew. Vamoose! Fuck off! Get lost!"

At that moment, an old white lady came out of the barracks. She wore a wide- **11** brimmed straw hat, dark glasses, a T-shirt, and black pants. She must have been seventy. From the doorway she called, "Carlos! How dare you speak to a young lady in such a despicable fashion. She asked for water—well, get her water, man!"

She came to me and put her hands on my shoulders. "Child! What is it? You're **12** trembling." She led me to the stairs and sat me down on the middle one. "What in God's name is this country coming to!" She stood and clapped her hands and shouted out a series of names or commands in a rapid language. Soon, a woman appeared with food on a paper plate and a plastic fork. It was the first hot, prepared food I'd had in over a month. But when I laid a forkful of it on my tongue, I nearly passed out with pain. The woman walked me to her car.

"My name is Lillian Gordon," she said. "I won't ask yours because it's probably a **13** fake. *This* I take it—she was feeling my kameez—isn't Guatemalan, is it? Are we talking India here? Punjab? Are you Sikh?"

I managed only to shake my head vigorously, no. "Hin—du," I finally said.   **14**

Gurkhas warlike people of Nepal, near India

"Lord. Well, there's nothing we can do here, is there? And I suppose those chap- 15
pies from the INS would leap at the sight of you in those sandals." She motioned me
to get in the station wagon.

Lillian Gordon took me home with her. Home was a wooden house on stilts on 16
blackish swampy ground. But over there, she said, over the black muck and just
beyond a fringe of bent Sabal palms, was the Gulf. I got her older daughter's bedroom. Framed, amateurish photos lined the walls. "Kate took those in high school,"
Lillian said. Sunsets on the beach, a dog. Pretty, but not special. In college she'd
come back one summer and shot* in a migrant-worker camp. Five years later she'd
done work with the Kanjobals in Florida, the basis of a book that had won a prize.
Lillian showed me the book. The pictures brought back such memories of
Hasnapur, I wept. That daughter now lived in New York and was a professional pho-
tographer. Another daughter was in Guatemala working with Kanjobal Indians.
Three Kanjobal women slept in bunk beds in that daughter's room.

I didn't tell Mrs. Gordon what she'd rescued me from. In some fundamental 17
way, she didn't care. I was no threat, and I was in need. The world's misery was a challenge to her ingenuity. She brought a doctor in to sew my tongue. The Kanjobal
women in her house had all lost their husbands and children to an army massacre.
She forbade all discussion of it. She had a low tolerance for reminiscence, bitterness
or nostalgia. Let the past make you wary, by all means. But do not let it deform you.
Had I said, "I murdered a man last night," she might have said, "I'm sure you had an
excellent reason. Next time, please, less salt in the eggplant." If I had said, "He raped
me," she certainly would have squinted sympathetically, then said, "You're not the
first and you won't be the last. Will you be needing an abortion?" She wasn't a mis-
sionary dispensing new visions and stamping out the old; she was a facilitator who
made possible the lives of absolute *ordinariness* that we ached for.

I was lucky, she said, that India had once been a British colony. Can you imag- 18
ine being stuck with a language like Dutch or Portuguese? "Look at these poor
Kanjobal—they barely speak Spanish!" Lillian, of course, had taught herself
Kanjobal. She felt it was the least she could do.

She gave me her daughter's high-school clothes: blouses with Peter Pan collars, 19
maxi shirts, T-shirts with washed-out pictures, sweaters, cords, and loafers. But
beware the shoes, she said, shoes are the biggest giveaway. Undocumented aliens
wear boxy shoes with ambitious heels. She opened her thumb and index finger a
good six inches like a crocodile's mouth.

Suddenly it all came back: Jullundhar, Prakash, a day just before the end, at Bata 20
Shoes. An image triggered the tears, the screams. The Kanjobal women left the
room; Lillian stayed with me, brewing tea.

Prakash in his peach-colored bell-bottomed slacks, kicking off his chappals and 21
asking to see their best "Western" burra sahib leather shoes. Oh, he looked so tall,
so proud, lifted in those shoes that gleamed like oiled hair in their boxy brilliance.

"See how tall I am, Jasmine?" 22

---

*A term used in photography meaning to take a picture or a series of pictures.

"Put these things away," he said to me back in the apartment. "No more chap- **23** pals for me." I felt love like a razor slash across my eyes and tongue, and now with a touch of shame.

"My daughter calls them Third World heels," Lillian said, laughed, after the tea **24** had calmed me down. Walk American, she exhorted me, and she showed me how. I worked hard on the walk and deportment. Within a week she said I'd lost my shy sidle. She said I walked like one of those Trinidad Indian girls, all thrust and cheek-iness. She meant it as a compliment.

"Tone it down, girl!" She clapped as I took a turn between the kitchen and bath. **25** I checked myself in the mirror, shocked at the transformation. Jazzy in a T-shirt, tight cords, and running shoes. I couldn't tell if with the Hasnapuri sidle I'd also aban-doned my Hasnapuri modesty.

We drove into a mall in Clearwater for the test. Time to try out my American talk **26** and walk. Lillian called me "Jazzy." In one of the department stores I saw my first revolving door. How could something be always open and at the same time always closed? She had me try out my first escalator. How could something be always mov-ing and always still?

At the bottom of the escalator she said, "They pick up dark people like you **27** who're afraid to get on or off." I shut my eyes and stepped forward and kept my eyes closed all the way to the top. I waited for the hairy arm of the law to haul me in. Instead, Lillian said, "You pass, Jazzy." She gave me two dollars. "Now, how about buy-ing me a Dairy Queen?"

I remember Dairy Queen as my first true American food. How it soothed my **28** still-raw tongue. I thought of it as healing food.

approximately 1600 words

Excerpted from Bharati Mukherjee, *Jasmine,* (New York: Globe Weidenfeld, 1989), pp. 127–33. Copyright © by Bharati Mukherjee. Reprinted with permission of Grove/Atlantic, Inc. and Janklow & Nesbitt Associates.

Questions for Writing/Discussion

1. The skill of a writer is often evident by how she or he creates minor characters. How would you describe Lillian Gordon? What kind of a person is she? Why do you suppose she befriends Jasmine and others?

2. Why were the shoes and the walk an important part of Jasmine's transformation? How does Jasmine now see herself?

3. Why does Jasmine refer to a Dairy Queen as "healing food"? There is more than a simple explanation.

4. Part of a writer's skill is setting up conflict in a story. At this point in the novel, what is the major conflict in *Jasmine*?

JOURNAL ENTRY

The essay in this chapter, "How Women and Minorities Are Reshaping Corporate America," focused on underrepresentation of certain groups in business and politics. The textbook selection focused on sexual harassment in the workplace. Also included was an excerpt from the novel *Jasmine* about a young Hindu woman who comes to America. How do you see Jasmine's prospects in this country in the future? What are the opportunities that may or may not be available to her? Write a journal entry that expresses your feelings about these opportunities. Add a statement about how you view *your own* future opportunities.

4

From Sentence to Paragraph to the Main Idea: Steps to Eliminate Problems in Comprehension

This chapter will help you
◆ Understand the meaning of complicated sentences.
◆ Know the difference between a paragraph topic and a main idea.
◆ Recognize both stated and unstated (implied) main ideas in paragraphs.
◆ Separate major details from minor details.

❖❖❖

Before reading, think about this question.
◆ What is particularly troublesome for you in recognizing and restating the main idea?

❖❖❖

Jot down some of your thoughts about finding the main idea in what you read. _____

_____

_____

_____

In this chapter, we will examine why particular sentences and paragraphs may cause difficulty in determining the main points in reading, and we offer suggestions to make the task simpler. Additionally, we will continue to stress the importance of making notations by marking important points in paragraphs; ultimately, any organizational method starts with good notes. The difference in recognizing the main point of sentences, paragraphs, articles, and essays is essentially one of degree; the paragraph generally contains more information about an idea than a sentence, while an essay or article elaborates even further on an idea than a paragraph.

❖ Sentences and Their Relationships

Most sentences have at least one key idea and generally contain two parts, a subject and a verb. The subject, usually a noun or noun phrase, identifies the main person or thing in the sentence. A verb or verb phrase* indicates what the person or thing is doing or has done. Additional information about the subject and verb may also be included.

> Example: The <u>American economy,</u> though weakened, still <u>grew significantly</u> in the past few years.

The key idea of this sentence is the *American economy grew significantly.*
The subject, *American economy,* tells what the sentence is about. The words *though weakened* add more information about the economy.
The verb phrase, *still grew significantly,* explains what the subject is doing. The words *in the past few years* simply add more information.

In longer sentences with combined ideas, the key idea is not always obvious.

> Extensive information networks continue to grow both inside and outside business organizations and require better writing skills from a growing number of American workers.

Two key questions help determine the key idea.

1. Who or what is the sentence chiefly about? *identifies the <u>subject</u>*
2. What is/was happening to the subject? *identifies <u>the verb or verb phrase/s</u>*

In the above sentence, the answer to the first question, "What is the sentence about?," is *extensive information networks.* The verb is more complex because it includes two ideas, *continues to grow* and *requires greater writing skills.* The key idea, then, is that *extensive information networks continue to grow and require better writing skills.* Longer sentences frequently have more than one main subject and more than one main verb.

*Also referred to as the *predicate.*

What Types of Sentences May Cause Difficulty?

In many sentences, particularly short ones, the key parts (the subject and verb) express a complete thought that is easily understood. In some sentences, however, intervening information separates the key parts. When the subject and the verb are split, you must find and recall the subject while reading the additional information so you can connect it to the verb. Some common types of sentences may interfere with comprehension.

1. Sentences with long introductions.
2. Sentences that are interrupted with paired dashes.
3. Sentences composed of many smaller sentences joined together.
4. Sentences with weak pronoun referents.

Sentences with Long Introductions

Some sentences contain much introductory information in phrases or clauses, modifying the key idea, which appears later. In the following examples, the introductory phrase is underlined; the key idea is in italics.

Less than a year after announcing they had found evidence of the missing piece of matter essential to understanding the universe, *scientists* this week *are expected to proclaim the discovery of the* elusive subatomic particle, the "*quark*."

Associated Press, March 1, 1995

If you search for an understanding of problems related to depletion of the ozone layer, or crystalline structures in rocks, or materials for superconductors, or metabolism and respiration, or the effects of medications on the body, *chemistry is there.*

Ralph A. Burns *Essentials of Chemistry*, p. 15

Sentences that Use Paired Dashes

To make longer sentences somewhat easier to read, writers often use dashes to break up the information. The sentence part enclosed with dashes *is never the key idea;* it simply provides related information. In the following example, the key idea is in italics.

Reports about the production of atomic fission from uranium written by famed mathematician Albert Einstein—who regarded the development of atomic warfare as a perversion of his life's efforts—*alerted the U.S. government* to potential military uses.

John Mack Faragher et al., *Out of Many*, p. 100

Sentences Composed of Many Short Sentences Joined Together

Another difficulty with reading some sentences is that short sentences are joined together through clauses and connecting words. In the following sentence from a sociology textbook, the key idea is italicized.

> Currently, *a heated debate is under way* between advocates of retaining our drug laws and their opponents, who believe that criminalization has failed and encourage adoption of a policy of decriminalization combined with an intensified emphasis on education and therapy.
>
> David Popenoe, *Sociology*, p. 176

The sentence includes the following ideas:

> Currently, a heated debate is under way between advocates of retaining our drug laws and their opponents.
> Opponents believe that criminalization has failed.
> They encourage adoption of a policy of decriminalization.
> They want this policy combined with an intensified emphasis on education and therapy.

Here is another example of ideas joined together in a sentence. Try to underline the key idea.

> Other researchers have found that disapproval of the marriage by friends and family is an important indicator of instability ahead, since this disapproval represents not only a prediction by people who know the couple but also a vote of non-confidence from those who could have helped bind the couple together.
>
> David Popenoe, *Sociology*, p. 319

Did you underline "Other researchers ... of instability ahead" as the key idea? How many ideas do you think have been combined? _____

Paraphrasing is one of the best things to do when sentences are particularly troublesome. To paraphrase this sentence, we might say, "Researchers have found that a marriage is unstable when those who know the couple disapprove of the union."

Pronoun Substitution in Sentences

Pronouns—words that take the place of nouns, such as *he, she, it, they,* and *them*— may serve as substitutions for other words and can be confusing. In the following sentence, note that the key idea includes the pronoun *they.*

> Example: More materialistic than the boomers but less so than the generation of the Reagan era, *they* see a real need for social reform but worry that the escalation of the national debt may make it impossible to implement needed changes.
>
> David Popenoe, *Sociology*, p. 123

The key idea is _____

In this sentence the *they* actually refers to America's adolescent and college-age peer group that appeared in the previous two paragraphs of the text!
Examine the following sentence, noting the pronouns in italics.

> Although the law is often slow to catch up with changing mores (customs), *it* usually does catch up with *them* in democratic societies because the legislators . . . change the laws to suit the voters' new goals and desires.
>
> Michael G. Roskin et al., *Political Science*, p. 431

Here you must determine what the pronouns stand for. Does *it* refer to mores (customs) or to the law? Does *them* refer to customs or to the law?

It refers to _____. *Them* refers to _____.

Careful reading reveals that *it* refers to the law while *them* refers to customs. In paraphrasing this sentence, the key idea is that *the law usually does catch up with changing customs*.

Reading Sentences that May Present Difficulty

Writers frequently combine related ideas into one sentence to clarify the key idea. To understand these sentences, you should

1. Identify the key idea.
2. Recognize how additional information relates to or modifies the meaning of the key idea.
3. Paraphrase the sentence, splitting it into several sentences if necessary.

With sentences that are particularly troubling, refer to the glossary or to a dictionary if the vocabulary is confusing.

ACTIVITY 4.1

Underline the key idea in the following sentences. Place one line under the subject (who or what the sentence is about) and two lines under the verb (what is happening to the subject). Look at the example first.

Example: Owing to its large prewar industry base, abundant natural resources (most of them free from interference by the war), and a civilian population sufficiently large enough to increase domestic labor without draining military energies, the nation rose to the challenge.

John Mack Faragher, *Out of Many p. 100*

1. Because smart "cards" contain a microprocessor that holds more information, has some processing capability, and is almost impossible to duplicate, smart cards may soon replace cards with magnetic strips.

   Larry Long, *Computer and Information Systems,* p. 410

2. But if literature can strip other cultures of their strangeness, unveiling what we have in common, it also has the important function of preserving the cultures.

   Carlos Fuentes, interview, *San Francisco Chronicle,* 14 May 1994, p. C-1

3. Having but limited success with the crude contraceptive techniques that were available to them, the ancients were much more likely to resort to abortion and **infanticide** in an effort to keep their population within the bounds of the existing food supply.

   Jedlicka and William M. Kephart, *The Family, Society, and the Individual*

4. Long accustomed to the assumption that each generation would be able to maintain a higher standard of living than its parents, children of the middle and working class are today facing the bleak reality that they may have to be fortunate as well as hardworking in order to do even as well as their parents did.

   David Popenoe, *Sociology,* p. 217

5. The need for physical contact is so great that when monkeys were placed in a cage with two substitute "mothers"—one made of wire and the other covered by soft cloth—the monkeys spent most of their time clinging to the soft-cloth mother.

   David Popenoe *Sociology,* p. 116

ACTIVITY 4.2

Underline the subject with one line, the verb with two lines.

1. The war that had begun at Pearl Harbor escalated into battles and strategic standoffs across a region of the world far larger than all of Europe, stretching from Southeast Asia to the Aleutian Islands.

   John Mack Faragher, *Out of Many*

2. One of the largest studies of air quality and health ever conducted shows that fine particles emitted by automobile engines, power plants and other sources can increase the risk of death 15 percent in the cities with the dirtiest air compared with the cleanest cities.

   The New York Times

---

infanticide (in fan´ tə cīd) murder of a baby

3. Japan's old guard—joylessly obsessed with exports, market shares, budgets, and trade wars, always emphasizing duty while subtly **derogating** leisure and pleasure, made nervous by creativity and individuality, scornful of small enterprise, hostile or indifferent to environmentalism and women's concerns—is increasingly alienated from a rising generation that it refers to as a "new species."

Alvin Toffler, *Christian Science Monitor*

4. A recently declassified intelligence document of April 30, 1946, concluded that "the dropping of the bomb" was the pretext seized upon by leaders as the reason for ending the war, but [even if the bomb had not been used] the Japanese would have **capitulated** upon the entry of Russia into the war.

John Mack Faragher *Out of Many*, p. 501

5. In their adolescence and early adulthood, many baby boomers, especially those born to middle-class families, strongly but temporarily embraced a variety of sharply counter-cultural patterns that seemed not only different but were actually opposed to the values accepted at the time by the adult world.

David Popenoe, *Sociology*, p. 127

❖ Punctuation: An Aid to Understanding Sentences

Punctuation can be a guide to sentence comprehension. To demonstrate how important punctuation is, try to read the following paragraph, from which all punctuation has been deleted.

Marriage both illustrates and reinforces the importance of thinking of others for as long as there has been human society men and women have recognized their need to mate to establish a lifelong bond that provides the essence of the support that each human being needs as he/she struggles to face the challenges of life throughout history it has been this union in which each partner is concerned with the good of the other which above all other forces has made it possible for men and women to experience their greatest joy it is this built in support system that enables them to be the best that that they can be sharing life's best and worst times increasing their ability to find meaning in life a sunset watched in solitude on a foreign shore only increases loneliness the same sight shared with a loved one is a special moment

Now, read the same material with punctuation and note the difference.

Marriage both illustrates and reinforces the importance of thinking of others. For as long as there has been human society, men and women have recognized their need to mate—

---

derogating (der´ ə gāt´ ng) detracting from
capitulated (kə pich´ ə lāt əd) gave up all resistance

to establish a lifelong bond that provides the essence of the support that each human being needs as he/she struggles to face the challenges of life. Throughout history, it has been this union—in which each partner is concerned with the good of the other—which above all other forces has made it possible for men and women to experience their greatest joy. It is this built-in support system that enables them to be the best that that they can be, sharing life's best and worst times, increasing their ability to find meaning in life. A sunset watched in solitude on a foreign shore only increases loneliness; the same sight shared with a loved one is a special moment.

McFarlane, "Meaning of Marriage"

Reading these two versions of the same paragraph illustrates that an awareness of punctuation while reading makes a real difference in understanding what is being stated. In addition to marking the end of sentences and separating them from each other, punctuation also separates other parts of a sentence. It indicates relationships, showing the relative importance of the various parts.

ACTIVITY 4.3

Read the following paragraph quickly, noting how you hesitate and are unsure where meaningful phrases begin and end because the paragraph lacks punctuation.

I was in the middle row of the formation slingshot in hand I had been grazed several times by rocks and bottles but fought on mothers called their sons home but we paid no heed amidst whistling yelling and cursing something whizzed past me barely missing my head but struck a barrel-chested thirteen-year-old boy to my left he clutched his face and shrieked the bastards theyve hurt my eye a couple of us rushed to his side someone said let go of your face and lets see he removed his bloodied hand from his face his right eye had been completely gouged out by a stone from a slingshot blood spurted out from the socket down his cheeks like giant teardrops there were no cars nearby no phones no means of getting him to the clinic he might bleed to death and he would be one-eyed for the rest of his life those thoughts numbed me then and there i decided to quit the gang permanently

Mark Mathabane, *Kaffir Boy*, p. 196

Now, add the correct punctuation to see how much easier it is to understand the paragraph's meaning.

What is the main idea? _____

_____

_____

_____

❖ Distinguishing the Topic from the Main Idea

It is important for readers to distinguish the topic from the main idea. The *topic* is the subject of a paragraph or passage and is most general in nature. On the other hand, *the main idea makes a particular statement or emphasizes a special aspect of the topic.* The topic may be stated in a word or short phrase and may often be mentioned over and over again, whereas the main idea is usually expressed as a complete thought. Some topic examples include the following:

1. Affirmative action
2. Child abuse
3. Ethnic diversity in television programming
4. Repressed memories
5. Space exploration
6. Sports in schools
7. Terrorism in the United States
8. Underwater treasure
9. Virtual reality
10. Widespread use of drugs

Notice that none of the topics is a complete idea or sentence but rather just the focus of some area, such as sports, drugs, child abuse, or terrorism. Any particular point developed from these topics could become a main idea. If you wanted to focus on the topic "sports in schools," for example, you could emphasize any of the following aspects:

1. Sports in schools create **elitist** groups among students.
2. Sports in schools build character among participants.
3. Sports in schools develop morale throughout the student body.
4. Sports in schools waste the taxpayers' money.
5. Sports in schools interfere with the learning process.

Simply asking one of the same questions that helps unlock sentence meaning—"What is it about?"—can help you determine the topic. For example, with each of the above titles to a selection, the answer to "What is it about?" would be "sports in school." That would be the topic but *not* the main idea.

---

elitist (a lēt´ ist) a person who considers himself or herself part of the best group

How Supporting Details Help Reveal the Topic

Many of the passage's specific supporting details should also help you form an impression that will reveal the topic. The support can take the form of examples, reasons, statistics, explanation, or simply relevant information. To see how this works, study the following example of a topic, its main idea, and specific support.

Topic: Development of English words

Main idea: Foreign languages are constantly acquiring English words and reworking them into their own language systems.

Support: (A) The Germans, for example, have words such as *Power stimmung,* meaning "great mood," and *relaxter,* meaning "more relaxed than their neighbors."

(B) The Japanese have imported the term *word processor* and changed it to *wa-pro,* adding another meaning later, "worst proportions," to describe a person with an unflattering figure.

(C) In the Philippines, an exciting close game is said to have a **cardiac** finish.

ACTIVITY 4.4

In the space provided, label each of the three items as the topic (T), the main idea (M), or the supporting statement (S). Look at the example first.

Example:

a. __T__ Business competition.

b. __S__ For example, if you decide to buy a pair of athletic shoes, you have a choice of several different stores in which to shop.

c. __M__ If profits motivate individuals to start businesses, competition motivates them to operate the businesses efficiently.

1. a. _____ The teaching of calculus—when to do it and even why to do it—has become a major issue in mathematics, inspiring a growing reform movement.

   b. _____ The necessity for calculus reform.

   c. _____ Calculus reform is considered urgent because of the course's demanding position in the early undergraduate experience of students hoping to go on to science, engineering, business, and other fields.

---

cardiac (kar´ dē ak´) of, near, or affecting the heart

2. a. _____ One of the biggest shortcomings of IQ tests is how deficient they are in probing the link between intelligence and everyday activity.

    b. _____ Recent IQ tests.

    c. _____ One study showed that homemakers who performed dismally in conventional mathematics tests were quite adept at doing comparison shopping.

3. a. _____ Witnessing a hanging.

    b. _____ When I saw the prisoner step aside to avoid the puddle, I saw the mystery, the unspeakable wrongness, of cutting a life short when it is in full tide.

    c. _____ His nails would still be growing when he stood on the drop, when he was falling through the air with a tenth of a second to live.

4. a. _____ People kiss **icons,** dice, and other objects, of course, in prayer, for luck, or as part of a ritual.

    b. _____ Among cultures of the West, the number of nonsexual uses of the kiss is staggering.

    c. _____ Kissing as a learned response.

5. a. _____ Native American culture has maintained a remarkable **resiliency,** continuity, and **mystical** determination to survive despite Westerners' attempts to eradicate it.

    b. _____ Native American culture.

    c. _____ For example, of the estimated 300 different languages spoken at the time of discovery by tribes in that portion of the New World that became the United States, at least half survive and are in current use.

ACTIVITY 4.5

Read the following paragraphs, and then, in the space provided, write the topic and the main idea and copy one supporting statement.

PASSAGE 1

Lack of self-esteem is a basic cause of failure. To be committed—indeed, to be successful at anything—you have to believe you can do it. Employers search for this as much as any other job qualification. People who lack self-esteem, although they may say all the right

---

icons (ī´ kans) religious images
resiliency (ri zil´ yən sē) ability to bounce or spring back
mystical (mis´ ti kəl) relating to something mysterious; of a spiritual nature

things, often say them with a question mark in their voices. You can get better at projecting a sense of self-esteem—even if you don't really feel it. Like an actor in a play, monitor your voice and actions to be sure you sound self-confident. Tape-record an imaginary interview and listen to yourself.

Carole Hyatt and Linda Gottlieb, *When Smart People Fail*

Topic: _____

Main idea: _____

Supporting statement: _____

PASSAGE 2

In much of the world male dominance has both existed and been reinforced by the writings of male philosophers and religious leaders. Sexist **ideology** is promoted in the sacred books of the world's three major religions, evoking supernatural justification for male supremacy. Islam's Koran states, "Men are superior to women on account of qualities in which God has given them pre-eminence." In the New Testament Saint Paul proclaims, "Let the woman learn in silence with all subjection. But I suffer not a woman to teach, nor to **usurp** authority over the man, but to be in silence . . . she shall be saved in childbearing, if they continue in faith and charity and holiness with sobriety." Finally, the morning prayer of the Orthodox Jews includes the line, "Blessed art Thou, oh Lord our God, King of the Universe, that I was not born a woman."

Vincent N. Parrillo, *Strangers to These Shores: Race and Ethnic Relations in the US*

Topic: _____

Main idea: _____

Supporting statement: _____

PASSAGE 3

Another promising approach to calculus reform is the introduction of writing as part of the mathematics curriculum. **Proponents** such as David Smith of Duke University stress the relationship between writing and reasoning. According to Smith, "failure to read and analyze instructions prevents students from getting started on a problem, and their ability to understand a solution process is related to their ability to explain in English what they have done." Robert Webber of Longwood College, for instance, requires students to write documentation of computer programs: explanations of what their programs are meant to do and how they work. He requires revision of any project that has inadequate documentation. Webber notes that about one quarter of the students receive a lower

---

ideology (ī dē al′ ə jē) way of thinking of an individual, class, etc.
usurp (yo͞o sərp′) to take or assume power or position
proponents (prō pō′ nənts) people who support a cause

letter grade because of their writing. He tells them that "if they don't write good documentation as professionals, they'll lose more than just a letter grade."

Barry A. Cipra, "Calculus: Crisis Looms in Mathematics' Future"

Topic: _____

Main idea: _____

Supporting statement: _____

PASSAGE 4

Prototypes of wearable computers, long a staple of science fiction, are already being promoted by Japan's NEC Corporation. In an effort to create truly personal computers that meld a computer and its user, NEC designers have divided the PC's components into cable-connected modules that fit into headsets, drape across shoulders, hang around the neck, and fasten around the waist, forearm, or wrist. Lightweight (about two pounds or less), the components would be covered in soft plastic and strapped on with Velcro.

Many of these prototypes combine existing or emerging technologies to create customized PCs for specific types of workers. The TLC (Tender Loving Care) PC for paramedics is a good example. At an accident scene, speech-recognition software would let the paramedic dictate symptoms and vital signs into a slender microphone hanging from a headset. The computer, draped across the medic's shoulders like a shawl, would compare this data to a CD-ROM medical directory in the shoulder unit. The computer would then project possible diagnoses and suggested treatments onto the headset's goggle-type display.

Larry Long, *Computers and Information Systems,* p. 22

Topic: _____

Main idea: _____

Supporting information: _____

PASSAGE 5

The power of speech, the freedom to engage our hearts and our bodies in dialogue is the most precious freedom of all. To secure all other rights granted to us by either our religions or our laws it is necessary to raise our voices. An idea inside our heads is, to our fellow humans, the same as no idea. It must be expressed if it is to have power. And the voice, the pen, is far mightier than any sword, any jail, any attempt to silence. Censorship is an **anathema** to a free people. We may not always like what we hear but we are always the poorer if we close down dialogue; if we **abrogate** free speech, and the open exchange of ideas.

Nikki Giovanni, *Sacred Cows and Other Edibles,* p. 86

_____

anathema (ən ath´ ə mə) a thing or person greatly detested

abrogate (ab´ rə gāt) to cancel or repeal by authority

Topic: _____

Main idea: _____

Supporting statement: _____

❖ Finding the Main Idea in a Paragraph

A paragraph is a group of related sentences that develops the same general topic. All the information regarding the topic, when summarized, helps to reinforce the writer's main point, generally referred to as the *main idea*. The main idea usually indicates the author's reason or purpose for writing and the message he or she wants to share with the reader.

A paragraph may contain anywhere from five to twelve sentences, but it is also possible for one sentence to stand alone as a paragraph. Within most paragraphs, there is often one sentence that specifically states the main idea. It can appear anywhere in the paragraph or can be implied, that is, suggested, rather than stated directly. The other sentences are the details or points that the author makes to support, reinforce, or add interest to the main idea.

Strategies to Use in Finding the Main Idea

Several strategies can be used to find and understand the main idea, the chief ones being

1. Asking key questions about the paragraph's content.
2. Locating a general statement within the paragraph that expresses the author's message.
3. Noting how the sum of the details emphasizes a main point.

We can begin finding the main idea by making use of what we have learned about the topic, and then asking, "What important thing is being said about the topic?" or "What is happening to the topic?" Words, phrases, or ideas that are repeated are *clues* to answering this question. Underlining these clues can sometimes help you see a main idea almost immediately.

Next, ask yourself, "How much support does the writer give for this idea?" The amount of detail and support mentioned by the writer will give you a general impression of his or her overall point. Remember, the writer can use examples, reasons, and situations to help develop or support the main point.

Let's examine how these questions can be applied to finding the main idea in the following paragraph.

Excess fat puts increased strain on the heart and circulatory system in two direct ways. First, the muscles of the body must work harder to carry the extra weight; the circulatory system, in turn, must work harder to meet the increased oxygen and nutritional demands of these muscles. Second, the extra fat cells themselves require oxygen and nutrients. It has been estimated that each pound of excess fat requires an extra mile of capillaries to nourish it. Thus, the heart must work harder to pump blood through an increased number of blood vessels.

John LaPlace, *Health*, p. 344

Answer the following questions in the space provided.

1. Who or what is the paragraph about? What is the topic?

    The topic is _____

2. What is stated about the topic? What is the topic's specific focus?

    The topic's specific focus is _____

The combined answers to these questions give you the author's main point: There are two ways in which excess fat adds an extra strain on the heart and circulatory system.

Although the author stated the main idea precisely in the first sentence, we have paraphrased it—changed several of the words and the word order. All the remaining sentences of this paragraph that deal with excess fat support the first sentence and answer a third key question.

3. With what specific details does the author support his point?
    Copy two supporting statements.

    a. _____

    b. _____

Did you include "The circulatory system must work harder" and "The extra fat cells themselves require oxygen and nutrients"? To help the reader follow the flow of ideas, the writer used (1) signal words, such as *first* and *second,* and (2) repetition of words like *extra* and *fat* to connect ideas.

Locating Stated Main Idea Sentences

The position of the stated main idea sentences in paragraphs can vary.

First and Last Sentence Main Idea

An important clue in locating the main idea is the position of the sentence. About 50 percent of the time, the first sentence of the paragraph contains the main idea. Actually, this makes reading easier; therefore, many essay and textbook paragraphs are written this way. Study the following paragraph for an illustration of a first sentence main idea. The *topic* is circled, the *main idea* sentence is underlined, and the *supporting statements* are italicized to help you recognize all three facets of the paragraph.

Researchers now believe that the most important influence on the emotional health of children is the quality of their relationships within their family, however that family might be structured, according to Robert Emery, a psychologist at the University of Virginia. For example, psychologists used to think that boys needed their father within the home until at least age 7 or 8. Now, they have discovered that the *physical presence of a father in the family is less important to boys than are warm and supporting adults.* . . . But the focus on relationships also means that *if divorced parents are angry and bitter, children will suffer and they will suffer more if they are exposed more to conflict through joint custody.*

Gina Kolata, *"Child Splitting"*

Rather than state the main idea at the beginning of a paragraph, some writers conclude a paragraph with the main idea sentence to create suspense or to challenge you to reason **inductively.** A concluding sentence often emphasizes how strongly the writer feels about an idea. Thus, the author presents supporting information at the beginning of the paragraph, leading you to the main idea in the final sentence. Although you may not ordinarily read the last sentence of a paragraph first, do so now. Then, read the entire paragraph. The paragraph has been marked to point out the topic, support, and main idea.

Our species evolved on the move. Recent research on the effects of exercise and the consequences of sedentary living has shown that physical activity is crucial to the proper processing of foods that we eat. In fact, most of the chronic and often life-threatening ailments that **besiege** Americans in epidemic proportions could be tempered by regular exercise. Among them are heart disease, diabetes, high blood pressure, arthritis, and **osteoporosis.** But let's face it: most people are not motivated to exercise by what it may do for them 20 years down the pike. *What gets people like me out moving every day is what exercise does for me right now, especially how it allows me to enjoy eating without gaining.* I, along with millions of Americans, have discovered that exercise is the key to permanent and painless weight control.

Jane Brody, "Exercise: A New Dietary Requirement"

---

inductively (in duc´ tiv lē) reasoning from a particular to the general
besiege (bē sēj´) to overwhelm; to crowd around
osteoporosis (ăs´ tē ō pə rō´ sis) a bone disorder

Grant Wood, "American Gothic." Courtesy of The Art Institute of Chicago.

Restated Main Idea in First and Last Sentence

Sometimes, writers help their readers grasp the main point by restating it at the end of a paragraph even though it was stated in the beginning. Read the following paragraph and then answer the questions.

Today *American Gothic* pervades our popular culture. Caricatures of the plain and nameless couple wish us well on anniversary cards or sell us cereal and cars on television. On dental hygiene posters the man holds a toothbrush instead of his pitchfork, urging us to brush our teeth; when the woman holds the pitchfork, she speaks for women's liberation. In political cartoons the rural couple becomes the nation's first family, posed in front of the White House rather than a tiny farmhouse. On homemade cards, husbands with wives, boyfriends with girlfriends, fathers with daughters, stand holding pitchforks, babies or drinks, against bungalows, ranch houses or churches. In short, *American Gothic* has become an infinitely variable mirror in which Americans can see themselves. It has become a kind of collective self-portrait, one which haunts and entertains us.

Wanda Corn, "The Painting That Became a Symbol of a Nation's Spirit," *Smithsonian*, Nov 1980 p. 84

1. What is the topic?_____

2. What main point is made about the topic? _____

3. What information is given in support of the main idea? _____

_____

Main Idea in the Middle

Sometimes, the writer first makes a broad statement or begins with a quotation or question, particularly when the main idea is stated in the second or third sentence.

Why do people fail to report so many crimes? *Studies show that they do not expect the police to be able to do anything, or that too much time and effort are required, especially for minor crimes.* Some people fear the criminal may take revenge on them. Some—rape victims, for example—fear insensitivity and harassment by the police. Also people are less likely to report crimes committed by friends and relatives than crimes committed by strangers. The poor report crimes less often than do middle-class victims. And commuters, tourists, and others passing through an area often fail to report crime because they do not have time to follow through with investigations. As a rule, the more serious a crime—if it involves a weapon, for example, or personal injury—the more likely the victim is to report it.

David Popenoe, *Sociology*, p. 180

Also, some authors begin with a statement to help create interest and get the reader involved before making the main point. As you read the following paragraphs, you may wish to circle words that are clues to the topic and underline some of the supporting details to help you find the precise main idea statement.

PASSAGE 1

[1]Not so long ago, the foods that people ate, the kind of exercise they got, the way they raised their children, and the quality of their sex lives were seen by most people as personal issues. [2]Today, to varying degrees, all these spheres of life, and many others as well, have come under medical jurisdiction. [3]That is, medical scientists have researched diet, exercise, child rearing, and sex, and have given physicians a store of knowledge on which to draw in recommending certain courses of action over others and in treating "problems" in these areas. [4]This expansion of medical jurisdiction to include problems that once were not regarded as medical has been termed the *medicalization of life.*

David Popenoe, *Sociology,* p. 275

Which sentence contains the main idea statement? _____

PASSAGE 2

[1]"We are Mexican," my mother and father would say. . . . [2]Yet regarding my family, I see faces that do not closely resemble my own. [3]Like some other Mexican families, my family suggests Mexico's confused colonial past. [4]My father's face recalls faces I have seen in France. [5]His complexion is white—he does not tan; he does not burn. [6]My mother . . . has an olive complexion; people have frequently wondered if, perhaps, she is Italian or Portuguese. [7]My older brother would come home from high school with girlfriends who seemed to me glamorous (because they were blonde); and during those years I envied him his skin that burned red and peeled like the skin of the **gringos.** [8]My youngest sister is **exotically** pale, almost ashen. [9]She is delicately featured, Near Eastern, people have said. [10]Only my older sister has a complexion as dark as mine, though her facial features are much less harshly defined than my own. [11]To many people meeting her, she seems (they say) Polynesian.

Richard Rodriguez, Hunger of Memory: *The Education of Richard Rodriguez,* p. 114

Which is the main idea sentence? _____

What sentences support it? _____

Main Idea in Several Sentences

Occasionally, writers state their main idea in several sentences. To understand the main point, you may have to piece together two **sequential** sentences or formulate the main point from several sentences scattered through the paragraph.

Read the following paragraph, underlining words that help to determine its main point.

Marilyn Monroe saw herself as clumsy, uncultured and unloved. Ann Landers tenses when she arrives at airports, afraid no one will be there to meet her. The great terror in Warren Beatty's life? Being considered dumb. Poor Marilyn, Ann and Warren: rich,

---

gringos (grēng´ gōs) a term, often considered offensive, for foreigners—especially Americans
exotically (ig zăt´ ik lē) fascinating or interesting because strange or different
sequential (si kwen´ chəl) following one after another

famous, talented—and insecure. It just doesn't make sense, you say. But that's often the thing about insecurity: It never makes sense for the other guy, who seems to have everything. You are the one who's different, who has a reason to feel insecure. But insecurity is something everyone experiences to some degree. To feel insecure is to be human.

Mary Long, "Ways to ... Insecurity," p. 75

The supporting details in the paragraph prove the point made in the last two sentences: *everyone experiences insecurity to some degree, for it is part of the makeup of human beings.* Notice how the writer leads you to this point by the repeated use of the words *insecure* and *insecurity.*

In the following selection, the main point is scattered throughout the paragraph. As you read, sort out what is most important. Then reread and underline the key words which, when pieced together, form the main idea. In the space provided, write a sentence or two, stating the main point in your own words.

The Greeks were skilled observers, and the detail included in their sculptures indicates that they had extensive anatomical knowledge. The Greek physician Hippocrates wrote a series of volumes dealing with medical and anatomical topics sometime around 400 B.C. The surviving manuscripts describe a number of surgical procedures, including an operation involving the opening of the skull. But the Greeks of this period tended to use observation as a means of revealing philosophical truths, and speculation rather than experimentation was the rule. Greek physicians spoke of four basic components or *humours* that composed the human body, blood, phlegm, yellow bile, and black bile. When all of these components were present in their proper amounts the individual was healthy, but if one became deficient or overabundant, disease would result.

Frederic H. Martini, *Fundamentals of Anatomy and Physiology,* p. 10

Main idea: _____

_____

Understanding the Implied Main Idea

In some paragraphs, especially in essay reading, you may have to supply the main idea if the author does not state it directly. This requires that you draw a conclusion based on the supporting statements that have been made. Try to draw a conclusion about the main point the writer makes about his alcoholic father in the following paragraph.

My father drank. He drank as a gut-punched boxer gasps for breath, as a starving dog gobbles food—compulsively, secretly, in pain and trembling. I use the past tense not because he ever quit drinking but because he quit living. That is how the story ends for my father, age sixty-four, heart bursting, body cooling, slumped and forsaken on the linoleum of my brother's trailer. The story continues for my brother, my sister, my mother, and me, and will continue as long as memory holds.

Scott Russell Sanders, "Under the Influence: Paying the Price," p. 360

In the above paragraph, there is no directly stated main idea, but the implied main idea is that *addictive drinking can have lifelong effects on the families of alcoholics.* Reread the last sentence to see how the main point has been suggested but not stated directly by the writer. Whenever you find a passage with no directly stated main idea, use your knowledge of finding the topic and support to conclude the main idea.

The following paragraph also has an implied main idea. As you read it, think about the topic and what the author is saying about it; then, write the implied main idea in the space provided.

> Alexander Graham Bell thought the telephone should properly be answered by saying, "Hoy! Hoy!"—an odd term from the Middle English that became the sailor's "ahoy!" and reflected Bell's sense that those speaking on early telephones were meeting like ships on a lonely and vast electronic sea. The world has now grown electronically dense, densest of all perhaps among the Japanese, who answer the telephone with a crowded, tender, almost cuddling quick-whispered *mushi-mushi.* The Russians say *slushaiyu* (I'm listening). The hipper Russians say *allo,* Italians say *pronto* (ready). The Chinese say *wei, wei* (with a pause between the words, unlike the Japanese mushi-mushi).
>
> Lance Morrow, *Time*

Main idea: _____

_____

_____

ACTIVITY 4.6 Practice Identifying the Main Idea

Read the paragraphs that follow to identify the topic, main idea, and important supporting points. Remember that the main idea may appear at the beginning, middle, or end of a paragraph. It may be scattered throughout the passage or stated in more than one sentence. In the case of an unstated main idea, the main point must be supplied by you, the reader.

In the space provided, write the topic, main idea, and at least one supporting statement for each passage. If the main idea appears in more than one sentence, write out a main idea summary statement. If the main idea is unstated, formulate it in your own words.

PASSAGE 1

American men don't cry because it is considered unmasculine to do so. Only sissies cry. Crying is a "weakness" characteristic of the female, and no American male wants to be identified with anything in the least weak or feminine. Crying, in our culture, is identified with childishness, with weakness and dependence. No one likes a crybaby, and we disapprove of crying even in children, discouraging it in them as early as possible. In a land so devoted to the pursuit of happiness as ours, crying really is rather un-American.

Adults must learn not to cry in situations in which it is permissible for a child to cry. Women being the "weaker" and "dependent" sex, it is only natural that they should cry in certain emotional situations. In women, crying is excusable. But in men, crying is a mark of weakness. So goes the American **credo** with regard to crying.

Ashley Montagu, "Don't Cry," p. 10

Topic: _____

Main idea: _____

Supporting statement: _____

PASSAGE 2

As far as we know, no society has ever advocated total **promiscuity.** But norms governing sexual behavior do vary widely from society to society and from one period of history to the next. For example, Denmark and Bangladesh represent two extremes regarding attitudes toward young people's sexuality. The Danes approve of adolescent sexual activity for both sexes. Concerned about the transmission of AIDS, Danish schools began in the late 1980s to distribute free condoms to adolescents as young as age 14. In Bangladesh, on the other hand, adolescent sexual activity among unmarried females is forbidden. If a young woman is not a virgin, she is labeled an outcast and considered unworthy of marriage. This is the case even if she has been raped.

David Popenoe, *Sociology,* p. 309

Topic: _____

Main idea: _____

Supporting statement: _____

PASSAGE 3

Good fathering is not an issue for teenage boys who avoid making babies in the first place. That is why many pregnancy prevention efforts are now targeting boys as well as girls. Planned Parenthood and other family planning clinics that were once considered "female" facilities are now reaching out more strongly to males. The most common advice given to boys is, in a word, condoms—the most effective preventative measure they can use, next to abstinence. Communities have also put pressure on school systems to balance their sex education curricula, which tend to focus on the female side of the issues. Boys are therefore less likely to sign up for the courses. But knowing the details about making babies is not enough. Boys as well as girls need to clearly understand that becoming parents too soon is not in their best interest.

Shelley Moore, "Father and Child," p. 301

---

credo (krē´ dō) a statement of belief

promiscuity (prä´ mis kyoo̅´ a tē) engaging in sexual practices indiscriminately

Topic: _____

Main idea: _____

Supporting statement: _____

PASSAGE 4

Was the **flapper** a genuine representative of the 1920s? Did she embody the "new morality" that was so widely discussed and chronicled in the media of the day? Historians have discovered that the flapper certainly did exist, but she was neither as new nor as widespread a phenomenon as the image would suggest. The delight in sensuality, individual pleasure, and rhythmically complex dance and music had long been key elements of subcultures on the fringes of middle-class society. In the 1920s these activities became **normative** for a growing number of white middle-class Americans, including women. Jazz, sexual experimentation, heavy use of makeup, and cigarette smoking spread to college campuses.

John M. Faragher et. al., Out of Many, p. 455

Topic: _____

Main idea: _____

Supporting statement: _____

PASSAGE 5

The yearning for "equal justice under law" is one of humankind's oldest aspirations. Justice Oliver Wendell Holmes once remarked, "My freedom to swing my arm stops where the other man's nose begins." Because humans are social beings, their freedom of action must have its limits if the freedom of all is to be preserved. But who decides what these limits are? Without a legal system, force alone would settle disputes. Even in primitive societies, two parties who disagree often look to an objective third party to provide a solution. Modern nations depend on laws to regulate human relations, and courts help to maintain order by enforcing these laws.

Michael J. Roskin et al. "Legal Systems and the Courts," Political Science, p. 57

Topic: _____

Main idea: _____

Supporting statement: _____

---

flapper (flap´ ər) a bold, unconventional young woman of the 1920s
normative (nor´ mə tiv) like the standard

ACTIVITY 4.7   Practice Understanding the Main Idea

As you read the following paragraphs, make mental or written notes to help you to identify the topic, main idea, and important supporting details. Then answer the questions that follow in the space provided.

PASSAGE 1

The crowds and speed of California life were only one of the many culture shocks Deborah had experienced since fleeing Kenya and seeking refuge here. There was so much that she didn't understand, and feared she never would—inside jokes and references which evoked responses from everyone else but which only left her baffled. She had once asked where the Twilight Zone* was, and everyone had laughed. She didn't ask questions after that. Eventually she had discovered that much of the California way was derived from television, something which, in all her life, Deborah had never seen. She felt as if she had missed out on a wedge of history, as if she were some sort of Rip Van Winkle[†] who had slept through a revolution. So much of what she observed and overheard seemed to be connected in some way to television or derived from it—language, mannerisms, jingles, even fashion and food. But more perplexing to her was that she had found, directly alongside this deep-rooted cultural anchor to television, a sweeping denial, by those same people, of ever watching it!

Barbara Wood, *Green City in the Sun*, p. 628

1. Why is neither the first nor the last sentence the precise main idea statement?

_____

2. Which supporting details help you to understand the writer's implied main idea—that Deborah's previous life experiences (she is from another country) had not prepared her to adjust easily to California living?_____

_____

PASSAGE 2

Imagine that your job is to monitor the operation of a vast telecommunications network. Cables snake underground and underwater. Data flows between communications satellites and earth and across wiring inside building walls. Now imagine that a graphic image of this vast grid and its data flows could be laid out below you, as you float above, an "infonaut" looking for the kink that is blocking service to millions of customers. Far below you see a pulsing light. There's the problem. With a gestured command, you fix it—without leaving your office. That's the promise of virtual reality, and it's quickly moving from computer fantasy to computer fact. In fact, US West and a number of other telecommunications firms are already experimenting with such systems.

Larry Long, *Introduction to Computers and Information Systems*, p. 44

The Twilight Zone was a TV series in which people found themselves in strange places and on other planets.

†Rip Van Winkle is the main character in a book by Washington Irving. He sleeps for several hundred years and awakens to find himself in a modern world.

1. Paraphrase the main idea. _____

    _____

2. What is *virtual reality?* An *infonaut?* _____

    _____

    _____

PASSAGE 3

Some people take abortion very lightly and measure its discomfort in physical or economic terms. For others, however, it involves a severe emotional trauma. People who long to be parents may make the extremely difficult decision to abort the fetus and may be surprised at their own anguish. As the offspring of efficient reproducers, we can expect that abortion would go against the grain to some degree, but for some, it can produce real agony. The agony of the woman has often been mentioned, but we may neglect the emotional upset of the man. No one is very happy about it, to say the least.

"Reproduction"

1. Paraphrase the main idea. _____

    _____

2. List two supporting statements that show why the second sentence, rather than

    the first, is the precise main idea statement. _____

    a. _____

    b. _____

PASSAGE 4

The Chinese were neither the first nor the last immigrants in America to **tote** their culture in their baggage. What set them apart—and this is true of other, more recent Asian immigrants to the United States as well—was the extent of their mutual support systems. They established their own schools taught in their own language, read their own newspapers and attended their own operas. Wherever possible they made a living working with, and selling to, one another. Groups of merchants organized **de facto** banks by putting money into a pool from which anybody in the group could borrow. They banded together in associations based on their home districts in China.

Donald Dale Jackson, "Sojourners Who Came to Stay," p. 118

---

tote (tōt) to carry
de facto (de fak´ tō) existing or being so in actual fact

1. Circle the correct letter for the topic for this paragraph.
   a. Mutual support systems of immigrants
   b. Recent Asian immigrants to the United States
   c. Chinese industries in the United States

2. Paraphrase the main idea. _____

   _____

3. List two supporting statements.

   a. _____

   b. _____

PASSAGE 5

[1]As previously mentioned, citizens watching out for each other is nothing new. [2]Back in the early 1800s, before the emergence of a police force, major cities like New York employed "citizen watches," consisting of citizens who strolled around all night and kept an eye out for fires or burglars or vandals. [3]They would sound an alarm or ring a bell to warn their sleeping neighbors of trouble. [4]Just keep in mind that there is a big difference between being vigilant and being a vigilante. [5]Both words are based upon the root word *vigil*, taken from the Latin, meaning to be awake. [6]A vigil is also a watch kept during night hours, or a surveillance. [7]Each of us should be *vigilant* in our homes and communities, in that we should keep watch against crime and help each other avoid becoming a victim. [8]The word *vigilante* means one who is a member of a vigilance committee—an organization that takes upon itself the power of pursuing and punishing criminals. [9]We, citizens, are not and should not be in the business of dealing out punishment, but we had better be in the business of watching out for criminals and alerting the authorities of their activities.

James D. Brewer, *The Danger from Strangers*, p. 235

1. What is the topic? _____
2. Two sentences in the paragraph must be combined in order to state the main idea. Write the numbers of these sentences.

   _____

3. Explain the difference between a *vigil* and a *vigilante,* according to the author.

   _____

4. Do you agree with the author that citizens should be *vigilant* but not *vigilantes?* Why or why not?

   _____

   _____

PASSAGE 6

[1]Through design and necessity, almost every workforce in America is more diverse today than it was just a decade ago. [2]Few companies, however, are capturing the benefits **inherent** in this diversity. [3]Most corporate cultures suppress nonconformity in employees, no matter what their **ethnicity**, gender, or experience. [4]Until we develop practices that encourage diversity of thought and action, employees who would present different points of view will suppress these views and be **homogenized** into the prevailing culture. [5]The successful organization of the future must incorporate diversity into its internal processes by rewarding the expression of internal differences. [6]The management of diversity must become a strategic issue.

Gary Heil, Tom Parker, and Rick Tate, *Leadership and the Customer Revolution*, p. 91

1. In which sentence is the main idea best expressed?_____
2. What must business leadership do to promote greater business success?

_____

_____

PASSAGE 7

On June 28, 1993 Kirk Bloodsworth walked out of a Jessup, Maryland, prison a free man—after serving nine years for a murder he did not commit. Standing before media cameras, Bloodsworth sobbed for his mother, who had died before seeing him cleared. Bloodsworth had been convicted in 1984 of the rape-murder of 9-year-old Dawn Hamilton and sentenced to die. He had consistently claimed he'd never met the girl. Recently, an FBI DNA test of semen found on the girl's underwear showed that Bloodsworth could not have been the killer. Were it not for modern technology, Bloodsworth would doubtlessly have remained imprisoned.

Modern technology will change many of the practical aspects of the criminal justice system of the twenty-first century—from the way in which evidence is gathered to the development of innovative forms of sentencing. Even so, the criminal justice system of the next century will look much like the system we know today. It will rest upon constitutional **mandates** and will be responsive to court **precedent**. The system itself will remain recognizable through its backbone of subsystems: the police, courts, and corrections. Deterrence, apprehension, and reformation will continue to serve as the philosophical trilogy guiding the day-to-day operations of criminal justice agencies. New issues will arise, but most of them will be resolved within the context of the question which has

---

inherent (in hir´ ənt) essential characteristic

ethnicity (eth nis´ i tē) belonging to a particular group

homogenized (ho moj ə nized) made uniform

mandates (man´ dāts) commands by authorities

precedent (pres´ i dint) a judicial decision that may be used as a standard in subsequent similar cases; custom

guided American criminal justice since its inception: how to ensure public safety while guaranteeing justice in a free society.

Frank Schmalleger, Criminal Justice Today, p. 664

1. Will the criminal justice system change much in the twenty-first century? Support your answer.

_____

_____

2. What will be the guiding principles of the criminal justice system in the twenty-first century?

_____

_____

PASSAGE 8

Read these paragraphs and determine the overall main idea.

The best ideas occur to me when my mind is otherwise unchallenged and there is no pressure to create. I have mentally composed whole articles while jogging, flashed upon the solution to a software dilemma while sitting in the steam room, come up with just the right opening line for a client's speech while pushing a vacuum. These were not problems I had set out to address at those particular times. Inventiveness came to my uncluttered mind in a random, unfocused moment.

The bonus is that creative thought is joyful. It doesn't matter if the idea is for a clever party decoration, a better way to rearrange the living-room furniture or the definitive antigravity machine. When a fine idea emerges there is a moment of "Eureka!" that simply beats all.

The simple fact is that time spent lost in thought isn't really lost at all. That's why "unplugged time" is vital. It's when new directions, different approaches and exciting solutions emerge from a place that can't be tapped at will.

It is unwise to take this resource for granted. Better to recognize it, understand something about where it resides and thereby ensure it is not lost.

Michele McCormick, "We're too Busy for Ideas," Newsweek, 121, (March 29, 1993), p. 10.
Copyright © 1993 by Newsweek, Inc. Reprinted with the permission of Newsweek.

1. Complete the main idea of this selection: *Creativity comes to us when* _____

_____

2. The writer owns a small public relations firm. Do you think the employees of her firm have a generous time-off period from work or a strict workday of 9 to 5 and a one-week vacation period? Support your answer.

_____

❖ Major Details/Minor Details

How Do You Recognize the Difference?

Details supporting a main idea are not of equal importance. For example, look at the following "to do" list:

Keep doctor's appointment
Wash car
Study for quiz
Attend final lab class
Check with Bill about Saturday night
Pick up dry cleaning

Which of the items are essential, and which are less important? Circle those of major importance, and draw a line through the others.

Did you circle "Keep doctor's appointment," "Study for quiz," and "Attend final lab class"? Similarly, all the facts, reasons, illustrations, and examples a writer includes in a passage may relate to the main idea but may not have the same significance. For example, the detail "Economists are in disagreement" is important in an evaluation of market conditions but is not important in considering where to obtain a degree in economics. Whether a particular detail is a major one depends on

a. The main point the writer is making, and
b. Whether the detail is essential in supporting, explaining, or changing the main idea in a significant way.

The following chart contrasts important differences between major and minor details.

Major Details	Minor Details
Directly support or explain the main idea	Often add information to a major detail
Are essential to the basic understanding of the paragraph or selection	Are not essential in developing a main idea—they simply help hold our attention and interest

When in doubt about whether a detail is major, first determine the main idea and then ask yourself these key questions:

Does the detail explain, support, or prove the main idea?

Does the detail add essential information or change the main idea in a major way?

ACTIVITY 4.8

For each of the following main idea statements (underlined), three details are given. Determine whether *each* detail is major (MJ) or minor (MN).

Example: Business letters must be concise and easily understood.

<u>MN</u> a. One communication specialist said, "We simply do not put up with wordy communication."

<u>MJ</u> b. The first paragraph of a business letter should state the main point clearly and in a **succinct** way.

<u>MJ</u> c. Business readers take charge of organizing the letter if the writer does not!

1. Many people who age well and live past 100 share certain characteristics.

_____ a. The first Briton who lived to be 100 died in 1967.

_____ b. Most of us have never met anyone who is 100 years old.

_____ c. Centenarians, those past 100, generally have superior intelligence, keen interest in current events, and a good memory.

2. Pen-based computers will be successful new additions to the computer market.

_____ a. Users report that the machines are easy to learn, reduce error, and save time.

_____ b. In other situations, typing on a laptop can be noisy.

_____ c. State Farm Insurance, for example, recently began testing notepads.

3. The organization and operation of American colleges differ from those of primary and secondary schools.

_____ a. In higher education, there is a definite hierarchy, with more money and more privilege going to instructors and administrators at the top.

_____ b. Faculty at colleges are freer to act than teachers in primary and secondary schools.

---

succinct (sək sinkt´) brief; concise

     _____ c. College presidents rarely supervise the teaching staff directly but are more concerned with public relations.

4. <u>Sociologists claim that self-fulfillment has become a predominant American value.</u>

     _____ a. Sociologists are concerned with social, economic, and political institutions.

     _____ b. Bell and Bellah collaborated on a recent book concerning American values.

     _____ c. A major problem with the self-fulfillment value is that people are less committed to the collective good of society.

5. <u>The geographer's task in studying the earth's landforms is not simple.</u>

     _____ a. Geographers are only marginally concerned with the Earth's interior.

     _____ b. The earth's surface is vast, complex, and often obscured.

     _____ c. But 70 percent of the earth's surface is covered by water.

ACTIVITY 4.9

Read the following paragraph and write the main idea on the line provided *before* answering the questions that follow.

Social Class and the Law

Extensive research strongly suggests that one's social class position affects how he or she is treated by the law. In principle, all Americans have the right to equal treatment. Yet this is sometimes not the case. Lower-class criminals are more likely to be caught than wealthy criminals and, once apprehended, are less likely to be able to afford highly skilled legal representation. When they appear in court, their life history—which often includes quitting school, unemployment, divorce, and an apparent lack of responsibility when judged by middle-class standards—may work against them. As a result, lower-income criminals are likely to receive heavier penalties than higher-income criminals for the same crime. And because they often cannot afford bail, lower-income criminals often have to wait for trial in jail cells rather than in the comforts of their own home.

David Popenoe, *Sociology*, p. 219

Main idea: _____

_____

_____

_____

Which of the following details support the author's main idea? Write major (MJ) or minor (MN) in the space provided.

_____ 1. All Americans have the right to equal treatment.

_____ 2. When they appear in court, their life history . . . may work against them.

_____ 3. Lower-class criminals are more likely to be caught than wealthy criminals.

_____ 4. They are less likely to be able to afford highly skilled legal representation.

_____ 5. They are likely to receive heavier penalties than higher-income criminals for the same crime.

Do you agree that the author's main idea is the first sentence, "Research strongly suggests that one's social class position affects how he or she is treated by the law"? Do the major details you chose support the main idea?

ACTIVITY 4.10

For each of the following paragraphs, determine the main idea and the major details. There may be more than one major detail.

PASSAGE 1

Gene Therapy

At first glance, her optimism [over gene therapy] seems well founded. For the past few years, the media and some physicians have relentlessly **touted** gene therapy's wonders. Recently, scientific articles have announced advances in gene therapies for cancer, heart disease, even AIDS. But some say this optimistic coverage is raising patients' hopes too high: Even its backers concede that gene therapy will not be arriving at your doctor's office anytime soon. Indeed, many scientists agree that gene therapy will never be a miracle cure. Instead, it will be just one more weapon against disease—and for some diseases, it simply won't work. "We've educated the lay public about the promise of gene therapy," says . . . a pioneer in the field. "But we haven't [had] a lot of success" in patients.

U.S. News and World Report, 14 Nov. 1994, p. 122

1. Circle the letter of the main idea.
   a. Gene therapy will be able to cure AIDS, heart disease, and cancer.
   b. Gene therapy as a miracle cure has not come to pass, nor will it produce miracle cures soon.
   c. Gene therapy will continue to be touted by doctors as a miracle of the times.

_____

touted (tout´ əd) highly praised or publicized

2. Circle the letters of the major detail/s.
   a. The lay public has been educated about the promise of gene therapy.
   b. Gene therapy will be one more weapon against disease.
   c. For some diseases, gene therapy will not work.

PASSAGE 2

Pleading the Fifth Amendment

The Fifth Amendment to the U.S. Constitution is one of the best known entries in the Bill of Rights. Television shows and crime novels have popularized phrases such as "pleading the Fifth," or "taking the Fifth." As these media recognize, the Fifth Amendment is a powerful ally of any criminal defendant. When the accused, generally upon the advice of counsel, decides to invoke the Fifth Amendment right against self-incrimination, the state cannot require the defendant to testify. In the past, defendants who refused to take the stand were often **denigrated** by comments the prosecution made to the jury. In 1965 the U.S. Supreme Court, in the case of *Griffin* v. *California,* ruled that the defendant's unwillingness to testify could not be interpreted as a sign of guilt. The Court reasoned that such interpretations forced the defendant to testify and effectively negated Fifth Amendment guarantees. Defendants who choose to testify, however, but who fail to adequately answer the questions put to them, may lawfully find themselves the target of a **prosecutorial** attack.

Frank Schmalleger, *Criminal Justice Today,* p. 353

1. Circle the letter of the main idea.
   a. The rights of those who plead the Fifth Amendment have been upheld by the Supreme Court.
   b. Defendants who choose to testify in court can face hard questions by the prosecutors.
   c. The accused take the advice of their counsel as to whether they will testify.
2. Circle the major detail/s.
   a. TV shows and crime novels have made phrases such as "taking the Fifth" popular.
   b. The Fifth Amendment is a powerful ally of the criminal defendant.
   c. In the past, defendants who refused to testify were denigrated by the prosecutors.

PASSAGE 3

Stalin of Russia; Truman of the United States

These two men, one the veteran revolutionary who had been in power for two decades, the other an untested leader in office for barely three months, symbolized the enormous differences that now separated the wartime allies. Stalin was above all, the realist. Brutal in securing total control at home, he was more flexible in his foreign policy, bent on exploiting Russia's victory in World War II rather than aiming at world domination.

---

denigrated (den´ i grāt əd) to be belittled; defamed
prosecutorial (pros i kyoo tor´ i əl) by legal action

Cunning and caution were the **hallmarks** of his diplomatic style. Small in stature, ungainly in build, he radiated a catlike quality as he waited behind his unassuming facade, ready to dazzle an opponent with his "Brilliant, terrifying tactical mastery." Truman, in contrast, personified traditional Wilsonian idealism. Lacking Roosevelt's **guile,** the new President placed his faith in international cooperation. Like many Americans, he believed implicitly in his country's **innate** goodness. Self-assured to the point of cockiness, he came to Potsdam clothed in the armor of self-righteousness.

Robert A. Divine, *America, Past and Present,* 31E, p. 806

1. Circle the letter of the main idea.
   a. One was a veteran revolutionary and the other an untested leader in office.
   b. The two leaders symbolized the enormous difference between Russia and the United States.
   c. Truman was self-assured to the point of cockiness when he came to meet Stalin.
2. Circle the major detail/s.
   a. Stalin, brutal in securing total control at home, was bent on exploiting Russia's victory in World War II.
   b. Truman placed his faith in international cooperation.
   c. Stalin was small in stature and ungainly in build.

PASSAGE 4

Jules Verne Predicted the Future in 1863 Novel

Jules Verne

An 1863 novel by science-fiction writer Jules Verne, containing prophetic descriptions of modern technology that a contemporary publisher rejected as far-fetched, has been published for the first time. In the novel, Verne predicted mass-transit trains, faxes, cars, and the electric chair.

Verne's great-grandson found the manuscript of *Paris in the 20th Century* in the family house in Toulon five years ago. It was published this week. It is believed to be the only novel by Verne—author of *Around the World in 80 Days* and *20,000 Leagues Under the Sea*—not published previously. Verne died in 1905.

Verne's publisher rejected the manuscript, writing in the margin, "My dear Verne, had you been a prophet, no one today would believe your prophecy." But the novel's hero, Michel, sees sights in the future Paris not so different from the reality today—cars running through the city, automated mass-transit trains suspended in the air, electric lights everywhere.

Money and technology are the guiding forces in Verne's bleak city, run by an all-powerful state seeking to erase the memory of classic culture.

Verne's book predicted the emergence of automobiles driven by the combustion engine, invented four years earlier. He also forecast the electric chair, which was invented in the United States in 1888, as a replacement for the guillotine.

Imagining the fax and the telephone, Verne wrote: "Photo-telegraphy allowed any

---

hallmarks (hôl´ marks) qualities or marks of excellence
guile (gīl) craftiness; cunning
innate (i nāt´) inborn

writing, signature or illustration to be sent far away, and any contract to be signed at a distance of (12,400 miles) . . . Every house was wired."

San Jose Mercury, Sept. 22, 1994, p. 9

1. Write the main idea of this short article.

_____

_____

2. Which details are major (MJ) and which are minor (MN)?

_____ a. Jules Verne's great-grandson found the manuscript five years ago.

_____ b. The manuscript was originally rejected as being too unrealistic.

_____ c. The importance of money and technology are themes in the novel.

_____ d. The electric chair has replaced the guillotine.

_____ e. The manuscript was published this week.

_____ f. Verne's book predicted the coming of the automobile with a combustion engine, the telephone, and the fax machine.

PASSAGE 5

Reforming the Juvenile Court System

The juvenile justice system is not without its critics. An emerging recognition of repetitive serious criminal activity by a small number of "hard-core" delinquents, combined with a concern for public safety has prompted efforts at reform. . . . Stiffer   penalties for some delinquents have been proposed by those who cite continued and frequent delinquent acts by a minority of **adjudicated** delinquents. The same critics argue that the present system is limited in its capacity to reform, often releasing dangerous juvenile offenders back to the streets. Evidence from the Habitual Serious and Violent Juvenile Offender Program, which targeted 13 cities for vigorous prosecution of violent and repeat offenders, tends to support such claims. The program combined careful case screening with victim/witness support to remove habitual juvenile offenders effectively from society. Supporting the movement toward stiffer penalties for delinquent youth, sentencing guidelines for juveniles proposed by the Justice Department recommend that state legislatures adopt fixed penalties for certain law violations. In a similar move, the Office of Juvenile Justice and Delinquency Prevention has developed a monetary and direct victim service **restitution** program for juvenile courts. Called RESTTA (for

---

adjudicated (ə jōō′ di kāt′ əd) settling by law
restitution (res′ ti tōō′ shən) act of restoring something to a rightful owner

Restitution Education, Specialized Training, and Technical Assistance Program) the program provides local juvenile courts with the information needed to make restitution a meaningful part of the dispositional process.

On the other side of the reform movement are those who argue for still greater protections on behalf of juveniles. Because they lack all the rights of adults, such critics say, juveniles are apt to be "railroaded" through a system which does not live up to its purpose of protecting children. Others cite the criminalizing influence of juvenile institutions and suggest that juveniles should be kept from institutionalization wherever possible. The National Council on Crime and Delinquency has identified four continuing problems in juvenile justice today.

approximately 275 words

Frank Schmalleger, *Criminal Justice Today*, p. 578

1. Write the main idea for this textbook passage. _____

_____

2. Indicate whether each detail is major (MJ) or minor (MN).

_____ a. Stiffer penalties have been proposed for some delinquents because the present system's reforms are not working.

_____ b. RESTTA is a program that provides local juvenile courts with information needed for restitution to the victims.

_____ c. On the other side of the reform movement are those who believe juveniles need greater protection.

_____ d. Evidence from thirteen cities supports claims for stiffer penalties.

_____ e. A past program used careful case screening with victim/witness support.

_____ f. Juveniles should not be institutionalized because it can make them criminals.

ACTIVITY 4.11

The following ideas were presented in earlier chapters. Chose one of them and write a paragraph that includes major and minor details. Underline the major details in your paragraph.

1. Knowledge about the Information Age has relevance for today's students.

2. Previewing can aid comprehension.

3. Improving vocabulary takes place over a period of time.

4. Study strategies can vary but are essential for college success.

5.   Successful students are generally successful at taking tests.

_____

_____

_____

_____

_____

_____

❖ A Note About the Main Idea in Reading Fiction

You may have noticed that many of the paragraphs you have read are taken from essays, articles, and textbooks—information-type reading rather than fiction. Novels and literary fiction seldom include topic or main idea sentences because the story or narrative usually moves in a time-order sequence. Sometimes, the writing is simply broken up into large and small paragraph chunks, conversation, and implied main ideas. Some paragraphs simply elaborate on what has already been presented. The following is an excerpt from a classic book of literary fiction, *An American Tragedy.* In this story set in the early 1900s, Clyde, the main character, has decided to "do away" with Roberta, a former girlfriend who is pregnant and stands in the way of a new love, a new career, and a better social position. The main idea in these paragraphs is simply to evoke a general feeling, to create a mood and tone as the reader senses Clyde's desperation in carrying out his plan to drown Roberta in the lake.

The stillness of these pines lining this damp yellow road along which they were traveling; the cool and the silence; the dark shadows and purple and gray depths and nooks in them, even at high noon. If one were slipping away at night or by day, who would encounter one here? A blue-jay far in the depths somewhere uttered its metallic shriek; a field sparrow, tremulous upon some distant twig, filled the silver shadows with its perfect song. And Roberta, as this heavy, covered bus crossed rill and thin stream, and then rough wooden bridges here and there, commented on the clarity and sparkle of the water: "Isn't that wonderful in there? Do you hear the tinkling of that water, Clyde? Oh, the freshness of this air!"

And yet she was going to die so soon!

God!

But supposing now, at Big Bittern—the lodge and boathouse there—there were many people. Or that the lake, peradventure, was literally dotted with those that were there—all fishermen and all fishing here and there, each one separate and alone—no privacy or a deserted spot anywhere. And how strange he had not thought of that. This lake was probably not nearly as deserted as he had imagined, or would not be today, any more than Grass Lake had proved. And then what?

Well, flight then—flight—and let it go at that. This strain was too much—hell—he would die, thinking thoughts like these. How could he have dreamed to better his fortunes by any so wild and brutal a scheme as this anyhow—to kill and then run away—or rather to kill and pretend that he and she had drowned—while he—the real murderer—slipped away to life and happiness. What a horrible plan! And yet how else? How? Had he not come all this way to do this? And was he going to turn back now?

approximately 375 words

Theodore Dreiser, *An American Tragedy*

ACTIVITY 4.12

We have stated that literature, with its narrative writing, often consists of paragraphs without stated main ideas. Instead, the central thought is implied through the details provided by the writer.

Read the following passage that introduces the short story "The First Seven Years," and note how the details add up to the central thought the writer wishes to convey. Then answer the questions.

Feld, the shoemaker, was annoyed that his helper, Sobel, was so insensitive to his reverie that he wouldn't for a minute cease his fanatic pounding at the other bench. He gave him a look, but Sobel's bald head was bent over the last as he worked, and he didn't notice. The shoemaker shrugged and continued to peer through the partly frosted window at the nearsighted haze of falling February snow. Neither the shifting white blur outside, nor the sudden deep remembrance of the snowy Polish village where he had wasted his youth, could turn his thoughts from Max the college boy (a constant visitor in the mind since early that morning when Feld saw him trudging through the snowdrifts on his way to school), whom he so much respected because of the sacrifices he had made throughout the years—in winter or direst heat—to further his education. An old wish returned to haunt the shoemaker: that he had had a son instead of a daughter, but this blew away in the snow, for Feld, if anything, was a practical man. Yet he could not help but contrast the diligence of the boy, who was a peddler's son, with Miriam's unconcern for an education. True, she was always with a book in her hand, yet when the opportunity arose for a college education, she had said no she would rather find a job. He had begged her to go, pointing out how many fathers could not afford to send their children to college, but she said she wanted to be independent. As for education, what was it, she asked, but books, which Sobel, who diligently read the classics, would as usual advise her on. Her answer greatly grieved her father.

A figure emerged from the snow and the door opened. At the counter the man withdrew from a wet paper bag a pair of battered shoes for repair. Who he was the shoemaker for a moment had no idea, then his heart trembled as he realized, before he had thoroughly discerned the face, that Max himself was standing there, embarrassedly explaining what he wanted done to his old shoes. Though Feld listened eagerly, he couldn't hear a word, for the opportunity that had burst upon him was deafening.

He couldn't exactly recall when the thought had occurred to him, because it was clear he had more than once considered suggesting to the boy that he go out with Miriam. But he had not dared speak, for if Max said no, how would he face him again? Or suppose Miriam, who harped so often on independence, blew up in anger and shouted at him for his meddling? Still, the chance was too good to let by: all it meant was an introduction. They might long ago have become friends had they happened to meet somewhere, therefore was it not his duty—an obligation—to bring them together, nothing more, a harmless connivance to replace an accidental encounter in the subway, let's say, or a mutual friend's introduction in the street? Just let him once see and talk to her and he would for sure be interested. As for Miriam, what possible harm for a working girl in an office, who met only loudmouthed salesmen and illiterate shipping clerks, to make the acquaintance of a fine scholarly boy? Maybe he would awaken in her a desire to go to college; if not—the shoemaker's mind at last came to grips with the truth—let her marry an educated man and live a better life.

approximately 600 words

Bernard Malamud, "The First Seven Years," *The Stories of Bernard Malamud*, pp. 13–14

1. Circle the letter of the main idea.
   a. Feld is anxious about repairing Max's shoes because they are too worn.
   b. Feld is an impossible dreamer with fanciful thoughts.
   c. Feld wants his daughter to improve her chances in life.

2. Write three major details that support the main idea you have chosen.

   _____

   _____

   _____

❖ Summary

It is necessary to make sense out of sentences and paragraphs in order to locate the main idea in extended readings. This chapter has shown that when the subject and verb of long sentences are separated, or when extensive introductory material precedes the subject and verb, the key idea may not be readily apparent. By asking key questions such as "Who or what is the sentence about?" (the *subject*) and "What is being said about the subject?" (the *verb*), you can make the meaning of that sentence become clearer.

In finding the main idea of paragraphs, it is important to distinguish the topic, which is general in nature, from the main idea, which makes a particular statement.

Strategies useful in finding the paragraph main idea include (1) asking key questions about the paragraph content, (2) locating a general statement within the paragraph that expresses the author's message, and (3) noting how a summary of the details can pinpoint the main idea of a paragraph.

The main idea may be found in different places in a paragraph. It is usually found in the first sentence in most informational paragraphs. Sometimes, however, it may be found in the last sentence. Main ideas are sometimes restated and found in both the first and last sentences, where they complement each other.

When writers use introductory information in paragraphs, the main idea is usually in the second or third sentence. In still other situations, the main idea is scattered throughout the paragraph. Last, the writer may not state a main idea directly, but may instead require you to draw a conclusion on the basis of other statements.

Major and minor details differ. Major details directly support or explain the main idea, while minor details are not essential to the main idea and simply help hold our attention and interest.

Novels and literary fiction sometimes use a different writing style, thereby limiting the use of sentence clues in finding the main idea.

Chapter 4 Vocabulary Review

A. **Using the Context:** Select the appropriate word from the words given below and write it in the space provided. Use the context to help determine the word's meaning.

proponents	**ideology**	**adjudicated**	**sequential**
besieged	**inductively**	**usurp**	

As the congresswoman arrived to speak about gun control at the rally, she

was suddenly (1) _____ by an angry group of citizens. These opponents of gun control shouted that she, as a member of the government, could

not (2) _____ their *right* to have all the guns and assault weapons they

wished. Meanwhile, the (3) _____ of stricter gun control laws were

peacefully waving white flags. What a difference in (4) _____ the two sides represented! A local dignitary walked to the podium and announced that each

side would take turns speaking and that the (5) _____ order had already been accepted by the leaders of both sides.

B. Answer *yes* or *no* to the following statements.

_____ 1. Are popular class members more likely to be members of an **elitist** group?

_____ 2. If a person is identified as being in **cardiac** arrest, is he or she going to prison?

_____ 3. Are **icons** likely to be found in churches?

_____ 4. Is **resiliency** important in running a marathon race?

_____ 5. Do the major religions employ **mystical** symbols?

Selection 7: **ESSAY**

☞ Preparation For Reading

Russell Baker, who wrote, "Hooked on Anger," has received many awards as both columnist and journalist, and in addition, he has written many books. He received two Pulitzer Prizes, one for a column he wrote in *The Observer* and a second one in 1982 for *Growing Up*, an autobiography of his bittersweet early years. For the past several seasons, he has replaced Alistar Cooke as the host of *Masterpiece Theater,* a PBS television program that performs English classics.

Preview the essay before reading, but first note these boldfaced words and their meanings. The words are underlined in the text.

vile speech	hateful; disgusting
rustic America	typical of country life; uncomplicated
inevitable **vagaries** of national life	odd, erratic, or freakish happenings
scowling models	looking angry or showing strong disapproval
obdurate government	unyielding; stubborn; obstinate
pursue war **ad infinitum**	without end; limitless
habituated to crying rage	accustomed by repetition
amenable to solution	responsive; open to suggestion

Hooked on Anger

Russell Baker

Anger has become the national habit. You see it on the sullen faces of fashion models who have obviously been told that anger sells. It pours out of the radio all day. Washington journalism hams snarl and shout at each other on television. Generations exchange sneers on TV and printed page. Ordinary people abuse congressmen and president with shockingly personal insults. Rudeness is a justifiable way of showing you can no longer control the fury within. <u>Vile</u> speech, justified on the same ground, is inescapable. 1

America is angry at Washington, angry at 2 the press, angry at immigrants, angry at television, angry at traffic, angry at people who are well off and angry at people who are poor, angry at blacks and angry at whites.

The old are angry at the young, the young 3 angry at the old. Suburbs are angry at cities, cities are angry at suburbs, and <u>rustic</u> America is angry at both whenever urban and suburban intruders threaten the peaceful rustic sense of having escaped from God's Angry Land.

Enough: A complete catalog of the varieties 4 of bile spoiling the American day would fill a library. The question is why. Why has anger become a reflexive response to the inevitable vagaries of national life?

Living perpetually at the boiling point seems to leave the country depressed and pessimistic. Study those scowling models wearing the latest clothes in the Sunday papers and magazines. Those are faces that expect only the worst. What a pity to waste such lovely new clothes on people so incapable of happiness. 5

The popularity of anger is doubly puzzling, not only because the American habit even in the worst of times has traditionally been mindless optimism, but also because there is relatively little nowadays for the nation to be angry about. 6

The country happily re-elected President Eisenhower in 1956 because it believed his campaign boast about giving it peace and prosperity. The "peace," of course, was life under the endless threat of nuclear devastation. 7

By contrast the country now, at last, really does enjoy peace, and if the prosperity is not so solid as it was in the 1950s, American wealth is still the world's vastest. So, with real peace and prosperity, what's to be furious about? 8

The explanation, I suspect, is that the country got itself addicted to anger and can't shake the habit. It was hooked long ago when there was very good reason for anger. 9

Massive, irritating and even scary expressions of it were vital in shaking an obdurate government, contemptuous of public opinion, from its determination to pursue war ad infinitum in Vietnam. 10

Massive, irritating and even scary expressions of anger—from Americans both black and white—were needed for the triumph of Martin Luther King and the civil rights movement. 11

These were monumental victories. If the nation had been unwilling to get mad—to shout, "We're not going to take it anymore!"—they might not have been won. 12

But what monumental struggle confronts us now? Giving young black people a stake in America is our most pressing problem, but nobody shouts much about that. Most other problems are so unmonumental that we might think the times ripe for greatness: an era of civility conducive to good feeling among neighbors of all races and persuasions, a golden age of progress in learning and the arts and science. 13

Is this making you angry? It's easy to imagine the cries of rage from a people habituated to crying rage: Are women not still oppressed by glass ceilings? Do black Americans no longer have to suffer the disrespect of a racist world? Who dares talk of prosperity when the wealth is distributed so unfairly? 14

True, all true. There is far too much poverty, racism remains an affliction, women still don't have economic equality with men. These present economists, philosophers and statesmen with exceedingly complex problems not amenable to solution by red-hot anger. 15

Politically minded people concerned with these issues have always known that low-grade anger must be maintained, that political feet must be kept to the fire, that the squeaky wheel gets the grease, and so on. The high-intensity fury now seething through the land on these and a hundred other issues, however, doesn't seem focused on any social or economic goal. It's as though the nation got mad as hell a long time ago, got good results, and now can't shake the anger habit. 16

approximately 800 words

Russell Baker, "Hooked on Anger," *San Jose Mercury News* Feb. 8, 1995, p. 7B. Reprinted by permission.

COMPREHENSION CHECK

Part I
General Comprehension Questions: Literal and Interpretive

Write the correct letter in the space provided.

_____ 1. Baker is puzzled by so many expressions of anger because
    a. of traditional mindlessness.
    b. the United States enjoys relative peace and prosperity.
    c. Americans are usually optimistic about the future.
    d. both b and c.

_____ 2. Baker points out that the United States under President Eisenhower had
    a. a fear of nuclear devastation.
    b. people angry at Congress and Washington.
    c. considerable racial tension.
    d. both a and b.

_____ 3. Baker believes that anger helped bring about
    a. the end of the Vietnam War.
    b. the election of Dwight D. Eisenhower.
    c. the triumph of the civil rights movement.
    d. both a and c.

_____ 4. He believes our most pressing problem today is
    a. depression and pessimism.
    b. our economy.
    c. improving opportunity for young black people.
    d. peaceful coexistence with other nations.

_____ 5. The author is surprised that
    a. today is not a time of greatness.
    b. we do not show great civility to one another.
    c. this is not a golden age of progress.
    d. all of the above.

_____ 6. The main idea of paragraph 15 is that
    a. serious problems are not solved by anger alone.
    b. racism is still a problem.
    c. women are still held back by the glass ceiling.
    d. we need better economists, statesmen, and philosophers.

7. State the main idea of paragraph 16. _____

_____

8. Indicate whether the following details are major (MJ) or minor (MN).

_____ a. Everyone today seems angry at everyone else.

_____ b. Anger is puzzling today because there is really little to be angry about.

_____ c. Our addiction to anger seems due to the fact that it was once necessary.

_____ d. Anger, by itself, will not solve our complex problems.

_____ e. We do not seem focused on any social or economic goals.

Part II
Application Questions for Writing/Discussion

9. Do you believe talk-show hosts are responsible for much of the hostility and anger prevalent in our country? _____ Support your answer.

_____

_____

10. Which group in the United States do you feel has the most justification to feel angry today?

_____

Support your answer. _____

Part III
Extend Your Vocabulary

Choose the correct word for the following sentences and write it in the space provided. You will not use all the words.

amenable   vile   vagaries   obdurate   rustic   ad infinitum

1. What a _____ speech! We were shocked to hear such language in a public place.

2. It reminded me of our farm in a nearby state—the scene was so _____.
3. We left the meeting in a happy mood because the change in plans had proved

    _____ to all parties.

4. The governor's _____ position on the budget angered the groups who had lobbied against the proposed cuts.

5. With the speaker rambling on _____, we left hurriedly, anxious to be spared any more of his repetitious remarks.

Selection 8: **TEXTBOOK**

 Preparation For Reading

While we have seen a lessening in the total number of crimes committed in the United States, the number of violent crimes has escalated. For example, every year more than 24,000 Americans are killed with guns. The number of homicides committed by adults age twenty-five or older declined 20 percent from 1985 to 1993, but the number of homicides committed by males age fourteen to seventeen rose 165 percent! Read about the American criminal justice system to find out what may be responsible for these changes in numbers.

Note the meaning of the boldfaced terms before reading. They are underlined in the text.

domestic squabbles	family arguments or fights
internalize the distinctions	taken into the mind
mediates the process	seeks to resolve the difficulty
felony indictments	serious crime
relative **lenience**	merciful; not strict
chivalry hypothesis	qualities of bravery and courteousness
many **jurisdictions**	territories controlled
traumatic for women	emotional shock

Preview, then read the selection.

Crime Control: The Criminal Justice System

David Popenoe

In the United States, the criminal justice system is an interlocking network of three distinct institutions: the police, the courts, and the correctional system. 1

THE POLICE

Crime control is the police function most in the public eye. Yet until the twentieth century, the major function of the police was to maintain order rather than to enforce the law. The maintenance of order—for example, police intervention in <u>domestic squabbles</u>—rarely leads to arrests. And even today, enforcing the criminal law probably occupies no more than 20 percent of police officers' time. The main activity of most local police forces is traffic control. 2

The police are always under great public pressure to "perform," a pressure that has pro- 3 moted the development of a distinct police subculture. One element of this subculture frequently noted by sociologists is a high level of suspiciousness—a belief that people cannot be trusted and are dangerous. Stemming from the danger that the police continually face as a part of their job, this belief sometimes colors their general attitudes, isolating them from the average citizen and confining them to their own special world.

While in training at a police academy, new 4 recruits undergo formal socialization processes. Among other things, they must learn the formal rules that govern the use of force, a right given exclusively to them by society. Yet society does little to help them make the often difficult decisions regarding when the use of force is warranted and just how much to use. They must internalize the distinctions between *legal force,* that which is sufficient to take a suspect into custody; *normal force,* that which is required under specific circumstances (though not always lawful or highly regarded); and *excessive force,* that which is brutal and unnecessary. In practice, much of the socialization of police officers is completed on the street—an informal learning process or "second training" that is as important as that in the academy.

THE COURTS

The second part of the criminal justice system is **5** the courts. In theory, the courts serve to determine the guilt or innocence of individuals accused of crimes and to decide on the punishment for those convicted. A prosecuting attorney represents the state; a defense attorney represents the defendant; and a judge mediates the process. A defendant who can afford to do so hires his or her own defense attorney; otherwise the court appoints one. If the defendant pleads guilty, there is no trial; the judge simply decides on the sentence. If the defendant pleads innocent, there may be a jury trial.

The popular image of the courts as a place **6** where the state and the defense present cases against and for the defendant is far from accurate, however. The court system is actually a complex bureaucracy, and most cases are settled through a process of negotiation. In order to handle the increasing number of cases, the courts have resorted more and more to *plea bargaining.* This is a process in which judges and prosecutors negotiate with defendants to get them to plead guilty to lesser crimes than the ones with which they are charged, thus avoiding jury trials, saving money, and taking some of the strain off an already overcrowded system. In many courts, more than 90 percent of all felony indictments are decided by plea bargaining.

The prevalence of plea bargaining proba- **7** bly contributes to growing public dissatisfaction with the criminal justice system. Dissatisfaction is also expressed with the courts' sentencing of criminals once they are convicted. Increasingly, people feel that sentences need to be tougher. One study of persons arrested on felony charges in 11 states found that 62 percent were convicted but that only 36 percent ended up serving time in jail. One-third of those convicted of violent crimes were sentenced to serve more than a year in prison.

The court system is not always adequately **8** prepared to handle new legal issues that arise as a result of technological innovation or cultural change. For example, 46 states enacted computer crime statutes between 1981 and 1985. Despite this concentrated legislative activity, a national survey of county prosecutors in states with computer laws found very low levels of prosecutorial activity. Why? There were no precedents for this new category of crime in the court cases. Consequently, it was difficult to know how to apply such traditional legal concepts as theft and fraud to computer abuse.

The court system has also been taken to **9** task in recent years for its treatment of women. Is the courts' traditional conception of what a "reasonable man" would do in a given set of circumstances fully applicable to what a "reasonable woman" would do? Aren't some current courtroom procedures biased against women? For example, some have argued that the requirement of giving testimony in public in front of a relatively large group of people may put some women at a disadvantage, because "domestic isolation will have given them fewer chances for public performances than men."

It is clear, however, that the women's move- **10** ment has had some impact on the treatment of women in the courts. In response to the feminist demand for equal treatment, there has been some movement away from the relative lenience with which courts have traditionally handled women—especially middle-class white women—who are accused of crimes. The "chivalry hypothesis" appears to be losing its validity. Furthermore, rape is punished more severely than it was previously, and a variety of steps have been taken in many jurisdictions to make it easier and less traumatic for women to prosecute men who rape them.

THE CORRECTIONAL SYSTEM

The correctional system was established to 11 apply sanctions and other measures to criminals convicted by the courts. At the heart of the correctional system in the United States are the prisons. This nation has the highest rate of imprisonment in the world; the number of imprisoned Americans increased from 196,000 in 1970 to 789,000 in 1991. The great majority of convicted criminals are either on probation or parole, however. *Probation* is a period of time during which offenders, instead of serving a prison term, are more or less closely supervised while continuing to live in the community. *Parole* is the conditional release of offenders from prison, usually for good behavior, before their full sentence is served.

A correctional system may, in theory, be 12 designed to accomplish one or more of four basic purposes: *retribution,* seeking revenge for a crime on behalf of both the victim and society as a whole; *incapacitation,* restricting the freedom of the offender so that he or she will be less able to commit further crimes; *rehabilitation,* seeking to reform the offender so that he or she will return to law-abiding ways; and *deterrence,* attempting to reduce criminal activity by instilling a fear of punishment. During the 1960s and early 1970s, there was a marked shift away from an emphasis on punishment and toward rehabilitation, but in the past 15 years the public's insistence that the criminal justice system "get tough" on crime has radically reduced the willingness of the prisons to attempt to reform their inmates.

Although humanitarians would like to see 13 additional emphasis placed on rehabilitation, many experts doubt that this goal is achievable in the prison setting. One review of rehabilitation programs in prisons concluded that no type of rehabilitation has been very successful because it is impossible to produce changes in unwilling individuals under the conditions of constraint or indifference prevalent in prisons.

Even changing the conditions of prisons 14 may not help. When prisons are changed to make them more humane, research suggests that no more rehabilitation takes place in them than in traditional penal institutions. If rehabilitation is to have a chance to become successful, it seems reasonable to suppose that correctional institutions should be better integrated into the community. As one researcher has noted, punishment must be coupled with fundamental changes in the prisoner's social environment in order to have any positive effect.

Deterrence has been the most widely 15 debated purpose of the correctional system in recent years; it has also been the subject of much research. Deterrence is based on the (not entirely realistic) idea that people are rational beings and calculate the risks versus the benefits of committing a particular crime. If deterrence is working, the crime rate should be low when the risk of punishment is high.

Punishment can vary according to *certainty* 16 (likelihood of imprisonment), *severity* (length of sentence), and *swiftness.* Each of these dimensions may play a role in deterrence. Some evidence suggests that crime can be reduced by making the punishment more severe and especially more certain. Other research has disputed these findings, however, and it is fair to say that at the present time no firm conclusions about deterrence can be drawn.

approximately 1450 words

COMPREHENSION CHECK

Part I
General Comprehension Questions: Literal and Interpretive

Write the correct letter in the space provided.

_____ 1. The main activity of most local police forces is to
   a. enforce the law.
   b. control domestic violence.
   c. maintain order.
   d. oversee traffic control.

_____ 2. Police develop a distinct subculture, part of which includes the idea that
   a. people are dangerous.
   b. training involves specific rules.
   c. people cannot be trusted.
   d. both a and c.

_____ 3. Defendants who plead not guilty
   a. may have a jury trial.
   b. always have a jury trial.
   c. seldom have a jury trial.
   d. none of the above.

_____ 4. Most court cases
   a. go to trial.
   b. are settled through negotiations.
   c. are decided by the judge.
   d. all of the above.

_____ 5. A major detail in paragraph 10 is that middle-class white women suffer
   a. a lesser penalty for crime.
   b. a greater penalty for crime.
   c. no penalty because of plea bargaining.
   d. punishment similar to that of men.

_____ 6. The main idea of paragraph 11 is that
   a. prisons are the heart of the correctional system.
   b. parole is time off for good behavior.
   c. the great majority of prisoners are either on probation or on parole.
   d. probation requires rigid supervision.

7. What is the meaning of the following sentence? "For example, some have argued that the requirement of giving testimony in public in front of a relatively

large group of people may put some women at a disadvantage, because 'domestic isolation will have given them fewer chances for public performances than men'" (paragraph 9)?

_____

_____

8. How effective are the courts in settling cases regarding theft and fraud in

computer abuse? _____

_____

Part II
Application Questions for Writing/Discussion

9. Are the courts today moving toward increasing punishment or rehabilitation?

Why? Do you agree with the trend?_____

_____

10. What changes do sociologists want for the court system? Do you agree with

their proposals? Why or why not?_____

_____

Part III
Extend Your Vocabulary

Use the context of the selection to define the following words.

1. plea bargaining _____

2. retribution _____

3. probation _____

4. rehabilitation _____

5. legal force _____

Selection 9: **LITERATURE**

☞ Preparation for Reading

One reason we enjoy literature is that we meet characters who, though imaginary, seem real. In the short story "El Patrón" that follows, the character development relates to generational differences between parents and children. "El Patrón" is from a collection of short stories, *Imagining America,* that reflects the diversity in American life.

The author of the story is a descendant of families who founded Albuquerque, New Mexico. He has been published in *Cuentos Chicanos* and has published a trilogy of New Mexican novels: *Memories of the Alhambra, Not by the Sword,* and *Inheritance of Strangers.*

Note the meaning of the boldfaced words before reading. They are underlined in the text.

talking **banalities**	of little interest; commonplace
belligerently received	in an aggressively hostile manner
impassioned call	filled with passion
perverse gourmet	away from what is right or good
summit meeting	the highest point
an **inanimate** warning	without spirit

El Patrón

Nash Candelaria

My father-in-law's hierarchy is, in descending order: Dios, El Papa, y el patrón.   1
It is to these that mere mortals bow, as in turn el patrón bows to El Papa, and El Papa bows to Dios.

God and the Pope are understandable enough. It's this el patrón, the boss, who causes most of our trouble. Whether it's the one who gives you work and for it pay, the lifeblood of hardworking little people, or others: our parents (fathers affectionately known as "jefe," mothers known merely as "Mamá"), military commanders ("el capitán"), or any of the big shots in the government ("el alcalde," el gobernador," "el presidente," and never forget "la policia"). It was about some such el patrón trouble that Señor Martínez boarded the bus in San Diego and headed north toward L.A.—and us.

Since I was lecturing to a midafternoon summer school class at Southwestern U, my wife Lola picked up her father at the station. When I arrived home, they were sitting politely in the living room talking <u>banalities</u>: "Yes, it does look like rain. But if it doesn't rain, it might be sunny. If only the clouds would blow away."

Lola had that dangerous look on her face that made me start talking too fast and too long in hope of shifting her focus. It never worked. She'd sit there with a face like a brown-skinned kewpie doll whose expression was slowly turning into that of an angry maniac. When she could no longer stand it, she'd give her father a blast: "You never talk to me about anything important, you macho, chauvinist jumping bean!" Then it would escalate to nastiness from there.

But tonight it didn't get that far. As I entered, Señor Martínez rose, dressed in his one suit as for a wedding or a funeral, and politely shook my hand. Without so much as a glance at Lola he said, "Why don't you go to the kitchen with the other women." 5

"There are no other women," Lola said coldly. She stood and <u>belligerently</u> received my kiss on the check before leaving.

Señor Martínez was oblivious to her reaction, sensing only the absence of "woman," at which he visibly relaxed.

"Rosca," he said, referring to me as he always did by my last name. "Tito is in trouble with the law."

His face struggled between anger and sadness, tinged with a crosscurrent of confusion. Tito was his pride and joy. His only son after four daughters. A twilight gift born to his wife at a time when he despaired of ever having a son, when their youngest daughter Lola was already ten years old and their oldest daughter twenty.

"He just finished his examinations at the state university. He was working this summer to save money for his second year when this terrible thing happened." 10

I could not in my wildest fantasies imagine young Vicente getting into trouble. He impressed me as a bright, polite young man who would inspire pride in any father. Even when he and old Vicente had quarreled about Tito going to college instead of working full time, the old man had grudgingly come around to seeing the wisdom of it. But now. The law! I was stunned.

"Where is he?" I asked, imagining the nineteen-year old in some filthy cell in the San Diego jail.

"I don't know." Then he looked over his shoulder toward the kitchen as if to be certain no one was eavesdropping. "I think he went underground."

Underground! I had visions of drug crazed revolutionary zealots. Bombs exploding in Federal Buildings. God knows what kind of madness.

"They're probably after him," he went on. Then he paused and stared at me as if trying to understand. "Tito always looked up to you and Lola. Of all the family it would be you he would try to contact. I want you to help me." Not help Tito, I thought, but help *me*. 15

I went to the cabinet and poured from the bottle that I keep for emergencies. I took a swallow to give me courage to ask the question. "What . . . did . . . he do?"

Señor Martínez stared limply at the glass in his hand. "You know," he said, "my father fought with Pancho Villa."

Jesus! I thought. If everyone who told me his father had fought with Pancho Villa was telling the truth, that army would have been big enough to conquer the world. Besides—what did this have to do with Tito?

"When my turn came," he continued. "I enlisted in the Marines at Camp Pendleton. Fought los japoneses in the Pacific." Finally he took a sip of his drink and sat stiffly as if at attention. "The men in our family have never shirked their duty!" He barked like the Marine corporal he had once been.

It slowly dawned on me what this was all about. It had been *the* topic during sum- **20** mer school at Southwestern U. Registration for the draft. "No blood for mideast oil!" the picket signs around the campus post office had shouted. "Boycott the Exxon army!"

"I should never have let him go to college," Señor Martínez said. "That's where he gets such crazy radical ideas. From those rich college boys whose parents can buy them out of all kinds of trouble."

"So he didn't register," I said.

"The FBI is probably after him right now. It's a Federal crime, you know. And the Canadians don't want draft dodgers either."

He took a deep swallow, polishing off the rest of his drink, and put the empty glass on the coffee table. There, his gesture seemed to say, now you know the worst.

Calmer now, he went on to tell me more. About the American Civil War: a **25** greater percentage of Spanish-speaking men of New Mexico had joined the Union Army than the men from any other group in any other state. About the Rough Riders, including young Mexican-Americans, born on horseback, riding roughest of all over the Spanish in Cuba. About the War-to-End-All-Wars, where tough, skinny, brown-faced doughboys from farms in Texas, New Mexico, Arizona, Colorado, and California gave their all "Over There." About World War II, from the New Mexico National Guard captured at Bataan to the tough little Marines whom he was proud to fight alongside; man for man there were more decorations for bravery among Mexican-Americans than among any other group. Then Korea, where his younger brother toughed it out in the infantry. Finally Vietnam, where kids like his nephew, Pablo, got it in some silent, dark jungle trying to save a small country from the Communists.

By now he had lost his calm. There were tears in his eyes, partly from the pride he felt in this tradition of valor. But partly for something else, I thought. I could almost hear his son's reply to his <u>impassioned</u> call to duty: "Yes, Papá. So we could come back, if we survive, to our jobs as busboys and ditch diggers; that's why I have to go to college. I don't want to go to the Middle East and fight and die for some oil company when you can't even afford to own a car. If the Russians invaded our country, I would defend it. If a robber broke into our house, I would fight him. If someone attacked you, I would save you. But this? No, Papá."

But now Tito was gone. God knows where. None of his three sisters in San Diego had seen him. Nor any of his friends in the neighborhood or school or work.

I could hear preparations for dinner from the kitchen. Señor Martínez and I had another traguito while Lolita and Junior ate their dinner early, the sounds of their childish voices piercing through the banging of pots and pans.

When Lola called me Emiliano instead of by my nickname, Pata, I knew we were in for a lousy meal. Everything her father disliked must have been served. It had taken a <u>perverse</u> gourmet expending a tremendous amount of energy to fix such rotten food. There was that nothing white bread that presses together into a doughy flat mess instead of the tortillas Papá thrived on. There was a funny little salad with chopped garbage in it covered by a blob of imitation goo. There was no meat. *No meat!* Just all those sliced vegetables in a big bowl. Not ordinary vegetables like beans and potatoes and carrots, but funny, wiggly long things like wild grass—or worms. And quivering cubes of what must have been whale blubber. But enough. You get the idea.

Halfway through the meal, as Señor Martínez shuffled the food around on his 30 plate like one of our kids resisting what was good for them, the doorbell rang.

"You'd better get that, Emiliano," Lola said, daring me to refuse by her tone of voice and dagger-throwing glance.

Who needs a fight? In a sense I was lucky because I could leave the table and that pot of mess-age. When I opened the door, a scraggly young man beamed at me. "I hitchhiked from San Diego," Tito said.

Before I could move onto the steps and close the door behind me, he stumbled past into the house. Tired as he was, he reacted instantly to seeing his father at the table. "You!" he shouted, then turned and bolted out the door.

Even tired he could run faster than me, so I hopped into the car and drove after him while Lola and Señor Martínez stood on the steps shouting words I couldn't hear.

Two blocks later Tito climbed into the car when I bribed him with a promise of 35 dinner at McDonald's. While his mouth was full I tried to talk some sense into him, but to no avail. He was just as stubborn as his father and sister. Finally, I drove him to the International House on campus where the housing manager, who owed me a favor, found him an empty bed.

"You should have made him come back with you," Lola nagged at me that night.

"He doesn't want to be under the same roof with his father." From her thoughtful silence I knew that she understood and felt the same way. When I explained to her what it was all about—her father had said nothing to her—it looked for a moment as if she would get out of bed, stomp to the guest room, and heave Señor Martínez out into the street.

The next day was an endless two-way shuttle between our house and the I House. First me. Then Lola. If Señor Martínez had had a car and could drive, he would have followed each of us.

Our shuttle diplomacy finally wore them down. At last there were cracks in father's and son's immovable positions.

"Yes. Yes. I love my son." 40

"I love my father."

"I know. I know. Adults should be able to sit down and talk about their differences, no matter how wrong he is."

"Maybe tomorrow. Give me a break. But definitely not at mealtime. I can't eat while my stomach is churning."

The difficulty for me, as always, was in keeping my opinions to myself. Lola didn't have that problem. After all, they were her brother and father, so she felt free to say whatever she pleased.

"The plan is to get them to talk," I said to her. "If they can talk, they can reach 45 some kind of understanding."

"Papá has to be set straight," she said. "As usual, he's wrong, but he always insists it's someone else who messed things up."

"He doesn't want Tito to go to jail."

"That's Tito's choice!" Of course she was right; they were both right.

The <u>summit</u> meeting was set for the next afternoon. Since I had only one late morning lecture, I would pick up Tito, feed him a Big Mac or two, then bring him to the house. Lola would fix Señor Martínez some nice tortillas and chili, making up for that abominable dinner of the night before last. Well fed, with two chaperones mediating, we thought they could work something out.

When Tito and I walked into the house, hope started to tremble and develop 50 goose bumps. It was deathly silent and formal. Lola had that dangerous look on her face again. The macho, chauvinist jumping bean sat stiffly in his suit that looked like it had just been pressed—all shiny and sharply creased, unapproachable and potentially cutting, an <u>inanimate</u> warning of what lay behind Señor Martínez's stone face.

Tito and I sat across from the sofa and faced them. Or rather I faced them. Both Tito and Señor Martínez were looking off at an angle from each other, not daring to touch glances. I smiled, but no one acknowledged it so I gave it up. Then Lola broke the silence.

"What this needs is a woman's point-of-view," she began.

That's all Señor Martínez needed. The blast his eyes shot at her left her openmouthed and silent as he interrupted. "I don't want you to go to jail!" He was looking at Lola, but he meant Tito.

Tito's response was barely audible, and I detected a trembling in his voice. "You'd rather I got killed on some Arabian desert."

The stone face cracked. For a moment it looked as if Señor Martínez would 55 burst into tears. He turned his puzzled face from Lola toward his son. "No," he said. "Is that what you think?" Then, when Tito did not answer, he said, "You're my only son. Damn it! Sons are supposed to obey their fathers!"

"El patrón, El Papa, and Dios," Tito said with a trace of bitterness.

But Lola could be denied no longer. "Papá, how old were you when you left Mexico for the U.S.?" She didn't expect an answer, so didn't give him time to reply. "Sixteen, wasn't it? And what did your father say?"

Thank God that smart-ass smile of hers was turned away from her father. She knew she had him, and he knew it too, but he didn't need her smirk to remind him.

He sighed. The look on his face showed that sometimes memories were best forgotten. He shook his head but did not speak. Lola had seen her father's reaction, and her voice lost its hard edge and became more sympathetic.

"He disowned you, didn't he? Grandpa disowned you. Called you a traitor to 60 your own country. A deserter when things got tough."

"I did not intend to stay in Mexico and starve," he said. He looked around at us one by one as if he had to justify himself. "He eventually came to Los Estados Unidos himself. He and Mamá died in that house in San Diego."

"What did you think when Grandpa did that to you?"

No answer was necessary. "Can't you see, Papá?" Lola pleaded.

Meanwhile Tito had been watching his father as if he had never seen him   **65**
before. Only the older children had heard Papá's story of how he left Mexico.

"I don't intend to go to jail, Papá," Tito said. "I just have to take a stand along
with thousands of others. In the past old men started wars in which young men died
in order to preserve old men's comforts. It just has to stop.

"There's never been a war without a draft. Never a draft without registration.
And this one is nothing but craziness by el patrón in Washington, D.C. If enough of
us protest, maybe he'll get the message."

"They almost declared it unconstitutional," I said. "They may yet."

"Because they aren't signing women," Papá said in disgust. But from the look on
Lola's face, I'd pick her over him in any war.

"If they come after me, I'll register," Tito said. "But in the meantime I have to   **70**
take this stand."

There. It was out. They had had their talk in spite of their disagreements.

"He's nineteen," Lola said. "Old enough to run his own life."

Señor Martínez was all talked out. He slumped against the back of the sofa. Even
the creases in his trousers sagged. Tito looked at his sister, and his face brightened.

"Papá," Tito said. "I—I'd like to go home if you want me to."

On Papá's puzzled face I imagined I could see the words: "My father fought with   **75**
Pancho Villa." But it was no longer an accusation, only a simple statement of fact.
Who knows what takes more courage: to fight or not to fight?

"There's a bus at four o'clock," Señor Martínez said.

Later I drove them in silence to the station. Though it was awkward, it wasn't a
bad silence. There are more important ways to speak than with words, and I could
feel that sitting shoulder to shoulder, father and son had reached some accord.

Papá still believed in el patrón, El Papa, and Dios. What I hoped they now saw
was that Tito did too. Only in his case, conscience overrode el patrón, maybe even
El Papa. In times past, Popes too declared holy wars that violated conscience. For
Tito, conscience was the same as Dios. And I saw, in their uneasy truce, that love
overrode their differences.

I shook their hands as they boarded the bus, and watched the two similar faces,
one old, one young, smile sadly at me through the window as the Greyhound pulled
away.

When I got back home, Junior and Lolita were squabbling over what channel to   **80**
watch on TV. I rolled my eyes in exasperation, ready to holler, but Lola spoke first.

"I'm glad Papá got straightened out. The hardest thing for parents is to let go of
their children."

Yeah, I started to say, but she stuck her head into the den and shouted at Junior
and Lolita to stop quarreling or they were going to get it.

approximately 1850 words

Nash Candelaria, "El Patrón," *The Day the Cisco Kid Shot John Wayne,* (Bilingual Press
Editorial Bilingüe, Arizona State University, 1988), pp. 23–30. Copyright © 1988 by
Bilingual Press. Reprinted by permission.

Questions for Writing/Discussion

1. What can you deduce about Senor Martinez from his remark to Rosca in paragraph 16, "I want you to help me"? Remember, Senor Martinez did not mention Tito.

2. What is the main idea of paragraph 26? Why did the author go to such great lengths with the details in this paragraph?

3. Did Rosca, the storyteller, handle the situation between the father and son well? What would you have done?

4. How did Lola's remark to her father in paragraph 58, "How old were you when you left Mexico?," help to bridge the difference between father and son?

5. Have you experienced a similar difficulty with your parents when your values were in disagreement? Explain.

JOURNAL ENTRY

The three selections at the end of this chapter emphasize the theme of anger: the anger of citizens, the anger that causes people to commit crimes, and the anger that often erupts when there are generation differences. Do you agree with Russell Baker (*Hooked on Anger*) that people today really have little to be angry about and, in actuality, there is *less* reason to be angry now than at any other time in history? What specifically angers you the most about our society today? About those close to you? How do you transcend your own anger when it surfaces?

Learning Paragraph Patterns

This chapter will help you

- recognize patterns used by writers to organize their ideas.
- understand how signal words are used to help connect ideas.
- identify the relationship between the topic, the main idea, and the writer's patterns of organization.
- practice notetaking for understanding and remembering information.

❖❖❖

Before reading, think about these questions.

- What do you imagine a writing pattern might be?
- What clues do authors use to show how their writing is organized?
- How might writing patterns be similar to speaking patterns?

❖❖❖

Jot down your thoughts about the above ideas in the space provided. _____

_____

_____

❖ Types of Writing

The *type* of writing found in essays, textbooks, and literature is generally classified into four broad categories.

1. *Narration:* The writer relates, or "narrates," events in some kind of sequence. In literature, this means the writer tells a story.
2. *Exposition:* The word *exposition* means "explanation." In expository writing, the author *exposes* information or ideas. The primary purpose of exposition is *not* to tell a story, as in narration, but rather to explain—for example, to describe how a computer works.
3. *Persuasion:* In persuasive writing, the author attempts to convince or persuade you of something, to think as he or she does, often trying to change your mind. Persuasive writing, which is most often found in essays and editorials, requires critical thinking, a skill emphasized in Part II.
4. *Description:* Description is generally used as a supporting device for any of the other three types of writing. Description is most helpful in creating a word picture of something concrete, such as a scene, a person, or a new technology. In textbooks, writers can describe abstract concepts, such as truth or justice.

❖ Understanding the Basic Patterns for Organizing Information

How do you normally go about explaining your ideas to someone? Most of us do pretty much the same thing. We use patterns of speech.

Patterns of Speech	An Example of the Pattern
Classifying and *enumerating* information or *dividing* it into parts	List class assignments.
Explaining the order in which something happened	Give directions.
Listing the steps in a process	Access computer information.
Giving *examples*	Discuss the kinds of exercises you do.
Comparing and *contrasting*	Decide whether to buy an American car or a foreign car.
Discussing a *cause* and its *effect*	Pass a course, because of diligent study.
Defining ideas or concepts	Explain your feelings about a career.

Although there are many ways to express ideas, writers usually use these seven basic patterns, generally mixing, overlapping, or combining them in paragraphs and passages. Therefore, the patterns can vary from page to page. Like computer programmers, writers create *programs* or *patterns* to communicate information to their readers. And after readers recognize the patterns, they are better able to process the information and think with the author. These patterns further help anticipate information, clarify topics or key ideas, and show the relationship of supporting statements.

The writer's purpose and the topic help determine the pattern or patterns to be used. Terms writers use to signal to the reader which pattern is being used should be familiar to you, since these are often the very words instructors use in exams and quizzes—for example, *define, compare, contrast, explain, list, describe, analyze.* You have probably encountered these words many times. Understanding writing patterns not only assists you in your reading/study tasks but also better prepares you to take examinations. These patterns can also serve as models or examples for your own writing tasks.

❖ Pattern 1: Classification

Information is often **categorized** or classified into groups on the basis of similarities and differences. The classification pattern is used extensively by textbook authors, especially in the sciences. Its purpose is to break down information into parts or to explain a series of things by discussing their individual **components.** The process used in classification often takes the form of an outline. The topic or main idea sentence usually helps identify the type of category. Writers often use numbers to signal a class or division, for example, *two classes,* or *three categories,* or *four divisions,* or *five groups.*

Signal or guide words are an obvious clue for this pattern. Study those listed here so you will recognize them when you are reading and so you will be able to use them when you write answers on examinations and in your general writing.

Signals for Classification

categories	features	sorts
characteristics	groups	types
classes	kinds	ways
classification	numbers	
elements	parts	

---

categorized (kat′ ə gə rīzd′) put into a specifically defined division
components (kəm pó nənts) part of a system or element

Generally, a writer classifies information in a series of statements giving supporting facts or details. The order in which the information is presented is usually not significant and can be switched around without changing the meaning. Read the following paragraph to see whether the meaning would change if the second and third sentences were switched. The signal words are circled.

The Chinese responded to prejudice and persecution in (two ways.) (First,) they created an insulated society-within-a-society that needed little from the dominant culture. (Second,) they displayed a **stoic** willingness to persevere, and to take without complaint or resistance whatever America dished out.

Donald Dale Jackson, "Sojourners Who Came to Stay," Smithsonian, Feb. 1991, p. 117

When studying textbook material, you may find it helpful to make some notations of the signal or guide words to assist you to understand information. Circling, highlighting, or underlining after an initial reading can help you recognize the parts of the classification. Then, outlining or mapping by creating a chart or diagram will simplify remembering the information when you study.

Read the following passage, marking the signal words as you do, and then study how it has been outlined on a chart.

Many people have to communicate and work with members of other cultures, and social skills training is now being given to some of these who are about to work abroad. Intercultural communication is necessary for several kinds of people:

1. Tourists are probably the largest category, though they stay for the shortest periods and need to master only a few simple situations—meals, travel, shopping, taxis, etc. To a large extent they are shielded from the local culture by the international hotel culture.

2. Business, governmental, and university visitors, on short business trips, have to cope with a wider range of problems, but are often accommodated in hotels or somewhere similar, and looked after by other expatriates. They, too, are somewhat shielded from the local culture; they rarely learn the language and are given a great deal of help.

3. Businessmen, or others on longer visits of up to five years, students who stay from one to three years, and members of the Peace Corps and Voluntary Service Overseas who stay for two years. This is much more demanding, involving living in a house or apartment, coping with many aspects of the local culture and learning at least some of the language.

Stephen Bochner (ed.), Cultures in Contact: Studies in Cross Cultures, in Larry A. Samovar and
Richard E. Porter, Intercultural Communication: A Reader, 6th ed. Wadsworth, 1991, p. 31

---

stoic (stō´ ik) displaying little emotion

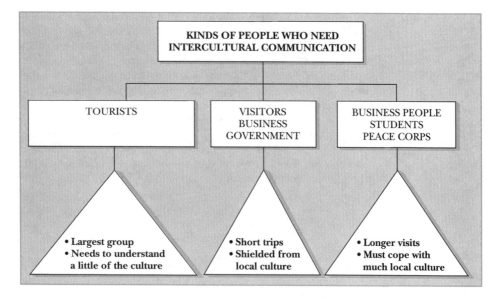

ACTIVITY 5.1

PASSAGE 1

After reading the passages that follow, make notes on the text itself of the main ideas and signal words. The first passage divides phobias (fears people experience) into three general categories. Which one of the fears do you believe would cause people the most anxiety? After reading the passage, without looking back, fill in the map to see what you can remember.

Basically phobias fall into three broad categories. Firstly, a fear of a specific object, such as a cat or spider. Secondly, a fear of a specific situation, such as being in a place, restaurant, school, or outside the home. Thirdly, and more abstract, a fear of a specific illness, or death.

Phobias in the first category—of a specific *object*—are often related to a previous, frightening incident. For example, a child who is already nervous of dogs could be knocked down or bitten by one, causing the fear to develop into a phobia. Or a child of a parent with a snake phobia may have modelled herself on the parent and "caught" it. Sometimes a child under stress at home or school may have an unpleasant experience with an insect or animal, and transfer its anxiety to the creature concerned. The insect or animal may then arouse the anxiety and fear. Fears of animals, birds, insects and so on are almost entirely confined to women—possibly because upbringing still dictates that boys should not show fear of such objects.

Phobias in the second category—of a specific *situation*—can also relate to a frightening incident. For example, a fear of being in a **lift** could be due to having been trapped

lift (lift) British term for elevator

in one once, or having been locked in a room. But social phobics—with their fear of social situations—and agoraphobics, with their fear of going out into the street, have more complex reasons connected with anxiety behind the onset of their phobia. Indeed, agoraphobia is known as the "calamity syndrome" because it is so often a reaction—sometimes delayed—to the shock of the death of a parent or an operation, or a change of life-style. Sometimes these events are the triggering point of the underlying stress, or depression.

The third category—fear of illness and death—often starts by a friend or relative contracting a particular illness, like cancer or heart trouble. Sometimes the phobic has nursed a dying parent and then becomes **morbidly** convinced he or she will now get the same illness. A specific fear of death—not necessarily tied up with illness—can be a continuation of a childhood fear.

approximately 400 words

Joy Melville, *Phobias and Obsessions, Goward, McCann & Gerghegan, Inc., New York, 1977,* pp. 170–171

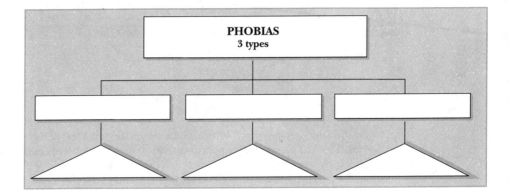

PHOBIAS
3 types

PASSAGE 2

Nine general types of prison life-styles are discussed in the following textbook passage.

a.   Mark the signal words and main idea sentences in the passage.

b.   After you complete the reading, write a paragraph in which you discuss which inmate types you think can best be **rehabilitated.**

Inmate Types

1. ***The Mean Dude.*** Some inmates adjust to prison by being mean. They are quick to fight, and when they fight, they fight like wild men (or women). . . . Other inmates know

morbidly (mor´ bid lē) preoccupied with unwholesome thoughts or matters
rehabilitated (rē hə bil´ ə tātid) a delinquent person restored to a useful life

that such prisoners are best left alone. The mean dude receives frequent write-ups and spends much time in solitary confinement.

A psychologist might say that the mean dude is acting out against the fact of captivity, striking out at anyone he (or she) can. This type of role performance is more common in male institutions and in maximum security prisons. It tends to become less common as inmates progress to lower security levels.

2. *The Hedonist.* Some inmates build their lives around the limited pleasures which can be had within the confines of prison. The smuggling of **contraband,** homosexuality, gambling, drug running, and other officially condemned activities provide the center of interest for prison hedonists. Hedonists generally have an abbreviated view of the future, living only for the "now." . . .

3. *The Opportunist.* The opportunist takes advantage of the positive experiences prison has to offer. Schooling, trade-training, counseling, and other self-improvement activities are the focal points of the opportunist's life in prison. Opportunists are the "do-gooders" of the prison subculture. They are generally well liked by prison staff, but shunned and mistrusted by other prisoners because they come closest to accepting the role which the staff defines as "model prisoner.". . .

4. *The Retreatist.* Prison life is rigorous and demanding. **Badgering** by the staff and actual or feared assaults by other inmates may cause some prisoners to attempt psychological retreat from the realities of imprisonment. Such inmates may experience neurotic or psychotic episodes, become heavily involved in drug and alcohol abuse, or even attempt suicide. Depression and mental illness are the hallmarks of the retreatist personality in prison. . . .

5. *The Legalist.* The legalist is the "jail house lawyer." Just like the mean dude, the legalist fights confinement. The weapons in this fight are not fists or clubs, however, but the legal "writ." Convicts facing long sentences, with little possibility for early release through the correctional system, are most likely to turn to the courts in their battle against confinement.

6. *The Radical.* Radical inmates picture themselves as political prisoners. Society, and the successful conformists who populate it, are seen as oppressors who have forced criminality upon many "good people" through the creation of a system which distributes wealth and power **inequitably.**

7. *The Colonist.* Some inmates think of prison as their home. They "know the ropes," have many "friends" inside, and may feel more comfortable institutionalized than on the streets. They typically hold either positions of power or respect (or both) among the inmate population. These are the prisoners who don't look forward to leaving prison.

8. *The Religious.* Some prisoners profess a strong religious faith. They may be "born again" Christians, committed Muslims, or even Hare Krishnas. Religious inmates frequently attend services, may form prayer groups, and sometimes ask the prison administration to allocate meeting facilities or create special diets to accommodate their claimed spiritual needs.

---

hedonist (hēd´ n ist) person who believes that pleasure or happiness is the greatest thing in life

contraband (kon´ trə band´) goods prohibited by law from being imported or exported

badgering (baj´ ə ring) tormenting by nagging or bullying

inequitably (in ek´ wə tə blē) unfairly; unjustly

9. *The Realist.* The realist is a prisoner who sees confinement as a natural consequence of criminal activity. Time spent in prison is an unfortunate "cost of doing business." This stoic attitude toward **incarceration** generally leads the realist to "pull his (or her) own time" and to make the best of it. Realists tend to know the inmate code, are able to avoid trouble, and continue in lives of crime once released.

approximately 570 words

Frank Schmalleger, *Criminal Justice Today*, pp. 498–500

Remember now to mark the main idea sentences and signal words, and then answer these questions.

1. Which inmate types do you think can best be rehabilitated? Why do you think so?

---

2. Do you agree with the classification of the last type as "the realist"? Why or why not?

❖ Pattern 2: Sequence or Time Order

In the sequence pattern, events are usually presented in the order in which they happened, that is, in **chronological** order. However, this pattern may also be organized in **spatial** order; that is, the details may be organized in order of their importance or by their relative position. A novelist can use spatial order to describe an indoor or outdoor setting—a room, a building, a forest.

Unlike the order in the classification pattern, the order in sequence is significant and cannot be **transposed.** For example, a history book can use time order to explain a series of events in a war, while a biology text can use a time sequence to show the evolutionary stages of animals. A manual on automotive transmissions can explain repairs in their order of importance, in a sequence of steps.

Generally, signal words help the reader see which important details will be developed in a sequential pattern. As with the classification pattern, numbers may be used, but for the purpose of showing time order or steps in a process, not for the

---

incarceration (in kär´ sə rā´ shun) being put in jail or shut in
chronological (krän əl aj´ ikəl) arrangement of events in order of occurrence
spatial (spā´ shəl) happening or existing in space
transposed (trans pōzd´) reversed

purpose of merely listing at random. Dates are also often a clue to time order. The major signal words to help you recognize the sequence pattern follow.

Signals for Sequence

first	now	later
second	after	stages
third	before	steps
next	finally	then
most important	furthermore	when
last		

Read the following paragraphs and note the circled signal words, which help the reader follow Hemingway's step-by-step analysis of what makes some Spainards declare a bullfighter's work to be "vulgar." Then, complete the outline of ideas.

The (three absolute) acts of the tragedy are (first) the entry of the bull when the **picadors** receive the shock of his attacks and attempt to protect their horses with their lances. (Then) the horses go out and the (second act) is the planting of the banderillos. This is one of the most interesting and difficult parts but among the easiest for a new bull fight fan to appreciate in technique. The banderillos are three-foot, gaily colored darts with a small fish hook prong in the end. The man who is going to plant them walks out into the arena alone with the bull. He lifts the banderillos at arm's length and points them toward the bull. (Then) he calls "Toro! Toro!" The bull charges and the **banderillero** rises to his toes, bends in a curve forward and (just) as the bull is about to hit him drops the darts into the bull's hump just back of his horns.

They must go in evenly, one on each side. They must not be shoved, or thrown or stuck in from the side. This is (the first time) the bull has been completely baffled, there is the prick of the darts that he cannot escape and there are no horses for him to charge into. But he charges the man again and again and each time he gets a pair of the long banderillas that hang from his hump by their tiny barbs and flop like porcupine quills.

(Last) is the death of the bull, which is in the hands of the **matador** who has had charge of the bull since his first attack. Each matador has two bulls in the afternoon. The death of the bull is most formal and can only be brought about in one way, directly from the front by the matador who must receive the bull in full charge and kill him with a sword thrust between the shoulders just back of the neck and between the horns. (Before) killing the bull he must (first) do a series of passes with the muleta, a piece of red cloth he carries about the size of a large napkin. With the muleta the torero must show his complete mastery of the bull, must make the bull miss him again and again by inches, before he is allowed to kill him. It is in (this phase) that most of the fatal accidents occur.

approximately 400 words

Mary Hemingway, *By- Line: Ernest Hemingway,* pp. 96–98

---

picadors (pik´ ə dôrs) horsemen who jab the bull with a lance to weaken its neck and shoulder muscles

banderillero (ban´ də rel yar´ ō) man who thrusts in the banderillas in a bullfight

matador (mat´ ə dôr) bullfighter who has the principal role in the fight

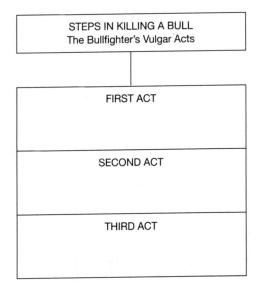

STEPS IN KILLING A BULL
The Bullfighter's Vulgar Acts

FIRST ACT

SECOND ACT

THIRD ACT

Questions for Discussion/Writing

1. Is bullfighting more barbaric than any sports followed in the United States? If so, which sports? Why do you think so? _____

_____

_____

2. Why do people attend events like the bullfight? _____

_____

3. Would you like to see a bullfight? Why, or why not? _____

_____

_____

ACTIVITY 5.2

PASSAGE 1

In the passage that follows, the history of public opinion polls is traced.

a. Circle the key dates and other important signal words as you read to help you recall their sequence.

b. List the significance of major dates in the space provided.

c. Decide after reading the passage whether public opinion polls are a good predictor of events.

The popular magazine *Literary Digest* was the first to develop a survey of great prestige. In the early years of this century, it earned itself quite a batting average, accurately predicting the 1916, 1920, 1924, 1928, and 1932 presidential elections. The guiding principle of the *Literary Digest* technique was to use a huge sample, on the notion that the more people questioned, the more dependable the result. All went well until 1936 when 2.4 million people replied that they wanted Franklin D. Roosevelt out of office. The *Literary Digest* predicted the Republican candidate, Alfred M. Landon, as victor with 59.1 percent of the vote. Franklin Roosevelt's landslide victory—with over 60 percent of the vote—signaled the . . . end of the straw-poll method of sampling.

As it happened, 1936 was also the first year that practitioners of the newly developed techniques of "scientific polling" were on the political scene, branching out from the field of market research. Several newspapers had begun **syndication** of George H. Gallup's survey results, which, in contrast to *Literary Digest,* forecast Roosevelt's victory. The guiding principle of the new technique used by Gallup was to select a sample as representative, rather than as large as possible.

This scientific sampling method has dominated the field since then with a very successful record. But even it met its match in the 1948 election when almost every poll predicted that Thomas Dewey would defeat Harry Truman by a landslide . . . Truman won with 49 percent. . . .

The major polls have further refined their methods since that time and today make special efforts to detect late swings to one candidate or the other. It should be noted, that they do not even claim to be able to predict divisions within closer than 2 or 3 percent.

approximately 300 words

Roskin et al., *Political Science,* pp.162–163

1. How reliable are public opinion polls? _____

_____

---

syndication (sin di cā´ shən) distribution of articles and features to newspapers

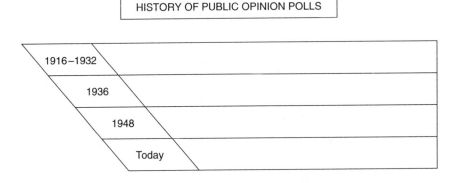

HISTORY OF PUBLIC OPINION POLLS

1916–1932

1936

1948

Today

2.   What is the major difference between polling in the 1920s and 1930s and now?

_____

PASSAGE 2

Choosing a mate or partner involves three stages, according to one textbook author.

a.   As you read the following passage, mark the signal word clues and main idea sentences.

b.   On the basis of your own experiences in selecting a mate, decide whether the order given is logical.

c.   List the three stages, and indicate which you believe is the most important one.

Several researchers have studied the mate-selection process, and according to a synthesis of their findings, choosing a mate occurs in three stages: the **stimulus** stage, the values stage, the roles stage.

In the first stage, one or more initiating stimuli—appearance, intellect, popularity, social status—make two parties notice each other. Physical attractiveness, of course, is a powerful stimulus, especially for men. Women look for attractiveness, too, but they are also drawn by status, preferring a leader over a follower, or a slightly older man over a slightly younger one, or a man with more education, or a better job. . . .

In the second stage, the couple compares their values. They discuss their attitudes toward work, marriage, religion, culture, and society. The more similar their views are, the more likely it is that the attraction will deepen, since such **concurrence** enhances each party's self-image. Similar values and interests also lead to shared activities through which the couple may further confirm their suitability.

_____

stimulus (stim´ yə ləs) action that causes an activity
concurrence (kən kʉr´ əns) agreement

Finally, as the couple interacts more frequently and becomes more intimate, they begin to develop their roles with each other. Role development is far deeper than the comparison of general values in the previous stage: it is a testing of the relationship in which each partner discovers how the other copes with the situations of daily life—finding out whether the other person shoulders or shirks responsibility, is honest or deceitful, is basically happy and stable or moody and unpredictable. . . .

Kathleen Berger, The Developing Person Through the Life Span, 1988, pp 438–439

1. The three stages in choosing a mate are as follows: _____

_____

_____

2. The most important stage is _____

3. Do you think the order is logical? _____

PASSAGE 3

As you read the following descriptive paragraph, use the marked phrases to help you follow the author's details. Try to visualize the kitchen, and then, make a simple sketch that shows you have pictured the spatial order that Kazin has presented.

The kitchen held our lives together. My mother worked in it all day long, we ate in it almost all meals except the Passover **seder,** I did my homework and first writing at the kitchen table, and in winter I often had a bed made up for me on three kitchen chairs near the stove. On the wall just over the table hung a long horizontal mirror that sloped to a ship's prow at each end and was lined in cherry wood. It took up the whole wall, and drew every object in the kitchen to itself. The walls were a fiercely **stippled** whitewash, so often rewhitened by my father in slack seasons that the paint looked as if it had been squeezed and cracked into the walls. A large electric bulb hung down the center of the kitchen at the end of a chain that had been hooked into the ceiling; the old gas ring and key still jutted out of the wall like antlers. In the corner next to the toilet was the sink at which we washed, and the square tub in which my mother did our clothes. Above it, tacked to the shelf on which were pleasantly ranged square, blue-bordered white sugar and spice jars, hung calendars from the Public National Bank on Pitkin Avenue and the Minsker Progressive Branch of the Workman's Circle; receipts for the payment of insurance premiums, and household bills on a spindle; two little boxes engraved with Hebrew letters. One of these was for the poor, the other to buy back the Land of Israel. Each spring a bearded little man would suddenly appear in our kitchen, salute us with a

_____

seder (sā´ dər) the feast commemorating the exodus of the Israelites from Egypt
stippled (stip´ əld) painted in dots or short touches

hurried Hebrew blessing, empty the boxes (sometimes with a sidelong look of **disdain** if they were not full), hurriedly bless us again for remembering our less fortunate Jewish brothers and sisters, and so take his departure until the next spring, after vainly trying to persuade my mother to take still another box.

approximately 325 words

Alfred Kazin, *A Walker in the City*

Sketch of the Kitchen

Question for Writing/Discussion

Is there a room or place that is special in your life? Using signal words that help show spatial order, write a paragraph describing your special place.

_____

_____

_____

_____

_____

_____

_____

disdain (dis dān´) to despise or treat with contempt

❖ Pattern 3: Simple Listing

There is a significant difference between using the patterns of classification and sequence and simply listing details.

In the classification pattern, numbers are used to designate various components— *two ways, three kinds,* and so on. The components are presented in random order.

In the sequence pattern, numbers are used to indicate a *particular* order and are not random: *the first step, the second step.*

In the simple listing pattern, writers develop their ideas by *listing* their supporting statements. They simply list or enumerate a series of details that support a point. The details may be examples, reasons, or types of things, and they are often, *but not always,* numbered.

Signals for Simple Listing

1, 2, 3, 4	another
a, b, c, d	moreover
first, second	next
also	then

Notice the random order of the following textbook details on drug problems in the workplace.

> Hoffman-LaRoche, Inc. made a study of drug problems in the workplace faced by 102 companies, and here is what was found:
>
> Almost 55 percent of all *absenteeism* was attributed to drug abuse.
>
> Nearly 40 percent of all *accidents* were drug related.
>
> *Medical expenses* increased an average of almost 40 percent as a result of drug abuse.
>
> Practically 40 percent of all *employee insubordination incidents* were drug related.
>
> About one-third of all *thefts* and *product or service problems* were the result of drug abuse.
>
> Stan Kossen, The Human Side of Organizations, p. 391

ACTIVITY 5.3

PASSAGE 1

Read the following textbook excerpt on the topic of listening to determine which pattern is being used in the section "Forms of Listening" and which in "Becoming an Effective Listener." Then answer the questions that follow.

---

insubordination (in´ sə bôr də nā´ shən) showing disobedience

Forms of Listening

Many types of listening behavior are as common in business as they are in personal communication.

- *Cynical listening* is a type of defensive listening that occurs when people fear that a message is intended to take advantage of them. . . .

- *Offensive listening* is listening that attempts to catch the speaker in a mistake or contradiction, much as a lawyer does when cross-examining a witness. . . .

- *Polite listening* is a kind of mechanical listening characterized by inattention. The listener really wants the speaker to stop talking so that he or she can begin. Because polite listeners often rehearse their own lines instead of paying attention, polite listening usually accomplishes very little. Many job applicants are guilty of polite listening. Instead of actively listening to what the job recruiter is saying, they are planning what to say next. . . .

- *Active listening,* on the other hand, is a form of listening that requires both sincere involvement with the information and **empathy** with the speaker's situation. . . . In business, active listening is the basis for effective communication.

Becoming an Effective Listener

You can improve your listening skills in both formal and informal business situations by applying the following principles. Many of the same principles can also be used to improve reading.

Learn the Art—and Wisdom—of Silence Silence not only gives someone else the opportunity to speak but gives you the opportunity to learn from another person's perspective. . . .

Be Aware of "Emotional Filters" Ask yourself whether you have strong opinions about the subject of the message or about the person to whom you are listening. Emotional reactions to words, people, or situations can cloud your thinking.

Be Slow to Judge If your natural tendency is to interrupt and argue when you disagree with what you hear, you may lose the opportunity to learn and, perhaps, to change your opinions for the better. Realizing that we all come to listening situations with preconceived viewpoints will help you avoid judging alternative ideas too quickly. Keeping an open mind often means being aware of your prejudices and seeking out evidence to disprove your own point of view.

Ask Questions to Focus Your Listening "The only dumb question is the question not asked." This **maxim** is as true in business as it is in personal communication. When you do not understand a concept, word, or phrase, be direct and ask, "What does that mean?" In the end, these interruptions are time savers, not time wasters. Listening patiently without understanding accomplishes little.

---

empathy (em´ pə thē) deep understanding of the feelings, thoughts, and motives of one person by another

maxim (mak´ sim) a short rule or principle of conduct

When you are finished asking questions, use clarifying statements to make sure that you have understood the message correctly. . . .

Focus on What Is Important It is estimated that only one in four people listening to a formal speech actually grasps the speaker's main idea. In normal business conversation as in public speaking, when poorly organized speakers intermingle unrelated facts with key points, it may be difficult to focus on critical issues. You can make listening easier by asking pointed questions, taking clear notes, being sensitive to repetition, and recognizing language transitions that focus attention on key concepts.

Be an Active Listener To avoid becoming an inattentive listener, focus your "extra" listening time—the time available to you because listening is faster than speaking—on the speaker's message: Try to anticipate what will be said next, review and summarize the points already made, evaluate and question the presentation, and listen between the lines (remember that changes in volume, tone, and body language can be more important than words). *Active concentration* is the key to effective listening.

approximately 600 words

Louis E. Boone and David L. Kurtz, *Contemporary Business Communication,* Copyright © 1994, Prentice Hall. pp. 60–61 Reprinted by permission.

1. The pattern used for "Forms of Listening" is _____

    Reason for choice: _____

2. The pattern used for "Becoming an Effective Listener" is _____

    Reason for choice: _____
3. Which principle of listening do you think most people find difficult to practice?

    _____

4. In what ways are the principles of listening related to reading improvement?

    _____

PASSAGE 2

Read the following article on how to find something you've misplaced. Notice the signal word *steps* as well as the numerical listing of the points. After reading the article, decide

a. Must the steps be followed in sequence?

b. Has the author used one particular pattern or several patterns in combination?

c. Has the writer of this article overlooked any steps that you would find helpful in locating a misplaced item?

Lose your car keys? Can't find your wallet? Have no clue what you did with that last Visa bill?

When in doubt, call on St. Anthony—patron saint of lost things. If you'd rather search in a more conventional fashion, call on Professor Solomon. Solomon—a sometimes bookstore clerk, substitute teacher, magician and actor—is the author of the newly published "How to Find Lost Objects."

Calling on his experience maintaining the lost-and-found box at a public high school, Solomon developed a method for finding lost stuff. Here are the steps:

1. Don't look for it. Though your first inclination might be to ransack your home, don't start searching until you have an idea where to look.
2. It's not lost—you are. There are no missing objects. Only unsystematic searchers.
3. Remember the three C's. Search with comfort, calmness and confidence.
4. It's where it's supposed to be. Or at least it might be. So look there first.
5. Domestic drift. Objects are often left where last used, instead of where they are normally kept.
6. You're looking right at it. An agitated mind would allow you to look right at an object and not see it.
7. The camouflage effect. Be sure to check under anything that might be camouflaging your object.
8. Think back. You were there when your object was misplaced, so you have to have some faint memory of what happened.
9. Look once. Look well. Check every place thoroughly once.
10. The Eureka Zone. Objects tend to travel no more than 18 inches from their original location.
11. Tail thyself. Recreate the scene of the crime.
12. It wasn't you. When all else fails, explore the possibility that your item was misappropriated, not misplaced.

approximately 280 words

Mary Jo Dilonardo, "Just Don't Misplace This Book," *The San Francisco Examiner,* 10 May 1995, p. C-5 Reprinted by permission of Scripps Howard News Service.

Answer these questions.

1. Must the steps be followed in sequence? _____

2. The pattern the writer used is _____

3. Are there any steps the writer overlooked that you use in finding lost or misplaced

   items? _____

   _____

   _____

PASSAGE 3

Mark the signal words that help you find the answer to this textbook question: "Why do some rich countries subsidize agriculture?"

Why Do Some Rich Countries Subsidize Agriculture?

Many rich countries subsidize their farmers and erect import barriers for several reasons. First, some countries pursue self-sufficiency in food production as a national security measure. The governments want some defense against grain **embargoes** and crop failures in those countries that normally have surpluses to market. Subsidizing a country's own farmers offers some protection against these threats. Following U.S. threats to halt grain shipments to the Mideast in the 1970s, for example, Saudi Arabia spent heavily to improve its agriculture. Iraq failed to do so, and by the time it occupied Kuwait in 1990, Iraq depended on imports for almost 80 percent of its nutritional needs.

Second, many rich countries, particularly in Europe, subsidize agriculture in order to keep their farmers from migrating to the cities in search of work. Rural-urban migration can overwhelm the ability of cities to absorb the new labor force, and it threatens the quality of life in the cities.

Third, rich countries may subsidize farming as part of national land-use plans. To them it is valuable in itself to have a farming countryside and to preserve green areas around cities, called *greenbelts*. Their urban citizens enjoy driving through or visiting convenient rural landscapes, and they are willing to subsidize farms in order to preserve them.

Fourth, many rich countries subsidize their farmers because their systems of political representation favor farmers. The farmers in the United States, Japan, and Europe constitute a decreasing percentage of the national populations, yet, particularly in Europe and Japan, the electoral districts have never been readjusted to the relative depopulation of the countryside and the urbanization of the populations. Thus, a rural vote may heavily outweigh an urban vote. Farmers enjoy **disproportionate** political power over urbanites. Most urban consumers remain unaware that food prices subsidize their nation's farmers, because the cost of food as a percentage of their incomes is falling anyway.

approximately 300 words

Edward F. Bergman, *Human Geography*, p. 219

_____ 1. One pattern the writer used is
   (a) classification   (b) listing   (c) sequence

2. Why do some rich countries subsidize agriculture? _____

_____

_____

embargoes (im bär´ gōz) legal prohibitions on commerce; stoppages
disproportionate (dis´ prə pōr´ shən it) out of proportion

❖ Pattern 4: Example

Examples that illustrate an idea are fairly easy to recognize. Example is one of the most common patterns of exposition. Often, one or more examples or illustrations will be used to support a main idea, explain or clarify a concept, or prove the **validity** of an argument. Good examples help to make general ideas more specific and also aid in holding the reader's interest. The following signal words often signal this pattern:

Signals for Example

for example
for instance
to illustrate
specifically
such as

Reread the two passages dealing with phobias and prison types (pp. 203-204 and 204-206) to see how each author gave numerous examples to develop the main point. If you first determine the main idea, you will readily see how examples are used to illustrate or clarify the important information. In textbook reading, examples are rarely the main point; rather, they support the major ideas.

Read the following selection, noting the important examples, and then answer the questions that follow.

> Most cultures have a number of forms of polite usage which may be misleading. These may take the form of exaggeration or modesty. Americans ask questions which are really orders or requests ("Would you like to ... ?"). In every culture, in many situations, there are special forms of words, or types of conversation, which are thought to be appropriate—to ask a girl for a date, to disagree with someone at a committee, to introduce people to each other, and so on. Americans prefer directness, but Mexicans regard openness as a form of weakness or treachery, and think one should not allow the outside world to penetrate their thoughts. Frankness by Peace Corps volunteers in the Philippines ... led to disruption of smooth social relationships.
>
> Larry A. Samovar & Richard E. Porter *Intercultural Communication: A Reader,* Stephen Bochner (ed.), *Intercultural Communication,* Wadsworth, 1991

1. What is the main idea? _____

_____

_____

validity (və lid´ ə tē) sound reasoning

2. List at least two examples that support the main idea.

_____

ACTIVITY 5.4

PASSAGE 1

In the following selection, the writer looks at the topic of Black English, examining why linguists—people who study language—consider the "so-called errors" made by African Americans an alternative form of acceptable English. Note and mark the signal clue. Then underline the important examples the writer uses to prove her point.

Black English used to be considered simply poor English until linguists realized that the so-called errors were actually consistent alternative grammatical forms, some of which originated in African linguistic patterns. For example, the word "be" in standard English is primarily used as part of the infinitive "to be." But in Black English, "be" can also be used to indicate a repeated action or **existential** state. Thus, in Black English, one can say, "I am sick" or "I be sick." The first means "I am sick at this present moment"; the second includes the recent past as well as the present. To express the second concept in standard English, one might say, "I have been sick for a while."

Another difference between Black English and standard English occurs in the expression of negation. Almost all children spontaneously use the double or even triple negative, saying "I don't want to see no doctor" or "Nobody never gives me nothing." But since these forms are wrong in standard English, middle-class children are usually corrected by their parents and older peers, and use only single-negative forms by middle childhood. However, consciously or unconsciously, speakers of Black English tend to resist such correction, perhaps because in Black English (as well as in many languages and dialects other than standard English) the double negative can be correct.

Kathleen Stassen Berger, *The Developing Person Through the Life Span*, p. 277

1. Restate the main idea in your own words. _____

_____

2. Do the examples convince you to accept the thesis that Black English is an

acceptable means of communication? Why or why not? _____

_____

_____

existential (eg´ zis ten´ shəl) of, based on, or expressing existence

PASSAGE 2

Writers sometime use very specific examples to give concrete form to their implied or abstract ideas. Use the specific examples given in the opening chapter of the book *The Peter Principle* to discover what the authors have to say about incompetence in our society, based on their experiences in Canada.

When I was a boy I was taught that the men upstairs knew what they were doing. I was told, "Peter, the more you know, the further you go." So I stayed in school until I graduated from college and then went forth into the world clutching firmly these ideas and my new teaching certificate. During the first year of teaching I was upset to find that a number of teachers, school principals, supervisors and superintendents appeared to be unaware of their professional responsibilities and incompetent in executing their duties. For example my principal's main concerns were that all window shades be at the same level, that classrooms should be quiet and that no one step on or near the rose beds. The superintendent's main concerns were that no minority group, no matter how fanatical, should ever be offended and that all official forms be submitted on time. The children's education appeared farthest from the administrator mind.

At first I thought this was a special weakness of the school system in which I taught so I applied for certification in another province. I filled out the special forms, enclosed the required documents and complied willingly with all the red tape. Several weeks later, back came my application and all the documents!

No, there was nothing wrong with my credentials; the forms were correctly filled out; an official departmental stamp showed that they had been received in good order. But an accompanying letter said, "The new regulations require that such forms cannot be accepted by the Department of Education unless they have been registered at the Post Office to ensure safe delivery. Will you please remail the forms to the Department, making sure to register them this time?"

I began to suspect that the local school system did not have a monopoly on incompetence.

As I looked further afield, I saw that every organization contained a number of persons who could not do their jobs.

approximately 400 words

Laurence J. Peter and Raymond Hull, *The Peter Principle*, William Morrow & Company, 1969

1. What is the authors' main point about the subject of incompetence?

   _____

   _____

2. Were the authors justified in being upset about how teachers and administrators

   handled their professional responsibilities? Explain your answer. _____

   _____

   _____

3. How effective is the second example regarding the author's application for

   certification? _____

   _____

   _____

4. Discuss an example of "incompetence" you have experienced in school or in

   your daily activities at home, at work, or in your community. _____

   _____

   _____

   _____

❖ Pattern 5: Comparison and Contrast

The comparison-and-contrast pattern is also usually easy to recognize. In comparing ideas or items, writers show similarities; in contrasting ideas or items, writers show differences. Frequently, writers make comparisons and contrasts within the same paragraph. Readers should be able to spot this pattern because of the terms used to signal likenesses and differences.

Signals for Comparison

compare	like/alike	resembles
in comparison	likewise	similar
in the same way/manner	parallels	similarly

Signals for Contrast

although	different	on the contrary
as opposed to	however	on the other hand
but	in contrast to	rather than
conversely	instead	unlike
difference	nevertheless	whereas
		yet

Writers often use the comparison-and-contrast method to show the positive and negative sides, or advantages and disadvantages, of an issue or an event. It is a useful pattern for you to learn to use when writing, whether your goal is to provide information or to emphasize, evaluate, or persuade. Listing similarities or differences in a column format is a good notemaking device, as it helps you sort out and remember points readily.

Read *only the first two sentences* of the following paragraph, noting the word *resemble,* which signals comparison.

Elephants are the biggest land creatures on Earth, and among the smartest and most endearing. In their lives and social dynamics they resemble humans in many ways.

1. Try to predict what similarities might be discussed.
2. List a few details you might expect to find in the paragraph on the following chart.

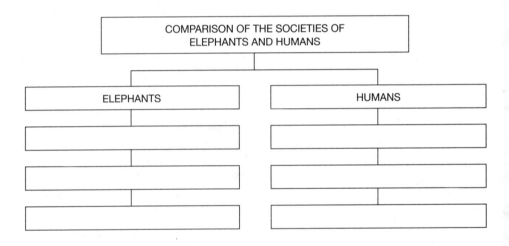

Now, finish reading the paragraph to see how well you anticipated the details.

They live in **matriarchal** societies—groups of sisters, aunts, nieces and nephews, often headed by a wise old grandmother. The bonds formed within an elephant family can last a lifetime that may span 60 or more years. Scientists who have studied elephants in the wild have noted in them such human-like characteristics as joy, grief, anger, loyalty, patience, playfulness, and sibling rivalry. To the 17th century poet John Donne, the elephant was "Nature's great masterpiece . . . the only harmless great thing."

Jim Merritt, "Requiem for a Heavyweight," *Modern Maturity,* April/May 1991, p. 54

---

matriarchal (mā trē är´ kəl) ruled by female

List three ways in which the author compared elephants and people.

1. _____

2. _____

3. _____

ACTIVITY 5.5

PASSAGE 1

The following news report uses a contrast pattern. The title suggests the main idea for the article.

a. Read *only the first two sentences* of the article to decide what is being contrasted.

b. Then write the main idea in the space provided after the passage.

Other Nations Are Tougher on Drunken Drivers

California lawmakers are congratulating themselves for toughening up the state's drunken driving laws by increasing the penalties.

But they may be shocked to find out that in other countries, if a drunk is caught behind the wheel for the first time the penalty could be anything from throwing his wife in jail to an execution.

In Malaysia, for example, the drunk driver is jailed and if he or she is married, the spouse also goes to jail on the first offense, according to research published by the National Traffic Safety Institute. In Finland, England and Sweden, drunken drivers are sentenced to one year in jail on their first conviction. In Germany, driving with a blood alcohol level of .08 percent requires that you lose your license for a year. (In California, the legal presumption for driving under the influence is .08 percent.) You would also receive a one-year minimum jail sentence if you are caught in Germany driving without a license.

Australia recently lowered their blood alcohol level to .05 percent, and they impose a $1000 fine and a one-year suspension of your driver's license for the first conviction.

South Africa is even tougher, with a 10-year prison term and a fine of $10,000 or both upon the first conviction.

In Bulgaria, your second conviction will be your last because the penalty is execution. In San Salvador, you may not get a second chance. There, drunken drivers can be executed immediately by a firing squad.

Ellen Norman, "Other Nations Are Tougher on Drunk Drivers," *The Peninsula Times Tribune,* 30 December 1981, p. A-6. Reprinted by permission of *The Peninsula Times Tribune*

1. The contrast being made is _____

_____

2. The main idea is _____

_____

3. Which nation imposes the toughest penalty on drunk drivers? Do you think the

punishment fits the crime? _____

_____

PASSAGE 2

Let's examine how writers can use both comparison and contrast within the same passage.

> The sex of the instructor affected the extent of active student participation. In classes taught by men with roughly equal proportions of male and female students, male students were responsible for about 75 percent of all class discussion; with women as instructors, female student participation rose from 25 percent to 42 percent, while male participation slipped from 75 percent to 58 percent. Many female students are apparently more comfortable in a class taught by a female instructor. Why? Perhaps because female instructors were as likely to direct specific questions to female students as to male students, while male teachers were more than twice as likely to direct questions to male students. Gender is, therefore, part of the interpersonal dynamics of the class.
>
> David Popenoe, *Sociology*, p. 417

1. In your own experience, have you found any difference in the way you respond to

male and female instructors? _____

_____

2. Does this paragraph seem to indicate that instructors prefer students of one sex

over the other? Which one?_____

_____

PASSAGE 3

Read the following passage, which contrasts envy and jealousy, and circle the signal words. Underline the important point that shows the difference between the two, and note whether there are any similarities. Then explain in a sentence whether envy or jealousy is the least desirable trait to possess.

> Long lumped together by ordinary folks and scholars alike, envy and jealousy are not a single, formless "super emotion." On the contrary, they are distinct, with different components, and are in fact elicited by completely different situations and in completely different settings.

According to a Georgetown University psychologist . . . envy occurs when a person lacks another person's superior quality, achievement, or possession, and desires it—or wishes that the other person lacked it.

Jealousy, by contrast, occurs in the context of a close relationship when a person fears losing an important other to a rival—in particular, losing a relationship that is important to one's sense of self.

For all their distinctiveness, envy and jealousy sometimes occur together. For instance, when a romantic partner gives attention to an attractive rival, a person may feel both jealous of that attention and envious of the rival for being so attractive. And since jealousy involves the loss of a personal relationship, it's usually more intense than envy.

"A Devastating Difference," *Psychology Today*, Jan./Feb. 1994, pp. 22–23

1. Which is the least desirable trait, envy or jealousy? Explain. _____

_____

_____

2. In what significant ways do envy and jealousy differ? _____

_____

3. Is there any way in which envy and jealousy are similar? _____

_____

_____

Look at the following chart.

ENVY	JEALOUSY
• Feelings of inferiority	• Fear of loss
• Longing	• Anxiety
• Resentment of circumstances	• Suspicion or anger about betrayal
• Ill will toward envied person, often accompanied by guilt about these feelings	• Low self-esteem and sadness over loss
• Motivation to improve	• Uncertainty and loneliness
• Desire to possess the attractive rival's qualities	• Fear of losing an important person to an attractive other
• Disapproval of feelings	• Distrust

4. Which is more destructive to one's personality—envy or jealousy? Discuss the

reasons. _____

_____

_____

PASSAGE 4

Read to understand the difference in emphasis on the individual versus the "group" in Eastern and Western society. What changes might occur in the United States if less stress were placed on the individual?

The single most important and fundamental difference between Chinese and **Occidental** peoples is undoubtedly the role played by the individual in the society. In the West, we place a strong emphasis on personal achievement, creativity, and **initiative.** We glory in our individual differences, nurture them, and value them as the essential features that make us unique. Indeed, uniqueness is a goal unto itself in the West; it's vitally important to us that we *not* be exactly like other people.

Who in the West hasn't been **admonished** to be your own person, or to look out for yourself because no one else can be counted on to look out for you? Who has never been praised for standing up for what you personally believe in, especially when the tide of opinion is flowing in the opposite direction? Among Western peoples, the premium is not on conformity; it is on individual expression and rugged independence.

In China, on the other hand—and no matter which side of the Taiwan strait—children are given an entirely different set of messages. Don't question the world around you or try to change it; accept it. Submit willingly and unquestioningly to authority. Your importance as an individual is not nearly as great as that of the role you play in a larger group.

That "larger group" may have appeared different in ancient China from what it looks like today. In Imperial China it would have been one's extended family—grandparents, father, mother, siblings, uncles, aunts, and cousins of all descriptions, all of whom might well have lived together in the same compound. In modern-day China the group might be one's nuclear family, one's class at school, one's military unit, fellow members of a delegation. . . . The situation varies; the dynamics, however, are much the same no matter what the group is.

Group process in China is not merely based on the authority of the leaders; there is a real premium on consensus. Matters are often debated at great length until agreement is reached on a course of action. And once a decision has been made, individual group members are expected to embrace it and act on it. This is one reason you will seldom hear a Chinese make an irreverent comment, or openly express a view at odds with that of his or her unit. Toeing the mark is important, and it is enforced.

Occidental (ăk´ sə den´ təl) pertaining to Europe and the Western Hemisphere
initiative (in ish´ ə tiv) determination; ability to begin and follow through with a plan or task
admonished (ad mon´ isht) warned; counseled against something

In essence, Chinese enter into a sort of compact with their groups; in exchange for obedience and loyalty, they can expect protection and support and be confident that their well-being will be a matter of concern to the group as a whole. Group membership requires that they subordinate their own wills to that of the whole and make decisions based on the best interests of the larger group, not personal selfishness. Chinese people must listen to those in authority and do as they say. And their actions, for good or ill, reflect not only on themselves but also on all of their compatriots. . . .

Telephone etiquette provides still another illustration of the preeminence of the group in Chinese society. You generally do not identify yourself personally when answering the telephone; what is deemed important is your work unit. The fact that common practice is to answer "I am the Ministry of Foreign Trade" rather than "I am Mr. Wang" speaks volumes about the relative importance of the individual and the group. So does the fact that it is units, and not individuals, that invite foreign guests, arrange activities for them, and sign contracts with them. . . .

Although Chinese people must be ever vigilant in fulfilling obligations to fellow group members, it's important to note that as a rule they feel no comparable responsibility toward outsiders. Courtesy and hospitality are frequently not forthcoming when Chinese deal with people with whom they have no connections. Indeed, they are capable of treating one another with indifference that can border on cruelty. The "us-them" **dichotomy** often surfaces in the work of the government in the form of **intractable** bureaucratic rivalries that impede progress and innovation. It has sometimes been pointed out that one of the Chinese culture's major failings is that its people just don't know how to treat outsiders. Ironically but luckily, foreigners are generally exempt from this kind of treatment, their very foreignness earning them favorable treatment as honored guests.

approximately 725 words

Scott Seligman, *Dealing with the Chinese: A Practical Guide to Etiquette in the People's Republic of China.* Copyright © Scott D. Seligman, 1989

1. How might Chinese cultural traditions impede business opportunities?

_____

2. Would you expect more or less family violence in China than in the United

States? Why or why not? _____

_____

_____

_____

dichotomy (dī kot´ ə mē) division into two contradictory parts or opinions
intractable (in´ trak´ tə bəl) stubborn; difficult to manage or govern

3. What can we learn from the Chinese?_____

_____

_____

4. What change might occur in the United States if less stress were placed on the

individual? Would you favor such a change? _____

_____

❖ Pattern 6: Cause-and-Effect Relationship

When writers present arguments or describe events, one of the most frequently used patterns is cause and effect. The writer discusses *why* or *how* something happened and *what* the results are or might be. The cause is the *reason* or *motive;* the effect is the *result, consequence,* or *outcome.*

This pattern is used extensively in scientific and technical textbooks. It is also one of the chief techniques of reasoning and, therefore, a common pattern found in persuasive and argumentative essays. Cause and effect can be used in various combinations to express a paragraph's main idea.

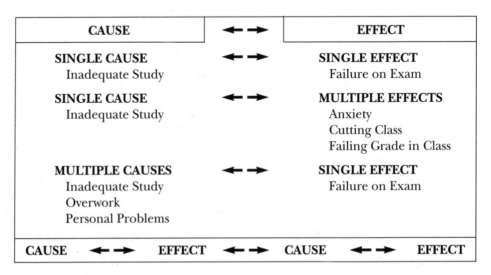

The cause-and-effect pattern can sometimes be recognized by signal words.

Signals for Cause

because	due to	on account of
cause	for this reason	since
		why

Signals for Effect

as a result	in effect	therefore
consequently	result	thus
hence	the outcome is	

Notice the various key words that signal a series of cause-and-effect relationships in the following paragraph. The notations in the margin will make these relationships clear to you.

Atherosclerosis is the (result) of the buildup of fat, fibrin (formed in clots), parts of dead cells and calcium on the inside of arteries. These substances reduce the elasticity of the vessel, and by decreasing the diameter of the vessel, they raise blood pressure, just as you would raise the pressure in a garden hose by holding your thumb over the end. If the artery is in the heart, the (result) can be heart failure. If it is in the brain, a stroke can result. No one knows what (causes) atherosclerosis, but a number of things can speed its development. These include smoking cigarettes and eating animal fat and cholesterol. (Other factors) include age, hypertension, diabetes, stress, heredity and sex (males have more heart attacks).

results { elasticity of blood vessels decreases

result { blood pressure rises

result { can be heart failure

result { stroke

other causes

Robert A. Wallace, *Biology: The World of Life*, p. 322

While textbook writers often use signal words to alert the reader to the cause-and-effect pattern, writers of articles and essayists do not always provide such signals; then you must analyze what is being said to recognize the pattern. If the writer explains *what* happened and *why* it happened, then the writing approach is usually cause and effect. Read the following passage, looking for the main idea based on the arguments the writer gives. Then, fill in the cause-and-effect chart that follows.

For years, trainers and coaches have wondered why certain athletes are able to shut out the noise, bright lights and frenzy that go along with competition, while their teammates are unnerved by such distractions. The answer, as it turns out, may have to do with psychological training. Some researchers believe that the ability to cope with stress makes the difference between giving a mediocre performance and a dazzler.

"It's the ability to take control of yourself—not to give in to the emotional factor in competition," says Dr. Thomas Tutko, a psychology professor at San Jose State University, co-author of *Sports Psyching: Playing Your Best Game All of the Time* and a firm believer in psychological conditioning in athletes. "After talking to literally thousands of athletes, we found that people who were successful practiced a certain kind of self-mind control, using any one of a series of techniques that got them to relax, concentrate or change their attitudes. These people were doing it automatically. They thought everybody did."

Nancy Josephson, "Why Some Athletes Excel," Family Weekly, 20 Dec. 1981

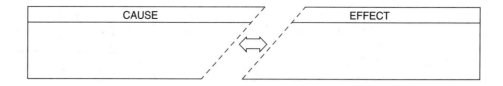

Do you agree with this author's thesis: "Some athletes excel because of their ability to handle stress"? List some causes and effects you feel were not included.

_____

_____

ACTIVITY 5.6

PASSAGE 1

As you read the following excerpt, mark any signal words that develop the cause-and-effect pattern. Then answer the questions that follow.

In many ways, immigrants know what Americanism is better than we do. They've paid us the profoundest compliment by leaving the land of their birth to come and spend their lives with us. And they didn't come here to join nothing, they came to join something— us at our best, us as they imagined us after a million movies and books and reports from relatives. They wanted to be part of our **raucous** drama, and they wanted the three m's— money, mobility, **meritocracy.**

Then there's what might simply be called the American style. For a lot of immigrants, America has a special quality reflected in a comment by a 21-year-old New Zealander I know. "Everything's happening here," she said. "America's just so—cool."

_____

raucous (rô´ kəs) loud and rowdy
meritocracy (mer ə täk´ rə sē) advancement of the most intelligent and talented in a society

Yes, indeed. We are, after all, the kind of people who'd send a volunteer army across the oceans to slam-dunk a dictator, liberate a nation and leave behind not an army of occupation but soldiers caring for starving refugees. In the 1960s some people accused America of being an imperialist nation; by now it's obvious that the only thing imperialistic about us is our culture, which has swept the world—but only because the world saw our movies and TV shows, loved our blue jeans and posters and fast food, listened to our jukeboxes and begged to be invaded. Deep in its heart the world thinks America is the bravest, sweetest, toughest, funniest place on earth, and for once the world is right.

Which is why the world comes here. And when immigrants arrive, some kind of magic happens: they do extraordinary things, things they couldn't do at home. In Indochina the Asians fight, rent by factionalism; here they build and get dressed up to go to the Westinghouse Awards and Ivy League commencements. In Greece the young are sunk in a funk, with widespread joblessness; here they become entrepreneurs.

Most of us see their coming as good news—immigration is affirmation, proof that we are still what we used to be, a haven for the bold and striving dispossessed. But we're concerned, too, about whether we are absorbing them into the country as successfully as we've done in the past. Which brings us to the old-fashioned idea of Americanism, and how to communicate it.

approximately 450 words

Peggy Noonan, "Why They Came Here," *The Reader's Digest,* July 1991, pp. 40–42 Copyright © by Peggy Noonan. Reprinted by permission.

1. State the main idea in your own words. _____

_____

2. List two details that support the main idea. _____

_____

3. Is it true that life is better in America than elsewhere? _____

_____

PASSAGE 2

The author of the next passage asks two questions at the end of the first paragraph. Read the passage and note the answers to these questions. Think about why rock concerts and rock stars appeal to different types of people.

If a **Mecca** exists for today's youth, it must take the form of a rock concert. Such a colossal event draws people from surprisingly distant places and from oddly diverging lifestyles. The sophisticated college student may be seated next to the wide-eyed junior high cheerleader, the latter showing fright at the approach of a wild-eyed freak. How do these

---

Mecca (mek´ ə) a place regarded as the center of an activity or interest

incompatible character types find a mutual appeal in rock concerts? What induces young people to exchange the few dollars earned through babysitting or car washing for a concert ticket?

To many, the answer is immediately obvious—the music is the source of appeal at a concert. The quality of the sound produced, however, frequently casts doubt on this explanation. Unquestionably, rock concerts are loud; the decibel level of some reportedly exceeds that attained by a jet plane on takeoff. In addition, this **aural** assault is often intensified by an out-of-tune guitar, by the faltering voice of the performer, or by the bad acoustics in the concert hall. Rock groups generally correct these problems in a studio; their recordings may even boast pleasing harmonies with intelligible lyrics. So why do we battle crowds to secure choice seating at a concert? . . .

A concert creates a magical, otherworldly atmosphere, reminiscent of a childhood never-never land. An eerie darkness shrouds the hall, and then, just as in our favorite fairy tale, the supernatural being (otherwise identified by the vulgar term, "rock star") appears in a burst of light. In another context he would have been known as a "god out of the machine." Bizarre lighting schemes and gimmicks such as mock hangings or fire-breathing contribute to the atmosphere of other-worldliness in some acts. The fans are permitted only a brief glimpse of the star before he vanishes once more in the darkness, only to materialize the following evening in a concert hall hundreds of miles away. The stage becomes the rock star's only natural habitat; for us, he can have no existence apart from it. We can scarcely conceive of our idols performing such mundane activities as going to the dentist, shopping for tuna fish, or changing the baby. Perhaps we have a need to believe in an illusory creature of the night, somehow different from ourselves. Who fits this description better than a rock star?

approximately 450 words

Jennifer McBride Young, "The Rock Fantasy," *The Essay Connection*

Why do rock concerts and rock stars have such appeal? _____

_____

PASSAGE 3

Read to find out why poor economic conditions result in hate violence.

Poor economic times contribute greatly to hate violence. In many areas of the country, when major industries such as steel and auto manufacturing have had downturns, go out of business, or relocate, the likelihood of economic distress among the low and unskilled increases. **Scapegoating** and blaming often results when blue-collar jobs are unavailable. The distress that accompanies unemployment and rising prices is often directed toward immigrants and minorities and manifests itself in harassment and violence. There seems to be a childlike tendency that exists within some people wherein they must blame oth-

---

aural (ar´ əl) received through the sense of hearing

scapegoating (skāp´ gō ting) blaming a person or thing for the mistakes of others

ers for their own misfortune or society's failings. New York City experienced an increase of 19 percent in reported hate crimes in 1988 after a recession hit the region following the stock market crash of 1987. In 1990, the Massachusetts unemployment rate had risen to a level of 8.6 percent, one of the highest rates in the nation. For the same year, the Boston police reported 273 bias crimes, which was up from 202 the previous year. . . . Los Angeles County reported an increase of 45 percent in bias crimes in 1990 after a nation-wide recession caused unemployment in the state to jump up to 7 percent, from under 6 percent one year earlier. Thus the frequency and intensity of such acts are shown to increase when the economy deteriorates.

Sociologists indicate that hate frequently stems from being deprived or having one's needs unsatisfied—so the poor can despise the rich, the uneducated ridicule the intellectual, the poor envy the **affluent,** and the established ghetto inhabitant can hate the new immigrant/refugee who moves into the area. Social scientists argue that the government definition of poverty does not measure the real depths or the changes taking place in inner cities (i.e., that, not only have the number of ghetto poor increased but the severity of economic deprivation among them has risen as well). Ghetto poverty and concentrations of large numbers of a diverse population in one area often lead to conflict in those neighborhoods. The stresses of urban life, especially in inner cities, give rise to increased incidents of violence, especially in depressed conditions and reduced space.

approximately 350 words

Robert M. Shusta et al., *Multicultural Law Enforcement,* pp. 275–276

1. Restate the main idea. _____

    _____

2. List two supporting details that help develop the main idea. _____

    _____

    _____

3. What can be done to help reduce the number of bias-related crimes nationwide?

    In your neighborhood? _____

    _____

    _____

    _____

    _____

_____

affluent (af´ loo ənt) having an abundance of money or property; wealthy; rich

❖ Pattern 7: Definition

At times you can figure out a word's meaning in a sentence by using context clues. Sometimes you need to refer to a dictionary. But a short definition in a dictionary may not convey the precise meaning of an idea. A writer may use an entire paragraph to describe the topic. Sometimes a title, a subtitle, or the first sentence of a paragraph, appearing in question form, indicates that the definition pattern will be used. Often, other writing patterns are incorporated into a passage where a definition is being presented.

In textbook writing, definitions tend to be **straightforward,** as in scientific textbooks. In other situations, authors use the definition pattern to explain technical language, important terminology, and concepts. **Abstract** terms, such as those used in sociology and philosophy, are less precise in meaning, however, and may require more lengthy explanations. The following paragraph demonstrates how even a simple term like *self-esteem* has its own special meaning in a contemporary textbook.

> By self-esteem, we refer to the evaluation which the individual makes and customarily maintains with regard to himself (or herself); it expresses an attitude of approval or disapproval, and indicates the extent to which an individual believes himself to be capable, significant, successful and worthy. In short, self-esteem is a personal judgment of worthiness and is expressed in the attitudes that the individual holds towards himself. It is a subjective experience which the individual conveys to others by verbal reports and other overt expressive behavior.
>
> H. Douglas Brown, *Principles of Language Learning and Teaching*, pp. 101–102

This definition can be mapped as follows.

```
                      TERM DEFINED
                      as in a textbook

                      SELF-ESTEEM

Evaluation an individual   Expresses attitude   Extent to which    Conveyed verbally
   makes of himself              of             he or she         and through other
     or herself          approval/disapproval   feels worthy      expressive behavior

                              DEFINITION
   Self-esteem is a personal judgment of worthiness expressed in one's attitude toward the
           self and conveyed verbally and through other expressive behavior.
```

straightforward (strāt fôr´ ward) direct; proceeding in a straight course
abstract (ab´ stract) not easily understood; not concrete

One way to recognize the writer's pattern is through signal or clue words. Signal words most commonly used to indicate the definition pattern include the following:

Signals for Definition

define	known as	we mean
is	that is, i.e.	we can state
is defined as	the term means	

ACTIVITY 5.7

PASSAGE 1

The question of doctor-assisted suicide is hotly debated. Read to determine the difference in meaning between *active* and *passive* euthanasia.

The most important individual in matters of life and death is you. Modern society gives you many options not only for life, but also for death. Euthanasia is the practice of ending a life for reasons of mercy. The word is derived from a Greek word meaning "good death." There are two kinds, active and passive. Active euthanasia involves an act that deliberately ends a life. One example would be purposely administering a lethal dose of medication. Passive euthanasia involves withholding a treatment that would probably prolong life. An example would be withholding chemotherapy from a cancer patient.

A controversial form of active euthanasia is assisting in someone's suicide. The Dutch Supreme Court allows physicians to perform such active euthanasia if five criteria are met: (1) The patient has no hope of improving from an intolerable condition; (2) there is no way to relieve the condition; (3) the patient is capable of making rational decisions; (4) the patient over time repeatedly requests assistance with ending his or her life; (5) two physicians agree with the patient's request. In contrast, the United States prosecutes physicians (and anyone else) for assisting in suicide. Dr. Jack Kevorkian, a Michigan physician, challenged this law by assisting in several suicides (New York Times, 1994). Neither the Dutch law nor the U.S. law has universal support.

Stephen Worchel and Wayne Shebilske, *Principles and Applications: Psychology,* p. 329

1. Explain what is meant by *active* euthanasia. _____

_____

_____

2. Do the Dutch Supreme Court's five criteria for assisting in someone's suicide help to explain why this act is considered active euthanasia? Why or why not?

_____

_____

3. Discuss whether physicians should be prosecuted for assisting in someone's

   suicide. _____

_____

_____

PASSAGE 2

Is causing harm to the environment a *crime?* See how the author's concept of crime has been applied to environmental harm, and decide whether you agree with his thesis.

Crime can be defined best as a violation of the criminal law. Looking behind most criminal **statutes,** however, we can generally catch a glimpse of the concept of harm. Criminal activity, such as theft and assault, most of us would agree, is harmful to others. Some crimes, however, such as drug abuse, prostitution, gambling, and pornography, are sometimes referred to as "victimless crimes" (or social order offenses) because the harm they cause is not readily identifiable at the individual level. Statutes outlawing social order offenses are rooted in the notion of social harm—that is, although no one who participates in prostitution, say, runs to the police to file a complaint (unless they are robbed, or in some other way directly victimized) lawmakers recognize that the act somehow lessens the quality of social life. Prostitution, many lawmakers argue, is harmful to the family and (in the case of heterosexual prostitution) **demeans** the status of women in society.

Today, a whole new class of criminal offenses is emerging based upon the notion of environmental damage. In what may be the best known environmental catastrophe to date, the Exxon *Valdez,* a 1,000-foot supertanker, ran aground in Alaska in 1989 and spilled 11 million gallons of crude oil over 1,700 miles of **pristine** coastline. Animal life in the area was devastated. The U.S. Fish and Wildlife Service reported **decimation** to salmon spawning grounds, the death of 580,000 birds (including 144 bald eagles), and the demise of an unknown, but presumably vast amount of sea life. . . . The initial cleanup involved over 10,000 people and cost more than $1 billion. Damages were estimated as high as $5 billion. . . .

---

statutes (stach´ o͞ots) laws enacted by the legislative branch of a government; a formally established rule
demeans (di mēnz´) lowers character, status, or reputation; humbles; degrades
pristine (pris´ tēn) remaining in a pure state; uncorrupted
decimation (des i mā´ shun) destruction of a large quantity of something

While the *Valdez* incident is still near the forefront of national consciousness, environmental crimes of all proportions are a common occurrence. Such crimes range from **ecological** terrorism, like that waged against Kuwait by Saddam Hussein, to small-scale recycling offenses which are frequently committed (sometimes unknowingly) by individual citizens. As ecological awareness continues to expand, new prohibitions are legislated and previously unheard-of offenses created. Today, a highly concerned society stands increasingly ready to define abuse of the environment in criminal terms. As a consequence, words like "curbside criminals," "recycling police," and "garbage crime" are becoming commonplace. The state of Pennsylvania, for example, recently enacted a recycling law which mandates stiff sanctions, including fines and jail sentences for violators. Under the law, what had formerly been routine daily activities (throwing out the trash) become criminal offenses unless properly conducted (plastics and glass separated from paper products, and lawn clippings and yard trash appropriately bagged).

While human beings have insulted the environment since before the dawn of history, it has only been in this century, as our dependence on the planet has become progressively obvious, that such activities have been ascribed criminal status. Hence, the question: What taken-for-granted aspects of our contemporary everyday lives will become subject to criminal sanctions in the twenty-first century?

approximately 550 words

Frank Schmalleger, "What Is Crime: The Example of Crimes Against the Environment," *Criminal Justice Today*, pp. 117–18.

1. Is harming the environment a "victimless crime"? Why, or why not? _____

_____

_____

2. What do terms like *curbside criminal, recycling police,* and *garbage crimes*

   reveal about society's attitude toward protecting the environment? _____

_____

_____

_____

3. Reread the last sentence of the passage. How would you answer the question

   posed by the author? _____

_____

_____

ecological (ēkʹ ə lojʹ i kəl) having to do with relationships between organisms and their environment

❖ Patterns in Combination

As you have seen in some of the passages we have been studying, although writers generally use a particular overall or dominant organizational pattern, they often mix or combine patterns to suit their writing purpose. Therefore, whether in a paragraph or passage, you should expect to find a good deal of overlap of patterns. Being aware that writers do this should prevent you from being confused when more than one pattern is present. *The purpose in learning these patterns has been to make you aware of the general organizing principles of writing as a means of aiding your comprehension, your retention of information, and your own writing.*

The following passage has been marked to show you the extent to which a writer can provide clues when a number of patterns are used. After reading the article and studying the notations, you should understand the role of sports and society.

A hundred years ago, when sport was confined largely to games played in the backyard or on the farm, one could hardly have imagined the attention that it has come to receive (in the twentieth century.) (Today,) the importance of sport in society is clearly demonstrated by the fact that even the CBS Evening News can be preempted for the finals of a tennis match or the airing of the Super Bowl. A survey conducted in the (late 1980s) revealed that fully 81 percent of all adults follow some organized sport, mostly on television. And the phenomenon of weekend "sports widows"—women abandoned by their husbands for weekend sports on television—is entering its (third generation.)

time order

THE FUNCTIONS OF SPORT

Sport is (defined) sociologically as competitive physical activity that is performed under established rules. Like all social institutions, sport serves (numerous) (functions) (First) it provides society with a vast array of leisure-time activities for all segments of the population. Although it is an overstatement to say that modern society is a leisure society, there has been a significant increase in the amount of nonwork time that most people have available. (Furthermore,) recreational activity has become increasingly necessary in a society in which the vast majority of jobs provide little or no physical activity.

(Second,) sport provides an outlet for energies that, if not diverted, could (cause) serious strain on the social order. For both fan and participant, sport per-

definition

simple listing

cause/effect

mits the expression of emotions (such as anger and frustration) in ways that are acceptable to, even encouraged by, society.

(Finally,) sport provides society with role models. Athletes at all levels, but especially famous athletes, provide (examples) of conduct and employment of skills that others can **emulate.** (For example,) many children's heroes today are professional football and baseball players.

example

THE CONFLICT PERSPECTIVE

(Although) sports promote many positive aspects of a society, conflict theorists are quick to point out that they also reflect society's inequalities. Like most other social institutions, sports are characterized by inequalities of class, race, and gender.

contrast

(For example,) certain sports—such as polo, tennis, and skiing—have traditionally appealed to the wealthy. People with lower incomes often simply cannot afford to purchase and maintain horses or expensive tennis and ski equipment. Other sports—such as boxing, which is often associated with urban poverty—are distinctly lower class in origin and participation. In general, members of the lower and working classes have tended to participate in sports (like) baseball and basketball: games that require little more than a field, a ball, and some players.

example

(Although) sport is sometimes considered exempt from racial inequality, sociological evidence has shown this not to be the case. (Although) it is true that nonwhites in American society have enjoyed greater opportunities for high incomes in professional sports than in other occupations, it is also true that virtually all managers and owners of sports teams are white. There are very few nonwhite sportscasters, administrators, umpires, or referees. Furthermore, nonwhites are all but absent (even as players) from all professional sports except baseball, basketball, boxing, and football.

contrast

The history of women in traditionally male-oriented sports is also one of discrimination and inequality. When the first modern Olympic Games were held in 1896, women were virtually excluded from all forms of competition. Until fairly recently, girls were not even allowed to play Little League

---

emulate (em´ yə lāt´) to try to equal or surpass another, especially through imitation

baseball. But the position of women in sports is cur- ⬭   *cause/effect*

tional "female" sports as gymnastics and figure skat-
ing but also in more aggressively "male" sports ⬭like⬭   *example*
race car driving and basketball.

approximately 625 words

David Popenoe, "Sports and Society: Using the Theoretical Perspectives," *Sociology*, pp.
18–19. Copyright © 1995 by Prentice Hall. Reprinted by permission.

1. Which writing pattern has the author used most extensively? _____

2. List three supporting details the writer provides to make the reader understand

   the important functions of sports in society. _____

   _____

   _____

   _____

3. In your own experience, have you found inequalities in sports because of your

   class, race, or gender? How do you react to such inequalities?_____

   _____

   _____

   _____

For easy reference, the paragraph patterns and their signal word clues are listed on
the chart on page 241.

❖ Summary

Although there are many ways to express ideas, writers usually use the basic methods we have discussed, often mixing or combining them in paragraphs and passages.
Recognizing the writer's pattern for developing ideas and being aware of signal
words can help you follow the flow of ideas, understand the main idea better, and
recognize the author's purpose. There are seven major writing patterns.

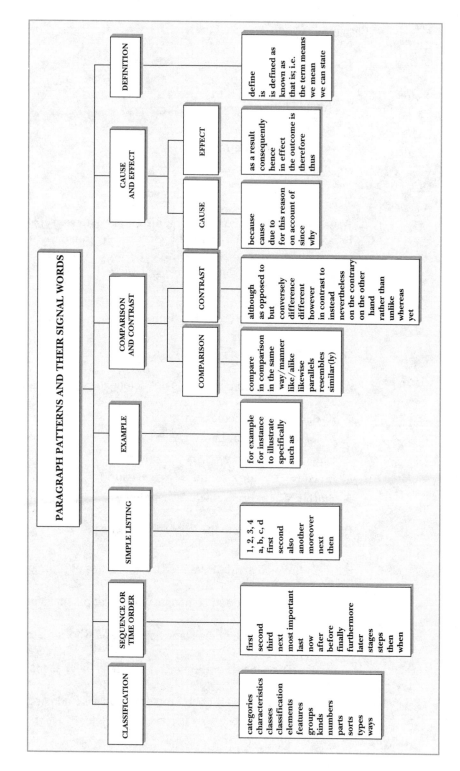

PARAGRAPH PATTERNS AND THEIR SIGNAL WORDS

CLASSIFICATION

categories
characteristics
classes
classification
elements
features
groups
kinds
numbers
parts
sorts
types
ways

SEQUENCE OR TIME ORDER

first
second
third
next
most important
last
now
after
before
finally
furthermore
later
stages
steps
then
when

SIMPLE LISTING

1, 2, 3, 4
a, b, c, d
first
second
also
another
moreover
next
then

EXAMPLE

for example
for instance
to illustrate
specifically
such as

COMPARISON AND CONTRAST

COMPARISON

compare
in comparison
in the same way/manner
like/alike
likewise
parallels
resembles
similar(ly)

CONTRAST

although
as opposed to
but
conversely
difference
different
however
in contrast to
instead
nevertheless
on the contrary
on the other hand
rather than
unlike
whereas
yet

CAUSE AND EFFECT

CAUSE

because
cause
due to
for this reason
on account of
since
why

EFFECT

as a result
consequently
hence
in effect
the outcome is
therefore
thus

DEFINITION

define
is
is defined as
known as
that is; i.e.
the term means
we mean
we can state

1. Classification

2. Sequence

3. Simple listing

4. Example

5. Comparison/contrast

6. Cause and effect

7. Definition

Writers can employ the seven organizational patterns separately or in combination. Be aware of the signal words so you can recognize them both in reading and in examinations. You need to realize, however, that signal words, like the patterns themselves, can overlap. This is the case with classification and sequence, which both use numbers (1, 2, 3; first, second, third). Also, numbers are used frequently when a writer wants to present a *list* of items. The different patterns that writers use are good models when you are composing your own essays.

Chapter 5 Vocabulary Review

A. Cross out the word that does not belong in defining the boldfaced words.

1. **disdain**	ridicule	scorn	regain	reject
2. **affluent**	wealthy	rich	influence	prosperous
3. **concur**	agree	consent	assent	deny
4. **raucous**	nice sound	bad sound	noisy sound	harsh sound
5. **morbidly**	gruesomely	hideously	frightfully	truthfully

B. Answer *yes* or *no* to the following statements:

_____ 1. Would an **abstract** idea be one that is easily understood?

_____ 2. If you **demean** someone, would that person's feelings be hurt?

_____ 3. Is a **hedonist** the same as someone who is a **stoic?**

_____ 4. Does **incarceration** mean the same thing as **insubordination**?

_____ 5. Do we usually try to **emulate** people we admire?

Selection 10: **ESSAY**

☛ Preparation for Reading

The following excerpt is from an essay about compulsive behavior. Much of the essay *defines* compulsiveness by the use of many *examples*. The essay further *compares* and *contrasts* destructive compulsiveness with a type that is "normal." It describes the *cause* of much compulsiveness and the *effect* that may follow.

While reading the essay, consider whether there are areas in your life that are controlled by compulsiveness. Is compulsiveness a positive or negative trait to possess?

The author uses the dash liberally, even though this is not considered a good writing style. After reading the selection, decide why she did so.

Note the meaning of the boldfaced words before reading. They are underlined in the text.

compulsive **chic**	smart elegance; stylish
the **mantra** of a whole generation	a hymn or portion of a text chanted as a prayer
to the **bizarre**	odd; strange
slightly obsessive, **meticulous**	extremely careful about details
ritualistic pattern	done like a solemn act
ironically, the more compulsive	opposite to what might be expected
frenetically neat people	frantically

Preview, then read the essay.

Control Freaks

Amanda Lovell

If it's possible for entire personality types to go in and out of fashion (remember when laid-back was in and uptight was out?) then the Nineties may well go down as the decade of Compulsive <u>Chic</u>. 1

People who used to go around saying, "I'm so disorganized" (code, as everyone knew, for "I'm so zany and creative and warm and wonderful") are piping down. The trendy plaint—if you haven't noticed—is "I'm so compulsive" (meaning: "I get things done"). At a time when being in control has become the <u>mantra</u> of a 2 whole generation, being compulsive is seen as the only way to achieve all one's goals.

In fact, "compulsive" means a lot of things, 3 ranging from the benign to the <u>bizarre,</u> from garden variety ashtray-emptying to nonstop shopping to the marathon hand washing of full-blown obsessive-compulsive disorder. All of these, oddly, appear to be either more in evidence or more talked about these days. Which raises a number of interesting questions.

When are compulsions—the hyper-neat 4 house, the never-missing-an-exercise-class, the need to shopshopshop—helpful and when are they over the top? Sometimes this is so obvious; sometimes it's a fine line. What might a bout of compulsive behavior symbolize—about an individual's emotional state? About our society? And what can be done about compulsiveness when it starts running amok?

Most experts agree that ordinary, everyday, half-of-us-have-it compulsiveness is a nonproblem. "What we call the compulsive character style—the perfectly normal but slightly obsessive, meticulous, perfectionistic approach to things—is often quite helpful and productive. Occasional checking, wondering if one has forgotten something—that's normal," says Dr. Joseph DeVeugh Geiss, a director of clinical research from Summit, New Jersey. 5

Maybe a little better than normal. "Compulsiveness correlates with intelligence and perfectionism," says New York psychologist Loretta Walder, PhD. "It's well-represented in the professions—in surgeons, lawyers, accountants, entrepreneurs, chefs." The word is that 70 percent of medical students have this character style—which may help to explain its good press among those who succeed in becoming doctors. 6

Walder claims, "What compulsive behavior does *for* a person is to organize chaos and reduce anxiety. If a woman has six thousand things to do, it helps to make lists, stick to schedules, prioritize; it's okay to be a little rigid. When someone's feeling overwhelmed, the routines of doing things in a set, ritualistic pattern can prevent confusion and scatteredness. In general, any high level achievement that requires a person to be compulsive in professional life has a carryover into one's personal life." 7

"Compulsive behavior is about control," asserts Sharon Hymer, an associate professor of psychology at New York University. "Ironically, the more compulsive the behavior, the more out of control the person probably feels deep 8

down. . . . However, one doesn't have to be a compulsive type to act compulsively. Just as even the most frenetically neat people often have little pockets of chaos in their lives—overflowing closets or handbags . . . so the generally laid-back have areas of drivenness. There's compulsive shopping, compulsive talking, compulsive eating, dieting, exercising, party going —you name it and someone has probably worked up a compulsion around it."

Strictly speaking, most of these urges aren't compulsions in the textbook sense. There's a distinct difference involved: True compulsions usually involve some form of counting, checking or cleaning—and no fun, only a grim sense of "gotta do it." But some of the features are similar: low self-esteem, a consequent need to assert control over some facet of one's life, stress acting as a trigger—and constant uncertainty, so that whatever one has, does or says never quite suffices. . . . 9

"Narrowing it down, the symbolism of one's unconscious choice is almost embarrassingly obvious," says Dr. Hymer. "The compulsive eater is trying to fill up a void in her life; . . . the compulsive talker is saying, "I don't think anyone will listen to me, so I have to control the situation by going on and on. The compulsive cleaner or exerciser is seeking self-esteem through a perfect body or pristine house. But it doesn't work, because too lean or too clean is never enough." 10

Still, one might not be a compulsive shopper, talker, party goer. One might merely be a passionate collector, a brilliant storyteller, a bon vivant . . . might one not? Georgia Witkin, Ph. D., assistant clinical professor of psychiatry at Mount Sinai School of Medicine in NYC and author of *Quick Fixes & Small Comforts,* suggests asking these questions: Is the behavior realistic? How does it leave you feeling afterward? What are the consequences? Is it possible to stop? And—since compulsions often start as anxiety reducers—is the hobby/passion/compulsion 1 covering up an underlying problem? If a person gets the feeling, he or she is winning the game but losing at real life, it's time to rethink.

When compulsiveness goes from being a 12 coping style—for good or ill—and takes over the entire persona, it becomes what psychiatrists call a compulsive personality. "It's the classic condition of someone who is cold, unemotional, rigid, moralistic and an unbearable perfectionist," so says Michael Liebowitz, M.D., director of the Columbia-Presbyterian Medical Center Anxiety Disorders Clinic.

"It's rampant right now," says Jay Lefer, 13 M.D., associate professor of psychiatry at New York Medical College. "It's really a consequence of how people adapt to society. The hysteria was nineteenth-century Vienna: the obsessive-compulsive is late-twentieth-century America. People feel helpless in urban society—and helplessness leads to a necessity to control oneself and others. The compulsive personality develops in an attempt to protect self-esteem."

approximately 800 words

Excerpted and adapted from Amanda Lovell, "Control Freaks," *Self,* Jan. 1989, pp. 81–84. Reprinted by permission.

COMPREHENSION CHECK

Part I
General Comprehension Questions: Literal and Interpretive

Write the correct letter in the space provided.

_____ 1. "The Nineties may well go down as the Decade of the Compulsive Chic." This means

a. it's not good to be compulsive.
b. it's a drug society.
c. it's better to be organized.
d. compulsiveness has become a way of life.

_____ 2. Ordinary compulsiveness

a. is still considered a problem by psychologists.
b. is not considered a problem by psychologists.
c. leads to more serious dangerous behavior.
d. can lead to drug abuse.

_____ 3. According to psychologists, there is a relationship between compulsiveness and

a. intelligence.
b. perfectionism.
c. the professions.
d. all of the above.

_____ 4. Professionals, according to the author, are well represented among the compulsives. Professionals who were not mentioned were

a. doctors.
b. lawyers.
c. engineers.
d. accountants.

_____ 5. According to one psychologist, the more compulsive the behavior,

    a. the more control one has over his or her actions.
    b. the less control one has over his or her actions.
    c. the more sleep is needed.
    d. the more often eating disorders appear.

_____ 6. Acting compulsively can be described as

    a. ritualistic behavior.
    b. a medical problem.
    c. animal-like behavior.
    d. both b and c.

7. What is the meaning of this sentence: "But it doesn't work, because too lean or too clean is never enough"? _____

    _____

8. What is the difference between a compulsion about something and a passionate interest in something? _____

    _____

Part II
Application Questions for Writing/Discussion

9. Define *compulsiveness.* What does compulsive behavior say about an individual's emotional state? _____

    _____

    _____

    _____

10. Why do you believe our present society produces so much more compulsive behavior? According to this article, are men or women more compulsive? Why do you think so? _____

_____

_____

_____

_____

_____

Part III
Extend Your Vocabulary

Use the context of the article and the sentence context to determine the meaning of the bold-faced word. Write the correct letter in the space provided.

_____ 1. What can be done about compulsiveness when it starts running **amok?**
a. backwards   b. wild   c. in a straight line   d. and stops

_____ 2. The compulsive cleaner is seeking self-esteem through a **pristine** house.
a. neat   b. perfectly clean   c. soiled   d. prim

_____ 3. It's well represented in the professions—in surgeons, lawyers, accountants, **entrepreneurs.**
a. blue-collar workers   b. sanitary engineers   c. secretaries
d. business organizers

_____ 4. One might merely be a passionate collector, a brilliant storyteller, or a **bon vivant.**
a. one who lives cautiously   b. one who lives fearfully
c. one who lives life fully   d. one who lives miserly

_____ 5. When compulsiveness goes from being a **coping** style—for good or evil—and takes over . . .
a. uplifting   b. successful handling   c. stylish trend   d. harmful look

Selection 11: **TEXTBOOK**

 # Preparation for Reading

Learn some of the ways researchers suggest that stress can best be handled, and evaluate the suggestions given for college students.

Before reading, note the meaning of the boldfaced words. They are underlined in the text.

finding is **correlational**	having a mutual relationship; parallel
an **aversive** event	causing strong dislike or unwillingness
level of **arousal**	stirred to action; excitement
increased **vulnerability**	sensitive to criticism; easy to attack or hurt
psychological effects of stress	derived from the mind or emotions

Preview the chapter excerpt before you begin reading it.

The Nature of Stress

John G. Seamon/Douglas T. Kendrick

Some researchers have studied the range of potentially stressful events, from losing a loved one to dropping the bag of garbage. . . .

LIFE CHANGES

In an effort to find out how stressful events are 1
linked to illness, Thomas Holmes and Richard Rahe asked tuberculosis patients about their lives just before they became ill. The researchers expected that unpleasant events would be linked with the onset of illness. Consistent with this expectation, many patients reported such things as the death of a spouse and the loss of a job. Unexpectedly, the patients also reported many seemingly neutral changes in recreational activities, sleep patterns, or domestic arrangements. Most unexpectedly, many of them reported seemingly positive events, including taking a vacation or getting married. From this information, the researchers developed the hypothesis that any disruption of our daily routine can be a stressor.

Following this hunch, Holmes and Rahe developed the Social Readjustment Rating Scale. The scale assigns readjustment values (or LCUs, "life change units") to 43 common life events. (See Table 5.1.)

In later studies, researchers found that 2
higher scores on the readjustment scale were associated with more illness. For instance, 79 percent of those who scored over 300 LCUs (and had therefore undergone major life stress) had had a serious illness during the year following the events. Fifty-one percent of those with moderate amounts of change (between 200 and 299 LCUs) had fallen ill, as had 37 percent of those with mild change (between 150 and 200 LCUs). Note that this finding is <u>correlational,</u> and does not prove that the stress led to illness. Perhaps the life changes were caused by other factors that also led to illness, or perhaps people recall more negative changes after they have fallen ill. There is some evidence that people with different dispositions bring different levels of stressful events on themselves.

TABLE 5.1

The Holmes and Rahe Social Readjustment Scale

Life Event	Mean Value
Death of spouse	100
Divorce	73
Marital separation	65
Jail term	63
Death of close family member	63
Personal injury or illness	53
Marriage	50
Fired at work	47
Marital reconciliation	45
Retirement	45
Change in health of family member	44
Pregnancy	40
Sex difficulties	39
Gain of new family member	39
Business readjustment	39
Change in financial state	38
Death of close friend	37
Change to different line of work	36
Change in number of arguments with spouse	35
Mortgage over $10,000*	31
Foreclosure of mortgage or loan	30
Change in responsibilities at work	29
Son or daughter leaving home	29
Trouble with in-laws	29
Outstanding personal achievement	28
Wife beginning or stopping work	26
Beginning or ending school	26
Change in living conditions	25
Revision of personal habits	24
Trouble with boss	23
Change in work hours or conditions	20
Change in residence	20
Change in schools	20
Change in recreation	19
Change in church activities	19
Change in social activities	18
Mortgage or loan less than $10,000*	17
Change in sleeping habits	16
Change in number of family get-togethers	15
Change in eating habits	15
Vacation	13
Christmas	12
Minor violations of the law	11

*Note: $10,000 was a figure based on the economy in the mid-1960s. An equivalent figure today would be $50,000.

MINOR EVERYDAY PROBLEMS

Instead of focusing on monumental stressors, **3** some psychologists believe that we can learn more about the effects of stress by studying what are sometimes called "daily hassles." These are the undramatic inconveniences of everyday life—returning to the car to find a parking ticket, arguing with your roommate about the dishes, or discovering that the cat has made a mess on the rug.

Researchers have asked subjects to record **4** these daily hassles, and found that, compared with major life changes, the minor inconveniences are actually better predictors of mental and physical distress. Obviously, some daily inconveniences are more relevant than others. Spilling the garbage is probably less upsetting than being stuck in traffic for an hour when you are already late for work. Psychologists Lee Anna Clark and David Watson found that arguments were the daily events most related to negative emotion. Having health problems, perhaps a cold or a flu, was also related to neg-

ative moods. Table 5.2 lists some common daily hassles found in a study of middle-aged adults, along with the things that were most likely to give them an "uplift."

Positive and negative daily events, and even **5** positive and negative daily moods, can occur at the same time. Good and bad things sometimes happen on the same day, and you can feel partly good and partly bad at the same moment. If you have an argument on Thursday, you are likely to rate yourself high on unpleasant moods, such as anger and depression. However, if you also get a good grade on the same day, you will rate your positive mood high as well. Research on college students' life events indicates that positive moods are related to such reinforcing events as getting a good grade or an unexpected gift, while negative moods are independently affected by painful events, including arguments with friends or parents. Positive events seem to raise our positive feelings but do not generally do much to erase the effects of painful experiences.

TABLE 5.2
A List of the Ten Most Frequent Daily Hassles and "Uplifts" Reported by Middle-Aged Adults over a Nine-Month Period

Hassles		Uplifts	
Item	% of Times Checked*	Item	% of Times Checked*
1. Concerns about weight	52.4	1. Relating well with your spouse or lover	76.3
2. Health of a family member	48.1	2. Relating well with friends	74.4
3. Rising prices of common goods	43.7	3. Completing a task	73.3
4. Home maintenance	42.8	4. Feeling healthy	72.7
5. Too many things to do	38.6	5. Getting enough sleep	69.7
6. Misplacing or losing things	38.1	6. Eating out	68.4
7. Yard work or outside home maintenance	38.1	7. Meeting your responsibilities	68.1
8. Property, investment, or taxes	37.6	8. Visiting, phoning, or writing someone	67.7
9. Crime	37.1	9. Spending time with family	66.7
10. Physical appearance	35.9	10. Home (inside) pleasing to you	65.5

*Note: The "% of times checked" figures represented the mean percentage of people checking the item each month averaged over the nine monthly administrations.

FEATURES OF STRESSFUL EVENTS: UNCERTAINTY AND LACK OF CONTROL

We are often confronted with stressors that are **6** outside of our control, from rare natural disasters to everyday traffic jams. There is a good deal of evidence that *uncontrollable events* are particularly stressful. The importance of controllability has been shown in studies of "executive rats," in which two rats receive exactly the same electric shock, but one is given a lever that could be used to turn the shock off after it occurs. Over a long series of such trials, the partner rat, helpless to do anything about its plight, is more likely to develop ulcers than is the "executive." In studies with humans, subjects are also more upset by electric shock if they have no means to control or prevent the shocks. In fact, subjects who simply *believe* that they can control the stressful events in their lives are less upset by unpleasant but naturally occurring life events. This research is closely related to the phenomenon of "learned helplessness," in which people give up in the face of stressors that seem to be uncontrollable.

An important aspect of having control over **7** the day-to-day inconveniences in your life, such as dental appointments, is that you know when they are going to occur. Animal studies indicate that *uncertainty* about an <u>aversive</u> event makes it much more disrupting. Human studies also show that uncertainty is aversive. One study found that subjects who were told that they had a 5 percent chance of receiving an electric shock were actually more aroused than those who were told that they had a 50 percent chance. Based on their discussions with the participants, the researchers concluded that those in the 50 percent group were resigned to receiving a shock, and could brace themselves. Those in the 5 percent group, on the other hand, were uncertain about how to prepare themselves.

In sum, then, there is evidence that certain **8** types of events are more stressful than others.

Major life changes, including divorce and the death of a spouse, are particularly stressful. Daily hassles, especially arguments, can also be quite stressful. Any given event is more stressful when it is novel, when it is uncertain, or when it cannot be controlled.

Stressful categories of events often involve **9** many of these stress-inducing features. For instance, the death of a spouse leaves the widowed person helpless to do anything about it and with a high degree of uncertainty about the future. It is important to keep in mind that the same event that is stressful to one person at one time may be exhilarating to that same person at another. . . . Totally familiar situations may be boring, while a certain amount of novelty causes a pleasant level of <u>arousal</u>. It is only when the arousal gets out of control that it is aversive. Recall also that some sensation-seeking individuals repeatedly seek out high levels of novelty and challenge in their lives.

> *Think about it . . .*
>
> If you fail an exam and call a friend for social support, is that an example of what Lazarus would call a "problem-focused" or an "emotion-focused" coping strategy? How would Lazarus categorize the use of a cognitive defense mechanism, such as rationalization?

COPING WITH STRESS

When grouchy bosses or difficult examinations **10** start to get on your nerves, you need not just sit passively as the fatty acids and catecholemines course through your arteries. If you are like the hardy executives in Suzanne Kobasa's research, you can try to take control and do something about it. Removing the cause of stress is probably the most effective coping strategy, but sometimes, . . . it is not possible. Barring an immediate solution to our problems, we may try a number of other strategies to make them less aversive—we may seek the support of friends, we may reinterpret our situation to make it seem less unpleasant, we may laugh or cry, go for a drink, and so on. These attempts to control stress are called *coping mechanisms.*

11 Richard Lazarus and his colleagues have made a useful distinction between problem-focused and emotion-focused coping strategies. Problem-focused strategies are those aimed at doing something to change the problem causing the distress (perhaps talking to the boss about what he or she expects of you). Problem-focused strategies tend to be used in situations that we regard as changeable. Emotion-focused strategies, used more in situations that are appraised as unchangeable, are aimed at regulating our distressing emotional responses. Compared with women, men are less likely to use emotion-focused strategies, such as seeking support from a friend.

12 Psychologists Susan Folkman and Richard Lazarus examined undergraduate students' coping strategies at three time periods—two days before a midterm examination; a week later, two days before the grades were announced; and five days after the grades were posted. Before the exam, students tended to use such problem-focused strategies as studying—a guaranteed way to reduce the potential problems caused by an upcoming exam. If they sought out others, it was more likely to be for information than for emotional support. After the exam, when their fates were sealed, they tended to use the emotion-focused cognitive strategy of "distancing" (measured by such phrases as "Try to forget the whole thing"). If they sought out others afterwards, it was for emotional support rather than for information. Our discussion will focus on these two related lines of defense in coping with stress: seeking social support from others and reinterpreting the meaning of a stressful situation to ourselves.

Social Support

13 Like other animals, humans have always been safer in groups. However, there is increasing evidence that people provide more than physical protection for one another. They provide emotional support and reassurance that can reduce the psychological and physiological symptoms of stress. A lack of support can increase our susceptibility to illness. For instance, short-term loneliness is associated with a decrease in immune response. This increased vulnerability can take a toll over time. Students who described themselves as "loners" in medical school had, compared with other medical students, the highest rates of cancer at a follow-up several decades later.

14 In contrast, people who get a lot of social support from their friends and co-workers are less upset by life changes and daily hassles. In the long run, those who have strong social ties are likely to be more resistant to disease and to live longer. For instance, after being diagnosed as having a life-threatening disease, married people are likely to survive longer than unmarried people with the same disease. One team of researchers found that those who lived alone after a heart attack had a 16 percent likelihood of a relapse, whereas those who lived with someone else had only a 9 percent relapse rate.

15 In addition to providing protection and emotional support, people give other types of support to one another. Several types of social support are listed in Table 5.3. For instance, other people may provide *appraisal support,* helping to evaluate and clarify how serious a problem is. If a professor tells you that he had also failed his first college algebra exam, the consequences of your failure will seem less devastating. Others can also provide *informational support,* giving advice about how to deal with the problem. In the search for solutions to problems at school or on the job, two heads are likely to be better than one.

16 Finally, friends and relatives may give us *instrumental support,* providing material goods or services to overcome the stress. If your father

TABLE 5.3

Different Types of Social Support

Type of Support	Example
1. Emotional	A sympathetic hug
2. Appraisal	A story about someone who did much worse than you did on the first math exam, and went on to get an A
3. Informational	A suggestion about where to get tutoring to help you pass a difficult course
4. Instrumental	A loan to help you pay for a tutor

Based on House (1981)

lends you some money when your car breaks down, you can stop tearing your hair out and just fix it. One way that relatives and friends may provide support is by facilitating laughter and tears. There is emerging evidence that both may reduce the physiological and psychological effects of distress.

Do we need another person to provide us with social support? Interestingly, recent research suggests that a pet dog may provide the same benefit, and sometimes the dog might be even better. Participants in one study were exposed to a stressful task either alone, in the presence of a friend, or with their pet dog around. The presence of a friend did not improve performance on a stressful task at all; it seemed to make matters worse. On the other hand, a pet dog seemed to have a significant calming effect. Over a period of years, elderly people with dogs make fewer contacts with doctors, and those who have a pet at home are more likely to survive a heart attack. From a social support perspective, then, a dog may serve at least as well as a best friend.

approximately 2700 words

Excerpted from John G. Seamon and Douglas T. Kenrick, "Stress, Coping, Health," *Psychology*, pp. 459–478. Copyright © by Prentice Hall, 1994. Reprinted by permission.

COMPREHENSION CHECK

Part I
General Comprehension Questions: Literal and Interpretive

Write the correct letter in the space provided.

_____ 1. Researchers have reported that

a. unpleasant events can trigger stress.
b. neutral changes can trigger stress.
c. positive events can trigger stress.
d. all of the above.

_____ 2. People who score very high on the Social Readjustment Scale would most likely have

a. less illness the following year.
b. more illness the following year.
c. several nervous breakdowns.
d. family adjustments.

_____ 3. The daily events most related to
negative emotions are

   a. inconveniences.
   b. arguments.
   c. misplaced things.
   d. relocations.

_____ 4. More stress is associated with
events that

   a. are uncertain.
   b. cannot be controlled.
   c. both a and b.
   d. are significant.

_____ 5. Of major life changes, the most
stressful is a

   a. first child.
   b. business readjustment.
   c. new marriage.
   d. spouse's death.

_____ 6. The most effective coping strategy
for stress is to

   a. get enough rest and relaxation.
   b. develop better eating habits.
   c. remove its cause.
   d. both a and b.

7. What is the relationship between stress and strong social ties? _____

_____

8. What basic organizational pattern do the writers use in discussing the nature of

stress and its consequences? _____

_____

Part II
Application Questions for Writing/Discussion

9. Describe a real or imaginary situation in which you used either problem-focused
coping strategies or emotion-focused coping strategies. Indicate which type you

described. _____

_____

_____

10. Which strategies are most effective in coping with stress? _____

_____

Part III
Extend Your Vocabulary

Change the part of speech of each italicized word to complete the phrases.

1. Change *aversive,* an adjective, to a noun.

   her _____ to taking an exam
2. Change *arousal* a noun, to a verb.

   had been _____ by a prowler
3. Change *cognitive,* an adjective, to a noun.

   when _____ is lacking
4. Change *psychological,* an adjective, to a noun.

   studying the _____ of stress
5. Change *correlational,* an adjective, to a noun.

   a direct _____ between cause and effect

Selection 12: **LITERATURE**

 # Preparation for Reading

The following short story was written by Tobias Wolff, who received the Pen-Faulkner award for "The Barracks Thief."

"The Rich Brother" first appeared in *Vanity Fair* and is part of a collection of short stories, *Back in the World*. Tobias Wolff teaches English at Syracuse University in upstate New York.

As you read, be aware of Wolff's major organizational writing pattern: comparison and contrast. Think about the description of the two brothers, Pete and Donald, to see in what ways their personalities are similar and how they differ. It is their differences that create the major conflict in the story. The setting of the story is Northern California.

Note the meaning of the boldfaced words before reading. They are underlined in the text.

an **ashram** in Berkeley	a communal retreat, often a secluded place
innuendo, looks of mild despair	indirect hint or suggestion, often meant to discredit someone
look of an **inquisitor**	official investigator
aware of Donald's **scrutiny**	close examination; careful inspection
"**Stygian,**" the man said.	dark; gloomy; of the lower world
tone was **sepulchral**	suggesting a tomb; dismal or gloomy
land and rights in **perpetuity**	existence forever

The Rich Brother

Tobias Wolff

There were two brothers, Pete and Donald.

Pete, the older brother, was in real estate. He and his wife had a Century 21 franchise in Santa Cruz. Pete worked hard and made a lot of money, but not any more than he thought he deserved. He had two daughters, a sailboat, a house from which he could see a thin slice of the ocean, and friends doing well enough in their own lives not to wish bad luck on him. Donald, the younger brother, was still single. He lived alone, painted houses when he found the work, and got deeper in debt to Pete when he didn't.

No one would have taken them for brothers. Where Pete was stout and hearty and at home in the world, Donald was bony, grave, and obsessed with the fate of his soul. Over the years Donald had worn the images of two different Perfect Masters around his neck. Out of devotion to the second of these he entered an <u>ashram</u> in Berkeley, where he nearly died of undiagnosed hepatitis. By the time Pete finished paying the medical bills Donald had become a Christian. He drifted from church to church, then joined a pentecostal community that met somewhere in the Mission District to sing in tongues and swap prophecies.

1

Pete couldn't make sense of it. Their parents were both dead, but while they were alive neither of them had found it necessary to believe in anything. They managed to be decent people without making fools of themselves, and Pete had the same ambition. He thought that the whole thing was an excuse for Donald to take himself seriously.

The trouble was that Donald couldn't content himself with worrying about his own soul. He had to worry about everyone else's, and especially Pete's. He handed down his judgments in ways that he seemed to consider subtle: through significant silence, <u>innuendo</u>, looks of mild despair that said, *Brother, what have you come to?* What Pete had come to, as far as he could tell, was prosperity. That was the real issue between them. Pete prospered and Donald did not prosper.

At the age of forty Pete took up sky diving. He made his first jump with two friends who'd started only a few months earlier and were already doing stunts. They were both coked to the gills when they jumped but Pete wanted to do it straight, at least the first time, and he was glad that he did. He would never have used the word "mystical," but that was how Pete felt about the experience. Later he made the mistake of trying to describe it to Donald, who kept asking how much it cost and then acted appalled when Pete told him.

"At least I'm trying something new," Pete said. "At least I'm breaking the pattern."

Not long after that conversation Donald also broke the pattern, by going to live on a farm outside of Paso Robles. The farm was owned by several members of Donald's community, who had bought it and moved there with the idea of forming a family of faith. That was how Donald explained it in the first letter he sent. Every week Pete heard how happy Donald was, how "in the Lord." He told Pete that he was praying for him, he and the rest of Pete's brothers and sisters on the farm.

"I only have one brother," Pete wanted to answer, "and that's enough." But he kept this thought to himself.

In November the letters stopped. Pete didn't worry about this at first, but when he called Donald at Thanksgiving Donald was grim. He tried to sound upbeat but he didn't try hard enough to make it convincing. "Now listen," Pete said, "you don't have to stay in that place if you don't want to."

"I'll be all right," Donald answered.

"That's not the point. Being all right is not the point. If you don't like what's going on up there, then get out."

"I'm all right," Donald said again, more firmly. "I'm doing fine."

But he called Pete a week later and said that he was quitting the farm. When Pete asked him where he intended to go, Donald admitted that he had no plan. His car had been repossessed just before he left the city, and he was flat broke.

"I guess you'll have to stay with us," Pete said.

Donald put up a show of resistance. Then he gave in. "Just until I get my feet on the ground," he said.

"Right," Pete said. "Check out your options." He told Donald he'd send him

5

10

15

money for a bus ticket, but as they were about to hang up Pete changed his mind. He knew that Donald would try hitchhiking to save the fare. Pete didn't want him out on the road all alone where some head case could pick him up, where anything could happen to him.

"Better yet," he said. "I'll come and get you."

"You don't have to do that. I didn't expect you to do that." Donald said. He added, "It's a pretty long drive."

"Just tell me how to get there."   20

But Donald wouldn't give him directions. He said that the farm was too depressing, that Pete wouldn't like it. Instead, he insisted on meeting Pete at a service station called Jonathan's Mechanical Emporium.

"You must be kidding," Pete said.

"It's close to the highway," Donald said. "I didn't name it."

"That's one for the collection," Pete said.

The day before he left to bring Donald home, Pete received a letter from a man who 25
described himself as "head of household" at the farm where Donald had been living. From this letter Pete learned that Donald had not quit the farm, but had been asked to leave. The letter was written on the back of a mimeographed survey form asking people to record their response to a ceremony of some kind. The last question said:

What did you feel during the liturgy?
a) Being
b) Becoming
c) Being and Becoming
d) None of the Above
e) All of the Above

Pete tried to forget the letter. But of course he couldn't. Each time he thought of it he felt crowded and breathless, a feeling that came over him again when he drove into the service station and saw Donald sitting against a wall with his head on his knees. It was late afternoon. A paper cup tumbled slowly past Donald's feet, pushed by the damp wind.

Pete honked and Donald raised his head. He smiled at Pete, then stood and stretched. His arms were long and thin and white. He wore a red bandanna across his forehead, a T-shirt with a couple of words on the front. Pete couldn't read them because the letters were inverted.

"Grow up," Pete yelled. "Get a Mercedes."

Donald came up to the window. He bent down and said, "Thanks for coming. You must be totally whipped."

"I'll make it." Pete pointed at Donald's T-shirt. "What's that supposed to say?"   30

Donald looked down at his shirt front. "Try God. I guess I put it on backwards. Pete, could I borrow a couple of dollars? I owe these people for coffee and sandwiches."

Pete took five twenties from his wallet and held them out the window.

Donald stepped back as if horrified. "I don't need that much."

"I can't keep track of all these nickels and dimes," Pete said. "Just pay me back when your ship comes in." He waved the bills impatiently. "Go on—take it."

"Only for now." Donald took the money and went into the service station office. 35 He came out carrying two orange sodas, one of which he gave to Pete as he got into the car. "My treat," he said.

"No bags?"

"Wow, thanks for reminding me," Donald said. He balanced his drink on the dashboard, but the slight rocking of the car as he got out tipped it onto the passenger's seat, where half its contents foamed over before Pete could snatch it up again. Donald looked on while Pete held the bottle out the window, soda running down his fingers.

"Wipe it up," Pete told him. "Quick!"

"With what?"

Pete stared at Donald. "That shirt. Use the shirt."   40

Donald pulled a long face but did as he was told, his pale skin puckering against the wind.

"Great, just great," Pete said. "We haven't even left the gas station yet."

Afterwards, on the highway, Donald said, "This is a new car, isn't it?"

"Yes. This is a new car."

"Is that why you're so upset about the seat?"   45

"Forget it, okay? Let's just forget about it."

"I said I was sorry."

Pete said, "I just wish you'd be more careful. These seats are made of leather. That stain won't come out, not to mention the smell. I don't see why I can't have leather seats that smell like leather instead of orange pop."

"What was wrong with the other car?"

Pete glanced over at Donald. Donald had raised the hood of the blue sweatshirt 50 he'd put on. The peaked hood above his gaunt, watchful face gave him the look of an inquisitor.

"There wasn't anything wrong with it," Pete said. "I just happened to like this one better."

Donald nodded.

There was a long silence between them as Pete drove on and the day darkened toward evening. On either side of the road lay stubble-covered fields. A line of low hills ran along the horizon, topped here and there with trees black against the gray sky. In the approaching line of cars a driver turned on his headlights. Pete did the same.

"So what happened?" he asked. "Farm life not your bag?"

Donald took some time to answer, and at last he said, simply, "It was my fault." 55

"What was your fault?"

"The whole thing. Don't play dumb, Pete. I know they wrote to you." Donald looked at Pete, then stared out the windshield again.

"I'm not playing dumb."

Donald shrugged.

"All I really know is they asked you to leave," Pete went on. "I don't know any of 60
the particulars."

"I blew it," Donald said. "Believe me, you don't want to hear the gory details."

"Sure I do," Pete said. He added, "Everybody likes the gory details."

"You mean everybody likes to hear how someone else messed up."

"Right," Pete said. "That's the way it is here on Spaceship Earth."

Donald bent one knee onto the front seat and leaned against the door so that 65
he was facing Pete instead of the windshield. Pete was aware of Donald's <u>scrutiny</u>. He
waited. Night was coming on in a rush now, filling the hollows of the land. Donald's
long cheeks and deep-set eyes were dark with shadow. His brow was white. "Do you
ever dream about me?" Donald asked.

"Do I ever dream about you? What kind of a question is that? Of course I don't
dream about you," Pete said, untruthfully.

"What do you dream about?"

"Sex and money. Mostly money. A nightmare is when I dream I don't have any."

"You're just making that up," Donald said.

Pete smiled.   70

"Sometimes I wake up at night," Donald went on, "and I can tell you're dreaming about me."

"We were talking about the farm," Pete said. "Let's finish that conversation and
then we can talk about our various out-of-body experiences and the interesting
things we did during previous incarnations."

For a moment Donald looked like a grinning skull; then he turned serious
again. "There's not that much to tell," he said. "I just didn't do anything right."

"That's a little vague," Pete said.

"Well, like the groceries. Whenever it was my turn to get the groceries I'd blow 75
it somehow. I'd bring the groceries home and half of them would be missing, or I'd
have all the wrong things, the wrong kind of flour or the wrong kind of chocolate or
whatever. One time I gave them away. It's not funny, Pete."

Pete said, "Who did you give the groceries to?"

"Just some people I picked up on the way home. Some fieldworkers. They had
about eight kids with them and they didn't even speak English—just nodded their
heads. Still, I shouldn't have given away the groceries. Not all of them, anyway. I
really learned my lesson about that. You have to be practical. You have to be fair to
yourself." Donald leaned forward, and Pete could sense his excitement. "There's
nothing actually wrong with being in business," he said. "As long as you're fair to
other people you can still be fair to yourself. I'm thinking of going into business,
Pete."

"We'll talk about it," Pete said. "So, that's the story? There isn't any more to it
than that?"

"What did they tell you?" Donald asked.

"Nothing."

80

"They must have told you something."

Pete shook his head.

"They didn't tell you about the fire?" When Pete shook his head again Donald regarded him for a time, then said, "I don't know. It was stupid. I just completely lost it." He folded his arms across his chest and slumped back into the corner. "Everybody had to take turns cooking dinner. I usually did tuna casserole or spaghetti with garlic bread. But this one night I thought I'd do something different, something really interesting." Donald looked sharply at Pete. "It's all a big laugh to you, isn't it?"

"I'm sorry," Pete said.

"You don't know when to quit. You just keep hitting away."   **85**

"Tell me about the fire, Donald."

Donald kept watching him. "You have this compulsion to make me look foolish."

"Come off it, Donald. Don't make a big thing out of this."

"I know why you do it. It's because you don't have any purpose in life. You're afraid to relate to people who do, so you make fun of them."

"Relate," Pete said softly.   **90**

"You're basically a very frightened individual," Donald said. "Very threatened. You've always been like that. Do you remember when you used to try to kill me?"

"I don't have any compulsion to make you look foolish, Donald—You do it yourself. You're doing it right now."

They ate dinner at a Denny's on the other side of King City. As Pete was paying the check he heard a man behind him say, "Excuse me, but I wonder if I might ask which way you're going?" and Donald answered, "Santa Cruz."

"Perfect," the man said.

Pete could see him in the fish-eye mirror above the cash register: a red blazer **95** with some kind of crest on the pocket, little black mustache, glossy black hair combed down on his forehead like a Roman emperor's. A rug, Pete thought. Definitely a rug.

Pete got his change and turned. "Why is that perfect?" he asked.

The man looked at Pete. He had a soft ruddy face that was doing its best to express pleasant surprise, as if this new wrinkle were all he could have wished for, but the eyes behind the aviator glasses showed signs of regret. His lips were moist and shiny. "I take it you're together," he said.

"You got it," Pete told him.

"All the better, then," the man went on. "It so happens I'm going to Santa Cruz myself. Had a spot of car trouble down the road. The old Caddy let me down."

"What kind of trouble?" Pete asked.   **100**

"Engine trouble," the man said. "I'm afraid it's a bit urgent. My daughter is sick. Urgently sick. I've got a telegram here." He patted the breast pocket of his blazer.

Pete grinned. Amazing, he thought, the old sick daughter ploy, but before he could say anything Donald got into the act again. "No problem," Donald said. "We've got tons of room."

"Not that much room," Pete said.

Donald nodded. "I'll put my things in the trunk."

"The trunk's full," Pete told him.   10

"It so happens I'm traveling light," the man said. "This leg of the trip anyway. In fact I don't have any luggage at this particular time."

Pete said, "Left it in the old Caddy, did you?"

"Exactly," the man said.

"No problem," Donald repeated. He walked outside and the man went with him. Together they strolled across the parking lot, Pete following at a distance. When they reached Pete's car Donald raised his face to the sky, and the man did the same. They stood there looking up. "Dark night," Donald said.

"Stygian," the man said.   11

Pete still had it in mind to brush him off, but he didn't do that. Instead he unlocked the door for him. He wanted to see what would happen. It was an adventure, but not a dangerous adventure. The man might steal Pete's ashtrays but he wouldn't kill him. If Pete got killed on the road it would be by some spiritual person in a sweatsuit, someone with his eyes on the far horizon and a wet Try God T-shirt in his duffel bag.

As soon as they left the parking lot the man lit a cigar. He blew a cloud of smoke over Pete's shoulder and sighed with pleasure. "Put it out," Pete told him.

"Of course," the man said. Pete looked into the rear-view mirror and saw the man take another long puff before dropping the cigar out the window. "Forgive me," he said. "I should have asked. Name's Webster, by the way."

Donald turned and looked back at him. "First name or last?"

The man hesitated. "Last," he said finally.   115

"I know a Webster," Donald said. "Mick Webster."

"There are many of us," Webster said.

"Big fellow, wooden leg," Pete said.

Donald gave Pete a look.

Webster shook his head. "Doesn't ring a bell. Still, I wouldn't deny the connec-   120
tion. Might be one of the cousinry."

"What's your daughter got?" Pete asked.

"That isn't clear," Webster answered. "It appears to be a female complaint of some nature. Then again it may be tropical." He was quiet for a moment, and then added: "If indeed it *is* tropical, I will have to assume some of the blame myself. It was my own vaulting ambition that first led us to the tropics and kept us in the tropics all those many years, exposed to every evil. Truly I have much to answer for. I left my wife there."

Donald said quietly, "You mean she died?"

"I buried her with these hands. The earth will be repaid, gold for gold."

"Which tropics?" Pete asked.   125

"The tropics of Peru."

"What part of Peru are they in?"

"The lowlands," Webster said.

Pete nodded. "What's it like down there?"

"Another world," Webster said. His tone was <u>sepulchral</u>. "A world better imag-   **130**
ined than described."

"Far out," Pete said.

The three men rode in silence for a time. A line of trucks went past in the other
direction, trailers festooned with running lights, engines roaring.

"Yes," Webster said at last, "I have much to answer for."

Pete smiled at Donald, but Donald had turned in his seat again and was gazing
at Webster. "I'm sorry about your wife," Donald said.

"What did she die of?" Pete asked.   **135**

"A wasting illness," Webster said. "The doctors have no name for it, but I do." He
leaned forward and said, fiercely, *"Greed."* Then he slumped back against his seat.
"My greed, not hers. She wanted no part of it."

Pete bit his lip. Webster was a find and Pete didn't want to scare him off by hoot-
ing at him. In a voice low and innocent of knowingness, he asked, "What took you
there?"

"It's difficult for me to talk about."

"Try," Pete told him.   **140**

"A cigar would make it easier."

Donald turned to Pete and said, "It's okay with me."

"All right," Pete said. "Go ahead. Just keep the window rolled down."

"Much obliged." A match flared. There were eager sucking sounds.

"Let's hear it," Pete said.

"I am by training an engineer," Webster began. "My work has exposed me to all   **145**
but one of the continents, to desert and alp and forest, to every terrain and season
of the earth. Some years ago I was hired by the Peruvian government to search for
tungsten in the tropics. My wife and daughter accompanied me. We were the only
white people for a thousand miles in any direction, and we had no choice but to live
as the Indians lived—to share their food and drink and even their culture."

Pete said, "You knew the lingo, did you?"

"We picked it up." The ember of the cigar bobbed up and down. "We were used
to learning as necessity decreed. At any rate, it became evident after a couple of years
that there was no tungsten to be found. My wife had fallen ill and was pleading to be
taken home. But I was deaf to her pleas, because by then I was on the trail of another
metal—a metal far more valuable than tungsten."

"Let me guess," Pete said, "Gold?"

Donald looked at Pete, then back at Webster.

"Gold," Webster said. "A vein of gold greater than the Mother Lode itself. After   **150**
I found the first traces of it nothing could tear me away from my search—not the
sickness of my wife nor anything else. I was determined to uncover the vein, and so
I did—but not before I laid my wife to rest. As I say, the earth will be repaid."

Webster was quiet. Then he said, "But life must go on. In the years since my
wife's death I have been making the arrangements necessary to open the mine. I
could have done it immediately, of course, enriching myself beyond measure, but I

knew what that would mean—the exploitation of our beloved Indians, the brutal destruction of their environment. I felt I had too much to atone for already." Webster paused, and when he spoke again his voice was dull and rushed, as if he had used up all the interest he had in his own words. "Instead I drew up a program for returning the bulk of the wealth to the Indians themselves. A kind of trust fund. The interest alone will allow them to secure their ancient lands and rights in <u>perpetuity</u>. At the same time, our investors will be rewarded a thousandfold. Two-thousandfold. Everyone will prosper together."

"That's great," Donald said. "That's the way it ought to be."

Pete said, "I'm willing to bet that you just happen to have a few shares left. Am I right?"

Webster made no reply.

"Well?" Pete knew that Webster was on to him now, but he didn't care. The story   155
had bored him. He'd expected something different, something original, and Webster had let him down. He hadn't even tried. Pete felt sour and stale. His eyes burned from cigar smoke and the high beams of road-hogging truckers. "Douse the stogie," he said to Webster. "I told you to keep the window down."

"Got a little nippy back there."

Donald said, "Hey, Pete. Lighten up."

"Douse it!"

Webster sighed. He got rid of the cigar.

"I'm a wreck," Pete said to Donald. "You want to drive for a while?"   160
Donald nodded.

Pete pulled over and they changed places.

Webster kept his counsel in the back seat. Donald hummed while he drove, until Pete told him to stop. Then everything was quiet.

Donald was humming again when Pete woke up. Pete stared sullenly at the road, at the white lines sliding past the car. After a few moments of this he turned and said, "How long have I been out?"
    165
Donald glanced at him. "Twenty, twenty-five minutes."

Pete looked behind him and saw that Webster was gone. "Where's our friend?"

"You just missed him. He got out in Soledad.* He told me to say thanks and goodbye."

"Soledad? What about his sick daughter? How did he explain her away?" Pete leaned over the seat. Both ashtrays were still in place. Floor mats. Door handles.

"He has a brother living there," He's going to borrow a car from him and drive the rest of the way in the morning."
    170
"I'll bet his brother's living there," Pete said. "Doing fifty concurrent life sentences. His brother and his sister and his mom and his dad."

"I kind of liked him," Donald said.

"I'm sure you did," Pete said wearily.

"He was interesting. He'd been places."

*Soledad is a city in California where a state prison is located.

"His cigars had been places, I'll give you that."

"Come on, Pete." 175

"Come on yourself. What a phony."

"You don't know that."

"Sure I do."

"How? How do you know?"

Pete stretched. "Brother, there are some things you're just born knowing. 180
What's the gas situation?"

"We're a little low."

"Then why didn't you get some more?"

"I wish you wouldn't snap at me like that," Donald said.

"Then why don't you use your head? What if we run out?"

"We'll make it," Donald said. "I'm pretty sure we've got enough to make it. You 185
didn't have to be so rude to him." Donald added.

Pete took a deep breath. "I don't feel like running out of gas tonight, okay?"

Donald pulled in at the next station they came to and filled the tank while Pete
went to the men's room. When Pete came back, Donald was sitting in the passenger's seat. The attendant came up to the driver's window as Pete got in behind the
wheel. He bent down and said, "Twenty-two fifty-five."

"You heard the man," Pete said to Donald.

Donald looked straight ahead. He didn't move.

"Cough up," Pete said. "This trip's on you." 190

Donald said, softly, "I can't."

"Sure you can. Break out that wad."

Donald glanced up at the attendant, then at Pete. "Please," he said. "Pete, I
don't have it anymore."

Pete took this in. He nodded, and paid the attendant.

Donald began to speak when they left the station but Pete cut him off. He said, 195
"I don't want to hear from you right now. You just keep quiet or I swear to God I
won't be responsible."

They left the fields and entered a tunnel of tall trees. The trees went on and on.
"Let me get this straight," Pete said at last. "You don't have the money I gave you."

"You treated him like a bug or something," Donald said.

"You don't have the money," Pete said again.

Donald shook his head.

"Since I bought dinner, and since we didn't stop anywhere in between, I assume 200
you gave it to Webster. Is that right? Is that what you did with it?"

"Yes."

Pete looked at Donald. His face was dark under the hood but he still managed
to convey a sense of remove, as if none of this had anything to do with him.

"Why?" Pete asked. "Why did you give it to him?" When Donald didn't answer,
Pete said, "A hundred dollars. Gone. Just like that. I *worked* for that money, Donald."

"I know, I know," Donald said.

"You don't know! How could you? You get money by holding out your hand." 205

"I work too," Donald said.

"You work too. Don't kid yourself, brother."

Donald leaned toward Pete, about to say something, but Pete cut him off again.

"You're not the only one on the payroll, Donald. I don't think you understand that. I have a family."

"Pete, I'll pay you back."

"Like hell you will. A hundred dollars!" Pete hit the steering wheel with the palm of his hand. "Just because you think I hurt some goofball's feelings. Jesus, Donald."

"That's not the reason," Donald said. "And I didn't just *give* him the money."

"What do you call it, then? What do you call what you did?"

"I *invested* it. I wanted a share, Pete." When Pete looked over at him Donald nodded and said again, "I wanted a share."

Pete said, "I take it you're referring to the gold mine in Peru."

"Yes," Donald said.

"You believe that such a gold mine exists?"

Donald looked at Pete, and Pete could see him just beginning to catch on. "You'll believe anything," Pete said. "Won't you? You really will believe anything at all."

"I'm sorry," Donald said, and turned away.

Pete drove on between the trees and considered the truth of what he had just said—that Donald would believe anything at all. And it came to him that it would be just like this unfair life for Donald to come out ahead in the end, by believing in some outrageous promise that would turn out to be true and that he, Pete, would reject out of hand because he was too wised up to listen to anybody's pitch anymore except for laughs. What a joke. What a joke if there really was a blessing to be had, and the blessing didn't come to the one who deserved it, the one who did all the work, but to the other.

And as if this had already happened Pete felt a shadow move upon him, darkening his thoughts. After a time he said, "I can see where all this is going, Donald."

"I'll pay you back," Donald said.

"No," Pete said. "You won't pay me back. You can't. You don't know how. All you've ever done is take. All your life."

Donald shook his head.

"I see exactly where this is going," Pete went on. "You can't work, you can't take care of yourself, you believe anything anyone tells you. I'm stuck with you, aren't I?" He looked over at Donald. "I've got you on my hands for good."

Donald pressed his fingers against the dashboard as if to brace himself. "I'll get out," he said.

Pete kept driving.

"Let me out," Donald said. "I mean it, Pete."

"Do you?"

Donald hesitated. "Yes," he said.

"Be sure," Pete told him. "This is it. This is for keeps."

"I mean it."

"All right. You made the choice." Pete braked the car sharply and swung it to the shoulder of the road. He turned off the engine and got out. Trees loomed on both sides, shutting out the sky. The air was cold and musty. Pete took Donald's duffel bag from the back seat and set it down behind the car. He stood there, facing Donald in the red glow of the taillights. "It's better this way," Pete said.

Donald just looked at him. **235**

"Better for you," Pete said.

Donald hugged himself. He was shaking. "You don't have to say all that," he told Pete. "I don't blame you."

"Blame me? What the hell are you talking about? Blame me for what?"

"For anything," Donald said.

"I want to know what you mean by blame me."

"Nothing. Nothing, Pete. You'd better get going. God bless you." **240**

"That's it," Pete said. He dropped to one knee, searching the packed dirt with his hands. He didn't know what he was looking for; his hands would know when they found it.

Donald touched Pete's shoulder. "You'd better go," he said.

Somewhere in the trees Pete heard a branch snap. He stood up. He looked at Donald, then went back to the car and drove away. He drove fast, hunched over the wheel, conscious of the way he was hunched and the shallowness of his breathing, refusing to look at the mirror above his head until there was nothing behind him but darkness.

Then he said, "A hundred dollars," as if there were someone to hear.

The trees gave way to fields. Metal fences ran beside the road, plastered with windblown scraps of paper. Tule fog hung above the ditches, spilling into the road, dimming the ghostly halogen lights that burned in the yards of the farms Pete passed. The fog left beads of water rolling up the windshield.

Pete rummaged among his cassettes. He found Pachelbel's Canon and pushed **245** it into the tape deck. When the violins began to play he leaned back and assumed an attentive expression as if he were really listening to them. He smiled to himself like a man at liberty to enjoy music, a man who has finished his work and settled his debts, done all things meet and due.

And in this way, smiling, nodding to the music, he went another mile or so and pretended that he was not already slowing down, that he was not going to turn back, that he would be able to drive on like this, alone, and have the right answer when his wife stood before him in the doorway of his home and asked, Where is he? Where is your brother?

approximately 5100 words

Tobias Wolff, "The Rich Brother," *Back in the World,* (New York: Houghton Mifflin, 1985) pp. 197–221. Copyright © by Tobias Wolff. Reprinted by permission of International Creative Management, Inc.

Questions for Writing/Discussion

1. In what ways are Pete and Donald alike? How are they different from each other?

2. Which of the two brothers did you find more admirable? Why?

3. What is the story's *theme?* How does the value system of each brother help develop the theme?

4. How realistically is the relationship of the two brothers portrayed? How does it compare to your own relationship with siblings? With acquaintances or close friends?

5. The story's ending is indefinite, allowing the reader to reach his or her own conclusion. Rewrite the ending. Decide whether Pete actually does go back and get Donald, or if he is going to sever his ties with Donald completely.

JOURNAL ENTRY

All of us live with some degree of stress. Sometimes, as indicated in the essay "Control Freaks," we create our own stresses. The textbook selection "Personality, Stress, and Health" discussed ways to handle stress. In "The Rich Brother," Pete experiences obvious stress in trying to "take care of" his brother. Write a journal entry discussing how you react to stressful situations and describing the coping strategies that work best for you.

chapter

6

Refining Reading Style
and Improving Rate

This chapter will help you

◆   Assess your current reading rate.
◆   Dispel some of the myths about the reading process and reading rate.
◆   Learn strategies for becoming a faster, more dynamic reader.

❖❖❖

Before reading, think about these questions.

◆   Do you want to become a faster reader?
◆   What are some of your present reading habits that prevent you from reading
    more rapidly?
◆   What steps could you take to increase your reading rate?

❖❖❖

Jot down your thoughts about reading as you consider
improving your rate. _____

_____

_____

❖ Facts And Myths

Fast and Slow Readers

In Chapter 1, we emphasized the vast amount of printed material that our Information Age is producing at speeds seemingly impossible for the average reader to handle. To cope with the mounting paper blitz, speed-reading classes are popular on many college campuses. These can be very valuable, time permitting, but the major thrust of these courses is getting students to practice, practice, and practice. We can reduce their philosophy to a reading rate improvement formula:

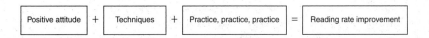

Slow readers usually dislike reading because for them it is so time-consuming. Therefore, they read very little and consequently never practice enough to improve. This, in turn, compounds the problem because they also fail to improve their vocabulary. An enriched vocabulary helps in reading faster because the printed page contains a much broader vocabulary than the spoken words heard and used. On the other hand, better readers usually read a great deal, enjoy reading, and are constantly improving both their vocabulary and reading skills. As a result, those who are good readers get better while those who aren't, don't.

So you need to begin this chapter by wanting to read faster and trust that you can do it. You have already engaged in strategies such as previewing and predicting ideas that assist you in reading more quickly. Now, developing a positive attitude and learning some simple techniques will markedly improve your rate while you maintain good comprehension.

Reading Rate Evaluation

Read the following article at your normal reading speed. Record your reading time (in minutes and seconds) in the space provided at the end of the article. Then, without referring back to the article, answer the questions that follow. After you answer the questions, use the chart provided to convert your time into a reading rate of words per minute. To find out your comprehension, check your answers with those at the end of this chapter. By knowing both your present reading rate and your comprehension at that rate, you can best use the information that follows.

The author of the following article has written more than forty books and is a well-known philosopher. In this essay, he outlines his secrets of success.

Success Means Never Feeling Tired

Mortimer J. Adler

Failure is probably the most fatiguing experi- **1** ence a person ever has. There is nothing more enervating than not succeeding—being blocked, not moving ahead. It is a vicious circle. Failure breeds fatigue, and the fatigue makes it harder to get to work, which compounds the failure.

We experience this tiredness in two main **2** ways: as start-up fatigue and performance fatigue. In the former case, we keep putting off a task that we are under some compulsion to discharge. Either because it is too tedious or too difficult, we shirk it. And the longer we postpone it, the more tired we feel.

Such start-up fatigue is very real, even if not **3** actually physical, not something in our muscles and bones. The remedy is obvious, though perhaps not easy to apply: an exertion of willpower. The moment I find myself turning away from a job, or putting it under a pile of other things I have to do, I clear my desk of everything else and attack the objectionable item first. To prevent start-up fatigue, always tackle the most difficult job first.

Years ago, when editing *Great Books of the* **4** *Western World,* I undertook to write 102 essays, one on each of the great ideas discussed by the authors of those books. The writing took me two and one-half years, working at it—among my other tasks—seven days a week. I would never have finished if I had allowed myself to write first about the ideas I found easiest to expound. Applying my own rule, I determined to write the essays in strict alphabetical order, from ANGEL TO WORLD, never letting myself skip a tough idea. And I always started the day's work with the difficult task of essay-writing. Experience proved, once again, that the rule works.

Performance fatigue is more difficult to **5** handle. Here we are not reluctant to get started, but we cannot seem to do the job right. Its difficulties appear insurmountable and, however hard we work, we fail again and again. That mounting experience of failure carries with it an ever-increasing burden of mental fatigue. In such a situation, I work as hard as I can—then let the unconscious take over.

When I was planning the 15th edition of **6** *Encyclopedia Britannica,* I had to create a topical table of contents for its alphabetically arranged articles. Nothing like this had ever been done before, and day after day I kept coming up with solutions that fell short. My fatigue became almost overpowering.

One day, mentally exhausted, I put down **7** on paper all the reasons why this problem could *not* be solved. I tried to convince myself that what appeared insoluble really *was* insoluble, that the trouble was with the problem, not me. Having gained some relief, I sat back in an easy chair and went to sleep.

An hour or so later, I woke up suddenly **8** with the solution clearly in mind. In the weeks that followed, the correctness of the solution summoned up by my unconscious mind was confirmed at every step. Though I worked every bit as hard, if not harder, than before, my work was not attended by any weariness or fatigue. Success was now as exhilarating as failure had been depressing. I was experiencing the joy of what psychologists today call "flow." Life offers few pleasures more invigorating than the successful exercise of our faculties. It unleashes energies for additional work.

Sometimes the snare is not in the problem **9** itself, but in the social situation—or so it appears. Other people somehow seem to prevent us from succeeding. But, as Shakespeare wrote, "The fault, dear Brutus, is not in our stars but in ourselves." Why blame other people and shrug off our own responsibility for misunderstandings? Doing a job successfully means doing whatever is necessary—and that *includes* winning the cooperation of others.

More often, the snare that blocks us is purely personal. Subject to human distractions, we let personal problems weigh on us, producing a fatigue-failure that blocks our productivity in every sphere. **10**

A friend of mine went into a decline over a family problem that she had let slide. Her daughter had secretly married a man she thought her father would disapprove of. The daughter told her mother but made her promise to keep silent. Worrying about the problem, and carrying a burden of guilt over the secrecy, exhausted the mother. Her fatigue spilled over into her job and turned her usual successes there into failures. She was saved from serious depression only when other people intervened and told the father—who didn't display any of the anticipated negative reaction. It seems incredible that a person can allow his or her life to get snarled up in this fashion, but that is how problems can fester if they aren't solved as they come along. **11**

So, our first step should be to use inexplicable fatigue that has no physical base as a radar—an early-warning system—and trace the fatigue to its source; to find the defeat we are papering over and not admitting. Then we must diagnose the cause of this failure. In rare cases, it may be that the task really is too difficult for us, that we are in over our head. If so, we can acknowledge the fact and bow out. Or the block may simply be in refusing to confront the problem. In most cases, it can be solved by patient attention to the task at hand—with all the skill and resolution we can muster. That, plus the inspired help of the unconscious. **12**

I have already given an example of one way of achieving a breakthrough. First, put down all the reasons why the problem is insoluble. Try to box yourself in, like Houdini, so no escape appears possible. Only then, like Houdini, can you break out. Having tied yourself up in knots, stop thinking consciously about the problem for a while. Let your unconscious work on untying the knots. Nine times out of ten, it will come up with a solution. **13**

The worst mistake we can make is to regard mental fatigue as if it were physical fatigue. We can recuperate from the latter by giving our bodies a chance to rest. But mental fatigue that results from failure cannot be removed by giving in to it and taking a rest. That just makes matters worse. Whatever the specific stumbling block is, it must be cleared up, and fast, before the fatigue of failure swamps us. **14**

Human beings, I believe, *must* try to succeed. This necessity is built into our biological background. Without trying to define success, it's enough to say that it is related to continuous peak performance, to doing tasks and solving problems as they come along. It is experiencing the exuberance, the joy, the "flow" that goes with the unimpeded exercise of one's human capabilities. **15**

Success, then, means never feeling tired. **16**

approximately 1100 words

Reading Time: _____ min. _____ sec.

Answer the comprehension questions that follow, and refer to the reading rate chart to find your words per minute.

COMPREHENSION CHECK

Write the letter that indicates the best possible answer in the space provided.

_____ 1. The main idea of this article is that

    a. mental fatigue is a normal experience.
    b. success cannot be defined or explained.
    c. failure is the result of mental and physical fatigue.
    d. positive attitudes about tasks foster success and help lessen fatigue.

_____ 2. Start-up fatigue is caused by

    a. putting off a task that must be done.
    b. getting tired quickly.
    c. feeling pressure as soon as a task is started.
    d. being bored.

_____ 3. Performance fatigue results from

    a. not having all needed supplies handy.
    b. fear of what others will say.
    c. a seeming inability to do the job right.
    d. a lack of cooperation.

_____ 4. The amount of time it took Adler to complete writing 102 essays for the Great Books series was

    a. one year.
    b. two and a half years.
    c. five and a half years.
    d. ten years.

_____ 5. Adler indicates that in problem solving

    a. the unconscious plays an important role.
    b. the unconscious plays a minor role.
    c. we need the cooperation of family and friends.
    d. mental and physical fatigue are inevitable.

_____ 6. The author believes that

    a. success exhilarates us.
    b. success makes us feel more energetic.
    c. success creates blocks in problem solving.
    d. both a and b.

_____ 7. Fatigue-failure can result from
    a. productivity.
    b. reasoning.
    c. willingness.
    d. personal problems.

Answer the next three questions in complete sentences.

8. Explain how the title of the article is related to the main idea. _____

_____

_____

9. Why does Adler think we blunder greatly if we treat mental fatigue as if it were physical fatigue?

_____

_____

10. Why does Adler state in the first line of paragraph 15 that "human beings ... must try to succeed"?

_____

_____

Check your responses at the end of this chapter.

"THE BOOK YOU TOOK OUT ON SPEED READING IS 12 MONTHS OVERDUE."

Reading time (min. & sec.)	Rate (words per minute)	Reading time (min. & sec.)	Rate (words per minute)
1:00	1100	5:30	200
1:15	880	5:45	191
1:30	733	6:00	183
1:45	639	6:15	176
2:00	550	6:30	169
2:15	489	6:45	163
2:30	440	7:00	157
2:45	400	7:15	152
3:00	367	7:30	147
3:15	338	7:45	142
3:30	314	8:00	138
3:45	293	8:15	133
4:00	275	8:30	129
4:15	259	8:45	126
4:30	244	9:00	122
4:45	232	9:15	119
5:00	220	9:30	116
5:15	210	9:45	113

Convert your reading time (minutes and seconds) to your reading rate (words per minute) by checking the rate chart above. Fill in your words per minute. _____

Now you have a base reading rate to measure against as you work to improve it.

Myths and Misconceptions

How many of the following myths about reading have influenced your reading rate?

Myth 1: Concentrating on Each Word in Print Aids Comprehension and Memory

If you concentrate on each separate word while reading, you create comprehension problems for yourself. In addition, often you may find that after you read a passage you cannot recall much of it. Research shows that in just one second, the brain can sort out 100 million separate messages, distinguishing between the important and the unimportant. The inefficient reader sends to the brain such "weak signals"—seemingly unrelated chunks of information—that the brain loses its focus on reading and gets distracted or bored. The eyes look at the print but the brain wanders: thinking, planning, daydreaming about unrelated topics. If you are unable to concentrate while reading or become easily bored or restless, you are probably reading too slowly to engage your mind in the reading material.

You do not speak in a faltering, robotlike fashion or pause after each word when you talk. You usually speak in groups of words. Since you think in similar fashion, why not read the same way—in idea clusters? It is the natural way to read. Your comprehension will improve if you learn to read for meaning and concentrate on ideas, not words. Recall that in Chapter 4 you noted how long, difficult sentences are more easily understood if you "chunk" the information into meaningful phrases. This practice, extended to all your reading, can help you read more rapidly.

Myth 2: The Only Way to Read Anything Is Slowly and Carefully

Many students read everything at the same habitual rate—slowly—whether it's the TV guide, the evening newspaper, a textbook, or a novel. In Chapter 1, we emphasized that efficient readers, however, learn that there is more than just one way to read. They are flexible; that is, they read different kinds of material in different ways. They vary their rate, depending on two main factors: the difficulty of the material and their purpose in reading.

While reading, do you silently say the words or need to hear each word? Then you are limiting yourself to a speed at which average people speak—fewer than 200 words a minute. You may either be vocalizing—moving your lips and saying the words in a whisper—or subvocalizing—hearing them in your head. While you cannot eliminate mentally hearing all words when you read, too much subvocalization reduces your reading rate by as much as 50 percent. Good readers tend to concentrate only on *key words,* those words that give important meaning to the passage. For example, read these two versions of the same sentence. Notice that the first sentence containing only key words can be understood as readily as the sentence in its entirety.

Important part of rocket probe—window through pictures and measurements taken

One of the most important parts of this rocket probe was the window through which many pictures and measurements would be taken.

Can you mark the key terms in the next sentence? "The window had to be extremely strong, and diamond was the only thing in the world that could do the job."*

Myth 3: Going Back Over Just-Read Material Improves Understanding

If you have the habit of "regression," constantly and needlessly going back and rereading parts of the sentences, not only will you be reading slowly but you may also have trouble understanding what you are reading. Here's what your reading may actually be like.

If you have the . . . If you have the habit of "regression," "regression," the habit of "regression," constantly and needlessly going back and "regression," constantly and needlessly going . . .

*window extremely strong/diamond could do job

The smooth, logical flow of thought is broken if you continually regress while reading. Additionally, you more than double your reading time to get through a passage.

Many people regress because they have developed this habit and lack the confidence to believe they can understand what they read the first time. At times, rereading is necessary to understand difficult material and to remember additional details. But the regression discussed here is an unnecessary, unconscious *habit*.

Myth 4: Comprehension Decreases as Rate Increases

Often students say with great pride that they read slowly because they want to be sure to get the full meaning and remember every single word. Actually, by trying to digest every word, these students read so slowly they **hamper** their comprehension and often find themselves confused and disinterested.

Readers who absorb 80 percent of what they read have very good comprehension. Striving for 100 percent all the time makes you read much more slowly than is necessary. If you try to remember everything, you can wind up remembering very little and become frustrated because of the tremendous task you have imposed on yourself. The faster, more efficient reader usually has far better comprehension than the very slow reader because the efficient reader focuses on *ideas* while reading.

Myth 5: It Is Physically Impossible to Read Rapidly Because Your Eyes Cannot Move that Quickly

Eye movement studies disprove this notion. The average first-year college student reads around 200 to 250 words per minute, but these studies indicate that it is physically possible for the eyes to see and transmit printed information to the brain at rates as high as 900 to 1000 words per minute. Beyond this rate students engage in subskills of reading: scanning (searching for a fact or item), skimming, and skipping (getting an overview). People who use the three S's are not engaged in thorough reading, but they are often using reading skills in a highly efficient way.

Our eyes do not really "read"; we read with our minds. Reading takes place when the eyes and mind work together: the eyes do 5 to 10 percent of the work, and the brain does the remaining 90 or 95 percent. The brain scans, sorts, selects, samples, and finally **assimilates** information. So the main limitations in rapid reading are our own physically imposed slow eye movements and a lack of belief that we can read faster.

Myth 6: Faster Reading Takes the Pleasure Out of Reading

It is wrong to assume that fast readers move so rapidly through print they never stop to reflect and "drink in" a favorite passage or a difficult one. Efficient readers

---

hamper (ham´ per) hinder
assimilates (ə sim´ ə lāts) absorbs, takes in, and makes part of oneself

have learned how to speed up or slow down at will, while slow readers are prisoners to slowness.

Slow readers rarely have the experience of reading a novel or a short story at one sitting. Have you ever watched a favorite movie, one you had seen in the theater, on TV? Aren't the intensity of the mood, the flow of the dialogue, the interaction of the characters, and the action of the plot rudely disturbed by all those commercials? The same can be true when a novel is read too slowly—if you always need to put it down after reading a small portion of the story. When reading more rapidly becomes automatic, you derive more pleasure from reading.

Reading Style Flexibility

Carefully study the mode and strategy chart that follows on page 280. It is an extension of the chart in Chapter 1 which pointed out how reading purpose is related to rate. In this chart, note the different strategies to use in reading, depending on your purpose and mode.

❖ Practical Strategies to Help Refine Your Reading Efficiency

Step 1: Raise Your Reading Consciousness

After reviewing the myths and misconceptions about reading discussed above, describe how you might change your previously held ideas about reading, and indicate your goals for improvement.

To refine my reading style and improve my reading rate, I should

1. _____

   _____

2. _____

   _____

As we have noted, the key to success is positive thinking. Believe in yourself and your ability to improve. Think: "I *can* read faster and better," "I *will* improve my reading rate and comprehension," "I *am* a good reader." From now on, every time you engage in the reading process, make a conscious effort to read faster and understand more. Each time you make that effort, you will push against your current reading barrier. Learn to compete with yourself, rather than against your classmates.

Mode and Strategy for Reading Different Materials

Mode	Material/Purpose	Strategy
Analytical Reading	Complex essays, technical reports, legal contracts.	Previewing; read to identify inference, make conclusions, and evaluate logic and the writer's craft. Reading and marginal notations, underlining.
Study Reading	Textbooks, problem-solving material; information to be recalled for testing; literature.	Previewing; reading and outlining; notemaking; mapping.
General Reading	Any nontechnical material read for enjoyment or good understanding of content.	Read actively with an inquiring mind, recognizing main idea and important details.
Skimming	Any printed material: a. When minimal comprehension is satisfactory for general information in newspapers, magazine articles, "junk mail," correspondence. b. For a preliminary familiarity with format and organization of lengthy or difficult material in textbook chapters, novels, instructional manuals. c. To get the gist or main idea of essays, editorials, reports.	Read titles and subtitles. Then read introductory paragraphs, opening sentences of all other paragraphs, and concluding paragraphs or summary.
Scanning	Any printed materials when looking for specific information or pertinent facts like names, dates, quantities, places. Also used for information from reference guides: Table of contents Index Appendix Dictionary Telephone directory TV schedule Want ads	Examine organization of information first—alphabetical, chronological, conceptual. Look for key ideas or words that guide rapid location of information. When looking up dates or quantity, visualize numbers. When looking for names or particular places, think of capital letters.

Step 2: Make Eye Movements Work for You

As you read, your eyes move along the lines of print in quick, jerking movements; that is, they move and then stop, move and then stop. Your eyes must stop in order to read. They cannot see the print when they are moving. The movement is so rapid, and the "stops," or "fixations," each taking a fraction of a second, are so brief, that the average person is totally unaware of this **sporadic** movement. The asterisks (*) in the following three passages represent the fixations for slow (passage 1), average (passage 2), and good (passage 3) readers. Read each passage aloud to become aware of how the number of fixations affects comprehension. Into which category of reader would you place yourself?

Passage 1: Slow Reader

A   very   slow   reader   who   often   also   has

poor   compre   hension   fixates   or   stops   at

every   single   word   and   even   divides   words

into   syllables   if   the   words   seem   too

long.   The   word   by   word   reader

plods   through   print   with   little   under

standing   of   what   is   read.

Passage 2: Average Reader

The average   reader,   on the   other hand,   tries to

see a   few words   each time   the eyes   stop

but does   so   in a helter-   skelter   way   and does

not get   much better   comprehension   than the

slow reader.   The average   reader stops   at

---

sporadic (spō rad´ ik) appearing or happening at irregular intervals

•   •   •   •

every few   words and   tries to   get meaning

•   •

from   them.

Passage 3: Good Reader

•   •   •

The efficient reader   usually fixates   in the middle

•   •

of a group of words   and reads thought units

•   •   •

during each fixation.   Better readers   do not read

•   •   •

single words.   They do not look   at the printed material

•   •   •

in a helter-skelter way.   They have trained   their eyes to work

•   •   •

in such a way   as to perceive ideas   in chunks or groups.

•   •

These are   smooth, rhythmical readers.

•   •

They read in clusters   connecting ideas naturally.

The fewer fixations you make, the more rapidly you read. To become an efficient reader, you need to look for meaningful groups of words and train your eyes and brain to fixate within the groups rather than to stop at every word or two. Take in as large a meaningful chunk of information as you can with each fixation. As you begin to practice idea clustering, you should be aware that many phrases, such as "for this reason" and "on the other hand," are often repeated and can be perceived by the mind as a single unit. Try reading this: "Inthepast whenIreadslowly I didnotsee groupsofwords." As you can see, it is possible to grasp meaning even when words are clustered together.

Practice more rapid idea clustering by separating the phrases below into meaningful groups.

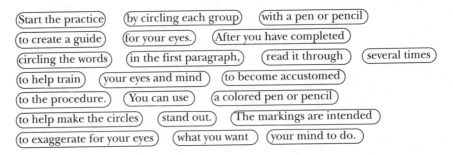

(Start the practice)   (by circling each group)   (with a pen or pencil)
(to create a guide)   (for your eyes.)   (After you have completed)
(circling the words)   (in the first paragraph,)   (read it through)   (several times)
(to help train)   (your eyes and mind)   (to become accustomed)
(to the procedure.)   (You can use)   (a colored pen or pencil)
(to help make the circles)   (stand out.)   (The markings are intended)
(to exaggerate for your eyes)   (what you want)   (your mind to do.)

The Miracle of Reading

As you effortlessly scan this paragraph, you are doing something absolutely remarkable: you're reading.

In an instant your eyes and mind are playing hunches, cutting corners, filling gaps, and dealing with an information processing task that would challenge the most ingenious computer.

For example, the eye doesn't register single letters. It takes in several at once, automatically selecting shorter or longer groupings depending on the complexity of the reading matter. A glance may cover a letter or two, or it can take in as many as 20. The average is about 7 letters at a time, with each stop taking less than a quarter of a second. For an accomplished reader to handle 350 words a minute, the eyes can linger no more than an average of four one-hundredths of a second on each letter.

From "The Miracle of Reading" in *Science Digest*, March 1981. Copyright © 1981, The Hearst Corporation

After reading the circled word groups becomes somewhat automatic for you, modify your practice by drawing slash marks between groups of words, trying to take in longer meaningful phrases.

Within a short while/ you should be able/ to read/ in groups of words/ without having to draw/ either the circles/ or slash marks./ Try using/ the slash mark method/ on these paragraphs/ from the article "The Miracle of Reading."

Scientists are intrigued by the eye's ability to speedily process unexpected information. "On the basis of computer models, we would predict that the eye can't read," says Caltech research scientist Dr. Raymond Briggs. But a computer, he points out, cannot cope with uncertainties, whereas the eye and the human brain can.

One reason, according to Briggs, is that the eye's job is done by a team: two parts of the eye communicating with two parts of the brain. The fovea, a small, specialized section of the retina, scrutinizes words for meaning and sends signals directly to the conscious, "thinking," part of the brain. But the fovea receives only a small part of the light entering the eye—usually no more than seven letters' worth at a time.

approximately 260 words

From "The Miracle of Reading" in *Science Digest*, March 1981. Copyright © 1981 by The Hearst Corporation

These practice exercises were intended to get you started in reading more than a word or two at a time. You should practice idea clustering daily on your own, until reading groups of words in longer thought units becomes an automatic procedure.

Step 3: Pace Yourself Through Print

To pace yourself through print, use a guide or marker when reading. Pacing can be done by using your finger, your entire hand, a pen or pencil, or an index card. It is an excellent way to break the habit of regression.

As you read, the eyes move from left to right to the end of one line to the beginning of the next. This movement from the end of one line to the beginning of the next is called "return sweep."

Eye movements are very much like the operation of a typewriter as the machine carriage returns to the left-hand margin. Some people do not complete the return sweep successfully. Instead, they repeatedly and continuously return to the same line.

Rereading is sometimes necessary to clarify ideas or remember information. But if you have developed the habit of regression, use your finger or hand to guide you through the lines of print. You can use an index card as a pacing device. Place your hand on the card as shown, and slide it down the column of a page of print as you read, covering the just-read material.

Why is the use of a pacer important? First, it forces you to attend to the reading instead of letting your mind wander. Second, it helps you to comprehend better after you become accustomed to it, because you are both physically and mentally involved. Again, improving rate is not something you do automatically because you have read that it is a good idea. Improving rate means practice, practice, and more practice.

How to Pace

Initially, use your whole hand. Sit in a relaxed position, moving your hand from left to right under each line as you read. What you are trying to do is get your eyes to move as rapidly as your hand. Again, you will be uncomfortable at first until you can pace rhythmically and smoothly.

Move your hand under each line and try to read that line faster than you ever have before. Practice for one minute. Now stop for a minute and try to mentally recall something of what you have read. At first you may not be able to recall much of anything because you are so involved with the mechanics of moving your hand! Each time you drill for a minute (increase it gradually to three minutes), begin reading the same information but try to take in an extra half page or more.

Always stop after each practice and try to recall what you read. Initially, this practice makes you aware of the tremendous potential you have to read faster than you do and accustoms you to the hand movements used in pacing. Gradually increase your practice time for longer periods. Also, set time goals for yourself and try to "beat the clock."

Newspapers and magazines like *Reader's Digest* are excellent to use for practice purposes. The columns are narrow and therefore the return sweep of the eye is shorter. The *Reader's Digest* has approximately 450 to 500 words on a full page with each column having between 225 and 250 words. When practicing, you can determine your words per minute with ease. For example, if you read one column in one minute, you read at approximately 225 to 250 words per minute. When reading longer selections, divide the total words read by the number of minutes used to determine your reading rate.

ACTIVITY 6.1 Pacing Practice

Practice pacing with the passage that follows. Experiment by trying to use your hand, finger, pen, pencil, or a pacing card to discover which guide best suits your own individual style. Then, answer the questions that follow the passage.

Looks Count, Says Study on Earning Power: Attractive People Are Rewarded with Higher Pay

Jonathan Marshall

1   Ten years ago, former TV news anchor Christine Craft sued a Kansas City station that demoted her for being "too ugly," a highly publicized and ultimately unsuccessful case that added "lookism" to the growing list of prejudices condemned by social critics.

2   Now the first full-blown study on the subject by economists shows that lookism carries a big price for its victims—and handsome economic rewards for those blessed with good looks.

3   The earnings gap between attractive and unattractive people, who otherwise share the same education, experience and other characteristics, rivals that between black and white or male and female workers, reported Daniel Hamermesh and Jeff Biddle, economists at the University of Texas and Michigan State University.

4   In a surprising departure from conventional wisdom, their research suggests that men earn even greater rewards for good looks and pay even greater penalties for ugliness than do women in our beauty-conscious society.

5   "The biggest effects are on the bad-looking, not the good-looking," said Hamermesh. "And the effects are if anything bigger for men than women, a result that's startling to me."

6   Attractive people tend to earn about 5 percent more per hour than those with average looks. Homely workers pull in about 7 percent less than average, other things being equal, the

researchers found. Men with below-average looks earned 9 percent less, compared with 5 percent for women.

The researchers also found that women 7 considered to be unattractive are less likely to work than other women and tend to marry men with lower levels of education.

These earnings gaps could be explained by 8 a variety of factors: employers showing simple favoritism toward attractive job applicants, a tendency by consumers or fellow employees to favor good-looking workers (thus making them more valuable to bosses) or the possibility that attractive workers have higher self-esteem and actually produce more.

PSYCHOLOGISTS' FINDINGS

Psychologists have found that attractive 9 people are widely regarded as being more intelligent, friendly, honest and confident than others—all traits that could influence employers and customers to discriminate in favor of them.

And attractive children are often rewarded 10 with more praise from parents and teachers, shaping their personality in ways that may boost their confidence and poise, both valued in the marketplace.

The economists found some evidence that 11 the earnings gap is caused by certain occupations catering to attractive employees more than others. But favoritism toward good looks and prejudice against homeliness is pervasive in most jobs, they determined.

"It's not just a matter of good-looking people 12 going to work in Hollywood and bad-looking people digging ditches," Hamermesh said. "Even within any given occupation, good-looking people make more."

THE INFLUENCE OF COSMETICS

. . . People can and do influence their looks by 13 spending on cosmetics, hair styling and fashionable clothes. In this sense "lookism" is more easily combatted than racism or sexism.

"People do intuitively understand these 14 results and invest in how well they look," Hamermesh said. "I fully expect that when these results are published, Revlon or some company will advertise that you can make 10 percent more if you buy their lipstick."

approximately 525 words

Jonathan Marshall, "Looks Count, Says Study on Earning Power," *San Francisco Chronicle*, 1 Nov. 1993

Write *Yes* or *No* in the space provided.

_____ 1. The TV news anchor who sued the station that demoted her won her case.

_____ 2. People with good looks earn more money than those who are unattractive.

_____ 3. Women pay greater penalties for ugliness than men.

_____ 4. Generally, good looks are not important or rewarding within most fields of employment.

_____ 5. It is just as difficult to combat the prejudice of "lookism" as it is to fight racism or sexism.

Check your answers at the end of the chapter.

Step 4: Stretch Your Eye Span and Expand Your Focus

An easy way to practice stretching your "eye span" and taking in longer thought units is with newspaper or magazine articles that have narrow columns of print, say five to six words on a line. Don't choose scientific or technical articles, the material should be easy so you can focus on the mechanics of reading without comprehension difficulties. Practice for about ten to fifteen minutes daily for at least a week.

Select a practice article, draw a line down the center of the column like the line drawn through "The Swelling Is Telling." Then, take a 3" × 5" card and draw a large arrow at the center from top to bottom as shown below.

Slide the card down the column of print from top to bottom, covering the previously read material and matching the arrow with the line you have drawn. You should be able to see all the words on each line and none of the white space outside the print.

This is also an excellent technique for eliminating regression. Your purpose is to force your eyes to focus on the center, yet see the entire line. At first, you may attain only limited comprehension but within a few practice sessions, you should be understanding nearly all of what you read. Within a few weeks, you will have trained your eyes and mind to simply focus in the center and read the print at either side.

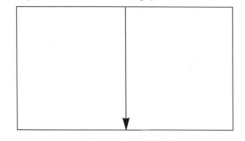

THE SWELLING IS TELLING

It seems that success can lead not only to a swollen head, but to a swollen signature as well. Students' signatures are found to be smaller after failure on a task, while after success they balloon.

As reported recently in *Psychology Today*, 28 Rhode Island college students signed their names and then had one minute to unscramble either five easy anagrams like "ohseu" (all succeeded) or five difficult ones like "crlufoneesec" (none got it right). The students then signed again. The successful students' signatures were now bigger by 45.21 square millimeters (multiplying length by

height) while the John Hancocks of those who
failed shrunk by 37.57 square millimeters.

And by the way, "ohseu" unscrambled is
"house," and "crlufoneesec" is really "fluores-
cence." O.K., now sign in please.

To further stretch your eye span, that is, to engage your peripheral vision, try a
technique called the Z-pattern. Try it now, using a pen, pencil, or your finger to follow the Z-lines drawn on the next passage. Notice that the position of the lines forces
you to begin reading about one-half inch in from each line and to make the return
sweep the same way. This helps you avoid the white space, the area on either side of
a page where no printed words appear.

When people are good-looking, we assume many other
good things about them. Because attractive people are
treated as if they have more to offer, they live up to our
positive expectations. Sadly, those less pleasing to look at
live down to our negative expectations.

In studies looking at the relationship between
attractiveness and personality, good-looking people turn
out to have higher self-esteem and to be happier, less
neurotic, and more resistant to peer pressure than those
who are less attractive. Those blessed with good looks
also have more influence on others, get higher salaries,
receive more lenient decisions in court, are thought by
their students to be superior teachers, and are more valued
as friends, colleagues, and lovers. The general pattern is
true of both men and women.

Beauty in our culture is clearly more than a superficial
matter.

Excerpt from David Popenoe, *Sociology*, p. 5

Step 5: Visualize Ideas While Reading Whenever Possible

To overcome two chronic barriers to efficient reading—vocalization (saying the words) and subvocalization (mentally hearing all the words)—try to channel your mind to think in pictures instead of words. Practice turning the printed words into images in your mind as you read, creating a mental television set for yourself. To see how this can be done, read the following excerpt.

> Joe Mondragón was thirty-six years old and for a long time he had held no steady job. He had a wife, Nancy, and three children, and his own house, which he had built with his own hands, a small tight adobe that required mudding every two or three autumns.
>
> Joe was always hard up, always hustling to make a buck. Over the years he had learned how to do almost any job. He knew everything about building houses, he knew how to mix mud and straw just right to make strong adobes that would not crumble. Though unlicensed, he could steal and lay his own plumbing, do all the electric fixtures in a house, and hire five peons at slave wages to install a septic tank that would not overflow until the day after Joe died or left town. Given half the necessary equipment, he could dig a well, and he understood everything there was to understand about pumps. He could tear down a useless tractor and piece it together again so niftily it would plow like balls of fire for at least a week before blowing up and maiming its driver; and he could disk and seed a field well and irrigate it properly.
>
> The Mondragón house was surrounded by junk, by old engines, by parts of motors, by automobile guts, refrigerator wiring, tractor innards. One shed was filled with wringer washing machines, and when Joe had the time he puttered over them until they were "running" again; then he tried—and often managed—to sell them . . . with pumps that went on the fritz (or wringer gears that neatly stripped themselves) ten minutes after Joe's three-month warranty (in writing) expired.

approximately 265 words

John Nichols, *The Milagro Beanfield War*, p. 197

As you read the above paragraph, images such as those illustrated on page 290 could come to mind, helping you to concentrate on ideas rather than words.

Put your visualization abilities to work as you read the following paragraph from Hernando Tellez's short story "Just Lather, That's All," trying to see images as if you were watching a movie. Tellez describes the thoughts of a barber who is shaving a longtime enemy.

> I could cut this throat just so, zip zip! I wouldn't give him time to complain and since he has his eyes closed he wouldn't see the glistening knife blade or my glistening eyes. But I'm trembling like a real murderer. Out of his neck a gush of blood would spout onto the sheet, on the chair, on my hands, on the floor. I would have to close the door. And the blood would keep inching along the floor, warm, **ineradicable,** uncontainable, until it

---

ineradicable (in i rad´ ə kə bəl) unable to be rooted out or got rid of

Yuk Hing Shum, DeAnza College, June 1995.
Reprinted by permission of the artist.

reached the street, like a little scarlet stream. I'm sure that one solid stroke, one deep incision, would prevent any pain. He wouldn't suffer. But what would I do with the body? Where would I hide it?

Hernando Tellez, "Just Lather, That's All" Américas

Were you able to picture the man being shaved and what would happen if the barber did cut his throat?

Step 6: Use Signal Words as Clues to Flexibility

Signal words are frequently guides to a passage's content—the writer's train of thought—as you discovered in Chapter 5. The good reader also uses these signposts to help determine how fast or how slowly to move through print. Recognizing these signals can help you become a more flexible and efficient reader.

The Fast Lane

1. *Go Words:* These words say to the reader, "More of what you just read is being continued." Therefore, you can sp—e—e—d up.

additionally, in addition	besides
again	correspondingly
also	further, furthermore
and, and so	likewise
another, other	more, moreover
as well	

2. *Examples Ahead:* These words tell you, "One or more examples will support, explain, or clarify what is being discussed." If more than one example is given, you can speed through the rest since examples usually are repetitive.

an illustration of, to illustrate	for this reason
as an example	specifically
for instance	such as

The Middle Lane—Yield Signs

With these words the author says, "Now I'm going to emphasize something important." The strategy here is to read carefully but be ready to pick up speed if conditions warrant it. While you can't race at your highest speed when you see these signals, you can venture a stop-and-go kind of action.

"Stay Alert" Signals

a central issue, concern, or factor	primarily
chiefly	the principal reason/cause
more important or significant	the basic fact, in fact
most of all	unquestionably, without question
particularly, pay particular attention	

WARNING!

The Slow Lane

1. *Caution Signals:* These signals mean, "There's a detour ahead; I'm going to change my mind, reverse my ideas, or say the opposite of what I just said." As the direction of the ideas change, you must slow down so as not to miss the shift in thought.

although, even though	on the contrary
but	otherwise
conversely	rather
despite, in spite of	unless
however, if	whether, whether or not
in contrast	while
nevertheless	

2. *Mile Markers:* Explanations may be listed in order. If this is the case, then the writer may use any of these signals.

first; second; third	first of all
last	in the first place
some of the advantages, causes	next

End-of-the-Road Signals—Stop

These signals warn the reader to slow down: "I've come to the end of explaining this idea and am going to summarize it for you or tell you what I think is most important." You should be anticipating important information at this point. The most important ideas are about to be presented in brief form or restated.

accordingly	last of all
basically	to summarize
consequently	therefore
finally	the effect
hence	the implication
in conclusion	the most important
in retrospect	thus
in summary	to recapitulate

❖ Summary

Through practice and the development of a positive attitude, you can become a better, faster reader. A good reader is one who is flexible, reads in idea clusters, and tries to avoid excessive vocalization, subvocalization, and regression, since these habits all hinder reading efficiency. At the same time, a good reader is always an active participant and is involved in what is being read.

Reading comprehension can actually improve as rate increases, and at the same time, reading can become more pleasurable.

We have suggested the following main techniques to improve reading rate:

1. Become aware of your reading habits and work to improve them.
2. Increase your eye span and read in idea clusters, grouping ideas.
3. Pace yourself through print.
4. Stretch your eye span and expand your focus.
5. Visualize ideas while reading whenever possible.
6. Use signal words as clues to improve rate, and practice, practice, practice!

ACTIVITY 6.2 Practice Improving Your Rate with Extended Readings

Begin to practice improving your reading rate with the selections that follow. Try the different techniques suggested in this chapter to see which ones best suit your reading style. *Remember to begin each practice by previewing.* After reading a selection, write down the time it took you in minutes and seconds. Then, answer the questions that follow the selection. Refer to the reading rate chart to find your rate in words per minute. Check your answers on page 305 to determine your comprehension at this reading rate.

Decide after reading the following article whether or not Elvis Presley was a "real" celebrity.

Elvis: Another Victim of Myth-Understanding

Richard Cohen

Elvis Presley, it seems, was a junkie. He was **1** allegedly cruel. He was supposedly dim-witted and not ambitious and spent money obscenely. He was sometimes violent and allegedly took unto himself as sexual toys a covey of near-adolescents whom he watched undress from behind a two-way mirror. I won't even tell you about the monkey.

But Albert Goldman will. Goldman is the **2** author of a new biography of Presley called *Elvis.* It is one of the few examples of a book that really tells you more than you want to know. Presley, Goldman says, had the emotional maturity of a 12-year-old and the appetite of a garbage disposal. He was a filthy man—literally. He hated to bathe.

What emerges from this book is a whole **3** new Presley, or if not that, at least a whole new Presley myth. It can take its place alongside the myth created by Elvis' long-time manager, Col. Tom Parker. That was the Elvis who was sweet to women, said sir and ma'am, loved his country and was in every way normal. With the book, the story of Presley comes full cycle—or almost full cycle. What comes next, of course, is the rehabilitation or, at least, an attempt to deal with the man as an entertainer. After all, he unquestionably had something.

For the moment, though, Elvis is just a cog **4** in the myth machine. He follows a pattern. First comes the making of the myth and then, sooner or later, comes the debunking of the myth. This happened to Joan Crawford, Tyrone Power, Judy Garland, John Kennedy and even Bing Crosby. They were all posthumously debunked. In the Soviet Union, people merely get dropped from the official encyclopedia.

The constant repetition of the process **5** makes you wonder what we expected in the first place. Did we think the values of these celebrities were unaffected by their (sudden) stupendous wealth and (sudden) fame? Did we think that all the money, all the adulation and all the power did not exaggerate what was worst in them? When it comes to Elvis, did we think that a man who dressed in rhinestones was in all other ways a diamond?

The answer is yes. In fact, it is the answer **6** that explains why we always fall for the myth. What we are doing is projecting, saying that if we were the ones who suddenly got rich and famous we would be unaffected. We would still keep the same old friends, and the same old values. We might get a pair of lizard cowboy boots and a Jacuzzi, but we would not throw out our morality with our old clothes. In this way, we can dream of fame but never pay its price.

But we have no idea if this is true. We are **7** not faced with the option of vast amounts of drugs or adoration—of more and more and more. Reality puts a limit on us. In a sense, we have the morality we can afford. The right combination of talent, timing and a marketing whiz like Col. Parker removed all the restrictions from Elvis' life. He was not prepared to deal with this and only he could have told us if it was worth it.

In the marketing of celebrities, everything **8**

about them gets sold. The celebrity becomes a product and is changed in the process. Everything is affected. Not just their talent, but their families and their background and their private lives get fed into the myth machine. A package is created and people buy in. They promote, they publicize, they manage, they invest the money, they secure the lovers or the limousines or the drugs.

A star becomes something of an industry, a cottage industry to the hangers-on, but something bigger to record studios, publishers, ball clubs, movie studios or television networks. They make money when the celebrity is on the way up, or on the way down. It is ironic, for 9 instance, that the same movie industry that told you Joan Crawford was such a star is now telling you what a bitch she was. Some people may now hate Crawford. Nobody, though, holds a grudge against the movie industry for lying one way or the other.

So here we have it happening to Elvis 10 Presley. He was an industry while he was alive and popular and he will continue to be one dead and infamous. In buying his records and his myth, we helped make him the person he was. Our money and our adoration took away the limitation. First we created the monster. Now we're paying to see it.

approximately 825 words

Reading Time: _____ min. _____ sec.

Richard Cohen, "Elvis: Another Victim of Myth-Understanding", *Washington Post*.
Copyright © 1980 by The Washington Post Company. Reprinted by permission.

Answer the comprehension questions that follow, and refer to the reading rate chart to find your words per minute.

COMPREHENSION CHECK

Write the letter that best completes each of the following ideas in the space provided. Remember not to look back, but to answer the questions as soon as you have finished reading.

_____ 1. The main topic of the article is

a. revealing Elvis as he was.
b. how myths about celebrities are made.
c. a final tribute to Elvis.
d. the magical life of celebrities.

_____ 2. The author's thesis is that

a. it is difficult to create myths about celebrities.
b. myths about celebrities replace their reality.
c. Elvis Presley and Colonel Parker always had numerous disagreements.
d. the public is also responsible for the myths that "make and break" celebrities.

_____ 3. The author claims that

    a. Elvis thought that fame and fortune were worth what he went through.

    b. Elvis did not believe that fame and fortune were worth what he went through.

    c. we will never know what Elvis thought about his fame and fortune.

    d. Colonel Parker stated that Elvis was satisfied with what fame and fortune had brought to him.

_____ 4. Which name was not mentioned as one who was affected by the myth machine?

    a. Joan Crawford

    b. Bing Crosby

    c. John Kennedy

    d. Joan Collins

_____ 5. The statement, "In the marketing of celebrities, everything about them gets sold," means

    a. a sale of their belongings takes place after their death.

    b. they are treated as a product and everything about them, including their private lives, gets sold.

    c. people buy the myth for their own selfish reasons.

    d. packaging and marketing go together.

_____ 6. The author's attitude is that sudden wealth and fame

    a. brings out the best in celebrities.

    b. can bring out the worst in celebrities.

    c. is not a factor to consider.

    d. does not affect celebrities who are already wealthy.

_____ 7. A statement such as "Elvis is just a cog in the myth machine" means that Elvis

    a. turns the myth machine.

    b. first fed the myth machine.

    c. created the myth machine.

    d. is just a tiny part of the myth machine.

_____ 8. We always fall for the myth about celebrities because

    a. the hype about them is contagious.

    b. celebrities are viewed as winners.

    c. we project ourselves as being "perfect" celebrities.

    d. celebrities make our lives more interesting.

_____ 9. The author finds it ironic that celebrities

a. make money for the media whether they are being admired or criticized.
b. don't always live up to their image.
c. prefer solitude to fame.
d. are unaware of their admirers and detractors.

_____ 10. Elvis continues to be "an industry" because

a. his daughter married Michael Jackson.
b. his ex-wife, Priscilla, has had many acting roles.
c. the myth of Elvis is still being exploited.
d. Graceland is visited by millions of Elvis fans.

Check your answers with those at the end of the chapter.

Reading time (min. & sec.)	Rate (words per minute)	Reading time (min. & sec.)	Rate (words per minute)
1:00	825	4:45	174
1:15	660	5:00	165
1:30	550	5:15	157
1:45	471	5:30	150
2:00	412	5:45	143
2:15	367	6:00	138
2:30	330	6:15	132
2:45	300	6:30	127
3:00	275	6:45	122
3:15	254	7:00	118
3:30	235	7:15	114
3:45	220	7:30	110
4:00	206	7:45	106
4:15	194	8:00	103
4:30	183		

Convert your reading time (minutes and seconds) to your reading rate (words per minute) by checking the rate chart above. Fill in your words per minute. _____

What are the latest findings about the math competency of U.S. students compared to students in other countries? Are American students really as "dumb" about math as the cartoon suggests?

"I wouldn't have taken Algebra if I had known there was math involved."

Bad at Math and Proud of It

Terry Tang

Millions of Americans shamelessly admit they hate mathematics. It's no wonder their kids do, too. **1**

"America 2000," [former] President Bush's education plan, aims to place U.S. students first in the world in math and science achievement by the year 2000. The latest report card makes Bush's goal seem like a bad joke. **2**

The NAEP test of 26,000 students found only 72 percent of 4th-graders can do simple addition and subtraction. One-third of 8th-graders can't multiply and divide. Fewer than half the 12th-graders can handle fractions, dec- **3**

imals, and two-step problems, and only 5 percent have a grasp of algebra and geometry.

The situation looks awful if American students are compared with those in other countries. A study by the Educational Testing Service comparing 13-year-olds in the United States, four Canadian provinces, and Great Britain, Ireland, Spain and Korea found U.S. math performance lowest overall. In a test of high-school seniors, the average Japanese student performed better in every math category than the top 5 percent of U.S. students. **4**

How does a work force so ill-prepared in **5**

math compete in the global economy? Can students who can't handle fractions hold on to jobs?

While employers struggle with incompetent workers, the National Council of Teachers of Mathematics (NCTM) and the National Research Council have been beating the drum for math-curriculum reform.   6

In 1981, the NCTM set goals for the decade. Teachers should be teaching children how to think. Math instruction should emphasize problem-solving rather than rote learning. Calculators and computers should be used at every grade level.   7

Those reforms have made little headway in 10 years. Most American students can compute, but $5 pocket calculators can perform faster than any 11-year-old. Even students who can multiply don't seem to know when to multiply.   8

Where to start?   9

Reform has to begin with parents' attitudes. Most are unaware of their children's math deficiencies. Campaigns have been waged against illiteracy, but "innumeracy" rarely gets public attention.   10

"Society says it's OK to be bad in math. It's almost a pride thing. Until we change, our kids will continue to fail. Japanese students are competent in math because their parents believe that all kids can do math," argues Jerry Johnson, a math-education professor at Western Washington University, north of Seattle.   11

Attachment to traditional ways of teaching also stymies reform. Parents who had a hard time learning math seem to believe that "what was good enough for me is good enough for my kid." Even young teachers, says Johnson, cling to methods their teachers used on them.   12

Resistance to change is nowhere more clear than in the fuss over using calculators in class.   13

"I ask parents when they last multiplied a four-digit number by a two-digit number with   14

pencil and paper. Usually they don't remember because they all use calculators. Yet people want kids to do drills because it's supposed to build character," says Reginald Waddoups, a junior-high-school math teacher in Kirkland, a Seattle suburb.

John Allen Paulos, mathematician and popular author of "Beyond Numeracy," compares the calculator quandary to debates in 15th-century Italy, where Arabic numerals replaced cumbersome Roman numerals in multiplication and division (try multiplying CXIV by LII without translating them). The academicians were wary of overreliance on the new "software."   15

Nationwide, only 3 percent of 4th-graders and 19 percent of 8th-graders are permitted free use of calculators even though reformers have pushed for calculators in all instruction.   16

Top math students are more likely to use calculators, according to the NAEP study. Lower achievers continue to work by hand basic arithmetic even in upper grades.   17

Some teachers—including Waddoups, Washington state winner of the Presidential Award for Excellence in Mathematics Teaching in 1984—moved away from repetitive drills long ago. Evidently, they're in the minority.   18

When Waddoups began teaching in the late 1960s, "new math" was gospel. Created in the 1950s by college mathematicians, new math was intended to prepare future scientists and engineers for the technology age.   19

Instead of memorizing rules, children spent time exploring the meaning behind math symbols and deriving the principles of arithmetic through deduction.   20

The aim was to improve reasoning and problem-solving skills. Beating the Soviets was the incentive, much as catching up to Japan drives reform now.   21

No curriculum change, before or since, has won such wide acceptance. Fueled by millions of dollars in grants from the National Science   22

Foundation, the movement reached nearly all classrooms—urban, suburban, rich and poor—by its second decade.

The baby-boom generation learned about **23** number theory, a topic explored in graduate school, along with arithmetic. Fourth-graders pondered the associative and commutative properties of addition, worked with number lines, and found the intersection of sets.

"Parents, however, were left out of the rev- **24** olution. A lot of parents simply gave up and told their kids, 'I can't help you,'" says Waddoups.

There were other problems. Many teachers **25** sabotaged the new curriculum by sticking to rote-memorization methods. Children who had good teachers developed insight into math principles; the less fortunate ended up without computational skills or conceptual understanding.

A backlash eventually led to the "Back to **26** Basics" movement of the 1970s. The counter-reform, a return to rigid workbooks, proved a catastrophe. Children trained to do pages of exercises froze at "word problems." Test scores, instead of rising, kept falling.

"Back to Basics was a response to what some **27** parents thought would be good for kids. It was awful, and it went too far. Many teachers saw a lot of value in new math, but by the 1970s, new math had such a bad reputation, those teachers were ignored," says Waddoups.

The pendulum may be swinging back. **28** Proposed reforms read very like goals from the 1950s, emphasizing problem-solving and discovery learning. Nostalgia for new math might even propel change. Baby-boomers, now helping their own 5th-graders with homework, are probably wondering why kids aren't being taught the distributive property of multiplication.

Of course, no one is advocating a return to **29** new math's abstraction. The key lesson from that failure—curriculum change—has to come up from teachers and parents, not down from university mathematicians.

The math crisis shows how tough reform in **30** even one subject area can be. Lack of money isn't the only, or even the biggest, obstacle.

New textbooks and more teacher training **31** would help. Ultimately, the only way to make a difference is to change what's taught and how it's taught.

Education reformers agree that elementary **32** math should include topics in geometry, measurement and probability as well as arithmetic.

Many experts believe too little new material **33** is introduced between 4th and 8th grades, making high-school math overly intensive. European schools, by contrast, teach algebra and geometry over four years instead of cramming them into two. Altering the pace could prevent kids from hitting the wall with algebra.

Too many students still approach math as **34** mind-numbing calculations that have no connection to the real world. Yet math is entirely a man-made language, based on reason.

Paulos, author and mathematician, says **35** people who hate math are usually surprised to learn that logic is math. "They're like the Molière character who was shocked to learn he had been speaking prose his whole life."

Daily life, after all, is full of "word prob- **36** lems." American students are failing because math to them exists only in books with answers in the back.

approximately 1100 words

Reading Time: _____ min. _____ sec.

Terry Tang, "Bad at Math and Proud of It," *The Seattle Times*, 14 July 1991, p. A13. Reprinted by permission.

Answer the comprehension questions that follow, and refer to the reading rate chart to find your words per minute.

COMPREHENSION CHECK

Write the letter that best completes each of the following ideas in the space provided. Remember not to look back, but to answer the questions as soon as you have finished reading.

_____ 1. It appears that Bush's goal of math excellence for students in the year 2000 will

  a. change.
  b. become a reality.
  c. not become a reality.
  d. be replaced by other goals.

_____ 2. In the United States, algebra and geometry seem to be mastered

  a. in special math classes with special math teachers.
  b. by boys chiefly.
  c. by less than a tenth of high school students.
  d. by about one-fourth of the high school students.

_____ 3. A comparison of American thirteen-year-old students to those in other countries showed that the scores for the Americans

  a. were similar.
  b. showed great variety.
  c. were in the middle.
  d. were at the bottom.

_____ 4. According to this author, attitudes about competency in math differ in the United States and

  a. Japan.
  b. England.
  c. Spain.
  d. Germany.

_____ 5. The failure of math teachers to use calculators in the classroom was compared to debates over the

  a. use of phonics.
  b. use of software.
  c. types of activities in physical education.
  d. use of Arabic numerals.

_____ 6. In the article, a math teacher claims parents believe that math drill and rote learning

  a. improve math proficiency.
  b. build character.
  c. help in problem solving.
  d. increase math accuracy.

_____ 7. The introduction of the "New Math" in the 1960s

  a. led to an end of the "Back to Basics" Movement.
  b. was meant to improve reasoning and problem-solving skills.
  c. was embraced by math teachers.
  d. was welcomed by parents.

_____ 8. The biggest obstacle to math
reform seems to be lack of

    a. money.
    b. enthusiastic students.
    c. interested parents.
    d. new textbooks and well-trained
       educators.

_____ 9. Those who favor "New Math"
in the elementary school
would include

    a. geometry.
    b. algebra.
    c. measurement.
    d. both a and c.

_____ 10. Students might view math
differently if they realized it is
based on

    a. statistics.
    b. reasoning.
    c. work force needs.
    d. simple formulas.

Check your answers with those at the end of the chapter.

Reading time (min. & sec.)	Rate (words per minute)	Reading time (min. & sec.)	Rate (words per minute)
1:00	1100	5:30	200
1:15	880	5:45	191
1:30	733	6:00	183
1:45	639	6:15	176
2:00	550	6:30	169
2:15	489	6:45	163
2:30	440	7:00	157
2:45	400	7:15	152
3:00	367	7:30	147
3:15	338	7:45	142
3:30	314	8:00	138
3:45	293	8:15	133
4:00	275	8:30	129
4:15	259	8:45	126
4:30	244	9:00	122
4:45	232	9:15	119
5:00	220	9:30	116
5:15	210	9:45	113

Convert your reading time (minutes and seconds) to your reading rate (words per minute) by checking the rate chart above. Fill in your words per minute. _____

Read the following textbook excerpt, and then try to decide whether repressed memories of childhood abuse are real or imagined.

Clashing Views in Delayed Memories of Childhood Trauma

Stephen Worchel and Wayne Shebilske

Are delayed memories of childhood trauma 1
real? The psychological community is debating
the dangers of being either too lenient or too
strict about the reliability of delayed memories
of childhood trauma. The debate ignited when
magazines, newspapers, and talk shows aroused
public interest in the topic. In 1991 *People* magazine carried stories of famous people who
reported such memories. One was Marilyn Van
Derbur, a former Miss America, who reported
that her father had sexually abused her when
she was a child and that she repressed the memory of the abuse until she was 24. Television star
Roseanne Barr Arnold told a similar story.
During psychological therapy as an adult, she
remembered that her mother had abused her
from infancy to age seven. Both parents deny
the charges. How skeptical should we be about
such delayed memories?

On one side, Elizabeth F. Loftus is a 2
spokesperson for those who stress the dangers
of being too lenient in accepting the reliability
of such memories. She warns that the memories
might be false and that accepting false memories is harmful to all concerned.

. . . Loftus reports that . . . leading state- 3
ments occur during therapy. One father hired a
private investigator to check out a therapist that
had allegedly uncovered his daughter's
repressed memory of incest. The investigator
pretended to be a patient. She complained of
nightmares and insomnia. The therapist said
that she may have hidden memories and recommended self-help books, including *Courage
to Heal: A Guide for Women and Survivors of Child
Sexual Abuse*. While the book comforts many
incest victims, however, it also includes statements that some fear could lead to false memories. The reader is told:

You may think you don't have memories, but
often as you begin to talk about what you do
remember, there emerges a constellation of
feelings, reactions, and recollections that add
up to substantial information. To say, "I was
abused" you don't need the kind of recall that
would stand up in a court of law. Often the
knowledge that you were abused starts with a
tiny feeling, an intuition. . . . Assume your feelings are valid. So far no one we have talked to
thought she might have been abused, and then
later discovered that she hadn't been. The progression always goes the other way, from suspi-
cion to confirmation. If you think you were
abused and your life shows the symptoms, then
you were.

Loftus fears that such statements might plant
false memories.

Loftus is concerned, therefore, about the 4
dangers of being too lenient about the reliability of delayed memories of childhood trauma.
She notes that false memories could destroy
families and damage the reputation of innocent people. She also worries that one person's
false memory will be used to discredit another
person's real memory.

On the other side of the issue, Judith L. 5
Herman and Mary R. Harvey are spokespersons
for the dangers of being too strict about the
reliability of delayed memories of childhood
trauma. They caution against overgeneralizing
from laboratory inductions of false childhood
memories. They reject four assumptions that
they say are needed to generalize: (1) that
patients would be as suggestible to a therapist as
they would be to a trusted brother or sister; (2)
that a therapist could plant false memories of a
detailed story without help from the family; (3)
that being influenced by false suggestions is as

likely when they concern the extreme trauma of sexual abuse as opposed to the mild trauma of being lost in a store; and (4) that therapist-induced false memories are probable enough to warrant extreme skepticism. Having rejected these assumptions about laboratory results, they look instead to clinical studies.

They review several studies. One attempted **6** to verify delayed memories of childhood sexual abuse in fifty-three women. Confirming evidence was found for 74%. Suggestive evidence was found for 9%. Only 6% could not find supporting evidence. And 11% did not try to confirm their memories.

Another study worked in the opposite **7** direction. It started with medical records of 200 children treated for childhood sexual abuse and asked the patients to recall the events 20 years later. One out of three patients did not recall the experiences that were documented in their records.

People who recall such memories after a **8** period of amnesia often seek help from therapists. Clinical experience suggests to Herman and Harvey that most patients in such cases have already recalled their delayed memories before they visit a therapist. But the patients

cling to doubts about the memories long after "most impartial observers would be convinced." That is why many therapists and self-help books encourage survivors to have confidence in their suspicions. . . . "

Herman and Harvey are concerned, there- **9** fore, about the dangers of being too skeptical about the reliability of delayed memories of childhood trauma. Sexual abuse victims have faced strong social pressures to remain silent or recant. Women's organizations have fought hard to reduce those pressures. Herman and Harvey fear that excessive skepticism will renew those pressures.

Despite many disagreements, the two sides **10** in these clashing views agree that childhood sexual abuse is a serious social problem. They also agree that children rarely make false claims. Another common theme emerges when both sides are considered together. Concerning the appropriate degree of skepticism about adult delayed memories, extremes are dangerous. Precise assessments of delayed memories are needed to reduce the human suffering that is caused by being either too lenient or too skeptical.

approximately 825 words

Reading Time: _____ min. _____ sec.

Stephen Worchel and Wayne Shebilske, "Memory and Cognition," *Principles and Applications: Psychology*, pp. 208–209. Copyright © by Prentice Hall, 1995. Reprinted by permission.

Answer the comprehension questions that follow, and refer to the reading rate chart to find your words per minute.

COMPREHENSION CHECK

Write the letter that best completes each of the following ideas in the space provided. Remember to answer the questions as soon as you have finished reading.

_____ 1. The debate over delayed memories of childhood trauma has not been sparked by
    a. magazines.
    b. newspapers.
    c. the Internet.
    d. talk shows.

_____ 2. Roseanne Arnold says she was abused until she was

    a. a television celebrity.
    b. a teenager.
    c. around seven years old.
    d. a stand-up comic.

_____ 3. Elizabeth Loftus stressed that we should

    a. believe claims of abuse.
    b. not believe claims of abuse.
    c. use caution and be skeptical of claims.
    d. allow children to sue their parents.

_____ 4. Loftus fears that self-help books on abuse may

    a. not help an abused victim to cope.
    b. point out the dangers of one's imagination.
    c. cause people to join support groups.
    d. encourage false memories.

_____ 5. Judith Herman and Mary Harvey's beliefs about repressed memory are based on

    a. self-help books.
    b. clinical studies.
    c. laboratory results.
    d. court cases.

_____ 6. In a study of 53 women to verified delayed memories of abuse, the percentage who did not try to confirm their memories was

    a. more than 15 percent.
    b. less than 15 percent.
    c. around 74 percent.
    d. between 6 and 9 percent.

_____ 7. In the study of 200 children asked to recall events twenty years later, the number who did not recall the experience was approximately

    a. 100.
    b. 85.
    c. 66.
    d. 40.

_____ 8. Therapists encourage survivors of abuse to have confidence in their suspicions because the survivors are often

    a. shy.
    b. doubtful.
    c. confused.
    d. afraid of their parents.

_____ 9. Both Loftus and Herman and Harvey would agree that childhood sexual abuse

    a. needs more media coverage.
    b. is a significant social issue.
    c. helps those who have been abused.
    d. is not debated sufficiently.

_____ 10. Regarding repressed memories, we can conclude that

    a. they will increase in the future.
    b. they will decrease in the future.
    c. accuracy in assessment is crucial.
    d. new psychological techniques are needed.

Check your answers at the end of the chapter.

Reading time (min. & sec.)	Rate (words per minute)	Reading time (min. & sec.)	Rate (words per minute)
1:00	825	4:45	174
1:15	660	5:00	165
1:30	550	5:15	157
1:45	471	5:30	150
2:00	412	5:45	143
2:15	367	6:00	138
2:30	330	6:15	132
2:45	300	6:30	127
3:00	275	6:45	122
3:15	254	7:00	118
3:30	235	7:15	114
3:45	220	7:30	110
4:00	206	7:45	106
4:15	194	8:00	103
4:30	183		

Convert your reading time (minutes and seconds) to your reading rate (words per minute) by checking the rate chart above. Fill in your words per minute. _____

Answers for Chapter 6

Reading Rate Evaluation:

"Success Means Never Feeling Tired," pp. 274-275
1. d   2. a.   3. c   4. b   5. a   6. d.   7. d
8. When we succeed at a task, we become more energetic so that we do not feel tired. The opposite occurs when we put off a task or are unsuccessful.
9. With physical fatigue, we can eliminate the problem by resting our bodies, but with mental fatigue, giving in makes it worse.
10. When we fail to succeed, it sets up a cycle of frustration that leads to a lack of energy and a sense of being tired.

Activity 6.1, p. 286

1. No   2. Yes   3. No   4. No   5. No

Activity 6.2

"Elvis: Another Victim of Myth-Understanding," pp. 294-296
1. b.   2. d.   3. c   4. d   5. b   6. b   7. d   8. c   9. a   10. c
"Bad at Math and Proud of It," pp. 300-301
1. c   2. c   3. d   4. a   5. d   6. b   7. b   8. d   9. d   10. b
"Clashing Views in Delayed Memories," pp. 303-304
1. c   2. c   3. c   4. d   5. b   6. b   7. c   8. b.   9. b   10. c

JOURNAL ENTRY

You have just completed practicing techniques that will help you to improve your present reading rate. Which of your present reading habits will you need to change in order to become a faster, more effective reader? Describe your feelings about reading faster, and write about how you plan to adopt some of the newly learned techniques to improve your reading rate.

Making Inferences and Drawing Conclusions

This chapter will help you

◆ Distinguish between a fact and an opinion.
◆ Understand the difference between valid and invalid inferences.
◆ Develop strategies for making logical inferences and drawing sound conclusions.
◆ Learn how a judgment and an **assumption** differ.

❖❖❖

Before reading, think about these questions.

◆ What criteria do you use when judging controversial issues?
◆ Why is it important to question your own conclusions about what you read?
◆ Why should you look beyond the literal meaning of what is written?

❖❖❖

Jot down your thoughts about how critically you evaluate

what you read._____

_____

_____

_____

assumption (ə sump´ shən) supposition; statement accepted as truth without proof

❖ Making Inferences: Daily Detective Work

One important aspect of critical comprehension involves making inferences while you read. *Making an inference means forming your own conclusion by reasoning on the basis of what has been suggested by a writer but not stated directly.* You practiced making inferences in earlier chapters by putting pieces of information together to draw reasonable conclusions. As a reader, you

Deduce word meanings from context.

Find unstated main ideas.

Determine a writer's implied thesis.

Recognize organizational patterns.

Inference, as it applies to reading, may be new to you, but we all make inferences daily using our intuition and feelings. We draw inferences from people's facial expressions, tone of voice, or body language. For instance, if your boss scowls at you when you arrive late for work, you can infer that she is unhappy with your tardiness. You infer from dark, gray, puffy clouds overhead that it may not be the best day for a picnic. In each case, you make an "educated," reasonable guess based on limited information, weighing known facts in light of your background knowledge and past experience. Making inferences is reasoning out what you see, or what you read.

To be a critical reader, you need to make connections between what the writer says *and* what the writer wants you to understand. When you are trying to interpret a writer's views on a topic, especially if the issue is political, economic, or social, your own cultural background and assumptions play a major role as you reason, make inferences, and draw conclusions.

Logical Reasoning Leads to Valid Inferences and Sound Conclusions

A *valid* inference is a conclusion or generalization based on clear evidence and logical reasoning about that evidence. An *invalid* inference is an assumption that is supported by inadequate evidence or arrived at through faulty logic. For example,

Most Americans get their political information from television and most say they believe information obtained from television more than that in newspapers.

Michael G. Roskin, et al. *Political Science*

Possible valid inferences from this statement might be

1. Television is shaping America's political views more than newspapers.
2. Most Americans place less value on newspaper reporting than on television news.
3. The outcome of the next presidential election will be influenced by television reporting.

Each of these inferences could be made from the statement. An inference, then, is not a statement that appears in print on the page but rather is formed through reasoning with what is given but not stated directly. In the example, the author suggests the popularity of television news over the newspaper, but none of the inferential statements are specifically expressed; they result from logically interpreting the textbook statement.

The following inferential statements would both be *invalid:*

1. It would be cheaper for Americans to buy a daily newspaper than a television set for getting the news.
2. The American public is illiterate and relies on television for information.

There is nothing in the textbook statement about cost or literacy. Usually, an invalid inference results either when a reader's thinking goes beyond what the writer has implied or when the reader's conclusion comes from his or her *own* preconceived ideas. We make sense of our world by thinking, and inferential thinking is actually reasoning and drawing conclusions from what is indirectly stated. In effect, inferential thinking is "detective thinking."

Critical readers try to uncover "hidden" or indirectly stated meanings, when they exist in much the way a detective looks for clues and evidence. When a writer suggests an idea indirectly, it is called an *implication*. The reader's inferences are attempts to understand a writer's implications. A reader *infers;* a writer *implies*. Some people refer to inference as "reading between the lines."

Reading Between the Lines

Why do writers sometimes "hide" their ideas and imply them rather than express them directly? They do so for a variety of reasons.

1. To avoid stating the obvious and to make the reading more interesting and stimulating.
2. To encourage readers to do their own thinking and draw their own conclusions.
3. To create or intensify emotions in a more artistic, literary way.
4. To conceal an unpopular notion, a biased opinion, or a persuasive appeal.
5. To manipulate the unsuspecting reader, as in cases of advertising where an association is made between a product and a desirable quality.

❖ Strategies for Making Valid Inferences

Many of the reading skills you have already acquired can be helpful as you use the following strategies to make valid inferences and draw sound conclusions.

Strategy 1: Separate the facts from the opinions.
Strategy 2: Evaluate the main ideas and supporting details.
Strategy 3: Test the logic of your inferences.

Let's begin looking at the first strategy.

Strategy 1: Separating the Facts from the Opinions

Much of what you read is designed to influence your thinking. The critical reader judges which statements to accept and which to question further by first distinguishing facts from opinions. It is not always easy to recognize whether a statement is a fact, an opinion, or a combination of both. Writers are influenced by their own opinions as they write and interpret information. Moreover, as they try to persuade you to their way of thinking, they sometimes word their opinions to appear as facts.

Additionally, your own opinions can influence you when you are evaluating persuasive writing. You may tend to respond positively to ideas that confirm your own beliefs or deny ideas contrary to your belief system. In fairness to the writer, you need to be open-minded while weighing the merits of arguments; but, at the same time, you must always examine ideas carefully so you do not accept everything in print to be truthful. When evaluating what you read, ask yourself

Is the author right about this?
Are there enough facts and valid arguments, or are the statements simply opinions?
Can the author's idea be proved?
Can it be supported?
Can anyone disagree with it?

Facts

What exactly is a fact, and how can a fact be distinguished from an opinion? *A statement of fact is one that can definitely be verified or proved or tested by experiment.* Facts can be verified, for example, in official documents, reference books, and legal records. They are based on some kind of direct evidence, experience, or observation.

All of the following statements are facts, and each can be verified.

Jonas Salk, who developed the polio vaccine, died in June 1995.

Light is essential to photosynthesis.

Every point on the circumference of a circle is the same distance from the center.

As a critical reader, you should evaluate statements of fact to determine whether they are current, **relevant,** and representative. A statement of fact may be true or false, since facts about the world change as scientists and scholars discover more information and gain new insights. The following news clipping illustrates this.

> In fourteen hundred and ninety-two, Columbus sailed the ocean blue. That much is true. But much else commonly held to be *fact* about Columbus and his four voyages to the New World is *myth,* says William Fowler, a marine historian at Northeastern University. Some popular misconceptions, Fowler says:
>
> - Columbus had to fight the accepted notion that the world was flat. The truth: "Every educated European knew the world was round by that time."
> - Queen Isabella of Spain had to sell her jewels to finance Columbus' expedition. The truth: "Spain was at the height of her power and could easily afford the expedition."
> - Columbus sailed to the New World in the Niña, Pinta and Santa Maria. The truth: Santa Maria is the correct name, but the Niña's real name was the Santa Clara, and the Pinta's real name is lost in obscurity.
>
> "1492: It's Not All True," *USA Today,* Oct. 10, 1983, p. 1

ACTIVITY 7.1

Test your current thinking by completing the following quiz prepared by psychologists Eleanor Macoby and Carol Jacklin, based on beliefs about sex differences. The psychologists examined more than 2000 books and articles dealing with sexual differences in social behavior, intellectual ability, and motivation. From this research, they determined which beliefs are backed up by evidence, which are not, and which are still inadequately tested.

On the list of twelve beliefs that follows, mark those that you think are fact (F) and those that you believe are myth (M). Compare your answers with Macoby and Jacklin's findings.

_____   1.   Girls are more "social" than boys.

_____   2.   Boys excel in mathematical ability.

_____   3.   Girls are more affected by heredity; boys by environment.

_____   4.   Boys excel in visual-spatial ability.

_____   5.   Girls have greater verbal ability than boys.

_____

relevant (rel´ ə vent) relating to the matter under consideration

_____   6.   Girls are "auditory," boys "visual."

_____   7.   Girls are better at rote learning and simple tasks. Boys are better at high-level tasks.

_____   8.   Males are more aggressive than females.

_____   9.   Boys are more analytic than girls.

_____ 10.   Girls are more suggestible than boys.

_____ 11.   Girls have lower self-esteem than boys.

_____ 12.   Girls lack motivation to achieve.

John Darley, et al. *Psychology*, Prentice Hall, 1990

Opinions

A statement of opinion cannot be proved true or false. It may not necessarily be incorrect; it just has not been proved and cannot be objectively verified. Statements of opinion usually express personal beliefs, feelings, attitudes, values, interpretations, or judgments that someone has about a subject or topic. Opinions are often based on inferences, hunches, guesses, or conclusions.

All of the following statements are opinions:

Christian Dior was the most outstanding dress designer of this century.
(*Most* outstanding? What about Coco Chanel? Liz Claiborne? Donna Karan?)
Premarital sex is the norm today.
(For whom? Everyone?)
April is the cruelest month because it is time to pay income taxes.
(The government might not agree.)

Although opinions cannot be checked for accuracy, writers need to support or back their opinions with evidence, facts, and reasons before they can convince readers. You need to determine whether stated opinions are reasonable, based on available information. The beginning of an essay on taxes illustrates this.

If April really is the cruelest month, it's not just because of the inevitability of you-know-what. Almost as bad as paying federal income taxes is having to endure all the newspaper and television reports whining about who collects them: the Internal Revenue Service. This is the month everyone takes aim at the IRS, from **civil libertarians** outraged about invasions of privacy to standard-issue libertarians outraged about taxes period. At this very moment, any newspaper editor worth his salt is on the lookout for that "IRS Hounds Elderly Widow for $2.49" story.

Richard Meyer, "Debt, Where Is Thy Sting?" p. 87

_____

civil libertarians (lib ər ter´ ē ənz) those who want full civil liberties

The author makes four statements. Are any of them supported?

_____

What does this say about much of what we read?

_____

An Informed Opinion

To strengthen an opinion, a writer may base it on facts, in which case it is considered an *informed opinion*. The reader must determine whether the thesis is presented honestly or has been slanted. If it is slanted, only favorable or unfavorable points will be presented in order to distort the truth of the situation. In an article about nuclear power plants, for example, the author may discuss only the unfavorable points to sway your thinking: "Nuclear power plants are bad because of their damaging effect on all aspects of the environment."

Finally, you must realize that most writing contains statements that combine both facts and opinions. A good reader knows where the fact ends and the opinion begins in any given statement.

Word Watch

The critical reader notices words that signal opinions rather than facts.

I believe	I suggest	She alleged	It apparently is
I conclude	I surmise	He appeared to	It seems that
I feel/think	I hold that	They usually	It probably will

A note of caution: Do not be misled into accepting statements as facts simply because they have been prefaced with any of the following expressions:

As a matter of fact	The fact of the matter is
In fact	The point is
It is a fact that	The truth is

Many times these words or phrases are followed by an opinion, as in the following statement: "The point is that not everyone should learn a foreign language." There is no fact in the statement, and whether everyone *should* learn a foreign language or not is one person's opinion.

Review the difference between a statement of fact and opinion by studying the following map before completing the next practice activity.

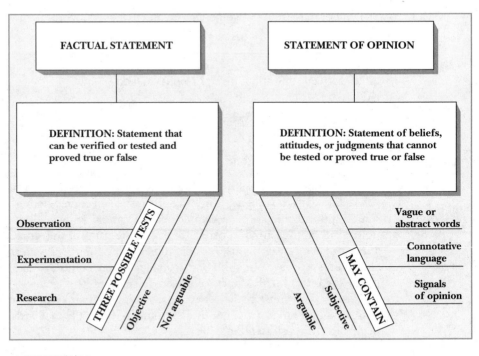

ACTIVITY 7.2

Circle the words in each of the following sentences that help you decide whether the statement is a fact, and underline the ones that signal an opinion. Then, in the space provided, place an F for a statement of fact and an O for a statement of opinion.

_____ 1. The fact is: you can have self-confidence for the asking.

"The Self-Confident Woman," New Woman, July 1985, p. 60

_____ 2. Healthy marriages are the single strongest **antidote** to many social ills—from poor school performance to teen pregnancy to poverty and crime.

"The Marriage Makeover," San Jose Mercury, 6 June 1995

_____ 3. Justice Oliver Wendell Holmes once remarked, "My freedom to swing my arm stops where the other man's nose begins."

Michael G. Roskin, et al Political Science, Prentice Hall, 1991, p. 336.

_____ 4. The technology that will predict your baby's health, either before conception or shortly after, probably can be used to produce identical copies of human embryos—that is, to clone humans.

Chicago Tribune, April 1990

---

antidote (an´ ti dōt) anything that relieves or counteracts an injurious effect

_____ 5. It is generally now agreed by scientists and philosophers of science that theories may have considerable evidence supporting them, but no theory can be said to be true.

Carol R. Ember and Melvin Ember, Anthropology

ACTIVITY 7.3

Judge whether the following statements are facts (F), opinions (O), or combinations of both (F/O). If a statement is a direct quotation, do not consider it a fact simply because someone has said it. The person making the statement may be merely expressing his or her opinion.

If a statement contains an opinion, indicate whether you can accept what is said because it reveals an informed, not a personal, opinion.

_____ 1. The valuable contribution early childhood programs can make by fostering mental health has been emphasized in a recent report by the Joint Commission on the Mental Health of Children.

Joanne Hendrick, The Whole Child: Trends in Early Education

_____ 2. The researchers found that joint custody was actually worse for children than sole custody.

Psychology Today, p. 32

_____ 3. The National Rifle Association remains one of the enduring **paradoxes** of American politics.

U.S. News & World Report, 1989

_____ 4. In spite of the reams that have been written on the subject, it may come as a surprise to learn that contraceptive techniques are age-old.

The Family, Society, and the Individual

---

paradoxes (par´ ə dăks´ əs) statements that are self-contradictory

_____ 5. Men are limited in their emotional response to anger and lust. They don't know how to express themselves when they feel confused by changing roles.

Psychology Today, Mar./Apr. 1995, p. 47

_____

_____

Making Inferences from Facts and Opinions

You will be faced with quite a challenging task when reading critically and making inferences from passages and essays rather than from simple sentences or short paragraphs.

ACTIVITY 7.4

The author makes some interesting observations about what he labels as today's "trash." Note the italicized words as you read. They should help you decide which statements are basically fact and which are opinion before you answer the questions that follow the selection. Remember to *preview* before you begin to examine the article closely.

We Love Trash

Neal Gabler

This, at least, conservatives and liberals seem to agree on: American culture is in a perilous state. Assaulted by rap music and heavy metal, made soft-headed by the novels of Robert James Waller and Danielle Steele, stimulated by violent films, narcotized by mindless TV programs and obsessed with O.J. Simpson, we slide ever closer to a cultural **abyss** filled with trash and nothing but trash.

Long before O.J. Simpson, however, Americans craved trash. The scandalous penny press, which sprang into existence in the 1830s as a vehicle for the working class, subsisted on juicy tales of criminal conduct. The case of Helen Jewitt, a young prostitute *allegedly* murdered by a rich client named Richard Robinson, held New York City rapt for months as newspapers screamed the **lurid** details and ordinary citizens debated the evidence.

It didn't take long for other **accoutrements** of trash culture to surface. In short order, violence was joined by pornography, scandal, exploitation and the mindless celebration of fame for fame's sake. By the 1870s, the **protago-**

---

abyss (ə bis´) a bottomless pit; hell

lurid (loor´ id) causing shock or horror

accoutrements (ə koo´ trə mənts) furnishings; clothes or equipment

nists of real-life crime and moral transgression were appearing on the vaudeville stage as similar protagonists today appear on tabloid TV shows: human commodities of trash.

Many conservatives concluded that democracy itself was at fault. Give people what they want, and you will get trash. As a remedy, these cultural custodians promoted **genteel** literature—stories of domesticity or aristocracy or chaste romance illustrating good and decent values. They felt the masses would learn from these as we are supposed to learn from William Bennett's* "Book of Virtues." We would uplift ourselves. **4**

To read trash, to flaunt trash, to prefer trash to "better" literature was a not-so-**subtle** way of asserting one's independence against one's social superiors. *It was a way of saying* that we are masters of our own culture. *It was a way of saying* that we are Americans. **5**

It still is. From crime pamphlets to dime novels to the "yellow press" to the movies to the tabloids to the trash of today, one theme keeps emerging. In a world culturally divided between the genteel and everything else, Americans opt for trash over art that is supposed to be good for them as much because they resent being told what they should like as because they like trash. *Seen this way*, trash is not an escape from life, as some would have it; it is an escape from seriousness, which is *no doubt why* trash in the form of our movies, TV shows, **6**

music and popular literature has become one of our chief exports. You don't have to be American to want to play hooky from high culture, though *Americans may be* prouder of it than anyone else.

To its defenders, trash has the virtue of honesty—of not **purporting** to be anything other than what it is, which is, well, trash. . . . **7**

Today's American culture, from exploitalk programs to tabloid TV to Howard Stern, is perceived as more honest and democratic than the **turgid,** domesticated arts and amusements that cultural conservatives believe *we should like*—and *would like*—if we weren't being shovel-fed trash. **8**

Trash is subversive that way. It exists to taunt. **9**

No doubt that is why cultural conservatives . . . hate it so. It is not because they want to save us from **perdition** that they rail against junk. *I suspect* it is because they want to reassert their dominance over a culture that long ago slipped out of their control even as conservatives have come to dominate politics. **10**

Damning trash and pretending that it is being **foisted** upon us by media conspirators is a clever technique—and a very old one. **11**

Most Americans, however, *know better.* Trash is how we distinguish ourselves from all the things others want us to be. Trash may not be good for us, but this we know: It is ours. **12**

approximately 675 words

Neal Gabler, "We Love Trash," *San Jose Mercury News.* Originally published in the *Los Angeles Times,* (June 6, 1995), p. 7B Copyright © by Neal Gabler. Reprinted by permission of the author.

protagonists (prō tag´ ə nists) leading characters
genteel (jen tēl´) refined in manner; polite
subtle (sut´ l) not immediately obvious; difficult to detect
purporting (pər pôrt´ ing) claiming to be or do something
turgid (tur´ jid) overornate in style or language; using big words
perdition (pər dish´ ən) eternal damnation; complete ruin
foisted (foist´ id) imposed on someone by force or deceit
*William Bennett headed the "War on Drugs" and is a leading national conservative.

1. Write whether each of the sentences in paragraph 2 is a statement of fact, (F), opinion, (O), or combined fact and opinion (F/O).

   Sentence 1: _____ Sentence 2: _____ Sentence 3: _____

2. a. Why does the author include information about "trash" from the 1800s?
   b. What inference can you make from this information?

   _____

   _____

   _____

3. Reread paragraph 3. Who are some of today's "similar protagonists" who appear on tabloid TV?

   _____

   _____

4. What facts have been included in paragraphs 5 and 6?

   _____

   _____

   What inferences does the writer want you to make from these two paragraphs?

   _____

   Do you agree with the writer's conclusions?

   _____

   _____

5. According to the author, what are the differences between the "cultural custodians" of the 1800s and the "cultural conservatives" of today?

   _____

   _____

6. Do you "love trash"? Why, or why not?

   _____

   _____

ACTIVITY 7.5

Having read about Americans' love affair with "trash," now examine the cartoon titled "U.S. Currency Redesign." On the basis of what you see and read, indicate which of the statements following the cartoon are facts (F) and which are opinions (O).

_____ 1. Pat Robertson demanded that his name appear on the redesign of the dollar bill.

_____ 2. O. J. Simpson's name is signed on the redesigned bill.

_____ 3. Cindy Crawford has more appeal than George Washington.

_____ 4. You should put an X on the bill if you want to donate to Bill Clinton's legal fund.

_____ 5. Instead of saying "ONE DOLLAR," the redesign says "ONE BUCK."

Now, let's see how many valid inferences you can draw from examining the cartoon. Write V if the inference given is valid and I if it is invalid. Write the support for the valid inferences in the space provided.

_____ 6. An extremist group is probably responsible for redesigning the dollar bill.

Support: _____

_____ 7. The cartoonist is being critical of some American values.

Support:_____

_____ 8. A dollar bill has more value when marijuana leaves are printed on it.

Support:_____

_____ 9. The cartoonist shows disapproval of the study claiming that Americans eat junk food that is far too fattening at movie theaters.

Support:_____

_____ 10. What item would you include on the redesigned bill to illustrate some American obsession that you think deserves criticism?

Notice that the ideas we call "inferences" are not stated anywhere in the picture, but you, the reader, made the inferences on the basis of *factual* evidence gathered. Inferences, then, cannot be proved true or false but are supported by the factual evidence that is directly present or stated. Using facts to make inferences about printed matter is similar to making inferences from photos.

ACTIVITY 7.6

PASSAGE 1

Read the following passages, and then mark the inferences that follow V (valid) or I (invalid). Write the *fact* or *facts* that support your valid inference below each statement in the space provided.

The uppermost **echelon** of women in corporate America have seen their salaries double over the past 10 years, to an average of $187,000, according to a 1993 study. Yet only 69 percent of the female movers and shakers at major U.S. corporations are married, versus 91 percent of males. Sure, getting to the top requires a sacrifice of time that might otherwise be spent cultivating intimate relationships; what's not clear is how much of the marriage gap reflects relationship difficulties high-earning women face just because of their salaries.

Among those who marry, female executives now pull in 66 percent of their household income. But all families increasingly rely on the woman's paycheck to keep the household humming. Layoffs, the high cost of living, medical expenses, falling male wages, the desire for a better lifestyle, and assorted other economic factors have made dual-income families a reality for 59 percent of married couples in the United States.

Working women report that their ability to bring home a paycheck increases feelings

---

echelon (esh´ ə lon) ranking of groups, units, or individuals of power, improves self-esteem, and gives them fulfillment and independence. But they also sense that society as a whole has yet to embrace female earning power as a positive.

Christy Casamassima, "Love and Work," *Psychology Today,* Mar./Apr. 1995, p. 43

_____ 1. The amount of money earned by women in powerful positions in corporate America has significantly increased over the last ten years.

Support: _____

_____ 2. The percentage of men and women who are married and who occupy powerful positions is about equal.

Support: _____

_____ 3. There is "marriage anxiety" among women in powerful positions.

Support: _____

_____ 4. Divorce occurs more often among married couples with dual incomes.

Support: _____

_____ 5. Society approves of high-salaried women in business.

Support: _____

PASSAGE 2

The Misuse of Personal Information

Sources of Personal Data

The issue with the greatest **ethical** overtones is the privacy of personal information. Some people fear that computer-based record-keeping offers too much of an opportunity for the invasion of an individual's privacy. There is indeed reason for concern. For example, credit-card users unknowingly leave a "trail" of activities and interests that, when examined and evaluated, can provide a surprisingly comprehensive personal profile.

The date and location of all credit-card transactions are recorded. In effect, when you charge lunch, gasoline, or clothing, you are creating a chronological record of where you have been and your spending habits. From this information, a good analyst could compile a very accurate profile of your lifestyle. For example, the analyst could predict how you dress by knowing the type of clothing stores you patronize. On a more personal level, records are kept that detail the duration, time, and numbers of all your telephone calls. With computers, these numbers easily can be matched to people, businesses, institutions, and telephone services. So each time you make a phone call, you also leave a record of whom or what you call. Enormous amounts of personal data are maintained on everyone by the IRS, your college, your employer, your creditors, your hospital, your insurance company, your broker, and on and on.

_____

ethical (eth´ i kəl) guided by principles of right and wrong governing the conduct of a group

We hope that information about us is up-to-date and accurate. Unfortunately, much of it is not. Laws permit us to examine our records, but first we must find them. You cannot just write to the federal government and request to see your files. To be completely sure that you examine all your federal records for completeness and accuracy, you would have to write and probably visit more than 5000 agencies that each maintain computer-based files on individuals. The same is true of computer-based personal data maintained in the private sector.

approximately 280 words

Larry Long, *Introduction to Computers and Information Systems*, pp. 440–41

_____ 1. There is potential for abuse within our present credit card system.

Support: _____

_____ 2. Pay cash—do not use credit cards.

Support: _____

_____ 3. It is difficult to find out whether information recorded about you is correct.

Support: _____

_____ 4. Considerable information has been compiled on people without their knowledge.

Support: _____

_____ 5. Congress should investigate the credit card issue.

Support: _____

PASSAGE 3

One significant difference between traditional downtowns and most new villages and suburban malls is that the latter are private property. People cannot be banned from a traditional downtown, and the right to petition on a public sidewalk is constitutionally protected. People may, however, be banned from private property, and constitutional rights, such as political pamphleteering, may be restricted. In many communities today, malls are the only public gathering places, so if the mall owners are allowed to decide who may speak in them, mall owners can determine the public's access to ideas. Candidates for political office have been banned from busy malls owned by their opponents, and so have labor union organizers.

U.S. law recognizes that private properties can perform functions traditionally associated with government. This is called the *public function doctrine*. The U.S. Supreme Court has ruled that the Constitution does not protect citizens' access to shopping centers against the wishes of the owners. Some states, however, have upheld the right of public access under their state constitutions. Each state has balanced public and private rights differently.

Edward F. Bergman, *Human Geography*, p. 320

_____ 1. Political discussions are limited at shopping malls since their owners' concern is making money.

Support: _____

_____ 2. American citizens do not have a constitutional right to campaign for office at a shopping mall.

Support: _____

_____ 3. The opinions of the Supreme Court and some states differ on the constitutional rights of citizens to public access.

Support: _____

_____ 4. Shopping malls, as gathering places, should permit the exchange of various political views.

Support: _____

_____ 5. Banning the right to petition is un-American.

Support: _____

Strategy 2: Evaluating the Main Idea and Supporting Details

Making inferences from the main ideas and supporting details is somewhat similar to making inferences from facts. You need also, however, to pay particular attention to the sequence of thought in support of the views expressed. To guide yourself in following the sequence, make marginal notations of the most important ideas, such as those you make in locating the main idea, and then evaluate these notations.

In the following passage on our competitive society, marginal notations have been made to assist you in making valid inferences. Also, important qualifying terms have been circled.

In our highly competitive society we compete for grades, athletic honors, jobs, marital partners, and almost everything else we want. (Although) we endorse certain rules for playing the game and may give grudging credit for effort, it is success that gains the rewards. The losing football team does not attract crowds or gain **plaudits** for its performance; the company that fails to gain contracts in competition with other companies is likely to go bankrupt. It is the students with superior records who win the com-

society stresses competition—only success gets rewards

Ex. of competition:

sports
business   stress
school
job

_____
plaudits (plô´ dits) rounds of applause; praise

petition for college entrance and later the competition for selection for advanced training.
(Nor) does the strain of sustained effort usually
cease when the individual leaves school. At
(almost) any occupational level a person (may be)
under considerable pressure to advance and
make the increased income often needed to
support a family. In general, most of us are
encouraged to be ambitious and "think big."
(Yet) not everyone can come in first, and striving
to do the impossible invites frustration and self-
devaluation.

James C. Coleman and Constance L. Hammen, *Contemporary Psychology and Effective Behavior*

One can infer from the paragraph that Americans are not interested in losers.
This is supported by the author's statements that "the losing team does not attract
crowds or gain plaudits." A second valid inference, based on the writer's assertion
that "striving to do the impossible invites frustration and self-devaluation," is that
competition negatively changes our self-perception.

Notice that it becomes easier to make inferences once you understand the
stated ideas and have examined the particular supporting details that develop these
ideas.

ACTIVITY 7.7

Read the following essay, separating the facts from the opinions as you make marginal notes.
On the basis of your notations, decide which of the inferences that appear after the essay are
valid. Then, write out one inference of your own.

Drug Peace

Joseph D. McNamara*

It was clear that the police chiefs were fed up 1
with the drug war. "How," the chief asked, "can
we get out of the drug war without evoking such
a vivid symbol of surrender and defeat?"

He was speaking the thoughts of many of 2
the 50 law enforcement leaders participating in

a two-day conference on drug policy held . . . at
the Hoover Institution at Stanford University.
. . . The group concluded that studying a medical and public health approach to drug control
does not mean putting rock cocaine on store
shelves next to soda pop. An evaluation of the

*Joseph D. McNamara served with the New York City Police Department and as police chief in Kansas City, Mo., and
San Jose. He is now a research fellow at the Hoover Institution, studying the effectiveness of government programs
against crime and violence.

drug war and a study of alternative methods of drug control is the way to an honorable peace.

The suggestion sends a powerful message 3 to the politicians trying to outdo each other in being tough on drugs. Ninety percent of the chiefs do not support the federal war against drugs. And the few who do support the war, nevertheless, were part of a **unanimous** vote saying that treatment, education and prevention are more useful than arrests and prison sentences.

The law enforcement leaders were also 4 unanimous in calling for a blue ribbon commission to evaluate the drug war and to study alternative methods of controlling drugs. The message to the politicians is that your political opponent cannot accuse you of being soft on drugs if you are following the recommendations of the majority of America's cops.

Ethan Nadelmann, formerly a Princeton 5 professor, opened the conference with an overview of the drug war's failure to reduce drug use and a challenge to the participants to put aside their moral views on drug use and to consider ways to minimize the harm being done to drug users and society.

Nadelmann was followed by professor 6 Jerome Skolnick of UC-Berkeley, who described studies showing that successful prosecutions of drug rings led to increased homicides and that successful seizures of drugs by the government sometimes led drug users to experiment with even more dangerous drugs.

Former Secretary of State George Shultz 7 reminded the group that powerful economic forces are at work in the illegal drug market and that it is essential to find a way to reduce the demand that leads to such **exorbitant** profits for drug dealers.

Baltimore Mayor Kurt Schmoke was the 8

show stopper. He described how his **constituents,** most of whom are African-Americans, re-elected him after he had called for the "medicalization" of anti-drug efforts—treating users as people needing help instead of merely jailing them as criminals . . . . Schmoke also described a school visit during which children told him that most of the youngsters dropping out of school did so not because they were hooked on drugs—they were hooked on easy drug money. Schmoke, because of his closeness to African-American neighborhoods, was able to counter Congressman Charles Rangel's charges that it is genocide to consider medicalization approaches to drug control. Schmoke said the drug war itself has a negative effect on African-Americans.

. . . Two federal judges, Vaughn Walker 9 and Robert Sweet, spoke of the inappropriateness of relying upon criminal law enforcement to control the personal behavior of drug use and the cruelty of imposing 10-year mandatory sentences on first-time drug offenders who had committed no other crime.

[Former] San Francisco Mayor Frank 10 Jordan told how his program of sterile needle exchange had lessened the danger of AIDS not only for intravenous drug users but also for the public and police officers. Professor Alfred Blumstein of Carnegie-Mellon University provided a **somber** description of how the illegal drug market had caused the juvenile homicide rate to explode. Easy availability of guns and dope money resulted in the juvenile murder rate by firearms more than doubling nationally since 1985. Blumstein also reported that drug enforcement and punishment fell disproportionately on non-whites.

I pointed out that truth is another casualty 11

---

unanimous (yōō nan´ ə məs) sharing the same opinions or views; in complete agreement
exorbitant (eg zor´ bə tənt) excessive; extravagant
constituents (kən stich´ ōō ənts) voters; serving as part of a whole
somber (som´ bər) dismal; gloomy

in the drug war. During my 18 years as a police chief and more than 35 years in law enforcement, we often celebrated "victories," yet almost everyone in law enforcement believes the drug problem is worse now. Furthermore, it does not make sense to have peace officers in a war.

Gen. Colin Powell once said a soldier's duty 12 is to kill the enemy. The first duty of the police is to protect human lives, including the lives of people unfortunate enough to be addicted to drugs. In addition, every week somewhere across the country there is another police scan- dal related to the drug war—corruption, bru- tality and even armed robberies by cops in uni- form, as well as consistent violations of civil rights by officers who feel that anything goes in a war.

It is not surprising that when law enforce- 13 ment leaders spend two days analyzing the drug problem, they conclude that the drug war is **futile.** If the president and Congress take the time to reflect on drugs the way the top cops did, they too, would support a study of how to find peace, and an honorable end to the war on drugs.

approximately 825 words

Joseph D. McNamara, "Drug Peace," *San Jose Mercury,* 17 May, p. 7-B. Copyright © 1995. Reprinted by permission.

Write V (valid) or I (invalid) for each of the following inferences based on "Drug Peace." Space is provided after each statement for your support.

_____ 1. Law enforcement leaders disagree as to whether education and treatment of drug users is more beneficial than arrest and imprisonment of drug sellers.

Support: _____

_____ 2. The author has failed to support his main ideas and thesis.

Support: _____

_____ 3. The "war on drugs" will be won only if the government's present methods continue.

Support: _____

_____ 4. Needle exchange among drug users in one city appears to be working.

Support: _____

_____ 5. The American people agree with and support the approach of drug enforcement leaders in controlling drugs.

Support: _____

_____ 6. Your inference:

_____

Support: _____

_____

futile (fyo͞o´ təl) useless; ineffective

Be Aware of Signal Words That Qualify the Meaning of the Main Idea

As you recall from your study of fact and opinion, you need to be aware of words that qualify meanings. The chart following groups the major signal words into four categories according to how they qualify a statement or what they imply about the author's attitude toward his or her statements.

Signal Words That Qualify Meaning

Signal Words of Inference		
The following words may signal an implication *by the writer.* Recall that the writer implies, and the reader infers.		
assumption	it is assumed; one can assume; the assumption is	
implication	this implies; it may be implied; the result implies	
inference	one can infer; this may infer; the inference is	
suggestion	this may suggest; it could be suggested; the suggestion here is	
Absolute Signal Words		
These words should make the reader reject a statement unless there is strong support.		
always	definitely	irrefutably
assuredly	indisputably	undeniably
certainly	invariably	without question
Probability Signal Words		
These words suggest that the information may be accurate but that other possibilities may exist.		
almost	probably	
presumably	there is little question	
Possibility Signal Words		
These words suggest that the ideas are subject to debate and that there is doubt as to their complete validity.		
apparently	perhaps	
could be	possibly	
likely	seems	
may/maybe	seemingly	
might	somewhat	

ACTIVITY 7.8

Underline the qualifying word(s) in each sentence. In the space provided, explain what the term implies, and write why you do or do not agree with what is stated.

1. The telephone as we know it today will probably disappear and be replaced by a multifunctional communication workstation.

   Ricky W. Griffin and Ronald J. Ebert *Business*

   Qualifying term implies: _____

2. Becoming the largest group of oppressed people is always frightening for those above you, those under you, and those who have been at your side.

   Felix Jiminez, "Dangerous Liaisons," *Hispanic*, April 1990

   Qualifying term implies: _____

3. The emerging field of human gene therapy offers perhaps the most exciting possibilities for profound and painless treatment of human ills.

   Michael Schrage, "If Market Won't Pay for Gene Therapy," *San Jose Mercury*, 2 Nov. 1990, p. 1

   Qualifying term implies: _____

4. If ten percent of the 1992 high school class is black and thirty percent is Hispanic, the University of California, the state colleges and the community colleges would presumably have to try to get the same proportion in their graduating classes four or five years later.

   "Worship of Ethnic Diversity," *Peninsula Times Tribune*, 18 July 1991, p. B-4

   Qualifying term implies: _____

5. While a victim of sexual assault may come out of the ordeal without a scrape, the psychological scars are inescapable.

   "A Conspiracy of Silent Abuse . . . " *USA Today*, May 1988, p. 1

   Qualifying term implies: _____

ACTIVITY 7.9 **Finding the Significance of Signal Words in Textbook Passages**

Read the following textbook selection about ancient civilizations. Underline each of the qualifying terms, which will help you determine how valid the writers' implications and how sound the conclusions are. Then answer the questions that follow.

Archeological Inferences About Civilization

The most ancient civilizations have been studied by archeologists rather than historians because those civilizations evolved before the advent of writing. How do archeologists infer that a particular people in the preliterate past had social classes, cities, or centralized government?

As we have noted, it appears that the earliest Neolithic societies were *egalitarian:* people did not differ much in wealth, prestige, or power. Some later societies show signs of social inequality. One kind of evidence of inequality in an ancient society is provided by burial finds. Archeologists generally assume that inequality in death reflects inequality in life, at least in status and perhaps also in wealth and power. Thus, we can be fairly sure that a society had differences in status if only some people were buried with special objects, such as jewelry or pots filled with food. And we can be fairly sure that high status was assigned at birth rather than achieved in later life if we find noticeable differences in children's tombs. For example, some (but not all) child burials from as early as 5500 to 5000 B.C. at Tell es-Sawwan in Iraq, and from about 800 B.C. at La Venta in Mexico, are filled with statues and ornaments suggesting that some children had high status from birth. But burials indicating differences in status do not necessarily mean a society had significant differences in wealth. It is only when archeologists find other substantial differences, as in house size and furnishings, that we can be sure the society had different socioeconomic classes of people.

approximately 250 words

Carol R. Ember and Melvin Ember, *Anthropology,* pp. 154–155

1. State at least one conclusion that archeologists have reached about people who lived in the period before writing was invented.

_____

_____

2. Is the archeologists' assumption that "inequality in death reflects inequality in life" a valid one? Why or why not?

_____

_____

3. What inferences can you make from paragraph 2, where the authors use the qualifying term "fairly sure" about conclusions you should reach?

_____

_____

_____

Strategy 3: Assessing the Logic of Your Inferences and Sound Conclusions

You can assess the logic of your inferences by making a check mark in the margin by the evidence that supports it. If you can find no support, the inference is probably unreliable. The more support presented for the inference, the more likely it is to be valid.

Use two key questions to help you judge the logic of your inferences.

• What support validates my inference?

Ask: Is this what has been suggested? Can this inference be justified?
- Is my inference a valid one?

Ask: Does it make sense? Is it reasonable based on the facts? Is the development of ideas logical?

Use these same key questions when drawing conclusions from inferences you have made, substituting the word *conclusion.*

- What support has the author provided for the conclusion I have drawn?
- Is my conclusion valid?

ACTIVITY 7.10 **Practice Using All the Strategies to Make Valid Inferences and to Draw Sound Conclusions**

Read each of the following passages, making marginal notations and circling words that may qualify the writer's assertions and implications. Place check marks by phrases that may lead to conclusions.

1. For each statement, circle the letter that makes it a valid inference.
2. Answer the questions that help in assessing whether your reasoning is logical.

PASSAGE 1

Does the threat of the death penalty deter people from murderous behavior more than the threat of imprisonment for life? We do not yet know with anything even approaching certainty whether the death penalty does or does not deter. The question is clearly **empirical,** and it is likely that sophisticated statistical techniques will eventually permit us an answer.

Professor Isaac Ehrlich and his colleagues, utilizing his statistical techniques, argue that there can be little doubt about the ability of the death penalty to deter. Ehrlich concludes that each additional execution prevents about seven or eight people from committing murder. All statistical arguments on the death penalty are, however, excruciatingly complex. Some critics, for example, have argued that increased likelihood of execution leads juries to convict fewer people, thereby offsetting the deterrent effect. If anything, the empirical evidence is that the death penalty *does* deter. But this is inevitably open to dispute. As a result, firm conclusions that the death penalty either does or does not deter are unwarranted and usually determined by one's psychological and moral leanings.

Steven Goldberg, "So What if the Death Penalty Deters," *National Review,* 30 June 1989, p. 42

---

empirical (em pir´ i kəl) relying or based on experiment or experience

1. The author implies that the death penalty
   a. definitely deters crime.
   b. probably deters crime.
   c. may possibly deter crime.
   d. allegedly deters crime.

   Support: _____

   _____

2. The author reasons and concludes that
   a. life imprisonment is a stronger deterrent to crime than the death penalty.
   b. statistical studies can give us the answers.
   c. the more people are executed, the more juries impose heavier sentences on people.
   d. there is no basis for arriving at a definite conclusion about the effectiveness of the death penalty.

   Support: _____

   _____

3. List three qualifying terms you needed to be aware of that the writer used.

   _____   _____   _____

PASSAGE 2

International Business

It is not surprising, then, that the annals of business abound in legends about managers who made foolish decisions because they failed to familiarize themselves with the foreign markets in which they hoped to do business. Estée Lauder, for example, launched an Italian cosmetics line with a picture of a model holding some flowers. The approach was conventional—and seemingly harmless—enough. Unfortunately, the flowers chosen were the kind traditionally used at Italian funerals—hardly the image that Lauder intended to communicate. Another U.S. firm introduced a cooking oil into South America with a Spanish name that translated as "jackass oil." Because of such misadventures, before Marriott opens a hotel in a foreign country, it sends a team of managers to study every facet of the economy and business system for several months.

Planning difficulties, of course, are compounded by difficulties in organizing, leading, and controlling. An organizational structure that works well in one country may not work as well in others. Management techniques that lead to high worker productivity in the United States may offend workers in Japan or the United Kingdom. Accounting and other control systems are well developed in U.S. firms but may be unsophisticated or even nonexistent in developing nations.

Ronald J. Ebert and Ricky W. Griffin, *Business Essentials*, p. 76

1. The author implies that
   a. business in foreign countries requires much cash flow.
   b. prejudice creates problems in foreign trade.
   c. it takes skillful management to achieve success in foreign trade.
   d. business abroad may be harmful to business at home.

   Support: _____

   _____

2. It is reasonable to conclude that in business dealings in foreign countries,
   a. it is easy to make errors.
   b. cosmetics and flowers are two industries to avoid.
   c. the American government should play a stronger legal role.
   d. difficulties between countries should be settled in courts.

   Support: _____

   _____

3. Is it wise to assume that knowledge of what works best in one country will
   transfer to another country? Why, or why not?

   _____

4. What "business misadventure" did you find most amusing?

   _____

PASSAGE 3

Read about what some parents may consider a "desirable" marriage.

Turning now to heterosexual behavior, what kinds of societies are more permissive than others? Although we do not as yet understand the reasons, we do know that greater restrictiveness toward premarital sex tends to occur in more complex societies—societies that have hierarchies of political officials, part-time or full-time craft specialists, cities and towns, and class **stratification.** It may be that as social inequality increases and various groups come to have differential wealth, parents become more concerned with preventing their children from marrying "beneath them." Permissiveness toward premarital sexual relationships might lead a person to become attached to someone who would not be considered a desirable marriage partner. Even worse (from the family's point of view), such "unsuitable" sexual **liaisons** might result in a pregnancy that could make it impossible for a girl to marry "well." Controlling mating, then, may be a way of trying to control property.

"Sex and Culture," Carol R. Ember and Melvin Ember, *Anthropology,* p. 323

_____

stratification (strat´ ə fi cá shən) arrangement in layers
liaisons (lē´ ə zänz´) links between two units

1. Concerning heterosexual behavior, the author wants you to conclude that
   a. sociologists understand the reasons for permissive sexual behavior.
   b. permissive sexual behavior is the result of too much wealth.
   c. whether or not a society is permissive as to sexual behavior may depend on economic factors.
   d. restrictive sexual **mores** lead to rebellion by adolescents.

   Support: _____

   _____

2. After considering the informed opinion of the author, you could conclude that
   a. primitive societies have many restrictions concerning sex.
   b. industrialized nations have more restrictions concerning sex than developing nations.
   c. different religions have different sexual taboos.
   d. permissiveness towards sex is a biological question.

   Support: _____

   _____

3. List several qualifying terms from this passage.

   _____

4. The United States fits the writer's criteria for a type of society with specific sexual mores. Think of the American sexual revolution of the last twenty years. Does this "revolution" strengthen or diminish the author's conclusions?

   _____

   _____

PASSAGE 4

Read to decide whether militia groups are a serious threat to the American government and its citizens.

The Mind of the Militias

Peter Doshock

. . . However concerned they may be about defending the Bill of Rights, militias aren't running through the woods waving copies of the Constitution.

---

mores (môr´ āz) traditional rules or customs of a group

"They want access to weapons," says Greg Moffat, Sheriff of Idaho's Madison County, "and I'm not talking about small arms: tanks, missiles, high explosives." Some groups acquire special equipment like night-vision goggles; the Florida State Militia is allegedly capable of defending themselves against chemical and biological warfare.

Extreme as that sounds, experts say it's just an extension of America's love affair with guns. And it has less to do with our frontier past—after all, Canada was founded in a similar fashion—than with a cultural vacuum. "The American obsession with guns and violence is a partial substitute for a traditional cultural base," Lifton says. If you're living in a remote region of Montana, visiting the local museum—or even checking out what's on cable—simply isn't an option. So why not shoot beer cans off a rock with a .22?

And throw in Rambo fantasies as well. The U.S. withdrawal from Vietnam was a crushing blow to men who equated American military might with their own masculine identity. . . . Blaming defeat on bureaucrats and politicians, they rejected the John Wayne model of soldiering in favor of a new American warrior: one who fights outside a corrupt political system. Thus was born the American paramilitary movement, laying the foundation for the militias who would adopt the antigovernment **rhetoric intact.**

But while a fondness for firearms and warrior fantasies might be a prerequisite for militiahood, it's by no means sufficient. "I think a lot of people joined thinking, 'Let's grab rifles, go out in the trees, and play games,'" says Moffat. "Then they found out it's a bit more than that, that they'd have to support theories that they didn't want to support."

. . . So what should we do about the militia movement? Gibson* says that it's crucial "not to **demonize** the demonizers." By expressing strong disapproval toward militia members, but not **ostracizing** them, we may be able to pull back toward the mainstream those who have one foot in the warrior world and the other in the world of job and family. The horror of the Oklahoma bombing may also bring some back: "Dead babies and social security clerks is not an image of heroic violence."

. . . The militia movement may lose steam once the new century begins—provided the government does not overreact in the interim. Most experts agree that given the militia's fears, cracking down or infiltrating them is the *worst* thing to do.

"If Congress makes militias illegal, if they pass more gun control laws, we could see these groups grow in size and scope," warns Smith.** "It's important that the government not overreact. We need to prosecute terrorist incidents, but we don't need to expand the ATF so that it becomes the Bureau of Alcohol, Tobacco, Firearms, and Fertilizer." . . .

approximately 400 words

Excerpted from Peter Doshock, "The Mind of the Militias," *Psychology Today,* (July/Aug. 1995), pp. 12–14, 70. Copyright © 1970 by Sussex Publishers. Reprinted with the permission of *Psychology Today.*

rhetoric (ret´ ər ik) way of speaking to persuade or influence someone
intact (in takt´) whole; having all parts
demonize (dē´ mə nīz) to turn into an evil person
ostracizing (os´ trə sīz ing) shutting out or banishing; excluding
*James Gibson, author of *Warrior Dreams: Paramilitary Culturel in Post-Vietnam America*
**Brent L. Smith, author of *Terrorism in America*

Lyle Cox, The Bulletin/API Wide World Photos

"Let's grab rifles, go out in the trees, and play games."

1. We can infer that members of paramilitary groups
   a. have been formed because of the *Rambo* movies.
   b. feel it is their patriotic duty to bear arms.
   c. are trying to change a political system they believe is corrupt.
   d. do not take owning firearms seriously.

   Support: _____

2. We can conclude that
   a. militia groups will disappear in the twenty-first century.
   b. militia groups will increase in the twenty-first century.
   c. Congress should outlaw military groups.
   d. We should be tough, but not extreme, with militia groups.

   Support: _____

3. List one important qualifying term from the passage.

   _____

4. Should militia groups be outlawed? Why, or why not?

   _____

ACTIVITY 7.11

In addition to making inferences and drawing conclusions from written text, you can draw inferences from poetry. What inference can be made from the following poem by Maya Angelou?

> . . . Mirror twins are different
> although their features jibe,
> and lovers think quite different
> thoughts
> while lying side by side.
>
> We love and lose in China,
> we weep on England's moors,
> and laugh and moan in Guinea,
> and thrive on Spanish shores.
>
> We seek success in Finland,
> are born and die in Maine.
> In minor ways we differ,
> in major we're the same.
>
> I note the obvious differences
> between each sort and type,
> but we are more alike, my friends,
> than we are unalike.
>
> We are more alike, my friends,
> than we are unalike.
> We are more alike, my friends,
> than we are unalike.

Maya Angelou, untitled poem from *Wouldn't Take Nothing for My Journey Now*, pp. 124-125. Copyright © 1993 by Maya Angelou. Reprinted with the permission of Random House, Inc.

1. What does the writer suggest about human beings and their differences?

   _____

2. State one conclusion you can reach from the poem.

   _____

Inferences can also be made from cartoons dealing with social and political issues.

3. What can you infer from this cartoon? _____

_____

4. What can you infer from this cartoon? _____

_____

Scott Willis, Mercury News

5. What can you infer from this cartoon? _____

_____

ACTIVITY 7.12 **Drawing Inferences from an Essay**

The same strategies you have learned for drawing inferences and conclusions in short passages can be applied to longer ones. Read the following essay on date rape to discover the writer's position and conclusions. To help you gather evidence, marginal notes are included, and qualifying terms are circled. Study the notations after reading each paragraph.

Crisis on Campus

Avery Corman

A couple of years ago I decided to write a novel about a campus date rape. Little did I know that by the time *Prized Possessions* was published, the subject would be a burning issue at colleges and in the media—and that some critics would say that even by using the label "date rape" I was lessening the crime and blaming the victim. "Rape is rape," the staunch feminists

critics say the term "date rape" lessens the crime & blames the victim

insist. They make no distinction between **pathological** criminals leaping from behind bushes and college students who find themselves in situations where sex goes wrong on a date. Demonstrations are being waged on campuses large and small to "take back the night" from fellow students who are defined as "rapists." On one campus activists besieged men walking alone and slapped "Gotcha" stickers on them—to show what it's like to be a potential victim.

Date rape is a dreadful, disturbing crime. But if we place the solution in the hands of extremists with a rigid political agenda tailored to blame men as the historic victimizers of women, we could end up souring the relationships between a whole generation of our young people.

Before we go any further here, what exactly is going on? Did an epidemic of date rape suddenly break out across the country? Some social observers say date rapes have always been underreported and we're finally hearing the bad news. Others, the writer Stephanie Guttman chief among them, say the only epidemic is of media coverage—that date-rape surveys are seriously flawed and that rape is being redefined to include behavior that isn't rape at all. Logic tells us that more young women are now willing to come forward and say they were raped, and that date rape, a relatively new designation, catches in its net behavior that was never so identified in years past.

In my novel a character says, "One rape is too many." That's pretty much how I feel about debating the numbers. The real issue is how to eliminate the crimes.

I think one reason young men persist when they don't have consent is that in these sexually liberated times some simply refuse to hear the word "no." They say to themselves: "What's the big deal? She's not a virgin anyway." And some have been so indulged in their lives that they're not accustomed to hearing *any* kind of "no."

But what of young women? Don't they bear any responsibility? One important survey indicated that in nearly half the alleged campus date rapes, the woman had been drinking. If you raise that issue, however, many activists regard it as blaming the

---

extremists make little distinction between a criminal and when sex goes wrong

extremists have a political agenda (author's opinion)

2 views:
  a. previously underreported
  b. media hype plus cases that are not true rape

author says—more women are "coming forward"

author says young men today not accustomed to hearing "no"

survey
1/2 of alleged date rapes—women had been drinking
Paglia says women have responsibility

---

pathological (pá thə läj´ i kəl) relating to any abnormal condition

victim. Yet, the **iconoclastic** author and professor Camille Paglia has written: "Every woman must be prudent and cautious about where she goes and with whom. The (only) solution to date rape is female self-awareness and self-control. A woman's number one line of defense against rape is herself."

Well, (I think) you should include men in that line of defense. To involve women *and* men, colleges need to do what they are in business to do: educate. You need a true dialogue between the sexes on campus. You need discussion of the nature of consent. You need to raise the question of drinking and self-control. You need to do this with *all* students.

needed—
education
dialogue
discussion
all students

Camille Paglia

I don't see how you can succeed with that educational process if you begin with the view that "rape is rape," pure and simple—that men are historic victimizers and women always their victims. It (seems to) (me) the goal should be change, not blame. How are you going to get any young man to change his thinking, to raise his consciousness, if your starting point is to equate him with a stranger wielding a knife? Inevitably, the result will be resentment and anger on both sides, and this coming at a very impressionable time in the lives of young men and women.

need for change

accusations lead
to anger & frustration

Many college students today (seem) bewildered by their sexual freedom. Back in pre-sexual-revolution days when I was first dating, men were eager and women were virgins, more or less. Turning back the clock is no solution, but neither is a political war between the sexes. Open, constructive dialogue might do it. It has to. One rape is too many.

cannot turn
back the clock

approximately 800 words

Avery Corman, "Crisis on Campus," *Family Circle*, (August 13, 1991), p. 132 Copyright © 1991 by Avery Corman. Reprinted by permission of the author.

One of Corman's main ideas is that the recent upsurge in date rape as reported in surveys may need to be assessed as to its accuracy. In the first few paragraphs he says that critics of a more balanced view of looking at responsibility for date rape are often extremists with their own political agenda. He says they wage demonstrations on campuses large and small. He says that on one campus "men were harassed—to show what it's like to be a potential victim of rape." (Does he mention any campuses by name?)

1. Has Corman given factual evidence about the activities of extremist groups?

_____

_____

iconoclastic (ī kän´ ə klas´ tik) attacking established ideas

2. What group is he implying has "a political agenda?" _____

_____

In paragraph 3 Corman presents two views on the reported increase in date rape: flawed surveys and media hype on the one hand versus underreporting of date rape in the past on the other hand. He states that some social observers say that "date rapes have always been underreported." But then he adds that Stephanie Guttman, chief among them, says it is the media coverage causing the figures to soar and that the figures include behavior that isn't rape at all. What is his purpose in including her remark? What inference can you draw from it about his attitude toward critics of a more balanced approach to eliminating date rape?

3. I can infer that _____

_____

In paragraph 4 Corman states a part of his thesis: "The real issue is how to eliminate the crimes." The next four paragraphs address what needs to be done, such as educating both men and women to be responsible. He includes a statement that a recent survey "indicated that in nearly half the alleged campus date rapes, the woman had been drinking." Note the qualifying word *nearly*, the absence of the name of the survey, and the statement "the woman had been drinking," not "drunk."

4. What conclusions can you draw from this evidence? _____

_____

The writer quotes the iconoclastic author and professor Camille Paglia, who wrote, "Every woman must be prudent and cautious about where she goes and with whom. The only solution to date rape is female self-awareness and self-control. A woman's number one line of defense against rape is herself." Why does he include this quote and choose Ms. Paglia? What implication does this choice have for the reader?

5. I can infer that _____

_____

The writer addresses many questions to the reader as he builds a case for his thesis.

6. Why does he ask so many questions? _____

_____

He concludes the essay by stating that turning back the clock is not the solution and that college students are bewildered by their sexual freedom—that constructive dialogue is the key. In spite of a limited amount of actual factual statements, do you agree with his thesis that "constructive" dialogue is the key to the elimination of date rape?

7. I agree/disagree with his conclusions because _____

_____

8. What criteria would you include in a "constructive dialogue"?

_____

❖ Fallacies in Reasoning

A sound argument is one in which a conclusion or inference is *logical*. If the argument made is based on false beliefs or mistaken ideas, it is called a *fallacy*. Fallacious arguments are incorrect but can seem quite persuasive and can "sound right," particularly when they affirm your own opinions.

These are some of the most common types of fallacious reasoning used by speakers and writers in their attempt to disguise the truth.

· Appeal to Authority

This fallacy is not always easy to pinpoint. Writers may attempt to prove or disprove an argument by referring to well-known personalities who are not actually authorities on the subject being argued. Sometimes the reader does not realize how unqualified these famous people are to discuss such subjects. For example, a so-called expert from Harvard who knew nothing about teaching young children and had never taught them wrote a widely publicized book about how it should be done.

An appeal to authority is also made when celebrities endorse products or political candidates to persuade you to do the same.

· Appeal Based on Statistics

The old saying "Figures don't lie, but liars figure" applies to the use of statistics. Often, statistics presented to support an argument are insufficient, or they may be "weighted" by leaving out important information. Additionally, some statistics are almost impossible to verify. Consider the following:

> You may have read such startling statements as "Fifteen million whiteflies are being hatched every day." Can such a figure be verified? How does anyone count the number of whiteflies?

· Bandwagon—Everybody Does It, Everybody Agrees with It

The use of statements such as "Everyone agrees that we must eliminate welfare" is merely an attempt to avoid discussing the issue. The purpose in bandwagon is to make readers feel they are the only ones out of step with current thinking if their ideas on an issue differ.

· Begging the Question

Circular reasoning is another way of saying someone has "begged a question." That is, the writer supports an argument by simply repeating in different words what he or she is trying to prove. The statement says the same thing in two ways. For example, if tutors teaching you to speed-read said, "The main reason you read so slowly is that you *spend too much time on each word;* to read faster, you should practice *spending less time on each word*—that's all there is to speed-reading," they have given you the cause of slow reading twice and have offered no real solution.

· Card Stacking

With card stacking, writers ignore conflicting facts that contradict their position. Most people naturally emphasize certain facts over others, but "stacking the cards" occurs when someone deliberately fails to include crucial facts that may weaken an argument. For example, in trying to sell a house, a real estate agent may fail to inform a prospective buyer that a shopping center or a superhighway is to be built directly opposite the intended home, which will lessen the home's value.

· Either-Or Position

The fallacy of *false dilemma,* also known as "either-or," occurs when we are asked to choose between two extremes without being able to consider additional options. If you are given only two choices, both of which are unpleasant or unsatisfactory, you have a true dilemma. For example, if a jury decides a convicted murderer should *either* be sent to the gas chamber *or* be put to death by lethal injection, no choice has been given to continue life.

· Hasty Generalization

Many generalizations are made on the basis of either one or only a few examples. When writers make a generalization, it must be based on both a sufficient number of instances and a representative sample. For instance, if someone says, "The Senate investigation proves all politicians are untrustworthy and self-serving," you must question whether all members of the Senate can be labeled "untrustworthy" on the basis of this single incident.

· Questionable Cause

Consider the controversy over the increase in pregnancy among unmarried teenagers and the cause given as a "lack of responsibility on their part." This is not likely to be the only reason, but it is much easier to blame teenagers than to admit that our entire social system may need to be examined. What about lack of parental supervision? Family breakups? The influence of films and videos?

· Red Herring

The red herring is a technique for diverting attention from the main issue by introducing an irrelevant or unrelated point. The purpose, of course, is to distract the reader from the real concern. For example, if a large corporation is accused of trying to put smaller ones out of business, the corporation's CEO may argue that her corporation pays its employees more and offers extensive health care benefits. These benefits divert attention from the fact that the corporation is trying to become a monopoly.

- **Ad Hominem: "To the Man"**

  This fallacy occurs when attention is directed to the *person* making an argument rather than to the *issue*. For example, if a state official proposes cutting certain programs because of budgetary problems, he could be attacked as being insensitive and uncaring, or the official's own personal wealth could be cited in an argument against the proposal. Opponents would not even mention the fact that no money is available or that the state is on the verge of bankruptcy.

- **Ad Populum: "To the People"**

  A writer may evade the real issue by appealing to people's emotions. The writer may use positive words or phrases, such as "the American way," "our flag," or "peacekeepers," to show love of country or may resort to negative words or phrases, such as "villains," "fools," or "flag-burning nerds," to show opposition.

❖ Using Unbiased Judgments

When you make a statement such as "Good looks are important to career goals," it is an assumption—opinion you believe to be true. In contrast, when you make a judgment, you evaluate whether a statement deserves support or has merit in a particular situation. For example, are good looks important in becoming a qualified pilot, doctor, or accountant? Certainly for a model, a movie star, and a TV personality, physical appearance is important. Therefore, judgments are *reasoned* evaluations of particular ideas, concepts, and situations.

As you read, engage in a dialogue with the author, questioning whether the author is correct about his or her beliefs. At the same time, be open-minded to new ideas that may challenge those you hold. Remember that your own experience and what you know about a topic may sometimes be limited, and you may have to reevaluate some of your previously held ideas.

The following chart lists steps in arriving at valid inferences, sound conclusions, and unbiased judgments. After you have studied it, complete the final activity in this chapter.

Making Valid Inferences, Drawing Sound Conclusions, and Forming Unbiased Judgments

UNDERSTAND THE ISSUE AND PROBLEM.	Identify the thesis and supporting evidence.
↓	
SEPARATE THE FACTS FROM OPINIONS.	Verify the facts. Note whether the opinions are informed or simply the author's assumptions.
↓	
BEWARE OF BIAS.	Identify the author's bias or biases concerning the issue. Identify your own bias or biases concerning the issue.
↓	
USE YOUR EXPERIENCE.	Look to your own experience, but evaluate how limited it might be in regard to the issue.
↓	
REASON AND THINK ABOUT THE ISSUE.	Identify fallacies in the writer's arguments. Identify fallacies in your *own* reasoning.
↓	
BECOME A CRITICAL READER.	Make valid inferences. Draw sound conclusions. Form unbiased judgments.

ACTIVITY 7.13

Read the following statements, all of which are assumptions by an author. Judge whether the author's statement has any fallacies. State whether you agree or disagree with the assumption, and why. Use the space provided.

1. Physical attractiveness, of course, is a powerful stimulus, especially for men. Women look for attractiveness, too, but they are also drawn by status, preferring a leader over a follower, or a slightly older man over a slightly younger one, or a man with more education, or a better job.

   Kathleen Stassen Berger, *The Developing Person Through the Life Span*, Ch. 19

_____

_____

_____

2. It has been suggested that all young Americans be required to perform a year of national service: helping the young, the old, the homeless, the environment . . . they owe something for the freedom they enjoy—and surely nothing would spark an appreciation of personal liberty as much as a term of involuntary **servitude.**

Peter Tauber, "A Free Country," *Family Circle*, p. 130, Sept. 1, 1991

3. Since antiquity, scholars have noted that . . . prejudice always seems to burst during times of social and political upheaval. Now, new psychological research suggests that by persecuting . . . those they consider as outsiders, a people or culture is acting to **alleviate** its own fears about survival.

Alison Bass, "A Malice Driven by Fear," *Boston Globe*, May 14, 1990, pp. 29–30

4. Opponents of abortion worry that once abortion is permissible immediately after conception, no argument will restrict it at any later time in the pregnancy. Then, they fear, one day it will be permissible to murder a fetus that is **unambiguously** a human being. Both pro-choice and pro-lifers (at least some of them) are pushed towards absolutist positions by parallel fears of the slippery slope.

Stuart James Kolner, M.D., *Pharos*, Spring 1990, pp. 34–37

5. AIDS is like a modern form of leprosy. Persons with AIDS are rejected by the community, not only for their life-style (since the disease is one that first hit homosexual men), but also because the disease is incurable . . . AIDS is often perceived as a threat to the health, well-being, and economic viability of our modern society.

David C. Thomasma and Thomas K. McElkinney, "Ethical Concerns About AIDS," copyright by ALPHA OMEGA ALPHA HONOR MEDICAL SOCIETY, Spring 1990

servitude (sûr´ və tōod) bondage; acting like a slave

alleviate (ə lē´ vē āt´) lessen or relieve

unambiguously (ən am big´ yōo əs lē) absolutely clear

_____

_____

6. The good Joe is friendly and easy; he fits in and likes people . . . with Europeans, he sometimes seems to have a kind of inferiority complex—foreigners tell him he is an "ugly American," "go home Yankee," and he may say conscientiously, "You are probably right," or "Everyone's opinion is worth listening to."

Orrin E. Klapp, *Heroes, Villains, and Fools: The Changing American Character,* p. 95

_____

_____

_____

7. Denouncing paramilitary groups as terrorists—or hailing them as patriots—ignores the often-subtle interplay of forces that have led to their rebirth some two centuries after Lexington and Concord. The psychological and cultural dynamics behind this resurrection can't be reduced to a catchy sound bite. But either we understand them—or we risk more Oklahoma **conflagrations.**

Peter Doshock, "The Mind of the Militias," *Psychology Today,* July/Aug. 1995, p. 70

_____

_____

_____

8. Clearly, the U.N. is a complaint desk where many customers leave dissatisfied. . . . It is a favorite target of nationalistic conservatives. . . . The American people seem to know better. A Times-Mirror poll showed that even though the ranks of the critics have increased, more Americans still view the U.N. favorably than approve of the work of Congress or the Courts.

David Broder, "Evaluated Over 50 Years, the UN Is Extraordinary," *Washington Post,* 27 June 1995

_____

_____

_____

_____

conflagrations (kon flə grā´ shənz) large and destructive fires

❖ Summary

Drawing conclusions based on valid inferences is an important aspect of critical reading because much of what we read consists simply of assumptions made by writers. We need to engage in a dialogue with authors, questioning whether they are correct in their beliefs. At the same time, we need to be open-minded to new ideas that challenge those we hold.

You make inferences by reasoning, forming your own conclusions or opinions based on what has been suggested but not stated directly by the writer. Inferences can be valid, based on clear evidence and logical reasoning. On the other hand, inferences can be invalid and merely assumptions resulting from inadequate evidence or arrived at through faulty logic.

Three strategies can assist you in making valid inferences and therefore drawing sound conclusions.

1. Separate the facts from the opinions.
2. Evaluate the main idea and supporting evidence.
3. Test the logic of your inferences and conclusion.

Critical readers who form unbiased judgments

1. Understand the issue and recognize the facts.
2. Become aware of the author's fallacies and their own biases.
3. Reason through their experiences and the use of logic.

Chapter 7 Vocabulary Review

Introduction to Word Analogy

College entrance exams and qualifying tests for some occupations and professions frequently contain vocabulary test items that require inferential thinking. These tests make use of the relationship of words through *analogy*. An analogy is an implied or unstated relationship between pairs of words. Many relationships can exist between words: a pair of words may be synonyms, antonyms, or homonyms, or they may be related through cause/effect, degree, characteristics, parts of speech, and so on. In analogy, you try to associate one paired item with another. Vocabulary analogies use the colon (:) as a type of shorthand. For example, if pairs of words use the relationship of synonyms, they appear as follows:

adversary:enemy::confidant: _____
(*Friend* is a word that could complete the analogy.)

Steps in Solving Analogies

1. Consider the above example as A:B::C:?
2. Identify the items in the first part of the analogy (A and B).
3. Determine how these items are related.
4. Consider the items in the second part (C:?) in terms of this relationship.
5. Determine the missing item in the second part (?) to complete the analogy.

A. The following practice exercise uses the relationship of synonyms. The first set contains a review word from previous chapters. You are to complete the second pair with a word from Chapter 7; select it from the list of boldfaced words. You will not use all the words listed.

somber   unanimous   constituents   futile   lurid   perdition   plaudits

1. hate:anathema::ruin: _____

2. disillusion:disenchant::useless: _____

3. awards:accolades::praise: _____

4. sepulchral:gloomy::grim: _____

5. willing:amenable::agreement: _____

B. Choose the correct word, and write it in the space provided.

1. Is an **exorbitant** price expensive or inexpensive? _____

2. Are **subtle** remarks easy or difficult to understand? _____

3. If one's headache is **alleviated,** is it better or worse? _____

4. In business, is it better to be at the top of the **echelon** or in the center?

_____

5. Are **relevant** details important or unimportant? _____

Selection 13: Article

 Preparation For Reading

The following article, "The Prenuptial Agreement," discusses why contracting for such an agreement before marriage creates a dilemma for many couples considering it. The following words are underlined in the article.

the **prerogative**	right or privilege
a **facet**	aspect or phase
primogeniture in England	the first-born has a right to inherit money and property
and not **unconscionable**	not guided or restrained by conscience
equitable distribution	fair; just
disillusioning day	disappointing
the **proverbial** ostrich	expressing a well-known truth or fact (in this case that the ostrich is a "stupid" bird)
a **bulwark** of open-minded fairness	strong defense

Preview, then read the article.

The Prenuptial Agreement

Elaine Louie

The prenuptial agreement isn't just the <u>prerogative</u> of the very rich. It's also becoming a <u>facet</u> of middle-class marriages, even those made in the rosy bloom of youth. It is a tradition that is as old as <u>primogeniture</u> in England. There, it was the parents who decided the terms, and seldom the young couple. The French also have a law that distinguishes between separate and marital property. In the United States, it was usually the wealthy who signed these agreements, either to protect inheritances or, on their second and later marriages, to protect the family interests and money for their children.

WHAT IS A PRENUPTIAL AGREEMENT?

Prenuptial agreements are legal, signed contracts of the partners' rights to all sorts of items

1

2

in the event of a divorce: pets, paintings, property, alimony or maintenance, children (whether or not to have them and after a divorce, who gets them), jewelry, silverware, and business interests. One lawyer had a client who negotiated the pick of the litter. In New York State, you cannot contract to divorce a spouse. Neither can you contract to commit adultery nor dissolve a marriage which would make the other a public charge, the responsibility of the state. Agreements can be short or long, but as matrimonial lawyer Eleanor Alter says, "In New York, terms must be fair when made and not <u>unconscionable</u>." She cites an example. "If when a couple first got married, he made $20,000 and she was to receive $5,000 a year in support, but when they divorce 20 years later, he is making $400,000, that $5,000 support has become unconscionable, and can be disputed in court."

WHY DO PEOPLE SIGN THEM?

One rather romantic reason people sign these 3 agreements, says attorney Morton Geller, "is that it's an opportunity to control your own destiny." Put another way, in the light of women's consciousness, matrimonial lawyer Rona Shays says, "Young women are beginning to believe the equality of their relationship. For a young couple starting out, economics are not the real thrust of the antenuptial agreement. They sign agreements for personal reasons. They want to define the roles of their relationships rather than economics. They do not want to talk about maintenance if they break up. They ask questions like what if his next stage is a step up on the corporate ladder but her next promotion might mean a move to California." Shays wonders why these young people need a lawyer to talk through ideas on career moves. "Shouldn't they be able to discuss with each other their expectations? Are they unable to communicate directly?" Still, for the young, the prenuptial agreement is precisely that—the vehicle for communication and a quest for independence within the structure of a marriage.

The prenuptial agreement can have a 4 stigma of distrust that is just now beginning to be erased. The San Francisco criminal lawyer Melvin Belli says that some people want their fiancés to sign them because "they're stingy, selfish, and mean." And many people are afraid that to disclose expectations and sign a contract will turn a romantic relationship into a business one. . . . A prenuptial agreement can be a test of insecurity as well as security. What motivates people to signing these contracts is as complex as the people themselves. However, prenuptial agreements come attached with symbolism as well as advantages and disadvantages.

Prenuptial agreements reveal an eye-open- 5 ing on the part of the women. Previously, many women who have been divorced have been shocked to discover that they were victims of their husbands, and perhaps the courts, and that they were not recipients of anything remotely resembling equitable distribution. Prenuptial agreements are preventive medicine against a disillusioning day in court. For a woman to ask a man to disclose his finances at the onset of a marriage, and vice versa, is a sign of greater, not lesser, communication. It also indicates a smarter woman. Attorney Alter deals with 200 divorces a year. . . .

"There are still a lot of women who say they 6 don't want to know about money, that they can say to the man, 'I trust you.' But at the time of divorce, for every woman who says that the man wouldn't explain his finances to her, there were an equal number of women who didn't want to hear about it." To not know the spouse's income is to function like the proverbial ostrich. If ignorance is bliss on the wedding day, why not have bliss at the divorce court?

For the young couple, Shays does not rec- 7 ommend writing custodial clauses for children that have not yet been born. "Custody depends on the nurturing quality of the parent, and to advise on cultural stereotypes—of who has traditionally been the stereotypical nurturer—is terribly wrong." She points out the obvious facts that people change in five years and that men can be as good nurturers of children as women. To decide who is the better nurturer for a child who is unborn and who may be born a boy, a girl, handsome or ugly, brilliant or retarded, is to make a premature, ignorant decision based entirely on the unknown. . . .

THE SECOND MARRIAGES: A LITTLE LESS ROMANCE?

Traditionally, the wealthy man who was burned 8 by his wife at the dissolution of his first marriage is the first to ask the second wife to sign a prenuptial agreement. It is assumed that he has been mortally wounded, taken financially to the cleaners, and that he needs the second wife's signature on the contract as proof that she loves him for himself, and not for his money. . . .

The problem then is not that these agreements exist, but whether one or the other is humiliated by it, in the event of a divorce. All the lawyers echo the same advice to anyone, man or woman, young or old, who is asked to sign a prenuptial agreement: Find an independent lawyer who will advise you of your rights. **9**

Just because a wealthy person—insecure about whether that person loves him or whether the marriage will endure—has the less monied fiancé sign an agreement does not mean that this agreement has to stay as it is, proof of someone's insecurity. Attorney Belli says, "Sign agreements for three or four years, then get it reviewed. Relationships last such a short time, or they change." People sometimes get more generous with each other, as the marriage goes on. That is the usual hope of the woman whose fiancé says, "Sign this agreement or I won't marry you." He is interpreted to be either extremely insecure, scared, or dominating and controlling. She signs, hoping that he will relax, once married. **10**

While lawyers have seen the most cynical and the most romantic couples sign these agreements, they do not, as a rule, like to negotiate the prenuptial contracts. "I prefer to negotiate separation agreements," says attorney Alter. . . . For young people, too, it's hard to talk about divorce and maintenance when they haven't even been married." **11**

Rona Shays says, "The psychology of dealing with people going into their first marriage and asking them to talk about business is **12**

against the American ideal of marriage, that it's for better or worse. It's tricky emotionally. People are either not trained or don't want to consider their finances in event of a divorce."

Women as Instigators of Agreements

Traditionally, more men than women have asked the future spouse to sign the agreements. This is because men had the larger fortunes. There are widows with inheritances from their own families or a previous spouse who sometimes ask new husbands to sign prenuptial agreements. "But you don't find too many women saying to the man, 'If you don't sign this, I won't marry you,'" says Shays. "Women still feel dependent. You don't cure this emotional dependency with sex-neutral statutes." **13**

Prenuptial agreements can be rendered null and void during an ongoing marriage. They can also be held up in a divorce court as a legal document. Still, judges who preside over divorces have their own biases, and some prenuptial agreements can be contested. Courts do not like to rewrite contracts, but if one party says the prenuptial agreement is now unconscionable, the judge will look carefully at the contract. Attorney Alter says, "Professional women are signing prenuptial agreements, and as a matter of principle they say that they don't want alimony. They don't know that the principle may fall by the wayside." A woman might get sick. Her job may disappear. Nothing, not even legal contracts, are certain. But a prenuptial agreement can be a <u>bulwark</u> of open-minded fairness against an eventual, bitter day in divorce court. It can be a covenant of romance and commitment. It can be a weapon of dominance. It is whatever you make it to be. **14**

approximately 1575 words

COMPREHENSION CHECK

Part I
General Comprehension Questions: Literal and Interpretive

Write the correct letter in the space provided.

_____ 1. Shays does not recommend that children be included in prenuptial agreements because

a. women are better at bringing up children.
b. men should have custody of their sons.
c. people change and the unborn child is an unknown.
d. prenuptial agreements should focus on money matters.

_____ 2. You can characterize prenuptial agreements as legal documents that protect a spouse's

a. career change.
b. job.
c. diverse items.
d. character.

_____ 3. The main idea of this article is that

a. although prenuptial agreements are soaring in numbers, they are ineffective.
b. these agreements cause more problems than solutions.
c. lawyers dislike handling prenuptial agreements and do a poor job.
d. these agreements are a form of self-protection and deserve consideration, especially by women.

_____ 4. The author concludes that

a. women should protect their economic situation.
b. partners should be able to get out of a relationship.
c. you should be wary about asking about your partner's income.
d. high income will lead to high alimony.

_____ 5. The writer implies that prenuptial agreements in New York

a. are superior to those of other states.
b. are unnecessary because laws already exist.
c. require that a sense of ethics and fair play be taken into consideration.
d. are always open to renegotiation.

_____ 6. The implication to draw from the comparison of one who does not know what a spouse earns and the "proverbial ostrich" is that

    a. animals would have better sense in handling money matters.

    b. a spouse's income is a personal matter.

    c. ignorance about money matters is absurd.

    d. prenuptial agreements sour romantic love.

_____ 7. From the statement "prenuptial agreements are tricky emotionally. People are either not trained or don't want to consider their finances in case of divorce," you can infer that

    a. people don't have time to arrange agreements.

    b. people cannot afford legal counsel.

    c. people still feel romantic about marriage.

    d. people don't listen to a marriage counselor.

8. Write F, for fact, O, for opinion, or C for a combination of fact and opinion in the space provided. Write your support.

_____ a. "Relationships last such a short time or they change."

Support: _____

_____ b. "All the lawyers echo the same advice to anyone . . . who is asked to sign a prenuptial agreement: Find an independent lawyer who will advise you of your rights."

Support: _____

9. What inferences can you make from the statement "[prenuptial agreements] are becoming a facet of middle-class marriages"?

_____

_____

10. Contrast reasons for the prenuptial agreements of earlier times and societies to reasons given today in the United States.

_____

_____

Part II
Application Questions for Writing/Discussion

11. The reading says, "For a woman to ask a man to disclose his finances at the onset of marriage . . . is a sign of greater, not lesser communication; it also indicates a smarter woman." Do you agree? Explain.

_____

_____

_____

_____

12. What conclusions have you drawn about a prenuptial agreement? What would you want to see included in one? Do you plan to have one, or have you ever had one? Why, or why not?

_____

_____

_____

_____

Part III
Extend Your Vocabulary

Circle the correct letter, using the context to determine the meaning of the boldfaced words. The sentences have been taken from the selection.

1. "The prenuptial agreement can have a **stigma** of distrust that is just now beginning to be erased"
   (a) finance   (b) lawyer fee   (c) a sign of disgrace   (d) settlement
2. "Shays does not recommend writing **custodial** clauses for children that have not yet been born."
   (a) monied   (b) price   (c) separate   (d) caring, keeping safe
3. "Men can be as good **nurturers** of children as women."
   (a) mothers   (b) at storytelling   (c) loving providers   (d) at fashions
4. "**Traditionally** . . . the wealthy man who was burned by his first wife . . . is the first to ask the second wife to sign a prenuptial agreement."
   (a) according to established custom   (b) at the present time
   (c) only once in a while   (d) in spite of
5. "There are widows with inheritances from their own families or a previous **spouse** who sometimes ask new husbands to sign prenuptial agreements."
   (a) husband   (b) friend   (c) brother   (d) companion

Selection 14: **TEXTBOOK**

The following textbook chapter excerpt focuses on both marriage and divorce. With the changing customs and values of today's society, marriage has placed greater demands on both partners. As you read, decide whether these changes offer marriage partners a better, more fulfilling, relationship. The boldfaced words are underlined in the essay.

their roles **diverging**	moving in a different direction
particularly **detrimental**	damaging
confrontation that women . . . seek	coming face to face with opposition
may **converge** more strongly	to come toward a common point
to restore the **mutuality**	having the same feelings
the present **cohort** of young adults	companions or associates

Survey, then read the chapter.

The Developmental Course of Love and Marriage

Kathleen Stassen Berger

Marriages, just like people, develop with time. Obviously, each marital relationship is different, and much depends on the personality and history of the individuals involved. However, some general trends can be identified.

One of the clearest is that marriages between people who have a lot in common are more likely to be satisfying and long-lasting than marriages between people who are quite different. Of course, it is not always the case, but all other things being equal, homogamy, that is, marriage between individuals who are similar in age, socioeconomic background, religion, ethnic group, and the like, has a better chance of survival than heterogamy, that is, marriage between individuals who are dissimilar on those variables.

Another factor that strongly affects the likelihood of a marriage's enduring is the maturity of the individuals who enter the relationship. At least until young adults are in their mid-20s, the younger marriage partners are when they wed, the less their chances of having a successful marriage. One reason for this is that, as Erikson explains, intimacy is hard to establish until identity is reached. Many older adolescents and young adults are still figuring out their values and roles, so a young couple might initially see themselves as compatible only to find their values and roles <u>diverging</u> as they become more mature. Further, the compromise and interdependence that are part of establishing intimacy are hard to achieve until one has a clear notion of self and has experienced independence.

More practical reasons are also apparent. Both partners are generally happier in marriage when the husband, in particular, has some financial security, and most young men have little until their mid-20s. This factor can be particularly <u>detrimental</u> when the reason for the marriage is a pregnancy. A disproportionate number of marriages between younger people do, in fact, occur because the bride is pregnant, and almost half of such marriages break up within five years.

Whatever the age of the newly wed couple, in the early months and years, marriage is at its most intense, which can be a good or bad thing. During this "honeymoon period," newly married people typically spend more time together, talking, going out, establishing their marital roles and routines, arguing, making up, and making love. When the marriage is going well, the intensity of the honeymoon period results in a higher rate of reported bliss. In fact, marriages characterized by extreme closeness, in which the partners share many activities and are open to new experiences together, tend to be most satisfactory to both husband and wife in the early years. When the marriage is troubled, however, this high intensity can lead to greater unhappiness. **5**

One of the major tasks for the couple during the honeymoon period is adjusting to the different perceptions and expectations that each partner may have of their life together. For example, women often are much more concerned about maintaining close relationships with their friends and relatives than men think is necessary or wise. Women are also more likely to find problems in the marriage relationship and to want to talk about them. Men are not as likely to recognize problems, and when they see them, tend to avoid the very <u>confrontation</u> that women seem to seek. The couple may also have to adjust to differences in the way they handle confrontation. Women typically try to evoke sympathy, while men use logic and get angry, to win an argument. Thus a wife might start to talk about an issue and begin to cry, provoking the husband to leave the room in a huff, telling her to stop sobbing and start thinking as he slams the door behind him. This pattern is obviously counterproductive, and successful couples usually find more constructive ways to resolve disputes. **6**

After the honeymoon period, intensity diminishes and satisfaction with marriage generally dips, especially for wives. The most commonly cited reason for this change is the arrival of children. For most couples, the time and effort spent on parenting usually comes out of the marital relationship. As Norval Glenn explains: **7**

> Negative effects of children on marital happiness grow to a large extent out of interference with the companionship and intimate interaction of the spouses. Taking care of children requires time and energy which the husband and wife could use to sustain their own relationship. Also conflict may ensue from disagreements concerning child-rearing, and of course, adding persons to a dyad creates a more complex social system in which the potential for jealousy and competition is greater.

Does this mean that marriages without children are more satisfying? This, of course, is a complicated question. In general, when both partners agree to postpone or avoid child-raising, they tend to be much more pleased with each other than couples who have several young children. On the other hand, those couples who are involuntarily childless experience considerable stress until they decide what to do—adopt, discover the reason for their infertility and attempt to remedy it, develop an alternative plan for their life together, or divorce. **8**

As time goes on, the interests and needs of the partners may move in different directions or they may <u>converge</u> more strongly, and the marriage relationship may evolve along new lines. . . . An intensive study of more than 400 "successful" marriages (ones that had lasted ten years or more) found five quite different patterns: **9**

1. *Conflict-habituated.* Husband and wife constantly argue, nag, fight, and belittle each other. Such battling is not considered a rea-

son for divorce, however. On the contrary, for some couples, conflict may be a way of expressing their attachment to each other. When one woman was asked if she ever considered divorce, she answered, "Divorce never. Murder, every day."

2. *Devitalized.* The husband and wife, once loving and close, have drifted apart. They continue to get along with each other, but share few activities and interests.

3. *Passive-congenial.* For these couples, marriage is, and was from the start, comfortable and convenient. They seem more like compatible roommates than lovers.

4. *Vital.* Both spouses are very involved in all the family activities, economic and emotional, recreational and social.

5. *Total.* These couples are very involved, not only with the family activities but with each other's lives, sharing work interests, personal confidences, fantasies.

According to this study, about 80 percent of all marriages fall into one of the first three categories.

Much of the pattern of a particular marriage over the years is determined by the nature of the dependence of each spouse on the other. When dependence is high, and each spouse is equally dependent on the other, the marriage is usually close and strong. However, when the dependence of one partner is much higher than that of the other, the marriage is likely to be characterized by conflict, stress, and anger. Changes in individual lives over the life span often make one partner more dependent, and the other more independent, than originally. If one partner becomes much better educated or gains higher social status, or conversely, if one becomes significantly less healthy, less attractive, or loses status, the balance between them may suffer. In some couples, such imbalance is endured with resignation; in others, a way is found to restore the <u>mutuality</u>; in many others, the inequality leads to divorce.

DIVORCE

Divorce statistics worldwide, and from different decades, reveal that, in general, marriages founder rather quickly. Internationally, the peak time for divorce is three or four years after the wedding; in addition, divorce is most likely to occur when the couple are in their late 20s. The United States shows similar trends, with half of all divorces occurring in the first seven years.

Although the stage of marriage at which divorce may occur seems to follow universal patterns, how frequently divorce actually does occur seems to be affected by specific historical and cultural conditions. Married adults are now divorcing two and a half times as often as adults did twenty years ago, and four times as often as fifty years ago. In fact, for every two American marriages that occurred in 1985, there was approximately one divorce.

Does this increase in failed marriages mean that the present <u>cohort</u> of young adults is less able than earlier cohorts to maintain a good marriage relationship? In fact, the case is probably the opposite. A study comparing families in the 1920s with their counterparts in the 1970s found substantial improvement in the communication and affection between spouses.

What accounts for the rise in divorce, then? One major factor, clearly, is that spouses today expect a great deal more from each other than spouses in the past did. In earlier decades, earning the money was considered the man's responsibility, and housework and child care, the woman's. As long as both partners did their jobs, the marriage usually survived. As one woman, married in 1909, advised newlyweds on her seventy-first wedding anniversary:

Don't stop on the little things. Be satisfied whatever happens. Ben didn't commit adultery, he's not a gambler, not a liar . . . So what's there to complain about?

In addition, husbands and wives in the past **15** usually did not expect to really understand each other: they generally assumed that masculinity and femininity are opposites, and that the sexes therefore are naturally a mystery to each other. Today, marriage partners have a much more flexible view of marriage roles and responsibilities and are likely to expect each other to be a friend, lover, and confidant as well as a wage-earner and care-giver.

Evidence for this shift in what is expected **16** from marriage partners is seen in the changing reasons given for divorce. In 1948, recently divorced women were asked what had caused the break-up of their marriage. Cruelty, excessive drinking, and nonsupport were among the most common reasons cited. A comparable survey in 1975 found lack of communication and poor understanding to be the most common reasons.

Research suggests that now both sexes have **17** quite similar complaints. For example, in one county in Wisconsin, everyone who files for divorce is asked the reasons the marriage failed. Table 7-1 [below] lists the ten most common reasons cited by each sex and the percentages of respondents of each sex citing those reasons.

It should be noted that, while women generally cited more reasons than men, both men **18** and women tended to see their marriage problems in similar terms. Two notable exceptions to this pattern may be accounted for by the persistence of some men's stereotypic views regarding appropriate sex roles: whereas 22 percent of the women considered physical abuse a significant cause of their divorce, only 3 percent of the men did; and whereas 15 percent of the men considered women's liberation a significant cause of their divorce, only 3 percent of the women did.

approximately 2000 words

Kathleen Stassen Berger, "The Developmental Course of Love and Marriage," *The Developing Person Through the Life Span*, 2nd ed., Copyright © 1988 by Worth Publishers, Inc. Reprinted by permission of the publisher.

TABLE 7-1

Reasons Given for Divorcing

Women		Men	
1. Communication problems	70%	1. Communication problems	59%
2. Basic unhappiness	60%	2. Basic unhappiness	47%
3. Incompatibility	56%	3. Incompatibility	45%
4. Emotional abuse	56%	4. Sexual problems	30%
5. Financial problems	33%	5. Financial problems	29%
6. Sexual problems	32%	6. Emotional abuse	25%
7. Alcohol abuse—spouse	30%	7. Women's liberation	15%
8. Infidelity—spouse	25%	8. In-laws	12%
9. Physical abuse	22%	9. Infidelity—spouse	11%
10. In-laws	11%	10. Alcohol abuse—self	9%

Cleek and Pearson

COMPREHENSION CHECK

Part I
General Comprehension Questions: Literal and Interpretive

Write the correct letter in the space provided.

_____ 1. A factor not mentioned as contributing to a happy marriage is

    a. similarity in background.
    b. maturity of the partners.
    c. beauty and handsomeness.
    d. shared values.

_____ 2. According to this excerpt, pregnancy before marriage increases chances of

    a. a quick divorce.
    b. a more stable marriage.
    c. financial difficulties.
    d. breakup within a few years.

_____ 3. Marriage at its most "intense" time

    a. can be a period of bliss or of unhappiness
    b. can be detrimental to a career.
    c. leads to in-law difficulties.
    d. is likely to occur during the wife's first pregnancy.

_____ 4. It can be inferred from this chapter that

    a. married couples are very much involved in all family activities.
    b. married couples are very much involved in each other's lives.
    c. married couples are constantly having problems.
    d. none of the above.

_____ 5. Which one of these statements pertaining to divorce is untrue?

    a. Divorce occurs most often when couples are in their late twenties.
    b. Half of all divorces takes place in the first seven years.
    c. The lessening of affection between spouses leads to more divorces.
    d. One of two marriages now ends in divorce.

_____ 6. A research study that evaluated the complaints voiced by both husbands and wives showed

    a. wide differences in complaints.
    b. an emphasis on problems caused by excessive drinking.
    c. a similarity of complaints, with some differences.
    d. an increase in mental cruelty.

7. What conclusions about marriage can you draw from this statement: "Divorce never. Murder every day"? How does this conflict with *compromise* and *interdependence*, two essentials the author claims are necessary in a good marriage?

_____

_____

_____

8. The author discusses dependence and independence. What is the difference? Does she use facts or opinions in support of her comments? Do you agree with her conclusions?

_____

_____

_____

Part II
Application Questions for Writing/Discussion

9. Expectations of marriage have changed. What are these expectations today? What has contributed to this shift? Is society as a whole better off or worse off?

_____

_____

_____

_____

_____

10. Which spouse (husband or wife) is more likely to want to talk about marital problems? What is often the outcome of this discussion? Pretend you are married and having a disagreement with your mate over a money matter. How would reading this chapter help you to handle it better?

_____

_____

_____

_____

Part III
Extend Your Vocabulary

Note the boldfaced word in the first sentence of each set, quoted directly from the chapter. In the second sentence, fill in a different suffixed form of that word to complete the sentence. The first word is completed for you.

1. "Men may use **logic** and get angry, to win an argument."

   Although she presented the reasons ___*logically*___ he failed to agree to the plan.
2. "A young couple might see themselves initially as **compatible,** only to find their . . . roles diverging as they become more mature."

   Early in marriage there may have been _____ between them, but that has all changed.
3. "A **disproportionate** number of marriages . . . occur because the bride is pregnant."

   They divided the estate _____ after the divorce.
4. "[M]arriages **characterized** by extreme closeness . . . tend to be most satisfying."

   The _____ of that marriage as ideal was far from the truth.
5. "[F]or every two American marriages that occurred in 1985, there was **approximately** one divorce."

   Only an _____ of the number of marriages could be made from the last report.

Selection 15: **LITERATURE**

Amy Tan has had a meteoric rise to fame as a result of her first book, *The Joy Luck Club,* from which the selection which follows has been excerpted. Her second book, *The Kitchen God's Wife,* was published in 1991.

In this excerpt from *The Joy Luck Club,* Waverly Jong, a thirtyish Chinese-American lawyer, is in a quandry over how to inform her traditionally minded Chinese parents that she plans to marry Rich, a red-haired, freckle-faced Caucasian with whom she works. Read the selection to see what develops as Waverly introduces Rich to her parents.

Amy Tan

The Joy Luck Club

Amy Tan

"You know, I really don't understand you," said Marlene when I called her the night   1
after I had shown my mother the mink jacket. "You can tell the IRS to piss up a rope, but you can't stand up to your own mother."

"I always intend to and then she says these little sneaky things, smoke bombs and little barbs, and . . ."

"Why don't you tell her to stop torturing you," said Marlene. "Tell her to stop ruining your life. Tell her to shut up."

"That's hilarious," I said with a half-laugh. "You want me to tell my mother to shut up?"

"Sure, why not?"   5

"Well, I don't know if it's explicitly stated in the law, but you can't *ever* tell a Chinese mother to shut up. You could be charged as an accessory to your own murder."

I wasn't so much afraid of my mother as I was afraid for Rich. I already knew what she would do, how she would attack him, how she would criticize him. She would be quiet at first. Then she would say a word about something small, something she had noticed, and then another word, and another, each one flung out like a little piece of sand, one from this direction, another from behind, more and more, until his looks, his character, his soul would have eroded away. And even if I recognized her strategy, her sneak attack, I was afraid that some unseen speck of truth would fly into my eye, blur what I was seeing and transform him from the divine man I thought he was into someone quite mundane, mortally wounded with tiresome habits and irritating imperfections.

This happened to my first marriage, to Marvin Chen, with whom I had eloped when I was eighteen and he was nineteen. When I was in love with Marvin, he was nearly perfect. He graduated third in his class at Lowell and got a full scholarship to Stanford. He played tennis. He had bulging calf muscles and one hundred forty-six straight black hairs on his chest. He made everyone laugh and his own laugh was deep, sonorous, masculinely sexy. He prided himself on having favorite love positions for different days and hours of the week; all he had to whisper was "Wednesday afternoon" and I'd shiver.

But by the time my mother had had her say about him, I saw his brain had shrunk from laziness, so that now it was good only for thinking up excuses. He chased golf and tennis balls to run away from family responsibilities. His eye wandered up and down other girls' legs, so he didn't know how to drive straight home anymore. He liked to tell big jokes to make other people feel little. He made a loud show of leaving ten-dollar tips to strangers but was stingy with presents to family. He thought waxing his red sports car all afternoon was more important than taking his wife somewhere in it.

My feelings for Marvin never reached the level of hate. No, it was worse in a way. **10** It went from disappointment to contempt to apathetic boredom. It wasn't until after we separated, on nights when Shoshana was asleep and I was lonely, that I wondered if perhaps my mother had poisoned my marriage.

Thank God, her poison didn't affect my daughter, Shoshana. I almost aborted her, though. When I found out I was pregnant, I was furious. I secretly referred to my pregnancy as my "growing resentment," and I dragged Marvin down to the clinic so he would have to suffer through this too. It turned out we went to the wrong kind of clinic. They made us watch a film, a terrible bit of puritanical brainwash. I saw those little things, babies they called them even at seven weeks, and they had tiny, tiny fingers. And the film said the baby's translucent fingers could *move*, that we should imagine them clinging for life, grasping for a chance, this miracle of life. If they had shown *anything else* except tiny fingers—so thank God they did. Because Shoshana really was a miracle. She was perfect. I found every detail about her to be remarkable, especially the way she flexed and curled her fingers. From the very moment she flung her fist away from her mouth to cry, I knew my feelings for her were inviolable.

But I worried for Rich. Because I knew my feelings for him were vulnerable to being felled by my mother's suspicions, passing remarks, and innuendos. And I was afraid of what I would then lose, because Rich Schields adored me in the same way I adored Shoshana. His love was unequivocal. Nothing could change it. He expected nothing from me; my mere existence was enough. And at the same time, he said that he had changed—for the *better*—because of me. He was embarrassingly romantic; he insisted he never was until he met me. And this confession made his romantic gestures all the more ennobling. At work, for example, when he would staple "FYI—For Your Information" notes to legal briefs and corporate returns that I had to review, he signed them at the bottom: "FYI—Forever You & I." The firm didn't know about our relationship, and so that kind of reckless behavior on his part thrilled me.

The sexual chemistry was what really surprised me, though. I thought he'd be one of those quiet types who was awkwardly gentle and clumsy, the kind of mild-mannered guy who says, "Am I hurting you?" when I can't feel a thing. But he was so attuned to my every movement I was sure he was reading my mind. He had no inhibitions, and whatever ones he discovered I had he'd pry away from me like little treasures. He saw all those private aspects of me—and I mean not just sexual private parts, but my darker side, my meanness, my pettiness, my self-loathing—all the things I kept hidden. So that with him I was completely naked, and when I was, when I was feeling the most vulnerable—when the wrong word would have sent me flying out the door forever—he always said exactly the right thing at the right moment. He didn't allow me to cover myself up. He would grab my hands, look me straight in the eye and tell me something new about why he loved me.

I'd never known love so pure, and I was afraid that it would become sullied by my mother. So I tried to store every one of these endearments about Rich in my memory, and I planned to call upon them again when the time was necessary.

After much thought, I came up with a brilliant plan. I concocted a way for Rich 15
to meet my mother and win her over. In fact, I arranged it so my mother would want to cook a meal especially for him. I had some help from Auntie Suyuan. Auntie Su was my mother's friend from way back. They were very close, which meant they were ceaselessly tormenting each other with boasts and secrets. And I gave Auntie Su a secret to boast about.

After walking through North Beach one Sunday, I suggested to Rich that we stop by for a surprise visit to my Auntie Su and Uncle Canning. They lived on Leavenworth, just a few blocks west of my mother's apartment. It was late afternoon, just in time to catch Auntie Su preparing Sunday dinner.

"Stay! Stay!" she had insisted.

"No, no. It's just that we were walking by," I said.

"Already cooked enough for you. See? One soup, four dishes. You don't eat it, only have to throw it away. Wasted!"

How could we refuse? Three days later, Auntie Suyuan had a thank-you letter 20
from Rich and me. "Rich said it was the best Chinese food he has ever tasted," I wrote.

And the next day, my mother called me, to invite me to a belated birthday dinner for my father. My brother Vincent was bringing his girlfriend, Lisa Lum. I could bring a friend, too.

I knew she would do this, because cooking was how my mother expressed her love, her pride, her power, her proof that she knew more than Auntie Su. "Just be sure to tell her later that her cooking was the best you ever tasted, that it was far better than Auntie Su's," I told Rich. "Believe me."

The night of the dinner, I sat in the kitchen watching her cook, waiting for the right moment to tell her about our marriage plans, that we had decided to get married next July, about seven months away. She was chopping eggplant into wedges, chattering at the same time about Auntie Suyuan: "She can only cook looking at a recipe. My instructions are in my fingers. I know what secret ingredients to put in just by using my nose!" And she was slicing with such a ferocity, seemingly inattentive to her sharp cleaver, that I was afraid her fingertips would become one of the ingredients of the red-cooked eggplant and shredded pork dish.

I was hoping she would say something first about Rich. I had seen her expression when she opened the door, her forced smile as she scrutinized him from head to toe, checking her appraisal of him against that already given to her by Auntie Suyuan. I tried to anticipate what criticisms she would have.

Rich was not only *not* Chinese, he was a few years younger than I was. And unfor- 25
tunately, he looked much younger with his curly red hair, smooth pale skin, and the

splash of orange freckles across his nose. He was a bit on the short side, compactly built. In his dark business suits, he looked nice but easily forgettable, like somebody's nephew at a funeral. Which was why I didn't notice him the first year we worked together at the firm. But my mother noticed everything.

"So what do you think of Rich?" I finally asked, holding my breath.

She tossed the eggplant in the hot oil and it made a loud, angry hissing sound. "So many spots on his face," she said.

I could feel the pinpricks on my back. "They're freckles. Freckles are good luck, you know," I said a bit too heatedly in trying to raise my voice above the din of the kitchen.

"Oh?" she said innocently.

"Yes, the more spots the better. Everybody knows that."   30

She considered this a moment and then smiled and spoke in Chinese: "Maybe this is true. When you were young, you got the chicken pox. So many spots, you had to stay home for ten days. So lucky, you thought."

I couldn't save Rich in the kitchen. And I couldn't save him later at the dinner table.

He had brought a bottle of French wine, something he did not know my parents could not appreciate. My parents did not even own wineglasses. And then he also made the mistake of drinking not one but two frosted glasses full, while everybody else had a half-inch "just for taste."

When I offered Rich a fork, he insisted on using the slippery ivory chopsticks. He held them splayed like the knock-kneed legs of an ostrich while picking up a large chunk of sauce-coated eggplant. Halfway between his plate and his open mouth, the chunk fell on his crisp white shirt and then slid into his crotch. It took several minutes to get Shoshana to stop shrieking with laughter.

And then he had helped himself to big portions of the shrimp and snow peas,   35 not realizing he should have taken only a polite spoonful, until everybody had had a morsel.

He had declined the sautéed new greens, the tender and expensive leaves of bean plants plucked before the sprouts turn into beans. And Shoshana refused to eat them also, pointing to Rich: "He didn't eat them! He didn't eat them!"

He thought he was being polite by refusing seconds, when he should have followed my father's example, who made a big show of taking small portions of seconds, thirds, and even fourths, always saying he could not resist another bite of something or other, and then groaning that he was so full he thought he would burst.

But the worst was when Rich criticized my mother's cooking, and he didn't even know what he had done. As is the Chinese cook's custom, my mother always made disparaging remarks about her own cooking. That night she chose to direct it toward her famous steamed pork and preserved vegetable dish, which she always served with special pride.

"Ai! This dish not salty enough, no flavor," she complained, after tasting a small bite. "It is too bad to eat."

This was our family's cue to eat some and proclaim it the best she had ever   40 made. But before we could do so, Rich said, "You know, all it needs is a little soy sauce." And he proceeded to pour a riverful of the salty black stuff on the platter, right before my mother's horrified eyes.

And even though I was hoping throughout the dinner that my mother would somehow see Rich's kindness, his sense of humor and boyish charm, I knew he had failed miserably in her eyes.

Rich obviously had had a different opinion on how the evening had gone. When we got home that night, after we put Shoshana to bed, he said modestly, "Well. I think we hit it off *A-o-kay.*" He had the look of a dalmatian, panting, loyal, waiting to be petted.

"Uh-hmm," I said, I was putting on an old nightgown, a hint that I was not feeling amorous. I was still shuddering, remembering how Rich had firmly shaken both my parents' hands with that same easy familiarity he used with nervous new clients. "Linda, Tim," he said, "we'll see you again soon, I'm sure." My parents' names are Lindo and Tin Jong, and nobody, except a few older family friends, ever calls them by their first names.

"So what did she say when you told her?" And I knew he was referring to our getting married. I had told Rich earlier that I would tell my mother first and let her break the news to my father.

"I never had a chance," I said, which was true. How could I have told my mother   45 I was getting married, when at every possible moment we were alone, she seemed to remark on how much expensive wine Rich liked to drink, or how pale and ill he looked, or how sad Shoshana seemed to be.

Rich was smiling. "How long does it take to say, Mom, Dad, I'm getting married?"

"You don't understand. You don't understand my mother."

Rich shook his head. "Whew! You can say that again. Her English was *so* bad. You know, when she was talking about that dead guy showing up on *Dynasty,* I thought she was talking about something that happened in China a long time ago."

approximately 2200 words

Amy Tan, "Four Directions," *The Joy Luck Club* pp. 173–79, Copyright © 1989 by Amy Tan. Reprinted by permission of The Putnam Publishing Group.

Questions for Writing/Discussion

1. What are some of the previous assumptions held by Waverly's mother that complicate the present situation?

2. What conclusion can you draw about Rich's personality based on Waverly's description of him: "He had the look of a dalmatian, panting, loyal, waiting to be petted"? How does Rich's personality complicate his relationship with Waverly?

3. If you were Waverly's friend, what advice would you have given her prior to the introduction of Rich to her parents? What advice might you have also offered Rich?

4. Why does the writer include the episode with Waverly's aunt?

JOURNAL ENTRY

The three selections you read—the article "The Prenuptial Agreement," the text-book selection "The Developmental Course of Love and Marriage," and the literature selection from *The Joy Luck Club*—all deal with difficulties involved in lasting relationships. Discuss how the status of marriage might be viewed in the next century. What important changes do you see in the future? What kind of marriage would you want to have, and why?

Understanding the Power of Persuasive Language

This chapter will help you

◆ Learn to differentiate between denotative and connotative language.
◆ Understand the persuasive power of words.
◆ Become aware of figurative and euphemistic language.

❖❖❖

Before reading, think about these questions.

◆ What are some ways writers of essays and articles slant what they write?
◆ How many of your daily decisions are influenced by commercial advertising in newspapers and magazines and on television?
◆ Do governments sometimes abuse the power of persuasive language?

❖❖❖

Jot down your thoughts about how critically you evaluate what you read. _____

_____

_____

_____

❖ The Two Dimensions of Word Meanings: Denotation and Connotation

During your college years, you will add many new words to your vocabulary. As you have learned, a strong vocabulary is essential in adult and college reading. But it is not enough to know the dictionary definition of words; you must also understand their *suggested* meaning to avoid being manipulated by writers with a particular bias or attitude.

Word choice is often an indication of the writer's attitude toward the subject and should provide you with yet another clue for making valid inferences and drawing reasonable conclusions. When you are reading, it is important to recognize both the denotative and connotative language chosen to express ideas and opinions.

Denotation

Denotation refers to a word's literal meaning, its accepted dictionary definition. *Denotation is the meaning of a word independent of any emotional association.*

Textbook writers generally use denotative language as in the following example:

> The world's two most populous countries, India and China, will heavily influence future prospects for global overpopulation. These two countries, together encompassing more than one-third of the world's population, have adopted different policies to control population growth. In the absence of strong family-planning programs, India adds about 4 million more people each year than China. At current rates of natural increase, India will surpass China as the world's most populous country by the middle of the twenty-first century.
>
> William H. Renwick and James M. Rubenstein, *Introduction to Geography*, p. 287

Connotation

When the meaning of a word goes beyond its accepted, agreed-upon dictionary definition, it becomes the *connotation* of the word. *The connotation of a word includes all the ideas, associations, and implications suggested above and beyond the dictionary definition.* Connotations may be either positive or negative. Depending on how they are used, many words can **evoke** an emotional response in the reader, stir up the reader's feelings, or create a visual image. Some words, however, are stronger in connotation than others. For example, the word *relax* generally suggests taking time off to rest. The word *loaf*, on the other hand, also refers to taking time off, but the connotative meaning implies that the time off is spent idly or wastefully. A clear example of how the connotation of words can be shifted in emphasis is found in the famous remark

---

evoke (i vōk´) to call forth; to produce or elicit a reaction, emotion, or response

Bertrand Russell, the philosopher and author, once made: "I am *firm;* you are *stubborn;* he is *pig-headed.*" While all three terms have a similar denotative meaning, their connotations are obviously quite different.

ACTIVITY 8.1 Practice Distinguishing Denotative and Connotative Language

To develop your awareness of the two dimensions of words, complete the following activity. First, note the denotative or dictionary meaning of the words in the first column. Then, for each of these words, read the two additional words opposite them, both with connotative meanings. While the denotations of all three words are often quite similar, the words clearly connote different things. Indicate whether you believe the connotations are positive (P) or negative (N). The first one is done for you.

Term	Denotation	Connotation
1. home	the place where one lives	mansion <u>P</u> shack <u>N</u>
2. prison	a place where persons are confined	jail _____ correctional facility _____
3. intoxicated	without control	inebriated _____ drunk _____
4. automobile	a passenger car	gas guzzler _____ Mercedes _____
5. war	armed conflict	freedom fighting _____ massacre _____
6. fear	anxiety caused by danger	reverence _____ dread _____
7. talk	exchange ideas by spoken words	discussion _____ gossip _____
8. love	a deep and tender feeling	infatuation _____ devotion _____
9. frugal	not wasteful; living simply	thrifty _____ cheap _____
10. inquisitive	seeking information	curious _____ prying _____

❖ The Persuasive Power of Words

While denotative language is commonly used in informational writing such as textbooks, connotative language is frequently used in the persuasive writing of editorials, book and film reviews, advertisements, and political speeches. These written forms rely on words with strong connotations to influence the reader and what the reader may infer.

Depending on their purpose, writers select words that create either pleasant or unpleasant responses. Someone writing an ad for a breakfast cereal, for example, would most likely say things like "the cereal that fits your light, active life-style," "wholesome crunchy taste of sunny corn," and "goodness in every bite," positive and pleasing words that encourage you to purchase the product.

ACTIVITY 8.2 Practice Finding Connotative Words in Ads

Study the Smith Corona ad and circle the descriptive words used to try to convince you how their products can enhance learning.

Power tools for the mind.

If you want to do a job right, you need the right tools. Fortunately, there are no tools more perfect for communicating, creating and computing than Smith Corona typewriters, personal word processors and personal computers.

Every feature is designed to help you, not confuse you. Fear of technology is replaced by the freedom to think.

And with that freedom, you'll find that suddenly writing becomes easier. Work becomes more enjoyable. Your brain shifts into high gear.

So if you want to turn on your mind, the answer is exceedingly simple. Just turn on a Smith Corona.

For more information on these products, write to Smith Corona Corporation, 65 Locust Avenue, New Canaan, CT 06840 or Smith Corona Canada, 440 Tapscott Road, Scarborough, Ontario, Canada M1B 1Y4.

TYPEWRITERS PERSONAL WORD PROCESSORS PERSONAL COMPUTERS TYPEWRITERS PERSONAL WORD PROCESSORS

Courtesy Smith Corona Corporation

You should have circled phrases like "do a job right," "no tools more perfect," "Work becomes more enjoyable," "Fear of technology is replaced by freedom to think," "turn on your mind," "exceedingly simple," and "writing becomes easier." What does the ad imply that Smith Corona products can do?

_____

_____

Circle the descriptive words and phrases used in the ad to try to convince you to apply for a job with United Technologies.

UNITED BY DIVERSITY
At United Technologies, it's the differences among us that empower us as one.

Otis elevators. Carrier air conditioning units. Pratt & Whitney aircraft engines. At United Technologies, the parent company to these and other international leaders, our diversity goes far beyond our business mix.

We're committed to developing and using the full potential of our multiracial, multi-cultural work force around the world. From Sikorsky helicopters to Hamilton Standard aerospace systems, our companies have created work environments that value people.

If you are interested in working for a Fortune 50 leader with opportunities as diverse as our product mix, send your resume to: Diversity Programs Office, United Technologies Corporation, One Financial Plaza, Hartford, CT 06101. We are an equal opportunity employer.

UNITED TECHNOLOGIES

Carrier • Hamilton Standard • Norden Systems • Otis Elevator • Pratt & Whitney • Sikorsky Aircraft • UT Automotive • UT Research

Courtesy United Technologies

1. Did you circle phrases such as "empower us," "international leaders," and "full potential"?

_____

2. What other words or phrases did you circle?

_____

3. What can you infer to be the attitude of the management at United Technology regarding affirmative action?

_____

Like writers of advertisements, essayists imply approval of their ideas by using words with positive connotations, words that flatter or even exaggerate, such as *excellent*, *superb*, and *outstanding*. While these words imply approval, negative words that **disparage** or criticize—*foolish*, *awkward*, and *ignorant*—imply disapproval.

Ask this key question to evaluate writers' attempts to influence your thinking by the importance or slant of their words.

Are the descriptive words used primarily positive or negative, favorable or unfavorable, pleasant or unpleasant?

❖ Connotative Language

After you have identified the connotative language used, you can more accurately understand an author's attitude toward a subject, even if you disagree with that opinion. In order to distinguish positive or negative connotations and the writer's slant, we can map the connotative terms. By the end of the reading, we have a visual record of the essential words chosen, and we can more readily infer how the writer feels about the topic. The following movie review, for example, begins on a negative note.

It's hard to imagine a more appalling start for the movie year than "Not Without My Daughter," a crudely made, **xenophobic** and racist would-be thriller.

Here is a film that plays into its audiences' prejudices, confirming long-held beliefs that foreigners—particularly those whose cultures we don't understand—are not to be trusted. It will stir up hatred. . . .

In other words, the film is every bit as small-minded and bigoted as the . . . Islamic attitude it so rightly condemns. And on top of that, it's boring.

Peninsula Times Tribune, 19 Jan. 1991, p. C-1

The descriptive terms can be mapped like this.

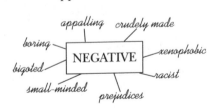

These negative words indicate that the reviewer finds the movie distasteful, so you can infer that watching it may not be worth your while.

To see how the slant of the message can be reversed, substitute *positive* connotative words in the spaces provided.

---

disparage (dis par´ ij) discredit; belittle
xenophobic (zen ə fō bik) fearing or hating strangers or foreigners

It's hard to imagine a more _____ start for the movie year than "Not Without My

Daughter," a _____ made _____, _____, and _____ thriller.

ACTIVITY 8.3   Practice Finding Connotative Terms in Passages

PASSAGE 1

Read the following passage about one aspect of the lives of celebrities. Circle the descriptive words and phrases, and write them in and around the boxes. Are these connotative words chiefly negative or positive? Place a check mark in the appropriate box.

> For celebrities, especially in the entertainment field, the pressure is always on to turn in a perfect performance, to be better than before, to constantly hit the mark. At the same time, artists tend to be sensitive souls, in touch with naked emotions they mine for our **perusal.**
>
> "Artists are the lenses through which life is transmitted. They show us what we think and feel in a way that is profound, intense, and highly emotional," [a professor of psychiatry] says. "They experience life more clearly than the rest of us." Drugs are a way to mute these feelings, which threaten to overwhelm.
>
> And with the riches that accompany their fame, drugs are an escape route celebrities can afford—at least for a while. The list of celebrity deaths from drugs is long, and continually updated—Elvis Presley, Judy Garland, Marilyn Monroe, Jim Morrison, Janis Joplin, Scott Newman, David Kennedy, John Belushi, River Phoenix.
>
> "I think it has to be remembered that he was 23 and he made the choice," said Judy Davis, who was set to star opposite Phoenix in his next movie. "There's something about stardom and the way it empowers people—he thought he was immune." Fame, therapists agree, can draw stars into a kind of magical thinking, wherein the laws of humankind are suspended.

Mary Loftus, "The Other Side of Fame," *Psychology Today,* May/June 1995, p. 72

1. What do the words you circled suggest about celebrities?

_____

_____

---

perusal (pə rōō´ zəl) careful examination

2. What inference can you make about the role fans play in creating the problems that celebrities face?

_____

_____

PASSAGE 2

Read the passage, and circle the connotative words. Are the words chiefly positive or negative? Check the appropriate box, and then answer the question below.

Strength of a Single Syllable

When you speak and write, no law says you have to use big words. Short words are as good as long ones, and short, old words like *sun* and *grass* and *home* are best of all. A lot of small words, more than you might think, can meet your needs with a strength, grace and charm that large words lack.

Big words can make the way dark for those who hear what you say and read what you write. They add fat to your prose. Small words are the ones we seem to have known from birth. They are like the hearth fire that warms the home, and they cast a clear light on big things: night and day, love and hate, war and peace, life and death.

Short words are bright, like sparks that glow in the night; sharp like the blade of a knife; hot like salt tears that scald the cheek; quick like moths that flit from flame to flame; and terse like the dart and sting of a bee.

If a long word says just what you want, do not fear to use it. But know that our tongue is rich in crisp, brisk, swift, short words. Make them the spine and the heart of what you speak and write. Like fast friends, they will not let you down.

Richard Lederer, "Strength of a Single Syllable," *The Miracle of Language. Reader's Digest,* 7 Nov. 1991, p. 7

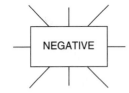

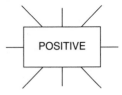

What do the descriptive words suggest?

_____

_____

_____

PASSAGE 3

Analyze the language in the paragraphs that follow, circling positive and negative words and phrases. These words should help you infer the young writer's attitude toward who is to blame for teenagers' use of drugs.

Teens Take Drugs Because There's Nothing Else to Do

The only way to get teens to stop using drugs is to make reality more appealing.

It is natural for everyone to experiment when they are young, but as a 19-year-old, I can tell you that people I know use drugs mainly because they're *bored*. And I don't blame them.

The measures that have been adopted to control the "problem"—closing beaches at night, curfews, closing clubs to those under 21, persecution of youth-oriented businesses and police patrols harassing youths in public areas—may make supplying drugs more difficult. But they only end up *increasing* demand and inspiring fear and contempt among teens of senseless authoritarian law enforcement that jumps down their throats every time they try to have a little fun.

If as much effort and money were spent on things for young people to *do* at night as has been wasted on jailing users and **draconian** efforts to stop the supply of drugs, nobody would *want* to use drugs because there would be so many other, more fun, alternatives.

It would probably have the added benefit of cutting down on teen pregnancy and sexually transmitted disease, sex being the other big time-killer among bored teens.

Society will never be able to protect us from the supposed evils of drug use through fear and restricted freedoms. It's about time we addressed the problem of *why* everyone is so desperate to get high.

Brad Hill, "Teens Take Drugs Because There's Nothing Else to Do," *San Jose Mercury,* July 23, 1995, p. A3. Copyright © 1995. Reprinted by permission.

1. What do the connotative words you circled suggest about the author's feelings for "authoritarian law enforcement"?

_____

_____

2. Do you agree with the writer that teens turn to drugs out of boredom?

_____

---

draconian (dra kō´ nē ən) a law or code that is extremely severe or harsh

PASSAGE 4

Is an Obsession with Health a Sign of Sickness?

Day after day this spring, the gyms, pools and Nautilus machines of the city pulse with the thud, splash and grunt of innumerable Americans who claim fervently that they live more healthily than ever.

But the same cannot be said for the society that surrounds them. When it comes to the elusive goal of perfect physical condition, the United States is deluded, uptight and confused, jogging and lifting and power-walking on a joyless quest for an unavailable immortality.

The prospect of 40 million "serious" joggers is bad enough. But what's worse is the creation of a religion of running, a philosophy of fitness that leaves its adherents without the deeper consolations of a true philosophy that reconciles them to their mortal selves.

True, Americans have emerged as among the healthiest people of all time. The average child born in 1984 can expect to live to the age of 74.7. In 1900, the life expectancy was only 47.3 years.

Yet, even so, all this fitness appears not to have bought even short-term happiness. People spend $6 billion a year on running shoes, yet worry constantly about heart fibrillations. They pump iron on the $738 million worth of exercise machines they bought last year, yet read electrocardiograms like horoscopes.

Indeed, so anxious and preoccupied have we become with being healthy that we appear incapable of even enjoying the benefits of good health. No wonder that after 15 years of intense health mania, during which life expectancy increased a staggering 3.8 years, polls show that the numbers of those satisfied with their health have actually dropped.

approximately 375 words

Mark Muro, "Is an Obsession with Health a Sign of Sickness?" *Boston Globe* SM, June 7, 1989, p. 30

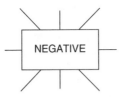

1. What does the author's choice of words like *thud, splash,* and *grunt* imply about his attitude toward exercise?

_____

_____

2. Why does the author think the United States is "deluded, uptight and confused" about the status of its physical well-being?

_____

_____

3. Is the author's conclusion that jogging is a "religion" justified?

_____

_____

4. Is the author's conclusion that there is "an intense health mania" valid or invalid? Defend your opinion.

_____

_____

_____

ACTIVITY 8.4 Practice Finding Connotative Language in Essays

Practice finding the connotative terms in the selections that follow. Analyze the language, circling positive and negative words. Then, infer the author's attitude toward society and answer the questions.

The first essay concerns the idea that we are becoming less like humans; in other words, we are being *dehumanized*.

PASSAGE 1

Dehumanization Happens

Listen closely to this story. A drunk on the subway wants desperately to impress a woman. He wants to impress her so desperately that he takes it upon himself to open the doors of the train while mumbling some **incoherent** advances, and through a combination of unfortunate mishaps and drunken stupidity, he ends up on the tracks and is **decapitated.**

No one—certainly not the woman—is impressed. She is hysterical.

Can you find any humor whatsoever in this true-life story? If you responded, "No. I see absolutely nothing funny about that story. It's sickening and tragic, what you'd expect to see sensationalized on the evening news," you flunked the test by the standards of modern society.

However, you may still be one of the few thinking human beings left in America. You

---

incoherent (in´ kō hir´ ənt) unable to express one's thoughts in an orderly manner
decapitated (dē kap´ ə tāt´ əd) beheaded

have not yet passed over to the dark side—where countless others have gone quite willingly.

I heard the account of the decapitated subway rider on morning talk radio, where taste is clearly not a criterion for success and where vulgarity is a **prerequisite** for popularity among the "shock jocks."

The rhinoceros in the radio studio tried to extract every possible ounce of sick humor from the story. He and his colleagues **guffawed** and cackled and made indecent quips. It made me momentarily wonder whether I perhaps was too prudish. You see, your sense of good taste gets jaded very easily in our culture, and you begin to ignore things that clearly would have sickened you in another decade.

Whether it involves the **misogyny** or violence of gangsta rap, the vulgarity of drive-time radio, or any of the other curious manifestations that make modern America look like Fellini's "Satyricon" or "A Clockwork Orange," we can only shrug over the indignities. They have become so commonplace we are beyond the point of outrage. That's the first sign you are changing.

approximately 315 words

Joe Pisani, "Dehumanization Happens," *San Jose Mercury*, March 5, 1995, p. 14

1. What do the circled words imply about the author's attitude?

_____

_____

2. What do you dislike most about particular news stories on TV?

_____

_____

Read the following essay concerning writing letters to decide whether the change is significant for the future of business communication. Circle the connotative words and phrases, and then answer the questions that follow.

PASSAGE 2

Why Computers Can't Write

Recently, newspaper columnist Russell Baker applied his nationally syndicated wit to the subject of the relationship between poor letter writing and computer technology. In Baker's opinion, word processors make graceless writing all too easy. Here are some of his observations:

---

prerequisite (prē rek´ wi zit) requirement
guffawed (gǝ fod´) hearty or coarse burst of laughter
misogyny (mi sôj´ ǝ nē) hatred of women

After using my powerful word processor to write a letter. . . . , I printed it on my state-of-the-art laser printer. What a professional look it had! It didn't look like a letter at all. It looked like a piece of junk mail.

Every day brings a dozen documents that look exactly like this letter. Every day they flutter into my trash can unread. One knows their messages too well:

An astounding new shampoo is available. An officeholder praises his own achievements. A sales pitch disguised as a lottery advises the recipient to steel himself for the arrival of an armored truck full of dollars. A friend of the President says a contribution of $10,000 is **imperative** in this critical year though $25 will not be sneered at.

My beautifully printed letter showed me caught in the American comedy about the silliness of progress. Just look at this letter: Writing it required several thousand dollars' worth of electronic machinery, not to mention a supply of electricity provided by vast corporations whose hot wiry **tentacles** stretched across thousands of miles.

With all these resources, what emerged? A letter that looked so like junk mail that [the recipient] would probably toss it away unread.

What's more, it was a poorly written letter—not a graceful phrase in it, too much stiffness in the prose joints, and twice as long as it needed to be.

Such gassiness is characteristic of writing done on computers. Computers make the physical toil of writing so negligible that the writer can write on forever, and often does, as I am currently doing at this very particular and precious point in time, a.k.a. now. . . .

My second-rate letter with the junk-mail look is a typical child of progress. With a goose quill, Thomas Jefferson could have written a letter at a fraction of the cost. It would have looked like the work of a human being, and it would have been a better letter than mine.

It would have been better not only because Jefferson had the more interesting mind but also because writing with goose feathers is such messy work that a writer has to put his mind in order before starting. With a computer, he merely flips a switch, then lets his brain mosey around in the fog on the chance it may bump into an idea. . . .

approximately 400 words

Russell Baker, "Ruled by Tools," *The New York Times,* May 12, 1992, p. A23.
Louis E. Boone and David L. Kurtz, *Contemporary Business Communication,* p. 194

1. What is the writer's opinion of letter writing with a computer?

_____

_____

2. Would you infer that the writer uses a computer to write his many essays and books?

Support: _____

_____

_____

---

imperative (im per´ ə tiv) expressing a command or having power to control
tentacles (ten´ tə kəlz) grasping fingers or arms like those of an octopus

3. What does Baker mean by "lets his brain mosey around in the fog"?

_____

_____

PASSAGE 3

Read the following article, "Civil Liberties Watch." The author takes a firm stand on what she believes is an **erosion** of our civil liberties and attacks many of our institutions. Circle all the connotative words and phrases, and then answer the questions that follow the essay.

Civil Liberties Watch

Barbara Dority

. . . As the lengthening tentacles of censorship crept down alleys and under back doors, civil libertarians did not sleep well. We became increasingly alarmed by the relentless erosion of our intellectual and personal freedoms. . . .

Many of us tried to sound an alarm. "Wake up!" we cried. "We're losing our liberties bit by bit. Look there! The monster is creeping upon us, shrouded in the fog. Can't you see it?"

Most people thought we were alarmists—until recently. Feeding on its many "small" successes, the **insidious** monster has grown bold and confident, revealing itself for all to see.

No medium is safe. Individuals and groups seeking to restrict the flow of information, images, and ideas are targeting public libraries, school classrooms, and resource centers. Motion pictures and television programs are policed by such groups as the American Family Association. Librarians, educators, school boards, publishers, bookstores, theaters, video stores, artists, musicians, and the electronic media are under persistent and organized attack. Under threats of legal action and boycott, many are capitulating to pressure tactics. America's marketplace of ideas is shrinking on a daily basis.

Artists, previously unconcerned, have been rudely awakened. They no longer believe that censorship only happens to other people. With the visual and performing arts under fire, the National Endowment for the Arts has been forced to implement funding restrictions on "offensive" works. Musicians and music distributors have been arrested and charged with violation of **obscenity** laws. Record companies have been pressured into censorship and labeling. The government restricts foreign educational films and speakers. The Supreme Court expands the definition of libel. The Freedom of Information Act slowly continues to erode.

Sexually explicit publications and information about sexuality are subject to severe restrictions. Magazines such as *Playboy* and *Penthouse* have been pulled from many retail shelves. Public school health and sex education books

---

erosion (i rō´ zhən) a wearing away
insidious (in sid´ ē əs) sly; crafty
obscenity (ăb sen´ ə tē) disgusting words or actions

are being challenged and, all too often, banned. In many school districts, opponents of sex education have succeeded in implementing programs based solely upon abstinence—programs which contain no information on prevention of pregnancy or sexually transmitted diseases.

In short, our public schools are under **siege** and held hostage by those who would impose a narrow view of life on all our children. Orchestrated censorship campaigns by highly organized and well-funded conservative groups are successful in over one-third of reported cases.

As a result of this hysterical climate, many are engaging in self-censorship. Librarians don't order "possibly controversial" books, school administrators censor student publications, and textbook publishers remove "controversial" materials from reading and science texts.

Liberty is like good health: we take it for granted until we lose it. During the past year, scores of "ordinary Americans" have seen the face of the monster. . . . They know that we can't sit around the kitchen table agreeing that censorship is wrong and waiting for someone else to do something about it. We can no longer afford to say we support freedom of expression while maintaining serious reservations about the Larry Flynts and the neo-Nazi skinheads.

It is our responsibility to organize and instruct these newly activated individuals. What we do not understand, we cannot effectively combat. Thus, it is essential that we possess and pass on an understanding of the pro-censorship mindset.

The pro-censorship mindset has remained the same throughout the history of civilization. The censors always aim at protecting us from the **perceived** harmful effects of what we read, see, and hear.

approximately 600 words

Barbara Dority, "Civil Liberties Watch," *The Humanist*, Vol. 51, No. 1 (Jan/February 1991) p. 43. Reprinted with permission of the publisher.

1. List the institutions and areas of our society the writer states are under attack.

   _____

   _____

2. Do you agree with the author? Has her choice of words influenced your opinion about our "loss of civil liberties"?

   _____

   _____

   _____

   _____

_____

siege (sēj) a long distressing period
perceived (pər sēvd´) recognized

3. Can you think of a serious instance where violations of civil liberties occurred in your state or country? Are there instances occurring today that you would consider violations of someone's civil liberties?

_____

_____

_____

❖ Figurative Language

Figures of speech are expressions that mean something other than what is actually stated. They are not meant to be interpreted literally but rather carry implied meanings. Figurative language gives stronger impact to ideas and opinions, often using *comparisons* to clarify or enrich abstract ideas, create emotional responses, or make ideas more interesting and colorful. We use figures of speech so much we often take their implied meaning for granted. If someone says, "This assignment is driving me up a wall," the exaggerated expression is not taken literally—the person is not sitting in a car being driven vertically up a wall! The expression means the assignment is creating some kind of anxiety or frustration. Whether in speaking or writing, when figurative expressions are used, they say one thing but mean another.

The following examples illustrate the difference between figurative and literal language:

> Figurative:　I *bombed* on the physics test.
> Literal:　　 The terrorists *bombed* the bank building.

> Figurative:　I'll see to it that you *eat* those words.
> Literal:　　 They will *eat* their meals in the new facility.

ACTIVITY 8.5 Distinguishing Literal and Figurative Expressions

In the following exercise, decide whether the statement can be read literally (L), meaning precisely what it states, or figuratively (F). If you decide the statement is figurative, ask yourself

What is being compared?

What is the association?

Write L or F in the space provided. For those you mark F, write out the implied meaning. Study the example first.

Example:

___F___ The blue eyes are frosted, looking inward like the windows of a snowbound cottage.

Richard Selzer, "The Discus Thrower"

Meaning: *Someone's eyes are clouded, and the person is unable to see clearly in the same way that one cannot see clearly out of an icy window.*

_____ 1. Human beings are restless and dissatisfied, always in search of new experiences, seldom content with the familiar.

L. Rust Hills, "How to Eat an Ice Cream Cone"

Meaning: _____

_____

_____ 2. Before the girls got to the porch, I heard their laughter crackling and popping like pine logs in a cooking stove.

Maya Angelou, "Grandmother's Victory"

Meaning: _____

_____

_____ 3. The story of Wing Biddlebaum is a story of hands. Their restless activity, like unto the beating of the wings of an imprisoned bird, had given him his name.

Sherwood Anderson, "Hands," *Winesburg, Ohio*

Meaning: _____

_____

_____ 4. A great deal of confusion and misinformation exists about just how science "works," and people make unwise and even dangerous decisions as a result.

Fundamentals of Anatomy

Meaning: _____

_____

_____ 5. Florida is like a sunny old playroom with several generations of wallpaper pasted one atop the other. As the layers peel away, it's startling to find what rests underneath: someone else's idea of fun or beauty or exotica.

Modern Maturity, April 1995

Meaning: _____

_____

_____ 6. The tiny foreigner tensed like a viper at the first provocation, ready to lash out at anyone who stood in his way.

Isabel Allende, *The Stories of Eva Luna*

Meaning: _____

_____

_____ 7. Waves, tired and angry and carrying their own weight over so many uninterrupted miles of water, unburden themselves in a tantrum of surf on the tiny cove.

Susan Hand Schetterly, *Pitcairn Island*

Meaning: _____

_____

_____ 8. The language of the conquering Europeans became the language of government, law, and usually education, and when the colonies gained their independence and chose an official language, many chose their former ruler's language.

Edward F. Bergman, *Human Geography*

Meaning: _____

_____

❖ Figuring Out Figures of Speech

Similes and Metaphors

Many figures of speech use comparison, which may be stated directly in the form of a *simile* or indirectly in the form of a *metaphor. A simile is a definitely stated comparison between two unlike objects and signaled by words such as* like *or* as. We can say of a quiet person, "Marc is *as* quiet *as* a fading sunset"; of an angry person, "He burst out the door *like* an explosion"; or of a contented person, "She acts *like* a cat with her soft purring words." Although the comparison is directly stated in the simile, there is also an implied meaning that changes the way you feel about the subject. For example, Marc is quiet but in a gentle way; "bursting out the door like an explosion" suggests a loud, sudden noise; and "purring words" have the effect of soothing and comforting tones.

Do not assume that whenever you see *like* or *as* in a sentence, it is a simile. To be a simile, a sentence must state a comparison between unlike things. For example, there is no simile present in "My house is like your house."

Comparisons using figures of speech can often be made indirectly in the form of a metaphor. *A metaphor is an implied comparison of unlike objects with some point in common without using the signal words* like *or* as. To say, "The salesperson is a sly fox" is to imply the person is crafty or clever like a fox. To describe *rage*, one might say, "The anger of the man was a consuming fire." Carl Sandburg used a metaphor to describe slang: "Slang is language that rolls up its sleeves, spits on its hands, and gets down to business."

Personification

Personification is another type of figurative language. *In personification the writer gives an inanimate object human qualities, emotions, or characteristics.* Examples include saying that the ocean *roared,* the wind *howled,* or the clock *struck* one.

Four key questions can help the reader understand the implied meanings usually found in figurative language.

1. What qualities are being compared?
2. What is implied in the comparison?
3. Why is the writer making the comparison?
4. Does the writer create a positive or negative image?

ACTIVITY 8.6 **Making Comparisons Using Figurative Language**

Explain what is meant by each of the following statements.

1. Kindness is a language the deaf can hear and the blind can read.

Mark Twain

Kindness is compared to _____ in two ways:

a. _____

b. _____

2. The sad thing about truth is that it keeps changing its clothes.

Curtis Bok

a. Truth is said to be similar to _____

b. Its literal meaning is _____

3. Her ideas dried up like a raisin in the sun. What is meant by an idea drying up?

_____

4. An aged man is but a paltry thing, a tattered coat upon a stick.

William Butler Yeats, "Sailing to Byzantium"

In comparing an old man to a "tattered coat upon a stick," the poet creates the image of a

_____

5. It is clear that being a spy is rather like riding a bicycle; once you have learned how, you never forget.

Time Nov. 18, 1985

What likeness does a spy bear to riding a bicycle? _____

ACTIVITY 8.7   Making Comparisons with Figurative Language in Short Selections

Consider the ideas suggested by the use of figurative language in the following passages. Then answer the questions that follow. The first one has been done for you as an example.

PASSAGE 1

[1] . . . enthusiasm for the death penalty seems based less on facts than on superstition. [2] By some kind of ritual magic, the killing of murderers is supposed to ward off burglars, thieves, muggers, rapists and armed robbers who prey on the innocent citizen minding his own business. [3] Our Supreme Court Justices, like cynical witch doctors in some primitive society, seem to agree among themselves that this magic may not be much good, but it vents frustration and makes people feel that the Government is doing its job. [4] What it's doing is **condoning** murder as an appropriate response to a terrible grievance, instead of correcting the problems in our society, our courts and our criminal-justice system.

Playboy, Jan. 1977

_____ 1. The figure of speech used in the third sentence, "Our Supreme Court Justices, like cynical witch doctors in some primitive society," is an example of
   a. simile   b. metaphor   c. personification

---

condoning (kon dōn´ ing) forgiving or overlooking an offense

Answer: a. Two clues help. The first is the use of *like* in the sentence, and the second, the comparison of Supreme Court justices to witch doctors.

2. What does the use of this and other figurative language imply about the writer's attitude toward capital punishment?

Answer: The writer suggests from the first sentence with the word *superstition* a lack of respect for people who favor the death penalty and further suggests that "this magic" is used to appease people's desire for justice but is itself a form of murder.

PASSAGE 2

Genetic engineering, the upstart young science that dares to tinker with the building blocks of life, is suddenly out of its diapers and into a business suit.

Ready or not, it is knocking at the door, carrying a sample case full of wonders both exciting and disturbing:

Soon we will be able to know if our babies will be healthy—before pregnancy.

We will be treated or cured of diseases once considered hopeless. We will even know how likely we are to get certain illnesses during our lifetimes.

We will shop in supermarkets where the pork is as lean as chicken, the tomatoes are perfect and the produce is free of viruses and pesticides.

Along with its bright promises, genetic engineering is lugging around some heavier baggage: the legacy of Nazi **eugenics** atrocities, fears of runaway mutant microbes, suspicions that a powerful technology will fall into the hands of crackpots and tyrants.

As it has matured over the past decade, genetic engineering has put some of these fears to rest by showing it can work within regulatory limits and without unpleasant surprises.

For genetics researchers, whose crowning achievement formerly was a Nobel Prize, the marriage of laboratory discoveries with **entrepreneurship** means they can become rich by discovering a new gene that can be used to make a valuable product.

> Ronald Kotulak and Peter Gomer, "The Gene is Out of the Bottle," *Chicago Tribune*, Apr. 8, 1990, p. C-5

_____ 1. In the first paragraph, the metaphor describing genetic engineering implies that
   a. genetic engineers are now businesspeople.
   b. the baby boomers have become genetic engineers.
   c. genetic engineering has matured and is making some medical advances.
   d. genetic engineering is useful for infertile couples.

   Support: _____

---

eugenics (yoō jen´ iks) movement to improve the human condition by controlling heredity
entrepreneurship (ăn trə prə nur´ ship) organizing a business undertaking

_____ 2. The phrase "it is knocking at the door" in paragraph 2 is an example of
a. simile
b. metaphor
c. personification

Support: _____

_____ 3. What is the literal meaning of "The marriage of laboratory discoveries with entrepreneurship means they can become rich by discovering a new gene that can be used to make a valuable product"?

_____

PASSAGE 3

The following passage is a partial transcript of the speech John F. Kennedy gave when he was sworn in as president and voiced his interest in creating the Peace Corps.

In your hands, my fellow citizens, more than in mine, will rest the final success or failure of our course. Since this country was founded, each generation has been summoned to give testimony to its national loyalty. The graves of young Americans who answered that call encircle the globe. Now the trumpet summons us again—not as a call to bear arms, though arms we need—not as a call to battle, though embattled we are—but a call to bear the burden of a long twilight struggle, year in and year out, "rejoicing in hope, patient in tribulation"—a struggle against the common enemies of man: tyranny, poverty, disease and war itself. Can we forge against these enemies a grand and global alliance, north and south, east and west, that can assure a more fruitful life for all mankind? Will you join in that historic effort? In the long history of the world, only a few generations have been granted the role of defending freedom in its hour of maximum danger. I do not shrink from this responsibility—I welcome it. I do not believe that any of us would exchange places with any other people or any other generation. The energy, the faith, and the devotion which we bring to this endeavor will light our country and all who serve it—and the glow from that fire can truly light the world. And so, my fellow Americans: Ask not what your country can do for you—ask what you can do for your country. My fellow citizens of the world: Ask not what America will do for you, but what together we can do for the freedom of man.

John F. Kennedy, Inaugural Address, 20 Jan. 1961

_____ 1. "And the glow from that fire would truly light the world" is an example of
a. simile   b. metaphor   c. personification

2. What is the literal meaning of "Now the trumpet summons us again"?

_____

3. Is the use of the word *light* in the sentence "The energy, the faith, and the devotion which we bring to this endeavor will light our country and all who serve it" a good choice? Why or why not?

ACTIVITY 8.8 Figurative Language in Literature

Read the following excerpts, the first from Eudora Welty's story *Losing Battles,* and the second from Julia Sorel's novel *Rocky*. After reading them, go back and underline the figures of speech. Then answer the questions that follow.

PASSAGE 1

When the rooster crowed, the moon had still not left the world but was going down on flushed cheek, one day short of the full. A long thin cloud crossed it slowly, drawing itself out like a name being called. The air changed, as if a mile or so away a wooden door had swung open, and a smell, more of warmth than wet, from a river at low stage, moved upward into the clay hills that stood in darkness.

Then a house appeared on its ridge, like an old man's silver watch pulled once more out of its pocket. A dog leaped up from where he'd lain like a stone and began barking for today as if he meant never to stop.

Then a baby bolted naked out of the house. She monkey-climbed down the steps and ran open-armed into the yard, knocking at the walls of flowers still colorless as faces, tagging in turn the four big trees that marked off the corners of the yard, tagging the gatepost, the well-piece, the bird-house, the bell post, a log seat, a rope swing, and then, rounding the house, she used all her strength to push over a crate that let a stream of white Plymouth Rocks loose on the world. The chickens rushed ahead of the baby, running frantic, and behind the baby came a girl in a petticoat. A wide circle of curl-papers, paler than the streak of dawn, bounced around her head, but she ran on confident tiptoe as though she believed no eye could see her. She caught the baby and carried her back inside, the baby with her little legs still running like a windmill.

Eudora Welty, *Losing Battles*

PASSAGE 2

Read about a brutal boxing match.

Insanely, Rocky got to his feet and tensed with renewed energy. He was a wounded, wild animal. The tide had suddenly turned and washed Rocky up on Apollo Creed. Rocky dropped low and caught Apollo with a pair of terrific body punches that seemed to drive Apollo's diaphragm up to his throat. A loud crack was heard. A glaze of pain covered Apollo's eyes with the jellied aspic of cruel reality. It was only by a supreme effort that the champion stayed upright. He was so badly hurt that he began to bend in the middle, like store-away furniture: Pretty soon, if he didn't rally, there'd be no room for him, and he'd be put away. Rocky kept coming; he imagined that Apollo was a frozen side of beef just waiting for Rocky to tenderize its dark flesh. But Apollo defrosted like a flash, flicked dread jabs into Rocky's eyes. Still, Rocky waded in with punches that seemed to bulge out Apollo's back. Creed took the punishment like a stoic. He had picked the Italian Stallion, and now that the horse was running wild, stampeding all over him, it was up to him to tame the wild beast or kill it in the name of sport. Blood, like dampened flame, or the soft tongue of the sanguinary soul, ran from Apollo's mouth. He didn't like losing it—blood was personal, his Universal O automotive fuel. In the clinch he leaned over Rocky, and it dripped down the Italian's neck and shoulders like a mantle. Apollo shielded his wound from the ringside judges and continued to fight.

Julia Sorel, *Rocky,* p. 130

1. Both writers use many figurative expressions. Select two from each passage that you felt were very effective, and explain their literal meanings.

Losing Battles   a. _____

                  b. _____

Rocky   a. _____

                  b. _____

2. Which of the two passages affected you more emotionally? Why?

_____

PASSAGE 3

Read about the feelings one may experience while looking at a volcano.

Kilauea

The volcano is on Hawaii, the largest island of the group. You land at Hilo and drive up, first through fields of rice and sugar-cane and then, climbing all the time, through a forest of great tree-ferns. They are weird and strange like the imaginations of some **draughtsman** of the horrible. All manner of climbing plants wind around the trees in an impenetrable tangle. Gradually the vegetation stops and you come to the lava field, grey, dead, silent; here no plants grow and no birds sing; you see the smoke rising, here and there thickly, in other places ascending thin and straight like the smoke from a cottage chimney. You get out and walk. The lava crunches under your feet. Now and then you step over narrow fissures from which the **sulphurous** smoke rises, making you cough. You come to the jagged edge of the crater. Nothing has prepared you for the sight. It is stupendous and alarming. You look down upon a vast sea of lava. It is black and heavy. It is in perpetual movement. The lava is only a thin crust and it is broken at irregular inter-

---

draughtsman (drats´ man) British term for a draftsman
sulphurous (sul´ fə rəs); a variant spelling for *sulfurous,* a pale yellow nonmetallic substance

vals by gashes of red fire, and here and there again are geysers of flame rising into the air, thirty, or forty or fifty feet. They spurt up, white hot, like artificial fountains. The two most impressive things are the roar: it is like the roar of surf on a gloomy day, as unceasing, or like the roar of a **cataract**, as **formidable;** and secondly the movement: the lava moves on, on, all the time, with a stealthy movement in which you may almost see the purpose of a living thing. There is something strangely determined about its quiet progress, it has a **malign** tenacity; and yet it transcends anything living, it has the inevitableness of fate and the ruthlessness of time. The lava is like some huge formless creature born of **primeval** slime crawling slowly in pursuit of some loathsome prey. The lava moves forward steadily towards a fiery gap and then seems to fall into a bottomless cavern of flame. You see vast holes of fire, great caves of flame. A man standing near said: "Gosh, it's like hell," but a priest beside him turned and said: "No, it is like the face of God."

approximately 350 words

W. Somerset Maugham, *A Writer's Notebook*, pp. 105–106

1. The author wishes to create a certain mood or effect with phrases such as "here no plants grow and no birds sing" and "it is like the roar of surf on a gloomy day, as unceasing, or like the roar of a cataract, as formidable." What feeling does the author try to convey? Why?

   _____

   _____

2. Figurative language is found throughout this selection. For example, smoke from the fissures is compared to smoke from a cottage chimney. List three other figures of speech you found especially descriptive.

   a. _____

   b. _____

   c. _____

3. Rewrite two sentences of the selection, using denotative language to make them as objective as possible.

   _____

   _____

---

cataract (kat´ ə rakt) a great waterfall

formidable (fôr´ mə də bəl) arousing fear and dread

malign (mə līn´) to speak evil or slander

primeval (prī´ mē vəl) belonging to the earliest ages; original

Euphemisms

Euphemisms are still another form of figurative language used when writers wish to describe an unpleasant subject or situation. They use indirect, less objectionable, more pleasant-sounding words to tell it "like it isn't" rather than "like it is"! Thus, by definition, *a euphemism is a softer or less offensive word or phrase used to replace one that is unpleasant, stronger or harsher.* Its original meaning, from the Greek, is "to use words of good **omen.**"

Euphemistic terms abound in our everyday speaking and writing. We often refer to old people as "senior citizens," their time as the "golden years." We say that someone's "employment has been terminated" or that a company is "managing staff resources" instead of saying someone has been fired. Euphemisms are frequently used in job descriptions to elevate a seemingly inferior position: a dogcatcher becomes an "animal control officer," a secretary becomes an "administrative assistant," a garbage collector a "sanitation engineer," and a housewife a "domestic engineer"!

The critical reader checks to see whether the writer has used euphemisms to disguise feelings or develop implications since euphemisms are frequently used to deceive and manipulate thinking. In his classic essay "Politics and the English Language," George Orwell wrote, "political language has to consist largely of euphemism, question-begging and sheer cloudy vagueness."

The use of euphemisms is sometimes referred to as "doublespeak."

ACTIVITY 8.9 Recognizing Euphemistic Expressions

Match the euphemistic expression in the first column with its corresponding intended meaning in the second.

Expression	Intended Meaning
____ 1. stretch the truth	a. broke
____ 2. temporarily without funds	b. have a facelift
____ 3. rejuvenate one's appearance with cosmetic manipulations	c. vending machine
	d. lie
____ 4. previously owned vehicle	e. suicidal
____ 5. misappropriate the company's funds	f. salesperson
____ 6. politically correct	g. inoffensive
____ 7. terminally disenchanted	h. steal
____ 8. habitual offender	i. criminal
____ 9. customer service representative	j. used car
____ 10. electronic merchandise device	

omen (ō´ men) something supposed to tell a future happening

ACTIVITY 8.10

As you read the next essay, underline the euphemisms (doublespeak) used by the Pentagon. When you have finished reading the selection, complete the matching exercise. Before you begin reading, think about what the following cartoon implies about euphemisms.

MICROSERFS

(FORMERLY THE 7 DWARFS)

T.O. Sylvester, "Microserfs" *San Francisco Chronicle and Examiner*, (October 23, 1994). Copyright © 1994 by T.O. Sylvester. Reprinted by permission.

No Ordinary Nut

William Lutz

. . . Doublespeak—whether jargon, euphemisms or bureaucratese—is not a slip of the tongue but a conscious use of language as both a tool and a weapon. It is language that conceals or manipulates thought. It makes the bad seem good, the negative appear positive, the unpleasant appear attractive or at least tolerable.

There is doublespeak in everyday life ("nondairy creamer"), business ("nonperforming assets") and government (the Internal Revenue Service). But when it comes to doublespeak, the military has a way with words that is unmatched. Only the military could call a tent a "frame-supported tension structure"; a parachute an "aerodynamic personnel decelerator"; and a zipper an "interlocking slide fastener."

Others may call it a bomb, but to the Army it's a "vertically deployed anti-personnel device."

NO MORE WAR

Military doublespeak starts at the top. From the founding of our republic, there has been a Department of War. Until 1947, that is, when the military pulled off the doublespeak **coup** of

---

coup (ko͞o) a brilliant action; clever move

the century. On July 27 President Harry S. Truman signed the National Security Act of 1947, an act that completely reorganized the armed forces. Section 202 establishes the post of secretary of Defense, while Section 205(a) eliminates the Department of War. Thus, war became "defense."

At first glance this change might not seem all that significant, but examine the implications. Now members of Congress campaign to spend more on "defense." Candidates for public office charge their opponents with wanting to cut the $300 billion defense budget, not the $300 billion war budget.

Doublespeak also is useful when the Pentagon wants expensive items to sound very complicated and worth their high price. It's not an ordinary steel nut; it's a "hexiform rotatable surface compression unit," which is why it cost $2,043 for just one of them. This little piece of doublespeak also allows the military to say that the equipment "suffered dramatically degraded useful operational life owing to the fact that a $2,000 hexiform rotatable surface compression unit underwent catastrophic stress-related shaft detachment," which sounds a lot more impressive than saying it won't work because a 13-cent nut broke.

Some penny-pinchers may think that $31,672 is a lot to pay for a couch, a love seat and 20 dining room chairs (or almost $1,500 for each piece of furniture), but not if you think of it the way the Navy does. All that money was spent on "habitability improvements" for the destroyer USS Kidd.

Nothing is ever simple with the Pentagon. Even a newly designed bayonet becomes a "weapons system," while the smoke used in smoke bombs becomes a "universal obscurant." Even that favorite of the GI, field rations or C-rations, has now become MRE or "meal, ready

to eat," though changing the name won't make it taste any better.

Then there is the "survivable enduring shelter," or SES, designed by Goodyear Aerospace to be placed on an existing truck chassis. Equipped with a 5,000-pound-plus payload, armor-plated shielding capable of stopping .30 caliber "projectiles" (Pentagon doublespeak for bullets) and an "intrusion detection system" (meaning a burglar alarm), the SES is designed "to meet the most stringent technical requirements for survival during a nuclear event," meaning it's supposed to be able to survive a nuclear bomb attack. . . .

IN OTHER WORDS, IT BLEW UP

With doublespeak, weapons never fail. The Pentagon can explain that the cruise missile didn't fly out of control and crash in three pieces during a test flight in Canada. According to the Air Force, the missile merely "impacted with the ground prematurely." Not to be outdone by their U.S. counterparts, an official of the Canadian forces said the test flight was simply "terminated five minutes earlier than planned." When an unarmed Minuteman III intercontinental ballistic missile developed problems after launch and had to be destroyed by commands radioed from the ground, the U.S. Air Force announced, "An **anomaly** occurred during the flight which caused the early termination." Although the Bigeye aerial nerve-gas bomb has been on the drawing boards for more than 20 years, it still doesn't work and, during one test drop in 1982, the bomb malfunctioned, producing what the Pentagon called "a forcible ejection of the internal bomb components." In other words, the bomb blew up.

With doublespeak, the missile can miss the target but the test can still be a success. "We did

---

anomaly (ə nom´ ə lē) abnormal event

acquire the target, but we did not hit it. . . . We achieved our objectives," said Jim Kittinger, an official in the air-to-surface guided weapons office at Elgin Air Force Base. . . .

approximately 600 words

Pentagon Doublespeak: Match the Euphemism with the Actual Meaning.

_____ 1. kill the enemy   a. weapon impacted with the ground prematurely

_____ 2. bayonet   b. vertically deployed anti-personnel device

_____ 3. weapon failure   c. habitability improvements

_____ 4. bomb   d. weapons system

_____ 5. exorbitant money   e. service the target
for furnishings

2. Is the Pentagon justified in using euphemisms and doublespeak?

Why, or why not? _____

_____

3. What is the author's chief complaint about the military?

_____

❖ Summary

The critical reader must be aware of the writer's use of denotative and connotative language because writers frequently choose the latter, which carries implied meanings. Denotative language can be taken literally since the words mean exactly what they say, while connotative language uses words that carry suggested meanings and are designed to arouse or allay certain emotions. Recognizing whether words have implied meanings helps the reader comprehend the writer's message and therefore reach sound conclusions and form unbiased judgments about issues.

Figures of speech are one way of using connotative language. Examples of figurative language include simile, metaphor, and personification.

1. A *simile* is a direct comparison of two unlike objects that have one point or trait in common, signaled with words such as *like* or *as*.

2. A *metaphor* is an implied comparison of two unlike objects that have one point or trait in common.

3. *Personification* expresses a comparison in which an inanimate object is given life-like qualities.

Euphemisms, sometimes referred to as doublespeak, may also be used when a writer wants to say one thing but mean another. In euphemistic writing, a softer or less offensive word or phrase replaces one that is unpleasant, stronger, or harsher.

Chapter 8 Vocabulary Review
Word Analogy

At the end of Chapter 7, you were introduced to the concept of word analogies with synonyms, relationships in which words have similarity in meaning. Another relationship involving analogies is through *antonyms,* words related through differences in meaning.

A. The following practice exercise uses the relationship of antonyms. The first set contains a review word from previous chapters. You are to complete the second pair with a word from Chapter 8; select it from the list of boldfaced words below. You will not use all the words. Look at the example before beginning the exercise.

> Example: ordinary:bizarre::normal: _____
> (*Anomalous* is a word that could complete the analogy.)

disparaging   condone   imperative   obscenity   incoherent   formidable

1. accolade:belittle::harmless: _____

2. clarify:confusing::clearness: _____

3. admonish:praise::scold: _____

4. irrelevant:relevant::unnecessary: _____

5. modest:iconoclastic::encouraging: _____

B. Answer *true* (T) or *false* (F) for each of the following statements.

_____ 1. If someone has been **decapitated,** they have lost their capital investment.

_____ 2. When you have **guffawed** at a joke, you've laughed loudly.

_____ 3. To **malign** someone is to show them courtesy while waiting in line.

_____ 4. A **misogynous** person does not like women.

_____ 5. **Xenophobic** people have no fears.

Selection 16: **ESSAY**

 ## Preparation For Reading

The following essay discusses the effects of a consumer-driven society on the environment. The author makes suggestions for change that are not the ordinary ones we read about in newspapers or hear on television. While reading the essay, decide whether you agree with his conclusions. The following words are underlined in the essay.

so **acquisitive**	eager to acquire money and things; grasping
and **profligate**	recklessly wasteful
the **biosphere** can sustain	earth
the **avarice** of mankind	greed for wealth
is **insatiable**	never satisfied
and **insidiously**	working or spreading harmfully
such as **integrity**	honesty; sincerity

Preview, then read the essay.

How Much Is Enough?

Alan Durning

1 Early in the post-World War II age of affluence, a U.S. retailing analyst named Victor Lebow proclaimed, "Our enormously productive economy . . . demands that we make consumption our way of life, that we convert the buying and use of goods into rituals, that we seek our spiritual satisfaction, our ego satisfaction, in consumption. . . . We need things consumed, burned up, worn out, replaced, and discarded at an ever increasing rate." Americans have risen to Mr. Lebow's call, and much of the world has followed.

2 Since 1950, American consumption has soared. Per capita, energy use climbed 60 percent, car travel more than doubled, plastics use multiplied 20-fold, and air travel jumped 25-fold.

3 We are wealthy beyond the wildest dreams of our ancestors; the average human living today is four-and-a-half times richer than his or her great-grandparents, and the factor is larger still among the world's consuming class. American children under the age of 13 have more spending money—$230 a year—than the 300 million poorest people in the world.

4 The richest billion people in the world have created a form of civilization so <u>acquisitive</u> and <u>profligate</u> that the planet is in danger. The lifestyle of this top echelon—the car drivers, beef eaters, soda drinkers, and throwaway consumers—constitutes an ecological threat unmatched in severity by anything but perhaps population growth. The wealthiest fifth of humankind pumps out more than half of the greenhouse gases that threaten the earth's climate and almost 90 percent of the chlorofluo-

rocarbons that are destroying the earth's protective ozone layer.

Ironically, abundance has not even made people terribly happy. In the United States, repeated opinion polls of people's sense of well-being show that no more Americans are satisfied with their lot now than they were in 1957. Despite phenomenal growth in consumption, the list of wants has grown faster still. 5

Of course, the other extreme from over-consumption—poverty—is no solution to environmental or human problems: it is infinitely worse for people and equally bad for the environment. Dispossessed peasants slash-and-burn their way into the rain forests of Latin America, and hungry nomads turn their herds out onto fragile African range land, reducing it to desert. If environmental decline results when people have either too little or too much, we must ask ourselves: How much is enough? What level of consumption can the earth support? When does consumption cease to add appreciably to human satisfaction? 6

Answering these questions definitively is impossible, but for each of us in the world's consuming class, seeking answers may be a prerequisite to transforming our civilization into one the biosphere can sustain. 7

THE COMPULSION TO CONSUME

"The avarice of mankind is insatiable," declared Aristotle 23 centuries ago, setting off a debate that has raged ever since among human hearts. But whatever share of our acquisitiveness is part of our nature, the compulsion to have more has never been so actively promoted, nor so easily acted upon, as it is today. 8

We are encouraged to consume at every turn by the advertising industry, which annually spends nearly $500 per U.S. citizen, by the commercialization of everything from sporting events to public spaces, and, insidiously, by the 9

spread of the mass market into realms once dominated by family members and local enterprises. Cooking from scratch is replaced by heating prepared foods in the microwave; the neighborhood baker and greengrocer are driven out by the 24-hour supermarket at the mall. As our day-to-day interactions with the economy lose the face-to-face character that prevails in surviving communities, buying things becomes a substitute source of self-worth.

Traditional measures of success, such as integrity, honesty, skill and hard work, are gradually supplanted by a simple, universally recognizable indicator of achievement—money. One Wall Street banker put it bluntly to the *New York Times:* "net worth equals self-worth." Under this definition, there is no such thing as enough. Consumption becomes a treadmill with everyone judging their status by who's ahead of them and who's behind. 10

ETHICS FOR SUSTAINABILITY

The basic value of a sustainable society, the ecological equivalent of the Golden Rule, is simple: Each generation should meet its needs without jeopardizing the prospects of future generations. What is lacking is the practical knowledge—at each level of society—of what living by that principle means. 11

In a fragile biosphere, the ultimate fate of humanity may depend on whether we can cultivate a deeper sense of self-restraint, founded on a widespread ethic of limiting consumption and finding nonmaterial enrichment. 12

Those who seek to rise to this environmental challenge may find encouragement in the body of human wisdom passed down from antiquity. To seek out sufficiency is to follow the path of voluntary simplicity preached by all the sages from Buddha to Mohammed. Typical of these pronouncements is this passage from the Bible: "What shall it profit a man if he shall 13 gain the whole world and lose his own soul?"

Living by this credo is not easy. As historian David Shi of Davidson College in North Carolina chronicles, the call for a simpler life is perennial through the history of the North American continent: the Puritans of Massachusetts Bay, the Quakers of Philadelphia, the Amish, the Shakers, the experimental utopian communities of the 1830s, the hippies of the 1960s, and the back-to-the-land movement of the 1970s. **14**

None of these movements ever gained more than a slim minority of adherents. Elsewhere in the world, entire nations have dedicated themselves to rebuilding human character—sometimes through brutal techniques—in a less self-centered mold, and nowhere have they succeeded with more than a token few of their citizens. **15**

It would be hopelessly naive to believe that entire populations will suddenly experience a moral awakening, renouncing greed, envy, and avarice. The best that can be hoped for is a gradual widening of the circle of those practicing voluntary simplicity. The goal of creating a sustainable culture, that is, a culture of permanence, is best thought of as a challenge that will last several generations. **16**

Voluntary simplicity, or personal restraint, will do little good, however, if it is not wedded to bold political steps that confront the forces advocating consumption. Beyond the oft-repeated agenda of environmental and social reforms necessary to achieve sustainability, such as overhauling energy systems, stabilizing population, and ending poverty, action is needed to restrain the excesses of advertising, to curb the shopping culture, and to revitalize household and community economies as human-scale alternatives to the high-consumption lifestyle. **17**

For example, if fairly distributed between the sexes, cooking from scratch can be digni- **18**

fied and use fewer resources than the frozen instant meal. Just so, communities that turn main streets into walking zones where local artisans and farmers display their products while artists, musicians, and theater troupes perform can provide a richness of human interaction that shopping malls will never match.

There could be many more people ready to begin saying "enough" than prevailing opinion suggests. After all, much of what we consume is wasted or unwanted in the first place. How much of the packaging that wraps products we consume each year—462 pounds per capita in the United States—would we rather never see? How many of the distant farms turned to suburban housing developments could have been left in crops if we insisted on well-planned land use inside city limits? **19**

How many of the unsolicited sales pitches each American receives each day in the mail—37 percent of all mail—are nothing but bothersome junk? How much of the advertising in our morning newspaper—covering 65 percent of the newsprint in American papers—would we not gladly see left out? **20**

How many of the miles we drive—almost 6,000 a year apiece in the United States—would we not happily give up if livable neighborhoods were closer to work, a variety of local merchants closer to home, streets safe to walk and bicycle, and public transit easier and faster? How much of the fossil energy we use is wasted because utility companies fail to put money into efficient renewable energy systems before building new coal plants? **21**

In the final analysis, accepting and living by sufficiency rather than excess offers a return to what is, culturally speaking, the human home: the ancient order of family, community, good work and good life; to a reverence for excellence of craftsmanship; to a true materialism that does not just care *about* things but cares *for* **22** them; to communities worth spending a lifetime in.

Maybe Henry David Thoreau had it right **23** when he scribbled in his notebook beside Walden Pond, "A man is rich in proportion to the things he can afford to let alone."

approximately 1500 words

Alan Durning, "How Much Is Enough?" *Worldwatch 3*, no. 6, Nov/Dec, 1990, pp. 12–19. Copyright © 1990 by Worldwatch Institute. Reprinted with the permission of Worldwatch Institute and W. W. Norton & Company, Inc.

COMPREHENSION CHECK

Part I
General Comprehension Questions: Literal and Interpretive

A. Write the correct letter in the space provided.

_____ 1. Which of the following statements best expresses the author's thesis?

    a. Governments must dictate a simpler life-style for their citizens.
    b. A simpler life-style would eliminate car drivers, beef eaters, and throwaway consumers.
    c. We need to return to the biblical ways of the Puritans and Quakers.
    d. A simpler life-style based on sufficiency, not excess, is needed to save our biosphere.

_____ 2. The statement by Aristotle, "The avarice of mankind is insatiable," strengthens Durning's thesis because it means

    a. people live by greed.
    b. human greed can never be satisfied.
    c. people should have no part of greed.
    d. human greed is natural.

_____ 3. The author believes the real culprits in this difficult situation are

    a. advertising industries and mass marketing.
    b. consumers.
    c. poor nations.
    d. all of the above.

_____ 4. In terms of success, Durning concludes we are measured

    a. by the position we hold.
    b. by the clothes we wear.
    c. by the amount of money we have.
    d. by our life-style.

B.

5. Fact, Opinion, or Combination: Write F, O, or F/O in the space provided. Write your support.

a. "American children under the age of 13 have more spending money—$230— a year than the 300 million poorest people in the world."

_____

Support: _____

b. "The richest billion people in the world have created a form of civilization so acquisitive and profligate that the planet is in danger."

_____

Support: _____

c. "None of these movements [that called for a simpler life] ever gained more than a slim minority of adherents."

_____

Support: _____

6. Connotative/Denotative Language: Determine whether the following statements contain connotative language. Write *yes* or *no* in the space provided. Underline the connotative phrase.

a. "The lifestyle of this top echelon—the car drivers, beef eaters, soda drinkers, and throwaway consumers—constitutes an ecological threat unmatched in severity."

_____

b. "We are encouraged to consume at every turn by the advertising industry . . . and, insidiously, by the spread of the mass market."

_____

c. "In a fragile biosphere, the ultimate fate of humanity may depend on whether we can cultivate a deeper sense of self-restraint."

_____

7. Figurative Language: In the space provided, indicate what is being compared, what type of figurative language is being used, and what the author actually means.

a. "Consumption becomes a treadmill with everyone judging their status by who's ahead of them and who's behind."

_____

b. "Voluntary simplicity or personal restraint will do little good, however, if it is not wedded to bold political steps."

_____

_____

8. Judge the merits of these statements, the first by the author, the second a quote from Thoreau. Are they valid or invalid? Write a V or I in the space provided.
   a. "Buying things becomes a substitute for self-worth." _____

   _____

   Reason: _____
   b. "A man is rich in proportion to the things he can afford to let alone." _____

   _____

   Reason: _____
9. Explain how paragraph 1, with a quote by Victor Lebow, strengthens Durning's thesis statement.

   _____

   _____

10. The author states "Elsewhere in the world, entire nations have dedicated themselves to rebuilding human character—sometimes through brutal techniques—in a less self-centered mold, and nowhere have they succeeded with more than a token few of their citizens." What nations could he have been referring to? Are there any such nations today?

   _____

   _____

Part II
Application Questions for Writing/Discussion

11. The author states that "action is needed to restrain the excesses of advertisers, to curb the shopping culture, and to revitalize household and community economies." How realistic are his suggestions?

   _____

   _____

   _____

12. What steps would you consider taking to eliminate some of the excesses of materialism in our society?

_____

_____

Part III
Extend Your Vocabulary

Match these terms. Write the correct letter in the space provided.

_____ 1. profligate   a. working or spreading harmfully

_____ 2. insatiable   b. never satisfied

_____ 3. insidiously   c. recklessly wasteful

_____ 4. echelon   d. eager to acquire money and things

_____ 5. acquisitive   e. level of responsibility in an organization

Selection 17: **TEXTBOOK**

☞ Preparation For Reading

Attitudes toward alcoholism have changed, but it still continues to be a major problem, not only in the United States but worldwide. While the proportion of those who drink in the United States has declined, **paradoxically** the number of those addicted appears to have increased! As you read, consider some of the staggering costs to society as a whole that are the direct result of alcoholism. The boldfaced words are underlined in the text.

other types of **hallucinogens**	drugs producing sights and sounds not present
the **infamous** disaster	having a very bad reputation
stimulated a **radical** departure	favoring basic change
moral **degradation**	dishonor
notorious public outcry	widely known, but unfavorably
today's **zealots**	fanatics

Preview, then read the selection. Note the author's questions to the reader in the margin. Some textbooks use this technique to alert the student to read with a questioning mind.

Problems of Substance Abuse

Stan Kossen

The problems of alcoholism and drug abuse, regardless of what many persons would prefer to believe, are considerable. Society, both by custom and law, defines what is meant by "drugs," and some authorities claim that alcohol, an intoxicant, should be classified as a drug, just like other types of stimulants, depressants, hallucinogens, and narcotics. **1**

ALCOHOLISM—A MAJOR HEALTH PROBLEM

Alcoholism is recognized as a major health problem. After heart disease and cancer, it is the third greatest killer in the United States. The National Institute on **2**

---

paradoxically (par´ ə doks´ ik lē) seemingly contradictory

Alcohol Abuse and Alcoholism estimates that nearly 18 *million persons* suffer from problems related to alcohol. Years ago, the typical stereotype of the alcoholic was the intoxicated derelict staggering clumsily through skid row. This view is *not* a realistic reflection; such persons are said to represent only about 3–5 percent of all persons with alcohol-related problems in the United States.

A study of 519,000 elementary and high school **3** students by the staff of *My Weekly Reader* revealed that among fourth-graders, 26 percent said "many" of their peers have tried wine coolers. Only 26 percent thought a cooler a day was harmful. The National Institute on Alcohol Abuse and Alcoholism estimates that 4.6 million high school students, or 30 percent, have alcohol-related problems, not quite the image of the "wino" hunched in a downtown doorway.

WHAT CONSTITUTES A DRINKING PROBLEM?

When might drinking be a problem?

We should be clear about what is generally meant by **4** a drinking problem. In all cases related to alcohol abuse, a common factor is the unfavorable effect alcohol has on the *health* or *well-being* of the *drinker* and his or her *associates*. According to more detailed information distributed by the National Institute on Alcohol Abuse and Alcoholism, the following are criteria for drinking problems:

1. Anyone who must drink to function or to cope with life has a severe drinking problem.

2. Anyone who by his or her own personal definition, or that of his or her family and friends, frequently drinks to a state of intoxication has a drinking problem.

3. Anyone who goes to work intoxicated has a drinking problem.

4. Anyone who is intoxicated while driving a car has a drinking problem.

5. Anyone who sustains a bodily injury that requires medical attention as a consequence of an intoxicated state has a drinking problem.

6. Anyone who comes into conflict with the law as a consequence of an intoxicated state has a drinking problem.

7. Anyone who, under the influence of alcohol, does something he or she avows would never occur without alcohol has a drinking problem.

ALCOHOLIC DEFINED

A person could experience some isolated examples **5** of such drinking problems without necessarily being an alcoholic. The term *alcoholic* generally refers to the person who *habitually lacks self-control in the use of alcoholic beverages,* or who drinks to the extent that his or her *health is adversely affected,* or that his or her *social or economic functioning is significantly disrupted.*

DRINKING PROBLEMS AMONG THE WORK FORCE

People drink for a variety of social, cultural, reli- **6** gious, or medical reasons. Approximately 68 percent of American adults are said to drink at least occasionally. Unfortunately, some persons reach the stage where they feel that they cannot do without alcohol, and many such individuals are employed in industry.

How extensive is the drinking problem?

The National Council on Alcoholism estimates **7** that 10 percent of the work force can be classified as alcoholics, with another 10 percent borderline alcoholics. Studies indicate that there are variations within specific companies, ranging from as little as *3 percent* of the employee population to as much as *12 percent.* The Associated Builders and Contractors estimates that at least 20 percent of all construction workers in the United States have an alcohol or drug abuse problem. And here's a shocker: A study done of 234,000 railroad employees for the Federal Railroad Administration by University Research Corporation concluded that:

"Shhaay, fella, why's that other train on our track?"

1. On any given day there were 33 "very drunk" workers on several railway company lines.

2. An estimated 19 percent of the workers (23 percent of those actually operating railways) could be called problem drinkers.

3. Only 4 percent of the problem drinkers were getting professional help.

4. Between 1975 and 1986, about 50 train accidents were attributed to drug- or alcohol-

impaired workers. In those mishaps, 37 people were killed, 80 injured, and $34 million worth of property destroyed. Would you care to dwell on that study during your next train ride?

Pretty slick method of distributing energy, eh?

The <u>infamous</u> 1989 disaster, the Exxon oil spill, **8** that occurred after the tanker *Valdez* struck a reef in Alaska's Prince William Sound and leaked 11 million gallons of crude oil into the clear, cool waters, was believed by many authorities to be alcohol-related. Although later acquitted, the ship's captain, Joseph Hazelwood, an alleged alcoholic, was found to have a blood-alcohol level 50 percent higher than the drunk-driving limit set by the Coast Guard for seamen operating a moving ship. An interesting sidelight is that Exxon supplied low-alcohol beer to tanker crewmen despite its policy of banning drinking aboard its ships.

The nation's "big hangover."

The alcohol problem is costly to industry and **9** society in terms of *lost work time* of employed alcoholics, *health and medical care expenses, property damage, wage losses,* and other costs associated with *traffic accidents.*

The National Council on Alcoholism has gath- **10** ered the following information on alcoholism in industry:

1. The alcoholic employee is absent two to four times more often than the nonalcoholic.
2. On-the-job accidents for alcoholic employees are two to four times more frequent than for nonalcoholics. Off-the-job accidents are four to six times more numerous.
3. Sickness and accident benefits paid out for alcoholic employees are three times greater than for the average nonalcoholic.
4. The alcoholic employee files four times more grievances than nonalcoholic employees.

Other costs of alcohol abuse are shocking. **11** Cirrhosis of the liver kills at least 14,000 alcoholics a year. Drunk drivers were responsible for approximately half of the 46,000 driving fatalities in the United States in 1986. Alcohol was blamed for about 70 percent of the 4,000 drowning deaths in 1988 and for about 30 percent of the nearly 30,000 suicides. A Department of Justice study estimates that almost one-third of the 523,000 state-prison inmates drank excessively before committing rapes, burglaries, and assaults. And an estimated 45 percent of the more than 250,000 of the nation's homeless are said to be alcoholics.

EASY TO COVER UP?

Alcoholic employees can sometimes go undetected for years. Fellow workers cover up for employees unable to perform their jobs because of drunkenness. Even managers may be adept at concealing their alcohol abuse problems. Their secretaries or loyal associates may cover up for them. Alcoholics can be clever at inventing "credible" excuses when detected. "I must have a drink or two when I'm entertaining customers, of course." 12

Who, me? Never touch the stuff.

VIEWPOINTS TOWARD ALCOHOL USE AND ABUSE

Alcohol abuse in the United States until the mid 1960s was customarily administered as a criminal act. Although some states had enacted treatment legislation, the laws in those states received scant attention and were largely ignored. In 1966, however, some significant court decisions stimulated a <u>radical</u> departure from previously held attitudes. 13

Since 1966, considerable progress has been made in the direction of treatment and rehabilitation. This trend seems likely to continue as a result of the passage of the Hughes Act (Comprehensive Alcohol Abuse and Alcoholism Prevention, Treatment and Rehabilitation Act of 1970) by Congress in 1970, an act that created the National Institute of Alcohol Abuse and Alcoholism, whose function is to engage in research and provide assistance to managers in establishing alcoholism programs. 14

The American Medical Association has helped to foster the trend toward considering alcoholism a treatable disease rather than a criminal act. The association's *Manual on Alcoholism* states that "alcoholics are treatable patients. Because their illness is a chronic disorder with tendency toward relapse, it should be approached in much the same manner as are other chronic and relapsing medical conditions. The aim of treatment is then viewed more as one of control than cure." 15

Note the use of the phrase *more as control than cure*. Both the American Medical Association and Alcoholics Anonymous take the position that a former alcoholic is never completely cured. The term *recovering alcoholic* is typically used. The American Medical Association further contends that the best reason to define alcoholism as a disease is that it is impractical to do otherwise. Calling alcohol abuse a moral problem tends to feed the guilt, fear, and anger felt by alcoholics, driving many of them into alcohol abuse. **16**

A 1987 Gallup poll found that a large majority of American adults are now convinced that alcoholism is truly an illness rather than solely a moral <u>degradation</u>. **17**

Regardless of a more enlightened attitude by the medical profession and a large proportion of the general public, an influential and vocal segment of the population moved during the 1980s in a less tolerant direction toward drinkers of alcoholic beverages. This new "temperance movement" in the United States, however, differs from the <u>notorious</u> public outcry that won a 1919 constitutional amendment outlawing the manufacture and sale of all intoxicating liquors, a shortlived period referred to as "prohibition." The current movement appears more concerned with limiting drinking under *specified conditions*. Rather than saving the drinkers' souls, today's <u>zealots</u> want to guarantee their neighbors' safety. **18**

Down with beer! Up with celery!

The proportion of Americans who drink peaked in the 1970s and has declined ever since. In 1978, 70 percent of Americans drank. The percentage declined to 63 percent in 1988. These changing views toward alcohol use are believed to be partially a result of the physical fitness craze, along with a highly effective campaign conducted by Mothers Against Drunk Drivers (MADD), with 1.1 million members and supporters in about 400 chapters, Students Against Drunk Drivers (SADD), with 15,000 chapters and about 4 million members in junior high and high schools and colleges, and other public groups. **19**

In spite of these changing attitudes, however, the National Institute on Alcohol Abuse and Alcoholism reports that the number of people who are addicted to alcohol has increased substantially **20** during the past decade, and now stands at 18 million persons. It is now estimated that alcoholism costs the United States over $117 billion per year in everything from medical bills to lost workdays.

approximately 1800 words

Stan Kossen, "Problems of Substance Abuse," *The Human Side of Organizations,* 5th ed. pp. 387–392. Copyright © 1991 by HarperCollins Publishers. Reprinted by permission of the publishers.

COMPREHENSION CHECK

Part I
General Comprehension Questions: Literal and Interpretive

Write the correct letter in the space provided.

_____ 1. Today, alcoholics can be best described as

   a. highly competitive individuals.
   b. having a treatable disease.
   c. staggering around drunk.
   d. winos hunched in doorways.

_____ 2. According to the National Institute on Alcohol Abuse, what proportion of high school students have alcohol-related problems?

   a. half
   b. one-third
   c. one-tenth
   d. a small number

_____ 3. Alcoholism in the workplace

   a. is not easily detected.
   b. is impossible to detect.
   c. is against the law to test for.
   d. is easily detected.

_____ 4. Among railroad workers

   a. alcoholism has not surfaced as a problem.
   b. those few who are alcoholics receive professional help.
   c. property damage caused by their drinking causes losses in millions of dollars.
   d. reforms in alcohol abuse have been undertaken.

_____ 5. The National Council on Alcoholism reports that alcoholics on the job are found to

   a. have more absenteeism and accidents.
   b. file more grievances than nonalcoholics.
   c. be less creative.
   d. both a and b.

_____ 6. One reason not given for the declining proportion of people who use alcohol today is

    a. the cost of alcohol.
    b. the efforts of MADD.
    c. the efforts of SADD.
    d. the physical fitness craze.

Persuasive Language

7. a. The American Medical Association defines alcoholism as "a treatable disease." How does this language change our perception of the alcoholic? Do you agree with this definition, and if so, why?

_____

_____

_____

_____

   b. Today there is a new "temperance movement." How does it differ from the old one? How does the new movement reflect the difference in our society today?

_____

_____

_____

8. What inference and conclusion can you draw from the statistics quoted here?
   a. Cirrhosis of the liver kills at least 14,000 alcoholics a year.
   b. Drunk drivers were responsible for approximately half of the 46,000 driving fatalities in the United States in 1986.
   c. Seventy percent of the drowning deaths in 1988 were due to alcoholism, and 30 percent of the suicides were due to alcoholism.

_____

_____

_____

Part II
Application Questions for Writing/Discussion

9. In view of Joseph Hazelwoods's blood-alcohol level at the time of the *Valdez* disaster, do you believe his initial acquittal was justified, and if so, why?*

_____

_____

_____

_____

_____

10. Given the staggering cost to society of dealing with alcoholism, who should bear the financial cost: the alcoholic, the taxpayers, businesses, or the government? Should cases be resolved in the courts or by the medical profession?

_____

_____

_____

_____

Part III
Extend Your Vocabulary

Note the boldfaced word in the first sentence of each set, quoted directly from the chapter. In the second sentence, fill in a different suffixed form of that word to complete the second sentence.

1. "[S]ome authorities claim that alcohol, an **intoxicant,** should be classified as a drug."
   Because of her chronic _____ while discussing claims with clients, she was removed from her job.

2. "Anyone who . . . does something he or she **avows** would never occur without alcohol has a drinking problem."

   His _____ that he would stop drinking came too late.

*Joseph Hazelwood was eventually retried and found guilty.

3. "[T]he ship's captain, Joseph Hazelwood, an **alleged** alcoholic, was found to have a blood-alcohol level 50 percent higher than the drunk-driving limit."

While _____ her blood-alcohol level was incorrectly determined, she staggered around in a drunken stupor.

4. "[C]onsiderable progress has been made in the direction of treatment and **rehabilitation."**

Only through _____ the alcoholic can part of the problem be solved.

5. "It should be approached in much the same manner as are other chronic and **relapsing** medical conditions."

Three _____ are three too many, so she lost her job.

Selection 18: **LITERATURE**

 Preparation for Reading

José Vasconcelos, author of *The Boar Hunt,* was an educator, a journalist, a prolific writer of essays, a politician, and a longtime public figure in Mexico. At one time, he was a presidential candidate. Although born at a time when such ideas were unpopular in his country (he died in 1959), he declared that

Latin America needed to do something about its soaring birthrate.
People of all races should be treated fairly and should have equal opportunity rights.
Every individual is obligated to contribute his or her talents to the betterment of society.

In a manner of speaking, we can say that the short story that follows, *The Boar Hunt,* is actually an essay on human behavior. Four hunters engage in what they believe will be an exhilarating experience. They are to explore territory that they have always dreamed about, and they believe their dreams are about to come true. Read to find out if their dreams actually do become a reality or if there is irony in the adventure.

Note the meaning of the boldfaced words before reading. They are underlined in the text.

assured ourselves **reciprocally**	performing or having an experience by both sides
lethargy of the jungle	lazy stupor; sluggish indifference
prevent the **methodical** killing	done in a systematic or regular order
infamy of the hunter	evil fame or reputation

The Boar Hunt

José Vasconcelos

We were four companions, and we went by the names of our respective nationalities: 1
the Columbian, the Peruvian, the Mexican; the fourth, a native of Ecuador, was
called Quito for short. Unforeseen chance had joined us together a few years ago on
a large sugar plantation on the Peruvian coast. We worked at different occupations
during the day and met during the evening in our off time. Not being Englishmen,
we did not play cards. Instead, our constant discussions led to disputes. These
didn't stop us from wanting to see each other the next night, however, to continue
the interrupted debates and support them with new arguments. Nor did the rough

sentences of the preceding wrangles indicate a lessening of our affection, of which we assured ourselves <u>reciprocally</u> with the clasping of hands and a look. On Sundays we used to go on hunting parties. We roamed the fertile glens, stalking, generally with poor results, the game of the warm region around the coast, or we entertained ourselves killing birds that flew in the sunlight during the siesta hour.

We came to be tireless wanderers and excellent marksmen. Whenever we 2 climbed a hill and gazed at the imposing range of mountains in the interior, its attractiveness stirred us and we wanted to climb it. What attracted us more was the trans-Andean region: fertile plateaus extending on the other side of the range in the direction of the Atlantic toward the immense land of Brazil. It was as if primitive nature called us to her breast. The vigor of the fertile, untouched jungles promised to rejuvenate our minds, the same vigor which rejuvenates the strength and the thickness of the trees each year. At times we devised crazy plans. As with all things that are given a lot of thought, these schemes generally materialized. Ultimately nature and events are largely what our imaginations make them out to be. And so we went ahead planning and acting. At the end of the year, with arranged vacations, accumulated money, good rifles, abundant munitions, stone- and mud-proof boots, four hammocks, and a half dozen faithful Indians, our caravan descended the Andean slopes, leading to the endless green ocean.

At last we came upon a village at the edge of the Marañón River. Here we 3 changed our safari. The region we were going to penetrate had no roads. It was unexplored underbrush into which we could enter only by going down the river in a canoe. In time we came to the area where we proposed to carry out the purpose of our journey, the hunting of wild boars.

We had been informed that boars travel in herds of several thousands, occupy- 4 ing a region, eating grass and staying together, exploiting the grazing areas, organized just like an army. They are very easy to kill if one attacks them when they are scattered out satisfying their appetites—an army given over to the delights of victory. When they march about hungry, on the other hand, they are usually vicious. In our search we glided down river between imposing jungles with our provisions and the company of three faithful Indian oarsmen.

One morning we stopped at some huts near the river. Thanks to the informa- 5 tion gathered there, we decided to disembark a little farther on in order to spend the night on land and continue the hunt for the boars in the thicket the following day.

Sheltered in a backwater, we came ashore, and after a short exploration found 6 a clearing in which to make camp. We unloaded the provisions and the rifles, tied the boat securely, then with the help of the Indians set up our camp one-half kilometer from the riverbank. In marking the path to the landing, we were careful not to lose ourselves in the thicket. The Indians withdrew toward their huts, promising to return two days later. At dawn we would set out in search of the prey.

Though night had scarcely come and the heat was great, we gathered at the fire 7 to see each other's faces, to look instinctively for protection. We talked a little, confessed to being tired, and decided to go to bed. Each hammock had been tied by one end to a single tree, firm though not very thick in the trunk. Stretching out from this axis in different directions, the hammocks were supported by the other end on other trunks. Each of us carried his rifle, cartridges, and some provisions which couldn't remain exposed on the ground. The sight of the weapons made us consider the place where we were, surrounded by the unknown. A slight feeling of terror made us laugh, cough, and talk. But fatigue overcame us, that heavy fatigue which compels the soldier to scorn danger, to put down his rifle, and to fall asleep though the most persistent enemy pursues him. We scarcely noticed the supreme grandeur of that remote tropical night.

8   I don't know whether it was the light of the magnificent dawn or the strange noises which awakened me and made me sit up in my hammock and look carefully at my surroundings. I saw nothing but the awakening of that life which at night falls into the lethargy of the jungle. I called my sleeping companions and, alert and seated in our hanging beds, we dressed ourselves. We were preparing to jump to the ground when we clearly heard a somewhat distant, sudden sound of rustling branches. Since it did not continue, however, we descended confidently, washed our faces with water from our canteens, and slowly prepared and served breakfast. By about 11:00 in the morning we were armed and bold and preparing to make our way through the jungle.

9   But then the sound again. Its persistence and proximity in the thicket made us change our minds. An instinct made us take refuge in our hammocks. We cautiously moved our cartridges and rifles into them again, and without consulting each other we agreed on the idea of putting our firearms safely away. We passed them up into the hammocks, and we ourselves finally climbed in. Stretched out face down, comfortably suspended with rifles in hand, we did not have to wait long. Black, agile boars quickly appeared from all directions. We welcomed them with shouts of joy and well-aimed shots. Some fell immediately, giving comical snorts, but many more came out of the jungle. We shot again, spending all the cartridges in the magazine. Then we stopped to reload. Finding ourselves safe in the height of our hammocks, we continued after a pause.

10   We counted dozens of them. At a glance we made rapid calculations of the magnitude of the destruction, while the boars continued to come out of the jungle in uncountable numbers. Instead of going on their way or fleeing, they seemed confused. All of them emerged from the jungle where it was easy for us to shoot them. Occasionally we had to stop firing because the frequent shooting heated the barrels of our rifles. While they were cooling we were able to joke, celebrating our good fortune. The impotent anger of the boars amazed us. They raised their tusks in our direction, uselessly threatening us. We laughed at their snorts, quietly aimed at those who were near, and Bang! a dead boar. We carefully studied the angle of the shoulder blade so that the bullet would cross the heart. The slaughter lasted for hours.

11   At 4:00 P.M. we noticed an alarming shortage of our ammunition. We had been well supplied and had shot at will. Though the slaughter was gratifying, the boars

must have numbered, as we had been informed previously, several thousands, because their hordes didn't diminish. On the contrary, they gathered directly beneath our hammocks in increasing groups. They slashed furiously at the trunk of the tree which held the four points of the hammocks. The marks of the tusks remained on the hard bark. Not without a certain fear we watched them gather compactly, tenaciously, in tight masses against the resisting trunk. We wondered what would happen to a man who fell within their reach. Our shots were now sporadic, well aimed, carefully husbanded. They did not drive away the aggressive beasts, but only redoubled their fury. One of us ironically noted that from being the attackers we had gone on the defensive. We did not laugh very long at the joke. Now we hardly shot at all. We needed to save our cartridges.

The afternoon waned and evening came upon us. After consulting each other, **12** we decided to eat in our hammocks. We applauded ourselves for taking the food up—meat, bread, and bottles of water. Stretching ourselves on our hammocks, we passed things to each other, sharing what we needed. The boars deafened us with their angry snorts.

After eating, we began to feel calm. We lit cigars. Surely the boars would go. **13** Their numbers were great, but they would finally leave peacefully. As we said so, however, we looked with greedy eyes at the few unused cartridges that remained. Our enemies, like enormous angry ants, stirred beneath us, encouraged by the ceasing of our fire. From time to time we carefully aimed and killed one or two of them, driving off the huge group of uselessly enraged boars at the base of the trunk which served as a prop for our hammocks.

Night enveloped us almost without our noticing the change from twilight. **14** Anxiety also overtook us. When would the cursed boars leave? Already there were enough dead to serve as trophies to several dozen hunters. Our feat would be talked about; we had to show ourselves worthy of such fame. Since there was nothing else to do, it was necessary to sleep. Even if we had had enough bullets it would have been impossible to continue the fight in the darkness. It occurred to us to start a fire to drive the herd off with flames, but apart from the fact that we couldn't leave the place in which we were suspended, there were no dry branches in the lush forest. Finally, we slept.

We woke up a little after midnight. The darkness was profound, but the well- **15** known noise made us aware that our enemies were still there. We imagined they must be the last ones which were leaving, however. If a good army needs several hours to break camp and march off, what can be expected of a vile army of boars but disorder and delay? The following morning we would fire upon the stragglers, but this painful thought bothered us: they were in large and apparently active numbers. What were they up to? Why didn't they leave? We thus spent long hours of worry. Dawn finally came, splendid in the sky but noisy in the jungle still enveloped inwardly in shadows. We eagerly waited for the sun to penetrate the foliage in order to survey the appearance of the field of battle of the day before.

What we finally saw made us gasp. It terrified us. The boars were painstakingly **16** continuing the work which they had engaged in throughout the entire night. Guided by some extraordinary instinct, with their tusks they were digging out the ground underneath the tree from which our hammocks hung; they gnawed the roots and continued to undermine them like large, industrious rats. Presently the tree was bound to fall and we with it, among the beasts. From that moment we neither thought nor talked. In desperation we used up our last shots, killing more ferocious beasts. Still, the rest renewed their activity. They seemed to be endowed with intelligence. However much we concentrated our fire against them, they did not stop their attack against the tree.

Soon our shots stopped. We emptied our pistols, and then silently listened to the tusks gnawing beneath the soft, wet, pleasant-smelling earth. From time to time the boars pressed against the tree, pushing it and making it creak, eager to smash it quickly. We looked on, hypnotized by their devilish activity. It was impossible to flee because the black monsters covered every inch in sight. It seemed to us that, by a sudden inspiration, they were preparing to take revenge on us for the ruthless nature of man, the unpunished destroyer of animals since the beginning of time. Our imagination, distorted by fear, showed us our fate as an atonement for the unpardonable crimes implicit in the struggle of biological selection. Before my eyes passed the vision of sacred India, where the believer refuses to eat meat in order to prevent the <u>methodical</u> killing of beasts and in order to atone for man's evil, bloody, treacherous slaughter, such as ours, for mere vicious pleasure. I felt that the multitude of boars was raising its accusing voice against me. I now understood the <u>infamy</u> of the hunter, but what was repentance worth if I was going to die with my companions, hopelessly devoured by that horde of brutes with demonlike eyes? **17**

Stirred by terror and without realizing what I was doing, I hung from the upper end of my hammock, I balanced myself in the air, I swung in a long leap, I grasped a branch of a tree facing the one on which the boars were digging. From there I leaped to other branches and to others, reviving in myself habits which the species had forgotten. **18**

The next moment a terrifying sound and unforgettable cries told me of the fall of the tree and the end of my companions. I clung to a trunk, trembling and listening to the chattering of my jaws. Later, the desire to flee gave me back my strength. Leaning out over the foliage, I looked for a path, and I saw boars in the distance, marching in compressed ranks and holding their insolent snouts in the air. I knew that they were now withdrawing, and I got down from the tree. Horror overwhelmed me as I approached the site of our encampment, but some idea of duty made me return there. Perhaps one of my friends had managed to save himself. I approached hesitantly. Each dead boar made me tremble with fear. **19**

But what I saw next was so frightful that I could not fix it clearly in my mind: remains of clothing—and footwear. There was no doubt; the boars had devoured them. Then I ran toward the river, following the tracks we had made two days before. I fled with great haste, limbs stiff from panic. **20**

Running with long strides, I came upon the boat. With a great effort, I managed 21
to row to the huts. There I went to bed with a high fever which lasted many days.

I will participate in no more hunts. I will contribute, if I have to, to the exter- 22
mination of harmful beasts. But I will not kill for pleasure. I will not amuse myself
with the ignoble pleasure of the hunt.

approximately 2500 words

José Vasconcelos, "The Boar Hunt," translated by Paul Waldorf from *The Muse in Mexico: A Mid-Century Miscellany,* Supplement to the *Texas Quarterly,* Vol. 11, No. 1, (Spring 1959), pp. 64–69. Copyright © 1959 by The University of Texas Press. Reprinted by permission of the publisher.

Questions for Writing/Discussion

1. What were some important facts the hunters failed to consider that might have prevented the final outcome of the hunt?

2. Contrast the difference in the narrator's attitude toward the hunt at the beginning of the story, in the middle, and at the end.

3. The author uses the word "slaughter" several times in detailing his adventure. How is this choice related to the author's message and conclusion?

JOURNAL ENTRY

In the essay "How Much Is Enough?," the textbook selection "The Prevalence of Alcohol in the Workplace," and the literature selection "The Boar Hunt," the subject of *excess* is a common theme. Which selection affected you the most? Write a journal entry, and describe whether or not these reading experiences have changed any of your views concerning your role and responsibility both in society and to the environment.

9

Recognizing Tone, Purpose, and Point of View: Aids to Critical Thinking

This chapter will help you to

- Understand the relationship between tone, purpose, and style.
- Learn key terms and descriptive words useful in identifying tone.
- Recognize different points of view.
- Develop the ability to evaluate a writer's credibility.

❖❖❖

Before reading, think about these questions.

- What purpose might a writer have besides informing or entertaining the reader?
- How does tone of voice differ from tone in writing?
- Why is it important to examine an author's credentials and background?

❖❖❖

Jot down how you go about deciding what to believe when

you read. _____

_____

_____

❖ Tuning in to Tone

When people speak, we generally recognize their attitude, feelings, or point of view by their tone of voice and physical gestures. Tone of voice can include loudness, pitch, inflection, choice of words, and speed of delivery. Physical gestures refer to body language: the smile on a face, a raised eyebrow, a wink, a frown, the speaker's stance. Whether the speaker is pleased, angry, serious, or sad is indicated by voice and gestures.

In writing, the tone is chiefly controlled by the words the writer chooses, words that color ideas, evoke desired emotions, and imply judgments. Recognizing a writer's tone is a valuable clue to determining purpose (*why* the writer says something) and point of view (*how* the writer looks at a topic), both important in critical reading.

Tone is the manner in which writers express themselves and convey their feelings. It is the emotional message behind their words, reflecting their attitude toward the subject matter. As you learned in Chapter 8, the writer's intent when choosing emotional words is to influence the reader's thinking. "An important function of language," says Richard Altick in his *Preface to Critical Reading,* "is to mold the reader's attitude towards the subject discussed. Tone determines just what that attitude should be."

Style, on the other hand, is the manner in which people say what they want to communicate. What may make a particular author or writer unique is known as that person's writing *style.* It is an overall effect and consists of a person's choice of words, arrangements of ideas through sentence formation, and level of language as well as point of view, purpose, and tone. In other words, the "voice" or personality of the writer is found in his or her style.

Writers generally have to vary their style to suit their intended audience just as people shift their style in speaking. For example, parents speak differently to their children than they do to co-workers, to family members, and to friends. So, too, with writers—for newspaper and magazine articles, for example, writers select an informal style to appeal to the general public. For textbook writing, the style is often more scholarly or learned. If the writer wants to target a particular group (religious or political, for instance) or profession (medical or legal) the style will change. Being aware of the writer's style helps the critical reader focus on the intended purpose as well as recognize the writer's tone.

In literary writing, such as short stories, novels, and plays, the tone is referred to as the *atmosphere* or *mood.* Atmosphere can be created by a writer's description or the choice of words used by the characters. The mood in stories, for example, can make the setting exciting, romantic, frightening, or gloomy and is based on the writer's purpose in developing the story's plot.

Depending on the purpose, an author's tone will vary. For example, if the purpose is to entertain, a humorous tone might be used. If the purpose is to voice disapproval, a sarcastic, bitter tone is displayed. When writing seriously, an author may use a **sentimental** tone to express nostalgic feelings. Often, more than one tone is used in a passage, essay, or story.

To determine the author's tone, a critical reader can ask these two key questions.

1. *How does the writer use words?*

   Note that emotional words not only help you to recognize the writer's true feelings but can be used to express anger or show positive support of an issue.

2. *What is the writer's attitude?*

   To a large extent, tone is based on attitude, the way an author feels about the topic because of his or her background and experience. For example, given the topic "Living in a Big City," one writer may use humor to describe amusing experiences he or she had while living there, another may wish to be sentimental because of a romance while living there, and a third may be sarcastic because of personal unpleasant experiences associated with a stay there.

❖ Major Tones in Writing

Writers often use these eight tones.

1. *Serious or neutral tone:* This tone is used in writing that focuses on important topics and is presented in a straightforward manner without hidden meaning. It is typically found in textbooks and often in newspaper and magazine articles. The term *neutral* is sometimes used to indicate the author is being objective in presenting both sides of an issue.

2. *Solemn tone:* The writer is extremely serious and uses formal language. His or her attitude is dignified or grave. When the writer's tone is solemn, there are usually no humorous or informal expressions. Generally, funeral orations or **eulogies,** a governor's state address, or a presidential message on a very serious matter are expressed solemnly.

3. *Critical tone:* The writer expresses judgments on what is good or bad about something. When criticizing, the writer may directly state approval or disapproval. For example, if a writer states, "*Scarlett* (the sequel to *Gone with the Wind*) is a spellbinding and powerful novel that I highly recommend," the criticism is positive and shows approval. But if the writer says, "*Scarlett* is highly overrated and not worth a reader's time," the critic shows a negative reaction and disapproval. Sometimes authors color a critical tone with sarcasm and even cynicism.

---

sentimental (sen´ tə men´ təl) showing tender feelings

eulogies (yōō´ lə jēz) speeches or written tributes praising one recently deceased; high tributes

4. *Cynical tone:* The writer is not only negatively critical but also expresses doubt about the goodness of human actions or motives or even the essential worth of a subject. Words used are often angry and **pessimistic.** The author's attitude is that humankind is selfish and corrupt and always acts out of self-interest.

5. *Sarcastic tone:* Like cynicism, sarcasm too is negatively critical and, here, words used are often harsh and bitter. While cynicism tries to show that people are selfish, sarcasm tries to show that people are foolish. The writer's attitude is cruel, brutal, and sometimes downright nasty. The purpose is to hurt and **belittle** rather than simply state disagreement or disapproval. While a sarcastic remark may appear to be funny on the surface, it generally expresses anger, spite, or contempt.

6. *Ironic tone:* In irony, the writer's true feelings are not obvious. The author says the opposite of what he or she feels or thinks, and the attitude is generally stated indirectly. For example, if the writer says, "We wore a gas mask for most of the day to enjoy the gorgeous weather," the writer wants the reader to understand the air was polluted and that the weather was terrible! In addition to irony in language, irony can also be situational. An essay written about how a fire station burned down might be extremely ironic.

7. *Humorous and witty tone:* A humorous tone is intended to create laughter and to entertain or amuse. Sometimes, humor can point out the foolishness or stupidity of humankind in a gentle way. When humor is used with irony or sarcasm, however, its intention usually is to ridicule.

    Writing that expresses humor that is **sophisticated** is said to be witty. For example, when author Dorothy Parker was informed that President Coolidge, an extremely quiet and reserved man, had died, she remarked, "How can they tell?" A witty tone is often clever and thought-provoking, while a humorous tone is simply enjoyable.

8. *Satiric tone:* In satire, the tone is often a blend of sarcasm, irony, wit, or humor. As in irony, a writer's true feelings are not obvious; the writer does not mean exactly what is stated. When authors use satire, they are often being critical, but their intention is not only to show disapproval but also to look for a remedy to a situation. They may use gross exaggeration, expressing disapproval of something in hopes of its being changed for the better. The **satirist** may direct comments at one individual, at a class in society, or at people with a specific ideology.

---

pessimistic (pes´ ə mis´ tik) always expecting the worst
belittle (bi lit´ l) to speak of as being unimportant
sophisticated (sə fis´ tə kāt əd) worldly-wise; knowledgeable
satirist (sat´ ə rist) someone who writes satire

ACTIVITY 9.1 **Select a Tone for a Topic**

For each of the topics listed below, indicate what tone a writer might choose to develop an essay. More than one tone may be appropriate, depending on the writer's purpose and attitude. Refer to the map on page 428 for concise definitions of the various tones.

1. Standardized college and graduate school aptitude tests _____

2. A town meeting on affirmative action _____

3. A bungled response to a three-alarm fire _____

4. Among students, murder becoming more popular than sex _____

5. A train accident resulting in many deaths, caused by a drunken engineer

    _____

6. The destruction of the ozone layer _____

7. A violin recital by children in a local elementary school _____

8. Trying to fix the welfare mess _____

9. A former prostitute running for town mayor _____

10. A doctor using medical technology to help people commit suicide

    _____

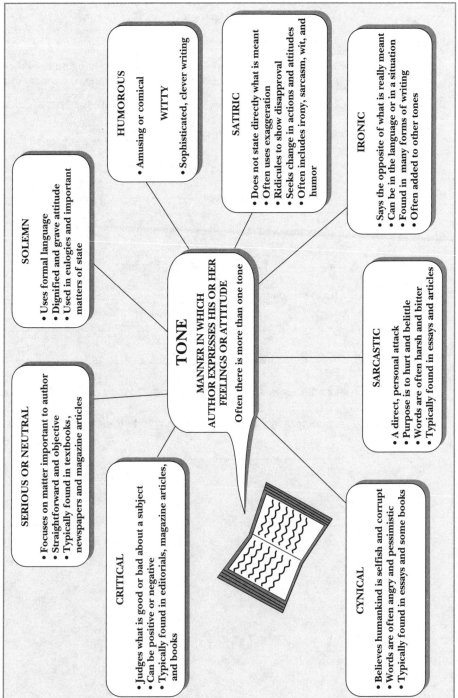

TONE

MANNER IN WHICH AUTHOR EXPRESSES HIS OR HER FEELINGS OR ATTITUDE

Often there is more than one tone

HUMOROUS
- Amusing or comical

WITTY
- Sophisticated, clever writing

SATIRIC
- Does not state directly what is meant
- Often uses exaggeration
- Ridicules to show disapproval
- Seeks change in actions and attitudes
- Often includes irony, sarcasm, wit, and humor

IRONIC
- Says the opposite of what is really meant
- Can be in the language or in a situation
- Found in many forms of writing
- Often added to other tones

SOLEMN
- Uses formal language
- Dignified and grave attitude
- Used in eulogies and important matters of state

SERIOUS OR NEUTRAL
- Focuses on matter important to author
- Straightforward and objective
- Typically found in textbooks, newspapers and magazine articles

CRITICAL
- Judges what is good or bad about a subject
- Can be positive or negative
- Typically found in editorials, magazine articles, and books

SARCASTIC
- A direct, personal attack
- Purpose is to hurt and belittle
- Words are often harsh and bitter
- Typically found in essays and articles

CYNICAL
- Believes humankind is selfish and corrupt
- Words are often angry and pessimistic
- Typically found in essays and some books

Adapted from an idea developed by Sally Wood, De Anza College.

Words Used to Describe Tone

Although we have classified into eight major categories the most widely used descriptive terms to explain a writer's tone, countless other words may also be used to express it. As you can see from the list that follows, most of these words are adjectives that identify a person's emotions, attitude, or feelings.

Words that Express Tone			
absurd	depressing	honest	outspoken
accusing	detached	hopeful	passionate
amused	dignified	impassioned	pathetic
angry	distressed	incredulous	persuasive
arrogant	earnest	indignant	pessimistic
authoritative	enthusiastic	insulting	playful
bitter	evasive	intense	positive
caustic	excited	irreverent	proud
cheerful	fair	joking	righteous
comical	fearful	joyful	romantic
compassionate	fervent	mocking	scornful
condescending	foolish	morbid	sentimental
contradictory	funny	nostalgic	sympathetic
cruel	gentle	optimistic	uneasy
delightful	grim	outraged	unrealistic

Add four descriptive words not included in the list that can indicate a person's feelings or attitude.

_____   _____   _____   _____

Examples of Various Tones

You have read many examples of serious, neutral, and even critical tone in this textbook. Now, let's analyze these as well as some of the additional types.

ACTIVITY 9.2

PASSAGE 1

Read passage 1, a commentary on the welfare system. Decide whether the language is positive or negative in demonstrating how the writer feels about the social welfare system. Circle any descriptive words that indicate the writer's feelings or attitude.

The social welfare system is a runaway **juggernaut.** It has devoured more than $5 trillion in hundreds of programs since 1965. . . . But the staggering cost is only part of the story. If all this treasure had given us happy, healthy families in our low-income neighborhoods, millions of hard-working Americans would have judged the sacrifice in taxes a badge of honor. The tragedy is that the reverse is the case. The welfare system has deterred parents from marrying. It has **consigned** untold children to lives of bitterness and failure; dismaying numbers of them have sought revenge on the society that intended to help.

The sentiment for stopping the juggernaut is overwhelming. Over two thirds of all Americans are skeptical about the needs of most welfare recipients. They are appalled to be subsidizing out-of-wedlock childbearing, and they resent the abuse of their goodwill.

Today, most women on welfare have not been married but go on receiving benefits for years. The system has become a holding pen for the poor, not a helping hand for the dependent to become independent. It has been transformed from a remedy for poverty into a cause of it, from a stimulus to social **cohesion** into a destroyer of it. These malign consequences arise because welfare **frays** the fabric of a family and undermines the role of a father.

Mortimer B. Zuckerman, "Fixing the Welfare Mess," *U.S. News & World Report,* 16 Jan. 1995, p. 68

By comparing the welfare system to a juggernaut, the writer reveals his disapproval of today's program. He could simply have said, "I think the welfare system needs improvement," but with this comparison and phrases like "holding pen for the poor" and "frays the fabric of a family," he has made a far stronger criticism. Essentially, the writer's tone is serious and critical; he finds faults and complains. It is also sarcastic; remember, there can be more than one tone.

With these comments in mind, answer the following questions.

1. What words or phrases does the writer use in paragraph 2 that reveal his negative attitude?

_____

_____

---

juggernaut (jug´ ər nôt) a frightening force that destroys everything it encounters
consigned (kən sīnd´) given over to the care of another
cohesion (kō hē´ zhən) force that holds things together
frays (frāz) wears away; unravels

2. In the last paragraph, "The system has become a holding pen for the poor, not a helping hand for the dependent to become independent" is an ironic statement. What does the writer mean by this?

____

____

PASSAGE 2

Read the following selection to discover how the writer incorporates several tones to develop her thesis. Pay particular attention to the title of the essay, the italicized words, and the marginal notations. Her attitude toward this subject will be quite evident!

Defining Lite, Ultra-Lite and Truth

The story began like a typical American breakfast, with a bracing dose of orange juice. Back in April, the Food and Drug Administration seized a batch of o.j. saying that it carried a false label. Citrus Hill Fresh Choice wasn't "fresh," dear Breakfast Clubbers and Wordsmiths, it was concentrated. Having gotten the *business folk to swallow that,* the regulators went after cooking oil next. In May they told three manufacturers they couldn't put *those cute little hearts* and no-cholesterol signs on bottles of high-fat vegetable oil. The labels weren't exactly false, but they were misleading. *They suggested that you could fry a path to good health.*

Sarcastic

Ironic

These two moves sent a message that the regulators are back in the business of regulating. And that it isn't only **linguists** who are interested in the labels. Soon, *we may be unraveling the mysteries of Low-fat, Low-salt, and Lite confusion that reign in the marketplace.*

Sarcastic

But there is still a missing entree in the regulatory menu. Every day 50 million Americans put something into their mouths that is exempt from the safety, health or truth-in-labeling laws that affect virtually every other product: Tobacco.

Tobacco remains the glaring renegade. *It is the absolute outlaw on the American market.* Consider, for example, NEXT cigarettes which are **brazenly** promoted for their "de-nicotined" tobacco. *De-Nic has that nice de-caf ring about its name. It promises all the flavor with none of the evil buzz.*

Critical

Sarcastic

But NEXT has nicotine, .1 milligrams a smoke, about the same amount as the older cigarettes, Carlton and NOW. In short, the makers of low-tar and low-nicotine cigarettes do precisely what the vegetable-oil folk did. They make an implied health claim in their ads. *But they get away with it. . . .*

Critical

Tobacco, the love child of politics, has been exempt from every federal health and safety act since the surgeon general's first report on the dangers of smoking. By now, we just assume everyone knows what the tobacco companies deny: that smoking is addictive and **lethal.** *There is an almost casually judgmental attitude toward people who are dumb or dependent enough to keep*

---

linguists (lin´ gwists) specialists in the study of language
brazenly (brā´ zən lē) shamelessly and boldly
lethal (lē´ thəl) causing death; fatal

smoking. On the other side, those who want to regulate cigarettes and cigarette advertising are often regarded as closet **prohibitionists** . . . .

Serious

If the government can define what's Lite, then it can define what's Ultra-Lite. If ads for cholesterol-free make false safety claims, what about the ads for Merit Free? And how about the ads that associate Virginia with slimness, and Camels with cartoons aimed at kids?

Ironic

At the moment, there is one cigarette manufacturer who tells it like it is in smoking country. From California, we have a brand bearing its dire message in a neat black pack with a skull and crossbones. It's called "Death." Now that's truth in advertising.

approximately 440 words

Ellen Goodman, "Defining Lite, Ultra-Lite and Truth," Copyright © 1991, *The Boston Globe Newspaper Co./Washington Post Writers Group.* Reprinted by permission of the Washington Post Writers Group.

1. How does the writer's use of several tones help to strengthen her criticism of product advertising?

_____

2. Specifically, what does she want the government to do?

_____

"Ugh! Marlboro Country!"

"*This isn't so bad, considering some companies have banned smoking areas altogether.*"

The next passage is a satire that demonstrates how a writer can use humor, exaggeration, and sarcasm in combination. This is how satire is created. The writer, Art Buchwald, has been a columnist for the *Washington Post* for several decades and is a world-renowned political and social satirist. Although the essay is funny, underlying the humor are criticism and exaggeration, which make it satiric. As you read, think about what Art Buchwald is *really* saying.

_____

prohibitionists (prō´ ə bish´ ən ists) those who wish to forbid by law

PASSAGE 3

Acid Indigestion

Art Buchwald

America is an abundant land that seems to have more of everything than anybody else. And if one were to ask what we have the most of the answer would be acid indigestion.

No country can touch us when it comes to heartburn and upset stomachs. This nation, under God, with liberty and justice for all, neutralizes more stomach acid in one day than the Soviet Union does in a year. We give more relief from discomfort of the intestinal tract than China and Japan combined.

They can say what they will about us, but we Americans know what to do with our excess gas.

It is no accident that the United States became the largest producer of acid indigestion in the world. When the first settlers came to the New World they found their lives fraught with danger. First they had to worry about Indians, then they had to worry about their crops. Afterward they had to worry about witches. This played hell with everyone's stomach and the early settlers realized if they ever hoped to survive they would have to come up with a cure for acid indigestion.

Providence was on their side, because amongst the early settlers were two brothers, Alka and Bromo Seltzer. They were both chemists who had experimented with various potions that had been given to them by the Indians.

One potion was a white powder that the Indians used for athlete's foot. Why, asked the Seltzer brothers, couldn't the same powder be used for upset stomachs. Al was neater than Bromo and rolled his powder into a tablet which he then dropped into a mug of water where it immediately fizzed. Bromo said it was too expensive to make tablets, and it was much easier just to dump the powder into the water, which would produce the same effect.

The brothers split in anger, and Al put out his product under the name Alka-Seltzer, while Bromo put his out as Bromo-Seltzer. Fortunately for the country, both methods worked, and as soon as the cure for acid indigestion had been concocted the New World could be settled once and for all.

You would think that after we killed all the Indians and won the West and became a large industrial nation, Americans would have stopped having queasy stomachs. But the truth is we suffer more from the blaahhs now than we ever did before. Some of it still comes from fear, some of it comes from ambition, and some of it comes from eating the whole thing.

As a people who strive for the best we must accept the fact that it takes a cup of acid for every step we take up the ladder of success. It is no accident that the men and women who run our corporations and our advertising agencies and our networks and our government are the same people who keep the Maalox, Pepto-Bismol, Bisodol tum and Rolaid companies alive.

Show me a man who has to drink milk instead of wine with his meals and I'll show you a **titan** of American industry.

For years other nations have tried to catch up with us when it came to sour stomachs and heartburn. But they never had the drive to produce a good case of acid indigestion. They never understood what it takes to keep up with the Joneses or outdo the Smiths.

---

titan (tī tan) giant

They don't realize that in order to live in the best of all possible worlds you have to have a certain amount of stomach discomfort to go with it.

Acid indigestion is as American as Mom's apple pie (which is one of the reasons we get it) and as long as there is enough heartburn to go around, we, as a great nation, will survive.

approximately 600 words

Art Buchwald, "Acid Indigestion," *Esquire*, December 1974. Reprinted by permission of *Esquire*

What is Buchwald really making fun of? What does he want us to change?

_____

_____

_____

ACTIVITY 9.3 Practice Recognizing Tone

As you read the following selections, you may wish to refer back to the tone chart on page 428. Remember that more than one tone may be used in a passage, but look first for the dominant tone.

PASSAGE 1

Read the following selection on *procrastinators*, people who put things off or delay doing them, and decide whether you should take the writer seriously.

And Tomorrow and Tomorrow

Procrastinators are simply less intimidated by time. . . . people like Les Waas, president of the Procrastinators Club of America. (Motto: "We're Behind you all the way.") Founded in 1956, the club numbers a half million, though Waas says only 12,000 have signed up. It even boasts two members who have missed planes that crashed. . . . Waas loathes people who lay out their next day's clothes before bed, who dream of 21,000-mile car tuneups at 20,000 miles, and who fancy themselves (more often than not) "morning people." Waas calls them "Anticrastinators." He avoids them as he would oven-cleaning.

"These are nervous and uptight folks," he says. "They're too high-strung and usually leave the world earlier than the rest of us. Then they're referred to as 'the late so and so.'"

"It's the ultimate irony."

. . . We gather each year at the Post Office, near midnight, on April 15, Tax Day. Our expressions mingle the harried relief and quiet satisfaction that is our badge of honor.

We'll reunite (in spirit if not body) at the auto registry the day our licenses expire, or at the airport terminal seconds before take-off. And our endgame **regimen** will work for us. No late fines accrued (if we're lucky). No planes missed (usually). No sweat (well, maybe a little).

. . . I live with a procrastinator. (You should see our bathroom!) I'm even marrying her this summer. We were engaged three years before we set a wedding date, which should tell you all you need to know about our procrastinating compatibility. Call us a Match Delayed in Heaven.

Nuptials are a procrastinator's bounty. Take, for instance, the rule that **sanctions** a year's leeway for wedding gifts. It supports the philosophy embraced by procrastinators and Chicago Cubs fans alike: "Wait Till Next Year."

Except I usually take a decade. I've attended 10 weddings in the last four years, which puts me eight gifts behind the curve today (thanks to two early divorces). But here's the upside: Now that I'm getting married, I tell the couples I'm indebted to to just forget my gift and we'll call it even. It spares me the guilt.

And the thank-you notes.

approximately 370 words

Mark Leibovich, "And Tomorrow and Tomorrow," *San Jose Mercury News.* (Mar. 15, 1994), p. 7
Copyright © 1994 by San Jose Mercury News. Reprinted by permission.

1. Is the writing basically an example of irony or humor? _____
2. Give two examples from the selection to support your analysis of the tone.

   _____

   _____

3. Discuss one situation that often causes you to procrastinate.

   _____

   _____

PASSAGE 2

Read the following selection by Mark Twain to understand how he felt about humankind.

Cats are loose in their morals, but not consciously so. Man, in his descent from the cat, has brought the cat's looseness with him but has left the unconsciousness behind—the saving grace which excuses the cat. The cat is innocent, man is not.

The higher animals engage in individual fights, but never in organized masses. Man is the only animal that deals in that atrocity of atrocities, WAR. He is the only one that gathers his brethren about him and goes forth in cold blood and with calm pulse to exterminate his kind. He is the only animal that for **sordid** wages will march out and help to

_____

regimen (rej´ i mən) set of habits or rules; systematic procedure
sanctions (sangk´ shənz) allows or permits
sordid (sôr´ did) dirty, filthy

slaughter strangers of his own species who have done him no harm and with whom he has no quarrel.

Man is the only animal that robs his helpless fellow of his country—takes possession of it and drives him out of it or destroys him. Man has done this in all the ages. There is not an acre of ground on the globe that is in possession of its rightful owner, or that has not been taken away from owner after owner, cycle after cycle, by force and bloodshed.

Mark Twain, *Letters from the Earth*

1. What tone does Mark Twain use?

_____

2. Explain your choice.

_____

3. Does Mark Twain say anything redeeming about people? Support your answer.

_____

_____

PASSAGE 3

Forests Under Siege

Americans clamor for an end to worldwide deforestation. Yet, while our accusing eyes turn toward the tropical regions of the globe, chainsaws scream virtually unchecked through the Earth's last vestiges of temperate rain forests in our own country. Today, less than five percent of this nation's original, native forests remain unharmed by human intrusion, and they continue to topple at the rate of 240 acres a day. While the waxing wave of environmentalism largely neglects their liquidation by a profit-crazed timber industry, the forest ecologies suffer **irreconcilable** damage with global **ramifications.**

Jeffrey L. Chapman, "Forests Under Siege," *USA Today*, March 1991, pp. 17–21

1. What tone does the writer use?

_____

2. Support your choice.

_____

3. What groups are at fault?

_____

---

irreconcilable (ir rek´ ən sīl´ ə bl) unable to be brought into agreement
ramifications (ram ə fi kā´ shəns) consequences

The next two passages discuss the topic of peace. Read the selections to determine which employs a serious tone and which uses a solemn tone.

PASSAGE 4

With malice toward none, with charity for all, with firmness in the right as God gives us to see the right, let us strive on to finish the work we are in, to bind up the nation's wounds, to care for him who shall have borne the battle and for his widow and his orphan, to do all which may achieve and cherish a just and lasting peace among ourselves and with all nations.

Abraham Lincoln, Second Inaugural Address

1. The tone of this passage is _____

PASSAGE 5

For in the final analysis, our most basic common link is that we all live on this small planet. We all breathe the same air. We all cherish our children's future. And we are all mortal. . . . And is not peace . . . basically a matter of human rights—rights to live out our lives without fear of devastation—the right to breathe air as nature provided—the right of future generations to a healthy existence.

John F. Kennedy, Commencement Address at American University, 1963

2. The tone of this passage is _____

Having just read quotations from two former Presidents, now examine how a cartoonist employs tone to specify a message.

Jack Ohman, *The Oregonian*

3. Is the cartoonist mainly sarcastic, serious, or ironic about presidential hopefuls?

_____

Support: _____

_____

4. Select one word from the list of words on page 429 that best illustrates the cartoonist's feelings.

_____

PASSAGE 6

"Mea culpa," the title of the following passage, is a Latin expression meaning "It's my fault." You have read several passages dealing with women and minority rights. Now look at the issue of "rights" from a white man's perspective.

Mea Culpa

In the first meeting of my Harvard class on African American writers, an argument erupted over whether the reading list was sexist.

"Why are there no *women* writers on this syllabus?" asked one student, a white man.

The professor said that the major black authors of the period happened to be men.

Big mistake. For the next half hour or so, I learned that maybe we just weren't *aware* of black women writers in the mid-twentieth century. If they were considered unimportant, it was because white men determined what was thought significant about black culture and, deep down, white men want black women only for clandestine mistresses.

I sat quietly through the hubbub. Anything I said would have been automatically discounted. And that's not because I'm a conservative, you understand. On a quick checklist of liberal credentials, I have a pretty high rating. I'm pro-choice, pro-affirmative action, pro-gay rights, and pro-social spending, and I've never voted Republican in my life (except for William Weld). But none of that counts, because for reasons beyond my control I'm the **archetype** of political incorrectness. I grew up in Fairfield, Connecticut, where the country clubs have no black members because the town has no black citizens. My ancestors didn't come over on the Mayflower, but close enough. I attended prep school (Groton) and an Ivy League college (Yale). I'm not differently abled. I was born with a politically incorrect sexual orientation. What right do I have to complain?

Some of this isn't just well-deserved psychological **retribution** for all my previous advantages. Female and minority applicants get into graduate school over a white male with equal or better qualifications. "Sometimes minority applicants are almost dragged in kicking and screaming and told that this will be a great experience for them," says one admissions officer. I did get in, but because I'm a white male it's harder to stay here. Harvard gives full financial aid to all minority graduate students regardless of need. I pay about $8,000 a year, not including living expenses. This breeds cynicism, even among those who benefit from it. . . .

_____

archetype (är kə tīp) an original pattern or model
retribution (ret´ rə byōō´ shən) deserved punishment

If I weren't a white male, I'd have little difficulty getting a teaching job when I finish my dissertation. Female and minority Ph.D.s are so much in demand, they're courted like baseball's free agents. My female and minority peers will be snapped up as soon as they enter the job market. Merit is moot. This hiring is based on the idea that one can teach only what one is. That knocks me out of the ring: white men have nothing of value to impart.

But a lot to atone for. As a straight white man, I've probably committed date rape, seeing as it's now defined so loosely as to include a peck on the cheek that's not explicitly demanded. My whiteness has contributed to the oppression of non-whites since the beginning of history. I crushed the proletariat, shackled the slaves, exterminated the Indi—Native Americans, I mean . . . .

In this environment, keeping one's liberal convictions takes work. I have to remind myself that I *believe* in affirmative action, I support opening up the literary canon. I know I've had a privileged life. But that isn't enough for my correcter colleagues. Their idea of diversity is a chorus of voices all saying the same thing.

But maybe I shouldn't say that.

approximately 450 words

1. Select one word from the list of words on page 429 that best illustrates how you think the *writer* feels.

   _____

2. Choose one word that expresses how *you* felt after reading the selection.

   _____

3. State the thesis and explain how the writer's tone strengthens the thesis.

   _____

   _____

PASSAGE 7

Read to analyze what John Steinbeck, one of America's best story writers, said about Americans in general more than thirty years ago.

One of the generalities most often noted about Americans is that we are a restless, a dissatisfied, a searching people. We spend our time searching for security, and hate it when we get it. For the most part we are an **intemperate** people: We eat too much when we can, drink too much, indulge our senses too much. Even in our so-called virtues we are intemperate: A teetotaler is not content not to drink—he must stop all the drinking in the world; a vegetarian among us would outlaw the eating of meat. We work too hard, and many die under the strain; and then to make up for that we play with a violence just as

_____

intemperate (in tem´ pər it) lacking in self-control; not moderate

suicidal. The result is that we seem to be in a state of turmoil all the time, both physically and mentally. We are able to believe that our Government is weak, stupid, overbearing, dishonest, and inefficient, and at the same time we are deeply convinced that it is the best Government in the world, and we would like to impose it upon everyone else.

Americans overindulge their children and do not like them; the children in turn are overly dependent and full of hate for their parents. Americans are remarkably kind and hospitable and open with both guests and strangers; and yet they will make a wide circle around a man dying on the pavement rather than become involved. Fortunes are spent getting cats out of trees and dogs out of sewer pipes; but a girl screaming for help in the street draws only slammed doors, closed windows and silence.

Americans seem to live and breathe and function by paradox; but in nothing are we so paradoxical as in our passionate belief in our own myths. We truly believe ourselves to be natural-born mechanics and do-it-yourselfers. We spend our lives in motorcars, yet most of us—a great many of us at least—do not know enough about a car to check the gas tank when the motor fails. Our believed myths are everywhere: We shout that we are a nation of laws, not men—and then proceed to break every law we can if we can get away with it. From **puberty** we are preoccupied with sex; but our courts, our counselors, and our psychiatrists are dealing constantly with cases of sexual failure or charges of frigidity or impotence, which amounts to the same thing.

approximately 370 words

John Steinbeck, *America and Americans*, Viking Press, 1966

1. Is Steinbeck's tone sarcastic, critical, or ironic? _____

2. Give two examples of the paradoxes, that is, the contradictions, that Steinbeck cites about the behavior of Americans in general.

_____

_____

3. With which of Steinbeck's statements about Americans do you disagree?

_____

4. Is the behavior of Americans in the 1990s any different than it was when Steinbeck wrote this in the 1960s?

_____

Explain your answer.

_____

---

puberty (pyo͞o bər tē) age of becoming first able to product offspring; the physical beginning of manhood or womanhood

The next passage is slanted toward courses some university professors offer to college students. Analyze the writer's remarks to learn how she feels about these "enlightened" course offerings, reflected by her choice of tone.

PASSAGE 8

Madonna

Finally, Educators Figure Out What's Interesting

I used to worry about the hole in the ozone. Not any more. I don't worry about the greenhouse effect, lead in the air, nuclear waste or the loss of biodiversity. The energy problem? No problem. I know our future is in good hands because our college students are finally studying the right stuff: Madonna.

We don't need to administer national tests to our schoolchildren. We don't need to throw more money into the endless drain of our school districts. We don't need to pay teachers higher salaries. We need more videos.

Professor Jesse Nash is teaching a course in Madonna at Loyola University, where tuition is $10,000 per year. If you get what you pay for, it must be a good school. And if it is a good school it must know what it is doing when it offers courses in Madonna.

Those who have plowed through Western Civilization as college freshmen may think it is a joke, but I am not making this up. Professor Cathy Schwictenberg at the University of Massachusetts says it is significant to study Madonna because she's part of our culture.

A graduate student at the University of Florida is doing his master's thesis on her. He says that you can learn the same things by studying the Material Girl that you can by perusing Aristotle, Plato and Socrates. Who needs physics and philosophy? They're so boring.

Since Madonna's musical masturbatory expressionism, so un-Like a Virgin, is the new university equivalent of Plato's *Theaetetus*, surely there are other, more interesting substitutions for such dull courses as history, math and biology. High school dropouts would flock to higher education if we offered credit in finite mathematics in exchange for viewing a Marilyn Monroe retrospective. I guess that would show those study-mad Japanese a thing or two!

Wouldn't you be reassured to know your cardiologist studied M.C. Hammer and Vanilla Ice as an undergraduate? When assessing heart function, the doctor who studied Tina Turner wouldn't be tempted to wonder what love's got to do with it. If I needed bypass surgery I'd want the steady hands that must inevitably emerge from years of immersion in dependable iambic rap. It must at least be the equivalent of a semester of anatomy.

Since Madonna is equivalent to the Greek philosophers, surely Judy Garland films could replace Constitutional law. We could throw in a few Busby Berkeley extravaganzas for the intellectually hungry, and judging from the decisions handed down by the current Supreme Court, a refresher course on Ginger Rogers musicals couldn't hurt.

But law and medicine are not the only areas that could be improved by enlightened course offerings. Think of the kinds of weapons Silicon Valley engineers could turn out by studying Madonna. We could admit women to combat positions, dress them in pointed aluminum bras and let them hurl themselves at the enemy.

Besides achieving educational excellence and eliminating dropouts, we could reduce the budgets for elementary and high schools and eliminate the hassle of a national test. After all, you don't need to read or write to watch videos.

By integrating the educational trends of our universities into primary and secondary schools we will produce a generation of students qualified for admission to those universities. I guess that ought to prove to the rest of the world we're still Number One!

approximately 570 words

Ruth Priest, "Finally, Educators Figure Out What's Interesting," *San Jose Mercury News*, (July 10, 1991). Copyright © 1991. Reprinted by the permission of the author.

1. What words in the first paragraph help you to realize the writer is being satiric rather than serious?

   _____

2. Does the writer actually believe we need more videos rather than providing more money for education?

   _____

3. Is the remark in paragraph 3, "If you get what you pay for, it must be a good school," sarcastic? Why, or why not?

   _____

   _____

4. List three examples of exaggeration the writer uses to help the reader understand that she is ridiculing the course offering at Loyola.

   _____

5. The writer never states her thesis directly but implies it throughout the essay, particularly in the last paragraph. What is the thesis?

   _____

   _____

PASSAGE 9

Elvis 101 Is Now in Session

Not long before Elvis Presley died in 1977, he bought a machine that allowed him to view microfilm.

His longtime friend Janelle McComb saw the device at his home, Graceland, and told him, "You know, one day you're going to be a part of history . . . . One day, kids are going to be studying about you."

"And now," says McComb, "it's true."

The official name of the course being taught at the University of Mississippi is "In Search of Elvis: Music, Race, Religion, Art, Performance."

The text is pure Presley.

No grades are being given at the International Conference on Elvis Presley, which is expected to be an annual event. The course lasts only six days. And at least one-third of the 150 participants are members of the media. The other two-thirds include an odd assortment of scholars, fans and men in spangled jumpsuits who fervently believe Elvis is still the King.

Many of the scholars at the conference believe the study of Presley and his impact on popular culture is here to stay.

Already, there's a course at Ole Miss, taught during the regular semester, that compares Presley's Hawaiian movies to author Herman Melville's books set in Polynesia.

Other Elvis courses are being taught or planned at such institutions of higher learning as Emory University in Atlanta; Mercer University in Macon, Ga.; Alcorn State University in Lorman, Miss.; and Birmingham (Ala.) Southern College.

William Ferris; director of the Center for the Study of Southern Culture, a sponsor of the conference, makes no apologies for scholarly study of the singer.

"He's the most popular entertainer of the 20th century," says Ferris. "This is a world-class opportunity to talk about someone that everyone is interested in."

Some lecturers at the conference believe Presley is worthy of study because of his role in race relations. They say his music, which relied heavily on blues music of the Mississippi Delta, opened opportunities for black artists.

approximately 310 words

Clifford Pugh, "Elvis 101 Is Now in Session," *San Francisco Examiner,* 10 August 1995, C-13. Copyright © 1991. Reprinted by permission.

1. How does the tone in this article differ from the tone in passage 8 on Madonna?

   _____

2. Based on the tone, which passage, 8 or 9, did you find more interesting to read? Why?

   _____

3. Do you think celebrities should be used as the basis for college course offerings? Why, or why not?

   _____

   _____

❖ Understanding the Author's Purpose

Tone and purpose are closely related, so when we examine an author's tone, we also look at his or her purpose. In the passage you just read on education, the purpose is to ridicule course offerings on topics like Madonna, in order to *persuade* both administrators and interested citizens to do something about such courses. The language relies on the connotative meanings of emotional statements such as "show those study-mad Japanese a thing or two!" The writer's purpose becomes apparent once you examine the words and determine their tone.

At times, writers want to influence your beliefs, emotions, or actions: *to persuade you.* Sometimes, they write to help you learn: *to inform you.* Or, they may try to amuse you: *to entertain you.* But they can also combine their purposes. Entertaining writing can be used to persuade, for example. Even in textbook writing, where the main purpose is to provide information, the writer can shift from facts (informing you) to a personal anecdote (to amuse you). A writer's purpose or reason for writing an essay, article, or literary piece will vary and may include any of the following:

1. Telling a story (Entertain)
2. Explaining a theory (Inform)
3. Describing something (Inform or entertain)
4. Persuading or influencing you to believe something (Persuade)
5. Defending or attacking something (Persuade)
6. Amusing you (Entertain)

Since a writer does not usually say, "In this article, I intend to amuse you or prove to you or argue that . . . ," it is up to the reader to discover or infer the purpose. The reader must look at the language and decide whether the author intends to inform, persuade, entertain, or combine purposes.

To find the writer's purpose, the critical reader asks these key questions.

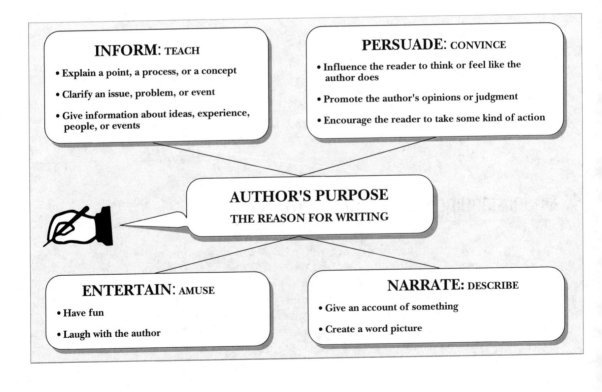

INFORM: TEACH

• Explain a point, a process, or a concept

• Clarify an issue, problem, or event

• Give information about ideas, experience, people, or events

PERSUADE: CONVINCE

• Influence the reader to think or feel like the author does

• Promote the author's opinions or judgment

• Encourage the reader to take some kind of action

AUTHOR'S PURPOSE
THE REASON FOR WRITING

ENTERTAIN: AMUSE

• Have fun

• Laugh with the author

NARRATE: DESCRIBE

• Give an account of something

• Create a word picture

1. What is the writer's reason for making these statements?
2. Why does the writer use these particular words?
3. What is the author's attitude about the topic?
4. What is the writer trying to convince me of or prove to me?

ACTIVITY 9.4   **Finding the Purpose**

Use the terms *inform, persuade,* and *entertain* as you select the author's purpose in the following selections. The commentary preceding each selection will assist you in determining purpose.

PASSAGE 1

Read to decide whether the writer is trying to persuade you to consider the pitfalls of fad diets, to inform you about vegetarianism, and/or to poke fun at addiction recovery programs and health-conscious Americans. Is the writer's intention to be serious or amusing?

The Unmaking of a Vegetarian—Or Why I'm Full of Bologna

I am a recovering vegetarian. The road to recovery is not an easy one, and it was a long while before I could admit that I had a problem. Even after my worst binges—those three- and four-day fruit fasts, or that night when the waiters had to throw me out of the macrobiotic restaurant so they could close and go home—even then I would not acknowledge what was obvious to everyone else, that I was powerless over vegetables.

I denied any connection between my long hours hanging out in health food stores and the drastic changes in my home life. It was about the time I started to cook tofu burgers out on our backyard grill that my son decided to get his own apartment, my marriage broke up and the neighbors began giving me strange looks on the street.

I was hitting the skids. Ordinary vegetables no longer satisfied my cravings. I tried gourmet greens like arugula and began to see weeds as delicacies, sating myself on dandelion shoots and burdock root. I can't say exactly when I bottomed out, but it may have been the day I noticed my skin yellowing—the result of belting down too much carrot juice. It was definitely a shock, a sobering glimpse of myself stumbling down the garden path to oblivion.

It was about this time that a friend confided that he was a member of Vegetarians Anonymous and dragged me to a meeting. One by one the group members told their stories of vegetable abuse and shared their progress along the 12 steps to recovery. Right then, I took the first step. I admitted I was powerless over vegetables, that my life had become unmanageable. That was as far as I got. The other 11 steps to recovery (I won't burden you with the details by listing them) looked to me like a mountain that I would never be able to climb. . . .

approximately 275 words

1. What are the author's tone and purpose?

_____

_____

2. How did you detect this tone?

_____

_____

3. With what group does the author compare his vegetable addiction in developing the essay?

_____

_____

PASSAGE 2

Read the following passage, which compares the attitudes of men and women toward each other, to see whether the writer is being critical or informative.

Mr. Fix-it and the Home-Improvement Committee

The most frequently expressed complaint women have about men is that men don't listen. Either a man completely ignores her when she speaks to him, or he listens for a few beats, assesses what is bothering her, and then proudly puts on his Mr. Fix-It cap and offers her a solution to make her feel better. He is confused when she doesn't appreciate this gesture of love. No matter how many times she tells him that he's not listening, he doesn't get it and keeps doing the same thing. She wants empathy, but he thinks she wants solutions.

The most frequently expressed complaint men have about women is that women are always trying to change them. When a woman loves a man she feels responsible to assist him in growing and tries to help him improve the way he does things. She forms a home-improvement committee, and he becomes her primary focus. No matter how much he resists her help, she persists—waiting for any opportunity to help him or tell him what to do. She thinks she's nurturing him, while he feels he's being controlled. Instead, he wants her acceptance.

These two problems can finally be solved by first understanding why men offer solutions and why women seek to improve. . . .

John Gray, *Men Are from Mars, Women Are from Venus*, p. 15

1. What are the author's tone and purpose?

_____

2. What language helped you arrive at this conclusion?

_____

3. Do you agree with the author's basic premise about the attitudes of women and men? Why, or why not?

_____

_____

PASSAGE 3

Think about what the author is actually criticizing in the following satire.

One Angry Man

It was 1999, and the O.J. Simpson trial had reached the halfway mark. The prediction was that by the year 2000 the defense would call its first witness.

Judge Ito had been appointed to the U.S. Supreme Court and had withdrawn from the case. He was replaced by Judge Geraldo Rivera, who had earned a law degree in 1996 and had been appointed to the bench by Gov. Sonny Bono.

By this time there was only one juror left.

Everyone else had been eliminated for one reason or another. Some had had nervous breakdowns, six had been shot by marshals when they rioted over the quality of the food, two had been discovered trying to get O.J. to autograph their footballs and one juror was caught kicking Marcia Clark in the shins.

The final juror was Larry Siegel, who had managed to survive by never talking to the other jurors and sticking cotton in his ears during the trial in the courtroom.

Ordinarily, the judge would have preferred 12 jurors, as would the defense and prosecution, but neither side wanted a mistrial, and so they agreed to try the case with only Larry.

Siegel was disappointed with their decision, particularly since his wife had stopped coming to the hotel for conjugal visits, claiming that the thrill was gone. He was also tired of the case itself. During the five years of the trial he had been permitted to hear only 15 minutes of evidence. The rest of the time he was sequestered while the lawyers argued their points before the judge.

There were some advantages to Larry being the solitary juror. He had the entire hotel floor set aside for the Simpson jury all to himself. His first request had been for a table-tennis paddle so he could play ping-pong against the wall.

Another advantage was that, even though he was alone, the hotel continued to send up 12 meals to the suite, so he had a big choice of desserts.

Every so often a marshal would report to the judge that Larry was talking to himself and kept asking to see President Clinton. Nobody was permitted to tell Larry that Clinton was no longer president and had been replaced by Steven Spielberg.

Finally, it was Larry's birthday. His mother baked him a beautiful Key lime pie with a single candle on it.

She also put a hacksaw blade at the bottom.

That evening Larry sawed his way out of the hotel bedroom window and, with sheets tied together, climbed down to the street. He ran into the first bar he saw and asked them to turn on Court TV so that he could watch its team of experts.

After an hour he knew that he was compromised and the judge had to throw him off the jury. Thus on April 30, 1999, with a complete lack of a jury, Judge Rivera was forced to call a mistrial, and everyone involved in the most famous trial of our time had to start all over again.

approximately 480 words

1. What is Buchwald's purpose in this article?

_____

2. Why does Buchwald use the names of people like Geraldo Rivera, Sonny Bono, and Steven Spielberg?

_____

3. What conclusion can you reach about Buchwald's feelings about the O. J. Simpson case from the last paragraph?

_____

Compare the next two passages on the subject of overpopulation, which is at times referred to as the *population bomb*. Passage 4 is from an interview with Ted Turner, billionaire entrepreneur. Passage 5 quotes Ben J. Wattenberg, a conservative New York columnist, whose perspective is quite different.

PASSAGE 4

Humanism's Fighting Chance

But the environmental degradation that's occurring now and the overpopulation—that's the real danger. Take a look at the planetary timeline. The world has been here for over four billion years; life on this planet, 3.5 billion years; human-like creatures, four million years; and Homo sapiens, 50,000 years. The start of agriculture was 15,000 years ago; the start of recorded history, 5,000 years ago; the Industrial Revolution, less than 200 years ago. And world population since then has increased tremendously. In 1830, it was one billion people; when I was born, it was two billion; now, it's 5.3 billion; and by the time I'm 60, it will be six billion. In 60 short years, the number of humans will have tripled. That's basically what the real problem with the environment is: there's too many people and they're using too much water, too much space, too much food—there's not enough land for anything else. . . .

Ted Turner

1. What are the tone and purpose?

   _____

2. What is Turner's position?

   _____

3. Why did Turner include so many figures and examples?

   _____

PASSAGE 5

The Anti-Malthus[1]

Among the big **demographic** trends that **undergird** Wattenberg's optimism, perhaps one of the most significant is the U.S.'s increasing population, the result of both rising immigration and higher fertility rates.

Wattenberg argues that the immigration of smart, hardworking, ambitious foreigners has long been the U.S.'s single most valuable comparative advantage in our competitive struggle in the global economy. Far from weighing down the economy, immigrants tend to be young workers who in the beginning take jobs many Americans consider undesirable. ... "Unless there's immigration, a country with fertility below replacement levels is slowly going out of business," says Wattenberg. ... Wattenberg points to census data that indicate the U.S. fertility rate—currently 2.1 children per woman—is actually increasing. That's the highest fertility rate in the U.S. since 1971. So if, as Wattenberg believes, global dominance has some relationship to population size, the U.S. is better positioned to benefit from this than any other major industrial country.

Eric Hardy

1. What are the tone and purpose of the essay?

   _____

2. Whose position on population growth do you find to be most acceptable, Ted Turner's or Ben Wattenberg's? Why?

   _____

   _____

---

demographic (di mag´ raf˘ ic) statistical study of people
undergird (un´ dər gird) surround and strengthen

[1]Malthus was a scientist who warned about the effects of overpopulation.

❖ Assessing the Author's Reliability

In addition to determining an author's tone and purpose, the critical reader questions the writer's reliability—his or her credentials and background as they relate to the information presented. It is important to determine whether the writer is an expert in the field, has had professional training or experience, and has quoted reliable sources in developing the thesis of an essay or textbook passage. Sometimes, facts about the writer are given at the bottom of the page or at the end of the essay or may be included in the introduction of the textbook. If no information is provided about the author, you must be especially careful when reading critically; the information presented should be based on facts and reasoned opinions, and it should be backed by evidence from authoritative sources.

Be on guard for vague references such as "reliable sources said," "reports point out," and "a survey shows" if no actual name is given for the source. Ask, "Who is the reliable source?" "Which specific report or survey is cited?" Do not accept information as factual where the identification of the source is missing.

If a writer presents both sides of an issue fairly, the writing is considered *objective* or *neutral* since it provides information readers can use to form their own opinions on the subject. It excludes any personal references or bias; the writer simply presents the information. But if the writing includes many personal opinions or slanted information to favor one side, we say it is *subjective* with the writer trying to influence the reader's thinking.

In order to determine how reliable the information is, the critical reader asks these key questions.

1. What is the author's background? Is he or she qualified to discuss the topic?
2. How much evidence is provided to support the point of view?
3. Are all aspects of the subject treated fairly?
4. Are reliable sources quoted?
5. Does the author ask for the reader's agreement?

The map that follows details the main differences between objective and subjective writing.

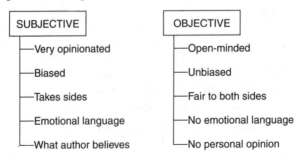

SUBJECTIVE	OBJECTIVE
Very opinionated	Open-minded
Biased	Unbiased
Takes sides	Fair to both sides
Emotional language	No emotional language
What author believes	No personal opinion

The paragraphs that follow are the conclusion to a selection on student **passivity** in college. Determine whether the information presented is objective and neutral or subjective and biased.

> [Social scientists,] Karp and Yoels systematically observed classes and conducted a survey of students at a coeducational university. They included various disciplines in their research, and studied both small (under forty students) and large (over forty students) classes. Although the small classes were characterized by slightly more student participation, in no case were more than a few students active. In small classes, only four or five students typically made more than one comment during a class period, and these few students were responsible for three-fourths of all interaction in the class. In larger classes, only two or three students were active participants; their discussion accounted for more than half of all class interaction. These results contradict the familiar argument that smaller classes encourage extensive student participation in classes of *all* sizes; however the vast majority of students are passive.
>
> Karp and Yoels also found that students themselves became irritated when one of their number was especially active in a class discussion. More than 60 percent of both male and female students reported that they were annoyed by students who "talked too much."
>
> John J. Macionis, Sociology

The excerpt is objective since the writer does not attempt to influence the reader to believe that student passivity is either good or bad. The writer quotes a source and presents information without using emotional language or stating opinions. The reader is free to draw his or her own conclusions about student passivity in the classroom. Therefore, this passage is objective and neutral.

ACTIVITY 9.5   Practice Assessing the Author's Reliability

Read the following article, which first appeared in *The New York Times*, to determine the author's reliability and degree of objectivity about brief, early marriages. Decide whether the information is backed by statistics, quotations, and people who are experts in assessing the success or failure of marriages.

"Starter" Marriages Often End

Deborah Schupack

Tim Barnard married when he was 25, fresh out of graduate school. His wife was a 21-year-old college student. "At that age," recalled Barnard, now 36, "I didn't comprehend what it took to

John Blanchard, *San Francisco Chronicle*

---

passivity (pas iv´ ə tē) inactivity; submissive stance

stay in a long-lasting relationship. It seemed that if you're in a serious relationship and you're committed to another person, the next logical step is to get married."

Four years later, they were divorced. He got the credit-card debt and she got the washer and dryer.

Barnard's marriage was typical of the many brief, early marriages that end in divorce by age 30, with no children and little more joint property than wedding gifts and a stereo. While couples in these marriages do not wed with the intention of divorcing, their temporary stay in marriage is much like the starter home of a generation ago, shed as the family outgrew it.

"The idea of a starter marriage is a fascinating one," said Dr. Constance Ahrons, professor of sociology at the University of Southern California in Los Angeles and associate director of its marriage and family therapy doctoral program. "These marriages are very common, but they are not given much credibility. ..."

BAROMETER OF SOCIETY

Marriage and family experts—psychologists, sociologists, lawyers and clergy—are beginning to look at these brief young unions, seeing in their implications a barometer of society's attitudes about marriage and divorce.

Some say starter marriages signal the need for more premarital counseling. Others have begun to rethink the whole notion of early, pre-children marriages, suggesting that it may be time to lessen the legal and social burdens of divorce for couples at this stage.

No statistics are kept on such marriages, but according to the Census Bureau, in 1992 there were 1.3 million divorces among people age 25 to 29, up from 253,000 in 1962—a five-fold increase—while the population for that age group did not even double in that time period.

Psychotherapists say brief, early marriages have been around as long as divorce has, although they often are overlooked in studies. "There may be no children, no property, and the marriage doesn't make headlines," said Ahrons, [who wrote] "The Good Divorce.". . . "But people still enter marriage with expectations, with dreams, with fantasies of the house we're going to buy, the children we're going to have." . . .

There is debate about how much people should pay in brief marriages without children. Margaret Mead recommended in the 1960s that such unions be codified as "trial marriages." Believing that it is the presence of children that should render a marriage lifelong, Mead described an alternative relationship that would last for a finite period, whereupon the couple would decide whether to have children and enter what she viewed as the more permanent stage of matrimony—or not. . . .

MORE COHABITATION

Mead's views on trial marriages came before the **proliferation** of **cohabitation**. In 1990, 2.9 million unmarried couples were living together, up 80 percent from 1980 and up 454 percent from 1970, according to the Census Bureau. Some of those couples may be replacing couples who could find themselves in a starter marriage, but cohabitation has not reduced the divorce rate.

---

proliferation (prō lif´ ə rā´ shən) rapid spread or increase
cohabitation (kō hab´ i tā shən) living together in a sexual relationship when not legally married

Society has a vested interest in making the breakup of a marriage difficult, said Michael Albano, president of the American Academy of Matrimonial Lawyers. . . .

Religious beliefs, too, tend to hold marriage as a **linchpin** of community, and many churches and synagogues offer marital counseling. In the Roman Catholic Church, for instance, couples undergo pre-wedding counseling on the specifics of married life, such as raising children and handling finances, said the Rev. Francis Muller, a judge with the Marriage Tribunal of the Archdiocese of New York. . . .

All marriages go through stages of evaluation, typically in the first year or two after marriage and again after seven years or so, said Dr. Anna Beth Benningfield, president of the American Association for Marriage and Family Therapy, a professional organization of therapists. At these junctures, the challenges of one's 20s—living independently for the first time, beginning a career—can strain a marriage to the breaking point. . . .

Those who have been through young marriages point to the divorce—not the wedding—as the real rite of passage of their 20s. "Marriage is very easy; divorce is very hard," said Pachett. . . .

Albano, the lawyer, . . . speaks to high school classes about the need to communicate in a marriage, about changing gender roles of spouses and parents, and about weathering the inevitable bad times.

"They really don't know that there are going to be days when he's obnoxious or she's so tired she can't deal with him, or the fact that she may make more money than he does" he said. "The Church tells them marriages are made in heaven, but so are thunder and lightning."

approximately 700 words

Deborah Schupack, " 'Starter' Marriages Often End," *The New York Times,* Home Section. (July 13, 1994). Copyright © 1994 by The New York Times Company. Reprinted by permission.

1. What is the author's purpose?

2. How reliable are the sources quoted to support the writer's thesis? Give some specific examples to support your answer.

3. Is the information presented objectively or subjectively?

Explain your answer.

---

linchpin (linch´ pin) pin that holds a wheel to its axle; any person, thing, or place that holds together the elements of a group

4. Are the statistics about divorces in 1992 relevant? Why, or why not?

_____

5. According to the author, why do starter marriages often fail?

_____

_____

❖ Looking at the Author's Point of View

Writers' beliefs often influence their point of view. In **colloquial** terms, point of view tells the reader "where the author is coming from." It is in effect the writer's particular *bias,* the angle from which he or she views things—the position or stance the writer takes. Both readers and writers have biases, preconceived ideas or judgments.

It is only natural that a person's background would influence his or her views or opinions on a particular topic. For example, would not an article written on alcoholism have a different degree of credibility if written by a member of Alcoholics Anonymous? A doctor? A priest? You should therefore examine the writer's point of view so as to recognize what bias or prejudice the writer expresses. The critical reader asks these key questions.

1. Is the writer's position for or against an issue?
2. What does the position imply about the writer?
3. How do the biases and beliefs of the author affect the presentation of ideas?

Always determine which side the writer is on. Remember, if the writer presents only one side of an argument, the passage is subjective and probably biased. If all sides of an issue are presented, it is neutral and objective.

A note of caution: In reading literature, the term *point of view* is quite different, with a specialized meaning: who is telling the story. Although someone writes the story, the point of view in novels and short stories refers to the "voice" in the story, or the person through whose eyes events are seen. Point of view can be first person (the word *I* is used by either a major or minor character, and the teller is subjective), third person (words like *he, she, it,* or *they* are used, and the teller is objective or detached), or **omniscient** (here, the author's story moves from one character's thinking to another's, and both the writer and reader know everything that is happening in the story, even when some of the characters do not).

---

colloquial (kə lō´ kwē əl) characteristic of informal speech
omniscient (ăm nish´ ənt) knowing all things

ACTIVITY 9.6 Assessing Author's Bias

Identify the author's bias in the following selections.

1. God bless me, my country, and its flag. I am not a Communist, and by most people's standards I am not even a radical, but I am angry because I stand with a healthy majority of my fellow Americans who cannot sing—standing *or* seated—our national anthem. Folks, to face facts, "The Star-Spangled Banner" is a real SOB to sing. There. It's been said. I have spoken my vicious, unpatriotic piece. I do not like the national anthem, and I hold that there are plenty of reasons and a good number of alternatives that would justify a change.

   What is the author's bias? _____

2. Many who hunt do so in ways that are irresponsible if not reprehensible. People shoot deer out of season, or illegally from cars as the deer freeze at night in the glare of the headlights. Others leave dead game in the woods, or perversely take aim at a domesticated animal such as cows or dogs, particularly if they've had a bad luck day.

   Leslie R. Gould, Jr., "Liberals: The NRA's Best Friends," *Washington Monthly,* April 1983, p. 95

   What is the author's bias? _____

3. Johnny Owen was the latest of approximately 330 men who have died since 1945 of injuries sustained in the boxing ring. If reason and humanity prevailed, he would be the last. The "sport" of boxing is a barbaric, brutal anachronism that has no place in modern civilized society.

   H. Bruce Miller, "Boxing Is a Barbarism Civilization Can Do Without," *San Jose Mercury News,* Nov. 15, 1980, p. D-2

   What is the author's bias? _____

4. To me any call for the abolishment of affirmative action sounds like a sneering pronouncement from 19th-century **potentates.**

   West Magazine, *San Jose Mercury,* May 21, 1995, p. 6

   What is the writer's position on affirmative action?

   _____

   _____

   _____

   potentates (pōt´ n tāts) those who have rule or power over others

5. Yale University psychologist Robert Sternberg says that one big part of what makes people smart is called *tacit knowledge.* "Unlike IQ, which involves the mental power to manipulate symbols, tacit knowledge is closer to 'practical' intelligence, or common sense. . . . Our studies suggest that not having common sense can hamper your career," says Sternberg. "As an employer, I'd take common sense over a few IQ points."

"Why IQ Isn't Destiny," *U.S. News & World Report,* October 24, 1994, p. 76

How does the writer feel about IQ compared to common sense?

_____

_____

ACTIVITY 9.7 **Looking at Point of View**

Examine what the cartoonist is saying about one's point of view.

"*It's all according to your point of view: To me, you're a monster.*"

Modern Maturity, (March/April, 1995), p. 56. Copyright © 1995 by American Association of Retired Persons.

Explain what the cartoonist implies about one's point of view.

_____

_____

ACTIVITY 9.8 **Looking at Point of View**

The following is an introduction to an interview held with many important world leaders:

> Since the Constitution was drafted, Americans have been engaged in an ongoing, often heated debate about its meaning and value. Both in the U.S. and abroad, students of democracy have puzzled over the document's contradictory roles as the chief focus of contention and the enduring symbol of cultural and political unity.
>
> Excerpted from "Contention and Continuity," Time, July 6, 1987, pp. 56–57

Read the following differing points of view of particular people in connection with the Constitution. Note the descriptions of the authors at the time they made the statements, and then answer the questions that follow.

POINTS OF VIEW ON ECONOMIC RIGHTS

T. Boone Pickens, a Texas millionaire

Through my experience with free enterprise, my appreciation continues to grow for the Constitution's principles of limited government and the freedom of individuals to achieve their maximum potential.

Ralph Nader, a consumer advocate

There should be a constitutional amendment that forbids a corporation from being treated as a person. You can't have equal protection of the laws when an individual is contesting against an Exxon.

Bernie Sanders, socialist mayor of Burlington, Vermont

The most obvious weakness of our Constitution is that the economic rights of our citizens are not adequately addressed. Freedom must mean more than the right to vote every four years for a candidate for President. Freedom must also mean the right of a citizen to decent income, decent shelter, decent health care, decent educational opportunity and decent retirement benefits. One is not free sleeping out in the streets. One is not free eating cat food in order to survive.

1. How do the three views differ? What are the particular biases of each?

_____

_____

_____

POINTS OF VIEW BY MINORITY MEMBERS

Antonia Hernandez, president, Mexican American Legal Defense and Educational Fund

Not having been born in the United States, I had to go through the process of becoming a citizen. I didn't think that the ceremony would have such an impact on me. But it really gave me the feeling that the Constitution was a part of me and I was a part of it.

Roger Wilkins, African-American political commentator

I was very young when I learned that although white people wrote rules that were grossly unfair, there were some limits that were imposed on them by the Constitution. What I appreciate most about the document is the 13th Amendment (abolishing slavery). If you have to go back to basics, that's it. The fact is that the 13th Amendment is the single most significant thing about the document to me and the thing that has the most meaning in my daily life.

Gordon Hirabayashi, jailed during World War II for challenging the internment of his fellow Japanese Americans

My objection has been not so much with the Constitution but with the people administering it, who either manipulated the Constitution or had a different view of it than I have. The Constitution is just a scrap of paper unless people care enough to make it work.

2. How do the three views differ? What are the particular biases of each?

_____

_____

POINTS OF VIEW FROM ABROAD

Raul Alfonsin, president of Argentina

The U.S. Constitution represents the most successful and lasting attempt to organize the history of a people around deliberate and rational principles of justice and social well-being. It constitutes a victory of reason and will over tradition and inherited custom, introducing transcendental ideas in a very concise text with considerable flexibility.

Antonio LaPergola, outgoing president of Italy's Constitutional Court

The process of judicial review is a miraculous contribution from the U.S. to democracies and political systems throughout the world. It is the way in which the Constitution is translated every day into a living set of rules. The process of judicial review has caught on in many of Europe's newer democracies, usually after long spells of dictatorship.

Georgi Arbatov, a Russian writer on American issues

I have great respect for your Constitution and your forefathers, but I think a lot of things are not going according to the way they wanted their nation to go. I think you need your own *perestroika* [reconstruction], your own *glasnost* [openness].

3. How do the three views differ? What are the particular biases of each?

_____

_____

ACTIVITY 9.8 Thinking Critically While You Read

After you read contrasting viewpoints on the following issue, in the columns provided, list the most significant points presented by each author. Then, based on your critical analysis, act as a judge, writing down your "verdict" of the issue. In so doing, consider the following:

Which writer's position is based chiefly on facts, sounder logic, and reasoning?
What is each author's purpose? How reliable are the author and the publication?
What are the biases of each author and publication?

Also consider these questions:

Can inferences be drawn from some of their statements?
Is the choice of language chiefly objective or subjective? Denotative or connotative?
Does either author omit or suppress any information that would help you reach a valid conclusion?

The Environment vs. the Lumber Industry

Concern for the environment becomes especially heated when it affects our own national forests, as many people consider them a nonrenewable national treasure. Others, however, claim that we depend on wood products and that these products produce jobs and bolster our economy. Laws to limit cutting of the giant trees are entangled in court proceedings. Environmental groups attack the lumber industry as greedy and insensitive while the lumber industry attacks the environmental groups as zealots who know little about forestry and logging. Again, this is a complex issue, and it is necessary to be a critical reader to judge it fairly.

The first article, in support of the preservation of our national forests, was written by Harry Lonsdale. At the time the article was written, Mr. Lonsdale was chairman of Bend (Oregon) Research, Inc., and former chairman of the Native Forest Council. He also was a candidate for the U.S. Senate in 1990. The article appeared in *USA Today.*

Can We Save Our National Forests?

Harry Lonsdale

If we don't act soon, the last of our native forests 1 will be destroyed. The trouble is, most Americans don't even know that their forests are being cut down. We tend to think of our woodlands as national parks, as preserves where the deer and the antelope play, birds sing, and clear water flows. In fact, they long ago were declared to be areas of "multiple use," where logging as well as recreational and other values supposedly could be sustained indefinitely. However, at the current rate of timber extraction, the last of the most valuable trees—the "old growth"—will be gone in a couple of decades. In even less time, those forests may be fragmented beyond the point of no return.

. . . John Muir at the beginning of this cen- 2 tury introduced the concept that, simply left alone, the natural world and especially the wilderness areas had a priceless and irreplaceable ecological value that science has yet to comprehend. In his words, "In wildness is the preservation of the world."

However, that same wildness also harbors 3 vast wealth. Because of the fine, clear grain of the wood in the ancient trees, those forests are extremely valuable when reduced to lumber. The remaining woodlands of the Pacific Northwest contain a preponderance of trees with 100 feet or more of branchless trunks, which yield some of the most highly valued lumber in the world. An acre of such old growth can have a value in excess of $100,000 to the timber industry. Thus, the millions of acres of ancient, publicly owned forests in Oregon and Washington alone are worth hundreds of billions of dollars in the open marketplace.

What those trees are worth if left standing 4 is a much harder figure to arrive at, and almost

any reasonable method of calculation comes up far short of the purely utilitarian value. Thomas Power, an economist at the University of Montana, and a team at Colorado State University headed by Richard Walsh have attempted to put a value on forests. One of the preferred methods of evaluation is to ask campers and hikers what they would pay to spend a day in the woods, or how much they expended as a part of their annual vacation costs to get to and enjoy the forests. Others, like Randall O'Toole of Cascade Holistic Economic Consultants, Corvallis, Ore., would have us pay the true costs of a forest experience with a fairly high annual user fee. Whatever the logic or method, it quickly becomes abundantly clear that there's much more money in lumber than in forests.

So, do we chop them all down and grow 5 trees on farms as they do in Europe? The Forest Service is planning just that. Its "tree of the future" will grow in rows and be cut down, or "harvested," when it reaches a diameter of 17 inches. If all we want is trees, that will give us enough forever, or at least until the soil is so depleted of nutrients that it won't support them any more. Chris Maser, a forest ecologist who for many years was on the staff of the Bureau of Land Management, believes that only about three such "crops" can be grown on a patch of land before the soil is depleted irreparably.

It well may be that all of this ecology vs. 6 economy talk soon will have become irrelevant. There's a new thinking loose in the world that says we must preserve and restore this planet before it's too late. Such thoughts may turn out to be irrepressible. As more Americans become aware of the fact that, somewhere on Earth, an acre of ancient forests is being destroyed every second, around the clock, the pressure to preserve what's left will mount irresistibly.

Before we throw up our hands, let's recognize that there is plenty of timber to go around, at least for our own country's needs. Over 72% of the nation's supply is privately owned and, while it's true that most of the country's native forests now are gone, we still have the capacity to grow more trees for all the 2x4s, newsprint, and toilet paper we'll ever need, if we manage those woodlands wisely. In 1976, Congress passed the National Forest Management Act (NFMA '76). That law provides, in part, that the national forests shall be managed so as to supply us with a minimum amount of timber "in perpetuity." That sounds reassuring, but NFMA '76 has been interpreted by the Forest Service to mean that they will produce at least a minimum amount of wood fiber per year, without regard to what the forests look like. Thus, because we've been overcutting for decades and because younger trees add more fiber per year than older ones, in order to meet the requirements of NFMA '76, we're heading for those tree farms—unless we change the law. 7

WE CAN'T SUPPLY THE WORLD

While we have plenty of timber for our own needs, we don't have enough to supply the world. Other countries, notably Japan, see our timber as grossly underpriced and are buying our logs as fast as we can cut them down. The world price of raw logs is greatly in excess of our domestic price. Thus, industry giants like Weyerhaeuser sell logs off their own lands to Japan while, at the same time, supplying logs to their U.S. mills from trees cut in our forests. The direct export of most logs cut in our national forests is illegal, but there's a huge loophole that allows this substitution that circumvents the spirit of the law. 8

Every time we export raw logs, we export the jobs that their processing would have produced. With a dwindling supply of ancient trees and with more improvements in automation, employment in the timber industry actually is contracting, just as production and corporate profits are at all-time highs. The industry, in a major national public relations campaign, unfairly is blaming the loss of jobs on the environmentalists who want to save the ancient forests. The timber industry is after short-term profits, and it wants to continue to earn them by continuing what it has been doing quite legally for years—chopping down our national forests. When the present trees in our national forests are gone, it plans to grow its own or cut those grown on national forest tree farms. It's been the tradition in that industry to "cut and move on," but we have reached the point where there's no place left to move on *to*. 9

If we'd stop the exports, we would have plenty of timber for our domestic use. After all, we now export more raw logs and other barely processed wood products from Northwest ports than we cut on all the national forests in Oregon and Washington. If we'd get smart and start exporting value-added wood products, we could create enough new jobs to more than replace those that might be lost due to a decrease in timber production that is inevitable at our present pace of overcutting. Only by stretching out the cutting of those forests can we produce wood products and the jobs that go with them indefinitely. The Swiss sell a cuckoo clock for more than we Americans sell a five-ton log! The wood products companies of the future in the Pacific Northwest will be those that manufacture furniture, doors and windows, and modular homes for domestic and foreign markets. 10

How can we bring about this change in a powerful, entrenched, and politically astute industry which is so strong that not one 11

Congressperson from Idaho, Oregon, or Washington dares to antagonize it by suggesting that we manage our national forests on a truly sustainable basis? By virtue of their wealth, the timber barons are represented on every major corporate and charitable foundation board in the Northwest. . . .

Our ancient forests provide us with pure 13 water, clean air, wildlife habitat, and, most importantly, a tranquil sanctuary. We can't let the search for profit lead us into the equivalent of the last buffalo hunt.

approximately 1370 words

Harry Lonsdale, "Can We Save Our National Forest?" *USA Today* (March 1991), pp. 22–24. Copyright © 1991 by the Society for the Advancement of Education. Reprinted by permission of *USA Today*.

The second article, in defense of the lumber industry, appeared in *Newsweek* magazine. At the time she wrote this article, Leila Kysar was the business manager of a tree-farm-management business in Washington state.

A Logger's Lament

Leila L. Kysar

My father was a logger. My husband is a logger. 1 My sons will not be loggers. Loggers are an endangered species, but the environmental groups, which so righteously protect endangered species in the animal kingdom, have no concern for their fellow human beings under siege. Loggers are a much misunderstood people, pictured as brutal rapists of our planet, out to denude it of trees and, as a result, of wildlife.

It is time to set the record straight. Loggers 2 take great pride in the old-growth trees, the dinosaurs of the forests, and would be sorry to see them all cut. There are in the national forests in Washington and Oregon (not to mention other states) approximately 8.5 million acres of forested land, mostly old growth set aside, never to be used for timber production. In order to see it all, a man would have to spend every weekend and holiday for 60 years looking at timber at a rate of more than 1,000 acres per day. This does not include acreage to be set aside for spotted-owl protection.

In addition to this huge amount of forested 3 land never to be logged, the State of Washington Forest Practices Act, established in 1973, specifies that all land that is clear-cut of trees must be replanted unless converted to some other use. As a tree farmer generally plants more trees per acre than he removes, more trees are being planted than are being cut. In the last 20 years in Clark County, Wash., alone, the Department of Natural Resources has overseen the planting of at least 15,000 acres of previously unforested private lands.

The term logger applies to the person har- 4 vesting trees. A tree farmer is the one who owns the land and determines what is to be done with it. To a tree farmer, clear-cutting is no more than the final harvest of that generation of trees. The next spring, he reforests the land. To the public, clear-cutting is a bad word. Does the public cry shame when a wheat farmer harvests his crop and leaves a field of stubble in place of the beautiful wheat?

In the Pacific Northwest, in five years, the newly planted trees will grow taller than the farmer's head; in 10 years, more than 15 feet tall; and in 20 to 30 years, the trees will be ready for the first commercial harvest. The farmer then thins the trees to make room for better growth. In 40 to 50 years, he will be ready to clear-cut his farm and replant again. Contrary to public opinion, it does *not* take 300 to 400 years to grow a Douglas fir tree to harvestable age.

Tree farming keeps us in wood products. We build with wood, write on paper and even use the unmentionable in the bathroom. But in order to keep this flow of wood products available, we need to keep it economically feasible to grow trees. If we restrict the tree-farming practices because we do not like clear-cuts or because some animal might (and probably might not) become extinct, or we restrict markets for the timber by banning log exports or overtax the farmer, we are creating a situation where the farmer will no longer grow trees. If he cannot make money, he will not tree-farm. He will sell his tree farm so that it can grow houses. The *land* that grows trees is the natural resource; the *trees* are just a crop.

Legislation is constantly being introduced to take away the private-property rights of tree farmers. They are beleaguered by the public, who believe that any forest belongs to the public. Who, after all, buys the land and pays the taxes? Who invests money in property that will yield them an income only once every 20 to 30 years? Would John Q. Public picnic in a farmer's wheat field?

The tree farmer must have a diversified market. When there is a building slump in this country, it is vital to the industry to have an export market. Earlier recessions were devastating to tree farmers until markets were developed overseas. Some trees have little market value in the United States. The logs China and Korea bought in the late '80s could not be sold here to cover the cost of delivery.

As to the wildlife becoming extinct, that is a joke that is not very funny. Animals thrive in clear-cuts better than in old-growth timber. Look at the Mount St. Helens blast area. Nature created an immense clearing and now deer, elk and other wildlife are returning in numbers. Why? Because there is more food growing in an open area than under the tall trees. And as for the spotted owl, surely the 8.5 million acres set aside is enough to maintain quite a respectable owl population. Numerous recent observations show that the owl lives in second-growth timber as well as in old growth. In the Wenatchie National Forest there are more than 250 examples of spotted owls living in other than old-growth timber. The owl is a tool of the environmentalist groups to get what they want: the complete eradication of the species *Logger.*

Beautiful new trees: Consider the scenic value of a preserved old-growth forest versus a managed stand of timber. In Glacier National Park, Mont., for example, which is totally untouched, one sees the old trees, the dead and dying trees, the windfalls crisscrossing the forest. In a managed forest, one sees the older stands with the forest floor cleared of the dead windfalls, leaving a more parklike setting. In the younger stands, one sees the beautiful new trees with their brilliant greens thrusting their tops to the sky and, in the clear-cuts, before the new trees obscure the view, one sees the huckleberry bushes with their luscious-tasting berries, the bright pink of fireweed and deer and elk feeding. True environmentalists husband the land; they do not let the crops stagnate and rot. Tree farming regenerates the trees *and* utilizes the product.

A tree farmer from Sweden (where they are fined if they do *not* tree-farm their forests) asked me recently why we do not just explain these facts to the environmental groups so that they will work *with* us instead of against us. Well, do you know the difference between a terrorist and an environmentalist? It is easier to reason with the terrorist.

approximately 1040 words

Leila L. Kysar, "A Logger's Lament," *Newsweek* (October 22, 1990), p. 10

List the most significant points made in each of the two essays. Remember to consider the author's thesis, purpose, objectivity, reliability, and language.

Significant Points *For* Prohibiting the Cutting of Our National Forests	Significant Points *Against* Prohibiting the Cutting of Our National Forests

Arguments not included:

What is your verdict on the pros and cons of legalizing the cutting of lumber on our national forests?

_____

_____

What are your reasons for your decision?

_____

_____

❖ Summary

A writer's tone, purpose, reliability, point of view, and bias are factors to consider when reading critically. While many tones are used by writers, eight major tones predominate:

1. Serious or neutral (straightforward and objective)
2. Solemn (dignified and grave)
3. Critical (good or bad features considered)
4. Sarcastic (harsh, bitter words that hurt and belittle)
5. Ironic (opposite of what is really intended)
6. Satiric (exaggeration and ridicule to bring about change)
7. Cynical (pessimistic and doubtful about humankind)
8. Humorous (amusing and comical writing; a witty tone has sophisticated, clever writing)

An author may use more than one tone, and the tone or tones are related to the author's purpose for writing. Writers do not state their purpose; the reader infers or discovers it. These purposes consist primarily of entertaining, informing, or persuading the reader, but as with tone, writers may have more than one purpose for writing. For example, entertaining writing also can be meant to persuade.

Critical readers also question the writer's reliability, his or her credentials and background, as they analyze the issue or information presented. The personal beliefs and background of an author influence his or her point of view. Critical readers note whether only one side of an argument is presented and whether the writing is subjective and therefore probably biased, or whether the writer presents both sides of an issue and lets the reader determine the merits of each.

Chapter 9 Vocabulary Review
Word Analogies

For this final practice with analogies, you are to decide whether the paired words are related by similarities *(synonyms)* or differences *(antonyms)*.

A. In this practice, the first set contains a review word from previous chapters. Complete the second pair with a word from Chapter 9. Select it from the list of boldfaced words below. You will not use all the words listed. In completing the practice, indicate the relationship of the pairs of words in the space provided, determining whether they are synonyms or antonyms as shown in the following example.

discredit: disparage: :run down: _____

(Belittle is a word that could complete the analogy.)

Relationship: *synonyms* _____

intemperance   proliferation   passive   lethal   frays   sordid   archetype

1. self-denial:hedonist: :self-control: _____

   Relationship: _____

2. inactive:dynamic: :lively: _____

   Relationship: _____

3. sensational:lurid: :contemptible: _____

   Relationship: _____

4. destroy:decimate: :deadly: _____

   Relationship: _____

5. increase:diminish: :reduction: _____

   Relationship: _____

B. For this last review practice, use the *context clues* to determine which of the words listed is appropriate in each sentence. You will not use all the words.

   regimen   cohabitation   pessimistic   colloquial   satirist   titan

1. Their parents disapproved of the young, unmarried couple's _____.

2. Using _____ language and slang in formal essays is generally considered inappropriate.

3. Voters were _____ and doubted that the proposed state tax decrease would appear on the ballot.

4. Bill Gates, the billionaire entrepreneur and _____ of the computer industry, has influenced business operations in the United States and abroad.

5. Essays by Art Buchwald, a well-known _____ and critic of politics, appear weekly in newspapers nationwide.

Selection 19: **ESSAY**

☛ Preparation for Reading

The following biographical essay was written by a young man who is of mixed parentage, being both Jewish and African American. From his particular vantage point, he is able to be very sensitive to the issue of race relations although this in no way prepared him for the prejudice he encounters over the years. Read to see how he learned that the "problem" was not his, but their problem and to see if you agree with him that today he is a better person for these experiences.

These words are underlined in the essay:

ambivalence about color	conflicting feelings
a nation of **apartheid**	strict racial segregation
assuaged the rage	calmed
heaped **invectives** upon whites	violent verbal attack
some minor **digressions**	wanderings from the main subject
inalienable rights	that which cannot be taken away or transferred
coerced into taking either side	forced or compelled

Preview, then read the essay.

Who I Am

Dexter Jeffries

It is a common practice to look back at one's 1 life and search for some thread, some theme that has run through it. For me, fortunately or unfortunately, color is the cord that ties up most of my life's successes, failures and contradictions. When Thoreau stumbled upon the gravestone of a slave, he ruminated on the words "a man of color" and remarked to himself, "As though he were discolored." That is how America has always made me feel: discolored. American <u>ambivalence</u> about color has followed me wherever I have traveled. That ambivalence—and my attempts to cope with it—have formed a major part of my life. Yet I feel that I am a richer person for this struggle, a better teacher, writer and friend because of it.

My parents, who were married in 1936 and 2 remained so until my father's death in 1977, always had difficulty in finding suitable housing. They were an interracial couple, a real anomaly for their times. My father was a black from Virginia, and my mother was the daughter of Russian Jews from Odessa. They suffered. America was a nation of <u>apartheid</u> in the 1930s. Separate facilities in all areas of society were common. Practically everything worked to keep them apart. When they lived in Washington, D.C., for instance, whenever they attended the movies, my father would have to sit in the balcony, which was for "Colored Only," while my mother sat down in the orchestra. They endured.

I have often wondered about the source of their courage and strength. Many of my peers, black and white, have suggested that even now . . . they would not venture into an interracial relationship because of the inevitable psychological hardships, particularly raising the children of such a union. They are frightened. So were my parents. . . . **3**

My sister, Elizabeth, my brother, Gregory, and I quickly became aware of our place in society. We were not wanted. We were not desirable. The problem was compounded by our not being dark enough to be taken as Negro nor light enough to be accepted as white. To this day, people are still confused by my appearance. Students at the college where I teach have asked about my identity. Am I black? White? Am I Hispanic? Because of the recent influx of new immigrants, the guesses are sometimes more exotic. Am I Egyptian? Am I Iranian? No one ever enunciates what I would really like to hear: human, *Homo erectus,* a member of the species, just like you. **4**

As an adult, I am politely asked questions. As youngsters, my sister, brother and I were usually expected to behave in a manner consistent with how we were perceived. If people thought we were white, we were expected to act "white." If neighbors suggested that we were black, we were expected to act "black." We all made feeble attempts at dealing with a society that thrives on racial and ethnic identification. My sister suffered the most because she was the oldest and therefore born a bit too soon as far as American history was concerned. **5**

I was born eight years after my sister, and there were some events that occurred that perceptibly changed the general social climate of race relations in the United States and the course of our lives. In 1947, Jackie Robinson joined the Brooklyn Dodgers and sports would never be the same. In 1948, the Armed Forces of the United States were integrated, and mil- **6**

lions of volunteers and draftees were exposed to the idea of blacks and whites working together. Finally, in 1954, *Brown v. Topeka* was a phrase on the lips of many people who lived thousands of miles from Kansas. These events made a difference. . . .

My brother was not born at the right time in history either. He felt the full brunt of discrimination as he was not permitted ever to become a part of the youthful male community of Springfield Gardens. Whether it was Little League, Davy Crockett and the Alamo, Boy Scouts or afterschool activities, he was always aware that something was wrong. Some children are too fat, too skinny, too short or too tall. You can also be too dark. One of the confounding problems of this situation is the realization that the bearer of this problem can do nothing about it. . . . **7**

Things had begun to change by the middle and late 1950s. Certain progressive ideals and notions had started to take hold. There were small and evolving changes, but they <u>assuaged</u> the rage and mistrust between whites and blacks just enough so that I did not have to suffer all of the racial indignities that my brother and sister were forced to brave. It might have been the elementary school teacher who acknowledged Negro History Week in the class and spoke about Paul Robeson, Negro soldiers in the Civil War and Dr. Ralph Bunche. Or it could have been a young white boy who uttered words evocative of a heroic Huck Finn, "Ah, let the colored guy play. They're pretty good sometimes." These were events that would never enter a history text, but they changed my present and future. **8**

However, for the most part, I was a bit befuddled as a youngster, since my parents had never prepared me for—nor could they forsee—the problems I would meet. I loved them, of course, and I did not see them as black or white. They were my mother and father. The **9** issue of race did arise, but it was always in a positive historical and social vein. My father would become rhapsodic as he spoke about his heroes, Paul Robeson, Duke Ellington, Alexandre Dumas, Pushkin and Charlie Parker. My mother was also well versed in Afro-American history. Elizabeth, Gregory and I now know that the education we received from our parents about Negro history was more comprehensive than any book written or documentary produced by the late 1960s, when black awareness became a facet of American culture.

I remember loving school and very 10 earnestly digesting everything that was dished out. One day, a neighbor asked me what I was. In kindergarten I had just learned about the Pilgrims . . . and I replied quickly, with all the confidence and innocence of that age, "I'm an Englishman." That was the last time I ever answered that question so quickly and unwittingly. With just as much confidence and a trace of contempt, this blond Irishwoman said, "Ah, no. You're a little Puerto Rican or maybe colored." It was on that day that the "veil," as W.E.B. Du Bois labeled it, was cast over me. I have never forgotten it. Du Bois also wrote: "The problem of the twentieth century is the problem of the color line."

As I grew older, I developed a dualistic view 11 of the world. I viewed things literally in black and white. People were quick to label me, and I spent a great deal of time and energy attempting to live out their visions. This manner of existence would make life bearable for two or three months, but the inevitable would always occur: a joke about niggers or a frenetic speech about the cheapness of Jews in which the speaker demonstrated that, in the American black ghetto, the Jew was supposedly the cause of all the misery. These insults caused a physical reaction. I would feel faint for a few moments as I realized that the person whom I had befriended had betrayed me. The friends with whom I had eaten hamburgers, played ball and shared the intimate moments of growing up had torn me asunder. With clenched fists, I wept.

Because I had my secret and extraordinary 12 vantage point—black and Jewish—one that allowed me access to the inner recesses of whites and blacks, there was a part of me that felt the jokes I heard were actually on the people who told them. They had taken me into their confidence and believed that I was just like them, black or white. And perhaps I was the one who was the betrayer of trust and faith, for I listened and never said a word. I listened to whites assault blacks and remained silent. Blacks heaped <u>invectives</u> upon whites, usually selecting Jews as the specific enemy, and I listened and nodded my head. During the 1960s, I had a front row seat on one of the most momentous social struggles in America, but the price of the ticket left me reeling. Every derogatory remark about blacks left me weaker. Every anti-Semitic remark left me sadder. . . .

I would think, and if they really knew . . . I 13 sometimes toyed with that idea. Tell them. Don't hide. Just tell them the truth and see what they say. I am ashamed to say that impotence and paralysis prevented me from taking such action for most of my life. It is difficult to discard love and affection even if it is tainted, to surrender friendship and its bonds for principles when you are confused about the principles yourselves. . . .

By college, where social relationships have 14 the potential to play such a major role in one's life, I realized that a human being could survive this sort of misery for only a limited time. A crisis brought on a final scream for help. I was dating a Greek girl at Queens College. She had met my family on numerous occasions, but I noticed that this exchange was not reciprocal. One night, just out of curiosity, I asked her why she had never invited me to her house. She avoided the question. I should have known. I pushed hard for an answer. She burst into tears. After she cried for a while, we hugged and then she said, "Dexter, my mom said it's all right to bring anyone home, anyone. Jewish, Italian, Irish, anyone. She said I can bring any boy home as long as he's not colored."

15 This event forced me into therapy. I had intentionally avoided this one possibility of help. . . .

16 Lying: That's how I spent my first six months in therapy. It was a waste of valuable time and energy, but I imagined it was the normal course of affairs, particularly for someone who had already lived a lie. I walked into the office. The therapist, a middle-aged woman, asked me what I would like to accomplish, talk about or discuss. I said, with dispatch and confidence in my voice, "I have this problem, something to do with identity. I'm sure you've handled many cases like it. . . ."

17 Dr. Hannah Sallinger smiled at me, leaned back in her chair, and said, "Well, it's good that you know what you want to talk about, but do you really think that I should do all the work, read the books, go to the library, research articles? What will you do? Don't you think we could solve your problem a little more quickly if we worked together, like a team, same goals?" Yes, I was to find out that we would work together, a lot of work, many discoveries, exploring, crying, reflecting and mourning. It's a long story with so many different facets and anecdotes. . . .

18 I kept on the main track with only some minor digressions. She helped me understand who I was, from a human point of view. And when it comes down to it, race is not human; it's an artificial categorization employed to justify what is inherently human: weakness, fear, diffidence and timidity. By focusing on the human side—my family, my relationships with my father, mother, brother and sister—I was able to make some substantial progress in consolidating a genuine identity.

19 In addition, there were other cures that worked in conjunction with therapy and helped bring about my emancipation: friends, my fellow soldiers when I was in the Army, lovers, radical politics, jazz and literature. It was in the last years of high school and then during college that I discovered books. It was on pages with words composed by Camus, Wright, Woolf, Kesey, Kafka, Ellison and Dostoyevski that a voice sounded like my voice. I embraced fictional characters as I watched them confront a world similar to mine, no matter if they were white, black, insane, women or Russian. Books made me feel whole and instilled in me a feeling that I was part of something much larger and more important than Queens, than being white, black or even American. No matter what shape or form the writer's pronouncement took, the message was always the same: Do not allow the external world to denigrate you. Create your own identity. I heard it in Joyce, Thoreau and Du Bois. Literature always affirmed what was best in men and women, and with that affirmation I was able, for the first time, to withstand the onslaught threatened by the world.

20 It was in the army that I began to take stands. By that time I had been through college, had received my degree in English and had had therapy. My first night in the barracks I talked to young men from California, Texas and Maine. There were Indians, Mexican-Americans, Samoans, farm boys and city toughs. Some were racist, some not. Some were anti-Semitic, some not. However, by that time I refused to tolerate anyone who harbored any prejudice. When someone said the word "nigger" I would tell that person to "get the hell out of here," and if a soldier started to inform me that "Jews shouldn't tell white people what to do," I would say, "Well, you're talking to

one now and he's telling you what to do."

I began to write. I kept journals and wrote short stories. I reread my favorite books again and again. I was so moved by the ideas and feelings in these books that I sought opportunities to thank their authors for what they had done, for liberating me, for showing me another way to live, hope, think and feel. When I was teaching at Queens College, I went to hear Ralph Ellison read from his work. The English department managed the affair, and I was happy knowing that I would actually meet one of my heroes. After the reading, I waited on line anticipating the handshake and the few brief words. The chairman and the upper ranks of the department stood by Ellison's side while teachers filed by. I was excited, much like the boy with a Pilgrim hat at Thanksgiving time. It was finally my turn. I shook his hand and said, "I want you to know that *Invisible Man*, especially the part about 'I yam what I yam,' really changed my life for the better." The chairman looked at me as though I had embarrassed him, and the others shook their heads and smiled. I felt foolish for being who I was. But as I walked away, Ellison touched my shoulder lightly and said, "That's the greatest compliment an author can ever receive."

I have frequently thought about what 22 Ellison said to me that evening and other evenings while I was reading his novel and his essays. He not only gave me strength to see and accept myself as a whole human being with inalienable rights to just as much self-worth and integrity as anyone else; Ellison, along with other writers, prepared me for America's continual problem of racial strife.

These times are difficult for the country 23 and particularly for New York City, my home. It seems as if the Kerner Commission's prediction of a racially divided society has arrived. I have heard and witnessed much hate in the last four years. People—whites and blacks—seem always to be on the edge of reacting violently. Which side should I take, white or black?

No American should be coerced into tak- 24 ing either side because both are inherently racist. Those who force us to take sides make things extremely difficult for people like me— black, Jewish and American—people caught in the middle of their ambivalence, their lost dreams and aspirations.

approximately 2550 words

COMPREHENSION CHECK

Part I General Comprehension Questions: Literal and Interpretive

A. Write the correct letter in the space provided.

_____ 1. Dexter Jeffries grew up in a neighborhood that could be characterized as

    a. the inner city.
    b. urban.
    c. suburban.
    d. a farming community.

_____ 2. His parents

    a. had limited education.
    b. could be considered middle class.
    c. worked at menial jobs.
    d. were quite poor.

_____ 3. Jeffries had less difficulty than his sister because

    a. he was more motivated.
    b. the racial climate had improved somewhat.
    c. he liked school.
    d. his parents favored him over his sister.

_____ 4. The event that forced Jeffries into therapy was

    a. his relationship with a girl of Greek nationality.
    b. a quarrel with his parents.
    c. a visit to his doctor.
    d. a fight with a buddy in the Army.

_____ 5. Jeffries was able to create an identity for himself through

    a. reading literature.
    b. taking a stand for what he believed.
    c. counseling.
    d. all of the above.

6. Why do you believe Jeffries states in the first paragraph that America's ambivalence and his attempt to cope with it have made him a better teacher, writer, and friend?

_____

_____

Part I

B.

7. Inferences/Conclusions
   a. What inference can you draw about Ralph Ellison from his statement to Jeffries in paragraph 21: "That's the greatest compliment an author can ever receive"?

   _____

   b. What do immediate questions like "Are you Egyptian, Iranian, Hispanic?" imply about the person asking the question? (See paragraph 4.)

   _____

   c. What can you conclude about Jeffries from his statement in paragraph 12: "Because I had my secret and extraordinary vantage point—black and Jewish—one that allowed me access to the inner recesses of whites and blacks, there was a part of me that felt the jokes I heard were actually on the people who told them"?

   _____

   _____

8. Figurative Language: Write the literal meaning of the following sentences.

   a. "It was on that day that the'veil,' " as W. E. B. DuBois labeled it, was cast over me." (paragraph 10).

   _____

   _____

   b. "During the 1960s, I had a front row seat on one of the most momentous social struggles in America, but the price of the ticket left me reeling". (paragraph 12).

   _____

9. Denotative/Connotative Language: Is this biographical essay primarily denotative or connotative? Why do you think so?

   _____

10. What is the overall tone of the essay?

   _____

11. Is the author's purpose directly related to the tone? Explain.

   _____

12. Is the author objective or subjective about his topic? Explain.

   _____

13. Does the author provide sufficient evidence to convince you of his thesis? Explain.

   _____

Part II
Application Questions for Writing/Discussion

14. Do you agree with Jeffries when he states in paragraph 13, "It is difficult to discard love and affection even if it is tainted, to surrender friendship and its bonds for principles when you are confused about the principles yourselves?"

   _____

   _____

   _____

15. In paragraph 24 the author makes the statement "No American should be coerced into taking either side because both are inherently racist." Apply this statement to your own background and present situation. Imagine yourself in a dialogue with Jeffries.

_____

_____

_____

_____

Part III
Extend Your Vocabulary

You have read these words and sentences in the context of the essay. Determine the meaning of the boldfaced word, and select the best definition from the choices given. Circle the correct letter.

1. "Every **derogatory** remark about Blacks left me weaker."
   (a) belittling   (b) pleasing   (c) cordial   (d) friendly

2. "I am ashamed to say that **impotence** and paralysis prevented me from taking such action for most of my life."
   (a) lack of money   (b) lack of friendship   (c) lack of opportunity
   (d) lack of physical strength

3. "[T]here were some events that **perceptibly** changed the general social climate of race relations."
   (a) youthfully   (b) understandably   (c) swiftly   (d) simply

4. "That was the last time I answered that question so quickly and **unwittingly**."
   (a) without talking   (b) without thinking   (c) without gesturing
   (d) without smiling

5. "As I grew older, I developed a **dualistic** view of the world. I viewed things literally in black and white."
   (a) three-sided   (b) two-sided   (c) sensible   (d) strange

Selection 20: **TEXTBOOK**

☛ Preparation for Reading

The following textbook selection deals with social class in the United States. Despite the fact that we are considered a democracy with equal opportunity for all, the actual distribution of wealth among the classes is far from equal.

Read to see where you can place yourself in the suggested class hierarchy. At the same time, note the range in social prestige in our country as defined by the different occupations.

The following words are underlined in the text.

turbulent life	wild or disorderly
pervasive power	quality of spreading throughout
social **stratification**	arrangement in layers
aristocracy	a ruling class of wealthy nobles
individual **autonomy** and achievement	independence
economic **disparity**	inequality

Preview, then read the selection.

Social Class in the United States

John J. Macionis

1   Nigeria Collins died one month and one day after she was born. She lies today in a corner of Evergreen Cemetery in Camden, New Jersey, a small city across the river from Philadelphia. She is not the only infant buried in this patch of scrub grass littered with trash and broken glass. Hundreds of other babies lie here in a place that should guard the remains of people who grew up, grew old, and eventually died.

2   A half-century ago, Camden was one of the busiest industrial cities in the United States. Its shipyard built battleships, its factories turned out record players and other consumer goods, and its processing plants canned soup and other foods.

3   But today Camden is perhaps the most down-and-out city in the country. The slide started in the 1950s, as people with the initiative and the cash were lured to the leafy green of the surrounding suburbs, leaving behind the poor, especially the minority poor. Today, two-thirds of the city's households live in poverty, and block upon block of housing is falling down, burned out, or boarded up. Camden also bears other familiar marks of cities in crisis: some two hundred liquor stores but not a single movie theater, a flourishing drug trade but no safe park, and street violence that erupts everywhere, often, and without warning.

4   The tragedy of Camden is all the more wrenching because this is a city of children: About half of its people (now numbering barely 100,000) are under the age of twenty-one. These youngsters cope in a world twisted by poverty, one that claims many infants like Nigeria Collins before they are even old

enough to know what did them in. To the lucky survivors who reach their teens, the streets of Camden offer little hope, and many succumb to the turbulent life of drug dealing or prostitution (Fedarko, 1992).

The story of Camden is also stark evidence 5 of the pervasive power of social stratification to shape the lives of people throughout the United States. Whether individuals achieve great success or collapse with broken spirits is not simply a matter of their individual talents and ambitions. Our fate also reflects the distribution of wealth, power, and opportunity in our society.

DIMENSIONS OF SOCIAL INEQUALITY

The United States stands apart from Japan and 6 most of Europe in never having had a titled aristocracy. With the significant exception of our racial history, this nation has never known a caste system that rigidly ranks categories of people.

Even so, U.S. society is highly stratified. The 7 rich not only control most of the money, but they also benefit from the most schooling, they enjoy the best health, and they consume the greatest share of almost all goods and services. Such privilege contrasts sharply with the poverty of millions of women and men who struggle from day to day simply to survive. This chapter will explain that the popular portrayal of the United States as a "middle-class society" does not square with many important facts.

For several reasons, we generally underesti- 8 mate the extent of stratification in our society.

1. We embrace the legal principle of equality. Founded in the wake of the Enlightenment, the United States has steadily pursued the ideal of equal standing under the law for all people. This principle encourages us to view everyone as equal even though our society historically has denied people of color and women full participation.

2. Our culture celebrates individual autonomy and achievement. Our belief is that people are the authors of their own social positions. We tend to play up the effect of individual effort on social standing and to play down how birth confers on some people advantages and opportunities that others can barely imagine.

3. We tend to interact with people like ourselves. Throughout the United States, primary groups—including family, neighbors, and friends—typically are composed of people with similar social standing. While we may speak of "how the other half lives," generally we have only brief and impersonal encounters with people very different from ourselves.

4. The United States is an affluent society . . . The overall standard of living in the United States is extremely high in global perspective. This affluence leads us to imagine that everyone in our society is relatively well off.

When people do acknowledge their differ- 9 ences, they often speak of a "ladder of social class" as if inequality were a matter of a single factor such as money. More accurately, however, social class in the United States has several dimensions. *Socioeconomic status* (SES), . . . amounts to a composite measure of social position that encompasses not just money but power, occupational prestige, and schooling.

Income

One important dimension of inequality 1 involves income, *occupational wages or salaries and earnings from investments.* The Bureau of the Census reports that the median U.S. family income in 1992 was $36,812. The first part of Figure 9-1 illustrates the distribution of income among all families[1] in the country. The 20 percent of families with the highest earnings (at least $64,300 annually, with mean earnings of about $100,000) received 44.6 percent of all income, while the bottom 20 percent (earning less than $17,000, with a mean of about $9,700) received only about 4.4 percent.

At the top of the income pyramid, the high- 11 est paid 5 percent of U.S. families (earning at least $107,000 per year, with a median of about $156,000) secured 17.6 percent of all income, more than the earnings of the lowest-paid 40 percent. In short, the bulk of the nation's income is earned by a small proportion of families, while the rest of the population makes do with far less. . . .

Income disparity in the United States 12 increased during the 1980s as a result of changes in the economy, new tax policies, and cuts in social programs that assist low-income people . . . Since 1990, however, income disparity has eased downward, a trend accelerated by the 1993 income tax hikes proposed by the Clinton administration and enacted by Congress, which place most of the increase on the shoulders of the top-earning 5 percent.

. . . Generally speaking, income disparity 13 declines as industrialization proceeds . . . Figure 9-2 on page 478 confirms this trend, showing that disparities in standard of living are more pronounced in societies that are less developed economically. Looking only at industrial soci-

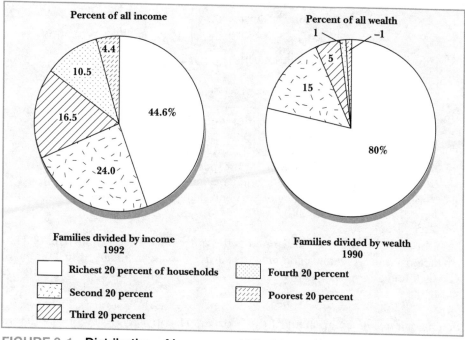

FIGURE 9-1   Distribution of Income and Wealth in the United States
(Income data from U.S. Bureau of the Census, 1993; wealth data are author estimates based on the Joint Economic Committee, 1986, and Kennickell & Shack-Marquez, 1992)

[1]Reported for households rather than families, median income is somewhat lower: $30,786 in 1992. The Census Bureau defines a household as one or more persons sharing a living unit; a family, by contrast, is two or more persons related by blood, marriage, or adoption. Most of the income difference between families and households is due to size: 1992 families contained, on average, 3.16 people compared to 2.63 people for households.

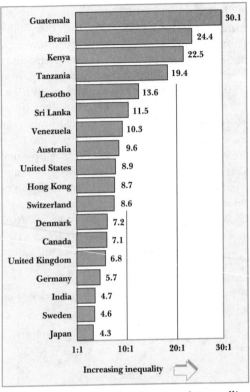

FIGURE 9-2   Extent of Income Inequality in Global Perspective

Ratios represent the standard of living, based on all consumption, for the most affluent 20 percent of the population as a multiple of the standard of living of the poorest 20 percent.

(The World Bank, 1993)

eties, however, we see that the United States is characterized by greater economic disparity than is found almost anywhere else.

Wealth

Income is but one component of the broader 14 economic factor of wealth, *the total amount of money and valuable goods that a person or family controls.* Wealth—in the form of stocks, bonds, real estate, and other privately owned property—is distributed even less equally than is income.

The second part of Figure 9-1 shows the 15 approximate distribution of wealth in the United States in 1990. The richest 20 percent of U.S. households own approximately 80 percent of the country's entire wealth. High up in this privileged category are the wealthiest 5 percent of households—the "super-rich"—who control more than half the nation's property. Richer still—with wealth into the tens of millions of dollars—1 percent of U.S. families possess about 30 percent of our nation's privately held resources. And at the very top of the wealth pyramid, the *three* richest U.S. families have a combined wealth in excess of $40 billion, which equals the total property of more than half a million average families, representing enough people to fill the cities of Boston, Milwaukee, and New Orleans . . .

The wealth of the typical U.S. family—the **16** median case—is about $40,000, roughly the same as median annual family income *(1991 Green Book)*. Lesser wealth is also different in *kind:* The richest people have most of their property in the form of stocks and other income-producing investments. The wealth of average people resides primarily in property that generates no income, such as a home.

When financial liabilities are balanced **17** against assets, the least affluent 40 percent of U.S. families have little or no wealth. The negative percentage shown in Figure 9-1 for the wealth of the poorest 20 percent of the population means that people in this bottom fifth actually live in debt.

Power

In the United States, as elsewhere, wealth **18** stands as an important source of power. People who own substantial shares of corporations, for example, make decisions that create jobs for ordinary people or scale back operations, putting men and women out of work.

More broadly, the small proportion of fam- **19** ilies who own most of the property in the United States also have a great deal of say about the national political agenda. Thomas Jefferson (1953; orig. 1785), the third U.S. president and a wealthy man himself, cautioned that the vitality of a democratic system depends on "subdividing property" so that the many, not just the few, have a strong voice in political affairs.

Occupational Prestige

Occupation, too, is an important dimension of **20** social standing, since one's job affects all the factors discussed thus far: income, wealth, and power. In addition, occupation is an important source of social prestige since we commonly evaluate each other according to the kind of work we do, envying and respecting some, shunning and looking down on others.

For more than half a century, sociologists **21** have measured the relative social prestige of various occupations. Table 9-1 presents the results of a recent survey involving a random sample of adults in the United States. In general, people accord high prestige to occupations—such as physicians, lawyers, and engineers—that also generate high income.

High prestige reflects more than just high **22** pay, however, since these occupations also typically require considerable ability and demand extensive education and training. By contrast, less prestigious work—as a waitress or janitor, for example—not only pays less but usually requires less ability and schooling. In global perspective, occupational prestige rankings are much the same in all industrial societies. . . .

White-collar work that involves mental **23** activity free from extensive supervision confers greater prestige than blue-collar occupations that require supervised, manual labor. There are exceptions to this pattern, however. As the table shows, for example, a blue-collar police officer enjoys greater social prestige than a white-collar bank teller.

In any society, privileged categories of peo- **24** ple tend to hold the occupations providing the greatest prestige. Reading down from the beginning of Table 9-1, one passes a dozen occupations before reaching "registered nurse," an occupation in which *most* workers are women. . . . Women are highly concentrated in so-called pink-collar occupations—the service work and clerical positions (including secretaries, waitresses, and beauticians) that provide little income and fall near the bottom of the prestige hierarchy.

Similarly, reading the table in reverse order **25** shows how many jobs that provide the least

TABLE 9-1

The Relative Social Prestige of Selected Occupations in the United States

White-collar Occupations	Prestige Score	Blue-collar Occupations	White-collar Occupations	Prestige Score	Blue-collar Occupations
Physician	86		Bookkeeper	47	
Lawyer	75			47	Machinist
College/university professor	74			47	Mail carrier
Architect	73		Musician/ composer	47	
Chemist	73			46	Secretary
Physicist/astronomer	73		Photographer	45	
Aerospace engineer	72		Bank teller	43	
Dentist	72			42	Tailor
Clergy	69			42	Welder
Psychologist	69			41	Apprentice electrician
Pharmacist	68			40	Farmer
Optometrist	67			40	Telephone operator
Registered nurse	66			39	Carpenter
Secondary-school teacher	66			38	TV repairperson
Accountant	65			37	Security guard
Athlete	65			36	Brick/stone mason
Electrical engineer	64		File clerk	36	Child care worker
Elementary school teacher	64			36	Hairdresser
Economist	63			35	Baker
Veterinarian	62			34	Bulldozer operator
Airplane pilot	61			34	Meter reader
Computer programmer	61			32	Bus driver
Sociologist	61			31	Auto body repairperson
Editor/reporter	60		Retail apparel salesperson	30	
	60	Police officer		30	Truck driver
Actor	58		Cashier	29	
Radiologic technician	58			28	Elevator operator
Dietician	56			28	Garbage collector
Radio/TV announcer	55			28	Taxi driver
Librarian	54			28	Waiter/waitress
	53	Aircraft mechanic		27	Bellhop
	53	Firefighter		25	Bartender
Dental hygienist	52			23	Farm laborer
Painter/sculptor	52			23	Household laborer
Social worker	52			23	Midwife
	51	Electrician		22	Door-to-door salesperson
Computer operator	50				
Funeral director	49			22	Janitor
Realtor	49			09	Shoe shiner

Source: Adapted from *General Social Surveys 1972-1993: Cumulative Codebook* (Chicago: National Opinion Research Center, 1993), pp. 937-45.

amount of prestige and income are commonly performed by people of color. The important point here is that social stratification typically involves various dimensions of inequality (based on income and work as well as sex and race) *that are superimposed on each other,* forming a complex, and often steep, hierarchy.

Schooling

Industrial societies generally define schooling **26** as necessary for all and offer primary, secondary, and some college education at public expense. Like other dimensions of inequality, however, schooling is a resource enjoyed in abundance by some and very little by others.

Table 9-2 indicates how much formal edu- **27** cation U.S. men and women aged twenty-five and over had acquired in 1991. According to the table, more than three-fourths had completed high school, although just over 20 percent were college graduates.

TABLE 9.2

Schooling of U.S. Adults, 1991 (aged 25 and over)

	Women	Men
Not a high-school graduate	21.7%	21.4%
8 years or less	10.3	11.0
9–11 years	11.4	10.4
High-school graduate	78.4	78.5
High school only	41.0	36.0
1–3 years college	18.6	18.2
College graduate or more	18.8	24.3

Source: U.S. Bureau of the Census, 1992.

Here, again, we see that dimensions of **28** inequality are linked. Schooling affects both occupation and income, since most (but not all) of the better paying, white-collar jobs shown in Table 9-1 require a college degree or other advanced study. Similarly, most of the blue-collar occupations that offer less income and social prestige demand less schooling.

approximately 1950 words

John J. Macionis, *Sociology,* 4/E. Copyright © 1995 by Prentice Hall, Inc. Reprinted by permission of publisher.

COMPREHENSION CHECK

Part I
General Comprehension Questions: Literal and Interpretive

A. Write the correct letter in the space provided.

_____ 1. Which of the following is *not* stated by the author as a reason for most people's failure to perceive the full range of social inequality?

    a. We believe that all are equal under the law.

    b. We interact with people of a similar social position.

    c. The United States is wealthy, and by world standards everyone seems reasonably well off.

    d. Most people do not read critically about issues related to social inequality.

_____ 2. Social class, and therefore social position in the U.S. encompasses

a. money and power.
b. occupational prestige.
c. schooling.
d. all of the above.

_____ 3. According to the government, statistics on economic power in the United States indicate that

a. the richest 20 percent of families receive one-third of all the income.
b. the poorest 20 percent receive about one-fourth of the total income.
c. the richest 5 percent of the population controls one-half of the nation's wealth.
d. the richest people do not pay their share of taxes.

_____ 4. Most industrial societies

a. cannot measure social prestige because changes have occurred.
b. generally disagree on which occupations have prestige.
c. generally agree on which occupations have prestige.
d. rely on statistics on prestige from the United Nations.

_____ 5. Which statement about the United States is correct?

a. Half of the population has a college education.
b. Less than one-fourth of the population has a college education.
c. Only 10 percent of the population has a college degree.
d. Two-year college degree programs are increasing.

Part I

B.

6. Inference/Conclusion:
What inference/conclusion can you draw from the fact that the disparity in the way wealth is distributed in the U.S. is far greater than the disparity in income?

_____

_____

_____

7. Denotative/Connotative Language: What does the author mean literally with the statement ". . . people with the initiative and cash were lured to the leafy green of the surrounding suburbs."

_____

_____

_____

8. Figurative Language: Explain the meaning of the following phrases.
   "Ladder of social class"

_____

_____

   "Pink-Collar Jobs"

_____

_____

9. Judgment: What change needs to be made so that one's forebears do not play such an important role in determining the future wealth of individuals in our society?

_____

_____

10. Author's Tone and Purpose
    a. How would you describe the tone and purpose of this selection?

_____

_____

    b. If you were writing an essay on this subject, what tone would you have selected, and why?

_____

_____

Part II
Application Questions for Writing/Discussion

11. Thomas Jefferson said that a democracy depends on "subdividing" property among people. Do you agree with this statement made more than 200 years ago?

_____

_____

_____

12. Which do you believe affords the greater social prestige in our country today—economic wealth or one's occupation? What kind of "prestige" is your goal for the future?

_____

_____

_____

_____

Part III
Extend Your Vocabulary

Note the boldfaced word in the first sentence of each set, quoted directly from the chapter. In the second sentence, fill in a different suffixed form of that word to complete the sentence.

1. "The U.S. has never had a feudal **aristocracy.**"

   Although he assumed an _____ manner, he came from a very humble background.

2. "The American emphasis on individual **autonomy** . . . frequently obscures the degree to which birth confers advantages."

   Many countries today are struggling to become _____.

3. "Income **disparity** increased during the 1980s."

   A _____ amount of work was allotted to various employees.

4. ". . . many succumb to the **turbulent** life of drug dealing or prostitution."

The police arrived to see why the _____ in the street had escalated.

5. "The United States is an **affluent** society."

Because of her _____ , she enjoyed great political power and prestige in the community.

Selection 21: **LITERATURE**

☞ Preparation for Reading

John Grisham

John Grisham is one of America's most prolific and successful contemporary novelists. He is best known for his legal thrillers. He said in a 1995 interview in *West,* a newsmagazine, that he had never planned to be a writer. He was a lawyer in Mississippi who was influenced to write *A Time to Kill* by a legal case he had heard about in the 1980s. Soon after its publication, he wrote *The Firm,* the first chapter of which is printed here. Grisham has also written *The Pelican Brief, The Client, The Chamber,* and *The Rainmaker.* His novel *The Client* became the basis for a television series in 1995.

The first chapter of *The Firm* gives us yet another view of social class in America and the materialism that motivates the decisions of many people.

Note the meaning of the boldfaced words before reading. These are underlined in the text.

that was **mandatory**	required or obligatory
studied a **dossier**	a collection of papers about a person; a file
most **prestigious** firms	having or bringing influence, honor, esteem
was **glib** and engaging	performing with ease and informality
braced for another **reprimand**	severe scolding; admonishment
She **deflected** this	turned aside; changed direction
treated him like a **leper**	a person afflicted with leprosy, a disfiguring disease

The Firm

John Grisham

The senior partner studied the résumé for the hundredth time and again found   1
nothing he disliked about Mitchell Y. McDeere, at least not on paper. He had the
brains, the ambition, the good looks. And he was hungry; with his background, he
had to be. He was married, and that was <u>mandatory</u>. The firm had never hired an
unmarried lawyer, and it frowned heavily on divorce, as well as womanizing and
drinking. Drug testing was in the contract. He had a degree in accounting, passed
the CPA exam the first time he took it and wanted to be a tax lawyer, which of course
was a requirement with a tax firm. He was white, and the firm had never hired a
black. They managed this by being secretive and clubbish and never soliciting job
applications. Other firms solicited, and hired blacks. This firm recruited, and
remained lily white. Plus, the firm was in Memphis, of all places, and the top blacks
wanted New York or Washington or Chicago. McDeere was a male, and there were

no women in the firm. That mistake had been made in the mid-seventies when they recruited the number one grad from Harvard, who happened to be a she and a wizard at taxation. She lasted four turbulent years and was killed in a car wreck.

He looked good, on paper. He was their top choice. In fact, for this year there were no other prospects. The list was very short. It was McDeere or no one.

The managing partner, Royce McKnight, studied a <u>dossier</u> labeled "Mitchell Y. McDeere—Harvard." An inch thick with small print and a few photographs, it had been prepared by some ex-CIA agents in a private intelligence outfit in Bethesda. They were clients of the firm and each year did the investigating for no fee. It was easy work, they said, checking out unsuspecting law students. They learned, for instance, that he preferred to leave the Northeast, that he was holding three job offers, two in New York and one in Chicago, and that the highest offer was $76,000 and the lowest was $68,000. He was in demand. He had been given the opportunity to cheat on a securities exam during his second year. He declined, and made the highest grade in the class. Two months ago he had been offered cocaine at a law school party. He said no and left when everyone began snorting. He drank an occasional beer, but drinking was expensive and he had no money. He owed close to $23,000 in student loans. He was hungry.

Royce McKnight flipped through the dossier and smiled. McDeere was their man.

Lamar Quin was thirty-two and not yet a partner. He had been brought along to   5
look young and act young and project a youthful image for Bendini, Lambert & Locke, which in fact was a young firm, since most of the partners retired in their late forties or early fifties with money to burn. He would make partner in this firm. With a six-figure income guaranteed for the rest of his life, Lamar could enjoy the twelve-hundred-dollar tailored suits that hung so comfortably from his tall, athletic frame. He strolled nonchalantly across the thousand-dollar-a-day suite and poured another cup of decaf. He checked his watch. He glanced at the two partners sitting at the small conference table near the windows.

Precisely at two-thirty someone knocked on the door. Lamar looked at the partners, who slid the résumé and dossier into an open briefcase. All three reached for their jackets. Lamar buttoned his top button and opened the door.

"Mitchell McDeere?" he asked with a huge smile and a hand thrust forward.

"Yes." They shook hands violently.

"Nice to meet you, Mitchell. I'm Lamar Quin."

"My pleasure. Please call me Mitch." He stepped inside and quickly surveyed the   10
spacious room.

"Sure, Mitch." Lamar grabbed his shoulder and led him across the suite, where the partners introduced themselves. They were exceedingly warm and cordial. They offered him coffee, then water. They sat around a shiny mahogany conference table and exchanged pleasantries. McDeere unbuttoned his coat and crossed his legs. He was now a seasoned veteran in the search of employment, and he knew they wanted him. He relaxed. With three job offers from three of the most <u>prestigious</u> firms in the country, he did not need this interview, this firm. He could afford to be a little overconfident now. He was there out of curiosity. And he longed for warmer weather.

Oliver Lambert, the senior partner, leaned forward on his elbows and took control of the preliminary chitchat. He was <u>glib</u> and engaging with a mellow, almost professional baritone. At sixty-one, he was the grandfather of the firm and spent most of his time administering and balancing the enormous egos of some of the richest lawyers in the country. He was the counselor, the one the younger associates went to with their troubles. Mr. Lambert also handled the recruiting, and it was his mission to sign Mitchell Y. McDeere.

"Are you tired of interviewing?" asked Oliver Lambert.

"Not really. It's part of it."

Yes, yes, they all agreed. Seemed like yesterday they were interviewing and submitting résumés and scared to death they wouldn't find a job and three years of sweat and torture would be down the drain. They knew what he was going through, all right. 15

"May I ask a question?" Mitch asked.

"Certainly."

"Sure."

"Anything."

"Why are we interviewing in this hotel room? The other firms interview on campus through the placement office." 20

"Good question." They all nodded and looked at each other and agreed it was a good question.

"Perhaps I can answer that, Mitch," said Royce McKnight, the managing partner. "You must understand our firm. We are different, and we take pride in that. We have forty-one lawyers, so we are small compared with other firms. We don't hire too many people; about one every other year. We offer the highest salary and fringes in the country, and I'm not exaggerating. So we are very selective. We selected you. The letter you received last month was sent after we screened over two thousand third-year law students at the best schools. Only one letter was sent. We don't advertise openings and we don't solicit applications. We keep a low profile, and we do things differently. That's our explanation."

"Fair enough. What kind of firm is it?"

"Tax. Some securities, real estate and banking, but eighty percent is tax work. That's why we wanted to meet you, Mitch. You have an incredibly strong tax background."

"Why'd you go to Western Kentucky?" asked Oliver Lambert. 25

"Simple. They offered me a full scholarship to play football. Had it not been for that, college would've been impossible."

"Tell us about your family."

"Why is that important?"

"It's very important to us, Mitch," Royce McKnight said warmly.

They all say that, thought McDeere. "Okay, my father was killed in the coal 30

©1997 Prentice-Hall, Inc.

mines when I was seven years old. My mother remarried and lives in Florida. I had two brothers. Rusty was killed in Vietnam. I have a brother named Ray McDeere."

"Where is he?"

"I'm afraid that's none of your business." He stared at Royce McKnight and exposed a mammoth chip on his shoulder. The dossier said little about Ray.

"I'm sorry," the managing partner said softly.

"Mitch, our firm is in Memphis," Lamar said. "Does that bother you?"

"Not at all. I'm not fond of cold weather."   **35**

"Have you ever been to Memphis?"

"No."

"We'll have you down soon. You'll love it."

Mitch smiled and nodded and played along. Were these guys serious? How could he consider such a small firm in such a small town when Wall Street was waiting?

"How are you ranked in your class?" Mr. Lambert asked.   **40**

"Top five." Not top five percent, but top five. That was enough of an answer for all of them. Top five out of three hundred. He could have said number three, a fraction away from number two, and within striking distance of number one. But he didn't. They came from inferior schools—Chicago, Columbia and Vanderbilt, as he recalled from a cursory examination of Martindale-Hubbell's Legal Directory. He knew they would not dwell on academics.

"Why did you select Harvard?"

"Actually, Harvard selected me. I applied at several schools and was accepted everywhere. Harvard offered more financial assistance. I thought it was the best school. Still do."

"You've done quite well here, Mitch," Mr. Lambert said, admiring the résumé. The dossier was in the briefcase, under the table.

"Thank you. I've worked hard."   **45**

"You made extremely high grades in your tax and securities courses."

"That's where my interest lies."

"We've reviewed your writing sample, and it's quite impressive."

"Thank you. I enjoy research."

They nodded and acknowledged this obvious lie. It was part of the ritual. No law **50** student or lawyer in his right mind enjoyed research, yet, without fail, every prospective associate professed a deep love for the library.

"Tell us about your wife," Royce McKnight said, almost meekly. They braced for another <u>reprimand</u>. But it was a standard, nonsacred area explored by every firm.

"Her name is Abby. She has a degree in elementary education from Western Kentucky. We graduated one week and got married the next. For the past three years she's taught at a private kindergarten near Boston College."

"And is the marriage—"

"We're very happy. We've known each other since high school."

"What position did you play?" asked Lamar, in the direction of less sensitive   **55** matters.

"Quarterback. I was heavily recruited until I messed up a knee in my last high school game. Everyone disappeared except Western Kentucky. I played off and on for four years, even started some as a junior, but the knee would never hold up."

"How'd you make straight A's and play football?"

"I put the books first."

"I don't imagine Western Kentucky is much of an academic school," Lamar blurted with a stupid grin, and immediately wished he could take it back. Lambert and McKnight frowned and acknowledged the mistake.

"Sort of like Kansas State," Mitch replied. They froze, all of them froze, and for   60 a few seconds stared incredulously at each other. This guy McDeere knew Lamar Quin went to Kansas State. He had never met Lamar Quin and had no idea who would appear on behalf of the firm and conduct the interview. Yet, he knew. He had gone to Martindale-Hubbell's and checked them out. He had read the biographical sketches of all of the forty-one lawyers in the firm, and in a split second he had recalled that Lamar Quin, just one of the forty-one, had gone to Kansas State. Damn, they were impressed.

"I guess that came out wrong," Lamar apologized.

"No problem." Mitch smiled warmly. It was forgotten.

Oliver Lambert cleared his throat and decided to get personal again. "Mitch, our firm frowns on drinking and chasing women. We're not a bunch of Holy Rollers, but we put business ahead of everything. We keep low profiles and we work very hard. And we make plenty of money."

"I can live with all that."   65

"We reserve the right to test any member of the firm for drug use."

"I don't use drugs."

"Good. What's your religious affiliation?"

"Methodist."

"Good. You'll find a wide variety in our firm. Catholics, Baptists, Episcopalians.   70 It's really none of our business, but we like to know. We want stable families. Happy lawyers are productive lawyers. That's why we ask these questions."

Mitch smiled and nodded. He'd heard this before.

The three looked at each other, then at Mitch. This meant they had reached the point in the interview where the interviewee was supposed to ask one or two intelligent questions. Mitch recrossed his legs. Money, that was the big question, particularly how it compared to his other offers. If it isn't enough, thought Mitch, then it was nice to meet you fellas. If the pay is attractive, *then* we can discuss families and marriages and football and churches. But, he knew, like all the other firms they had to shadowbox around the issue until things got awkward and it was apparent they had discussed everything in the world but money. So, hit them with a soft question first.

"What type of work will I do initially?"

They nodded and approved of the question. Lambert and McKnight looked at Lamar. This answer was his.

"We have something similar to a two-year apprenticeship, although we don't call   75 it that. We'll send you all over the country to tax seminars. Your education is far from over. You'll spend two weeks next winter in Washington at the American Tax Institute. We take great pride in our technical expertise, and the training is continual, for all of us. If you want to pursue a master's in taxation, we'll pay for it. As far as practicing law, it won't be very exciting for the first two years. You'll do a lot of research and generally boring stuff. But you'll be paid handsomely."

"How much?"

Lamar looked at Royce McKnight, who eyed Mitch and said, "We'll discuss the compensation and other benefits when you come to Memphis."

"I want a ballpark figure or I may not come to Memphis." He smiled, arrogant but cordial. He spoke like a man with three job offers.

The partners smiled at each other, and Mr. Lambert spoke first. "Okay. A base salary of eighty thousand the first year, plus bonuses. Eighty-five the second year, plus bonuses. A low-interest mortgage so you can buy a home. Two country club memberships. And a new BMW. You pick the color, of course."

They focused on his lips, and waited for the wrinkles to form on his cheeks and **80** the teeth to break through. He tried to conceal a smile, but it was impossible. He chuckled.

"That's incredible," he mumbled. Eighty thousand in Memphis equaled a hundred and twenty thousand in New York. Did the man say BMW! His Mazda hatchback had a million miles on it and for the moment had to be jump-started while he saved for a rebuilt starter.

"Plus a few more fringes we'll be glad to discuss in Memphis."

Suddenly he had a strong desire to visit Memphis. Wasn't it by the river?

The smile vanished and he regained his composure. He looked sternly, importantly at Oliver Lambert and said, as if he'd forgotten about the money and the home and the BMW, "Tell me about your firm."

"Forty-one lawyers. Last year we earned more per lawyer than any firm our size **85** or larger. That includes every big firm in the country. We take only rich clients—corporations, banks and wealthy people who pay our healthy fees and never complain. We've developed a specialty in international taxation, and it's both exciting and very profitable. We deal only with people who can pay."

"How long does it take to make partner?"

"On the average, ten years, and it's a hard ten years. It's not unusual for our partners to earn half a million a year, and most retire before they're fifty. You've got to pay your dues, put in eighty-hour weeks, but it's worth it when you make partner."

Lamar leaned forward. "You don't have to be a partner to earn six figures. I've been with the firm seven years, and went over a hundred thousand four years ago."

Mitch thought about this for a second and figured by the time he was thirty he could be well over a hundred thousand, maybe close to two hundred thousand. At the age of thirty!

They watched him carefully and knew exactly what he was calculating.

"What's an international tax firm doing in Memphis?" he asked.   **90**

That brought smiles. Mr. Lambert removed his reading glasses and twirled them. "Now that's a good question. Mr. Bendini founded the firm in 1944. He had been a tax lawyer in Philadelphia and had picked up some wealthy clients in the South. He got a wild hair and landed in Memphis. For twenty-five years he hired nothing but tax lawyers, and the firm prospered nicely down there. None of us are from Memphis, but we have grown to love it. It's a very pleasant old Southern town. By the way, Mr. Bendini died in 1970."

"How many partners in the firm?"

"Twenty, active. We try to keep a ratio of one partner for each associate. That's high for the industry, but we like it. Again, we do things differently."

"All of our partners are multimillionaires by the age of forty-five," Royce **95** McKnight said.

"All of them?"

"Yes, sir. We don't guarantee it, but if you join our firm, put in ten hard years, make partner and put in ten more years, and you're not a millionaire at the age of forty-five, you'll be the first in twenty years."

"That's an impressive statistic."

"It's an impressive firm, Mitch," Oliver Lambert said, "and we're very proud of it. We're a close-knit fraternity. We're small and we take care of each other. We don't have the cutthroat competition the big firms are famous for. We're very careful whom we hire, and our goal is for each new associate to become a partner as soon as possible. Toward that end we invest an enormous amount of time and money in ourselves, especially our new people. It is a rare, extremely rare occasion when a lawyer leaves our firm. It is simply unheard of. We go the extra mile to keep careers on track. We want our people happy. We think it is the most profitable way to operate."

"I have another impressive statistic," Mr. McKnight added. "Last year, for firms **100** our size or larger, the average turnover rate among associates was twenty-eight percent. At Bendini, Lambert & Locke, it was zero. Year before, zero. It's been a long time since a lawyer left our firm."

They watched him carefully to make sure all of this sank in. Each term and each condition of the employment was important, but the permanence, the finality of his acceptance overshadowed all other items on the checklist. They explained as best they could, for now. Further explanation would come later.

Of course, they knew much more than they could talk about. For instance, his mother lived in a cheap trailer park in Panama City Beach, remarried to a retired truck driver with a violent drinking problem. They knew she had received $41,000 from the mine explosion, squandered most of it, then went crazy after her oldest son was killed in Vietnam. They knew he had been neglected, raised in poverty by his brother Ray (whom they could not find) and some sympathetic relatives. The poverty hurt, and they assumed, correctly, it had bred the intense desire to succeed. He had worked thirty hours a week at an all-night convenience store while playing football and making perfect grades. They knew he seldom slept. They knew he was hungry. He was their man.

"Would you like to come visit us?" asked Oliver Lambert.

"When?" asked Mitch, dreaming of a black 318i with a sunroof.

The ancient Mazda hatchback with three hubcaps and a badly cracked windshield   105
hung in the gutter with its front wheels sideways, aiming at the curb, preventing a
roll down the hill. Abby grabbed the door handle on the inside, yanked twice and
opened the door. She inserted the key, pressed the clutch and turned the wheel. The
Mazda began a slow roll. As it gained speed, she held her breath, released the clutch
and bit her lip until the unmuffled rotary engine began whining.

With three job offers on the table, a new car was four months away. She could
last. For three years they had endured poverty in a two-room student apartment on
a campus covered with Porsches and little Mercedes convertibles. For the most part
they had ignored the snubs from the classmates and co-workers in this bastion of
East Coast snobbery. They were hillbillies from Kentucky, with few friends. But they
had endured and succeeded quite nicely all to themselves.

She preferred Chicago to New York, even for a lower salary, largely because it
was farther from Boston and closer to Kentucky. But Mitch remained noncommit-
tal, characteristically weighing it all carefully and keeping most of it to himself. She
had not been invited to visit New York and Chicago with her husband. And she was
tired of guessing. She wanted an answer.

She parked illegally on the hill nearest the apartment and walked two blocks.
Their unit was one of thirty in a two-story red-brick rectangle. Abby stood outside
her door and fumbled through the purse looking for keys. Suddenly, the door
jerked open. He grabbed her, yanked her inside the tiny apartment, threw her on
the sofa and attacked her neck with his lips. She yelled and giggled as arms and legs
thrashed about. They kissed, one of those long, wet, ten-minute embraces with grop-
ing and fondling and moaning, the kind they had enjoyed as teenagers when kiss-
ing was fun and mysterious and the ultimate.

"My goodness," she said when they finished. "What's the occasion?"

"Do you smell anything?" Mitch asked.   110

She looked away and sniffed. "Well, yes. What is it?"

"Chicken chow mein and egg foo yung. From Wong Boys."

"Okay, what's the occasion?"

"Plus an expensive bottle of Chablis. It's even got a cork."

"What have you done, Mitch?"   115

"Follow me." On the small, painted kitchen table, among the legal pads and
casebooks, sat a large bottle of wine and a sack of Chinese food. They shoved the law
school paraphernalia aside and spread the food. Mitch opened the wine and filled
two plastic wineglasses.

"I had a great interview today," he said.

"Who?"

"Remember that firm in Memphis I received a letter from last month?"

"Yes. You weren't too impressed."   120

"That's the one. I'm very impressed. It's all tax work and the money looks good."

"How good?"

He ceremoniously dipped chow mein from the container onto both plates, then ripped open the tiny packages of soy sauce. She waited for an answer. He opened another container and began dividing the egg foo yung. He sipped his wine and smacked his lips.

"How much?" she repeated.

"More than Chicago. More than Wall Street."

She took a long, deliberate drink of wine and eyed him suspiciously. Her brown eyes narrowed and glowed. The eyebrows lowered and the forehead wrinkled. She waited.

"How much?"

"Eighty thousand, first year, plus bonuses. Eighty-five, second year, plus bonuses." He said this nonchalantly while studying the celery bits in the chow mein.

"Eighty thousand," she repeated.

"Eighty thousand, babe. Eighty thousand bucks in Memphis, Tennessee, is about the same as a hundred and twenty thousand bucks in New York."

"Who wants New York?" she asked.

"Plus a low-interest mortgage loan."

That word—mortgage—had not been uttered in the apartment in a long time. In fact, she could not, at the moment, recall the last discussion about a home or anything related to one. For months now it had been accepted that they would *rent* some place until some distant, unimaginable point in the future when they achieved affluence and would then qualify for a large mortgage.

She sat her glass of wine on the table and said matter-of-factly, "I didn't hear that."

"A low-interest mortgage loan. The firm loans enough money to buy a house. It's very important to these guys that their associates look prosperous, so they give us the money at a much lower rate."

"You mean as in a *home*, with grass around it and shrubs?"

"Yep. Not some overpriced apartment in Manhattan, but a three-bedroom house in the suburbs with a driveway and a two-car garage where we can park the BMW."

The reaction was delayed by a second or two, but she finally said, "BMW? Whose BMW?"

"Ours, babe. Our BMW. The firm leases a new one and gives us the keys. It's sort of like a signing bonus for a first-round draft pick. It's worth another five thousand a year. We pick the color, of course. I think black would be nice. What do you think?"

"No more clunkers. No more leftovers. No more hand-me-downs," she said as she slowly shook her head.

He crunched on a mouthful of noodles and smiled at her. She was dreaming, he could tell, probably of furniture, and wallpaper, and perhaps a pool before too long. And babies, little dark-eyed children with light brown hair.

"And there are some other benefits to be discussed later."

"I don't understand, Mitch. Why are they so generous?"

"I asked that question. They're very selective, and they take a lot of pride in paying top dollar. They go for the best and don't mind shelling out the bucks. Their turnover rate is zero. Plus, I think it costs more to entice the top people to Memphis."

"It would be closer to home," she said without looking at him.   **145**

"I don't have a home. It would be closer to your parents, and that worries me."

She <u>deflected</u> this, as she did most of his comments about her family. "You'd be closer to Ray."

He nodded, bit into an egg roll and imagined her parents' first visit, that sweet moment when they pulled into the driveway in their well-used Cadillac and stared in shock at the new French colonial with two new cars in the garage. They would burn with envy and wonder how the poor kid with no family and no status could afford all this at twenty-five and fresh out of law school. They would force painful smiles and comment on how nice everything was, and before long Mr. Sutherland would break down and ask how much the house cost and Mitch would tell him to mind his own business, and it would drive the old man crazy. They'd leave after a short visit and return to Kentucky, where all their friends would hear how great the daughter and the son-in-law were doing down in Memphis. Abby would be sorry they couldn't get along but wouldn't say much. From the start they had treated him like a <u>leper</u>. He was so unworthy they had boycotted the small wedding.

"Have you ever been to Memphis?" he asked.

"Once when I was a little girl. Some kind of convention for the church. All I **150** remember is the river."

"They want us to visit."

"Us! You mean I'm invited?"

"Yes. They insist on you coming."

"When?"

"Couple of weeks. They'll fly us down Thursday afternoon for the weekend."   **155**

"I like this firm already."

approximately 3775 words

John Grisham, The Firm. Copyright © 1991 by John Grisham. Reprinted by permission of Bantam Doubleday Dell Publishing Group, Inc. pp. 1–14.

Questions for Writing/Discussion

1. a. What is the tone of the story during the interview between Mitch and the members of the firm?

   b. How does the tone change when Mitch arrives home and discusses his interview with his wife, Abby?

2. What does the author mean when he says the characters must "shadowbox" through the issues in the interview (paragraph 72)?

3. Why do you think the firm was seeking a man who was "hungry," and how did they know that Mitch was "their man"?

4. Why was money such a big issue for Mitch in selecting the firm? Is there anything he failed to realize about the price he was going to pay to achieve the status he desired?

5. What can you infer about a firm that is described as "lily white" and condones no drugs, drinking, or womanizing (paragraph 1)? Would you be willing to work for such a firm if offered a salary and benefits similar to those offered to Mitch? Why, or why not?

JOURNAL ENTRY

Compare the ways in which the social class status and life goals of Dexter Jeffries ("Who I Am") and Mitchell McDeere (*The Firm*) may be similar yet also so different.

After making your comparison, think about the social class into which you were born (lower, middle, upper) and the reaction of others to you. Were they pleasant or unpleasant? What is your social class standing now? Why might you want to change it, or why might you want to remain as you are?

10

Reading Visual Information

This chapter will help you to

- ◆ Understand how to read graphs, charts, tables, and diagrams.
- ◆ Learn the major purpose of graphic information.
- ◆ Learn how to integrate graphic information with the text.
- ◆ Appreciate the special use of graphics in the sciences and business.

❖❖❖

Before reading, think about these questions.

- ◆ How well do you read and analyze graphs, charts, and diagrams?
- ◆ What questions do you ask as you study graphic information?
- ◆ What may be the major purpose of graphic information?

❖❖❖

Jot down your own method of reading graphic information.

_____

_____

In the first chapter, we pointed out that we are living in an Information Age in which a vast array of new knowledge and information bombards us every day. As an effective reader of this information, you learned to think critically and judge issues on their merits and not on the presupposed assumptions that you held. In this final chapter, we examine how to become more effective readers of visual information. Reading, then, includes not only thinking critically about words but evaluating information from graphs, charts, diagrams, tables, illustrations, and photographs.

Visual literacy is important because much information can be condensed into a small amount of space. Moreover, visuals can dramatically show and summarize information. Business advertisements, for example, frequently compare products and use easy-to-read visuals to highlight the major selling points of a particular product. The media frequently use visuals, such as weather maps and tables, for comparison purposes. Political analysts use visuals to highlight information such as voting trends.

Perhaps most important for you at this time as a college student, effectively reading your college textbooks often means integrating a substantial amount of visual information with printed information. Tables, charts, diagrams, and graphs are included in textbooks to give you important information in condensed form. The illustrations often try to help you understand difficult concepts presented in the text in a simpler format. If you overlook "reading" visual aids, you are ignoring a valuable source of information.

Graphics are expensive to reproduce and are included in your textbook for several important reasons.

Graphics clarify concepts that are difficult to understand.
Graphics take the place of text in illustrating ideas or information.
Graphics add information to the text.

Although reading visual information is not the same as reading prose, similar strategies can be used. Looking over a graph initially to get an overall idea is comparable to previewing written text; examining facts and putting them together can be compared to getting the main idea; and noting trends, patterns, and relationships can be compared to making inferences and drawing conclusions. It is also possible to apply the information, where appropriate, to yourself and your life-style.

❖ Graphs

The major purpose of graphs is to show relationships. On the basis of these relationships, the reader then makes inferences and draws conclusions. Graphs consist of three types: the bar, the line, and the circle or pie graph.

Bar and Line Graphs

Bar and line graphs have the same underlying structure, as shown in Figure 10.1.

1. Both types of graphs have two lines drawn at right angles.

2. Each of these lines is referred to as an *axis*.

3. Each axis shows a measure of something.

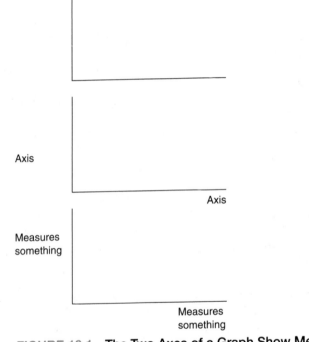

FIGURE 10.1   The Two Axes of a Graph Show Measures.

Bar Graphs

The purpose of a bar graph is to show the relationship between the two lines and, sometimes, the change over time, as in Figure 10.2.

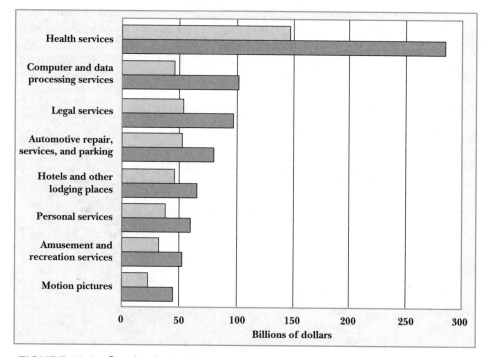

FIGURE 10.2   Service Industries—Annual Receipts of Taxable firms: 1985 and 1992

Source: Statistical Abstract of the United States, *1994*

The graph shows that the annual tax for service industries has increased steadily from 1985 to 1992. As can be noted, the greatest tax dollars are paid by health services while the least are paid by motion pictures. However, all firms involved in services are paying higher taxes.

Bar graphs often include more than one bar. Dots or stripes, or even color, can add to their impact. Bars can be placed either **vertically** or **horizontally,** as can be seen in the following graphs that show participation in sports activities (Figure 10.3) and attendance at various arts activities (Figure 10.4). Note that in Figure 10.3 the sex of the participants is distinguished by light and dark bars.

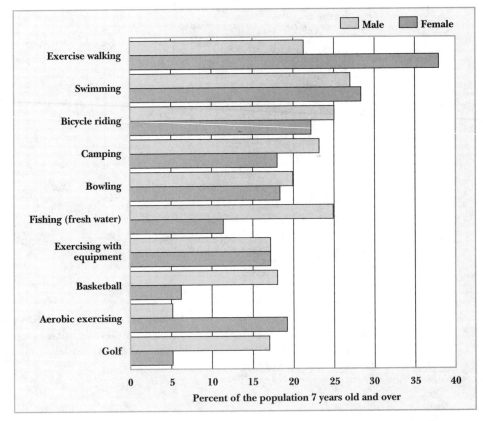

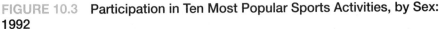

FIGURE 10.3   **Participation in Ten Most Popular Sports Activities, by Sex: 1992**

Source: Chart prepared by U.S. Bureau of the Census, 1994

---

vertically (vər´ tik lē) arranged from top to bottom
horizontally (hôr ə zänt´ ə lē) arranged from side to side

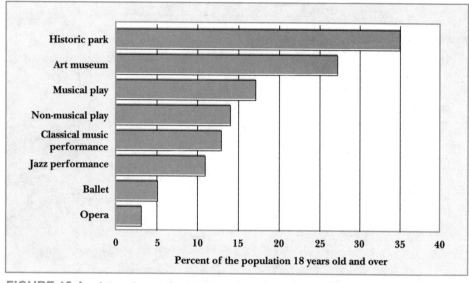

FIGURE 10.4 **Attendance for Various Arts Activities: 1992**

Source: Chart prepared by U.S. Bureau of the Census, 1994

Line Graphs

With a line graph, the relationship between two items is shown by a line (or several lines) plotted and then drawn on the graph. Note how Figure 10.5 on page 504 dramatizes the United States' **meteoric** rise as an economic power after World War I and adds substantially to the text below.

> **Gross National Product.**   If you add up the total value of all the goods and services produced by an economic system during a one-year period, the sum is the system's gross national product, or GNP. GNP is a useful indicator of economic growth because it allows us to track an economy's performance over time. Because inflation and other factors can change the value of the dollar, however, we compare economies based on an adjusted figure called real gross national product.

---

meteoric (mēt ē ôr´ ic) momentarily swift

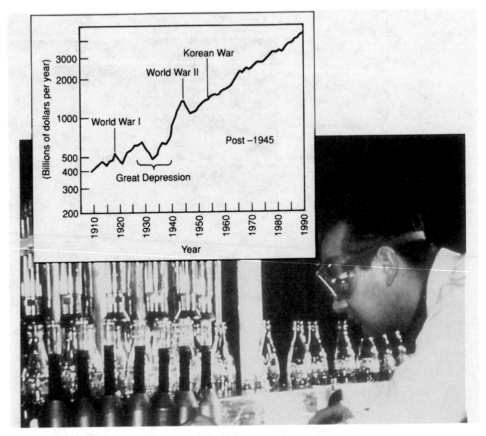

FIGURE 10.5
Real gross national product (GNP) growth is an important measure of economic health. The United States has the highest real GNP in the world, although other countries are gaining.

The United States has the highest real GNP of any industrial nation in the world, although some other countries are gaining on us. For example, real GNP in the United States was $4,864 billion in 1989, whereas Japan, the second largest economy in the world, had a real GNP of $2,858 billion that year. But during the 1980s the U.S. real GNP grew at a rate of 3.4 percent per year, while Japan's grew at a rate of 4.4 percent per year. Figure 10.5 illustrates changes in real GNP in the United States since 1980.

Business, p. 21

Circle or Pie Graphs

Circle graphs divide a quantity of something into its parts. When the parts are measured in percentages, the entire circle graph equals 100 percent. When fractions are used, the whole equals 1.

The graph in Figure 10.6 uses percentages to show the percentage of money invested in different areas of commerce. It is obvious that electronics (including computers) receives the lion's share of investment capital, or 56 percent of it, and that other areas of commerce receive far less.

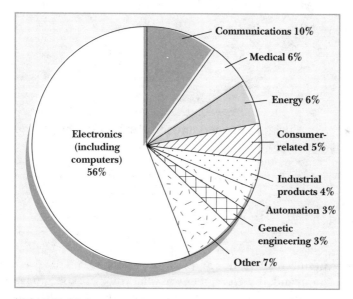

FIGURE 10.6

Capital is invested in many different areas of commerce. However, investment in electronics and communications businesses is especially high today.

Source: Ricky W. Griffin and Ronald J. Ebert, Business, *p. 152. Copyright © 1991 by Prentice Hall. Reprinted by permission of the publisher.*

The circle graph in Figure 10.7 indicates the actual amount of money spent by businesses in the year 1987 for employee insurance.

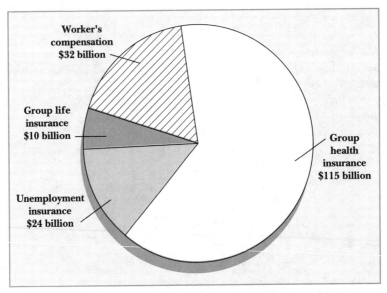

FIGURE 10.7 **Business Expenditures for Employees' Insurance**
Dollar outlay by employers for employee insurance coverage in 1987
(from total compensation).

Source: Ricky W. Griffin and Ronald J. Ebert, Business, p. 614. Copyright © 1991 by Prentice Hall. Reprinted by permission of the publisher.

❖ How to Read Graphic Information

1. First, carefully read the title and subtitles when given. This gives you the purpose of the graph and, therefore, tells you what you can expect to learn from it. With the preceding graphs, we supplied you with most of the information.

2. Next, read the legend (or caption) to learn how to interpret the details presented. Sometimes the legend is at the bottom of the graph. For example, the legend may help to clarify whether the numbers are in thousands, millions, or billions.

3. Check for other explanatory notes. These might include information on how the data was collected or may indicate whether the data is incomplete.

4. Then, skim the information up and down the vertical column (↕) as well as the information across the horizontal column (↔) for bar and line graphs. You will sometimes have to approximate the numbers; the bars or lines of many graphs fall between the numbers given. Find out what units of measurement have been used.

5. Finally, determine the relationship of the information shown in the horizontal and vertical columns. Understanding this relationship is the key to reading not only graphs but tables, charts, and some diagrams.

6. Ask yourself some key questions to understand the graphics.
    a. What general information is presented, and for what purpose?
    b. What relationship has been plotted?
    c. What inferences and conclusions can be made?

In making your inferences and drawing conclusions, ask yourself these questions:

Is the source of the data reliable?
How were the data gathered?
Is there any bias in how the data are presented?

ACTIVITY 10.1 **Examine the following graphs, applying the key questions. (The first one is done for you.)**

Federal and State Prisoners: 1970 to 1989

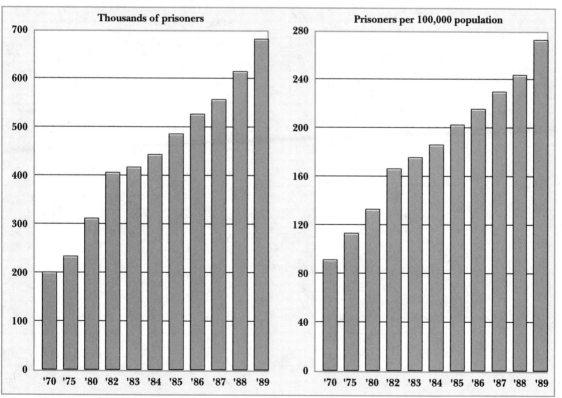

Source: Statistical Abstract of United States, *1991*

1. a. General information and purpose: _Shows the number of prisoners in both federal & state prisons._

   b. Relationship/s shown: _The numbers have consistently increased._

   c. Inferences and conclusions: _Steps need to be taken at the local, state, & federal levels to bring about change._

   d. Data: _Information obtained from the Statistical Abstract of the United States; no other info given._

Top Purchasers of U.S. Exports and Suppliers of U.S. General Imports: 1992

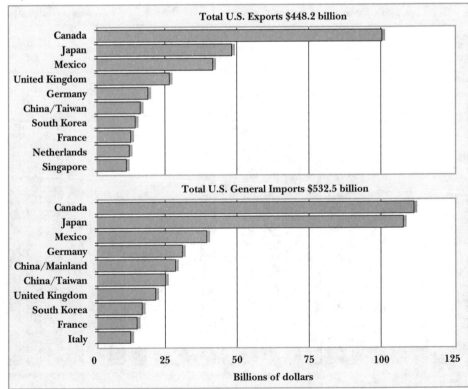

Source: Chart prepared by U.S. Bureau of the Census, 1994

2. a. General information and purpose:

_____

_____

b. Relationship/s shown:

_____

_____

c. Inferences and conclusions:

_____

_____

d. Data:

_____

_____

Consumer Complaints Against U.S. Airlines: 1986 to 1993

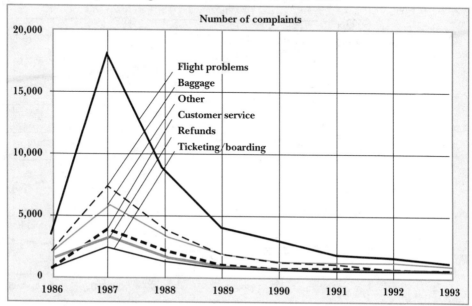

Source: Chart prepared by U.S. Bureau of the Census, 1994

3. a. General information and purpose:

_____

_____

b. Relationship/s shown:

_____

_____

c. Inferences and conclusions:

_____

_____

d. Data:

_____

_____

Selected Crime Rates: 1980 to 1989

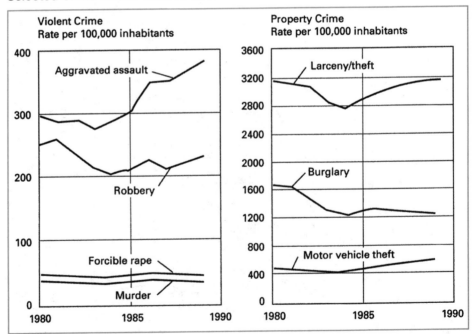

Source: Statistical Abstract of the United States, *1991*

4. a. General information and purpose:

_____

_____

b. Relationship/s shown:

_____

_____

c. Inferences and conclusions:

_____

_____

d. Data:

_____

_____

While there are fewer corporations than there are sole proprietorships, corporations earn most of the revenues in the United States. Indeed, in most years corporations earn over 90 percent of the sales revenues in this country.

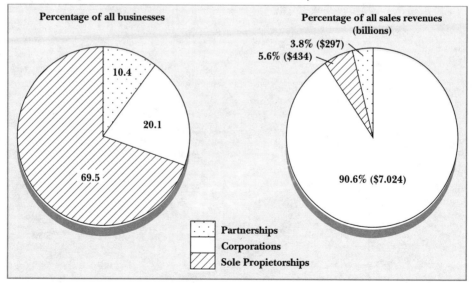

Source: Ricky W. Griffin and Ronald J. Ebert, Business, *2nd ed., p. 34. Copyright © 1991 by Prentice Hall, Inc. Reprinted by permission of the publisher.*

5. a. General information and purpose:

_____

_____

  b. Relationship/s shown:

_____

_____

  c. Inferences and conclusions:

_____

_____

  d. Data:

_____

_____

Distribution of AIDS Deaths, by Age: 1982 through 1992

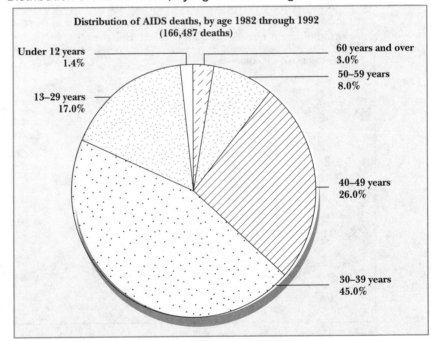

**Distribution of AIDS deaths, by age 1982 through 1992
(166,487 deaths)**

Under 12 years
1.4%

13–29 years
17.0%

60 years and over
3.0%

50–59 years
8.0%

40–49 years
26.0%

30–39 years
45.0%

Source: Statistical Abstract of the United States, *1994*

6. a. General information and purpose:

_____

_____

b. Relationship/s shown:

_____

_____

c. Inferences and conclusions:

_____

_____

d. Data:

_____

_____

❖ Tables

Tables, too, are often used to show comparisons. The following table details hazardous waste sites in the United States and includes both proposed and final sites of hazardous waste. Additionally, the table includes the number of sites in each state out of a total of 1207 and each state's percentage of the total.

ACTIVITY 10.2 **Examine the table and answer the questions that follow.**

Hazardous Waste Sites on the National Priority List, by State: 1990 [includes both proposed and final sites listed on the National Priorities List for the Superfund program as authorized by the Comprehensive Environmental Response, Compensation, and Liability Act of 1980 and the Superfund Amendments and Reauthorization Act of 1986]

State	Total Sites	Rank	Percent Distribution	State	Total Sites	Rank	Percent Distribution
Total	1,207	(x)	(x)	Missouri	24	15	2.0
				Montana	10	34	0.8
United States	1,197	(x)	100.0	Nebraska	6	43	0.5
Alabama	12	27	1.0	Nevada	1	50	0.1
Alaska	6	43	0.5	New Hampshire	16	22	1.3
Arizona	11	29	0.9	New Jersey	109	1	9.1
Arkansas	10	34	0.8	New Mexico	10	34	0.8
California	88	3	7.4	New York	83	4	6.9
Colorado	16	22	1.3	North Carolina	22	17	1.8
Connecticut	15	24	1.3	North Dakota	2	48	0.2
Delaware	20	19	1.7	Ohio	33	12	2.8
District of Columbia	–	(x)	–	Oklahoma	11	29	0.9
Florida	51	6	4.3	Oregon	8	40	0.7
Georgia	13	26	1.1	Pennsylvania	95	2	7.9
Hawaii	7	42	0.6	Rhode Island	11	29	0.9
Idaho	9	38	0.8	South Carolina	23	16	1.9
Illinois	37	10	3.1	South Dakota	3	46	0.3
Indiana	35	11	2.9	Tennessee	14	25	1.2
Iowa	21	18	1.8	Texas	28	13	2.3
Kansas	11	29	0.9	Utah	12	27	1.0
Kentucky	17	21	1.4	Vermont	8	40	0.7
Louisiana	11	29	0.9	Virginia	20	19	1.7
Maine	9	38	0.8	Washington	45	7	3.8
				West Virginia	5	45	0.4
Maryland	10	34	0.8	Wisconsin	39	9	3.3
Massachusetts	25	14	2.1	Wyoming	3	46	0.3
Michigan	78	5	6.5				
Minnesota	42	8	3.5	Guam	1	(x)	(x)
Mississippi	2	48	0.2	Puerto Rico	9	(x)	(x)

– Represents zero x Not applicable

U.S. Environmental Protection Agency, press release, August 1990 *Statistical Abstract of the United States,* 1991

1. Which three states have the largest total number of sites?

_____

2. Which three states have the lowest total number of sites?

_____

3. Which three states have the highest concentration of hazardous waste in terms of percentage of the total?

_____

4. Which three states have the lowest concentration of hazardous waste in terms of percentage of the total?

_____

❖ Diagrams

Diagrams can be used in diverse areas, from plotting how a plane flies to the stages an embryo goes through to become a fetus and eventually a newborn baby.

ACTIVITY 10.3

Maps are a type of diagram. This one illustrates exactly where hazardous waste sites are located in the United States.

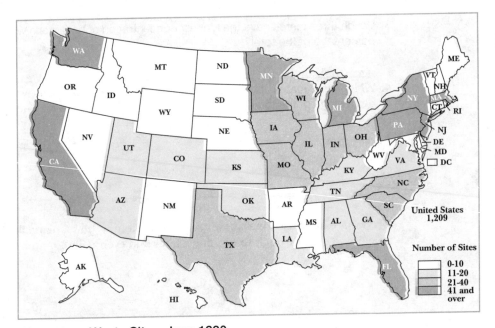

Hazardous Waste Sites: June 1990

Source: Statistical Abstract of the United States, *1991*

Based on this map and the table in Activity 10.2, what inferences and what conclusions can you draw about hazardous waste sites in the United States?

_____

_____

_____

Examining Information from Different Graphics

ACTIVITY 10.4

Study the following graphics that give a profile of how the U.S. population changed over a four-year period between 1990 and 1994. Then, answer the questions that follow.

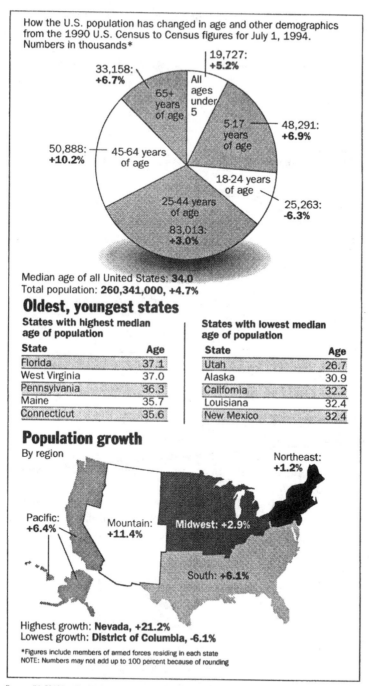

How the U.S. population has changed in age and other demographics from the 1990 U.S. Census to Census figures for July 1, 1994. Numbers in thousands*

19,727: +5.2% — All ages under 5

33,158: +6.7% — 65+ years of age

5-17 years of age — 48,291: +6.9%

50,888: +10.2% — 45-64 years of age

18-24 years of age — 25,263: -6.3%

25-44 years of age — 83,013: +3.0%

Median age of all United States: **34.0**
Total population: **260,341,000, +4.7%**

Oldest, youngest states

States with highest median age of population

State	Age
Florida	37.1
West Virginia	37.0
Pennsylvania	36.3
Maine	35.7
Connecticut	35.6

States with lowest median age of population

State	Age
Utah	26.7
Alaska	30.9
California	32.2
Louisiana	32.4
New Mexico	32.4

Population growth

By region

Northeast: **+1.2%**

Pacific: **+6.4%**

Mountain: **+11.4%**

Midwest: **+2.9%**

South: **+6.1%**

Highest growth: **Nevada, +21.2%**
Lowest growth: **District of Columbia, -6.1%**

*Figures include members of armed forces residing in each state
NOTE: Numbers may not add up to 100 percent because of rounding

Source: "A Shifting Profile," San Francisco Examiner, *(March 1, 1995), p. A-13 Copyright © 1995 by* the San Francisco Examiner. *Reprinted by permission of the publisher.*

1. a. Which age group has experienced the largest percentage of growth?

   _____

   b. Which age group has had the smallest percentage of growth?

   _____

2. a. Which State has the population with the highest median age?

   _____

   b. What is the lowest median age of population reported?

   _____

3. a. What region of the United States has the second-highest growth rate?

   _____

   b. What region of the United States has the next-to-lowest growth rate?

   _____

4. What inferences or conclusions can you reach about U.S. population changes between 1990 and 1994?

   _____

   _____

❖ Integrating Text and Graphics

When reading textbooks, especially in the sciences, economics, or business, you will often need to integrate the information in graphics and text. Sometimes, what you read is clarified or explained in a graphic, but other times the graphic simply adds more information to the text. You will need to go back and forth, integrating both sets of information. Some instructors refer to this as "two-finger" reading; that is, you

hold your place in the text while reading the graphic, moving back and forth through a chapter.

In reading math and science textbooks, since the information often builds on what has preceded it, you must read very carefully, not skipping anything. Science information is dense and requires very slow and deliberate concentration, with several rereadings and much notetaking. This is true even for those readers who may have some familiarity with the subject.

Atmospheric pressure is more easily understood by integrating the text and diagram in Figure 10.8.

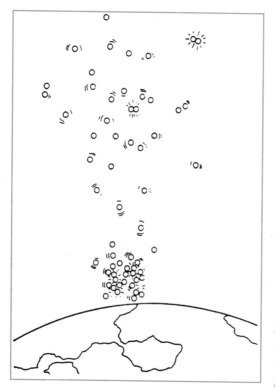

FIGURE 10.8

In the upper atmosphere, gaseous molecules are far apart and collide infrequently, which produces relatively low pressure. In lower layers, the molecules are closer together, and there are many more collisions, which produces higher pressure.

Source: Tom L. McKnight, "Atmospheric Pressure and Wind," Essentials of Physical Geography, p. 73. Copyright © 1992 by Prentice Hall, Inc. Reprinted by permission of the publisher.

The atmosphere is held to the Earth by the force of gravity, which prevents the gaseous molecules from escaping into space. At lower levels in the atmosphere, the molecules are packed more densely together because of the weight of the overlying air. Hence there are more molecular collisions and, therefore, higher pressure at lower levels. At higher elevations, the air is less dense, and there is a corresponding decrease in pressure. At any level in the atmosphere, then, the pressure is equivalent to the "weight" of the air directly above; thus the lower the elevation, the greater the pressure.

Why is atmospheric pressure greater at the earth's surface?

_____

_____

_____

ACTIVITY 10.5

Note how a combination of text and several graphics about tornadoes can help you understand the major ideas of a section of a physical geography textbook that deals with the weather.

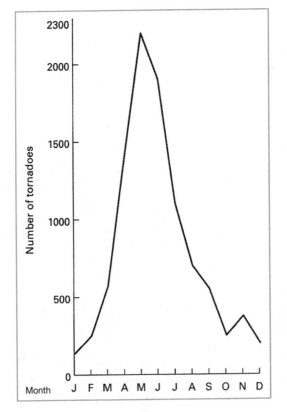

Seasonality of tornadoes in the United States, 1953–67. Late spring and early summer comprise the prime time.
Source: Tom L. McKnight, "Transient Atmospheric Flows and Disturbances," Essentials of Physical Geography, *pp. 150–51 Copyright © 1992 by Prentice Hall, Inc. Reprinted by permission of the publisher.*

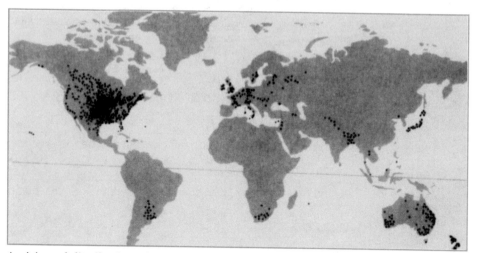

Anticipated distribution of tornadoes over the world in any given half-decade.

Large parcels of air in the troposphere that have relatively uniform horizontal physical characteristics are referred to as air masses. When air masses move away from their source regions, they cause significant weather changes as they go. When unlike air masses meet, a front is established between them, which is usually a zone of unsettled, sometimes stormy, weather.

Air masses and fronts are prominent components of major migratory pressure systems called extratropical cyclones and anticyclones that dominate midlatitude circula-

Distribution of tornadoes in the conterminous United States. Isolines refer to average number of observed tornadoes on an annual basis.

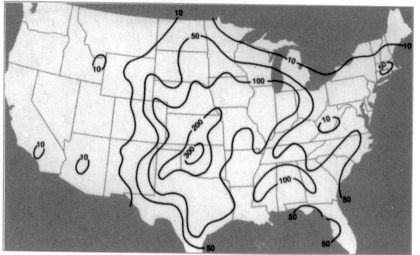

tion, particularly in winter. The former are battlegrounds of tropical and polar air with dynamically and dramatically changing weather conditions, whereas the latter represent stable, nonstormy interludes. Other notable storms include tropical cyclones (hurricanes), easterly waves, thunderstorms, and tornadoes.

1. What might be called the typical tornado season?

_____

2. What country will be subject to the greatest number of tornadoes?

_____

3. What particular areas of that country will have the greatest number of tornadoes?

_____

❖ Summary

Graphics may consist of graphs, charts, diagrams, tables, and photographs. They are common because considerable information can be condensed in a small space. Graphics are important parts of articles and textbook chapters, so the reader must integrate them with the text for better comprehension and understanding. Reading graphics demands careful attention and analysis. For college students, graphics are especially important in reading in the sciences and math-related areas such as business and economics.

The major purpose of reading graphics is to note trends and patterns and, after doing so, to draw inferences and conclusions about areas and issues.

Graphics enhance and dramatize the text, indicate trends and patterns, and, important for students, clarify the text and aid in the recall of particular pertinent information.

Selection 22: **TEXTBOOK**

☞ Preparation for Reading

What interests many people today is the state of our economy and those factors that can contribute to the growth of that economy. Many people are unaware of the major role in business and industry played by small businesses in the United States. Read to find out their importance and the difficulty in maintaining a small business profitably. Perhaps you have thought of someday starting such a small venture of your own.

Note while reading how the graphics help to summarize the major points. The boldfaced words are underlined in the selection.

innovation, and big business	a new method or device
extol the virtues	praise highly
impending problems	about to happen
disadvantages of **franchising**	marketing a parent company's goods or services

Preview, then read the selection.

Running the Small Business in the U.S. Economy

Ricky W. Griffin and Ronald J. Ebert

THE IMPORTANCE OF SMALL BUSINESS IN THE U.S. ECONOMY

As Figure 10.9 shows, more than 99 percent of 1 the nation's 16 million businesses employ fewer than 100 people. The vast majority of these companies are owner operated. Thus, just by sheer numbers alone, small business is a strong presence in the nation's economy. But small business is also a vital economic force because of its effect on job creation, <u>innovation</u>, and big business.

Job Creation

Economists and politicians alike <u>extol</u> the 2 virtues of small businesses as generators of jobs. In fact, studies show that over the last twenty years most new jobs have come not from big business but from small business. One study, for example, found that over a ten-year period, businesses with 20 or fewer employees created

66 percent of all new jobs nationwide and 99 percent of all new jobs in New England. Small, young, high-technology businesses create new jobs at a much faster rate than do older, larger businesses. High-technology businesses, especially those in chemistry or electronics, require individuals with a high degree of scientific or engineering knowledge to succeed. Thus, they continually need new people skilled in the latest breakthroughs.

POPULAR TYPES OF SMALL BUSINESS ENTERPRISE

Small businesses are also more common in 3 some industries than in others. Note in Figure 10.9 how five major industry groups—service, retailing, wholesaling, manufacturing, and agriculture—differ in terms of personnel, money, materials, and machines. The more resources an industry requires, the harder a business is to

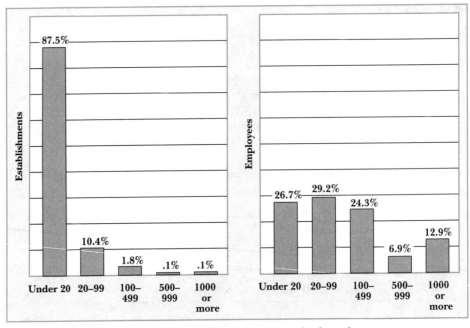

FIGURE 10.9   The Importance of Small Business in America

Source: *Chart prepared by U.S. Bureau of the Census*

start and the less likely the industry is to be dominated by small firms.

As a general rule, manufacturing busi- 4 nesses are the hardest to start, while service businesses are the easiest. To make sewing machines, for example, small businesses must invest not only in personnel but also in raw materials and machines. They must also develop an elaborate distribution network and advertise heavily. However, to prepare tax forms, small business-people need only invest in their own education and a few office supplies and reference books. They can run their businesses out of storefronts or even from their homes. (Though, as you will see later, ease of entry is no guarantee of success!)

Service Businesses

In part because they require a relatively low 5 level of resources, services are the largest and the fastest-growing segment of small business

enterprise today. Services also take advantage of small business-people's talent for innovation. No other industry group offers a higher return on time invested. The different services offered by small businesses number into the thousands, ranging from shoeshine parlors to car rental agencies, from marriage counselors to computer software, from legal advice to accounting and management consulting.

TRENDS IN SMALL BUSINESS START-UPS AND FAILURES

Approximately one half million new businesses 6 incorporate every year. This figure contrasts markedly with the 200,000 per year in the early 1960s. The rising tide of incorporations reflects an active small business community. Indeed, the economic boom of the 1980s resulted in more small businesses being formed than during any other decade in history.

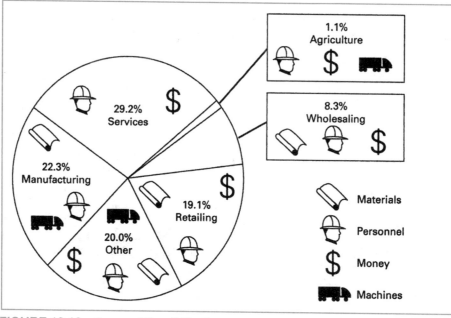

FIGURE 10.10   **Areas of Small Business and the Primary Resources They Require**

Economic prosperity also led to a reduction in the rate of small business failure. During the 1960s and 1970s, for example, less than half of the new businesses lasted more than 18 months and only one in five lasted ten years. New data, however, suggest a dramatic change. For example, one recent large study found that of new businesses started in the 1980s, over 77 percent were still in operation after three years. And recent SBA estimates suggest that at least 40 percent of all new businesses can expect to last at least six years.   **7**

REASONS FOR SUCCESSES AND FAILURES

Why do many small businesses succeed and others fail? While there is no set pattern, as Figure 10.11 shows, there are some common causes of both success and failure.   **8**

Reasons for Failure

Four common factors contribute to small business failure. One major problem is managerial incompetence or inexperience. If managers do not know how to make basic decisions, they are unlikely to make them effectively. A second contributor to failure is neglect. That is, after the glamour and excitement of the big grand opening, some entrepreneurs get discouraged and don't concentrate as much on their business as they should.   **9**

Third, weak control systems can also be a cause of failure. If control systems fail to alert managers to <u>impending</u> problems, they are likely to be caught unprepared to deal with them. Finally, many small businesses fail because the owner does not have enough capital to keep it going. New business owners are almost certain to fail if they expect to pay the   **10**

SUCCESS	FAILURE
Hard work, drive, and dedication Market demand for products/services Managerial competence Luck	Managerial incompetence Inexperience Neglect Weak control systems Under capitalization

FIGURE 10.11 **A variety of factors contribute to small business success and failure**

second month's rent from the first month's profits.

Figure 10.12 shows some advantages and disadvantages of <u>franchising</u>. On the plus side, franchising provides the entrepreneur with proven business methods, training, an established reputation, financial support, and reduced risk. There are also costs, however. Among the most major are the financial costs.

The costs of buying a franchise vary widely. Fantastic Sam's hair salon franchise fees are $20,000, but a Gingiss Formalwear franchise can run as much as $100,000! Very profitable hard-to-get franchises are even more expensive. A franchise for a McDonald's restaurant costs several hundred thousand dollars. A franchise for a professional sports team can run to several million dollars. Franchises may also have a con-

FIGURE 10.12 **Franchising has Both Advantages and Disadvantages for the Small Businessperson**

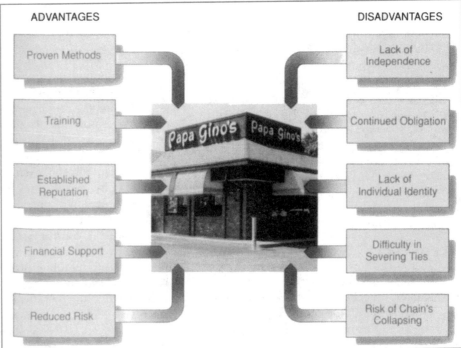

tinued obligation to contribute a percentage of sales to the parent corporation, reducing their own profits.

Buying a franchise entails less tangible **12** costs, too. For one, the small business-person sacrifices independence. A McDonald's franchisee, for example, cannot change the way hamburgers or milkshakes are made. Fran-chisees cannot create individual identities in the community. (Thus the owner of a McDonald's restaurant is, for all practical purposes, anonymous.) Many franchise agreements also are difficult to terminate.

Finally, while franchises minimize risks, **13** they are not a guarantee of success.

approximately 1000 words*

Ricky W. Griffin and Ronald J. Ebert, "Organizing and Managing Business," *Business*, 2nd ed., Prentice Hall, 1991, pp. 140, 145, 146, 152, and 159.

1. Why are small business ventures important in our country? In your answer, integrate the graphic information presented.

_____

_____

2. What is the major area of small businesses? What are the two major resources needed in whatever small business is undertaken? Use the graphics to help you to answer the question.

_____

_____

3. If you started a small business, which "success factor" would you be most certain of? What "failure factor" would you be especially careful of, knowing yourself and your business potential?

_____

_____

4. Would you consider buying a franchise? Why, or why not?

_____

_____

*The approximate word count does not include words in illustrations or tables.

Selection 23: **TEXTBOOK**

 Preparation for Reading

This selection deals with the body's response to injury and inflammation. As you read the text, note how the diagram and chart that follow make the process much clearer. You would have to have some familiarity with some of the specialized terms before you could begin to understand this chapter excerpt. Remember that in both math and science, information builds upon what has preceded it, so careful, deliberate study-type reading becomes essential.

You might have to refer to a glossary frequently while reading a science textbook. Glossary terms, written in academic language, must often be "translated" by you into everyday English as illustrated by the italics in the definitions below.

The following boldfaced terms from this selection were introduced in previous chapters of the textbook.

homeostasis	a constant internal environment *(you're healthy)*
bacterium	a single-celled microorganism, which may be pathogenic *(these guys can cause disease)*
mast cell	connective tissue cells that initiate the inflammatory response *(this starts getting rid of the problem)*
histamine and **heparin**	two chemicals released by mast cells to initiate the inflammatory response *(these two are needed to start the process)*
phagocytes (phagocytizing)	cells that engulf foreign or pathogenic materials for removal *(this is the "heavy hitter" in the process)*
macrophages	phagocytic cells *(this type is huge)*
lymphocytes	cells of the lymphatic system that participate in the inflammatory response *(these cells also help initially)*

Preview, noting the graphics, and then read the selection.

Homeostatis at the Tissue Level

Frederic Martini

THE INFLAMMATORY RESPONSE

Life is an adventure, and injuries often occur. The restoration of <u>homeostasis</u> following an injury involves two related processes. First the area is isolated, while damaged cells, tissue components, and dangerous microorganisms are cleaned up. Second, the damaged tissues are replaced or repaired. These two phases overlap. Isolation establishes a framework that guides the cells responsible for reconstruction, and repairs begin well before cleanup operations have ended. Unless unusual conditions exist, the repair leaves the tissue almost "good as new." In general, epithelia and connective tissues show the greatest abilities to restore homeostasis after injury.

Whenever tissue damage occurs, it triggers **2** an inflammatory response. Inflammation produces symptoms of swelling, redness, heat, tenderness, and reduced function. The stimulus provoking this response might be a mechanical stress, such as abrasion, chemical irritation, or a temperature extreme (hot or cold). An infection is an inflammation resulting from the presence of some biological invader, such as a bacterium.

The inflammatory response, diagrammed **3** in Figure 10.13 depends on the activities of mast cells in connective tissues. When stimulated by alterations in their environment, these cells release chemicals (histamine and heparin) that affect blood vessels in the immediate area. The vessels enlarge, or dilate, and as blood flow increases, the region becomes reddish in color and warm to the touch. The increased blood supply brings nutrients, oxygen, and cellular defenders into the area, and removes dissolved waste products and toxic chemicals.

These chemicals also make the capillary **4** walls more permeable, and fluid containing dissolved materials enters the injured tissue. The area then becomes swollen, and combined pressure and chemicals released by injured cells stimulate nerve endings that produce the sensation of pain. Some of the proteins introduced from the blood are dissolved molecules of fibrinogen (fī-BRIN-ō-jen; *gennan*, to produce). These proteins can interact to form large, insoluble fibers of fibrin. Fibrin formation at the injury site is slowed by the heparin released by mast cells, but around the edges of the affected area fibrin appears in a meshwork, or clot. Clot formation walls off the inflamed region, slowing the spread of cellular debris or bacteria into surrounding tissues.

Meanwhile, fixed macrophages and free **5** macrophages are phagocytizing the debris and bacteria. Chemicals released by mast cells, active macrophages, and injured cells attract other cellular defenders, and white blood cells

FIGURE 10.13   **The Inflammatory Response**
This diagram summarizes key features in the inflammatory response. The regulatory mechanism provides another example of homeostatic control through negative feedback.

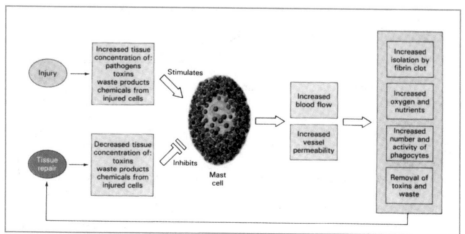

TABLE 10.1

A Summary of the Inflammatory Response

	Event	Primary Effect	Secondary Effect	Functional Significance
Step 1	Injury disrupts homeostasis.	Tissue damage with or without microorganisms.	Chemical change in interstitial fluids.	Triggers inflammatory response.
Step 2	Chemical change in interstitial fluids.	Mast cells release histamine and heparin.	Dilation of vessels, increase in blood flow and vessel permeability.	Area becomes red, swollen, and warm.
Step 3	Increased blood flow and vessel permeability.	Increased oxygen, nutrients; fewer toxins, wastes.	Slower spread of inflammation; abnormal chemicals appear in the bloodstream.	Increases metabolic activity of phagocytic and repair cells.
Step 4a	Increased permeability of vessels.	Leakage of fibrinogen from plasma.	Clot formation.	Encloses area, slows the spread of inflammation or infection.
Step 4b	Abnormal chemicals appear in bloodstream.	Stimulates plasma cells.	Production of antibodies.	Helps destroy or inactivate invading microorganisms or foreign toxins.
		Free macrophages and microphages attracted to area.	Migration of cells into inflammation site.	Removes cell debris, toxins, and microorganisms.
Step 5	Reduction in tissue concentrations of debris, toxins, microorganisms.	Histamine and heparin release by mast cells stops.	Reduction of inflammation.	Return to homeostasis.

squeeze through the capillary walls to join the attack. Some of the lymphocytes within the tissue differentiate into plasma cells that begin producing antibodies. Macrophages and microphages arriving from the blood increase the number of phagocytic cells in the region; the microphages known as neutrophils (NŪ-trō-filz) are most abundant. Actively phagocytic cells are short-lived, most surviving for just a few hours before dying and disintegrating. Pus is the mixture of living and dead cells and tissue debris that develops within an area of inflammation. The inflammatory response has been summarized in Table 10.1.

Tissues heal fastest in young and healthy **6**

individuals whose diet contains adequate amino acids, energy sources, and vitamins C, D, E, and K. Repairs are always slowed by poor health, infection, or an inadequate diet. Age is also a factor, for healing takes more time in elderly patients, even healthy ones.

approximately 600 words*

Frederic Martini, "Homeostasis at the Tissue Level," *Fundamentals of Anatomy and Physiology,* pp. 107–109. Copyright © 1989 by Prentice Hall, Inc. Reprinted by permission of the publisher.

1. Identify the two tissues that usually heal the quickest.

   _____

2. An infection is a particular type of inflammation. What characterizes it?

   _____

3. Complete the outline of the inflammatory response after injury occurs.

   I. Mast cells in the connective tissue release the chemicals _____

       and _____.

   II. These chemicals affect blood vessels in the immediate area.

       A. Blood flow increases and brings in _____.

       B. Blood flow then removes _____.

   III. Chemicals also make the walls of the blood vessel more _____,
        and fluids can enter the injured tissue.

       A. Within the fluids are molecules of _____.

       B. These help in _____ formation and keep surrounding
          tissue clear.

   IV. Joining the attack on the injured area are _____ that
       phagocytize the debris and bacteria.

   V. Production of antibodies is then caused by _____.

   VI. Removal of toxins and waste lead to a return to _____.

*The approximate word count does not include words in illustrations or tables.

Selection 24: **TEXTBOOK**

 Preparation for Reading

The first paragraph of the selection describes us as denizens of the atmosphere living at the bottom of the ocean of air much like the fish living at the bottom of the sea. Our atmosphere both nourishes and sustains us, and especially today, it is important for us to understand it.

As you read, integrate the graphic information with the text so you will be better prepared to answer the final question at the conclusion of this text. The bold-faced words are underlined in the selection.

hospitable **milieu** for life	environment, especially a social setting
denizen of the atmosphere	inhabitant of a particular place
inert gaseous element	inactive
inordinately significant	excessive
in **minuscule** quantities	tiny

Preview, then read the selection.

Constituents of the Atmosphere

Tom K. McKnight

The atmosphere interacts significantly with 1 other components of the earthly environment, and it is instrumental in providing a hospitable <u>milieu</u> for life. Whereas we often speak of human beings as creatures of the Earth, it is perhaps more accurate to consider them as creatures of the atmosphere. As surely as a crab crawling on the sea bottom is a resident of the ocean, so a person living at the bottom of the ocean of air is a <u>denizen</u> of the atmosphere.

CONSTITUENTS OF THE ATMOSPHERE

The atmosphere is composed of a mixture of 2 discrete gases and an immense number of tiny suspended particles in solid or liquid form. The chemical composition of pure, dry air at lower elevations is simple, uniform, and basically unvarying through time. Certain minor gases and nongaseous particles, however, vary markedly from place to place and from time to time, as does the amount of moisture in the air.

The Gases

Most of the volume of the atmosphere is 3 provided by two chemical elements: *nitrogen* and *oxygen*. Nitrogen comprises more than 78 percent of the total, and oxygen makes up nearly 21 percent. See Table 10.2 and Figure 10.14. Nitrogen is added to the air by the decay and burning of organic matter, by volcanic eruptions, and by the chemical breakdown of certain rocks. It is utilized in the atmosphere by certain biological processes and by being washed away in rain or snow. Overall, the addition and removal of nitrogen gas are balanced, and the quantity remains constant. Oxygen is produced by vegetation and is removed by a variety of organic and inorganic processes; its

TABLE 10.2

Principal Gases of Earth's Atmosphere

Component	Percent of Volume of Dry Air	Concentration in Parts per Million of Air
Uniform gases:		
Nitrogen (N_2)	78.084	
Oxygen (O_2)	20.948	
Argon (A)	0.934	
Neon (Ne)	0.00182	18.2
Helium (He)	0.00052	5.2
Methane (CH_4)	0.00015	1.5
Krypton (Kr)	0.00011	1.1
Hydrogen (H_2)	0.00005	0.5
Important variable gases:		
Water vapor (H_2O)	0–4	
Carbon dioxide (CO_2)	0.0353	353
Carbon monoxide (CO)		< 100
Ozone (O_3)		< 2
Sulfur dioxide (SO_2)		< 1
Nitrogen dioxide (NO_2)		< 0.2

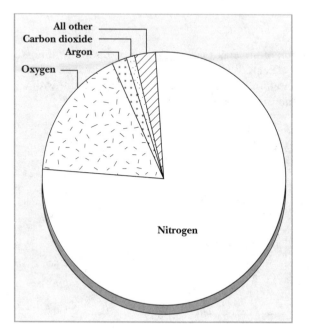

FIGURE 10.14

Proportional volume of the gaseous components of the atmosphere. Nitrogen and oxygen are the dominant elements.

total quantity also apparently remains stable. The remaining 1 percent of the atmosphere's volume consists mostly of the <u>inert</u> gaseous element *argon*. These three principal atmospheric elements—nitrogen, oxygen, argon—are of minimal importance in their effect on weather and climate and therefore need no further consideration here.

Several other gases occur in sparse, **4** although highly variable, quantities in the atmosphere, but their influence on weather and climate is prominent. See Figure 10.15. *Water vapor* is the gaseous phase of moisture in the air and represents the humidity of the atmosphere. It is largely absent from the upper atmosphere, but near the surface it is often present in notable proportions. It is most common in those portions of the atmosphere overlying warm, moist surface areas, such as tropical oceans, where it may amount to as much as 4 percent of total volume. Over deserts and in polar regions, the amount of water vapor is but a tiny fraction of 1 percent. For the atmosphere as a whole, the total component of water vapor

remains virtually constant. Water vapor is <u>inordinately</u> significant to weather and climate in that it is the source of all clouds and precipitation and is intimately involved in energy transfer (the storage, movement, and release of heat).

Carbon dioxide is important to life processes **5** because of its role in photosynthesis but it also has a significant influence on climate. This is primarily due to its potent ability to absorb infrared radiant energy, which maintains the warmth of the lower atmosphere. It is distributed fairly uniformly in the lower layers, but its accumulation has been increasing for the last century or so, and the rate of accumulation has been accelerating, presumably because of the increased burning of fossil fuels. The long-range effect of increasing amounts of carbon dioxide in the atmosphere is debatable, but many scientists believe that it will warm up the lower atmosphere sufficiently to produce major, and still unpredictable, global climatic changes. The proportion of carbon dioxide in the atmosphere has been increasing at a rate of

FIGURE 10.15
Vertical distribution of the major gaseous components in the atmosphere. The width of each column shows the relative distribution of that component by altitude. The columns are *not* comparable with one another volumetrically, only proportionally.

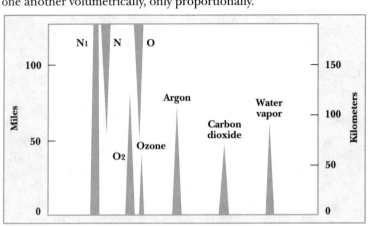

about 0.0007 percent (7 parts per million) per year, and at present is about 400 parts per million.

Another minor but vital gas in the atmos- 6 phere is ozone. For the most part, ozone is concentrated a few miles above the Earth, particularly between 9 and 30 miles (15 and 48 km) above the Earth. Ozone is an excellent absorber of ultraviolet solar radiation: it filters out enough of these burning rays to protect earthly life from potentially deadly effects.

Several other minor gases exist in the 7 atmosphere in <u>minuscule</u> quantities. Some of them—particularly carbon monoxide, sulfur dioxide, nitrogen oxides, and various hydrocarbons—are increasingly introduced into the atmosphere by emission from machines such as furnaces, factories, and automobiles. All these gaseous pollutants are hazardous to life and at least potentially influential on climate.

approximately 700 words*

Tom L. McKnight, "Introduction to the Atmosphere," *Essentials of Physical Geography,* Prentice Hall, © 1992 pp. 34–35.

1. What gases are of minimal importance to weather and climate?

_____

2. Why is water vapor very significant in weather patterns?

_____

3. CO_2 in the atmosphere can produce problems. Why?

_____

4. What is the major role of the ozone layer?

_____

5. What dangers do we encounter from other minor gases in the atmosphere?

_____

More and more, textbooks such as the physical geography text from which the following excerpt was taken are integrating essays along with graphics to make textbook reading relevant to today's concerns. As we have read and understood the complexity of our atmosphere with its finite gaseous components, we can appreciate the danger at present to our planet from the depletion of the ozone layer.

*The approximate word count does not include words in illustrations or tables.

☞ Reading About Our Changing World

Read this final essay to answer one last very important question in your journal.

People and the Environment: Depletion of the Ozone Layer

Tom L. McKnight

Only within the last two decades has the significance of the ozone layer been understood. Ozone is a form of the oxygen molecule that has three atoms (O_3) rather than the more common two (O_2). It is created in the upper atmosphere by the action of solar radiation on oxygen molecules; sunlight splits apart O_2 molecules, some of which recombine as O_3 molecules.

The concentration of ozone molecules in a definite layer serves as a shield for the Earth, absorbing most of the potentially dangerous ultraviolet radiation found in sunlight. Ultraviolet radiation is biologically destructive in many ways. It causes skin cancer and cataracts, it suppresses the human immune system, it diminishes the yield of many crops, it disrupts the aquatic food chain by killing microorganisms on the ocean surface, and doubtless causes other negative effects still undiscovered.

But the ozone layer is a fragile shield. It is paper-thin at best and has been thinning even more in recent years, apparently because of the release of certain human-produced synthetic chemicals into the air. These chemicals, classed as chlorofluorocarbons, or CFCs, are widely used in refrigeration and air conditioning (Freon), in foam and plastic manufacturing, and in aerosol sprays. They were thought to be exceedingly benign, for they are odorless, nonflammable, noncorrosive, and nontoxic.

Although extremely stable and inert in the lower atmosphere, at high levels CFCs are broken down by ultraviolet radiation, releasing chlorine and bromine. Under certain circumstances a chemical reaction occurs that destroys large quantities of ozone. As many as 100,000 ozone molecules can be removed from the atmosphere for every chlorine molecule released. [See Figure 10.16.]

Not only is the ozone layer thinning, in some places it has disappeared entirely, on a temporary basis. A "hole" in the ozone layer has developed over Antarctica every year since 1979, and the duration of the missing layer has increased every year. [See Figure 10.17.] In 1988 a second ozone hole was found over the Arctic for the first time.

In response to these alarming discoveries, several countries (including the United States) banned the use of CFCs in aerosol sprays in 1978. A major international treaty was promulgated in 1987 that would diminish the production of all ozone-depleting chemicals by 50 percent by 1999. The Du Pont Company, the world's largest producer of CFCs (25 percent of total world output), voluntarily decided in 1988 to phase out all production of chlorofluorocarbons.

Thus serious steps are now under way to control a global pollutant, for the first time. One hopes that it is not too late.

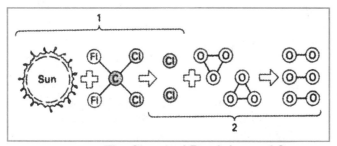

FIGURE 10.16   **The Chemical Breakdown of Ozone**

1. A typical CFC molecule has one carbon atom (C) bonded to two chlorine atoms (Cl) and two fluorine atoms (Fl). Sunlight breaks the bonds in CFCs, releasing chlorine atoms.
2. Chlorine atoms engage in a complex chemical reaction with ozone, resulting in the breakdown of ozone molecules into oxygen molecules. Chlorine atoms are unchanged by the reaction and can repeat the process. Thus a single chlorine atom can destroy tens of thousands of ozone molecules.

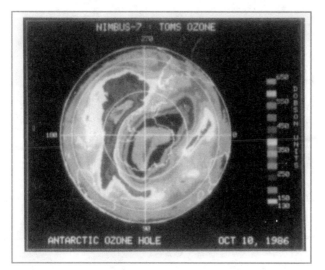

FIGURE 10.17

The Antarctic ozone hole as imaged from the Nimbus 7 satellite in 1986. The "hole" is the gray oval feature covering most of the Antarctic continent. (Courtesy of NASA.)

approximately 500 words

Tom L. McKnight, "Introduction to the Atmosphere," *Essentials of Physical Geography*, p. 37. Copyright © 1992 by Prentice Hall, Inc. Reprinted by permission of the publisher.

JOURNAL ENTRY

The last essay in this text explains the dangers to our environment from the depletion of the ozone layer. In this Information Age, does it appear that adequate technology exists to solve the problem? Are American citizens willing to change their behavior in order to reduce the risk of excessive radiation that results from the ozone layer's deterioration? What are our expectations from other countries in regard to this global environmental problem?

As a future citizen of the twenty-first century, how do you view your own responsibilities in this area? What are some positive steps you can take? As an effective reader, how do you plan to stay informed?

Vocabulary Words Defined as Bottom-Line Words

abridged
abrogate
abstract
abyss
accolades
accoutrements
acronyms
adjudicated
admonished
adversity
affluent
alleviate
amnesty
anathema
anomaly
antidote
antonyms
archetype
aspirations
assimilates
assumption
aural

❖

badgering
banderillero
belittle
besiege
brazenly
burgeoning

❖

calamitous
capitulated
cardiac
cataract
categorized
chronological
civil libertarians
clarify
climax
cohabitation
cohesion
colloquial

components
concisely
concurrence
condoning
conflagrations
conscientious
consigned
constituents
contraband
coup
credo
critical

❖

decapitated
decimation
de facto
demeans
demographers
demographic
demonize
denigrated
derogating
dichotomy
diminish
disdain
disparage
disproportionate
dissuade
draconian
draughtsman
dynamic

❖

echelon
ecological
elitist
emanate
embargoes
empathy
empirical
emulate
envisaged
entrepreneurship

erosion
erudite
ethical
ethnicity
eugenics
eulogies
evoke
existential
exorbitant
exotically

❖

facilitate
flapper
foisted
formidable
frays
futile

❖

genres
genteel
glossary
gringos
guffawed
guile

❖

hallmarks
hamper
hedonist
heighten
hierarchy
homogenized
horizontally

❖

iconoclastic
icons
ideology
imperative
implied
incarceration
incoherent

inductively
inequitably
ineradicable
infanticide
inference
inflections
inherent
initiative
innate
insidious
insubordination
intact
intemperate
interchangeably
intractable
irreconcilable

❖

juggernaut

❖

lethal
liaisons
lift
linchpin
linguists
literary
lurid

❖

malign
mandates
matador
matriarchal
maxim
mecca
meritocracy
metaphor
metaphorical
meteoric
misogyny
mnemonic
mobility
modes

morbidly
mores
mystical

❖

neurological
normative
nuance

❖

objective
obscenity
occidental
omen
omniscient
osteoporosis
ostracizing

❖

paradigm
paradoxes
paradoxically
passivity
pathological
perceived
perceptibly
perdition
periodicals
perusal
pessimistic
phonetic
picadors

plaudits
potentates
precedent
precise
prerequisite
primeval
pristine
prodigious
proficient
prohibitionists
proliferation
promiscuity
proponents
prosecutorial
protagonists
puberty
purporting

❖

quantum leap

❖

ramifications
randomly
raucous
regimen
rehabilitated
relevant
resiliency
restitution
retribution
rhetoric

rote

❖

salient
sanctions
satirist
scapegoating
seder
semantic
sentimental
sequential
servitude
siege
simultaneously
somber
sophisticated
sordid
spatial
sporadic
statutes
stimulus
stippled
stoic
straightforward
stratification
subjective
subtle
succinct
sulphurous
syndication
synonyms
syntactic

synthesize

❖

tentacles
titan
topical
tote
touted
transposed
turgid

❖

unabridged
unambiguously
unanimous
undergird
unique
unprecedented
usurp

❖

validity
vertically
vicariously

❖

xenophobic

❖

yeoman

Vocabulary Words Defined for Reading Selections

acquisition
acquisitive
acuity
ad infinitum
aggregate
ambivalence
amenable
anachronism
apartheid
arbitrary
aristocracy
arousal
ascribed
ashram
assuaged
autistic
autonomy
avarice
aversive

❖

bacterium
banalities
bastion
belligerently
bigotry
biosphere
bizarre
bulwark

❖

camouflage
chic
chivalry
coerced
cognitive
cohort
confrontation
consensus
constraints
converge
correlational

❖

deflected
degradation
deleterious
denizen

detrimental
deviant
digressions
disillusioning
disparity
diverging
diversity
domestic
dossier

❖

eloquently
endogamy
equitable
euphemistic
excruciating
extol

❖

facet
felony
feudalism
foraging
franchising
frenetically

❖

generate
glib

❖

habituate
hallucinogens
heparin
histamine
homeostasis
homogeneous
hysterically

❖

impassioned
impediments
impending
impoverished
inalienable
inanimate
ineluctably
inert
infamous
infamy

infusion
innovation
innuendo
inordinately
inquisitor
insatiable
insidiously
integrity
internalize
intimidating
introspective
invective
ironically
irreparable

❖

jurisdictions

❖

lenience
leper
lethargy
loathing
lurched
lymphocytes

❖

macrophages
mandatory
maneuvering
mantra
marginality
mast cells
mediates
methodical
meticulous
milieu
minuscule
mutuality

❖

notorious

❖

obdurate

❖

parity
perpetuity
pervasive

perverse
phagocytes
plausible
predisposed
prerogative
prestigious
primogeniture
profligate
prosecutorial
proverbial
psychological
pundits

❖

radical
reciprocally
relentless
renaissance
reprimand
ritualistic
rumble
rustic

❖

scowling
scrutiny
sepulchral
squabbles
stratification
stygian
summit

❖

traumatic
turbulent

❖

unconscionable

❖

vagaries
viability
vile
vulnerability

❖

zealots

Credits

Chapter 1

pp. 16–18 Marcia Kaplan, excerpts from "Illiteracy: a looming crisis in the information age," *San Francisco Examiner* (May 7, 1995). Copyright © 1995 by Marcia Kaplan. Reprinted with the permission of the author.

Chapter 2

pp. 40–41 Sydney J. Harris, excerpt from "Using Love in Whatever We Like" from *The Best of Sydney J. Harris* (New York: Houghton Mifflin, 1957). Originally appeared in the *Chicago Sun-Times*. Copyright © 1957 by Sydney J. Harris. Reprinted with the permission of the *Chicago Sun-Times*. **p. 59** Entries "boxcar" to "bourbon" from *The American Heritage Dictionary of the English Language,* Third College Paperback Edition, edited by Peter Davies. Copyright © 1993 by Houghton Mifflin Company. Reprinted with the permission of the publishers. **p. 60** Entries "carnival" to "carom" from *The American Heritage Dictionary of the English Language,* Third College Paperback Edition, edited by Peter Davies. Copyright © 1993 by Houghton Mifflin Company. Reprinted with the permission of the publishers. **pp. 62–63** Entries "astonish," "cruel," and "obedient" from *The American Heritage Dictionary of the English Language,* Third College Paperback Edition, edited by Peter Davies. Copyright © 1993 by Houghton Mifflin Company. **p. 64** Entry on "talk" from *The New Roget's Thesaurus in Dictionary Form,* edited by Norman Lewis. Copyright © 1978 by G. P. Putnam's Sons. Reprinted with the permission of The Putnam Publishing Group. **p. 65** Cartoon: T. O. Sylvester, "Roget's Thesaurus," *San Francisco Chronicle* (October 23, 1994). Copyright © 1994 by T. O. Sylvester. Reprinted by permission. **p. 68** Photo: Michael Ahearn. **pp. 68–69** William Lutz, "Double-Talk," *Family Circle* (November 26, 1991). Copyright © 1991 by William Lutz. Reprinted with the permission of the author, c/o Jean V. Naggar Literary Agency. **p. 71** Cartoon: Buddy Hickerson, "The Quigmans: Snow White and Seven Politically Correct Dwarves." Copyright © 1993 by Los Angeles Times Syndicate. Reprinted with the permission of Los Angeles Times Syndicate. **pp. 73–79** John G. Seamon and Douglas T. Kenrick, excerpts from "Language and Thought" and "The Nature of Stress" from *Psychology, Second Edition.* Copyright © 1994 by Prentice Hall. Reprinted with the permission of Prentice-Hall, Inc. **pp. 82–88** Evan Hunter, "On the Sidewalk, Bleeding" from *The Jungle Kids* (New York: Simon & Schuster, 1956). Copyright © 1956 by Evan Hunter. Reprinted with the permission of William Morris Agency Inc., on behalf of the author.

Chapter 3

pp. 93–95 Alice Steinbach, excerpts from "Reversal of fortune: Attitude can reroute adversity," *The Baltimore Sun* (January 13, 1991). Copyright © 1991. Reprinted with the permission of *The Baltimore Sun.* **pp. 99–101** Linda Winikow, "How Women and Minorities Are Reshaping Corporate America," *Vital Speeches of the Day* 57, no. 8 (February 1, 1991). Copyright © 1991 by Linda Winikow. Reprinted with the permission of the author. **pp. 109–110** John Mack Faragher, excerpts from *Out of Many: A History of the American People.* Copyright © 1994 by Prentice-Hall, Inc. Reprinted with the permission of the publishers. **pp. 110–112** John Mack Faragher, excerpts from *Out of Many: A History of the American People.* Copyright © 1994 by Prentice-Hall, Inc. Reprinted with the permission of the publishers. **pp. 120–123** Vincent N. Perrillo, "Sexual Harassment" from *Strangers to These Shores: Race & Ethnic Relations in the U.S., Third Edition.* Copyright © 1990 by Macmillan Publishing Company. Reprinted with the permission of Allyn & Bacon. **p. 124** Cartoon: Wayne Stayskal, "Watch It: I Hear He Just Took Out Sexual Harassment Insurance," *Peninsula Times Tribune* (December 7, 1991). Reprinted with the permission of Tribune Media Services. **p. 135** Photo: Judith Carlson/*San Jose Mercury News.* **pp. 135–138** Bharati Mukherjee, "Jasmine" from *Jasmine.* Copyright © 1989 by Bharati Mukherjee. Reprinted with the permission of Grove/Atlantic, Inc. and Penguin Books Canada Limited.

Chapter 4

p. 151 Vincent N. Perrillo, excerpt from *Strangers to These Shores: Race & Ethnic Relations in the U.S., Third Edition.* Copyright © 1990 by Macmillan Publishing Company. Reprinted with the permission of Allyn & Bacon. **p. 152** Larry Long, excerpts from *Introduction to Computers & Information Systems.* Copyright © 1994 by Prentice-Hall, Inc. Reprinted with the permission of the publishers. **p. 156** Grant Wood, "American Gothic." Courtesy of the Art Institute of Chicago. **pp. 157, 158** David Popenoe, excerpts from *Sociology.* Copyright © 1995 by Prentice-Hall, Inc. Reprinted with the permission of the publishers. **p. 161** David Popenoe, excerpts from *Sociology.* Copyright © 1995 by Prentice-Hall, Inc. Reprinted with the permission of the publishers. **p. 162** John Mack Faragher, excerpts from *Out of Many: A History of the American People.* Copyright © 1994 by Prentice-Hall, Inc. Reprinted with the permission of the publishers. **p. 163** Larry

Long, excerpts from *Introduction to Computers & Information Systems*. Copyright © 1994 by Prentice-Hall, Inc. Reprinted with the permission of the publishers. **pp. 166–167** Frank Schmalleger, excerpts from *Criminal Justice Today*. Copyright © 1995 by Prentice-Hall, Inc. Reprinted with the permission of the publishers. **p. 167** Michelle McCormick, "We're Too Busy for Ideas," *Newsweek* 121 (March 29, 1993), p. 10. Copyright © 1993 by Newsweek, Inc. Reprinted with the permission of *Newsweek*. **p. 170** David Popenoe, "Social Class and the Law" from *Sociology*. Copyright © 1995 by Prentice-Hall, Inc. Reprinted with the permission of the publishers. **p. 172** Frank Schmalleger, "Pleading the Fifth Amendment" from *Criminal Justice Today*. Copyright © 1995 by Prentice-Hall, Inc. Reprinted with the permission of the publishers. **p. 173** Photo: Bettmann. **pp. 173–174** "Jules Verne saw the future in 1863 novel," *San Jose Mercury News* (September 22, 1994). From Mercury News Wire Services. Reprinted by permission. **pp. 174–175** Frank Schmalleger, "Reforming the Juvenile Court System" from *Criminal Justice Today*. Copyright © 1995 by Prentice-Hall, Inc. Reprinted with the permission of the publishers. **pp. 177–178** Bernard Malamud, "The First Seven Years" from *The Stories of Bernard Malamud*. Copyright © 1988 by Bernard Malamud. Reprinted with the permission of Farrar, Straus & Giroux, Inc. **pp. 181–182** Russell Baker, "Hooked on anger," *The New York Times* (February 8, 1995). Copyright © 1995 by The New York Times Company. Reprinted with the permission of *The New York Times*. **pp. 186–188** David Popenoe, "Crime Control: The Criminal Justice System" from *Sociology*. Copyright © 1995 by Prentice-Hall, Inc. Reprinted with the permission of the publishers. **pp. 191–196** Nash Candeleria, "El Patrón" from *The Day the Cisco Kid Shot John Wayne* (Tempe, Ariz.: Bilingual Press/Editoria Bilingue, 1988). Copyright © 1988 by Nash Candeleria. Reprinted with the permission of the author and Bilingual Press/Editoria Bilingue, Hispanic Research Center Arizona State University.

Chapter 5

pp. 204–206 Frank Schmalleger, "Inmate Types" from *Criminal Justice Today*. Copyright © 1995 by Prentice-Hall, Inc. Reprinted with the permission of the publishers. **p. 207** Mary Hemingway, *By Line: Ernest Hemingway*, edited by William White. Originally published in *Toronto Star Weekly* (October 20, 1923). Copyright © 1967 by Mary Hemingway. Reprinted with the permission of Scribner's, a division of Simon & Schuster, Inc. **pp. 214–215** Louis E. Boone and David L. Kurtz, excerpts from *Contemporary Business Communication*. Copyright © 1994 by Prentice-Hall, Inc. Reprinted with the permission of the publishers. **p. 216** Mary Jo Dilonardo, "Just don't misplace this book," *San Francisco Examiner* (May 10, 1995). Originally in *The Cincinnati Post*, a Scripps Howard Newspaper. Copyright © 1995 by Mary Jo Dilonardo. Reprinted with the permission of Scripps Howard News Service. **p. 223** Ellen Norman, "Other Nations Are Tougher on Drunken Drivers," *The Peninsula Times Tribune* (December 30, 1981). Copyright © 1981. Reprinted with the permission of *The Peninsula Times Tribune*. **pp. 226–227** Scott Seligman, *Dealing With the Chinese: A Practical Guide to Etiquette in the People's Republic of China*. Copyright © 1989 by Scott D. Seligman. Reprinted with the permission of Warner Books, Inc. **pp. 230–231** Peggy Noonan, "Why They Came Here," *The Reader's Digest* (July 1991). Copyright © 1991 by Peggy Noonan. Reprinted with the permission of the author. **pp. 231–232** Jennifer McBride Young, "The Rock Fantasy" from *The Essay Connection, Third Edition*, edited by Lynn Z. Bloom (Lexington, Mass.: D. C. Heath and Company). Reprinted by permission. **p. 235** Stephen Worchel and Wayne Shebilske, excerpts from *Principles and Applications: Psychology*. Copyright © 1995 by Prentice-Hall, Inc. Reprinted with the permission of the publishers. **pp. 236-237** Frank Schmalleger, excerpts from *Criminal Justice Today*. Copyright © 1995 by Prentice-Hall, Inc. Reprinted with the permission of the publishers. **pp. 238–240** David Popenoe, excerpts from *Sociology*. Copyright © 1995 by Prentice-Hall, Inc. Reprinted with the permission of the publishers. **pp. 243–245** Amanda Lovell, "Control Freaks," *Self* (January 1989). Reprinted by permission. **pp. 248–253** John G. Seamon and Douglas T. Kenrick, excerpts from *Psychology, Second Edition*. Copyright © 1994 by Prentice-Hall. Reprinted with the permission of Prentice-Hall, Inc. **pp. 256–267** Tobias Wolff, "The Rich Brother" from *Back in the World* (New York: Houghton Mifflin Company, 1985). Copyright © 1985 by Tobias Wolff. Reprinted with the permission of International Creative Management, Inc.

Chapter 6

pp. 272–273 Mortimer J. Adler, "Success Means Never Feeling Tired," *Reader's Digest* (March 1979). Copyright © 1979 by The Reader's Digest Association. Reprinted with the permission of the author. **p. 275** Cartoon: Harley Schwadron, "The book you took out . . . " Reprinted with the permission of Harley Schwadron. **pp. 285–286** Jonathan Marshall, "Looks Count, Says Study on Earning Power," *San Francisco Chronicle* (November 1, 1993). Reprinted by permission. **p. 288** David Popenoe, excerpts from *Sociology*. Copyright © 1995 by Prentice-Hall, Inc. Reprinted with the permission of the publishers. **p. 290** Drawing: Yuk Hing Shum, DeAnza College, July 1995. Reprinted with the permission of the artist. **pp. 293–294** Richard Cohen: "Elvis: Another Victim of Myth-Understanding," *Washington Post* (1980). Copyright ©

1980 by Washington Post Writers Group. Reprinted with the permission of Washington Post Writers Group. **p. 297** Cartoon: Bunny Hoest, "I wouldn't have taken Algebra if I had known there was math involved," *Parade* (May 30, 1993). Copyright © 1993. Reprinted with the permission of Bunny Hoest and *Parade.* **pp. 297–299** Terry Tang, "Bad at Math and Proud of It," *The Seattle Times* (July 14, 1991). Copyright © 1991. Reprinted with the permission of *The Seattle Times.* **pp. 302–303** Stephen Worchel and Wayne Shebilske, "Clashing Views in Delayed Memories of Childhood Trauma" from *Principles and Applications: Psychology.* Copyright © 1995 by Prentice-Hall, Inc. Reprinted with the permission of the publishers.

Chapter 7

pp. 316–317 Neal Gabler, "We Love Trash (with a vengeance)," *San Jose Mercury News* (June 6, 1995). Originally published in the *Los Angeles Times.* Copyright © 1995 by Neal Gabler. Reprinted with the permission of the author. **p. 319** Cartoon: Mike Luckovich, "U.S. Currency Redesign," *Atlanta Constitution* (July 16, 1994). Reprinted with the permission of Creators Syndicate, Inc. **pp. 321–322** Larry Long, "Sources of Personal Data" from *Introduction to Computers & Information Systems.* Copyright © 1994 by Prentice-Hall, Inc. Reprinted with the permission of the publishers. **pp. 324–326** Joseph D. McNamara, "Drug peace," *San Jose Mercury News* (May 17, 1995). Copyright © 1995 by Joseph D. McNamara. Reprinted with the permission of the author. **pp. 333–334** Peter Doshock, "The Mind of the Militias," *Psychology Today* (July/August 1995). Copyright © 1995 by Sussex Publishers. Reprinted with the permission of *Psychology Today.* **p. 335** Photo: Lyle Cox/ *The Bulletin*/AP Wide World Photos. **p. 336** Maya Angelou, untitled poem (" . . . Mirror twins are different") from *Wouldn't Take Nothing for My Journey Now,* page 125. Copyright © 1993 by Maya Angelou. Reprinted with the permission of Random House, Inc. **p. 337** Cartoon (top): Signe Wilkinson, "Students Around the World," *Philadelphia Daily News.* Reprinted with the permission of Signe Wilkinson. **p. 337** Cartoon (bottom): Hitch "Contemporary Father's Day Cards," *San Francisco Examiner and Chronicle* (June 18, 1995). Reprinted by permission. **p. 338** Cartoon: Scott Willis, "Great American Gunworks," *San Jose Mercury News* (May 16, 1991). Reprinted with the permission of Scott Willis. **pp. 338–340** Avery Corman, "Crisis on Campus," *Family Circle* (August 13, 1991). Copyright © 1991 by Avery Corman. Reprinted with the permission of the author. **p. 340** Photo: Luca Babini. **pp. 350–352** Elaine Louie, "The Prenuptial Agreement," *House & Garden* (June 1981). Copyright © 1981 by Conde Nast Publications, Inc. Reprinted with the permission of the author. **pp. 356–359** Kathleen Stassen Berger, "The Developmental Course of Love and Marriage" from *The Developing Person Through the Life Span, Second Edition.* Copyright © 1988. Reprinted with the permission of Worth Publishers, Inc. **p. 363** Photo: Reid Schumann/Reuter/Bettmann. **pp. 363–367** Amy Tan, "Four Directions" from *The Joy Luck Club.* Copyright © 1989 by Amy Tan. Reprinted with the permission of The Putnam Publishing Group.

Chapter 8

p. 372 Smith Corona ad: "Power tools for the mind" from *People.* Courtesy Smith Corona Corporation. **p. 373** United Technologies ad: "United by Diversity." Courtesy United Technologies. **p. 377** Brad Hill, "Teens take drugs because there's nothing else to do," *San Jose Mercury News* (July 1995). Reprinted by permission. **pp. 380–381** Russell Baker, "Ruled By Tools," *The New York Times* (May 12, 1992). Copyright © 1992 by The New York Times Company. Reprinted with the permission of *The New York Times.* **pp. 382–383** Barbara Dority, "Civil Liberties Watch," *The Humanist* 51, no. 1 (January/February 1991). Copyright © 1991. Reprinted with the permission of the publisher. **p. 395** Cartoon: T. O. Sylvester, "Microserfs," *San Francisco Chronicle,* Book Review Section (August 13, 1995). Copyright © 1995 by T. O. Sylvester. Reprinted by permission. **pp. 395–397** William Lutz, "No Ordinary Nut," from *Doublespeak.* Copyright © 1989 by Blonde Bear, Inc. Reprinted with the permission of HarperCollins Publishers, Inc. **pp. 399–402** Alan Durning, "How Much is Enough?," *Worldwatch* 3, no. 6 (November/December 1990). Reprinted in *How Much Is Enough?: The Consumer Society and the Future of the Earth* (New York: W. W. Norton & Company, 1992). Copyright © 1990 by Worldwatch Institute. Reprinted with the permission of Worldwatch Institute and W. W. Norton & Company, Inc. **pp. 406–412** Stan Kossen, "Problems of Substance Abuse" from *The Human Side of Organizations, Fifth Edition.* Copyright © 1991 by HarperCollins Publishers, Inc. Reprinted with the permission of the publishers. **pp. 416–421** José Vasconcelos, "The Boar Hunt," translated by Paul Waldorf, from *The Muse in Mexico: A Mid-Century Miscellany,* supplment to *Texas Quarterly* 11, no. 1 (Spring 1959). Copyright © 1959 by The University of Texas Press. Reprinted with the permission of the publishers.

Chapter 9

pp. 431–432 Ellen Goodman, "Defining Lite, Ultra Lite, and Truth." Copyright © 1991 by The Boston Globe/Washington Post Writers Group. Reprinted with the permission of Washington Post Writers

Group. **p. 432** Cartoon: Toppix, "Ugh! Marlboro Country." Reprinted with the permission of Tribune Media Services. **p. 432** Cartoon: Wayne Stayskal, "This isn't so bad. . . . " Reprinted with permission of Tribune Media Services. **p. 433** Photo: Bill O'Leary/Los Angeles Times Syndicate. **pp. 433–434** Art Buchwald, "Acid Indigestion," *Esquire* (December 1974). Copyright © 1974. Reprinted with the permission of *Esquire*. **pp. 434–435** Mark Leibovich, "and tomorrow and tomorrow," *San Jose Mercury News* (May 15, 1994). Copyright © 1994 by San Jose Mercury News. Reprinted with the permission of *San Jose Mercury News*. **p. 437** Cartoon: Jack Ohman, "If These People Had Been Democratic Presidential Hopefuls," *The Oregonian* (1991). Reprinted with the permission of Tribune Media Services. **pp. 438–439** Richard Blow, "Mea Culpa," *The New Republic* (February 18, 1991). Copyright © 1991 by The New Republic. Reprinted with the permission of *The New Republic*. **p. 441** Photo: Ed Bailey/A/P Wide World Photos. **pp. 441–442** Ruth Priest, "Finally Educators Figure Out What's Interesting," *San Jose Mercury News* (July 10, 1991). Copyright © 1991. Reprinted with the permission of the author. **pp. 442–443** Clifford Pugh, "Elvis 101 is now in session," *Houston Chronicle* (1991). Copyright © 1991. Reprinted with the permission of *Houston Chronicle*. **p. 445** Paul Trachtman, "the unmaking of a vegetarian—or why I'm full of bologna," *Smithsonian* (April 1993). Copyright © 1993 by Paul Trachtman. Reprinted with the permission of the author. **pp. 447–448** Art Buchwald, "One Angry Man." Copyright © 1995 by Los Angeles Times Syndicate. Reprinted with the permission of the author. **pp. 451–453** Deborah Schupack, "'Starter' Marriages Often End," originally titled "'Starter' Marriages' So Early So Brief," *The New York Times,* Home Section (July 13, 1994). Copyright © 1994 by The New York Times Company. Reprinted with the permission of *The New York Times*. This selection is accompanied by a cartoon by John Blanchard—*San Francisco Chronicle*. Reprinted by permission. **p. 456** Cartoon: Handelsman: "It's all according to your point of view," *Modern Maturity* (March/April 1995). Copyright © 1995 by American Association of Retired Persons. Reprinted with the permission of *Modern Maturity*. **pp. 460–462** Harry Lonsdale, "Can We Save Our National Forests," *USA Today Magazine* (March 1991). Copyright © 1991 by the Society for the Advancement of Education. Reprinted with the permission of *USA Today*. **pp. 462–464** Leila L. Kysar, "A Logger's Lament," *Newsweek* (October 22, 1990). Reprinted by permission. **pp. 467–471** Dexter Jeffries, "Who I Am," *Present Tense* (August 1988). Copyright © 1988 by The American Jewish Committee. Reprinted with the permission of The American Jewish Committee. **pp. 475–481** John J. Macionis, "Social Class in the United States" from *Sociology, Fifth Edition.* Copyright © 1995 by Prentice-Hall, Inc. Reprinted with the permission of the publishers. **p. 486** Photo: Jane Rule Burdine. **pp. 486–495** John Grisham, excerpts from *The Firm.* Copyright © 1991 by John Grisham. Reprinted with the permission of Doubleday, a division of Bantam Doubleday Dell Publishing Group, Inc.

Chapter 10

pp. 503, 504, 505, 506, 511 Ricky W. Griffin and Ronald J. Ebert, excerpts and graphics from *Business, Second Edition.* Copyright © 1991 by Prentice-Hall, Inc. Reprinted with the permission of the publishers. **p. 517** Graphic: "A Shifting Profile" from *San Francisco Examiner* (March 1, 1995). Copyright © 1995 by San Francisco Examiner. Reprinted with the permission of the publishers. **pp. 519, 520, 522** Tom L. McKnight, excerpts from *Essentials of Physical Geography.* Copyright © 1992 by Prentice-Hall, Inc. Reprinted with the permission of the publishers. **pp. 523–527** Ricky W. Griffin and Ronald J. Ebert, excerpts from *Business, Second Edition.* Copyright © 1991 by Prentice-Hall, Inc. Reprinted with the permission of the publishers. **pp. 528–531** Frederic Martini, "Homeostasis at the Tissue Level" from *Fundamentals of Anatomy & Physiology.* Copyright © 1989 by Prentice-Hall, Inc. Reprinted with the permission of the publishers. **pp. 532–535** Tom L. McKnight, "Constituents of the Atmosphere" from *Essentials of Physical Geography.* Copyright © 1992 by Prentice-Hall, Inc. Reprinted with the permission of the publishers. **pp. 536–537** Tom L. McKnight, "People and the Environment: Depletion of the Ozone Layer" from *Essentials of Physical Geography.* Copyright © 1992 by Prentice-Hall, Inc. Reprinted with the permission of the publishers.

Index